In clear, direct language stripped of legal jargon and with carefully constructed illustrations, investment adviser and estate planning specialist Henry W. Abts III explains what probate is, why you want to avoid it, and how to do so with a Living Trust. Based on his experience in creating thousands of Living Trusts and giving countless seminars, *The Living Trust* is a complete course that answers every question in language you can readily understand. Now updated to reflect changes in the laws and expanded to cover topics of special interest, *The Living Trust* is chock-full of essential information:

- Why and how a Living Trust works, with illustrative examples for every size and type of estate

- Provisions to look for in a good Living Trust, with advice to help you screen out attorneys writing worthless documents from those who can create a personalized, ideally designed Living Trust

- Which special provisions to consider in specific circumstances: the Living Will (Right to Die), Durable Power of Attorney, Transfer of Personal Property, Appointment of Guardian, and others

- Plus up-to-date information about tax-saving provisions such as the Charitable Remainder Trust, Q-DOT Trust, Insurance Preservation Trust, Spousal and Family Support Trust, Gift Trust, Generation-Skipping Trust, and the Family Limited Partnership

Not a "do-it-yourself" substitute for proper legal advice, *The Living Trust* is designed to provide the information you need in order to work with a qualified professional to create a legally proper and specifically designed Living Trust.

The Living Trust is the first and last book that you need ever buy on the subject of avoiding probate. This is *the* definitive manuscript. Bar none. Buy this book, read its lucid prose, follow its logical examples and carefully implement its suggested steps and you'll not only save yourself, your estate, and your heirs 5 percent to 15 percent or more of the value of your estate but more important, you will save those you love the needless agony, delay, hardship, and publicity that are the inevitable hallmarks of probate.

—Charles Matthews
Attorney
Little Rock, Arkansas

CAN I BE OF MORE ASSISTANCE?

As a result of the overwhelming response to my bestselling books, I receive thousands of requests for additional information. To learn more about our Living Trust or my company, The Estate Plan, please call (800) 350-1234. If you prefer, you may E-mail me at info@the estateplan.com or visit our site at www.the estateplan.com.

BECOME A CERTIFIED ESTATE PLANNING PROFESSIONAL (CEPP)

I have spent well over a quarter of a century developing the finest wealth-preservation programs for my clients. At the same time, I have developed a nationwide network of independent Certified Estate Planning Professionals to assist people in need of quality estate planning. If you are interested in becoming a registered CEPP and joining me in this work, please call (800) 292-0223. You should be actively engaged in the fields of financial, insurance, and/or estate planning; ethical in your business dealings; and eager to serve your clients. I will teach you my estate-planning techniques, share with you my estate-planning programs, and include you in the network.

ABOUT THE AUTHOR

Henry W. Abts III is a graduate of USC and the Stanford Graduate School of Business. He is a noted economist with an impressive background as a financial consultant to individuals and corporations since 1971. For years, he was a registered principal and chairman of H. W. Abts & Associates, a Registered Investment Adviser firm.

He served his country during the Korean War as a naval officer and as chief engineering officer aboard destroyers. He returned with five battle stars.

Abts is a nationally recognized authority on the Living Trust and has given more than three thousand seminars on wealth preservation. He has dedicated the better part of his life to educating people about one of the most crucial and beneficial concepts to family wealth planning—the Living Trust. In 1982, he founded The Estate Plan, a corporation dedicated to bringing the finest Living Trust documents within financial reach of everyone.

As an opponent of probate, he wrote the book *The Living Trust*, first published in 1989 and updated in 1993, 1997, and again in 2002. *The Living Trust* has sold upwards of a million copies and is considered the standard in the industry. Concerned with the questions that can arise regarding settlement of these Living Trusts, he published *How to Settle Your Living Trust* in 1999.

As a tireless advocate for consumer interests, Abts founded The Abts Institute for Estate Preservation, a nonprofit organization dedicated to raising awareness of Living Trusts and other estate-preservation topics, techniques, and applications. This institute provides professional training in estate-preservation techniques. Graduates are awarded the title of Certified Estate Planning Professional.

Abts entered the financial planning field via insurance with New York Life. Prior to that, he gained financial experience as president and chief executive officer of Demonstration Enterprises, served as senior vice president of Merle Norman Cosmetics, and built a nationwide food division for Ralston Purina.

He was a senior consultant in New York with a leading management consulting firm, Cresap, McCormick, and Paget. He began his career with the American Can Company in sales, marketing, and new product development.

While he was with the American Can Company in New York, he taught marketing at New York University. He also has served as a guest lecturer at the Stanford Graduate School of Business.

Abts has been active in his community as an officer and member of the board of directors of the American Lung Association of Los Angeles, Big Brothers, and Guide Dogs for the Blind.

He was commodore of the Santa Monica Yacht Club and the Association of Santa Monica Bay Yacht Clubs, and founding commodore of the Marina Yacht Club. He was Yachtsman of the Year in 1973. He was a founding member of the Marina City Club and served on its board of governors.

He and his wife, Bonnie Jean, are the parents of four grown children and seven grandchildren.

The LIVING TRUST

REVISED & UPDATED EDITION

The LIVING TRUST

The Failproof Way to Pass Along Your Estate to Your Heirs Without Lawyers, Courts, or the Probate System

HENRY W. ABTS III

Contemporary Books

Chicago   New York   San Francisco   Lisbon   London   Madrid   Mexico City
Milan   New Delhi   San Juan   Seoul   Singapore   Sydney   Toronto

Library of Congress Cataloging-in-Publication Data

Abts, Henry W.
      The living trust / Henry W. Abts III. — revised and updated ed.
            p.   cm.
      "The failproof way to pass along your estate to your heirs without lawyers,
courts, or the probate system."
      Includes index.
      ISBN 0-07-138709-9
      1. Living trusts—United States.   2. Estate planning—United States.
   I. Title.

   KF734.A93   2002
   346.7305'2—dc21   2002067747

Unless indicated otherwise, all figures and tables copyright © 1989 by The Estate Plan. Excerpts from *A Report on Probate: Consumer Perspectives and Concerns* used by permission of the American Association of Retired Persons.

1 2 3 4 5 6 7 8 9 0   QPD/QPD   1 0 9 8 7 6 5 4 3 2

ISBN 0-07-138709-9

McGraw-Hill books are available at special quantity discounts to use as premiums and sales promotions, or for use in corporate training programs. For more information, please write to the Director of Special Sales, Professional Publishing, McGraw-Hill, Two Penn Plaza, New York, NY 10121-2298. Or contact your local bookstore.

The material contained in *The Living Trust* is intended to present a comprehensive overview of the advantages and mechanics of the Living Trust. This book is not intended to be a substitute for qualified counsel; rather, it is designed to help the reader work with a qualified attorney in creating a specifically designed, legally proper Living Trust. *The Living Trust* is sold with the understanding that the publisher is not engaged in rendering legal, accounting, estate-planning, or other professional services.

The information supplied has been reviewed and approved by estate planners. However, as no published work can be totally current, all information and statements should be checked against the most recent developments by a qualified estate-planning specialist.

While every attempt has been made to provide accurate information, neither the author nor the publisher can be held accountable for any error or omission.

This book is printed on acid-free paper.

The update to this book has been particularly trying and has taken considerable time and tribulation to complete. Its successful conclusion is due in great part to the continued support and devotion of my eternal companion—my bride of thirty-seven years. I thank the Lord each day for giving her to me, and I honor her as His daughter.

She has given us four wonderful children who make our life worthwhile—Henry W. Abts IV (Skip), Christopher Kendall Abts, Laurel Ashley Abts, and Jeremy Stephen Preston Abts. And they in turn have given us seven wonderful grandchildren. This is what life is really about.

Contents

Preface

My experiences led me, through frustration and a sense of duty, to write two books, *The Living Trust* and *How to Settle Your Living Trust*, and to establish two companies, The Estate Plan and The National Estate Plan. These companies were created to make a good Living Trust financially available to the general public throughout the United States.

MY FIRST EXPERIENCE WITH PROBATE

My first experience with the probate process was enough to last a lifetime. In 1966, my parents decided to sell their family home and move into smaller accommodations. However, a week before the close of escrow, my father died suddenly of a massive stroke. The sale of my parents' home was immediately suspended, and the estate that they had worked a lifetime to build was now entangled in the laborious grind of the probate process.

I spent the next several months dealing with an outdated bureaucracy, hopelessly trying to keep the sale of my parents' home from collapsing.

I spent the next several months dealing with an outdated bureaucracy, hopelessly trying to keep the sale of my parents' home from collapsing. The stress of these events began to take its toll on my mother, and I was forced to place her in the hospital while I alone buried my father.

I Discover the Living Trust

The feelings of hopelessness, frustration, and anguish were indelibly etched upon my mind. In 1970, four years later, I discovered the Living Trust, and because of my experience with the probate process, I immediately recognized its importance. At the time, I was pursuing my career in personal estate and financial planning with my own company, H. W. Abts & Associates. I named this company after my grandfather's company, which was once one of the largest food wholesaling companies in the Midwest. While I never knew my grandfather, I have always been impressed by his history of honesty and integrity—and I have tried to follow in his footsteps.

Within the provisions of a Living Trust are the keys to avoid probate, ease the transition of a loved one's passing, and preserve the family's estate.

Within the provisions of a Living Trust are the keys to avoid probate, ease the transition of a loved one's passing, and preserve the family's estate. Thereafter, I took every opportunity to advise and encourage all of my financial and insurance clients to adopt a Living Trust instead of relying on Wills and the probate process. I simply explained how the Living Trust worked and its advantages and recommended that they seek out an attorney to provide this Living Trust.

The Legal Community Was Disserving My Clients

As the years passed, I sadly discovered that the legal community was disserving my clients. There were four areas of client abuse:

- They were convinced that they didn't need a Living Trust and instead were sold a Will.
- They had been provided a Living Trust, but since they didn't understand it, they hadn't signed it.
- They had received their Living Trust, but it was unfunded.
- They had received a Living Trust that wasn't worth the paper on which it was written.

A Major Learning Experience

My worst learning experience came in 1978, when, within a three-month period, three corporate presidents separately and independently agreed with me that they should have Living Trusts. However, they felt obligated to have their corporate attorneys, with whom they had worked closely for some ten to twenty years, draw up their Living Trusts. Six months passed, and then, within a period of weeks, each corporate president asked me to review his new Living Trust. I naively agreed. Different attorneys, each unknown to the other, had drawn these Trusts. I reviewed the three Trusts, which, in 1978, had cost from $2,500 to $3,500. I was stunned to realize that not one of the Trusts was worth the paper on which it was written.

I suddenly had a serious problem on my hands: how could I tell these men that they had wasted substantial dollars on their Trusts—at my recommendation? I didn't care so much

about the current impact of the Trusts, since they were revocable while both husband and wife were living, but I was deeply concerned about the impact on these families when one of the spouses died and part of the Trust became irrevocable.

This attorney also concluded that these documents were "worthless."

To confirm my conclusion, I took the Trusts to one of the leading Trust attorneys and asked for his opinion. This attorney also concluded that these documents were "worthless." He wrote to each of these clients and stated his findings, and because he felt a professional responsibility to put things right, he went further. He said there was nothing he could do to fix their existing documents, but he offered to provide them with his own Living Trust (for which at that time he charged $450) for half of his cost—only $225. Each of my clients was embarrassed and ended up doing nothing. To my knowledge, they still have done nothing to this day.

I realized that I had unintentionally done these gentlemen a great disservice. I had assumed that, if an attorney said he or she could draw a Living Trust, the person was capable of doing so. Instead, these attorneys, who were obviously good at their corporate work, charged their clients for their learning experience and yet wrote documents of minimal value to their clients.

The Final Straw

Thereafter, I sought experienced attorneys who could create a well-written Living Trust. I established a list of five qualified professionals to whom I felt that I could refer my clients for a good Living Trust.

I discovered that the attorney often didn't communicate appropriately and, as a result, the clients didn't understand their Living Trust and therefore failed to put it into effect.

Even with these recommended attorneys, however, I discovered that the attorney often didn't communicate appropriately and, as a result, the clients didn't understand their Living Trust and therefore failed to put it into effect. Or, a client would leave the attorney's office with an unfunded Trust or one that didn't meet the family's needs. Clients would be frustrated and confused by the legal language and unable to understand what they had purchased.

THE COMPANY

Following these unfortunate experiences, I approached a knowledgeable attorney in the field of Living Trusts and asked him to help me create a company to produce Living Trust documents solely for my investment and insurance clients. I decided that the adage "If you want it done right, do it yourself" was very appropriate.

The Estate Plan

In conjunction with this attorney, in August of 1982, utilizing our years of research, knowledge, and experience with thousands of clients, I formed, in Westlake, California, a company called The Estate Plan. Our common goal was to understand our clients' unique situations and to develop together a comprehensive system to address their needs. We sought to bring the finest Living Trust program within reach of everyone.

We sought to bring the finest Living Trust program within reach of everyone.

As we met with clients, we identified their common problems and developed working solutions. Each new provision was included in our Trust documents so that future clients would not be subjected to the same problems. The Living Trust document and its supporting elements grew with our expanding client base, resulting in a set of documents designed to cover every contingency, developed from real-life experiences.

All of the pieces had come together, and we settled the estate in less than an hour!

The thoroughness of our program became evident in 1984 while we were helping a client settle her estate. We realized that there was really very little to do. All of the pieces had come together, and we settled the estate in less than an hour!

The Book—*The Living Trust*

The Living Trust did not just materialize overnight. The seeds germinated for many years and were influenced by situations that I encountered through personal experiences as well as a host of situations specific to my clients.

Meeting with thousands of clients gave me the opportunity to address their technical questions in terms they could understand. When they asked for written information to send to their parents in Florida or to their children in New York, I began writing my experiences down. As the years passed, many of my clients, and eventually a publishing agent, asked me to write a book about the Living Trust in layperson's terms. They felt I had a way of explaining complex concepts in simple and understandable terms. *The Living Trust* took four years of writing and a year of editing and was first published in June 1989. The book immediately became a nationwide success. It was updated in 1993, 1997, and now in 2002, and more than one million copies have been sold.

The National Estate Plan

Immediately following the publication of *The Living Trust* in 1989, the company became inundated with requests for our Living Trust documents from almost every state in the country. Shortly thereafter, I formed The National Estate Plan, doing business as The Estate Plan, a separate company, to meet this nationwide demand. Our challenge over the next several years was to find and train competent, ethical advisers and attorneys throughout the United States and to work out a legally acceptable method to serve our potential clients. (Why did we change the name to The National Estate Plan while operating as The Estate Plan? Simple! We incorporated the latter company in Nevada for tax purposes, and Nevada rejected the name The Estate Plan as being too generic.)

Our challenge over the next several years was to find and train competent, ethical advisers and attorneys throughout the United States and to work out a legally acceptable method to serve our potential clients.

The National Estate Plan is the only nationwide Living Trust company whose Trust documents are valid in all fifty states. Our clients enjoy the confidence and peace of mind that come from knowing that our company has produced more than sixty thousand Living Trusts nationwide and settled more than ten thousand of these Trusts without a problem.

The Seminars

After *The Living Trust* was published, I began a nationwide seminar tour to further spread the good word that probate was unnecessary. These seminars were simply an extension of the seminars that I had been giving in southern California since 1978. Since then, I have given more than three thousand seminars. However, as I traveled throughout the nation, I was continually confronted by seminar attendees who said, "Henry, I read your book and went to an attorney for my Living Trust, but my Trust turned out to be nothing like what you have talked about here today." I urge everyone to read Chapter 10, "Separating the Good from the Bad," and to use these 150-plus "must provisions" as your guide to a *good* Living Trust.

I urge everyone to read Chapter 10, "Separating the Good from the Bad," and to use these 150-plus "must provisions" as your guide to a good Living Trust.

THE AGONY OF PROBATE IS NO LONGER NECESSARY

Unfortunately, I have assisted many people through the endless maze of probate, those who did not plan well. Each case incurred the same result of agony and frustration. The surviving spouse or children going through probate tend to suspend their lives, career goals, and major decisions until the probate process is completed—which can often take eighteen months to two years. The survivors tend to put

their lives on hold in the interim. I refer to this period as the "agony of probate."

In contrast, survivors with a good Living Trust should be able to settle the significant issues of an estate within an hour, and then move forward with their lives without worry.

In contrast, survivors with a good Living Trust should be able to settle the significant issues of an estate within an hour, and then move forward with their lives without worry. Usually, within a few months, our clients' lives are back on track.

I feel this benefit far outweighs any other advantage. When people have a choice, I wonder . . . Why would anyone choose to put loved ones through the unnecessary turmoil and agony of probate?

THE AFTERMATH

When I first wrote *The Living Trust*, I sincerely felt that I had done something good by educating hundreds of thousands of people about Living Trusts. However, during my nationwide seminar tour I began to realize, sadly and with some alarm, that I was somehow letting my readers down. My elation quickly turned to concern.

Many Will and Probate attorneys decided not to fight the Living Trust, but to join our march—with the objective that they would inevitably get their excessive fees in the end, when one or both parties died.

As time went on, I began to hear terrible tales of wasted time, frustration, and the cost of settling an estate in a Living Trust. Initially, it seemed that the Will and Probate attorneys were doing everything possible to turn people away from the Living Trust; however, eventually many of these attorneys decided to stop their fight and simply offer the Living Trust themselves. Unfortunately, the content of *good* Living Trusts is not taught in law school, so the attorneys were, to a great degree, on their own and simply creating documents as best they could. Most of these documents were terribly inadequate, which meant that, upon the death of one or both trustors, the successor trustees of their Living Trust would have to appeal to the courts to rectify the areas of inadequacy in the Trust.

Such situations didn't bother these attorneys, because they would be the ones taking the Trust to court—and earning hefty fees in the process. If a person's Living Trust wasn't properly funded, that was all right, too, because the attorneys would be the ones taking the client through probate. If everything in the estate happened to be in order, so much the better, because there was less work for the attorneys to do, but their fees always seemed to parallel what a probate fee would have been. Therefore, many Will and Probate attorneys decided not to fight the Living Trust, but to join our march—with the objective that they would inevitably get their excessive fees in the end, when one or both parties died.

THE BOOK—*HOW TO SETTLE YOUR LIVING TRUST*

By the many letters, telephone calls, and personal comments that I received from all over the country, I learned that I had been able to help a great number of people—which was my original intent. However, I also realized that I had unfortunately, and inadvertently, left many people in the lurch: they now had Living Trusts, but they really didn't know what to do when a spouse died and how their Trusts should be used to drastically simplify the process of settling their estates.

Unfortunately, many Will and Probate attorneys are now taking unfair advantage of far too many people by settling Living Trusts in the same way as they would probate estates— and charging nearly the same (and totally unnecessary) fees.

The Unfulfilled Need and the Book
How to Settle Your Living Trust

Unfortunately, many Will and Probate attorneys are now taking unfair advantage of far too many people by settling Living Trusts in the same way as they would probate estates—and charging nearly the same *(and totally unneces-*

sary) fees. As a result, I wrote *How to Settle Your Living Trust*, which was published in 1999. The primary purpose of that book is to fill the void and to guide you, in simple step-by-step fashion, in the matters required to settle your estate. Don't be alarmed! Having a good Living Trust, instead of a Will, greatly simplifies the settling of an estate, keeps your financial matters private, and costs almost nothing— compared with the agony, lengthy time delays, and high cost of going through the probate process.

The American public no longer need be the unwilling (and often unknowing) victims of unscrupulous attorneys when the inevitable time comes to settle the estate of a loved one. By understanding the basic principles presented in *How to Settle Your Living Trust*, you will at least be familiar with the concepts of settling an estate in a Living Trust and, thus, better able to chart your own course.

As you will see as you read through the book, settling an estate in a Living Trust can be fast, easy, private, and done at almost no cost by the surviving family members themselves!

How to Settle Your Living Trust *is intended to show you that most estates can be easily settled, with complete privacy, and with little or no delay.*

How to Settle Your Living Trust is intended to show you that most estates can be easily settled, with complete privacy, and with little or no delay. The hope is that, through the book, you will come to understand the many benefits of having a *good* Living Trust, as well as how easily most estates can be settled—without going through the agony of probate, incurring unnecessary legal fees, and enduring long delays associated with the probate process.

The estates of most average Americans (which covers about 90 percent of the population) can be easily settled—by surviving family members themselves—by following the advice in Part I (Chapters 1 through 20) of How to Settle Your Living Trust.

WELCOME TO THE REVISED AND UPDATED EDITION OF *THE LIVING TRUST*

One of the primary reasons this book was initially written was to educate people on how to preserve their assets from the abusive probate process—by creating a Living Trust. My desire was to present the concept of the Living Trust in terms that the layperson could easily understand. With more than one million copies now in the hands of the public, the book has made a significant contribution to raising people's awareness level and knowledge of Living Trusts.

Over the years, I traveled throughout the United States and was gratified to see that so many people had become acquainted with the Living Trust. I found that people were more educated and sophisticated about Living Trusts and that they understood the significance of placing their assets in a Living Trust—in order to spare their children from having to run the gauntlet of the agonizing probate process.

As I was preparing the revision, I received the following E-mail message, which I thought would be most appropriate to include. It says who we are better than I ever could:

> My sincerest appreciation to you and all at The Estate Plan. Henry, I do not mean to sound overly flattering, but it is just so rare in this day and age to find an individual who has achieved your level of success to be so genuine, sincere, and caring.
>
> Given my experiences with you, sir, whenever I hear the name Henry Abts, I will have a smile come to my heart for your *absolute* support. I thought the strength of your program was your outstanding book, documents, and staff, but now I understand that the true success and strength of this program is the leadership and commitment to the highest standards by one Mr. Henry Abts III and which is now being carried on by his sons. It is a legacy I hope I can leave to my children and community.
>
> Tom Current, Your Adviser in Kentucky

In keeping with the public's rising level of knowledge about the Living Trust, this updated edition of *The Living Trust* addresses new issues, discusses other advantageous types of Trusts, and includes important changes—thus giving people more information to assist them in preserving and managing their estates. At the same time, since this book is a basic reference tool for the layperson desiring to expand his or her knowledge of the Living Trust, every effort has been made to retain the same easy-reading style, informative content, and level of simplicity of the first edition, so that the newcomer to the field of estate planning will be able to truly understand the significance of the Living Trust and its important ancillary documents.

Some significant events have occurred as a result of the publication of this book in 1989 and its subsequent revisions. This current revision incorporates important information concerning these happenings, including changes in the tax laws that affect Living Trusts.

One thing, however, hasn't changed: a Living Trust protects your estate *far better* than any Will. With the information provided herein, the issue is no longer whether or not you should have a Living Trust; the facts overwhelmingly justify this need. Now the crucial issue is how to choose a *good* Living Trust.

One thing, however, hasn't changed: a Living Trust protects your estate far better *than any Will.*

Important revisions have been incorporated throughout the book to bring it up-to-date and to make sure that it provides you with the most complete and current information on the Living Trust.

What's New
- The Economic Growth and Tax Relief Reconciliation Act of 2001 and how it will potentially impact your estate in the future. These are the areas of impact:
  - Estate Tax
  - Gift Tax
  - Generation-Skipping Tax
  - Stepped-Up Valuation
  - State Death Taxes

- A new chapter on the ignominious history of probate, titled "Lest We Forget."
- Two new probate studies—featuring the states of Maryland and New York—which parallel our earlier study of the state of Washington and the AARP study.
- An important Private Letter Ruling that now clarifies that the joint A-B and A-B-C Trusts are appropriate for separate property states.
- The terrible price of frivolous lawsuits that can engulf any one of us—or "What Price Integrity?"
- The Offshore Trust for asset protection.
- Lifetime settlements—don't give up that insurance policy before you know its true value.
- Parties to the Trust—the role of beneficiaries, contingent beneficiaries, and remainder beneficiaries.
- Qualified/IRA Trusts and why to avoid IRA Wills.
- Cost of a Living Trust updated with a price range.
- FDIC protection rules for insurance on bank deposits in a Living Trust.
- The Catastrophic Illness Trust—well and viable.
- Further clarification of the types of beneficiaries—primary, contingent, and remainder.
- The importance of placing your Living Will on file.

What's Changed

- The 150 must provisions of a *good* Living Trust have been added to and revised.
- The discussion of IRA beneficiaries has been changed to maximize income and estate taxes.
- Probate cost is now estimated to consume $50 billion annually.
- The "universal" Living Trust is now applicable in all fifty states.

Updates

- The nonsense of separate Trusts in a separate property state.
- Non-resident citizens qualify for the Living Trust and $1 million federal estate tax exclusion, but not for the Maximum Marital Deduction.

- Final instructions on how to settle your estate.
- Appropriate costs for estate-preservation vehicles and ancillary documents.

Sound Advice

- The necessity of a *good* Living Trust.
- Avoiding the administrative nightmare of separate Trusts for a married couple.
- Beware of the wolf in sheep's clothing offering cheap Living Trusts.
- Maximizing income and estate tax protection on your IRA.
- How to protect your estate against frivolous lawsuits.

INDEPENDENT STUDIES AND REPORTS

During the past few years, more and more articles have appeared in various publications that support the premise of this book—avoiding probate through the use of a Living Trust.

Recent independent studies and surveys have been conducted about the probate process and the inequities foisted on bereaved survivors by probate attorneys. The results of these studies universally establish that probate should be avoided and that a Living Trust is a far superior solution to passing on your estate to your heirs.

AARP Study

The American Association of Retired Persons (AARP) commissioned a two-year study on the probate process. Because of the numerous articles and publications written during the past few years that have recommended bypassing probate through the use of the Living Trust, AARP set out to determine whether these avoidance efforts were warranted. The principal question to be answered was: Is getting a Living Trust a valid recommendation? AARP's answer: Absolutely.

The AARP study, copyrighted in 1990 and titled *A Report on Probate: Consumer Perspectives and Concerns*, was the first formal study of probate in more than twenty years and is one of the most perceptive analyses of the probate system. This study deserves far more credit and publicity than it has been given to date.

The study, conducted by unbiased attorneys, analyzed three states—California, Wisconsin, and Delaware—as the most representative of the three different methods of charging probate fees nationwide. The study found that the average time in the probate process was fifteen months and the average cost of probate consumed 5 percent to 10 percent of the gross estate. (Gross estate is the total value of your estate prior to any reduction for liabilities such as mortgages or loans.)

The study found that the average time in the probate process was fifteen months and the average cost of probate consumed 5 percent to 10 percent of the gross estate.

The main purpose of probate, as identified in the study, is to establish clear title of a person's assets by paying off the creditors, or, restated, *the purpose of probate is to pay the creditors*. However, the study found that 95 percent of creditors do not use the probate process. In fact, most creditors do not even bother to read death notices; they simply send out the bills, and the survivors usually pay the bills.

This comprehensive study produced convincing evidence that the probate process is inflicting undue strain and emotional and financial duress on the unsuspecting public. The study concluded that probate is time-consuming, costly, and entirely unnecessary—and that a Living Trust is a valid solution. The study also presented a strong message that consumers should be educated about the evils of probate and about simple alternatives to avoid it. The study recommended that "state and local bar associations should require members of the probate bar, when drafting a will, to disclose the estimated cost of the eventual probate proceeding . . . and how this might affect the assets they intend to pass to survivors."

This comprehensive study produced convincing evidence that the probate process is inflicting undue strain and emotional and financial duress on the unsuspecting public. The study concluded that probate is time-consuming, costly, and entirely unnecessary—and that a Living Trust is a valid solution.

The AARP study made a significant comment about Wills versus Living Trusts:

> Generally, it costs more to set up a Living Trust than to draft a Will. But the cost for drafting a trust can be less in the long run than the combined cost of an inexpensive Will and the ensuing expense of probate. . . . Those who go to an attorney and merely ask for a Will may get less, and pay more, than they bargained for.

The AARP study established that a Living Trust "completely avoids probate's public scrutiny, delays, and costs." In addition, according to the study, the Living Trust is "a reasonably priced alternative to a will, and it avoids probate altogether." If you have any doubt about the value of a Living Trust in lieu of the probate process, I urge you to read the excerpt of the AARP study in Appendix H.

Personally Commissioned Study

In an effort to further validate the AARP study, our firm engaged the prestigious law firm of Lane, Powell, Spears, and Lubersky to conduct a survey of probate in the state of Washington, which is a Uniform Probate Code state. The key results of this survey indicated that probate took an average of thirteen months (with 22 percent of the cases still open after three and a half years), in contrast to the one to three months being trumpeted by most probate attorneys. Only 20 percent of the cases were closed within six months! Additionally, the cost of probate varied from an average of 4 percent to an unconscionably high 54 percent! This finding was again in sharp contrast to many probate attorneys' claim of "insignificant time and cost of probate."

The study also refuted the often-heard argument that "Your estate is too small for you to consider a revocable Living Trust." The study provided evidence that the greatest impact of probate costs was on estates of $100,000 and less.

The study also refuted the often-heard argument that "Your estate is too small for you to consider a revocable Living Trust." The study provided evidence that the greatest impact of probate costs was on estates of $100,000 and less. In fact, the study found that the impact on estates valued at less than $10,000 was so great that these estates were eliminated from the study to avoid skewing the results. For example, one $10,000 estate incurred probate costs of $7,400—leaving only $2,600 for the heirs! Furthermore, the study showed that the greatest percentage of the probate cost burden was borne by the smaller estates. Thus, smaller estates need the protection of a Living Trust even more than larger estates—because smaller estates can ill afford the erosion of their limited assets to the needlessly expensive probate process.

Maryland and New York Probate Studies

You will see in Chapter 3—"The Million-Dollar Lawsuit, or What Price Integrity?"—that we conducted two more independent studies. One was in Maryland, where the Maryland Bar Association has the statement on its website that estates up to $750,000 can be settled for $700. We also conducted a similar study in New York, where it has been touted that probate is typically settled in thirty to sixty days. In each case, we dispelled the myths and found that probate in Maryland and New York follows the same cost and time pattern as found in the other studies.

THE AWESOME POWER OF WILL AND PROBATE ATTORNEYS

As I traveled throughout the nation giving seminars on the power of the Living Trust and vital estate-preservation vehicles, I discovered the awesome clout wielded by many Will and Probate attorneys. I am convinced that they are willing to pay any price and go to any length—including the dissemination of misinformation even to their brethren—to protect their vested interests of $25 billion annually in probate fees taken at the expense of the general public.

Recent estimates are that my generation (age sixty and older) will pass $20 trillion to their heirs (the baby boomers) over the next twenty years. In the *AARP Bulletin* of April 1990, the association reported that it found that the average cost of probate was 5 to 10 percent. If we use the conservative figure of only 5 percent, and if we assume that the estates will go through probate only on the death of the second spouse (a highly unlikely proposition), *we are looking at a staggering fee to the Will and Probate attorneys of $25 billion annually*. That's an awfully big hand in the pockets of the American public—and one that is totally unnecessary with proper estate planning.

. . . we are looking at a staggering fee to the Will and Probate attorneys of $25 billion annually.

If these attorneys can create sufficient doubt in your mind about establishing a Living Trust, they have won their battle. Why? The reason is simple: If you choose either to create a Will or to do nothing, *you lose*, and the attorneys siphon money from *your* estate that would otherwise go to your heirs.

If you are confused, or have reason to question the validity of using a Living Trust to preserve your estate, I urge you to read Appendix I, "Fact vs. Fallacy: Misrepresentation by Will and Probate Attorneys." You have a right to know the facts.

State Bar Associations Are "Protecting Their Own"

Many state bar associations have joined forces with their Will and Probate brethren to help protect the vested interests of probate that they have enjoyed for centuries.

The Iowa Bar Association was the first to declare that any attorney who works with an organization outside the state offering the Living Trust would be disbarred. (Such tactics are effective deterrents to the legitimate inroads of the Living Trust.) Similar tactics were initiated in Colorado, but the actions were met by lawsuits filed by some of their own attorneys. Lawsuits have also been filed in Nebraska and Florida.

The Oregon Bar Association asked the state's attorney general to stop our company from providing Living Trusts in the state. We submitted every document asked for over an exhaustive two-year period. However, we refused to disclose our client names and client personal data. After two years of harassment, and having not prevailed, the attorney general threatened to sue us. I knew that, as with our experience in Washington, we would win, but I was in the process of writing my next book. I recognized that I must choose one or the other. I can't fight every battle, so I took the most important course and chose to accede to the pressure of the Oregon attorney general and write my book. I agreed that we would withdraw from Oregon even though we had done nothing wrong.

I hear from Oregon residents from time to time that they are disappointed that we cannot be of help to them. I wish I could, but the attorney general is an elected official, and they elected him. I feel that his position in this matter is illegal in that it supports the Oregon Bar Association in creating a monopoly and eliminates competition—but so goes the state of Oregon.

In Minnesota the Department of Commerce harassed our adviser, in Kentucky it was a witch-hunt by the Kentucky Bar Association, and again in Ohio it was pressure from the Cleveland Bar Association. These harassments usually begin with a disgruntled attorney who feels we might be taking business away from him or her and files a frivolous, meaningless complaint. While these complaints are all dismissed, they cost time, money, and frustration. On the other hand, they do clarify that we are doing something worthwhile, because if we weren't, the bar associations would ignore us. We are obviously making inroads into their potential $25 billion annual probate revenue.

Numerous other bar associations are rushing to the aid of their colleagues—to help protect their long-standing vested interest in probate at the expense of the consumer and to preserve their substantial annual income from probate fees.

As you can surmise, I have little respect for the legal industry. I believe that it is a shame that so many young great minds are pursuing law careers because of the money. These are great minds that are taken away from other fields that could be most productive to our economy. Sadly, the legal fraternity is extracting money and productivity from a society that badly needs their minds and skills. These resources could be used to contribute to our society rather than prey upon it. I do not condemn all attorneys; I have found many to be most reputable and to contribute to our society, but they are getting fewer and more difficult to find. I must leave you with the age-old adage "Let the buyer beware."

My wife tells me that this edition of the book will only anger attorneys more. I acknowledge that, but my frustration comes from more than thirty years of experience dealing with individuals driven by greed and ignorance. I write with a clear heart, knowing that I write what is true. I fear not death; I simply fear the continued attacks by the legal fraternity. I have lived my life well and, through this book, am trying to right a terrible wrong—the continued perpetration of probate on an unwitting public. I simply desire to help honest, hardworking people protect what they have labored to build.

Misleading Arguments

Two of the most common statements made by a Will and Probate attorney to a client are that "you don't need a Living Trust" and "your estate is not large enough to justify a Living Trust." An attorney once complained that our firm, The Estate Plan, had written a Living Trust for a widow who "had an estate of only $300,000." The attorney asserted that his state had a system called Adjudication of Intestacy (or Heirship) that could settle the estate without any probate cost. His state does have such a system—but it is applicable only to simple estates, which are typically under $100,000. Moreover, only the legal profession is aware of this system, and since there is no money to be made from it, the public is not told about it! Only one individual will gain from not using a Living Trust—the attorney.

Equally prevalent is the argument that probate *in this state* is simple and inexpensive. The Will and Probate attorneys in the state of Washington are typical of attorneys nationwide; their instant response has been that probate in Washington is incredibly easy, taking only a few months and costing very little. (Our independent study of probate in the state of Washington proved otherwise.)

It is interesting to note that Norman Dacey and I are from opposite ends of the nation, warning the public about the same concern—the evils of the probate system—over a time span of more than twenty-five years.

This misleading argument is an all-too-common technique of the Will and Probate attorneys throughout the nation. When Norman Dacey published his book *How to Avoid Probate* in 1965, the hue and cry from attorneys was that "he is from Connecticut, and his findings do not apply outside that state." Following publication of *The Living Trust* in 1989, the same familiar hue and cry was heard: "The author of *The Living Trust* is from California, and those conditions do not apply outside that state." It is interesting to note that Norman Dacey and I are from opposite ends of the nation, warning the public about the same concern—the evils of the probate system—over a time span of more than twenty-five years.

I hope that by becoming aware of these misleading arguments and tactics, you, *the consumer*, can make yourself heard and regain control of your destiny—and, ultimately, control of your estate.

THE OPENING OF PANDORA'S BOX

During the years that have elapsed since *The Living Trust* was first published, it's become clear to me that this book has done two things:

It has helped to educate many thousands of people about the advantages of a Living Trust and how to know a well-written Trust from a poorly written one.

At the same time, since so many people now want Living Trusts, it has prompted many unqualified individuals and firms to offer to fill the demand. As a result, many poorly qualified attorneys as well as financial planning institutions are now trumpeting the advantages of a Living Trust and offering to sell their often inadequately written documents to the unsuspecting public.

My good intentions of making everyone aware of the advantages of a good Living Trust have, in too many instances, done a disservice to the individuals who were persuaded to get Living Trusts but who were then victimized by individuals and institutions who preyed upon the unsuspecting public by selling them Living Trusts that were, in many cases, poorly written and almost worthless for protecting the estate of the trustees and beneficiaries.

Chapter 10, "Separating the Good from the Bad," contains information that is more important today than it was in 1989 when this book was first published!

A MOST DIFFICULT QUESTION

At almost every seminar I have given—to an average of two thousand people per month—I am faced with the following question: "How do I convince Mom and Dad that they need a Living Trust to avoid probate?"

I am continually asked this difficult question by younger adults who readily understand the many advantages of a Living Trust and who also are aware of the horrors of probate—and do not want to be subjected to it for settling their parents' estates. Probate is a critical family issue, since it is the surviving children who will suffer the agony of the probate process and who will forfeit a substantial share of the estate to the probate attorneys.

It is not always easy to get parents to realize that how their estate is settled—whether with a Will and the accompanying probate process or with a Living Trust and the simple matter of having the successor trustees assume their responsibilities for managing the estate—involves the family members (most often the adult children) who remain after the parents die.

Parents who have the foresight to place their assets in a Living Trust not only have the peace of mind of knowing that their affairs are in order, but they also show the ultimate consideration for their successor trustees (usually their children) by sparing them the agony and frustration of an unnecessary trip through the time-consuming probate process. The parents' estate will remain private (not open to public scrutiny), and the parents will have had the opportunity to make the decisions regarding their estate so that their wishes concerning allocation and distribution of their assets will be followed. Most important, parents will know that the estate that they have built through a lifetime of work will pass to their heirs without monies being needlessly siphoned off by probate attorneys.

Since the primary purpose of probate is to pay the creditors, and most creditors do not use the probate process to collect their funds, the key question is: Why should you use probate?

If I can convey any message to you, it would be that there is no need for probate. However, unless you choose the legal alternative of creating a revocable Living Trust, your family will *eventually* go through probate.

ADDRESSING YOUR NEEDS AND CONCERNS

Having listened to the questions and concerns voiced by our seminar attendees plus those of our attorneys and advisers nationwide, as well as the numerous readers of the previous editions of *The Living Trust*, I have taken the opportunity in this revised edition to address the areas of greatest consumer interest, as well as to keep you apprised of the latest changes pertaining to probate and smart estate planning.

For more than thirty years, my message has been the same: "If you love your spouse and/or children, avoid the time, cost, and agony of probate—give them the gift of a good Living Trust."

For more than thirty years, my message has been the same: "If you love your spouse and/or children, avoid the time, cost, and agony of probate—give them the gift of a good Living Trust."

If you would like further information, please call (800) 350-1234.

Acknowledgments

This book did not just happen; it took blood, sweat, and tears. Even though the book is the result of more than thirty years of experience and four years of writing, it never would have come to fruition without the dedication of many people. I would like to take this opportunity to thank those special individuals who breathed life into *The Living Trust*.

My sincere appreciation goes to Michael and Martha Desch (now deceased) for their magnificent job of editing. They took my language and converted it to readable form. Their probing questions and attention to detail ensured that the complex subject matter was adequately covered in an easy-to-understand form.

I particularly want to thank the thousands of clients who have met with me over the years to learn more about the Living Trust. Their innumerable questions provided the basis for writing the first edition of this book. These people, through their desire to learn about the many advantages of the Living Trust, made the book possible. Now, more than twelve years after the original publication of *The Living Trust*, I sincerely want to thank the thousands of new clients and the many hundreds of readers who offered their constructive comments about the book. In addition, our hundreds of advisers and attorneys throughout the nation also contributed suggestions for this edition.

Many fine attorneys made significant contributions and provided important input to much of the revised material in this edition of *The Living Trust*. Contributing to the effort were Richard Siefert of the law firm of Lane, Powell, Spears, and Lubersky. David Boerner, dean of the former Puget Sound School of Law (now the Seattle School of Law), contributed his expertise in legal ethics, and William Oltman, a leading Trust professor and nationally recognized author, enthusiastically shared his expertise in Trusts.

I would like to extend thanks to Charles Matthews, a special friend and an extremely competent Trust specialist who has carefully reviewed this book for legal correctness. I would also like to thank George Knapp, a good friend and very competent financial adviser, who goes out of his way to keep me abreast of changes that affect the Living Trust and its ancillary documents.

My most sincere gratitude belongs to my very special wife and companion, Bonnie Jean, who continually provided the encouragement, strength, and support needed to complete this overwhelming project.

I feel impressed to thank and recognize three outstanding doctors, for if it were not for them I would not be here today to update this book.

We lived in Thousand Oaks, California, for seventeen years before moving to Incline Village, Nevada. Irving Kent Loh, M.D., F.A.C.C., F.A.H.A., F.C.C.P., F.A.C.P., Medical Director, Ventura Heart Institute, Thousand Oaks, has been my cardiologist for over fifteen years. Once we moved, we also needed a cardiologist in this area and were fortunate enough to come under the care of John Speer Schroeder, M.D., Professor of Cardiology, Stanford University Medical Center. I have continued under the care of both cardiologists.

On a routine visit to Dr. Schroeder last year, he suggested that I have a sonogram of my carotid arteries. I had exhibited no adverse symptoms; this was simply a fine cardiologist doing what he thought would be in the best interest of his patient. The sonogram showed that my carotid arteries were 70 percent blocked, which was not unreasonable for someone who was seventy-two years old. But Dr. Loh wasn't satisfied. He suggested that Dr. Schroeder confirm this with a more definitive study, an MRI (magnetic resonance imaging) of my carotid arteries. Dr. Schroeder made the arrangements and I went through this simple exam believing all was well and returned home. A few days later, Dr. Schroeder called and asked how quickly I could return to Stanford. We were there the next afternoon, and I was in surgery the following day. The MRI showed that the carotid arteries were 90 percent blocked, and the surgeon reported that he found them to be 95 percent blocked.

Thanks to Dr. Schroeder, I had the finest surgeon, Gary K. Steinberg, M.D., Ph.D., Professor and Chairman, Department of Neurosurgery, Stanford University Medical Center. I am most grateful to Dr. Steinberg for clearing his calendar and taking me immediately into surgery. I am also most grateful to his coordinating nurse, Teresa E. Bell-Stephens, R.N., who cleared his calendar and watched over me like a mother. To this day she continues to see that I get proper care.

I am deeply grateful to the professionalism, experience, and dedication of these wonderful people. Were it not for them, and their inspiration, I might not be here today.

Introduction

Many people ask, "Why should I have a Living Trust?" As you will see, there are several reasons why a Living Trust is essential to good estate planning. A Living Trust eliminates the need for your heirs or surviving spouse to be subjected to the agony and unnecessary cost of probate; a Living Trust provides the entity to ensure that you either pay no estate and inheritance taxes or at least minimize those onerous taxes. In addition, a Living Trust establishes the means to provide for your needs in the event that you become incompetent; it provides the entity for the support and education of your minor children; it creates the vehicle to indirectly care for a handicapped child without jeopardizing his or her government benefits; and a Living Trust assures what all people want—*privacy* of their financial affairs. (Today, many young adults are deciding that a Living Trust for their mom and dad is a cost-effective way to preserve their own inheritance.)

Many people, with honest sincerity, say, "I have a Will, and therefore my estate will not go through probate." Unfortunately, that statement reflects one of the most common misconceptions of people in all walks of life. A special study conducted for our firm by Elway Research, Inc., showed that even though 53 percent of those surveyed had heard about the Living Trust, less than 4 percent of those people had one. This finding seems to indicate an alarming insecurity about where to get the right set of documents. The words *Will* and *probate* are synonymous, and the cost of probate can be very expensive, even to the smallest estates.

Another common misconception heard all too frequently is that people will avoid probate by having their assets in joint tenancy. You will learn later in this book that having your assets in joint tenancy only *postpones* the agony of probate. Yes, probate is avoided when the first spouse dies, but probate is inevitable—and when the second spouse dies, the *entire* estate must then go through probate.

This book is the result of more than thirty years of experience with the Living Trust. Having met with thousands of clients and prospective clients, I have seen that once they have been introduced to the concept of the Living Trust, they want to learn more about it. My intent, throughout this book, is to communicate to you, in simple and easy-to-understand language, five major topics related to a Living Trust:

- Why you should have a Living Trust
- How a Living Trust works
- How you can distinguish a good Living Trust from a bad one
- Why probate is unnecessary
- How to tell fact from fallacy about Living Trusts

Understanding the advantages of having a Living Trust and deciding that you (or you and your spouse) desire to get your own Living Trust is not enough. Unless you understand how a Living Trust works, along with the particular advantages it can bestow on your personal financial and estate-planning goals, the Trust cannot work for you to its best advantage.

Even more important, once you decide to get your own Living Trust, you must be able to distinguish a good Trust from a bad one. As the popularity of the Living Trust increases, more and more attorneys are offering to draw up Living Trust documents, but few of these attorneys are knowledgeable about Living Trusts. Without the proper knowledge on your part, it is just too easy for you to pay too much money for a poorly drawn Trust—which can often be worse than having no Trust at all. When you finish reading this book, you will not be at the mercy of the legal fraternity; you will know what provisions you should have in your Living Trust, and why.

I am deeply concerned about the increasing proliferation of Living Trusts being thrust on the public today, with a resultant dramatic reduction in the quality of these documents. My intent is not to condemn the legal profession but rather to raise its standards in drawing quality documents that contain the provisions most appropriate for each client's individual circumstances. Although everyone should have a Living Trust today, I would like to think that because of this book a client can now be assured that his or her Living Trust will meet his or her needs and will also be of the highest quality.

After years of assisting thousands of clients in creating Living Trusts and hundreds of clients in settling their estates upon the death of a spouse or parent, I have yet to find a single disadvantage to a properly drawn and funded Living Trust. Furthermore, the advantages of having a Living Trust are limitless.

I also have yet to see a client, having once understood the Trust, complete his or her Trust and then walk away without a feeling of absolute relief—and peace. The Living Trust is the finest gift that one spouse can give the other, or that parents can give their children.

I have never worked with any other document that is as versatile and that allows you to do with your assets whatever your heart most desires. Whether married or single, young or old, owner of a small estate or a large one, every person has the same need for a Living Trust.

As I noted in the Preface, to acquaint people with the many advantages of a well-drawn Living Trust, I have presented thousands of seminars on the Living Trust. The two most commonly asked questions at the seminars are, "Why doesn't everyone have a Living Trust?" and "How do I convince Mom and Dad that they need a Living Trust?" The answer to the first question is simple: The people either have not heard of the Living Trust or do not yet fully understand its benefits.

The answer to the second question is to make sure that Mom and Dad know the facts: Probate is unnecessary—and it is a family affair, because, unless a Living Trust is utilized, your children will forfeit a substantial part of their share of your estate to the Will and Probate attorneys. The smaller the estate, the greater will be the cost impact of probate. Without having a Living Trust, and if you are married and your estate ever exceeds $1 million, your children will pay an unnecessary estate tax. (I acknowledge that you can achieve the same saving of estate taxes with a Testamentary Trust, but then your estate must go through probate.)

Children might consider paying for their parents' Living Trust—since it is the children who will ultimately benefit from their parents'

Living Trust by avoiding the agony, time, and frustration of probate, as well as by avoiding the forfeiture of a substantial share of their rightful inheritance to the Will and Probate attorneys and possibly to the Internal Revenue Service in the form of estate taxes.

You should be aware that many Will and Probate attorneys are pursuing an aggressive campaign to intentionally mislead the public by spewing out articles and regularly making statements about the Living Trust that are wrong and are calculated to mislead the public. (See Appendix I, "Fact vs. Fallacy," for more information.) If, by their intentional misleading statements, they can get you to hesitate about implementing a Living Trust, then they have won, because without a Living Trust your estate will go through probate whether or not you have a Will. By their tactics, the attorneys are denying many people their right to choose how their estates eventually will be handled.

The questions most frequently asked are categorized and answered for you (along with the chapter reference to where the subject is covered in more detail) in Appendix G: "Everything You Always Wanted to Know About the Living Trust—But Were Afraid to Ask."

The intent of this book is to impart a clear understanding of the Living Trust, as well as to make you aware of the importance a Living Trust plays in sound estate planning.

Experience with thousands of clients has shown that, before you can fully understand the advantages that can be yours with a Living Trust, you need to be fully aware of the pitfalls that await your heirs and the adverse tax consequences that can accrue to your estate.

You need to know how to implement your Trust (i.e., how to transfer all of your assets into your Trust and how to maintain your assets in your Trust), lest you fall back into the probate trap.

You need to know how to organize your estate simply and to easily maintain such organization so that when needed your assets can be found and your estate settled swiftly. Our Estate Plan Binder is the key solution (see Chapter 13).

Equally important to the Living Trust are the many vital ancillary documents everyone should have in place today. These documents include:

- Living Will
- Durable Power of Attorney for Health Care
- Durable General Power of Attorney
- Competency Clause
- Assignment of Furniture, Furnishings, and Personal Effects
- Appointment of Guardian (where appropriate)
- Appointment of Conservator
- Separate Property Agreements (where appropriate)

You should not only have each of these documents in place today, but you should also clearly understand them and know when and how to use them.

The Living Trust is but the first step of many sophisticated but clearly understandable approaches to save what you have worked so hard to create. There is a whole quiver of estate-preservation tools that should be used where appropriate to further preserve estates that exceed the federal estate tax equivalent exemptions. These include the Insurance Preservation Trust, the Spousal and Family Support Trust, the Gift Trust, the Generation-Skipping Trust, the Spousal Gift, the Family Limited Partnership, and the Charitable Remainder Trust. Each of these documents can play a vital role in preserving your estate.

The last, and probably the most important, issue is the eventual settlement of your estate. There is an incredible proliferation of groups, firms, and individuals offering Living Trusts. The real questions are: Do they know how? Are they going to be there when you need them to help settle your estate? Will their fee be reasonable? Do you trust them? Settling an estate is now becoming a nightmare to far too many people. Our firm has settled more than two thousand Living Trusts gracefully and without incident.

Many examples are used throughout the book to illustrate various points in explaining how a Living Trust works for everyone—in all situations. All of the examples in the book are actual situations encountered by my clients. However, even though real-life situations are used, the names in the examples are fictitious to preserve the privacy of the individuals involved.

After untold years of estate planning, I believe that I have an important message to share with people everywhere:

Everyone needs a *good* Living Trust.

Indeed, everyone:

• Needs to be able to properly implement his or her Trust and to easily organize his or her estate
• Needs the appropriate ancillary documents—now

• Should consider the other numerous supplementary Trusts to further preserve the estate
• Needs to be assured that his or her estate will be settled timely and reasonably

Thus, the answer to sound estate planning and peace of mind for you and your heirs is very simple: a Living Trust (instead of the typical Will), along with the vital ancillary documents, and an organized estate (instead of a guessing game). The Living Trust becomes, in effect, your Will—and it specifically spells out to whom, and when, your assets are to be distributed. Most individuals do not plan to fail; they just fail to plan. Why not start planning now? Establishment of a Living Trust is a giant step in planning for the future.

1

Lest We Forget

All too often people are confronted with the state and county bar associations' disinformation campaign. These organizations assert that we don't need a Living Trust because the probate process is simple and quick, or that the Living Trust has been promoted as the answer to preserving federal estate taxes for both husband and wife, and now that the estate tax exclusion has been substantially increased (for the present), many estates are no longer subject to such taxes, so the Living Trust is unnecessary.

We tend to forget the primary purpose of the Living Trust: to avoid the cost, time, and agony of probate.

Thus, I would like to take this opportunity to give you an overview of the origins of the Living Trust, the more recent history of probate in this country and why you want to avoid it at all costs, why you want a Living Trust, and how to recognize some potentially serious pitfalls.

HUMBLE BEGINNINGS

We can trace the Living Trust back to Roman law. Its origins go as far back as A.D. 800.

Because the British Isles were long occupied by the Romans, English peasants adopted the Living Trust to protect their lands from abusive kings and nobles. It was common for the king or noble to accuse a peasant landowner of some crime so that the land could be appropriated. The peasants' answer to this practice was to place their land in a Living Trust where it was protected from seizure. Isn't that where we are today? We need to protect our hard-earned land and assets from the hands of the probate attorneys.

English peasants adopted the Living Trust to protect their lands from abusive kings and nobles.

The Source of Our Probate System

Our probate system comes from English law. At the time this country was formed, England had three systems of probate: the king's courts, also called "common law courts," which were the most complex, time-consuming, and costly, to handle land; "ecclesiastical courts," a vast improvement, to handle personal property; and "equity courts," an even greater improvement, to expedite transfer of fiduciary property such as stocks and bank accounts. We could have chosen any one or all three. We chose the most complex system—the king's court, or "common law court." It is also of note that while England has modernized its entire probate system, we remain in the dark ages. It is still an ordeal to go through probate in England, but according to one author, it takes seventeen times longer and costs one hundred times as much in the United States to transfer a deceased person's wealth to survivors.

We chose the most complex system—the king's court, or "common law court."

Norman Dacey as a Modern-Day Pioneer

The abuse of the probate system in this country defies imagination. In 1965, Norman Dacey published a book called *How to Avoid Probate*. He was our pioneer. This book was a masterpiece of probate horror stories. Dacey lived in Connecticut and worked in New York, so his accounts came from these Eastern states. In response to his book, the legal fraternity had him jailed for the unauthorized practice of law. He was released after three months on the basis of the first amendment—which he had not violated, but the legal system had. That incident turned out to be the best possible publicity for the book. For the first time, people began to read of the true horror stories that were happening to their estates in probate. Dacey recommended that people get a Living Trust. He eventually learned that this recommendation proved fruitless because he was relying on the legal fraternity to satisfy clients' requests.

The abuse of the probate system in this country defies imagination.

The Response of the American Bar Association

As a response to the growing anxiety of the American public regarding the probate process, the American Bar Association formed a committee to revise the probate system. In 1968, the committee completed its work, producing what is known as the Uniform Probate Code. It was designed to substantially simplify the probate process and, as a result, it would seriously reduce the time, cost, and agony of probate. The chairman, a well-known professor of law, declared that all states must adopt this code and that "failure to do so would bring the wrath of the American people down on the legal profession in twenty years." Most state legislatures rejected this revision outright. A few accepted it in name only, having emasculated all of its provisions.

Early Studies of Probate

Prior to and during this period, it was standard practice for local bar associations to poll their probate attorneys and ask them to review their files to determine the average fee they were charging for probate. Results of the poll were then published to all of the association's members. I remember seeing the results of the Los Angeles County Bar Association poll a number of times. The typical cost was 8 to 10 percent of the gross estate. (The gross estate is the total estate before deducting any liabilities, such as the mortgage on a home.)

The Antitrust Decision

In 1968, the Government Antitrust Division found that the bar associations were using this method as price-fixing. They were in essence telling their members what they were to charge for probate. This stung the legal profession—and they haven't conducted a probate study or published any results since.

Probate as a Monopoly

Settling estates through probate is a monopoly that attorneys are loath to give up without a fight. It is an example of what is very often a "simple" matter, of which Chief Justice Warren Burger commented, "There are a host of relatively simple transactions where ordinary folk must employ lawyers because our profession has a monopoly. In all too many cases . . . clients are 'ripped off' by fees that are greatly out of proportion to the complexity of the transaction of the time spent by the lawyers."

"There are a host of relatively simple transactions where ordinary folk must employ lawyers because our profession has a monopoly. In all too many cases . . . clients are 'ripped off' by fees that are greatly out of proportion to the complexity of the transaction of the time spent by the lawyers."

THE AARP STUDY—THE FIRST DEFINITIVE ANALYSIS OF THE PROBATE PROCESS

After the antitrust ruling of price-fixing against the bar associations, there were no more published reports on the time or cost of probate until the American Association of Retired Persons conducted an extensive two-year study of the probate system. The study was published in 1990 and is titled *A Report on Probate: Consumer Perspectives and Concerns*. Within months, AARP put the study on the back shelf after the Will and probate attorneys came in with big money to publish the ads in AARP's magazine declaring that probate wasn't really that bad.

AARP's study was exhaustive and condemning. Consider:

- The purpose of probate is to pay creditors, but according to Professor John Langbein, "Even creditors who traditionally use probate are now beginning to question the system's usefulness."
- Joint tenancy is not the answer. The study found that a startling 90 percent of all estates of widows and widowers age sixty and above would go through probate because their assets were held in joint tenancy or as community property. They also lose one of their federal estate tax exclusions because the assets of the deceased spouse passed to the surviving spouse.
- Probate is a "cash cow" for attorneys. Indeed, small firms of one to ten attorneys dominate the probate practice. Probate doesn't just pay their bills; they make a good living at it.
- The Will is the attorney's assurance that he or she will eventually probate the estate. These attorneys often write a Will as a "loss leader," knowing that they will more than make up the difference when they probate the estate. The study also established that many of these "loss leader" Wills were poorly drawn.
- The study concluded that the probate process is both costly and time-consuming. The average process took one year and five months and consumed 5 to 10 percent of the gross estate. AARP even documented cases in which attorney fees consumed 20 percent or more of the estate value.
- The study further concluded that time to completion is lengthened by redundant reporting requirements and flexible deadlines that are often unenforced or ignored.
- Education is needed. Specifically, the study recommended that "aging organizations should provide information to older consumers about estate-planning issues, including (1) information about the procedural and cost problems of probate . . . [and] (2) information about alternatives to probate such as living trusts." Among the study's recommendations was that "state and local bar associations should require members of the bar, when drafting a will, to disclose the ultimate cost of the probate proceeding."

Probate is a "cash cow" for attorneys. Indeed, small firms of one to ten attorneys dominate the probate practice. Probate doesn't just pay their bills; they make a good living at it.

The Cost of Probate to the American Public

AARP reported that the probate process, in 1989, cost the American public $25 billion annually. In 1997, our study concluded that the figure was more like *$50 billion annually*, but, because of the recent stock market debacle, I use the more conservative figure of $25 billion annually.

MY DISCOVERY OF THIS REMARKABLE SOLUTION TO PROBATE

In 1970, I learned about the Living Trust for the first time. Having just gone through the probate process for my father, I was incredibly impressed with the simplicity of a Living Trust. For the next ten years, I told all of my investment clients that they must go to their local attorney and get one of these great estate preservers. It took me those ten years to discover that in many cases, one of the following situations occurred:

- The attorney convinced the client that a Living Trust wasn't needed because the probate process was so quick and inexpensive.
- The attorney drew up a Living Trust that wasn't worth the paper on which it was written.
- The attorney didn't put the client's assets in the Living Trust.
- The client didn't put the Living Trust into effect because he or she didn't understand it.

I then tried to recommend specific attorneys who I felt drew a decent Living Trust. It was still to no avail.

If You Want to Do It Right, You Invariably Have to Do It Yourself

In August 1982, with the help of a very knowledgeable trust attorney, I formed a company in Westlake, California, called The Estate Plan, created for the sole purpose of providing the Living Trust for my investment clients.

I was a Registered Investment Advisor, and in those days I gave financial planning seminars and concluded each with an explanation of the need for a good Living Trust. As we reviewed the comments of the attendees, we realized that 70 percent of our audience were coming to the seminar to learn about the Living Trust. So, I changed my focus and began giving Living Trust seminars. To date, I have given more than three thousand Living Trust seminars nationwide.

The Emergence of *The Living Trust*

A publishing agent who attended one of my seminars suggested that I write a book. Urged on by both my clients and my agent, over the next few years I began to stay at the office for another hour or two each evening and simply dictated what my clients and I had discussed. From this, the book *The Living Trust* evolved.

Published in June 1989, it became a bestseller almost overnight and projected our Living Trust company nationwide. I revised the text in 1993, 1997, and, for this edition, in July 2002. In 1989, we created a new company, The National Estate Plan, to meet the overwhelming demand. To date, we have done more than sixty thousand Living Trusts nationwide through some five hundred advisers working with attorneys and have settled more than ten thousand Living Trusts with nary a problem.

We created a new company, The National Estate Plan, to meet the overwhelming demand. To date, we have done more than sixty thousand Living Trusts nationwide through some five hundred advisers working with attorneys and have settled more than ten thousand Living Trusts with nary a problem.

The Move to Reno

In 1994, I became very dissatisfied with California's antibusiness sentiment. Corporate and personal income taxes were strangling us, and California's workers' compensation program was completely out of control. The company looked at a number of states as possible relocation sites and chose Nevada because of the commitments made to us by state and county officials. I am happy to say that every one of those commitments has been more than fulfilled. Even more important, the company received an unexpected bonus: the Nevada people have that Midwest work ethic, a sharp contrast to the California worker's belief that "you owe me."

An attorney recently said to me, "What good can come out of Reno?" I didn't justify his comment with a retort—it didn't need any. We know what we have here, and we appreciate it. We also appreciate that our home in Incline Village, just forty-five minutes from Reno, is on the north shore of Lake Tahoe, one of the most beautiful locations in the nation.

THE BATTLE BEGINS

The story doesn't end there. The legal profession has done everything possible to try to stop us.

The legal profession has done everything possible to try to stop us.

In late 1991, I returned home from a series of seminars and found a fax from the attorney general of the state of Washington, who demanded that my wife and I appear in his office within the next few days with a list of all of our community property, which he purported to acquire because we were practicing law without a license.

We engaged the very reputable law firm of Lane, Powell, Spears, and Lubersky. With their astute guidance, David Boerner, an expert in legal ethics and dean of the Puget Sound School of Law (now the Seattle School of Law), established that our presentation was absolutely legal. Moreover, Professor William Oltman, an expert in Living Trusts, reviewed our documents and determined that they met all requirements.

The icing on the cake was an intensive study of probate in the state of Washington, conducted by Peterson Consulting. The report, titled *Study of the Average Cost and Average Length of Probate in the State of Washington*, was most revealing. The findings mirrored those of the AARP study. According to the researchers, the average cost of probate was 8 to 10 percent of the gross estate, with the average time of probate ranging from eighteen to twenty-four months. The study was conducted in 1992 and addressed probate cases opened in 1988, under the assumption that most would be closed by the time of this study. As it turned out, 22 percent of the 1988 cases remained open. We specifically researched estates that exceeded $10,000, but it was noted that estates under $10,000 had an average probate cost of 19.8 percent, with one as high as 75 percent. There was no way one could conclude that probate was anything but barbarous. As a result, the attorney general gave us a rare Letter of Assurance that our documents and process were appropriate.

Truth Isn't Necessarily the Byword
The challenges continue. In the early '90s, the California Bar Association formed a special committee called The Truth Squad. Its primary objective is to use every form of public communication to disinform the public about Living Trusts. Many other bar associations have followed with similar campaigns. Two examples are Maryland and New York. In Maryland, the bar association provides a manual and a website that state that probate is simple and economical, claiming that any estate up to $750,000 can be settled for only $700. Likewise, *Newsweek* and the *Kiplinger Letter* both published articles representing that probate was simple in New York, taking only thirty to sixty days. Last year, we conducted a probate study in Maryland, followed by another study this year in New York. The results were always the same: consumption of 8 to 10 percent of the gross estate and at least eighteen to twenty-four months to settle.

To this review I will add one more pertinent comment by Chief Justice Burger: "The greatest number of client complaints is about incompetence, neglect, and procrastination." Whitney North Seymour Jr. has reported that 80 percent of the client complaints to the Association of the Bar of the City of New York deal with the lawyer's failure to perform his or her professional responsibilities promptly, or at all.

"The greatest number of client complaints is about incompetence, neglect, and procrastination."

PROBATE IS TO BE AVOIDED AT ALL COSTS
The simple truth is that the probate process is a monster. It is costly, time-consuming, and agonizing. I've personally settled more than one hundred Living Trusts. I have seen what happens to widows with Living Trusts as opposed to those who go through probate. The widow going through probate puts her life on hold during the eighteen to twenty-four months of the probate process. It's only at the conclusion that she learns how much money she will have to live on. That's agony. In contrast, the widow with a Living Trust comes in a week to ten days following the death of her spouse, and within an hour we can resolve all

of the basic issues. Her typical question is, "Can I go and be with my children (typically in another state) to get my life in order?" The answer is always yes, and she'll return in four or five months with her life in order. That's why I do what I do.

The simple truth is that the probate process is a monster. It is costly, time-consuming, and agonizing.

Be on Your Guard

Unfortunately, there is not a happy ending. In recent years, numerous Trust mills have arisen to sell you an inexpensive Trust as the *basis* of ultimately selling you something else, such as poor quality annuities that pay the agent a large commission. These Trusts leave much to be desired. Often the assets are not placed in the Trust and, most important, the Trust mill is not going to be around when the Trust needs to be settled.

The California insurance commissioner recently issued a warning titled "Living Trust Mills and Pretext Interviews." This notice warns that individuals selling annuities are unlawfully using the offer of a Living Trust as the means of obtaining an interview with unsuspecting clients and then eliciting the client's financial data. The clear implication is that their disservice is in providing a Living Trust as well as poor annuities. I agree that Living Trust mills have done all of us a great disservice and bring discredit on our industry. In far too many cases, these individuals are using the Living Trust as their means of promoting less-than-acceptable annuities. Nevertheless, to condemn the industry as a whole is unjust. In the more than twenty years in which we have been in business, we have provided more than sixty thousand Living Trusts and have settled well in excess of ten thousand Living Trusts without any problem.

Of course, the very fact that these Trust mills have provided clients with a Living Trust is anathema to the legal profession. How dare anyone divert individuals from the probate process? That's an outright attack on the income of the legal fraternity. My concern with

the Living Trusts provided by the Trust mills is more to the point. I would ask the following questions:

- Are the provided Living Trusts competent?
- Are the assets placed in the Living Trust, including the home?
- Does the client understand the Living Trust?
- Will the individual or company be around to settle the Living Trust when the time comes?

Granted, using the Living Trust to sell bad annuities is a violation of business ethics and a disaster for the client, but let us not throw the baby out with the bathwater.

Beware of False Prophets

I recently issued the following warning to our clients: "There are numerous Trust mills operating throughout the country targeting seniors, using unscrupulous and aggressive telemarketers who have just enough knowledge to be dangerous. They will attack anyone's Living Trust and will use any scare tactic to get an appointment. The result is usually that an unaware buyer is sold a miserable Living Trust, with the ultimate objective being to market some other product of questionable quality (such as annuities). Don't be misled. If you are contacted, or harassed, by one of these telemarketers who tells you that your Trust should be replaced or changed—don't give the message any credence."

I suggest that you read the client letter included near the end of Chapter 3, which cites just this type of situation.

The Legal Fraternity Decides to Join the Living Trust League Rather than Fight

Many members of the legal fraternity have decided that it is easier to join the Living Trust forces rather than fight the Will and Probate battle. Most of the resulting Trusts are simplistic; if your heirs have a problem in the future, the attorney can always resolve it—for a fee. The most insidious feature, however, is the settlement process. It has become standard for an attorney to take a Living Trust through an unnecessary administrative procedure, much like the probate process. Not only does this step take unnecessary time, but also the typical fee is 5 percent of the gross estate. That's an improvement over the probate fee—but not by much. And it is totally unnecessary.

Many members of the legal fraternity have decided that it is easier to join the Living Trust forces rather than fight the Will and Probate battle.

Combating a National Disgrace
In an effort to improve our service to communities nationwide, I created a nonprofit corporation, The Abts Institute for Estate Preservation, through which we give our advisers the most extensive estate-planning training possible and then award them with the title of Certified Estate Planning Professional (CEPP). We follow up annually with advanced institutes. If an individual fails to continue his or her education or to maintain our standard of ethics, we withdraw the CEPP credential.

REVIEW YOUR TRUST
How is your Living Trust? My wife has an aunt whom we just moved into an assisted-living facility in southern California. Years ago, I offered to do her Living Trust, but I never force myself on family members—or anyone else. She chose instead to get her Living Trust from a close friend and church member. While this man is a fine attorney with impeccable credentials, the Living Trust is not his specialty. He did the very best he could. Some months ago, she asked me to review the Trust and make any appropriate changes. I have spent the last two months consumed with rewriting and undoing what could have been a disaster. This was particularly important to me because my brother-in-law, whom I love dearly, is the successor trustee. I wanted to spare him the months of pain that he would have had to endure. Again, I must ask, how is your Living Trust?

If you have a Living Trust now, maybe it's time to get it reviewed to be sure that it's going to accomplish the goals for which you created it. A key question to ask is, "What will it cost to settle the estate?" And if I were you, I would get the answer in writing.

2

The Agony of Probate

When most people die, their estates are settled via the frustrating and agonizing process of probate—a costly legal procedure that usually consumes at least a year or more. However, with proper estate planning, estates can be settled in less than an hour at little or no cost!

The question "Why should I have a Living Trust?" can best be answered first by showing you what can happen to your estate—the agony through which your heirs must suffer and the monetary consequences that can befall even the most meager estates—if you do not have a Living Trust. Then it will be much easier for you to understand the many tangible advantages that can accrue to your estate if you have a Living Trust. Later chapters will introduce you to several additional advantages a Living Trust can provide for your peace of mind. A well-written Trust will handle many contingencies that may occur during your lifetime. A Living Trust is just that—a Trust that is a living document providing many advantages to you while you are living as well as after you pass away.

THE MOST IMPORTANT ADVANTAGE OF A LIVING TRUST

The single most important reason for having a Living Trust is to *avoid probate*. Some years ago, the American Bar Association (ABA) strongly recommended that every state revise its probate code because these codes had become bureaucratic and abusive. A few states gave only lip service to the ABA's admonishment, and the rest of the states simply rejected outright the association's recommendation.

In the United States today, probate is one of the most agonizing and expensive experiences in which an individual can participate. To name someone as the executor of your Will (which means that the individual will eventually take part in the probate process) is to place an incredibly painful burden upon that individual. I would not wish that experience on my worst enemy.

The single most important reason to have a Living Trust is to avoid the cost and agony of probate.

Upon the death of a spouse or a parent, the surviving spouse and/or children, in effect, have to leave the past and start their lives anew. However, those people enduring the eighteen months to two years of probate remain suspended in the never-never land of their past. Only after the probate process is complete can the survivors really make a fresh start.

In contrast, the estates of clients who have established Living Trusts are settled within less than an hour. Within a week to ten days following the death of a spouse or parent, these people can stop mourning and realize that they can return to an active, productive way of life. Typically, the surviving spouse or children return to our office some four or five months after the estate is settled to reposition their assets (for example, change their stock portfolio from growth stocks to income stocks). By this time, the survivors' lives are usually back in order.

Our clients contrast sharply with people going through probate with their lives on hold—which is part of the agony of probate. Avoiding the probate process is the most important reason why the Living Trust is the best way to hold assets.

THE OLD WAY VS. THE NEW

In days gone by, almost everyone thought it was a good idea to have a Will, but now more and more people are becoming aware of the advantages of having a Living Trust rather than a Will. The following examples illustrate some startling differences between having a Will and having a Living Trust:

Laura Haines left an estate of $130,000 in cash. A year and a half later, the estate was finally settled and funds were released. Settlement of the estate cost $8,500. Howard Murphy, a grown man, broke down in tears over the sheer frustration of administering his father's estate of $600,000. Robert Courtland had to leave medical school while the administrators haggled over his father's estate of $8 million, which included funds for Robert's tuition.

In contrast, Mary Carson's estate of $180,000, Donald Scott's estate of $350,000, and Jim Boswell's estate of $1.4 million were each settled in less than an hour—and cost nothing to settle.

The estates in the second group were no less complex than the estates in the first group. The difference between the sets of examples is that each of the people in the second group had his or her assets in a Living Trust—and each estate was organized.

Most people spend their lifetimes putting assets together, but these people give little thought to how, upon their death, their assets will be transferred to their heirs. People assume that all of their personal assets, personal effects, business assets, insurance, and government benefits will go to their heirs. However, this presumption is not so, according to a study by the Estate Research Institute, an organization well known for its extensive research and professional publications in the area of estate planning. As shown in Figure 2-1, this study indicates that 10 percent to 70 percent of a deceased person's assets will be siphoned off by probate fees, federal estate taxes, state inheritance taxes, and other costs!

Unfortunately, the topic of probate results in more misinformation, myths, and just plain old wives' tales than any other subject I know. In fact, most people do not even have Wills. However, those people who do have Wills usually have outdated ones. Conversely, if a Living Trust is properly written (and covers the multitude of contingencies that could arise), it should not need to be updated except to meet changing personal situations, such as different successor trustees, a change in beneficiaries, or modifications to allocation and distribution of assets.

Everyone should know that the process of settling an estate can be incredibly costly, time-consuming, and frustrating. I have watched grown men cry over the sheer frustration of probate. I have watched stock values deteriorate while the legal process moved forward with laborious and painful slowness. I have watched valuable businesses, built through years of hard work, falter and die in the probate process. I have watched small estates be almost entirely consumed by legal fees. The tragedy is that none of this frustrating process is necessary—with proper estate planning.

The time and expense of preplanning—that is, creating a Living Trust—are minuscule in relation to the results of no planning. For example, having a Living Trust drawn up properly usually costs anywhere from $1,200 to $1,800, and occasionally as much as $3,500.

However, the probate cost of settling an estate even as small as $100,000 for a married couple would typically be $12,000 ($4,000 on the first person to die and $8,000 on the second person to die). These figures assume a probate cost of 8 percent, which is reasonably conservative. The probate cost for larger estates would be proportionately greater. Yet, regard-

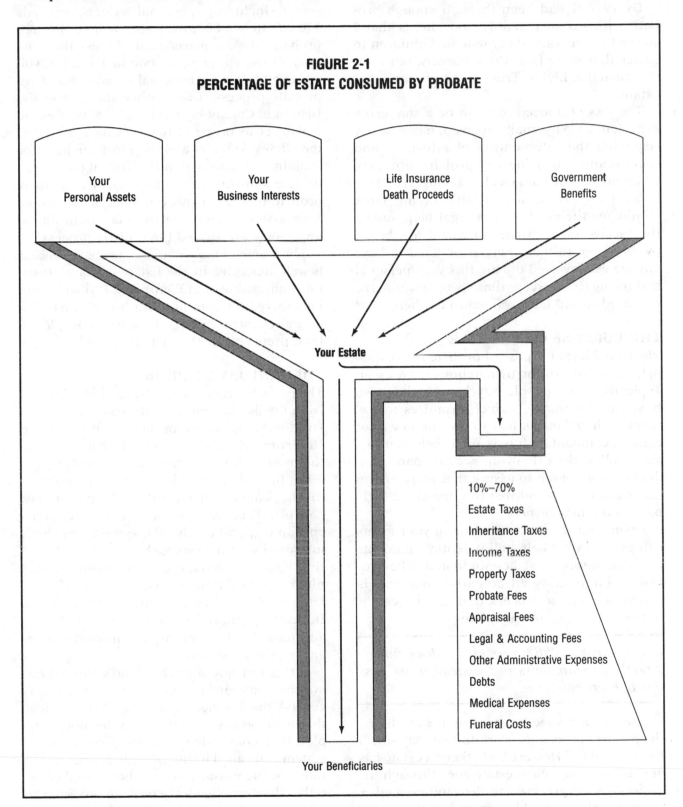

FIGURE 2-1
PERCENTAGE OF ESTATE CONSUMED BY PROBATE

Your Personal Assets

Your Business Interests

Life Insurance Death Proceeds

Government Benefits

Your Estate

10%–70%
Estate Taxes
Inheritance Taxes
Income Taxes
Property Taxes
Probate Fees
Appraisal Fees
Legal & Accounting Fees
Other Administrative Expenses
Debts
Medical Expenses
Funeral Costs

Your Beneficiaries

less of the amount of money involved in setting up a Trust, it is *insignificant* in relation to the human trauma of going through the probate process.

By 1974, I had been through enough probate with my own family and clients that I swore I never wanted my wife and children to suffer that same fate. Consequently, our family created a Living Trust and organized our estate.

The loss of a loved one can be a shattering experience. Why make it even more so by requiring the intervention of attorneys and accountants (in using the probate process), when none is needed (with a Living Trust)?

Most important, a revocable Living Trust eliminates the need to seek legal help, unless the survivor(s) or trustee(s) would feel better by doing so. In fact, there is no need to have anyone get involved during this very personal and trying time, except those people whom the deceased would have wanted to be there.

THE PURPOSE OF PROBATE

The stated legal purpose of probate is to establish clear title to, or ownership of, an asset. Typically, when people buy homes, they also buy "title insurance," which promises to pay them if their land is lost to an unknown but rightful claimant. Before issuing such an insurance policy, the title insurance company conducts a title search to assure that there are no other claimants—and that the title can clearly pass to the new owners.

Upon your death, before title to your assets can pass to your heirs, all potential claimants to those assets must be eliminated. The process of eliminating all potential claimants is called probate, a process that can be costly, time-consuming, and agonizing.

If you have a Will, your estate does not go directly to your heirs but instead must pass through probate.

Used as a protective process for creditors, the probate process is overkill. You may say, "I have no debts." However, whether an estate has any debts or not, each estate goes through the same probate process—to determine whether unknown claims could exist against the estate.

THE PROCESS OF PROBATE

The size of an estate determines whether an estate must be probated. For most states, if real estate holdings exceed $10,000 or if the total estate, including personal effects, exceeds $30,000 to $60,000, the estate will go through probate. If your gross estate is less than the amount shown for your state in Table 2-1, you are eligible for an informal or administrative probate process. In all other states, and the District of Columbia, every dollar of your estate is subject to probate! If your estate is within the allowable limits and therefore qualifies for avoiding probate, a simple affidavit procedure may be substituted for the lengthy and costly probate process. However, since most people have assets that exceed the maximum limits, few people are spared the probate process.

The tremendously complex probate process is well illustrated by the Estate Research Institute's chart shown in Figure 2-2. Probate is not only incredibly complex, but it is also psychologically destructive at a time when people are least prepared for the mental stress.

THE HISTORY OF PROBATE

The probate process came to the United States from English law, which is the basis for all constitutional and common law in this country. Unfortunately, the founding fathers adopted the most complex of the English probate systems. In medieval England, land was probated in the king's courts, called "common law courts." Proceedings were complex, time-consuming, and costly. The system was vastly improved with the establishment of "ecclesiastical courts" to handle personal property simply and expeditiously. "Equity courts" were later established to expedite title transfer of fiduciary property, such as stocks and bank accounts. England eventually modernized its entire probate system.

Instead of adopting England's three-court system (common law, ecclesiastical, and equity courts), the American founding fathers heaped the entire process together into the more complex, time-consuming, and costly common law system and called it the "probate court." Unfortunately, the passage of time has complicated, rather than simplified, the probate process. Our system of probate in the United States today

TABLE 2-1
MAXIMUM ESTATE VALUE TO AVOID PROBATE

	All Assets	Real Estate	Spouse		All Assets	Real Estate	Spouse
Alabama	$ 3,000			Montana	$ 7,500		
Alaska	$ 15,000			Nebraska	$ 10,000		
Arizona	$ 30,000	$50,000		Nevada	$ 25,000		
Arkansas	$ 50,000			New Hampshire	$ 10,000		
California	$100,000			New Jersey	$ 5,000		
Colorado	$ 27,000			New Mexico	$ 30,000		$30,000 + homestead
Connecticut	$ 20,000						
Delaware	$ 20,000			New York	$ 10,000		
D.C.	$ 15,000			North Carolina	$ 10,000		$20,000
Florida	$ 20,000			North Dakota	$ 15,000		
Georgia	$ 2,500			Ohio	$ 35,000		$85,000
Hawaii	$ 20,000			Oklahoma	$ 60,000		
Idaho	$ 25,000			Oregon	$140,000	$90,000	
Illinois	$ 50,000			Pennsylvania	$ 25,000		
Indiana	$ 15,000			Rhode Island	$ 10,000		
Iowa	$ 15,000			South Carolina	$ 10,000		
Kansas	$ 10,000			South Dakota	$ 10,000		
Kentucky	$ 10,000			Tennessee	$ 10,000		
Louisiana	$ 50,000	no real estate		Texas	$ 50,000		
Maine	$ 10,000			Utah	$ 25,000		
Maryland	$ 20,000			Vermont	$ 10,000		
Massachusetts	$ 15,000			Virginia	$ 10,000		
Michigan	$ 15,000			Washington	$ 60,000		
Minnesota	$ 20,000			West Virginia	$ 50,000		
Mississippi	$ 20,000			Wisconsin	$ 10,000		
Missouri	$ 40,000			Wyoming	$ 70,000		

takes seventeen times longer and costs one hundred times more to transfer a deceased person's wealth to survivors than the currently revised system in England.

In the mid-1960s, efforts to modernize the probate system through adoption of the so-called Uniform Probate Code were conceived as joint projects of the American Bar Association and the National Conference of Commissioners on Uniform State Laws. The project attempted to bring some order to a system that was so archaic and complex that few, if any, of the country's scholars of jurisprudence could find any redeeming value in it at all.

Unfortunately, the Uniform Probate Code ran into such universal opposition that it was either rejected outright or, where adopted by certain states, watered down to such an extent that one legal scholar said, "One wonders whether the original writers of the model code would recognize their own work."

THE COST OF PROBATE
As one legal scholar expressed it so well, "The cost of probate expands to consume the money available." Although said with tongue in cheek, the remark was also an attempt to encourage the legal profession to reform a system that has become scandalously consumptive.

A nationwide survey of probate and administrative costs was published in 1977 by the Estate Research Institute. Table 2-2 shows the relative consistency of the probate cost—as a percentage of the estate. Note that the fees are

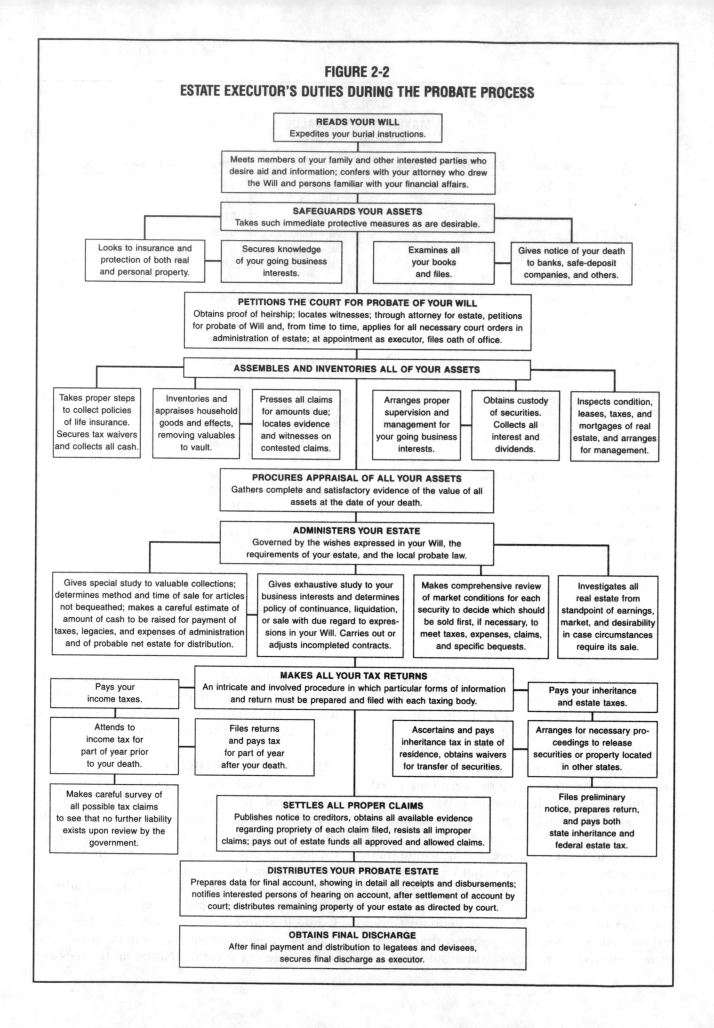

FIGURE 2-2
ESTATE EXECUTOR'S DUTIES DURING THE PROBATE PROCESS

READS YOUR WILL
Expedites your burial instructions.

Meets members of your family and other interested parties who desire aid and information; confers with your attorney who drew the Will and persons familiar with your financial affairs.

SAFEGUARDS YOUR ASSETS
Takes such immediate protective measures as are desirable.

Looks to insurance and protection of both real and personal property.

Secures knowledge of your going business interests.

Examines all your books and files.

Gives notice of your death to banks, safe-deposit companies, and others.

PETITIONS THE COURT FOR PROBATE OF YOUR WILL
Obtains proof of heirship; locates witnesses; through attorney for estate, petitions for probate of Will and, from time to time, applies for all necessary court orders in administration of estate; at appointment as executor, files oath of office.

ASSEMBLES AND INVENTORIES ALL OF YOUR ASSETS

Takes proper steps to collect policies of life insurance. Secures tax waivers and collects all cash.

Inventories and appraises household goods and effects, removing valuables to vault.

Presses all claims for amounts due; locates evidence and witnesses on contested claims.

Arranges proper supervision and management for your going business interests.

Obtains custody of securities. Collects all interest and dividends.

Inspects condition, leases, taxes, and mortgages of real estate, and arranges for management.

PROCURES APPRAISAL OF ALL YOUR ASSETS
Gathers complete and satisfactory evidence of the value of all assets at the date of your death.

ADMINISTERS YOUR ESTATE
Governed by the wishes expressed in your Will, the requirements of your estate, and the local probate law.

Gives special study to valuable collections; determines method and time of sale for articles not bequeathed; makes a careful estimate of amount of cash to be raised for payment of taxes, legacies, and expenses of administration and of probable net estate for distribution.

Gives exhaustive study to your business interests and determines policy of continuance, liquidation, or sale with due regard to expressions in your Will. Carries out or adjusts incompleted contracts.

Makes comprehensive review of market conditions for each security to decide which should be sold first, if necessary, to meet taxes, expenses, claims, and specific bequests.

Investigates all real estate from standpoint of earnings, market, and desirability in case circumstances require its sale.

MAKES ALL YOUR TAX RETURNS
An intricate and involved procedure in which particular forms of information and return must be prepared and filed with each taxing body.

Pays your income taxes.

Pays your inheritance and estate taxes.

Attends to income tax for part of year prior to your death.

Files returns and pays tax for part of year after your death.

Ascertains and pays inheritance tax in state of residence, obtains waivers for transfer of securities.

Arranges for necessary proceedings to release securities or property located in other states.

Makes careful survey of all possible tax claims to see that no further liability exists upon review by the government.

SETTLES ALL PROPER CLAIMS
Publishes notice to creditors, obtains all available evidence regarding propriety of each claim filed, resists all improper claims; pays out of estate funds all approved and allowed claims.

Files preliminary notice, prepares return, and pays both state inheritance and federal estate tax.

DISTRIBUTES YOUR PROBATE ESTATE
Prepares data for final account, showing in detail all receipts and disbursements; notifies interested persons of hearing on account, after settlement of account by court; distributes remaining property of your estate as directed by court.

OBTAINS FINAL DISCHARGE
After final payment and distribution to legatees and devisees, secures final discharge as executor.

TABLE 2-2
PROBATE AND ADMINISTRATIVE COSTS

Gross Estate	Probate and Administrative Expenses
$ 50,000	8.6%
$ 100,000	8.2
$ 200,000	7.7
$ 300,000	7.4
$ 400,000	7.2
$ 500,000	7.0
$ 600,000	6.8
$ 700,000	6.7
$ 800,000	6.6
$ 900,000	6.5
$ 1,000,000	6.4
$ 1,500,000	6.1
$ 2,000,000	6.0
$ 2,500,000	5.9
$ 5,000,000	5.8
$10,000,000	5.7

based on the *gross* estate, before any debts owed by the estate to other parties are deducted.

One of the leading county bar associations surveyed its membership of more than 23,000 attorneys about probate costs. The association, which published the survey results in its own journal, found that the cost of probate ranged from 8 percent to 10 percent of the gross estate.

Components of the Probate Fee

There may be two parts to the probate fee: *statutory fees* and *extraordinary fees*. Statutory fees are those fees established by a state legislature and readily referred to when someone asks an attorney about probate costs. Extraordinary fees are those fees charged for additional services—and approved by the probate court. It is common practice for attorneys to charge both statutory and extraordinary fees, and it is equally common for attorneys to receive approval, without question from the court, for these often outlandish fees. In legal jargon, the combination of these two types of fees is called *reasonable fees*. Some states allow attorneys to charge only reasonable fees. States that do not provide statutory fees allow attorneys to charge

by the hour. Unfortunately, it is very difficult to determine in advance the hours that an attorney may consume. In these cases, probate fees are unknown until it is too late. One scholar of the system reported that, in his fifteen years of active participation with the probate courts, he witnessed the reduction of only one extraordinary fee considered to be excessive—and that fee was reduced by only 25 percent!

All too often an attorney will downplay the cost of probate to a client. The attorney will show the client the statutory fees established by the state legislature and imply that these fees are the "maximum" fees. In actual practice, however, these statutory fees tend to serve as the "minimum" fees charged—with the unmentioned extraordinary fees added on to the total probate cost.

In addition, if a person happens to have a Testamentary Trust with a financial institution named as executor, the statutory fees apply both to the financial institution as executor and to the attorney who drew the Trust. In other words, the person gets to pay twice!

Basis for Computing Probate Cost

Actual costs of probate vary drastically. Costs run from 4 percent to 10 percent of the *gross* estate before any liabilities (such as mortgage or other debts) are subtracted. This cost of probate is substantiated by two nationwide studies, as well as interviews with numerous estate planners, probate attorneys, and trust officials. As a rule of thumb, many organizations simply use a flat fee of 5 percent of the estate. In calculating probate expenses, however, most authorities consider the 5 percent figure to be too conservative. Whether the probate fee is 4 percent, 8 percent, or 10 percent of the *gross* estate, such a probate cost is excessive.

The value of a gross estate and a net estate can differ significantly. Let me illustrate the difference between the two values.

Some years ago I did an estate analysis for the treasurer of a large corporation. As an executive benefit, the company provided investment opportunities for its key employees. The following example shows this particular individual's estate:

Gross estate	$5,000,000
Less: Loans outstanding	($4,500,000)
Net estate	$ 500,000

The income from the individual's investments would pay off the notes for the loans outstanding in five years—when his "net" estate would be worth $5 million. However, if the individual died before the loans were paid, a 10 percent probate fee would wipe out his entire estate ($5 million × 10 percent = $500,000)!

During the estate-planning process it was discovered that the individual had a previously unknown serious heart disease. A Living Trust was quickly established to eliminate the necessity of probate—a process that could have left this successful businessman's family destitute.

Enormity of Probate Fees

A California court recently found that $23 million was *not* an excessive probate fee! The heirs challenged the fee as excessive; however, the court ruled that it could find no "intent of malice towards the heirs" and let the probate fee stand. (Even though the estate was $1.4 billion, I still wonder how $23 million of legal expenses can possibly be justified.) Many people would thus believe the previously cited comment that the cost of probate expands to consume the funds available.

LENGTH OF PROBATE

Probate is time-consuming. Although this complex process usually takes at least one and a half to two years to complete, many cases take as long as three or four years and more. Most people assume that their individual estates are simple and therefore will pass through probate quickly. This assumption is simply false.

Some time ago an attorney and friend who had heard my frequent complaints about the probate system called to illustrate a typical case. The attorney had just left the courtroom where he had settled a widow's very simple estate worth $110,000. The estate consisted entirely of cash instruments such as savings accounts, but settling the estate had taken eighteen months, and the attorney's fee was $8,500—8 percent of the estate.

Remember that, regardless of how simple an estate appears to be, it is almost impossible to close an estate through the probate system in less than a year. Even though I occasionally do hear of an estate where probate closed in less time, far more often I hear of probates extending well beyond two years.

The main reason probate takes so long is that it is such a complex process. Summarizing the steps shown in Figure 2-3, the process can be broken down into the following sequence:

- Gathering material and filing petition
- Publishing notice to creditors
- Inventorying assets and obtaining appraisals
- Preparing accounting of assets and expenditures and filing petition for distribution and accounting
- Filing closing petition

Figure 2-3 indicates minimum and typical time periods required to accomplish each step in this sequence.

There are two other major reasons for the lengthy probate delays. First, attorneys have a natural inclination to procrastinate—put off until tomorrow what need not be done today. Many a client calls his or her attorney for a probate progress report only to hear that "it's moving along"—knowing full well that the attorney has set the case aside and is not actively working on it.

The second reason for delays in completing the probate process is more common than people would like to believe: the dishonesty of probate attorneys.

Following a television appearance, a desperate woman called me seeking any means to terminate her father's probate. The woman's father had died six years earlier, leaving her an estate of several million dollars. Sadly, the woman had yet to receive even a penny! The first attorney whom the woman had engaged

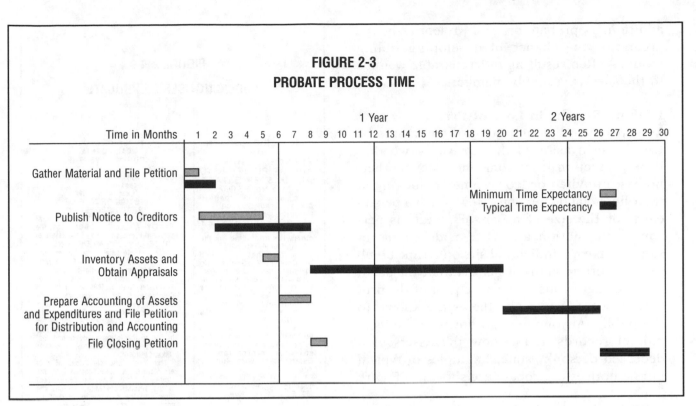

FIGURE 2-3
PROBATE PROCESS TIME

had charged enormous fees, paid from the estate, but had come nowhere close to settling the estate. The woman replaced the first attorney with another attorney, who proceeded to sue the first attorney for charging excessive fees. Six years had passed, the estate was no closer to settlement, and the woman was so frustrated with the whole process that she claimed she would gladly give up her inheritance—if only she could just extract herself from the probate process.

In this same vein, at one of my seminars a retired FBI officer told me that he had spent two years as a federal referee, investigating estates that were being exhausted of their assets by attorneys. By the time the investigations were completed, the estates were stripped bare—with nothing left for the heirs. The FBI agent saw the Living Trust as the legal means to prevent estates from being similarly drained in the future.

OTHER PROBLEMS
ASSOCIATED WITH PROBATE

Besides being cumbersome and time-consuming, the entire process of probate causes other,

related problems for individuals who must endure it.

Probate Cannot Be Stopped Once Begun
Once the probate process has started, there is no turning back. The process churns on with seemingly no end in sight. Similar to a Rube Goldberg invention, probate is a system that has grown topsy-turvy, makes little logical sense, creates work for many in the profession, and drones on without end.

Time and again I have been asked—in that special tone of anguish now so readily recognizable—whether there is any way that an individual can be extracted from the probate process. Can probate be shortened or even terminated? At seminar after seminar, I have asked hundreds of people who have gone through probate whether they would be willing to do so again, and I have always received an adamant "no!"

Probate Causes Discord
The probate process engenders contention among the family members involved. The longer the probate period continues, the greater the stress on the surviving spouse. In

addition, as probate drags on relentlessly, the greater is the chance of developing sibling rivalry—often resulting in irreparable wounds to the surviving family members.

Probate Results in Loss of Privacy

Most people religiously guard their right to be free from invasion of their privacy—whether it be protection from someone entering their homes uninvited or from someone looking at their financial documents. How much a person earns or the size of a person's estate is personal information and is considered sacrosanct. Yet, each individual sits on a time bomb set to go off upon his or her death or the death of his or her spouse—because part of the probate process is to make the estate known to the public. Anyone may go down to the local hall of records and review the assets of a deceased person's estate. Examples of typical public notices of probate are shown in Figure 2-4.

The Internet provides immediate access to some of the most famous Wills. We all remember how well Jacqueline Kennedy Onassis guarded her privacy, yet her Will is readily available on the Internet. Or how about Jerry Garcia's Will? The list goes on.

The estates of celebrities receive extensive news coverage. For example, the death in 1952 of Dixie Lee Crosby, Bing Crosby's first wife, resulted in the public's knowing about the estate. Everyone learned the size of the estate, the debts, and the cash available—as well as the cost to settle the estate. The public also learned that Bing had to sell his interest in the Del Mar racetrack, as well as his horses, in order to settle the estate and pay all of the resultant costs.

However, Mr. Crosby had learned a valuable lesson from his experience with the probate process: Within a few days of Bing's death, his legal firm in Beverly Hills announced that he had a Living Trust and that there would be no further comment. Consequently, no details of his estate have ever been made public. As a result of his Living Trust—which avoided probate—the public will never know the size of Bing Crosby's estate or who received what. Bing had learned how to preserve his privacy.

FIGURE 2-4

PUBLIC NOTICES OF PROBATE

NOTICE OF DEATH OF FRANCES L. HURLEY AND OF PETITION TO ADMINISTER ESTATE
Case No. P64967
To all heirs, beneficiaries, creditors and contingent creditors of FRANCES L. HURLEY and persons who may be otherwise interested in the will and/or estate:
A petition has been filed by Cheryl W. Graham in the Superior Court of Ventura County requesting that Cheryl W. Graham be appointed as personal representative(s) to administer the estate of FRANCES L. HURLEY.
The petition requests authority to administer the estate under the Independent Administration of Estates Act with limited authority.
The petition is set for hearing in Dept. No. 42 at 800 S. Victoria Ave., Ventura, CA 93009 on June 6, 1988, at 10:00.
IF YOU OBJECT to the granting of the petition, you should either appear at the hearing and state your objections or file written objections with the court before the hearing. Your appearance may be in person or by your attorney.
IF YOU ARE A CREDITOR or a contingent creditor of the deceased, you must file your claim with the court or present it to the personal representative appointed by the court within four months from the date of first issuance of letters as provided in Section 700 of the Probate Code of California. The time for filing claims will not expire prior to four months from the date of the hearing noticed above.
YOU MAY EXAMINE the file kept by the court. If you are interested in the estate, you may serve upon the executor or administrator, or upon the attorney for the executor or administrator, and file with the court with proof of service, a written request stating that you desire special notice of the filing of an inventory and appraisement of estate assets or of the petitions or accounts mentioned in sections 1200 and 1200.5 of the California Probate Code.
Cheryl W. Graham, Petitioner(s)
IRWIN D. GOLDRING, Esq.
Attorney(s) for Petitioner(s)
1888 Century Park East, #350
Los Angeles, CA 90067
81367
PUBLISH: May 27, 28, June 2, 1988
DV1-376476-0-9

SUPERIOR COURT OF CALIFORNIA, COUNTY OF VENTURA
In re the Estate of JOYCE D. DOBBIN, Deceased.
Case No. P 64394
NOTICE OF SALE OF REAL PRROPERTY
NOTICE IS HEREBY GIVEN that RANDY MILLER DOBBIN, as the personal representative of the estate of JOYCE D. DOBBIN, Deceased, will sell at private sale to the highest and best bidder, under the terms and conditions herein mentioned, and subject to confirmation by the Superior Court, on June 6, 1988, at 10 AM, in Courtroom 42, of the Ventura County Superior Court located at 800 S. Victoria Ave., Ventura, CA 93009, all the right, title, interest and estate of the Estate of Joyce D. Dobbin, deceased, in and to the following described real property: 626 Kendale Lane, Thousand Oaks, California.
The terms and conditions of sale are: cash, in lawful money of the United States of America. Ten percent of the amount bid to acrompany the offer and the balance to be paid on confirmation of sale by the court.
Bids or offers are invited for this property and must be in writing and will be received at the office of Pamela M. Hanover, attorney for the personal representative, at 141 Duesenberg Dr., #6, Westlake Village, CA 91362, or may be filed with the clerk of the Superior Court, at any time after first publication of this notice and before making the sale.
For further information and bid forms apply at the office of said attorney for the personal representative.
The first is reserved to reject any and all bids.
DATED: May 19, 1988.
/s/ Randy Miller Dobbin, Personal Representative of the Estate of Joyce D. Dobbin, Deceased
/s/ Pamela M. Hanover, Attorney for Personal Representative
141 Duesenberg Dr., #6
Westlake Village, CA 91362
PUBLISH: May 25, 29, June 1, 1988
DV1-376198-0-6

Probate Must Be Conducted in Every Jurisdiction Where You Own Real Estate

An area of potential frustration arises in owning real estate in more than one state. If you have property in more than one state or country, recognize that an *independent* probate will be conducted in each site on the portion of your estate that is located in that jurisdiction. If probate is costly, complex, and agonizing in your resident state, imagine what it is like in one or more absentee states or countries!

THE AGONY OF PROBATE

After seeing our audiovisual seminar on the Living Trust, an attorney said, in a manner of criticism, that he objected to the continual use of the phrase *the agony of probate*. In contrast, another attorney who participated in one of our seminars came away so moved by the intense anger expressed by so many people who had gone through probate that he summarized his feelings on paper and asked that he be given the opportunity to continue participating in the seminars. Even though the attorney professionally handled many probate cases, his attendance at the seminar was the first occasion where he had experienced being on the other side and had witnessed the sheer frustration and anger of so many people.

I have seen once-thriving businesses shrivel up and die as they were held in limbo by the probate process. I have watched large stock portfolios disintegrate to the point of being almost worthless. I have seen savings accounts remain locked in at 4 percent interest when the market rate (in 1979) was 16 percent to 20 percent. I have witnessed homes literally being given away in distress sales after standing unattended for two or more years. I have observed liquid assets being drained away by legal fees. Everything stands still—nothing can be sold— as the process of probate drones slowly on toward establishing clear title.

I watched as a widow was required to pay $6,000 for a bond in order to act as executor of her (and her deceased husband's) jewelry business. I watched as a son, a sole heir, almost had apoplexy as the court required him to purchase a bond in order to act as executor of his parents' estate.

Unfortunately, all of the mental trauma associated with probate happens during the worst period of an individual's life—following the loss of a beloved companion or parent.

For example, I remember a mother of seven young children who had recently lost her spouse. She not only had to be both mother and father, but she also had to return to college in order to complete her education, so that she could provide for her family. By day's end, the young woman was exhausted, lonely, and very frustrated over the legal paperwork of probate and over delay after frustrating delay. Too often, I found the young mother in tears. As if the loss of the woman's beloved companion were not enough, she continuously had to try to cope with an unreasonable legal system.

When a loved one dies, the survivor or survivors tend to put their lives on hold until the entire probate process is completed. However, when the probate lasts from one to two years, the process becomes excruciating.

In a study of people's perceptions of probate, 50 percent of the people interviewed, who had Wills, believed that *because they had a Will, they would avoid probate*. There is nothing further from the truth! The words *Will* and *probate* are synonymous: If thou has a Will, thou shall go through probate.

THE MYTH OF AVOIDING PROBATE

Even though probate is essentially unavoidable unless a person has a Living Trust, people are constantly relating stories about acquaintances who have avoided probate. However, such purported occurrences are almost always false. Probate *can be delayed*, but the process is inevitable.

Some Estates Avoid Probate

Occasionally, someone will mention that a parent or spouse died and the survivors did not have to go through probate. This circumstance usually means either that the estate was small—generally under $10,000 to $60,000, depending on the particular state—or that the assets were held in joint tenancy. However, even when the assets are held in joint tenancy, the estate will inevitably go through probate upon the death of the survivor. Therefore, if you are a surviving spouse, you need to create a Living Trust in order to prevent your entire estate from going through probate upon your death.

The next chapter will discuss the pitfalls of trying to use joint tenancy as a way to avoid probate.

Probate Is Not Required— Until an Asset Is to Be Sold

I am often asked whether there is a "Big Brother" standing over people to ensure that an estate goes through probate. The answer is no. No one *has* to go through probate—as long as the person does not want (or need) to sell an asset.

Many a widow or widower has come into our office to say that she or he has never gone through probate.

> A widower once told me that his wife had died seven years earlier, and he had never gone through probate. The man went on to say, "My attorney said that I didn't have to do anything." Then he asked, "Why does my tax bill still arrive with my wife's name on it?" (Obviously, his wife's name is still on the deed.)

All too often, the survivor does not realize that title to the assets still must be transferred into his or her name—until the survivor attempts to sell an asset. He or she will then quickly discover that the sale must remain on hold until completion of the lengthy process of probate—the steps of clearing title, clearing creditors, and transferring the cleared title in the name of the new owner.

MISGUIDED ADVICE

Our clients invariably ask, "Why didn't my attorney tell me about the Living Trust?" I used to believe that the reason was that the attorney would not get his or her probate fee. Attorneys talk among themselves about their "accumulated Wills," much as you and I would speak about retirement plans. The attorneys will comment to each other with pride, "I've got ten drawers of Wills," or "I've got seventeen drawers of Wills," or "I've got twenty-three drawers of Wills." Such Wills are an attorney's "retirement plan"!

However, after having given numerous three-day workshops on the Living Trust to attorneys, I have watched them become ecstatic by the third day, as they recognize the tremendous potential of the Living Trust. Most of the attorneys then admit that they had never been taught about the Living Trust in law school. Unlike the typical legal courses, which include Wills and torts, the Living Trust is included only in the extracurricular courses taught for attorneys who wish to specialize in estate planning. Consequently, even though human greed is a predominant reason why many attorneys do not steer clients away from probate, lack of knowledge or familiarity with the Living Trust can also be a major factor.

Occasionally, a client will turn to his or her certified public accountant (CPA) for confirmation about the advisability of having a Living Trust. Invariably, the CPA will respond that, since the client's estate is under $600,000, the client does not need a Living Trust. However, the CPA is talking about federal estate taxes, not about the probate process. Recognize also that a CPA's function is to account for the estate after death. In more than twenty years of practice, I have found very few CPAs who either were knowledgeable of or participated in estate planning—which is the function of reducing estate taxes and probate costs in the future. To be fair to the CPAs, however, I acknowledge that estate planning is not a normal function of a CPA.

Please remember this word of advice: If your attorney or CPA tells you that your estate will not have to go through probate or gives you a specific probate cost, ask him or her to put the statement in writing.

THE CONTESTED CREDITOR CLAIM

The probate court offers the estate a method to dispose of contested creditor claims—abnormal, frivolous, or false claims and lawsuits brought against an estate whose creditor is no longer alive to challenge them. Rather than subject the estate to a costly and long civil suit that will be heard by a jury, the probate judge, who is charged with protecting the estate, has the power to dismiss or settle such claims in only four months. However, contested creditor claims are rarely used. In fact, the AARP study stated the ". . . complicating factors, . . . such as contested creditor claims, occur in fewer than 2 percent of the cases."

To handle the rare occurrence of the contested creditor situation, a properly written Living Trust includes a provision that authorizes the trustees to withdraw any appropriate assets needed to satisfy such contested creditor claims and run them through the probate process. In this way, the probate process can be used, *but only if needed.* (In the thousands of Trusts written by The Estate Plan, we have yet to see this option exercised.)

Notice to Creditors—A New Concept

The California state legislature pioneered a new law that authorizes the trustee of a Living Trust to file a simple affidavit with the probate court and to file a notice to creditors in the newspaper to discharge any creditor claim. This law thus absolutely eliminates the need for probate, even under the possibility of a contested creditor claim. This legislation is quickly being adopted throughout the country. If you have a Living Trust and one of the parties to the Trust dies, either the husband or the wife, I suggest you contact your local probate court to see if such notice to creditors should be filed in your state. Remember, this is a major plus for a Living Trust.

THE GOOD NEWS

After having read about some of the many people who suffer so much, you can understand why I refer to the lengthy time delays, mental frustration, and costly process of establishing clear title to assets as "the agony of probate." However, the key message I wish to convey is that:

Probate is unnecessary!

With a Living Trust, upon the death of a spouse or loved one, the process of settling an estate is so simple that it may easily be done by the heirs without the intervention of attorneys or CPAs.

Every experienced estate-planning attorney I have ever met recommends the revocable Living Trust as the solution to avoiding the probate process. The following examples illustrate this point:

- George Turner, in his book *Revocable Trusts*, written for attorneys and published by McGraw-Hill, states, "[T]he most viable alternative presently available is the use of the revocable living trust."
- William Seligman wrote in the *Los Angeles Times*, "In most estates, the only one justification for not having a [living] trust is because the attorney will not get his probate fee."
- Max B. Lewis wrote in the *Reader's Digest*, "The living trust is the finest gift a husband can give his wife."
- One highly experienced estate-planning attorney feels quite strongly that attorneys who draw Wills for clients, and thus subject them to probate, should be sued for malpractice.

With these endorsements of the Living Trust in mind, I can only leave to your imagination the *real* motivation of the Will and Probate attorneys who insist that everyone should have a Will—rather than a Living Trust.

Remember: Probate is a family affair, because not only will the members of your family suffer the agony and time of probate (usually more than a year), but also the heirs will forfeit a substantial share of their inheritance—your hard-earned money—to the Will and Probate attorneys.

However, if the only purpose of probate is to pay the creditors, and the creditors do not use the process to collect debts owed them, then there really is no need for probate. Yet, unless you take action to create a Living Trust, your family will indeed go through probate. Consider my own experience: My father, who had a Will (but had no Living Trust), did not go through probate, but *I* did—for *his* estate. Similarly, if you have a Will rather than a Living Trust, you will not go through probate for your own estate, but your children will—an agonizing process that no loving parent should force on his or her children, and one that will cause your children to forfeit to the probate attorney a substantial share of what is rightfully theirs.

3

The Million-Dollar Lawsuit, or What Price Integrity?

Lawsuits of any kind can be devastating. Like the probate process, they can be extremely costly, time-consuming, and agonizing. The lawsuit that is the focus of this chapter became a challenge to my integrity, but it also yielded a powerful lesson.

From this experience I learned, for one thing, that life insurance policies, once considered valueless when the insured decides to let them lapse, can have substantial value if presented to a reputable company that offers "lifetime settlements." I also learned that attorneys can charge unconscionable rates to "settle" a Living Trust. An important development here was the Private Letter Ruling by the Internal Revenue Service that substantiates that joint (A-B and A-B-C) Living Trusts are viable in separate property states. Further, in contrast to what the bar would like you to believe about the cost, time, and agony of probate, the process in Maryland and New York follows the same pattern as in the other states. Even more important is the knowledge that litigation can be avoided and assets protected by utilizing the Offshore Trust. Finally, I learned that, in the end, even the worst situations have a silver lining.

A TERRIBLE DISCOVERY

It was the July 4 weekend, 1999. As my wife and I have done each year, we were celebrating the holiday with a family gathering and barbecue. With four children and their spouses, friends, and six grandchildren, this was a special occasion. In the midst of the festivities, the doorbell rang. I strode briskly downstairs to welcome, as I assumed, this newest guest to our party. Instead, I was greeted with a summons to appear in the Maryland Federal District Court, where my company The National Estate Plan, my book *The Living Trust*, and I were being sued for *$1 million plus punitive damages*.

The Client Was Knowledgeable

This is not the story of the little old widow. In this case, it was the daughter, who is an attorney. She bought my book and gave it to her father to read. He did so and said he "devoured it" and "was enthralled by it."

He is an educated man, a graduate of Marietta College, and a knowledgeable and successful businessman, having been the owner and president of S. T. Little Jewelry Company in Cumberland, Maryland, for some twenty years. He is also familiar with insurance and legal documents, having been the county commissioner for Allegany County, Maryland, for two terms, from 1962 to 1970. He had built a nice estate of around $1,500,000.

He is married and has three daughters, all of whom are well educated; two are attorneys, and one is a nurse with a degree in anthropology from Cornell University and a nursing degree from Maryland University. His wife, though competent, had been diagnosed with the onset of Alzheimer's disease.

The Client Seeks Our Living Trust
In the summer of 1991, he called our office and asked for a referral to one of our advisers in his area. Our office gave him the name of the nearest adviser at the time, who was located in Pennsylvania. In July of that year, the company received his workbook and prepared and sent him drafts of his A-B-C Living Trust, along with the appropriate ancillary documents. In December, we received name changes to some of the draft documents. Final documents were prepared and sent for execution. They were signed and notarized on December 23, 1991.

The Documents Must Be Approved by Local Legal Counsel
Since all of our documents must be reviewed and approved by local legal counsel representing the client, the documents were reviewed and approved by an attorney in Pennsylvania and then by the client's own attorney in Maryland. So, our documents were reviewed not just by one attorney but by two.

Our documents were reviewed not just by one attorney but by two.

Direct Communication Was Limited to One Phone Call
In the following years, our company had no further communication with this client, except for our periodic newsletter, "Living Trust Times." Then, in 1994, we sent him a letter advising that if he had one of our Insurance Trusts (which removes the insurance from the estate, as explained in Chapter 12) and had not received communication from us directly, he should let us know so that we could make a necessary amendment to meet IRS modified requirements. He recognized that he did not have our Insurance Trust and therefore did not respond to the letter. Thus, the only direct communication with this client was the one telephone call for the referral to an adviser. Personally, I had neither met nor talked to him. He knew me only through my book.

. . . the only direct communication with this client was the one telephone call for the referral to an adviser.

The Client's Objectives
This client told our adviser that he had three objectives:

- He wanted to avoid probate.
- He wanted to *eliminate* paying any federal estate or state inheritance taxes entirely.
- He wanted to provide for their children.

I must comment that while I recommend that we do everything possible to reduce the federal estate tax and state inheritance tax, I have never advocated complete avoidance. We all have an obligation to pay our rightful share of taxes, but we also have the right to appropriately reduce them.

Additional Estate-Planning Vehicles Were Recommended by the Adviser
Unbeknownst to our company or to me, the independent adviser also provided a whole panoply of estate-planning vehicles, which involved the following actions:

- August 1991, the client took a medical exam for an insurance policy.
- August 1991, he and his wife signed into effect a Foundation Trust, a special state preservation vehicle.

- August 1991, he and his wife signed into effect an Insurance Trust. (While we did not provide this Insurance Trust, it was an exact copy of our Insurance Trust.)
- December 1991, he applied for a $400,000 life insurance policy to be placed in the Insurance Trust.
- February 1992, he and his wife signed into effect a Charitable Remainder Trust (see Chapter 12).
- February 1992, Lincoln Benefit Life Insurance Company issued a $400,000 insurance policy to this individual, age seventy-six, and rated for reasons of health. (He had emphysema and was therefore considered to have a shorter life expectancy, which resulted in a higher insurance premium.) The premium was $40,000 annually for six years, and then it could rise to $68,000 for the remaining years. If interest rates were favorable, the premium could be reduced or phased out. In this case, the interest rates were not favorable.
- February 1992, he and his wife signed into effect an amendment that substantially altered our Living Trust and eliminated the C, or Q-TIP, Trust.
- They named their daughter, the nurse, as the trustee of the Insurance Trust. Each year, he would technically gift $40,000 to his children, and his nurse daughter, as trustee, would then pay the insurance premium.

The Wife Passes Away

In February 1998, the wife died of Alzheimer's disease. The following June, father and daughter took the Living Trust and other executed documents to a local Maryland attorney to have the estate settled for the wife's deceased interest. Then the fireworks began.

Insurance Is a Poor Investment

The attorney's first recommendation was to drop the insurance policy because "insurance is a poor investment." I must agree: insurance has never been a good investment. We take insurance to provide for our loved ones in the event of a premature death or to pay estate taxes to avoid substantial erosion of our estate, not as an investment. As a matter of course, I have always carried a $500,000 life insurance policy to provide for my beloved wife in the event of my demise. She is assured of this amount regardless of the circumstances, such as a stock market debacle or a significant lawsuit—as in this case. My annual insurance premium has been $50,000. It is my secure protection for my devoted companion of these many years.

Insurance has never been a good investment. We take insurance to provide for our loved ones in the event of a premature death or to pay estate taxes to avoid substantial erosion of our estate, not as an investment.

In this case, the husband had discovered in August 1992 that he had prostate cancer. Fortunately, radiation therapy was successful. Had he died, the insurance agent would have been considered a hero. According to the daughter's deposition, her father "was relieved that he had got the insurance, because he wouldn't have qualified for it after having been diagnosed with the prostate cancer."

LIFETIME SETTLEMENTS, OR DON'T FOOLISHLY GIVE UP YOUR LIFE INSURANCE BEFORE YOU KNOW ITS VALUE

While I don't wish to argue with the attorney's recommendation, I believe he did this client a great disservice. Instead of dropping the insurance policy, they should have sold it to a reputable company that offers lifetime settlements.

A number of good companies will buy existing insurance policies as an investment. Typically, they want policies of at least $100,000 from individuals with a life expectancy of thirteen years or less (as a general rule, people age sixty-five or older). The policy could be term, whole life, variable life, universal life, survivorship, adjustable life, joint first to die, or group—if convertible to an individual policy. Obviously, the larger the policy and the shorter the life expectancy, the greater will be the potential return. Here, the policy probably would have generated around $40,000, particularly since the insured was then age eighty-three.

I hope that this example will be good advice to all attorneys, CPAs, and financial advisers confronted with situations such as this in the future.

Instead of dropping the insurance policy, they should have sold it to a reputable company that offers lifetime settlements. This is not a viatical sale. A number of good companies will buy existing insurance policies as an investment.

Lifetime Settlements Are Good Investment Opportunities

A recent study by Conning & Company estimates that there is $57 billion of term insurance and $435 billion of permanent insurance in force for insureds age sixty-five and older, totaling a market of $492 billion. The researchers further estimate that $43 billion, or 75 percent, of the term insurance and $65 billion, or 15 percent, of the permanent insurance, totaling $108 billion of life insurance, is currently available for lifetime settlements. This is a nice way of saying that these policies are about to be dropped. The issuing insurance companies would like to see these policies lapse, since that is profit to them, but these are good investment opportunities for reputable investment companies. These companies can estimate when the client will die and, as the new owner of the policy, they can reasonably predict the return on their investment in the policy. A large company purchasing numerous policies will find that the insurance industry's life expectancy tables will work to their benefit.

If you—or your client—should decide to drop an insurance policy, seek a reputable lifetime settlement company. If you need help, call our customer service line, and we will be glad to direct you to the right company. Don't lose out as this individual did.

If you—or your client—should decide to drop an insurance policy, seek a reputable lifetime settlement company.

One company offers these examples of settlements:

- Universal Life policy, age seventy-seven, face amount $700,000, cash value $130,000—Policy sold for $160,000.
- Universal Life policy, age sixty-six, face amount $100,000, cash value $100,000—Policy sold for $200,000.
- Whole Life policy, age seventy-six, face amount $8,000,000, cash value $795,000—Policy sold for $2,300,000.
- Universal Life policy, age eighty-two, face amount $900,000, cash value $325,000—Policy sold for $425,000.
- Universal Life policy, age eighty-two, face amount $5,000,000, cash value $2,500—Policy sold for $700,000.

This individual failed to call us for help—and he paid a dear price. We invite our clients through our "Living Trust Times" newsletter to continue to use our company to help them resolve their estate needs. We are only a telephone call away—and we pay for the call—(800) 350-1234.

This individual failed to call us for help—and he paid a dear price.

They Want to Recover the Insurance Premiums

Presumably, the attorney was reflecting the interests of both father and daughter. Daughter, as trustee of the Insurance Trust, had said from the beginning that she felt uncomfortable paying so much in premiums to an insurance company. She said, "This is more money than I ever made in a year then." As for the father, his wife had died, his three daughters were independent, and his estate was intact. The insurance was no longer needed as a protective device.

To date (for six years), he had paid $240,000 in premiums, and they wanted the money back. They complained to the Maryland insurance commissioner, with no satisfaction. Lincoln Benefit Life Insurance Company, an affiliate of Sears, was no more helpful.

Their solution was to sue the insurance agent, the attorney who reviewed and approved the Living Trust in Pennsylvania, the attorney who reviewed and approved the Living Trust in Maryland, and of course, yours truly—as the author of *The Living Trust*—and our company, The National Estate Plan. We were supposedly the deep pocket (the potential source of big money).

HAVING AN ATTORNEY SETTLE A LIVING TRUST CAN BE A COSTLY MISTAKE

They also wanted to recover the $35,000 they had paid to the local Maryland attorney to settle the estate on the wife's behalf. This estate had not been settled per se. The attorney identified nine potential problem areas but did not seek actual resolution.

He did prepare a form for the husband to disclaim any interest in his wife's share of the estate and filed it with the registrar of Wills for Allegany County. The attorney's objective was to help protect the wife's federal estate tax exemption. However, if he felt this was an issue, he should have filed the disclaimer with the IRS. In fact, the simple solution would have been to file Forms 55 and 706 with the IRS, and the issue would have been resolved once and for all. I asked our attorney why this was not done. He said that attorneys like to identify potential problems—not necessarily solve them. It is the businessperson who seeks a solution.

Attorneys like to identify potential problems— not necessarily solve them. It is the businessperson who seeks a solution.

When I learned the amount of the fee charged to "settle" the estate, I did some quick math. The estate was worth $1,500,000. Half of that, or $750,000, would be attributed to the wife, and 5 percent of that half is $37,500. This is the typical fee charged by attorneys to settle a Living Trust. In his deposition, the attorney claimed that much of his chargeable time was attributable to discussing the case with the other attorneys in his office. If one of our advisers had settled the estate, I doubt that the fee would have exceeded $500. Then again, this Trust had been amended by someone else and was therefore no longer one of our Trusts.

The Attorney Identifies Three Potential Problems

The attorney identified three potential problems that could apply to our Living Trust:

- We used the term *tenancy by the entirety* instead of the preferred *tenancy in common*.
- Our documents elicited the age-old question of separate trusts for husband and wife versus a joint trust for husband and wife (our A-B and A-B-C Trusts) in a separate property state (as is Maryland).
- In some areas of the Living Trust, the word *he* was used inadvertently instead of *she*, and the plural pronoun was used instead of the singular.

These items were resolved as follows:

- One of the foremost authorities on Living Trusts in Maryland, George K. Reynolds III, of Miles and Stockbridge P.C., analyzed our Trust and issued an excellent ten-page analysis that concluded: "My review of the Trust document, the facts surrounding the creation and funding of the Trust, the intent of the parties in creating the Trust, and the applicable law leads to the conclusion that this Trust document was effective to obtain the federal estate tax benefits desired by the parties, and to pass assets at the death of both without the requirement to undertake any formal probate proceedings." In effect, whether the words *tenancy by the entirety* or *tenancy in common* were used was immaterial, since the construction of the Trust clearly established separate Trusts for husband and wife upon the demise of the first spouse.

- Private Letter Ruling 200101021, issued on January 5, 2001, asserted that a joint Living Trust (A-B and A-B-C) is appropriate in separate property states. This subject is discussed later in this book. We had sought our own Private Letter Ruling and were pleased to be preempted by this ruling.

- The problem with *he* versus *she*, and singular versus plural, is addressed and resolved in the "Glossary of Terms" section included at the end of each Trust. While this pronoun fault is common with computer-generated documents, we believe we essentially resolved it with our 1994 computer program.

Private Letter Ruling 200101021, issued on January 5, 2001, asserted that a joint Living Trust (A-B and A-B-C) is appropriate in separate property states.

MOTIVATION FOR THE LEGAL ATTACK WAS MY EXPOSURE OF THE PROBATE ILLS

I was attacked for the usual reason. In this book, *The Living Trust*, I openly condemn the probate process as being costly, time-consuming, and agonizing. Since probate provides the livelihood for many small law firms (one to ten attorneys—see the AARP study), I was a delicious target for these opposing attorneys. They licked their chops as they filed this lawsuit. If they could discredit me, they could discredit the Living Trust.

The Emperor's Dilemma

At this point, I must share with you the philosophy of the local Maryland attorney who had attempted to settle this estate and, in effect, generated the lawsuit. In his deposition, he cited the fairy tale of the emperor's clothes, by Hans Christian Andersen:

> I call it the emperor's dilemma.
>
> The emperor's dilemma harkens back to "The Emperor's New Clothes," where, you recall, the emperor had no new clothes, but it was told that anybody who couldn't see them was a fool or unfit for his position. So, the emperor's dilemma in these planning situations is: Do I dare tell the client, who is totally sold on probate avoidance and revocable trusts, that the emperor has no clothes? And the answer to that is yes, you tell the client, and you walk them through. And the reason I refer to that is I taught MICPEL* courses on this very subject and tried to deal with it, because attorneys really do, who are in this position, find themselves in a lot of pressure, because the clients come in with an expectation, and they can be absolutely convinced that that's what they need [a Living Trust]. . . .
>
> I've told you that I really don't think a revocable trust is necessary.

. . . in Maryland, probate avoidance, it's a red herring.

[*MICPEL is an acronym for the Maryland Institute for the Continuing Professional Education of Lawyers. This is what the attorneys in Maryland are being taught. If they are misinformed, it is because the Maryland State Bar Association is teaching them accordingly.]

From his standpoint, this frame of mind is understandable. The Maryland State Bar Association publishes brochures that say much the same thing. Included on its website under the title "Living Trusts: Get the Facts" are innumerable statements derogatory to Living Trusts. The most telling is this sentence: "In Maryland, for example, the probate fee for an estate of between $500,000 and $750,000 is $750." This was pulled off the Internet on July 25, 2000. In order to appreciate the level of disinformation of this website, consider that $750 is only *one-tenth of 1 percent* of $750,000.

The most telling is this sentence: "In Maryland, for example, the probate fee for an estate of between $500,000 and $750,000 is $750." This was pulled off the Internet on July 25, 2000.

The Maryland Probate Study

Unbeknownst to the plaintiff and his attorneys, we conducted a probate study in the state of Maryland. Dated December 2000, it was directed by Driven Business Solutions and is titled *Study of the Average Cost and Average Length of Probate in the State of Maryland*. The study reviewed 524 actual probate cases filed in 1996 and closed by October 13, 2000. In order to provide an accurate measurement of the state, five counties were reviewed: Allegany, Anne Arundel, Baltimore, Frederick, and Howard. Statistically, the confidence level of the study was 95 percent. That's as close as anyone needs to get in determining the actual time and cost of probate. We chose the year 1996 for probate filing under the assumption that most all of these cases would be closed within four years. What we found was that *18 percent of the probate estates were still open four years later.*

. . . 18 percent of the probate estates were still open four years later.

The results of this study were quite similar to those of the AARP nationwide study of 1990 and our study of Washington state probate in 1992. We found that Maryland's probate cost ranged as high as 61 percent, with two cases exceeding the reported value of the estate. Excluding these two cases, the average cost of probate ranged from 4 percent to 7 percent, depending on the size of the estate. The percentage of probate was highest for estates of $20,000 to $100,000 and lessened for larger estates.

The average cost of probate ranged from 4 percent to 7 percent. The percentage of probate was highest for estates of $20,000 to $100,000. . . .

This study flies in the face of the statement quoted from the Maryland Bar Association's website.

Why the Disparity?

The various state bar associations have actively pursued a course of disinformation to mislead the public in an effort to deter them from adopting a Living Trust. I suspect that even well-meaning attorneys begin to believe their own misinformation because they tell themselves over and over that probate is inconsequential. If we tell ourselves an untruth often enough, we begin to believe it. This was certainly true for the attorney settling the estate in this case. It is ironic that he used the story of the emperor's new clothes.

The various state bar associations have actively pursued a course of disinformation to mislead the public in an effort to deter them from adopting a Living Trust.

Hans Christian Andersen wrote about a self-centered, self-indulgent emperor who was swindled by two travelers. These travelers offered to make the emperor new clothes out of the finest material, which would become invisible to every person who was not fit for the office he held or was impossibly dull. The travelers acquired much wealth from the emperor but faked their making of the clothing. Then they urged him to dress in this new finery for his procession through the town. The emperor stood naked before his mirror but would not admit that he did not see his clothes, for that would mean he was not fit for office or was impossibly dull. His ministers, likewise, saw the ruler as naked but feared to admit that they too could not see the clothes. And so on down through all of the townspeople as the emperor paraded through the streets. Finally, it was an innocent child who called out, "But he has got nothing on."

While this story may have some merit in the attorney's quandary as to how to convince a client that he or she doesn't need a Living Trust because probate is supposedly inconsequential in Maryland, what struck me were the words that Hans Christian Andersen used to describe the travelers: *swindlers*, *crafty impostors*, and *rogues*. Given the statement on the Maryland Bar website and the Maryland probate study, I leave it to the reader to conclude how best to interpret the emperor's dilemma.

We discovered that New York has sealed its public probate records to anyone other than an attorney. This is a convenient method of avoiding any public oversight.

The New York Probate Study

Before leaving this subject, I should add that we also asked this same research firm to do a study of the cost and time of probate in the state of New York. Several years ago, *Newsweek* and later the *Kiplinger Letter* reported that probate in the state of New York was insignificant and took only sixty days to settle. We knew this was an obvious distortion, because Norman Dacey based his book, *How to Avoid Probate*, on the evils of probate, particularly in New York and Connecticut. In addition, I have the words of New York residents who have called me over the years to tell me that they went to numerous attorneys seeking a Living Trust and were rejected outright.

We discovered that New York has sealed its public probate records to anyone other than an attorney. This is a convenient method of avoiding any public oversight. In response, we hired attorneys, who did get reasonable access to many probate files, but they were stopped when it became known that the records were being sought for a probate study. Thus, we could not produce a thorough study, but we did obtain sufficient information to conclude that probate in the state of New York is at least as costly and time-consuming as was established in the other studies—if not more so.

Probate in the state of New York is at least as costly and time-consuming as was established in the other studies—if not more so.

STATE BAR ASSOCIATIONS AT WAR WITH THE LIVING TRUST

There is a determined effort on the part of state bar associations to stop the Living Trust. Many states have enacted laws that effectively prevent anyone except lawyers from writing Living Trusts. In any other form of business, we would call this antitrust discrimination or a monopoly. The sole purpose of such laws is to protect the small law firms from losing their probate business. While Europe is opening up legal documents to qualified individuals other than attorneys, U.S. attorneys are closing ranks and doing just the opposite. In many states, this has forced us to form alliances with attorneys and provide our Living Trust in an entirely different manner from the way we have done in the past.

This restriction would make sense if the attorneys were really that qualified—but most are not. Their mentality is still enmeshed in the probate concept. Moreover, they continue to aggressively disinform the public about the true cost, time, and agony of probate.

There is a determined effort on the part of state bar associations to stop the Living Trust.

Most Attorneys Are Not That Well Versed in the Living Trust

I was amazed at the deposition of the attorney who was hired by the client to review our trust,

especially given his background. This attorney attended law school at West Virginia University and graduated in May 1974. He said that his mentor was one of the leading estate planners and that he therefore geared his classes to specialize in his practice of business and estate planning. He said that he took estate-planning seminars, tax seminars, and tax classes—and had practiced law in the field of estate planning for twenty-seven years. He had attended some major conferences on estate planning, including an intensive weeklong conference in Madison, Wisconsin, sponsored by the American Law Institute and American Bar Association, and a similar conference in New Orleans. He also attended every estate-planning seminar or conference offered within driving distance. He has given lectures on postmortem estate planning, general estate planning, and use of insurance trusts—in effect, the general estate-administration planning process. In addition, he advised other lawyers and paralegals on assisting in the estate-planning administration process.

Based on this set of credentials, the person would appear to be the type of expert attorney with whom we would want to work. However, his deposition, parts of which are cited in Appendix J, leaves me with the impression that he would be one of the last individuals to whom I would want to turn for my estate planning.

The Primary Intent of the Lawsuit

The sum and substance of this lawsuit was that while an individual wanted to recover insurance premiums, this was a grand opportunity for two attorneys from two different law firms to attack and attempt to destroy me and my company—and in so doing, to discredit the Living Trust as a viable means to avoid probate. One attorney represented the client, and the other sought a class action suit.

The suit consumed almost two years of my time and cost me in excess of $300,000. They exhaustively examined our company, from its conception, including all of our policies and procedures—and found nothing wrong. They minutely examined our Living Trust and ancillary documents for any defect—with no success. Even their claimed problems were disproved.

In addition, they did a comprehensive search of my background to try to uncover any wrong that might be helpful. For one who was age seventy, that's a lot of ground to cover. At one point, my attorney asked me if I had done anything wrong in school that could be a concern, since they were pursuing those records.

I am sure they were disappointed to find that I really did graduate from the University of Southern California in 1951 with a B.S. and naval science degrees; that as a midshipman, I had been regimental commander during my senior summer cruise and battalion commander during my senior year at USC, and had received five awards upon graduation; that I had been commissioned an ensign in the U.S. Navy and served on destroyers during the Korean War, earning five battle stars and retiring as a lieutenant; and that I did attend Stanford Graduate School of Business and did graduate with my M.B.A. in 1956. This obviously did not help their cause.

The sum and substance of this lawsuit was that while an individual wanted to recover insurance premiums, this was a grand opportunity for two attorneys from two different law firms to attack and attempt to destroy me and my company—and in so doing, to discredit the Living Trust as a viable means to avoid probate.

Finally, they agreed that we had done nothing wrong and they could not find anything improper. Nevertheless, apparently attorneys cannot leave it there. There seems to be an unwritten law that plaintiff's attorneys, though having failed in the lawsuit, have a right to recover their expenses. As such, they called for a settlement agreement before a judge in which each party submits an estimate of their costs if the case went to trial. The judge acts as a mediator and each party agrees to pay the plaintiffs a fee substantially less than it would cost to pursue the case.

Prior thereto, we had to show the judge how much it could cost us if we went to court. My attorneys estimated that it would cost us $50,000 to $100,000 to try this case. I was tempted to take it all the way, to establish in court that we were right and to present our

probate studies and the Private Letter Ruling. However, I realized that we had already established that we had done nothing wrong. The lawsuit had cost some $300,000 to date, and to spend more would be imprudent and would accomplish nothing further. We had won—but it was a costly victory.

The Settlement Conference

At the settlement conference, the judge asked us to contribute $30,000 to the plaintiff's attorney's cost. I felt this was applying insult to injury, but I agreed to do so only if the client would sign a written agreement absolving us of any wrongdoing.

I required one stipulation: that the case not be sealed. In the future, anyone considering suing me or my company can go to the United States District Court for the District of Maryland (Northern Division) and look up the case of Robert L. Ebert, Individually, as Personal Representative of the Estate of the Late Elta Mae Ebert, and on behalf of all others similarly situated, Plaintiff, vs. The National Estate Plan, Inc., et al. Case No. WMN 99 CV 2596.

Establish the Facts vs. a Settlement

I cannot fault my attorneys for the time and cost of the lawsuit. I sought the best legal firm, Venable, Baetjer and Howard, LLP, and they gave me the best service ever. They clearly established that we had done no wrong, but the system is like a quagmire: once you're in it, there is no way out but through.

I was often asked by laypeople, "If they found nothing wrong, why didn't the plaintiff have to pay your legal fees?" That's the way English law works, but unfortunately, the trial attorneys are one of the strongest lobbies in the nation. To allow the English concept under which the loser pays all legal fees would be anathema to the trial attorneys. Frivolous lawsuits would cease.

The system is like a quagmire: once you're in it, there is no way out but through.

I WAS NAIVE—THE OFFSHORE TRUST

I admit my own naïveté. For years, our legal counsel had tried to convince me that I needed to protect myself, and my company, from a potential lawsuit, but I did nothing, because I couldn't imagine that anyone would sue me. After all, I had spent more than thirty years trying to help people preserve what they have worked so hard to build. Why would someone want to sue me for that? What a bitter lesson I had to learn.

From the outset, the opposing attorneys pursued me, and the company, as the deep pocket. They eventually discovered that while our company and my published books have been quite successful, I have historically reinvested the money in the company in the form of improving computer software for more accurate and better productivity of our products, for ongoing improvement of our documents, for various probate studies to justify our purpose, to defend our right to provide the Living Trust to the people in each state, and to bring the best Living Trust to our clients at the lowest cost possible. We were not the deep pocket they thought we were.

I Have Learned a Bitter Lesson

Acting on what I learned from this experience, I have now taken the company, along with its supporting organizations and my own assets, offshore. My intent is not to avoid income or estate taxes, but solely to protect these assets against future frivolous lawsuits.

I have now taken the company, along with its supporting organizations and my own assets, offshore. My intent is not to avoid income or estate taxes, but solely to protect these assets against future frivolous lawsuits.

The Offshore Trust for Asset Protection

I first learned about Offshore Trusts in 1978, when the federal estate tax was particularly abusive. I was given the history, the Offshore Trust documents, and the supporting documentation for review. I thought that if it worked, it could be an excellent estate-preservation vehicle for many of my clients. I took my material to three attorneys and asked them to review it and tell me if it would be feasible.

Three months later, I returned for an answer. Two of the attorneys told me emphatically that it wouldn't work. They hadn't done any research; they were just mouthing the general belief. The third attorney, however, had done his research and told me that if the Trust were properly drawn and administered, it would work well. Subsequently, with the adoption of President Reagan's Tax Reform Act of 1981, the Offshore Trust was no longer necessary to preserve estates from the formerly abusive and consumptive estate tax. Now, though, in today's excessively litigious society, the Offshore Trust becomes essential if one is to protect assets from frivolous lawsuits.

An Offshore Trust Requires a Knowledgeable, Competent, and Experienced Attorney

As the years passed, I became increasingly aware of the need for the Offshore Trust as an asset-protection device. On the downside, I also became aware of the many IRS regulations introduced over the years to prevent its use as a way to avoid income and estate taxes. Most important, I recognized that a knowledgeable, competent, and experienced attorney must be the one to create an Offshore Trust, in order to survive attack by the IRS.

For years, I sought such an attorney, and I finally found him in Los Angeles at the firm of Raiskin and Revitz. From now on, if anyone desires to sue me or my company, I will simply refer the party to Dan Raiskin, and that should be the end of it. I feel most comfortable in doing this now that we have been exhaustively examined and not found wanting. As noted, anyone who wants to find information about us can go to the case mentioned earlier—which will not be sealed.

THE LAWSUIT WAS COSTLY, TIME-CONSUMING, AND AGONIZING

The lawsuit cost me more than $300,000. Fortunately, I was able to borrow sufficient funds to cover it. I have since learned of others who lost their business and their home because of legal costs—and then had to default because they could not afford to continue. It's like playing a game of poker: how long can you afford to stay in the game?

The lawsuit consumed almost two years. Again, fortunately, my son was able to run the business while I concentrated entirely on the suit. My time was devoured with the required discovery, the depositions, and the documents continually filed with the court as part of the legal sparring. Instead of revising my books or contributing to the company, I was enmeshed in satisfying the legal game of survival. I consider those two years the worst waste of my time that I have ever spent. One morning, at the start of my deposition, I looked around the room and estimated that the cost of the attending attorneys was $1,250 per hour and thought, "What a waste of productivity."

The lawsuit was agonizing; it was the most draining experience that I have ever endured. After having experienced many a difficult challenge, that's saying a lot. I had spent the better part of my business life trying to help people, and now I was confronted regularly with documents alleging nearly every misdeed imaginable. Then there were the three days of deposition. I was obliged to defend myself against two opposing attorneys who were determined to destroy me. The adversary seated across from me badgered me with every conceivable ruse, guile, trick, distortion, and cunning tactic available to him. I answered the questions honestly and in detail, but that wasn't enough. They wanted answers to the hypothetical question "What if your Living Trust didn't have this wording?" I refused to answer their "what ifs?" and thus avoided falling into their traps.

The strain has taken its toll. I am still trying to recover from the deceitful allegations that I had to bear for those two years. I would do anything to avoid going through that degrading experience again. I now have an Offshore Trust as an asset-protection device.

The lawsuit was agonizing; it was the most draining experience that I have ever endured.

I recognized that ultimately the lawsuit was the result of my attacks on the Will and Probate attorneys. I don't regret the aggressive position that I have taken against these parasites on an individual's lifetime savings. Although I had been challenged time and again for some thirty years, I never realized how destructive a personal lawsuit can be. I know that it has taken years off my life. I also know that I will never go through it again, because of my Offshore Trust.

I had never met the plaintiff and his daughter until the settlement conference. When they walked in, I went over and introduced myself. His daughter made an interesting comment, "You are not what I expected." In other words, I was not the ogre that I had been made out to be.

But What About Your Built-In Legal Protections?

People knowledgeable about the law may ask why the plaintiff's case wasn't stopped because of the statute of limitations, the First Amendment right of free speech, the lack of agency, and numerous other legal defenses. The answer is that these arguments were all submitted to the assigned judge, but if the judge fails to read them or act, the arguments are simply a waste of paper and research unless and until the case goes to trial. The judge, in the meantime, hopes it will eventually go away of its own merit—as it finally did in this case.

Beware of the Frivolous Lawsuit— Anyone Is a Potential Target

I do not believe that anyone should be subject to a frivolous lawsuit. I am convinced that the only one who wins is the attorney. I therefore urge anyone who could conceivably be faced with such a suit to take the necessary steps to avoid it. I recommend the Offshore Trust as the most successful means of protecting your hard-earned assets—but most of all, to avoid the agony of actually going through the process of daily attack and deceitful allegations.

I recommend the Offshore Trust as the most successful means of protecting your hard-earned assets—but most of all, to avoid the agony of actually going through the process of daily attack and deceitful allegations.

"A Clear and Present Danger"

Stephen Moore, director of fiscal policy for the Cato Institute, astutely summarized today's trial lawyers as "a clear and present danger" to our nation's policy, to corporate income, to corporate investors, and to consumers. He notes that class action lawsuits are a boon to trial attorneys. These attorneys look for profitable companies to sue, and the rewards are unbelievable. They are effectively transferring corporate wealth from the corporations, investors, and consumers. Not only that, but also, they are doing it under the pretext that they are acting in the public interest by safeguarding the health and welfare of children, consumers, and workers. Moore points out that this money is being rechanneled back into the political system—to buy off politicians, special interest groups, and even judges. He goes on to state that the trial bar association has the financing to fundamentally transform American politics.

According to Michael Horowitz, of the Hudson Institute, "Tobacco case fees of $20 billion will alone soon give a small group of attorneys more disposable income to invest in politics than is now spent in all U.S. elections in any given year. That's $20 billion—with a 'b'— as compared to the $50 million that President [G. W.] Bush raised in his campaign for the presidency" (*Human Events*, December 17, 1999). He cites an example of the power of the legal rewards: "Sen. John Edwards of North Carolina, articulate and charming and hardworking enough to have made $40 million in accident cases, who spent $3.2 million of it to upset an incumbent." (Similar comments can be found in *U.S. News and World Report*, June 28, 1999.)

It seems that under our current form of litigation, everyone—as a consumer or stockholder—pays for the few successful attorneys in this legal warfare.

THE NEED TO CLEAR MY NAME, OR WHAT PRICE INTEGRITY?

At the onset of the case, I was introduced to an attorney with an impressive record of success. His goal was to settle the case as early as possible and for as little cost as possible. This would have been the logical approach and certainly would have saved me tens of thousands of dollars, but there was more at stake here than money: my reputation, my work over the past thirty years, my company that claimed to provide one of the finest Living Trusts, and my book that attacked the probate system. So, instead, I sought the best law firm that was knowledgeable about estate planning in order to prove that I had done nothing wrong. In other words, What price integrity?

After All of This, There Is Satisfaction

The other day, unexpectedly, I received the following letter. I appreciated this communication more than the writer could imagine, because it said so well what I have spent the better part of my business life trying to accomplish. It gave me the satisfaction of knowing that I do reach at least a few people.

In early 1998, I had read your first edition of *The Living Trust* book that I bought at Costco. I didn't know that there was a second edition.

Later in 1998, AARP sent us a letter in which we could request information on having a trust written for us. A person called, and we made an appointment. This person was an agent for a lawyer who was not connected with AARP. She showed us their services and would charge about $1,000 to write the trust—I knew from your book that this price was too low. Also, she said that they were selling an annuity that paid 18 percent a year. That raised a red flag because even in those days with a booming stock market, I thought that this was too good to be true. I believe that your book or your organization warned us that people claiming to write trusts would also try to sell such annuities.

I noticed that they didn't do A-B-C trusts and asked if they did them, and she said "No." I then showed her the list of the "Must Have Provisions" in your book and asked if their trusts contained these provisions, and she said that she didn't know but suggested that I could check with the lawyer if their trusts contained these provisions. I made contact with that office with questions about these "Must Have Provisions," and they never replied to me.

If it wasn't for your book, I wouldn't have known about A-B-C trusts and wouldn't have known about asking about these "Must Have Provisions" in your book. In November of 1998, we had our trust written by your organization.

Please feel free to use excerpts from this testimonial. . . .

Also, I believe that you have respect for AARP, because you quote from them in your book. Thus, I was surprised that they would refer us to a lawyer that didn't offer the service to write the kind of trust we wanted and that the agent they referred us to would try to sell us an 18 percent annuity.

Thank you very much.
Michael Thorner
Manhattan Beach, California

I must add here that many salespeople have falsely stated that they represent AARP, and when AARP is able to establish this deceit, it issues cease and desist orders. Unfortunately, Will and Probate attorneys exert a strong political and financial influence on AARP, and therefore, I would find this type of solicitation out of character for AARP.

A Lesson Learned

If I had it to do over, I would have established an Offshore Trust years ago. If any good has come out of this painful experience, it is that after an exhaustive examination, my company, my book *The Living Trust*, and my work over the past three decades are now unchallengeable. In addition, I have learned how to avoid lawsuits in the future. The principal lesson that I can pass on is that each one of us is potentially subject to a frivolous lawsuit—but you can do something to protect yourself and your assets. You too can protect your assets with an Offshore Trust. Remember also that before you drop your insurance policy, it can pay to check to see if it has a value.

4

Joint Tenancy: A Poor Alternative

All too often, individuals try to avoid probate by holding assets in joint tenancy. However, the use of joint tenancy has serious potential disadvantages:

- *Joint tenancy with children can be dangerous.* If you hold an asset in joint tenancy with one or more of your children, you could lose your asset. For example, if your child has an automobile accident that results in a lawsuit, the asset is subject to being lost as the result of a legal judgment, since the asset is a part of the child's estate.
- *Joint tenancy loses "stepped-up valuation."* When property is held in joint tenancy rather than as community property, half of the potential stepped-up valuation is lost. The loss of stepped-up valuation can result in very costly tax consequences.
- *Joint tenancy forfeits one of the $600,000 federal estate tax equivalent exemptions.* By passing all of your assets to your spouse through joint tenancy, you effectively "throw away" your $600,000 federal estate tax equivalent exemption (described in Chapter 5). Therefore, the surviving spouse is left with only one $600,000 exemption; then, on the death of the survivor, everything over $600,000 will be taxed, beginning at 37 percent—a very costly mistake.
- *Not all assets are held in joint tenancy.* Most estates fail to have the title to all of the assets in joint tenancy. Items that are not held in joint tenancy must go through probate.
- *Under joint tenancy, the survivor takes all.* When one of the joint tenants dies, the surviving joint tenant then owns the entire asset. Such a result may conflict with the desires of a person's Will, yet joint tenancy will always take precedence over a Will.
- *Joint tenancy does not eliminate cost.* Although joint tenancy can avoid the time and frustration of probate, it does not avoid legal costs. Most survivors will turn to an attorney to transfer the assets into the name of the survivor—at an exorbitant cost.
- *Joint tenancy does not eliminate probate.* With joint tenancy, probate is inevitable. Even though joint tenancy can avoid probate on the first spouse to die, the entire estate must go through probate upon the death of the survivor.

- *Gifted property forfeits stepped-up valuation.* When an individual gives his or her children a share of a jointly owned asset, the children forfeit the benefit of stepped-up valuation upon the parent's death. The children may also be subject to gift taxes and penalties.

JOINT TENANCY WITH CHILDREN CAN BE DANGEROUS

People should be cautious when they try to avoid probate by sharing ownership with their children as joint tenants. Entering into joint tenancy with your children will not avoid taxes that were originally due, because the practice is so common that this situation is one of the first areas looked at by the Internal Revenue Service. Entering into joint tenancy with children to avoid probate creates an additional set of problems.

- The children's share of the property becomes subject to the children's creditors—including people who win lawsuits and legal judgments against them.
- The children have an equal right to the enjoyment of the property. They may move in or create such untenable conditions that the parents are forced to move out or sell the property.

If one of the children were unable to pay his or her debts or were involved in an accident, for example, and had a lawsuit or judgment rendered against him or her, the parents' assets held in joint tenancy with the child would be subject to the child's creditors. Therefore, the parents could well lose their home (or other assets) in order to satisfy their child's creditors or judgment.

Over the past several years, seven clients of my legal associates lost their homes because they decided to go into joint tenancy to avoid probate. In these instances, the clients named their children as joint tenants. In more than one instance, a child had a serious automobile accident, and the child's interest in the home was considered to be a part of the child's assets. The family home had to be sold in order to satisfy a legal judgment against the child!

When people hold property in joint tenancy with one or more of their children, the children have an *equal* right to the enjoyment of the property.

In one particular incident, the children added on to the home, reportedly to move into the home; however, then the children decided that they would sell the home. Obviously, the mother and father refused, yet the children moved into the house and made life so miserable that the parents eventually had no alternative but to sell their home and move. For their efforts, the disillusioned parents ended up with only their share of ownership interest—one-half of the home—after the sale!

JOINT TENANCY LOSES STEPPED-UP VALUATION

Holding property in joint tenancy can be very costly to the survivor from a tax standpoint. Property held in joint tenancy loses *half* of the stepped-up valuation. However, there is a quirk in the joint tenancy law that does allow full stepped-up valuation—but *only* if the other joint tenant is a beneficiary other than the spouse and if the entire asset is included in the decedent's estate. Note that a spouse does not qualify for this tax-saving advantage! Specifically, the decedent must have gifted the specific share of the asset to the decedent's beneficiary while living, held the asset in joint tenancy, and then included the entire asset in the decedent's estate for estate tax purposes.

Property held in joint tenancy loses half *of the stepped-up valuation otherwise available.*

Stepped-Up Valuation

The concept of stepped-up valuation is almost totally unknown to most people, but it is one of the most important concepts that should be understood by all people who wish to preserve as much of their estates as possible for their heirs. Stepped-up valuation is one of the key reasons why a well-drawn Living Trust can minimize and, in most cases, eliminate capital gains taxes on the eventual sale of highly appreciated assets (such as the family home).

The term *stepped-up valuation* means that, upon the death of the owner of an asset, the cost basis of the asset (the price at which the asset was originally bought) is automatically "stepped up" to the market value of the asset (the price at which the asset could be sold today).

Stepped-up valuation is a key way in which a Living Trust can minimize or eliminate capital gains taxes upon the sale of assets.

Receiving full stepped-up valuation can have significant tax advantages by shrinking the size of capital gains. On the other hand, not receiving stepped-up valuation can mean that a large capital gain is realized upon the sale of an asset whose market value is much larger than its cost basis. If an asset is jointly owned—for example, by a husband and wife—typically only half of the asset will receive stepped-up valuation; the other half of the asset, when it is sold, will be subject to capital gain based on the original cost basis. Depending on how the couple held title to the property, the amount of stepped-up valuation attributed to the asset can be nothing, can be half the current market value, or can be all of the current market value. This concept applies not just to your home but to *all* of your assets.

JOINT TENANCY FORFEITS ONE OF THE $600,000 FEDERAL ESTATE TAX EQUIVALENT EXEMPTIONS

The AARP study mentioned in the Preface found that *90 percent of all estates of widows and widowers, age 60 and above, will go through probate.* This sad fact is the result of spouses holding property in joint tenancy (or where applicable, in community property), with the survivor taking all.

There are two flaws with this ill-advised approach to estate planning. First, the decedent spouse's $1 million federal estate tax exclusion is "thrown away" (i.e., cannot be claimed), potentially subjecting the estate to unnecessary estate taxes—with every dollar over $2 million being taxed. (This subject is discussed in Chapter 5.) Consequently, one of

the greatest disadvantages of a husband and wife holding assets in joint tenancy is that, upon the death of one spouse, the assets flow directly to the surviving spouse, causing one exemption to be lost.

Second, even though probate is avoided at the time the first spouse dies, the *entire estate* is subject to probate upon the death of the surviving spouse. When the first of the joint tenants dies, the survivor then has title to (i.e., owns) all assets that were held in joint tenancy—without the necessity of a probate proceeding. However, when the survivor dies, the entire estate must then go through probate to pass clear title to the beneficiaries.

The only way to preserve the $1 million federal estate tax exclusion of both individuals in a marriage (for a total federal estate tax equivalent exemption of $2 million) is to create an A-B Living Trust (discussed in Chapter 6).

NOT ALL ASSETS ARE HELD IN JOINT TENANCY

Even where clients decide that they are going to use the joint tenancy method to avoid probate, they never quite seem to get all of their assets into joint tenancy. As a result, even the best-intentioned people eventually have to take some of their assets through the frustrating probate process.

UNDER JOINT TENANCY THE SURVIVOR TAKES ALL

Another important aspect of joint tenancy is the concept of "the survivor takes all." This concept may be fine when the joint tenants are husband and wife. However, let's look at the situation where two brothers and their wives decide to pool their resources to buy a mountain cabin. The two families decide to hold title to the cabin in joint tenancy. The effect of this action is that, if one husband and wife die, the surviving couple will take all. However, this division of property certainly was not the real intention of the families. In such situations, it is usually the intention that each couple has the right to pass their share on to their children. Thus, in the case of two couples purchasing a cabin together, it would be most appropriate for them to hold title to the cabin as tenants in common, which allows each individual owner to "will" his or her interest in the property to whomever he or she desires. A Living Trust would accomplish the same thing.

JOINT TENANCY DOES NOT ELIMINATE COST

Joint tenancy does not necessarily avoid the high cost of settling an estate. The cost of probate can often be exorbitant, but so can the cost of transferring title under joint tenancy. *Estate Planning and Taxation Coordinator*, one of the authoritative publications of the estate-planning industry, makes the following observation:

> While overall estate administration costs may be reduced through joint ownership, attorneys' fees, fiduciary commissions and other costs relating specifically to jointly owned property may be incurred after a co-owner's death. Such costs could include fees for contesting inclusion of jointly owned property in the deceased co-owner's gross estate, determining death taxes apportioned against jointly owned property and collecting taxes from survivors, costs of securing tax waivers to permit transfer of jointly owned assets to the survivor, fees for reregistering jointly owned property in the sole name of the surviving joint tenant, recording fees, legal fees for establishing rights to joint bank account funds, etc.*

The abbreviation *etc.* at the end of the statement means that the attorney will obtain his or her fee one way or another.

A typical example of the onerous costs that can be charged for relatively simple actions associated with settling an estate was cited in an article that appeared on August 30, 1984, in the *Los Angeles Times*.

> In the article, the staff writer stated that she was dumbfounded when she was charged $850 for transferring her deed from joint tenancy into her name (a transaction that should have cost only about $50). The writer said that she did ask about the fee, but was never told what it would be. When the woman filed a complaint against the attorney, the complaint was dismissed on the basis that, since she had engaged an attorney, there need be no limit to his or her "fee for professional services." The attorney need only state that his fee was for "professional services," and therefore the fee must be paid!

JOINT TENANCY DOES NOT ELIMINATE PROBATE

Joint tenancy does not entirely eliminate the process of probate. Even though joint tenancy can avoid probate on the first spouse to die, the entire estate must go through probate upon the death of the survivor.

Joint tenancy avoids probate only on the first spouse to die; upon the death of the survivor, the entire estate must go through probate.

All too often, I hear attorneys say to a married couple, "You don't need a Living Trust; you can avoid probate by putting your assets into joint tenancy." However, I then have to pose the question, "What happens upon the death of the second spouse?" Later, after the death of one of the individuals, I hear these same attorneys say to the surviving spouse, "You don't need a Living Trust, because, since you are single, you now can't have an A-B Trust." What hypocrites! Too many unknowing people are swept up by this "logic," which is actually illogical. What a shame!

Having the entire estate go through probate upon the death of the second spouse is one of the strongest arguments against joint tenancy. At best, joint tenancy simply delays the inevitable probate cost on the second to die. It seems logical that, if probate is eventually certain (when the assets are held in joint tenancy) and if there is a better way to avoid probate entirely—and there definitely is a better way—then the time to act is now.

---

* *Estate Planning and Taxation Coordinator* (Paragraph 27, 105) (New York: Research Institute of America, 1988). Reprinted with permission.

GIFTED PROPERTY FORFEITS STEPPED-UP VALUATION

Another reason for parents not going into joint tenancy with one or more of their children is that they effectively *gift* to them that share of the parents' asset (or assets). When the child receives the parents' share of the asset as a gift, the value of the share is received at the parents' original cost basis (thus losing the tax benefit of stepped-up valuation).

For a brief clarification of this point, let's look at an example that, unfortunately, is fairly typical.

If you owned a home worth $200,000 (with a cost basis of $50,000) and decided to go into joint tenancy with one of your children, the child would end up with half a home worth $100,000 and a cost basis of only $25,000. Upon your death, your child would receive a $200,000 house but would retain the original cost basis (i.e., he or she would have a $200,000 house with a cost basis of only $50,000)—thus forfeiting stepped-up valuation. If the child had, instead, inherited the house after your death, the asset would have received stepped-up valuation, and the child then would have received the house with a new cost basis of $200,000.

In addition, be aware that, if the gift exceeds $1 million for a single person or $2 million for a married couple with an A-B Trust (explained later), a gift tax is imposed on the estate. Any taxes not paid at the date of gift are eventually due, with appropriate penalties.

METHODS OF HOLDING TITLE TO ASSETS

To understand why joint tenancy is a poor alternative to the Living Trust, you need to be familiar with some basic concepts concerning methods of holding title to your assets. There are several common ways of holding title to assets:

- Joint tenancy
- Tenancy in common
- Tenancy by the entirety
- Community property
- Separate property
- Living Trust

Joint tenancy is the most commonly used form of ownership throughout the United States. Until only a few years ago, most people were not even aware that alternative forms of ownership were available. Depending on your individual circumstances, however, the particular form of ownership by which you hold title to your assets can have very different effects on your estate when you die.

Co-Ownership

People who share ownership of an asset may choose joint tenancy, tenancy in common, or tenancy by the entirety. Under the joint tenancy form of ownership, two or more individuals jointly own an asset (such as a house). When one of the joint tenants dies, ownership of the property passes to the surviving joint tenant(s). The property will eventually pass to the last surviving party. Joint tenancy takes precedence over any existing Will or Trust.

Tenancy by the entirety is essentially the same as joint tenancy, except that tenancy by the entirety must involve a husband and wife and may be terminated only by the *joint* action of both owners during their lives, whereas joint tenancy may be terminated by either one of the parties. Tenancy by the entirety is commonly used as a joint form of ownership in separate property states, which will be discussed later.

A third form of co-ownership, tenancy in common, differs in terms of what happens to the property upon the death of an owner. If a tenant in common dies, that person's share of the property passes—through probate—to the heirs of the decedent, who may or may not be the other owners of the property.

Note that, in all of these cases, the share of ownership in the property that is inherited is not a specific physical part of the property. When an asset such as real estate has more than one owner, each person's interest in the property is usually considered to be an undivided interest. "Undivided" means that one owner cannot try to divide up the property and sell "his" or "her" share of it. The property is treated as an indivisible unit. For example, in the situation of the two couples who bought a cabin, the ownership of the property could be recorded in all the owners' names, and the brothers and sisters-in-law would each be part owners of the whole property. Each owner's interest in that property is known as an undivided interest.

From a tax standpoint, the Economic Recovery Tax Act of 1981 specifies that tenancy in common and tenancy by the entirety will be treated in the same manner as joint tenancy in separate property states.

Community Property and Separate Property

Ownership of assets by a married couple may be affected by whether those assets are legally considered community property or separate property. Under the community property form of ownership, all property attained prior to marriage and property that one spouse receives by gift or inheritance during the marriage is separate property. All other property acquired during marriage is community property and is attributed equally—one-half to each spouse. Regardless of whether one or both spouses are wage earners, each is considered to own half of these assets. In states that recognize community property, the community property form of ownership can yield significant tax advantages over joint tenancy, from the viewpoint of settling an estate.

The term *separate property* can easily be confused, because it can mean two entirely different things. In states that do not recognize community property, separate property usually refers to the property of a husband and wife, and all property acquired by a married couple is considered to have one owner (typically the husband, depending on the law of the state).

Transferring your undivided interest in property into your Trust has no effect on the other holders of undivided interests in the property.

The term *separate property* is also used, in community property states as well as in separate property states and particularly with Living Trusts, to denote property that was acquired by a spouse before marriage or property gifted to or inherited by one spouse. Such property is uniquely specified to be separate property (by using a Separate Property Agreement), and the other spouse has no claim to it.

Living Trust

With a Living Trust, property is owned by the Trust but is under the complete control of the trustees.

Clients who want Living Trusts often ask what they should do when real estate is held by more than one party. Let's return to the example of the two couples who purchased a cabin together. If one of the families had a Living Trust, a deed would be written that would transfer title of the family's one-half "undivided" interest into the name of the Living Trust.

Writing a deed to transfer an undivided interest into a Trust has no practical effect on the other real estate holders. If, for example, the other brother decides not to hold his share of the asset in a Trust, but chooses instead to leave title in joint tenancy with his wife, he may do so. If you place your interest in real estate in the name of your Living Trust, you sever the joint tenancy and create a tenancy in common. Therefore, you have the right to *will* your interest in the property as you desire and, at the same time, avoid probate for your heirs.

The most advantageous form of ownership is to hold assets in the name of your Living Trust and, wherever possible, to hold assets as community property—in order to get maximum stepped-up valuation upon the death of a spouse.

Community Property States vs. Separate Property States

It is easiest to arrange the most advantageous way to hold title to your property (as community property in a revocable Living Trust) if you live in a community property state. Community property states originate from Spanish or French law and provide certain tax advantages—especially the opportunity to attain full stepped-up valuation. There are eight original community property states: Arizona, California, Idaho, Louisiana, Nevada, New Mexico, Texas, and Washington.

Because of the particular tax advantages available to community property states, many state legislatures are in the process of declaring their states to be community property states. The Wisconsin legislature was the first to pass such a statute. All other states are separate property states and assume that the husband holds *sole* title to all property.

An understanding of community property has far greater application than one might think throughout the United States, because many people today move from state to state. Although community property states are few, the United States populace is transient, so people will often move to a community property state, if only for a short period of time. While residing in a community property state, people should take advantage of their right—*with the Living Trust*—to transfer their assets from separate property to quasi community property (effectively community property). Thereafter, those assets will have the community property benefit of stepped-up valuation and will also retain the community property characteristic, even if the individuals owning those assets move back to a separate property state.

If the individuals execute their Living Trusts in a community property state, all of their assets (except those assets specifically identified in the Trust as separate property in Separate Property Agreements) are considered to be community property.

COMMUNITY PROPERTY VS. JOINT TENANCY

Community property is not treated as community property if the characteristic of that property is modified by changing its title to joint tenancy, which takes precedence over the principles governing community property. Although the surviving spouse retains his or her rightful share of community property under state law, the surviving spouse will lose stepped-up valuation under Internal Revenue Service rules.

The tax implications of holding property in joint tenancy versus community property can thus be very different. The following examples illustrate the different tax implications affecting an estate when property is held as com-

munity property instead of in joint tenancy. The same tax implications apply to assets held in tenancy in common and tenancy by the entirety.

Let's assume that you are married and own a home that you purchased for $50,000. Let's further assume that it is many years later, and your home is now worth $200,000—which is not unusual in many of today's housing markets.

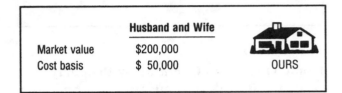

	Husband and Wife	
Market value	$200,000	
Cost basis	$ 50,000	OURS

Home Owned in Joint Tenancy

Let's see what happens under the assumption that you own your home in joint tenancy. If you do, the Internal Revenue Service says (for some unknown reason) it can effectively draw a line straight through the center of your home (for taxation purposes). This ruling means that you do not own a whole home; each spouse owns half a house worth $100,000, and each of you has a cost basis of $25,000 for your half of the house.

	Husband	Wife		
Market value	$100,000	$100,000		
Cost basis	$ 25,000	$ 25,000	HIS	HERS

Now, let's illustrate what would happen from a tax standpoint if the husband were the first to die. The husband's cost basis (on only *his* half of the house) would receive stepped-up valuation—simply meaning that his cost basis becomes market value at date of death. However, the same is *not* true for the wife's half of the house. The wife would inherit a home worth $200,000 (the current market value); however, she would also inherit her husband's new cost basis of $100,000 (whether she wants to or not), while still retaining her original cost basis of $25,000. Therefore, the wife would end up with a total cost basis of $125,000. If the wife were to sell the home, she would realize a taxable gain of $75,000!

	Husband	Wife	Survivor	
Market value	$100,000	$100,000	$200,000	HERS
Cost basis		$ 25,000	($ 25,000)	
Stepped-up valuation	$100,000		($100,000)	HIS
Taxable gain			$ 75,000	

Home Owned as Community Property

In contrast, let's assume that you and your spouse own the same house as community property. With community property, for some unknown reason, the IRS says that it *cannot* draw a line through the center of the house. Therefore, upon the death of one spouse, the entire cost basis (the original cost of $50,000) receives that special tax benefit called stepped-up valuation—meaning that cost basis ($50,000) becomes market value ($200,000) at the date of death. Under these circumstances, the surviving spouse would inherit a home worth $200,000, as well as the *new* cost basis of $200,000. If the surviving spouse were to sell the home, he or she would have a taxable gain of zero! Realize that nothing has changed, except the manner in which the title to the home is held.

	Husband and Wife	Survivor	
Market value	$200,000	$200,000	
Cost basis	$ 50,000	$ 25,000	
Stepped-up valuation		($200,000)	OURS
Taxable gain		-0-	

Even though the principle of stepped-up valuation has been described with regard to a home, the principle also applies to everything a person owns: stocks, bonds, mutual funds, Ginnie Maes, real estate, trust deeds, interest in a business, and so on.

Being able to receive full stepped-up valuation is almost a necessity when a person owns a privately held business. Typically, the cost basis is close to zero; yet, if the business owner is successful, the privately held business can become quite valuable. In this situation, being able to receive full stepped-up valuation (upon the death of a spouse) can be extremely valuable.

If, for some reason, you decide to share ownership of your business as joint tenants with your children, be aware that your children will receive the business at your *original* cost basis. Your children lose the opportunity of gaining stepped-up valuation (for those assets in which they are joint tenants) upon the death of their parent or parents.

PRESERVING YOUR ESTATE THROUGH STEPPED-UP VALUATION

Interestingly, there have been many cases where individuals whose assets are held in joint tenancy with their spouses have lost their spouses and then have elected to go through the probate process—specifically to *revoke* the joint tenancy and thus have the assets become community property (which can then receive the benefit of full stepped-up valuation).

Such an example is the case of Marian Trumble, who, many years ago with her husband, bought a small home in the Hollywood hills for $20,000. The husband and wife owned the home in joint tenancy. Many years later, the Trumbles' house was worth $500,000. Since the home was owned in joint tenancy, this situation meant that Mr. and Mrs. Trumble each owned half a house worth $250,000 (and each had a cost basis of $10,000).

	Husband	Wife
Current value of home	$250,000	$250,000
Original cost basis	$ 10,000	$ 10,000

When Mr. Trumble died, the cost basis for his half of the house received stepped-up valuation. However, because the house was held in joint tenancy, Mrs. Trumble's cost basis remained at the original $10,000. Mrs. Trumble inherited her husband's half of the house worth $250,000, along with her husband's new cost basis of $250,000; when Mrs. Trumble's original cost basis of $10,000 was added, she had a total cost basis of $260,000 (for a home worth $500,000).

	Survivor
Current value of home	$500,000
Cost basis	($500,000)
Taxable gain	-0-
Tax on gain	-0-

	Husband	Wife	Survivor
Current value of home	$250,000	$250,000	$500,000
Cost basis		$ 10,000	($260,000)
Stepped-up valuation	$250,000		
Taxable gain			$240,000

When Mrs. Trumble decided that she needed to sell the family home (in order to have sufficient funds to live on in the future), she had a taxable capital gain of $240,000. Since Mrs. Trumble was over the age of fifty-five, she could use her exemption of $125,000; however, she would still have a $115,000 taxable gain! (This exemption is now $250,000.)

	Survivor
Current value of home	$500,000
Cost basis	($260,000)
Gain	$240,000
Less: Once-in-a-lifetime exemption	($125,000)
Taxable gain	$115,000

In contrast, it would have been to Mrs. Trumble's financial benefit to elect to go through the agonizing and costly probate process in order to *revoke* the joint tenancy with her late husband. After the joint tenancy ownership was severed, Mrs. Trumble would have inherited the home and also would have gained *full* stepped-up valuation—thus inheriting a home with a new cost basis of $500,000. Then, when the family home was sold, the taxable gain would have been zero!

Why, you may then ask, have most people been told to hold their assets in joint tenancy even though, in most cases, this advice is now outdated? The answer is that in the earlier days of our country, holding property in joint tenancy was a good recommendation, because then, as now, few people had Wills, and joint tenancy, in effect, created a Will for that piece of property. Joint tenancy takes precedence over all other Wills and legally specifies that the survivor will be the recipient of the entire asset. Now, however, most real estate brokers and stockbrokers will no longer recommend joint tenancy. In 1978, stepped-up valuation was reinstated by the tax code, but it took the legal fraternity at least a year or two to recognize the value of stepped-up valuation. By 1984, most stockbrokers and real estate brokers had been specifically directed *not* to advise clients to place assets in joint tenancy.

When you now buy stocks or real estate, the broker usually asks you, "How would you like to hold title?" Unfortunately, most people today are so conditioned to placing their assets in joint tenancy that they simply respond, "Why, the same way we have always done it—in joint tenancy."

Joint Tenancy—An Example of the Consequences

At this point, let me illustrate another true story. Sometimes it helps to learn from another's sad experience.

Years ago, two clients, a husband and wife, built a home near Malibu, California, in an area called Big Rock, which was situated on a bluff overlooking the ocean. The clients built the house themselves, so their only cost was the materials—which amounted to $20,000. As the years passed, that location overlooking the ocean became more and more valuable, and the home was eventually worth $500,000. The home was held in joint tenancy when the wife died twelve years ago.

When the wife died, only her half of the house received stepped-up valuation. The husband's cost basis of $10,000 remained the same. Therefore, the husband ended up inheriting a home worth $500,000, but with a cost basis of only $260,000.

After Wife's Death—Joint Tenancy			
	Husband	Wife	Survivor
Market value	$250,000	$250,000	$500,000
Cost basis	$ 10,000	$250,000	$260,000

Some years later, the bluff overlooking the ocean began to slowly slide toward the ocean. It seems that far too many homes had been built on the mesa, and the irrigation and water flow from all of the homes percolated down into the rock, causing the bluff to begin slipping. With the use of submersible pumps embedded deeply into the bluff, the movement of the mesa has been slowed. However, even though the families are still living in their homes, the houses may *not* be sold!

As a result of the moratorium on the sale of the houses, the value of the client's $500,000 home has dropped to zero. Consequently, the client was able to write off his cost basis in the house as a loss against his taxable income. Unfortunately, because he held the home in joint tenancy, he could write off only $260,000.

If, instead, the clients had held their home as community property, upon the death of the wife, the entire cost basis would have received stepped-up valuation. The husband would have inherited a home worth $500,000 with a corresponding cost basis of $500,000. He could have then taken a tax loss against his income for the full $500,000. What a costly error!

A Living Trust—An Example of the Advantages

Now, let's look at a true-life example where the Living Trust with special provision allowed a surviving spouse not only to avoid the frus-

trating probate process, but also to avoid having to pay excessive taxes for capital gains.

A woman came to me for help. She told me her husband was dying of cancer. The couple desired to have a Living Trust, so the woman and I went to the hospital where her husband was confined. A Living Trust for the couple was executed, and then all of the couple's assets were transferred into the Trust. The husband died only six weeks after the Trust was created.

Several weeks after the husband's death, I met with the widow in her home; within an hour, the estate of her husband had been settled. There were no estate taxes to pay.

About six months later, the widow went home to Indiana for a visit. While back home, the woman met her former high-school sweetheart. The man was now a widower; before the woman left to return to California, her former beau asked her to marry him. When the woman returned, she called me—all excited—and advised me that she was going to sell her assets, move to Indiana, and start her life anew. I was delighted for her.

However, only two days later, the woman called in tears and told me that her CPA had advised her that she could not sell her rather substantial real estate holdings—because the capital gains tax would be prohibitive. The woman owned two apartment buildings and a home in Los Angeles, as well as a home in a nearby community where she and her deceased husband had planned to retire.

It was obvious to me that the woman's CPA did not understand how a Living Trust had allowed all of the assets to receive full stepped-up valuation at the time of the husband's death. I told the now-distraught woman to have her CPA call me, and that I would "read him chapter and verse." When the CPA called me, I carefully explained the tax consequences of the woman's Living Trust.

Because all of the assets had been transferred into the couple's Living Trust, all of the assets received full stepped-up valuation when the husband died. Therefore *no* capital gain would be realized when the real estate was sold! Shortly thereafter, the woman sold all of her real estate holdings and paid *no* capital gains tax.

JOINT TENANCY VS. SEPARATE PROPERTY

Although the usual means of ownership in the past was for a husband and wife to hold assets in joint tenancy, people living in community property states or who have a Living Trust with special provision in separate property states have a substantial advantage—if the assets are held as community property instead of in joint tenancy. However, you also need to be aware of what happens to separate property when a spouse dies.

Between Husband and Wife

You have already seen the tax consequences of owning an asset in joint tenancy. If, in contrast, all of the property were held as separate property in the name of either the husband or the wife, very different tax consequences would occur, depending on which person were the first to die. Assume, for purposes of the following example, that the property is held as separate property in the name of the husband. If the husband were the first to die, his cost basis would receive stepped-up valuation. Since the wife legally had no ownership in the house, the market value and cost basis attributable to the wife would both be zero.

In this situation, the wife would benefit by receiving a home worth $200,000, along with her husband's new stepped-up cost basis of $200,000. If the wife were to sell the home, she would have a taxable gain of zero (since the $200,000 market value would be offset by the $200,000 cost basis).

	Husband	Wife as Survivor	
Market value	$200,000	$200,000	
Stepped-up valuation	$200,000	($200,000)	
Gain		-0-	

However, let's now see what happens if the wife were to be the first to die. The results are very different! If the wife were the first to die, since she legally did not own any of the house (remember, the house is separate property held in her husband's name), the market value of the wife's share would be zero, and her cost basis would also be zero. Therefore, the surviving husband retains the home with a market value of $200,000 and retains the original cost basis of $50,000.

If the surviving husband were to sell the house, he would recognize a taxable gain of $150,000! The husband would receive no stepped-up valuation, since the home was held as separate property in the name of the surviving spouse.

	Wife	Husband as Survivor	
Market value	$200,000	$200,000	
Cost basis	-0-	($ 50,000)	
Gain		$150,000	

Between Parent and Child

In a manner similar to the previous example of husband and wife, joint tenancy of an asset held by a parent and child deprives the child of stepped-up valuation. From a tax-saving viewpoint, it is much better if the child receives the asset (after your death) as a distribution from your estate.

For example, assume that a parent had purchased a home for $50,000 (the cost basis) and that years later the home is worth $200,000. If the parent decides to avoid probate by gifting one-half interest in the house to a child, the child would receive the parent's cost basis. The parent and child each would own a one-half interest in the house.

	Parent	Child	
Market value	$100,000	$100,000	
Cost basis	$ 25,000	$ 25,000	

Upon the death of the parent, only the parent's half of the home would get the benefit of stepped-up valuation. The child would inherit a home worth $200,000 with the parent's stepped-up valuation of $100,000. The child would retain his or her original gifted cost basis of $25,000, which would yield a new cost basis for the entire house of $125,000. If the child were to decide to sell the home, he or she would realize a taxable gain of $75,000.

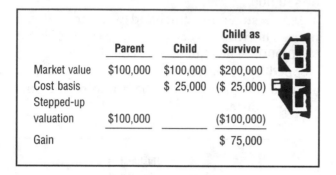

	Parent	Child	Child as Survivor
Market value	$100,000	$100,000	$200,000
Cost basis		$ 25,000	($ 25,000)
Stepped-up valuation	$100,000		($100,000)
Gain			$ 75,000

Now let's review the same situation, but assume that the home is held as separate property instead of in joint tenancy. Instead of gifting one-half interest in the home to the child, the parent retains the entire home as separate property. Upon the death of the parent, the entire cost basis of the home would receive the benefit of stepped-up valuation. The child would inherit a home worth $200,000 and a cost basis of $200,000. If the child were to decide to sell the home, he or she would recognize a taxable gain of zero.

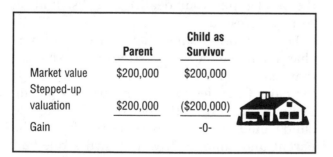

	Parent	Child as Survivor
Market value	$200,000	$200,000
Stepped-up valuation	$200,000	($200,000)
Gain		-0-

BETTER ALTERNATIVES

This chapter has introduced some very important concepts that help to set the stage for later, by showing you the many advantages of a Living Trust. One of the key contributions to minimizing unnecessary estate taxation is the special tax benefit of stepped-up valuation.

Remember that the concept of stepped-up valuation applies to more than just your home. This principle applies to everything you own: other real estate, stocks, bonds, mutual funds, Ginnie Maes, trust deeds, interest in a business, and so on.

You can see that joint tenancy can avoid probate, in certain instances, on the first to die; however, by holding property in joint tenancy, the owners lose the benefits of stepped-up valuation, as well as throw away one of their $600,000 federal estate tax equivalent exemptions. Many years of experience have repeatedly proven that joint tenancy can be an incredibly costly means of avoiding probate.

Community property allows for assets to receive full stepped-up valuation but does *not* avoid probate. Separate property, on the other hand, may gain full stepped-up valuation *if* the property is held by the decedent (the person who died), but the asset is subject to probate. However, if an asset were not held by the decedent, then there would be *no* tax benefit because of stepped-up valuation.

In contrast, a Living Trust with special provision for a married couple or a Living Trust with separate property for a single person, is the best of both worlds, because a Living Trust avoids probate, and a Living Trust with special provision for a married couple (or separate property for a single person) gains full stepped-up valuation. The Living Trust, *with special provision*, grants full stepped-up valuation to married couples living in separate property states, comparable to the rights of married couples living in a community property state. Putting your assets in the name of a Living Trust is so much simpler, affords greater security, and provides a much better solution to proper estate planning.

5

Estate and Inheritance Taxes

People often assume that their estates will pass intact to their heirs—but such an occurrence seldom happens. Upon your death, estate and inheritance taxes can destroy the estate that you have worked so diligently all your life to create. Few people are aware of these two most unpleasant taxes, which can, in effect, take away almost *half* of some estates. Typically, the last person to learn about these taxes is the surviving spouse (or children), who may be ill prepared to handle the tax aspects of settling an estate. As you will see as you progress through this book, however, payment of unnecessary estate taxes—an area that is so important to preserving your estate—can be reduced or eliminated altogether with a Living Trust.

The difference between federal estate tax and state inheritance tax is often misunderstood, and many people erroneously use the terms interchangeably. *Estate tax* is a federal tax levied on an estate when the owner dies. In effect, when a person begins life, Uncle Sam joins with that person in business; when the person dies, Uncle Sam wants out with his share of that person's estate—right away. If there is a tax to pay, the accounting must be completed within six months after the date of death, and any payment due must be made within three months thereafter.

Inheritance tax is a state tax on the right to inherit. Typically, each state imposes an inheritance tax on any property located within that state. This tax is not paid by the heirs but is instead paid by the estate *before* any assets are distributed to the heirs.

In the past, estate and inheritance taxes were largely confiscatory and often took from the surviving spouse the very funds that were necessary for survival.

Then came the Taxpayer Relief Act of 1997. And now we have the Economic Growth and Tax Relief Reconciliation Act of 2001.

THE ECONOMIC GROWTH AND TAX RELIEF RECONCILIATION ACT OF 2001

It has been my experience that Americans have not changed much from their predecessors—who, when eventually pressed too far by the crown's taxes, dumped the tea in Boston Harbor. Similarly, when the estate tax ultimately became too overwhelmingly confiscatory, the ire of the American public was stirred up, and Congress was forced to react. (Unfortunately, Congress seldom acts; it only reacts.)

Some twenty years ago, Americans received long-overdue estate tax reforms with the Economic Recovery Tax Act of 1981. The most significant estate tax reforms in the 1981 tax code were the Unlimited Marital Deduction, a larger and more meaningful Unified Credit, and a ceiling on the maximum federal estate tax rate.

The Unlimited Marital Deduction remains in effect and is just as important now as it was when it was first enacted. The Unified Credit, on the other hand, is no longer applicable. As for the maximum federal estate tax rate, it will be reduced to 49 percent by 2003 and is supposed to be further reduced to 45 percent by 2007, and then is supposed to be repealed in 2010.

Unlimited Marital Deduction

The Unlimited Marital Deduction (sometimes called the Maximum Marital Deduction) enables a spouse to pass his or her entire estate to the other spouse free of any gift or estate taxes. Thus, the surviving spouse would no longer be required to liquidate hard-earned lifetime assets in order to pay the estate taxes due. Many states soon followed with similar legislation for state inheritance tax.

Some caution is advised here, because the Unlimited Marital Deduction, even though a great benefit to the surviving spouse, can be a deceptive benefit. By using the Unlimited Marital Deduction, people end up losing one of their federal estate tax equivalent *exclusions*.

Maximum Federal Estate Taxes

The 1981 tax code gradually reduced the maximum tax from 70 percent to 55 percent. The Economic Growth and Tax Relief Reconciliation Act of 2001 reduces the maximum federal estate tax rate to 50 percent and is supposed to reduce it further to 45 percent by 2007, and then repeal it in 2010. The Act now gives each of us a federal estate tax exclusion of $1 million.

The 1981 tax code gradually reduced the maximum tax from 70 percent to 55 percent. The Economic Growth and Tax Relief Reconciliation Act of 2001 reduces the maximum federal estate tax rate to 50 percent and is supposed to reduce it further to 45 percent by 2007, and then repeal it in 2010.

Few, if any, estate planners who understand the history of the nation's confiscatory estate taxes and how Congress was eventually forced to react can foresee Congress returning to its former position of imposing such a confiscatory tax. Nevertheless, the pendulum of change swings back and forth. Therefore, if the Economic Growth and Tax Relief Reconciliation Act of 2001 is substantially altered or deleted, and the federal estate tax again becomes confiscatory, the pendulum will swing back, and Congress will again be forced to react. We can only hope and pray that Congress will retain the Act and then reinstate it in 2011.

Many people tend to look at the federal estate tax exclusion of $1 million and do nothing, because they think that their $300,000 estate will never exceed the exclusion limit. However, you are advised not to be complacent! Since Congress reacts rather than acts, it may be many years before these exclusions are again raised. In the meantime, inflation will reduce the real benefit of the exclusion by making its worth less relative to the size of a person's estate.

For example, inflation can double, triple, and quadruple an estate fairly quickly, as shown in Table 5-1. With an inflation rate of 7 percent per year, a $300,000 estate would be worth $600,000 in just ten years and would increase to a value of $1.2 million in twenty years. The tax bite from such an estate would be painful.

During 1980–81, I assisted three surviving spouses in settling their estates after their husbands had died. (Chapter 15 describes how to

TABLE 5-1
EFFECTS OF INFLATION ON AN ESTATE'S VALUE

Inflation Rate	Years to Double	Years to Quadruple
5%	14	28
6	12	24
7	10	20
8	9	18
9	8	16
10	7	14
11	6½	13
12	6	12

settle an estate.) The estates were valued at only $100,000, $125,000, and $150,000, respectively. Ten years later, I had the opportunity to review each of these estates, and the value of all three by then exceeded the federal estate tax exemption! The increased value was not based on the investing wisdom of the widow; it was due to inflation and real estate appreciation.

Unfortunately, each estate had only an A Trust, rather than an A-B Trust. (The different types of Trusts are explained in a later chapter.) Therefore, when the surviving spouse died, every dollar over the federal estate tax exemption was taxed, since only one federal estate tax equivalent exemption (now an *exclusion*) could be claimed. (Ten years ago, it was difficult to convince people of the need to anticipate the adverse effects of inflation—and the need to upgrade their A Trusts to A-B Trusts.)

As a result of this experience, I now always recommend an A-B Trust for a husband and wife, regardless of the size of their estate at the time their Living Trust is created.

A "do-nothing" approach can be costly to your heirs. Inflation causes estates to increase in value over the years. Therefore, you should do some realistic estate planning now.

Far too many people believe that this new tax law has solved their estate tax problems. Nothing could be further from the truth.

The Congressional Budget Act of 1974

Last year, in a letter to our clients, I wrote that the estate tax was a political football and that, as long as we had a divided Congress and administration, the federal estate tax would remain intact. Well, we had a Republican Congress and administration, and look at what we got. It sounds good, and it feels good, but it has serious consequences that can negatively affect the tax benefits of your Living Trust.

West Virginia Senator Robert Byrd (D) attached the Tax Act to the Congressional Budget Act of 1974. The significance of this move is that Congress can alter the Tax Act at any point. Right now it's congressional gamesmanship: the Democrats will simply outspend the budget—at which they are masters—and then blame the President for his tax bill. Then, they will attack the tax bill. Since its basis is the Congressional Budget Act of 1974, Congress can act with impunity—and it's anyone's guess what will come next.

It's Like Magic: Now You See It, Now You Don't

The Tax Act is a distorted mystery. It purports to give you one thing, while, by sleight of hand, it will almost certainly give you something entirely different.

The Economic Growth and Tax Relief Reconciliation Act of 2001 is staggeringly complex. It changes the federal estate tax from an *exemption* to an *exclusion* and *purportedly* phases it out over the next ten years. It repeals the entire estate tax in 2010, and then reinstates it at 55 percent in 2011. Similar significant changes are made to the gift tax, the generation-skipping transfer tax, stepped-up valuation, and state death taxes.

To refresh your mind, the following is a brief explanation of each of these tax areas:

- **Federal estate tax exclusion:** That part of the estate that may be exempted from federal estate taxes.
- **Gift tax:** Lifetime gifts that may ultimately become more tax beneficial than the federal estate tax exclusion. Each individual can now gift up to $1 million as a lifetime gift, which would escape estate taxation.
- **Generation-skipping transfer tax:** Tax penalty on assets passing to grandchildren.
- **Stepped-up valuation:** Valuation of assets upon the death of each trustor.
- **State death taxes:** Many states adopted the concept of the pickup tax, which is a percentage of the federal estate tax that may pass directly to the state. This new tax law phases out the state death tax credit over the next three years. What will the states do to recapture this lost revenue?

The problem is that not one tax expert believes this tax law as passed will ever come to fruition.

The problem is that not one tax expert believes this tax law as passed will ever come to fruition. So, what will we eventually have:

an exemption, an exclusion, an alteration, a repeal, a recision, or something else—and what will the figures be? No one has the answer. We all agree that the present Tax Act will not survive in its current state, and the best guess is that the first to go will be that political football—the estate tax.

Federal Exclusions and Exemptions

Table 5-2 summarizes the Economic Growth and Tax Relief Reconciliation Act of 2001 as it pertains to the federal estate and gift tax exclusion, and the generation-skipping transfer tax (GSTT) exemption. Included as a basis for comparison are the 2001 figures for the federal estate and gift tax exemptions—the tax law that was replaced.

To comply with the Congressional Budget Act of 1974, all of the changes, including both the income tax changes and the repeal of the estate tax, will *not* apply after December 31, 2010. These new provisions are (technically) only temporary and will expire after December 31, 2010, unless Congress reenacts them.

Marginal Estate Tax Rates

The marginal tax brackets for estate taxes under the Economic Growth and Tax Relief

Reconciliation Act of 2001 are shown in Table 5-3. Included for comparison are the marginal estate tax rates for the last year of the Taxpayer Relief Act of 1997 as it applied in 2001. As you can see, the marginal tax rate slowly phases down to 2007–2010 and then purportedly is reinstated at 55 percent in 2011.

STEPPED-UP VALUATION AND STATE DEATH TAX CREDITS

Stepped-up valuation and the state death tax credit will also be significantly changed. Both of these tax programs can have a dramatic impact on estates if they take effect as written. That is a very big "if," because it assumes that this Tax Act will continue on for its ten-year tenure without change.

Stepped-Up Valuation

The concept of stepped-up valuation came in with the 1981 Tax Reform Act. The objective was to try to introduce some fairness in estate taxation.

The concept of stepped-up valuation came in with the 1981 Tax Reform Act. The objective was to try to introduce some fairness in estate

---

TABLE 5-2
ECONOMIC GROWTH AND TAX RELIEF RECONCILIATION ACT OF 2001—MAXIMUM FEDERAL TAX RATE

| Year | Estate Tax & GSTT Exemption | | Gift Tax | |
	Exclusion[1]	Top Rate	Exclusion	Top Rate
2001	$ 675,000	55%	$1,060,000	55%
2002	$1,000,000	50%[2]	$1,000,000	50%
2003	$1,000,000	49%	$1,000,000	49%
2004[3]	$1,500,000	48%	$1,000,000	48%
2005	$1,500,000	47%	$1,000,000	47%
2006	$2,000,000	46%	$1,000,000	46%
2007	$2,000,000	45%	$1,000,000	45%
2008	$2,000,000	45%	$1,000,000	45%
2009	$3,500,000	45%	$1,000,000	45%
2010	N/A—Repealed (12/31/10)		$1,000,000	35%[4]
2011	Reinstated at	55%	$1,000,000	35%[4]

[1] Estate tax Unified Credit exclusion commences in 2002.
[2] 5% surcharge above $10,000 is eliminated.
[3] Family-owned business estate tax deduction is repealed.
[4] The gift tax is not repealed.

TABLE 5-3
MARGINAL TAX BRACKETS FOR ESTATE TAXES

Year	Estate Value	Marginal Estate Tax Rate
2001	$1,000,000 to $1,250,000	41%
	1,250,000 to 1,500,000	43%
	1,500,000 to 2,000,000	45%
	2,000,000 to 2,500,000	49%
	2,500,000 to 3,000,000	53%
	3,000,000 plus	55%
2002	$1,000,000 to $1,250,000	41%
	1,250,000 to 1,500,000	43%
	1,500,000 to 2,000,000	45%
	2,000,000 to 2,500,000	49%
	2,500,000 plus	50%
2003	$1,000,000 to $1,250,000	41%
	1,250,000 to 1,500,000	43%
	1,500,000 to 2,000,000	45%
	2,000,000 plus	49%
2004	$1,500,000 to $2,000,000	45%
	2,000,000 plus	48%
2005	$1,500,000 to $2,000,000	45%
	2,000,000 plus	47%
2006	$2,000,000 plus	46%
2007–10	$2,000,000 plus	45%
2011	Reinstated at	55%

These provisions will "sunset" and the existing estate tax will be reinstated in 2011.

The gift tax after 2009 will be a flat tax, with all gifts above $1,000,000 taxed at the top rate of 35%.

taxation. The reasoning was that since the estate tax was computed on the inflated current value of your assets, this new inflated value should become the new value of your assets for capital gains taxation when the assets are sold.

The inequity of *not* receiving stepped-up valuation is illustrated in the following account of clients with whom I worked in 1976.

A retired couple owned a 600-acre farm in Iowa, part of which the two had purchased for a small sum in 1929, with the balance being inherited, resulting in an almost zero cost basis. Too old now to work the farm, the couple leased it out to others. Their annual income was around $17,000—from the farm lease, a small pension, and social security benefits. The retired pair considered themselves poor, and both were in ill health.

Unfortunately for them, since they weren't interested in selling their farm—they just wanted to survive—the value of their land had increased considerably since they had acquired it. Farmland was now worth $1,000 per acre, and their 600 acres were therefore worth $600,000. The couple knew that when one of them died, the survivor would face estate taxes on half of the estate, or $300,000.

Let's assume that the federal estate taxes and state inheritance taxes would be $80,000. How is the survivor supposed to pay $80,000 in taxes when the only real asset in the estate is the farmland? It would not be possible to sell, say, just the back forty acres because a farm can't be sold in pieces. In this case, as was true of so many farmers, it would be necessary to sell the *entire* farm in order to pay the estate taxes when the husband or wife died. With a cost basis of zero and no stepped-up valuation, the entire sale of $600,000 would be subject to capital gains tax of 20 percent, or $120,000. Thus, the survivor would lose his or her home of a lifetime, as well as neighboring friends and surroundings, and be forced to find a new way of survival. Sadly, this story was being repeated daily.

Within the next few years, Congress changed the estate tax law to compel taxation only upon the death of the *second* spouse and gave us the concept of stepped basis. This concept is fair in that the government taxes our estates at current market value, which becomes our new cost basis.

The bad news now is that the *step-up* in basis at death will end with the federal estate tax beginning in 2010. Thereafter, the decedent's property will have a basis equal to the *lesser* of the decedent's basis or fair market value at death. This can be particularly onerous on assets held in community property states where, under current tax law, the marital assets receive full stepped-up valuation upon the death of the first spouse. (The assets of the second spouse to die would also receive stepped-up valuation.)

Beginning January 1, 2010, there will be a new step-up in basis for $1.3 million of property from the decedent—and an additional $3 million of new basis for the surviving spouse. Everything above that will be at cost basis. I know this sounds confusing, but it is not worth dwelling on at this point, since it does not come about until 2010. It is just one more reason to be concerned about what may happen in the interim.

Step-up basis will be extremely controversial. It was enacted as part of the Tax Reform Act of 1976 and then repealed retroactively in 1980 because it was far too complicated.

State Death Tax Credit

Historically, the federal tax code provides a state death tax credit. This credit works much like the state income tax allowance against federal income tax—with limitations. Whatever we pay in state income tax may be deducted from our gross income before we compute our federal income tax. This makes income taxation reasonably fair—assuming that we accept the burden of our income taxes as fair.

In the case of the federal estate tax computations, however, there is one enormous problem: the federal government limits the amount of state death tax that can be deducted from your gross estate before computing your federal estate tax. This limitation is called the state death tax credit and is found in the State Death Tax Credit Table of the federal tax code.

State Inheritance Tax Reforms

The state inheritance tax has also been confiscatory in many states, but, as in the federal government, state tax reform has been occurring in many states. California is an excellent example of state tax reform. Following on the heels of California's now-famous Proposition 13 property tax reform, the voters adopted Proposition A, a significant inheritance tax reform measure.

Prior to the adoption of Proposition A, the state inheritance tax on a $300,000 estate could be as high as $80,000. Unlike income taxes, federal laws disregarded the actual state inheritance tax paid and permitted only a nominal

deduction against the estate for the state inheritance taxes that were paid. The allowable federal deduction was taken from a table titled Maximum Credit for State Death Taxes.

Enacting California's Proposition A created two major reforms relating to the way the state handled inheritance taxes:

1. No state inheritance tax is due unless a federal estate tax is due.
2. If federal estate tax is due, the state inheritance tax will be the same as that allowed under the maximum credit for state death taxes (i.e., the state tax will not be greater than the deduction allowed by the IRS). Effectively, there is no additional tax for state inheritance.

With proper estate planning (such as with an appropriate Living Trust), no federal estate taxes and, in many states, no inheritance taxes will be due when the first spouse dies.

Many states have followed California's lead and have enacted similar tax reform measures.

The key to state inheritance tax reform is that, with proper estate planning (such as with an appropriate Living Trust), no federal estate taxes and, in many states, no inheritance taxes will be due when the first spouse dies. In addition, for the majority of estates, no federal estate or state inheritance taxes will be due when the second spouse dies—meaning that no "death taxes" need be paid.

Thirty states, plus the District of Columbia, have no direct inheritance tax, per se, as shown in Table 5-4.

Some of these states, however, do have a pickup tax—whereby the states "pick up" a portion of the estate tax that is owed to Uncle Sam. This pickup tax concept was conceived in the past eight years as a means of eliminating the onerous state inheritance tax by allocating a portion of the federal estate tax to the state. This action markedly reduced the amount of inheritance tax paid to the state.

The federal estate tax table allows you to deduct a state death tax credit from the amount of federal estate tax that is owed. The state then picks up this portion as its share of tax. The

TABLE 5-4

STATES WITH NO INHERITANCE TAX
(or Only a Pickup Tax)

Alabama	Missouri
Alaska	Nevada
Arizona	New Mexico
Arkansas	North Dakota
California	Oregon
Colorado	Rhode Island
District of Columbia	South Carolina
Florida	Texas
Georgia	Utah
Hawaii	Vermont
Idaho	Virginia
Illinois	Washington
Maine	West Virginia
Massachusetts	Wisconsin
Michigan	Wyoming
Minnesota	

TABLE 5-5

REDUCTION SCHEDULE FOR REPEAL
OF STATE DEATH TAX CREDIT

Year	Reduction
2002	25%
2003	50%
2004	75%
2005	Repealed—Replaced with a deduction for state death taxes paid.

total tax paid, to both the federal government and the state, equals the federal estate tax computation—so no *additional* tax is paid to the state. If no federal estate tax is owed, no tax is collected by the state.

All of this improvement in state taxation is about to be lost.

Historically, the trend has been for states to move away from imposing an inheritance tax, as well as to eliminate taxing the surviving spouse. Only twenty states had some form of state inheritance (or state estate) tax.

Reduction and Repeal of the State Death Tax Credit

Under the Economic Growth and Tax Relief Reconciliation Act of 2001, the state death tax credit is reduced over the next few years and then repealed. The proposed schedule for that reduction and repeal is shown in Table 5-5.

Under the Economic Growth and Tax Relief Reconciliation Act of 2001, the state death tax credit is reduced over the next few years and then repealed.

The impact will be striking on many states. Those that have enacted the pickup tax will lose

their state death taxes. As an example, Nevada never had an inheritance tax. It was for this reason that, just before his death, Howard Hughes was headed from Mexico City to Nevada, but he died en route when the plane landed to refuel in Texas. Eventually, Nevada adopted the pickup tax so that it would not be giving away a portion of the federal estate taxes. Now that benefit will disappear over the next few years.

What will the pickup tax states do? Obviously, many will reenact or adopt inheritance taxes. And how large will these new inheritance taxes be? These are questions that should be on everyone's mind. This is just one more example of the need to watch and be prepared to accommodate future tax changes that will affect your estate. Table 5-6 shows the states that have some form of state inheritance (or state estate) tax.

IRAs AND 401(k) PLANS

Included in the Economic Growth and Tax Relief Reconciliation Act of 2001 are changes to maximum allowable contributions to individual retirement accounts (IRAs) and 401(k) plans. The maximum IRA contribution will increase from $2,000 to $5,000 annually by 2008 ($6,000 for people age fifty and older). You can increase your contribution to an Education IRA from $500 to $2,000 annually as of 2002.

The allowed contribution to 401(k) plans will increase from $10,500 to $15,000 annually by 2006 ($20,000 for people age fifty and older).

I do not foresee the IRA or 401(k) allowed contributions being reduced or withdrawn over the coming years. The real challenge is to the estate tax, the gift tax, the generation-skipping

TABLE 5-6
STATES WITH INHERITANCE TAX

State	Children, Parents, Surviving Spouse	Brothers, Sisters, Grandparents	Aunts, Uncles	All Others
Connecticut	0	3–6%	4–10%	8–14%
Delaware	2–4%	1–6%	5–10%	10–16%
Indiana	0	1–10%	7–15%	10–20%
Iowa	0	1–8%	5–10%	10–15%
Kansas	0	1–5%	3–12.5%	10–15%
Kentucky	0	2–10%	4–16%	6–16%
Louisiana	2–3%	2–3%	5–7%	5–10%
Maryland	0	1%	10%	10%
Mississippi	0	1–16%	1–16%	1–16%
Montana	0	0	6–24%	8–32%
Nebraska	0	1%	6–9%	6–9%
New Hampshire	0	0	18%	18%
New Jersey	0	0	11–16%	15–16%
New York	0	2–21%	2–21%	2–21%
North Carolina	0	1–12%	4–16%	8–17%
Ohio	0	2–7%	2–7%	2–7%
Oklahoma	0	1–15%	1–15%	1–15%
Pennsylvania	0	6%	15%	15%
South Dakota	0	3.75–15%	4–25%	6–30%
Tennessee	0	9.50%	9.50%	9.50%

Column group header: **Relationship of Beneficiary***

*The general relationship categories may vary slightly from state to state.

transfer tax, stepped-up valuation, and state death taxes.

RESIDENT NON-CITIZENS

It is important to clear up one enormous misunderstanding. Numerous articles have been written stating that a non-citizen is not entitled to the federal estate tax equivalent exclusion. Not so! If the non-citizen is a *resident* (i.e., holds an Alien Registration Card, commonly referred to as a green card), he or she has the right to claim the federal estate tax equivalent exclusion.

If the non-citizen is a resident (i.e., holds an Alien Registration Card, commonly referred to as a green card), he or she has the right to claim the federal estate tax equivalent exclusion.

If you are a resident non-citizen whose spouse dies, and his or her share of the estate exceeds $1 million, every penny over $1 million will be taxed outright. The only way to avoid this outright taxation is by having a Living Trust along with a Q-DOT Trust. (See Chapter 7.) This taxation applies to both separate property and community property states.

An American citizen married to a resident non-citizen cannot utilize the Unlimited Marital Deduction. However, such a citizen does qualify to make an annual gift of $100,000 per year to his or her spouse without any gift or estate tax ramifications. In this manner, a citizen with wealth could marry a non-citizen with few assets and, within six years, could fully utilize the non-citizen spouse's $1 million federal estate tax exclusion. The spousal gift, in conjunction with a Living Trust, is an ideal vehicle to accomplish this annual transfer. The spousal gift is discussed in Chapter 12.

In addition, the fact that a non-citizen spouse cannot utilize the Unlimited Marital Deduction to receive a decedent spouse's assets tax-free demands that the non-citizen spouse's family utilize an A-B or A-B-C Living Trust as opposed to a Will.

DOES THIS TAX ACT NECESSITATE A CHANGE FOR EXISTING LIVING TRUSTS?

As stated earlier in this chapter, no tax expert believes that this tax law as passed will ever come to fruition. No one can confidently predict what we'll end up with, but it's likely that the first piece to go will be the estate tax.

Your Trust may not be designed to gain the most favorable tax benefits of this new Tax Act with its myriad potential changes to the estate tax, the gift tax, the generation-skipping transfer tax, stepped-up valuation, and state death taxes.

In order to benefit, your Living Trust must authorize the trustee to take advantage of the most favorable tax option available at any given time between now and 2011.

ONE OF THE GREATEST CHALLENGES TO AMERICA'S ECONOMY

I believe that one of the greatest challenges to this country's economy is the estate tax imposed on small businesses. The center of the economy is rapidly shifting from manufacturing to services. The present key to our nation's growth is the thousands of small businesses that are started every year. They are a major factor in employing millions of people. Their founders took the risks—and succeeded, most against overwhelming odds. Many fail, but many thrive and continue to make their special contribution to our nation's economy.

In the coming years, the founders of these great small businesses eventually will die, and so will their spouses. If this new Tax Act is repealed, these successful businesses, employing millions, will be subject to the formerly consumptive federal estate tax. Few businesses can remain operating when they have to pay a consumptive federal estate tax. It follows that when these small businesses begin to succumb, the employees lose their jobs, and the country loses their productivity. And so goes our economy—unless estate tax relief is maintained.

MINIMIZING TAXES WITH PROPER ESTATE PLANNING

Few people are really aware of how proper estate planning can minimize the bite that federal estate taxes and state inheritance taxes take from their estates. Everyone should be reasonably knowledgeable about these taxes. People need to know how to minimize these taxes and, where appropriate, how to eliminate them altogether. In addition, people should be aware of when their estates will be subject to estate and inheritance taxes and how much of their estates will be affected. Estate planning should then provide an appropriate means of having the needed liquidity to pay those taxes without selling major assets. Each of these important issues is addressed in subsequent chapters.

6

The Living Trust vs. a Will

Unfortunately, as noted, the word *Will* is synonymous with the process of probate. In my experience—confirmed by the recent Elway Research, Inc., study—more than 50 percent of the people who have Wills fervently believe that, because they have Wills, they will avoid probate. Not so! The good news, however, is that the Living Trust is an exception; it provides an alternative to the shortcomings of a Will.

The history of Wills is fraught with abuse. Thus, the laws pertaining to Wills are extremely rigid and vary widely from state to state. In fact, a person who moves to another state should have his or her Will reviewed for compliance with the new state's law and, in many cases, rewritten to bring it into conformance.

In early times, Wills were typically deathbed statements to the priest. Coincidentally, the church seemed to be receiving an inordinate amount of the estates. Eventually, two witnesses were required to be present for the deathbed statement. With the passage of time and further apparent abuse, it became customary for an individual to place in writing his

or her last Will and testament, which was then witnessed by two or three people.

At least one-third of all written Wills are successfully contested by heirs.

Even today, with all of the legal requirements necessary to adequately satisfy a Will, at least one-third of all written Wills are successfully contested by heirs. Why? After a person writes a Will, he or she typically places it in a safe-deposit box—seldom to be looked at again. As time passes, events occur in the person's life that "might" have caused the Will to be written differently. Thus, the contention is that, if the author of the Will could somehow be brought back to life in order to review the events that have taken place since the Will was written, he or she would change the contents of the Will.

Each person who does write a Will typically changes it about four times during his or her lifetime. A change to a Will is called a "codicil"; however, instead of writing a codicil, most attorneys find it easier to write an entirely new Will. This practice is not only more costly to the individual, but it is also more profitable to the attorney.

At a recent seminar, a woman handed me a copy of a check written to the IRS for $193,000 with the inscription "Warning: This is what happens with no estate planning!" The woman was going through the probate process for her mother, who had died eight months earlier, and the time had arrived to write the estate tax check. Her father had died two years earlier. She recognized that if her mother and father had done some basic estate planning when they were both living, this check would be entirely unnecessary.

In order to appreciate her dilemma, imagine for a moment that you have just received a check for $200,000. Think what you might do with that check—for yourself, your spouse, your children, your grandchildren. Then realize that you must take pen in hand and write a check for $193,000 to the Internal Revenue Service. However, if the parents, prior to their deaths, had done some estate planning and had created a simple A-B Living Trust, this check need not have been written.

You or your children could find yourselves in such a situation. However, with some simple, basic estate planning, your estate can be preserved.

INHERITANCE WITHOUT A WILL

Unfortunately, most people do not have written Wills, and, for those people who do have Wills, their Wills are usually neither current nor appropriate for their present estates. The results can be particularly tragic in second marriages following the death of a spouse.

Far too many people today have no written Will. However, never fear. The state has one for you—only far more complex and not necessarily written according to your desires.

Separate Property States

In separate property states, if two people are married and have children (and have no written Will), the results could be disastrous. If a married couple has one child, the surviving spouse typically will receive half the estate, and the child will receive the other half. If the mar-

ried couple has two or more children, however, the surviving spouse could receive substantially less. Unfortunately, the surviving spouse's share usually is entirely inadequate for his or her future security and well-being.

If the children are minors (younger than age eighteen), the court must create a Trust to handle the children's portion of the estate, and the surviving spouse is subject to court supervision in order to use the children's funds. Once the child attains legal age (eighteen years old), his or her share is distributed outright (handed over in one lump sum), *regardless* of the child's experience or judgment. The child's age, needs, and degree of competency are ignored by the court.

If you don't have a written Will, the state has one for you—but it might not be the one you want.

Community Property States

In community property states, if a married couple have children and leave no written Will, the community property will pass entirely to the surviving spouse. However, separate property will be treated as indicated above for separate property states.

INHERITANCE WITH A WILL

With a properly written Will, you make the decisions. You decide not only who gets what, but when the heirs will get their allocations. You are able to designate what happens to the assets in your estate.

The following sections will acquaint you with the three types of written Wills:

- Holographic Will
- Loving (or Attested) Will
- Testamentary Trust

Unfortunately, all Wills are destined for probate.

Holographic Will

A Holographic Will is a handwritten Will that is signed and dated by the person writing it.

This type of Will is not witnessed by anyone else.

Until recently, a Holographic Will had to be on plain paper with no other printing. There is an actual case of an unbalanced individual who rented a hotel room, sat down at the desk in his hotel room, and wrote out his Will on hotel stationery. After completing his Will, the individual then jumped out the window. The Will was successfully contested, because it was written on hotel stationery with the hotel name and address at the top of the page.

Many states have since eliminated the restriction about a Holographic Will needing to be on plain paper. However, if you decide to write a Holographic Will, you should still use plain paper until you are sure of the requirements in your own state. Be aware, though, that some states no longer recognize a Holographic Will as a valid legal document.

In a few specific situations, I have recommended Holographic Wills as a temporary expedient to young people who have minimal estates and who are just getting started with their careers and building their estates. I have also suggested this form of Will to young newlyweds. Yet, in every case, I have ardently admonished the young people to do formal estate planning with a Living Trust when they decide to start their families—regardless of the size of their estates.

Loving Will

A Loving Will (also known as an Attested Will) is the typical Will drawn up by an attorney and attested (that is, witnessed). I refer to this Will as a "Loving Will" because it usually leaves everything to the surviving spouse or children.

Testamentary Trust

The Testamentary Trust is a step in the right direction—but only a half step, because "testamentary" means that a person must *die* before the Trust goes into effect. Since the Trust is not in effect during a person's lifetime, none of his or her assets are in the Trust. Therefore, this situation means that, upon your death, your assets must go through probate *before* they can be placed in the Trust.

The Testamentary Trust is the best of both worlds for the attorney, who collects a substantial fee for drawing up the Trust now and a probate fee later.

Even though the Testamentary Trust does not avoid probate, it *will* avoid unnecessary estate taxes on the death of the second spouse. Unfortunately, I have yet to find a Testamentary Trust for an estate in excess of $1 million that contains the C Trust. The C Trust, also known as the Q-TIP Trust, is a legal device created by Congress in 1981 to permit avoidance of estate taxes on the estate of the first spouse to die. (A more detailed explanation of the Q-TIP Trust is presented in Chapter 7.)

The Testamentary Trust also suffers from the same potential challenge as a Will, since the Testamentary Trust, like a Will, is usually drawn up, placed in a safe-deposit box, and seldom reviewed again. Events that inevitably occur during a person's life after drawing a Testamentary Trust will permit the person's heirs to successfully contest his or her Trust for the same reason that the heirs are so frequently able to contest a Will.

The Testamentary Trust is, in effect, the best of all worlds for members of the legal profession. The attorney not only receives a substantial fee for drawing up the Testamentary Trust but also will eventually have the opportunity to collect the probate fee.

The best solution is the Living Trust.

LIVING TRUST

The knowledgeable family or individual will choose the Living Trust as the best solution to holding assets. Besides the benefits you have read about so far—especially avoiding probate—the Living Trust is, as you will learn in the next chapter, an excellent way to provide for the support and education of minor children. In addition, unlike other forms of written estate plans, a properly funded Living Trust is basically unchallengeable, because the Trust is "living" (that is, in existence) today and includes *all* of a person's assets. Unlike the Will, which has been badly abused, the Living Trust may be easily changed at any time by simply striking out or adding a section and initialing it.

It is a good idea to always keep an executed copy of your Living Trust at home, where you can make changes to the Trust whenever desired or whenever special circumstances dictate.

If a person makes any changes, it is strongly recommended that he or she eventually have these changes formalized as an amendment (to ensure that the changes are consistent throughout the document). However, such a simple change, without the formality of a legal amendment, *will* stand up in court. Since a person can easily and readily change his or her Living Trust document right up to the hour of death, the document is basically unchallengeable.

NO GREATER GIFT

I know of no greater gift one spouse can give the other, or parents can give their children, than a Living Trust. You need to go through probate only once to appreciate this statement.

The Living Trust has dramatic economic advantages over the Loving Will. To fully appreciate how a Living Trust can have a significant influence on preserving most, or all, of your estate for your heirs, you need to compare the economic differences between a Living Trust and a Loving Will.

The single most important reason for having a Living Trust is to avoid the cost and agony of probate. Attorneys and accountants often advise a client that he or she does not need a Living Trust if the person's estate is less than $1 million. However, the professionals are confusing the federal estate tax exclusion with the probate process, which is entirely separate. Most states require probate for an estate with real estate holdings that exceed $10,000 or total net assets, including personal effects, that exceed $10,000 to $100,000. (See Table 2-1 in Chapter 2.)

A second important reason for having a Living Trust is to avoid paying unnecessary estate taxes. Even though an estate of less than $1 million is not subject to the tax, few people seem to realize that an estate of only $300,000 will typically *double* in value in the next ten to twelve years, by inflation alone. In the past six months, I have reviewed numerous estates that were worth only $200,000 to $300,000 six to seven years ago when the first spouse died. Today, these estates exceed $600,000. Such an estate can avoid estate taxation if it is in a form of Living Trust called an A-B Trust. However, an A-B Trust can be created only while both spouses are living. This also assumes that Congress will not alter the Economic Growth and Tax Relief Reconciliation Act of 2001.

The different types of Living Trusts will be more fully explained in a later chapter. However, for now you need only know that there are four forms of a Living Trust, which will be referred to throughout this chapter: A Trust, A-B Trust, A-B-C Trust, and a Partner A-A Trust. The only other bit of knowledge you need at this point is to understand that a Trust is a legal entity that "owns" (holds title to) your assets, but since you are the trustee of the Trust, *you maintain full control over your assets*.

THE SIZE OF YOUR ESTATE

The size of an estate is of great importance in determining the type of Living Trust that is best for each individual or married couple. All too often, I have seen Living Trusts drawn by attorneys who may have understood the Trust, but who failed to sufficiently understand the client's financial estate and therefore recommended the wrong type of Trust. Such a situation is similar to going into a shoe store, buying a beautiful pair of shoes, and then getting home and finding that the shoes do not fit.

The gross value of an estate and its net value are both important. Probate fees are calculated on the *gross* value of an estate, whereas estate taxes are calculated on the net value of the estate. A net estate is the result of subtracting the liabilities from the assets of the estate. A gross estate is the assets without the liabilities being removed. The example in Figure 6-1 indicates the difference between a gross estate and a net estate.

Note that life insurance on both spouses has been included in Figure 6-1. The reason is that life insurance is included in your estate for

FIGURE 6-1
GROSS ESTATE AND NET ESTATE

Gross Estate

Checking and savings accounts	$ 10,000
Stocks and bonds	50,000
Home	200,000
Other real estate	100,000
Life insurance on both spouses	100,000
Total gross estate	$ 460,000

Net Estate

Checking and savings accounts		$ 10,000
Stocks and bonds		50,000
Home	$ 200,000	
Less: Mortgage	($ 120,000)	
Net value of home	$ 80,000	80,000
Other real estate	$ 100,000	
Less: Mortgage	($ 60,000)	
Net value of real estate	$ 40,000	40,000
Total net estate		$ 180,000
Plus: Life insurance on both spouses		100,000
Net estate plus life insurance		$ 280,000

estate tax purposes. For estates that contain large amounts of insurance, Chapter 12 will show how the insurance can be insulated from the estate by using an Insurance Preservation Trust.

Before proceeding, take a few moments to calculate the gross and net values of your estate. Several examples will be presented for various sizes of estates to illustrate the financial advantages of a Living Trust, and the examples will be much more meaningful when you can relate the most appropriate example to your own personal estate. If your own estate is larger than the value used in the most appropriate illustration, the beneficial effect of having a Living Trust will be the same—only proportionately greater.

The importance of a Living Trust can best be illustrated by showing how a Living Trust minimizes (and usually eliminates) the adverse financial impact of taxes on a person's estate.

The balance of this chapter is devoted to examples comparing the Living Trust with the Loving Will and to the Testamentary Trust. The Living Trust is compared with a Loving Will for the following types of estates:

- Single person with estate under $1 million
- Single person with estate over $1 million
- Married couple with estate under $1 million
- Married couple with estate over $1 million
- Married couple with estate over $2.5 million

The Living Trust is also compared with a Testamentary Trust for the following types of estates:

- Single person with estate under $1 million
- Married couple with estate under $1 million
- Married couple with estate over $2 million

For simplicity in reading, select the examples that best illustrate your estate. You can read those examples and ignore the others. Once you see how the examples work, you may want to turn to Appendices A through F, which provide comparisons for estates of varying sizes, to find a situation that more closely matches your own. The examples in the Appendices are computed in the same way as the examples in this chapter.

Please note that "arithmetic license" has been taken with all of the examples and illustrations; the figures have been rounded off to make the illustration easier to read. In many examples, a calculator will probably not come up with exactly the same numbers! In addition, although probate fees are calculated on the gross estate and federal estate taxes on the net estate, for simplicity of arithmetic calculations, all of the following examples use the net value of the estate in calculating *both* the probate fee and any estate taxes, thus substantially understating the estimated death costs. For the probate fee, all of the examples use a conservative 8 percent of the net estate.

THE LOVING WILL VS. THE LIVING TRUST

Since most people are accustomed to thinking of a Will as an estate-planning instrument, it is logical to first compare a Loving Will with a Living Trust. As pointed out earlier, everyone has a Will, whether it is written or not; if an individual does not have a written Will, the state mandates one for the person.

Single Person with Estate Under $1 Million

The following example illustrates the financial difference between a Loving Will and a Living Trust for a single person's estate valued at less than $1 million—in this case, an estate worth $100,000. The probate cost would be 8 percent of $100,000—which is $8,000. Subtracting the probate cost from the original value of the estate leaves only $92,000 for the heirs, as shown on the left of Figure 6-2. (In addition, the probate process may have taken as long as two years!) Because the value of the estate is less than $1 million, no federal estate tax would be due.

In contrast, if the same individual had a Living Trust, there would be no probate and no cost of probate. Therefore, the full $100,000 value of the estate would come down (that is, be passed on) to the heirs, as shown on the right of Figure 6-2. The Living Trust therefore provides an $8,000 gain for the heirs. However, the amount of money saved is inconsequential compared with the fact that the heirs have been spared the lengthy time period and sheer frustration of the probate process.

Appendix A applies these same principles to an estate of a single person having the following values:

- $100,000
- $200,000
- $300,000
- $400,000

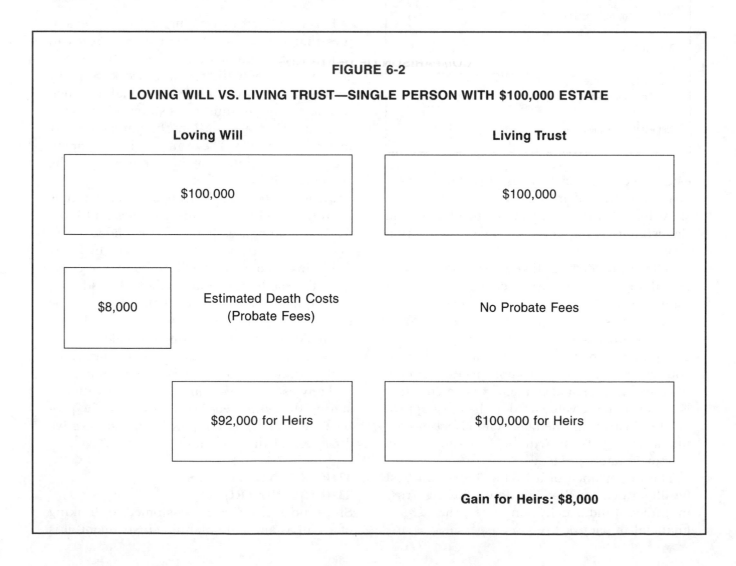

FIGURE 6-2

LOVING WILL VS. LIVING TRUST—SINGLE PERSON WITH $100,000 ESTATE

Loving Will	Living Trust
$100,000	$100,000
$8,000 — Estimated Death Costs (Probate Fees)	No Probate Fees
$92,000 for Heirs	$100,000 for Heirs
	Gain for Heirs: $8,000

- $500,000
- $600,000
- $800,000
- $1 million

- $1.2 million
- $1.5 million
- $2 million

Single Person with Estate Exceeding $1 Million

The following example illustrates the financial difference between a Loving Will and a Living Trust for a single person's estate valued at more than $1 million. Assume that a single person (unmarried or widowed) has an estate worth $1.2 million. An 8 percent probate cost would be $96,000.

In addition to the probate cost, the estate would owe federal estate tax because the value of the estate exceeds the current $1 million federal estate tax exclusion for a single person. The federal estate tax on this estate would be $43,000. (When calculating the federal estate tax in a real-life situation, keep in mind that the cost of probate is first subtracted from the value of the estate, so the federal estate tax in this example would be computed on an estate value of $1,104,000. A comparison of the estate tax computations for the Loving Will and a Living Trust is shown at the end of this example.)

The cost of probate and the expense of the estate tax would yield an estimated death cost of $139,000! After the $139,000 is subtracted from the original estate value of $1.2 million, only $1,061,000 would remain for the heirs, as shown on the left in Figure 6-3.

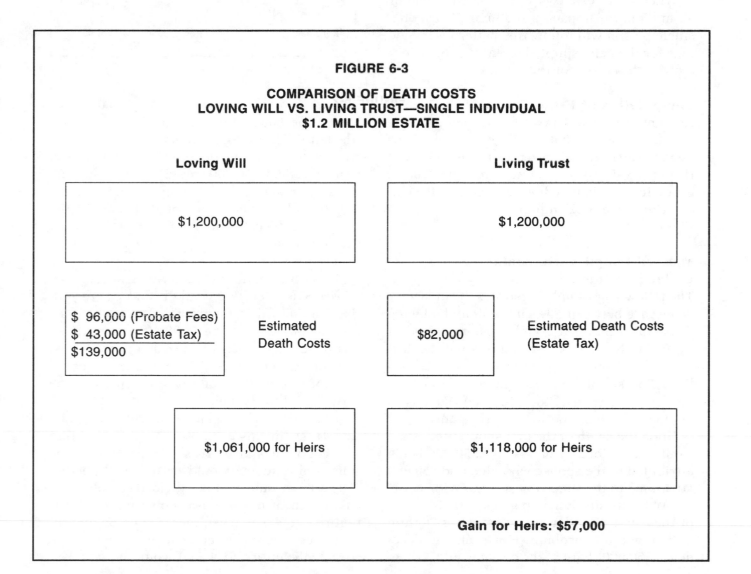

FIGURE 6-3

COMPARISON OF DEATH COSTS
LOVING WILL VS. LIVING TRUST—SINGLE INDIVIDUAL
$1.2 MILLION ESTATE

Loving Will

$1,200,000

$ 96,000 (Probate Fees)
$ 43,000 (Estate Tax)
$139,000

Estimated Death Costs

$1,061,000 for Heirs

Living Trust

$1,200,000

$82,000

Estimated Death Costs (Estate Tax)

$1,118,000 for Heirs

Gain for Heirs: $57,000

If the same person has a Living Trust, there would be no cost of probate. However, federal estate tax would again be due. There are no probate fees to deduct from the value of the estate; consequently, the federal estate tax would be based on the entire estate value of $1.2 million. As shown on the right in Figure 6-3, when the federal estate tax expense of $82,000 is deducted from the original $1.2 million value of the estate, the heirs would be left with $1,118,000.

As a result, even though the federal estate taxes would be higher with a Living Trust, the total death costs would be greater with a Will. The Living Trust would provide roughly an extra $57,000 for the heirs, as shown at the bottom of Figure 6-3.

Whether an estate is valued at $100,000 or $2 million, the impact of the Living Trust on a single person will follow this pattern. The savings for the heirs simply increases proportionately with the size of the estate.

Computation of Estate Taxes

In computing estate taxes for an estate having a Will, recognize that the attorney gets his or her share first. The probate fee is deducted from the value of the estate before the federal estate tax is calculated. An example of the calculation for a $1.2 million estate is shown in Figure 6-4.

Married Couple with Estate Under $1 Million

The following example illustrates the monetary difference between a Loving Will and a Living Trust for a married couple's estate valued at $100,000. No federal estate taxes will be due, since the estate is valued at less than $1 million. For simplicity, assume that, upon the death of one spouse, the $100,000 estate is to be divided equally between both spouses.

Upon the death of the first spouse, the estate would be divided in half—with $50,000 being attributed to the spouse who died and $50,000 attributed to the surviving spouse. With a Loving Will, the surviving spouse's $50,000 share of the estate would automatically pass to him or her without probate. However, the decedent's $50,000 share of the estate would be sub-

---

FIGURE 6-4

COMPARISON OF ESTATE TAX CALCULATIONS
Single Person with $1.2 Million Estate

	With a Will	With a Living Trust
Value of estate	$1,200,000	$1,200,000
Probate cost (8%)	($ 96,000)	-0-
Taxable estate	$1,104,000	$1,200,000
Federal estate tax exclusion	($1,000,000)	($1,000,000)
Net taxable estate	$ 104,000	$ 200,000
Federal estate tax	$ 43,000	$ 82,000
Total cost to estate (Probate fees and estate tax)	$ 139,000	$ 82,000
Net Estate	**$1,061,000**	**$1,118,000**

---

ject to probate. At 8 percent of $50,000, the cost of probate would be $4,000, as shown on the left in Figure 6-5. If this probate cost were subtracted from the decedent's $50,000 share, a net estate of $46,000 would be left. Thus, the surviving spouse eventually would receive $96,000—his or her own $50,000 share of the original $100,000 estate and $46,000 remaining from the decedent's share of the original estate.

Upon the death of the surviving spouse, the entire $96,000 estate would be subject to probate, as shown in Figure 6-5. The probate fee on this estate would be $8,000 (figure rounded off for clarity). When the $8,000 probate cost is subtracted from $96,000, only $88,000 of the original $100,000 estate would remain to be distributed to the heirs.

In contrast, if the married couple had a Living Trust (in this example, it is assumed that the couple has an A Trust, defined later), the financial outcome would be decidedly better. The estate would again be divided equally upon the death of one spouse; however, since the entire estate is in trust, there would be no probate and, therefore, no cost of probate. As a result, the entire $100,000 would come down

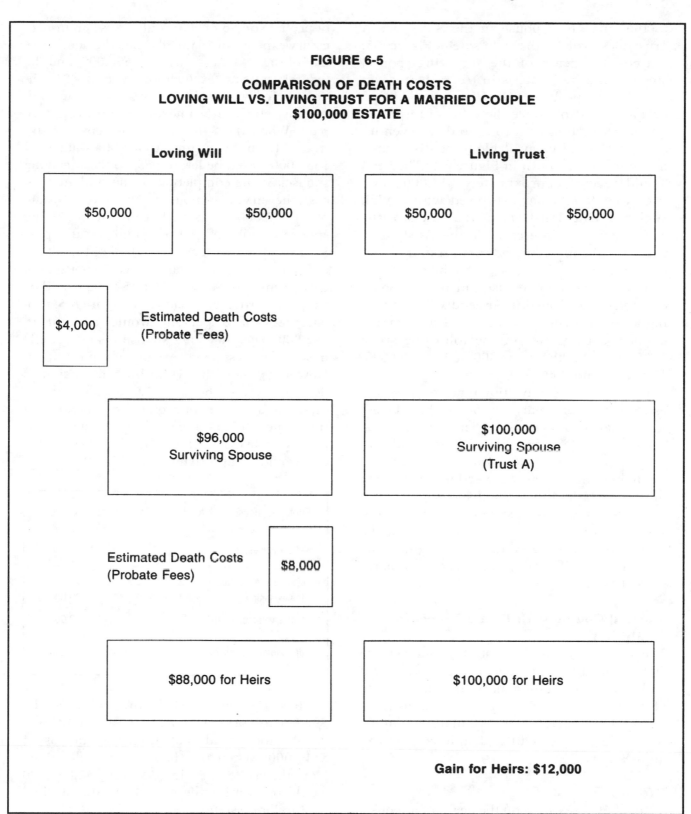

FIGURE 6-5

**COMPARISON OF DEATH COSTS
LOVING WILL VS. LIVING TRUST FOR A MARRIED COUPLE
$100,000 ESTATE**

Loving Will   **Living Trust**

$50,000 $50,000 $50,000 $50,000

$4,000   Estimated Death Costs
           (Probate Fees)

$96,000 $100,000
Surviving Spouse   Surviving Spouse
                                    (Trust A)

Estimated Death Costs $8,000
(Probate Fees)

$88,000 for Heirs $100,000 for Heirs

Gain for Heirs: $12,000

to the surviving spouse in the Survivor's A Trust, as shown on the right side in Figure 6-5.

Upon the death of the surviving spouse, since the entire estate is in trust, there *again* would be no probate. Since there would be no probate costs to reduce the value of the estate on either the first or second to die, the entire $100,000 would be available to be distributed to the heirs, as shown in Figure 6-5. The heirs would receive approximately $12,000 more than they would have received with a Will. With a Living Trust, *all* of the assets of the estate have been preserved in the Trust, to be used, for example, for the support and education of minor children or grandchildren.

The same principles used in the foregoing examples are applied in Appendix B, comparing a Loving Will and an A Trust for married couples with estates of the following sizes: $100,000, $200,000, $300,000, $400,000, $500,000, and $600,000.

It is my strong conviction that, regardless of estate size, every married couple should elect to have an A-B Trust, in order to protect the estate from the effects of inflation and real estate appreciation. Remember, with proper estate planning, estate tax need not be applied until the death of the *second* spouse, by which time the value of the estate can increase substantially. Since it is anyone's guess what the estate tax will bring eventually, any estate tax can take a significant tax bite out of your hard-earned estate.

Married Couple with Estate Exceeding $1 Million

The following example illustrates a much more significant difference between a Loving Will and a Living Trust for a married couple's estate of $1.2 million. This example demonstrates why it is important for any married couple with an estate exceeding $1 million to utilize an A-B Trust.

With a Loving Will

With a Loving Will, upon the death of a spouse, the estate would effectively be divided in half, as shown at the top of Figure 6-6. The decedent's half of the estate must pass through probate before being distributed. An 8 percent cost

of probate on $600,000 would cause an unnecessary expense of $48,000! Since the decedent's half of the estate is valued at $600,000, and the federal estate tax exclusion is currently $1 million, no federal estate taxes would be due, and, in most states, no inheritance tax would be paid. When the $48,000 probate cost is subtracted from the original $600,000 estate, only $552,000 would be left to pass to the surviving spouse. At the completion of the probate process, the surviving spouse would have an estate of $1,152,000—$600,000 from the surviving spouse's half of the original estate plus $552,000 from the decedent's half of the estate.

Upon the death of the surviving spouse, the entire remaining estate of $1,152,000 would be subject to probate, as shown in Figure 6-6. Probate fees of 8 percent would amount to $92,000. The surviving spouse also currently has a federal estate tax exclusion of $1 million. However, when the $1 million exclusion is deducted from the $1,152,000 value of the estate (less the cost of probate), the balance of the estate ($152,000) would be subject to federal estate tax. Therefore, the federal estate tax due would be approximately $25,000.

Surviving spouse's estate	$1,152,000
Less: Probate fees	($ 92,000)
Net taxable estate	$1,060,000
Less: Federal estate tax exclusion	($1,000,000)
Taxable value of estate	$ 60,000
Approximate estate tax	$ 25,000

Thus, the estimated death cost would be $92,000 of probate cost plus an additional $25,000 for federal estate taxes—a total cost of $117,000! When this hefty sum is deducted from the estate of $1,152,000, only $1,035,000 would remain for the heirs from the original $1.2 million estate.

With a Living Trust

If the same estate were held in a Living Trust, as shown in Figure 6-7, the estate would still

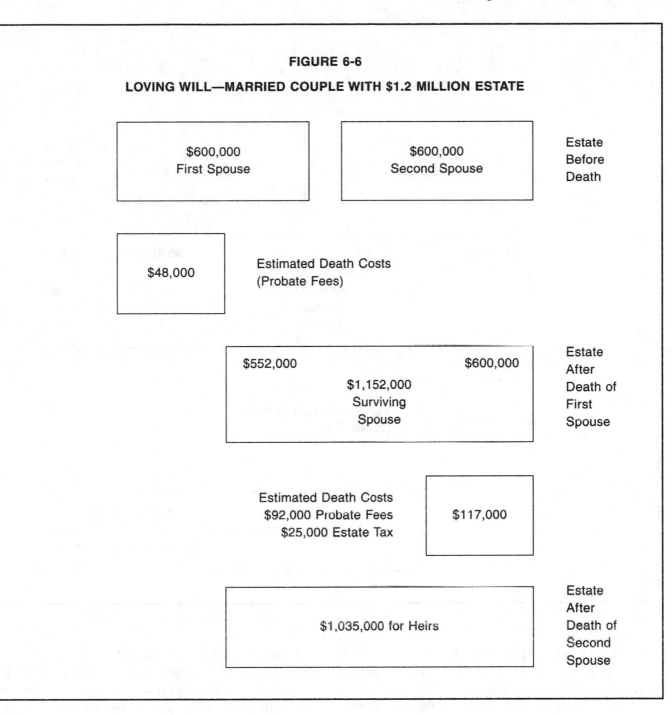

FIGURE 6-6

LOVING WILL—MARRIED COUPLE WITH $1.2 MILLION ESTATE

$600,000
First Spouse

$600,000
Second Spouse

Estate
Before
Death

$48,000

Estimated Death Costs
(Probate Fees)

$552,000 $600,000
$1,152,000
Surviving
Spouse

Estate
After
Death of
First
Spouse

Estimated Death Costs
$92,000 Probate Fees
$25,000 Estate Tax

$117,000

$1,035,000 for Heirs

Estate
After
Death of
Second
Spouse

be divided in half. However, since the entire estate is in trust, there would be no cost of probate. Since the surviving spouse has only one federal estate tax exclusion of $1 million, when he or she dies, $200,000 of the estate would be subject to federal estate tax. The federal estate tax would be $82,000, leaving only $1,118,000 for the heirs. With only an A Trust, the federal estate tax exclusion of the first spouse would go unused (effectively, *thrown away*).

The couple could benefit even more from a Living Trust if their assets were placed into an A-B Trust, a form of Trust in which each spouse's share of the assets comes down into a separate division of the same Trust, preserving both federal estate tax exclusions.

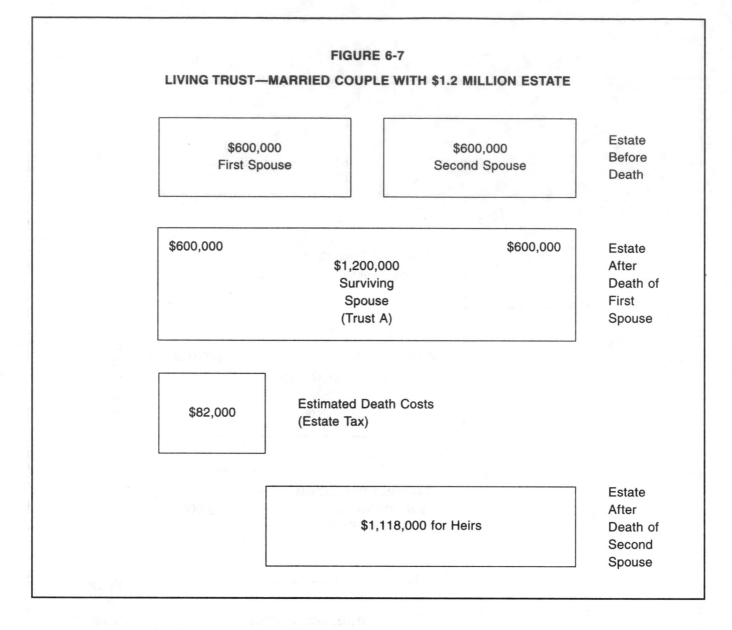

FIGURE 6-7

LIVING TRUST—MARRIED COUPLE WITH $1.2 MILLION ESTATE

| $600,000 First Spouse | $600,000 Second Spouse | Estate Before Death |

$600,000 $600,000   Estate
$1,200,000   After
Surviving   Death of
Spouse   First
(Trust A)   Spouse

$82,000   Estimated Death Costs (Estate Tax)

$1,118,000 for Heirs   Estate After Death of Second Spouse

As shown in Figure 6-8, the entire $1.2 million would come down to the surviving spouse in the following manner: The surviving spouse's half of the estate, $600,000, would come down to the surviving spouse in Trust A (the survivor's Trust). The other half of the estate, attributed to the spouse who died, would come down in Trust B (the decedent's Trust). The decedent's federal estate tax exclusion of $1 million would be deducted from the deceased spouse's half of the estate, yielding an estate tax of zero; in most states, there also would be no state inheritance tax to pay.

The assets in the Decedent's B Trust would thus be insulated from any further estate tax-ations, regardless of the value to which they may grow. This would therefore make Trust B an excellent estate-planning tool for sheltering growth items. (The use of the B Trust to shelter appreciating assets from unnecessary taxation is discussed more fully in Chapter 15.)

Since the entire estate is still in trust, there would be no probate cost upon the death of the surviving spouse. Once the surviving spouse has died, the assets in the Survivor's A Trust would be subject to estate tax. However, because the second spouse to die also has a federal estate tax exclusion of $1 million, the $600,000 in Trust A escapes estate taxation, and in most states, no state inheritance tax

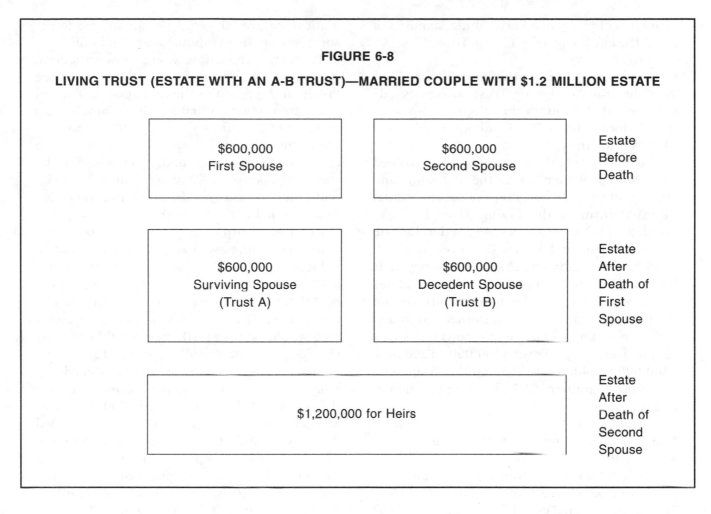

FIGURE 6-8

LIVING TRUST (ESTATE WITH AN A-B TRUST)—MARRIED COUPLE WITH $1.2 MILLION ESTATE

$600,000 First Spouse	$600,000 Second Spouse	Estate Before Death
$600,000 Surviving Spouse (Trust A)	$600,000 Decedent Spouse (Trust B)	Estate After Death of First Spouse
$1,200,000 for Heirs		Estate After Death of Second Spouse

would be due. As Figure 6-8 shows, the entire $1.2 million estate would be passed to the heirs.

Another way to compare the A Trust and A-B Trust is to say that, by passing the entire estate to the surviving spouse, the A Trust "throws away" the first spouse's federal estate tax exclusion of $1 million. For estates valued in excess of $1 million, this action would be a costly mistake. In contrast, the A-B Trust preserves the exclusion by putting the decedent's $600,000 into Trust B (the Decedent's B Trust), where that share of the estate would be insulated from further estate taxes (since, in effect, it has already been subjected to federal estate tax).

"Throwing away" the decedent's federal estate tax exclusion means that if the decedent's share of the estate were simply passed to the surviving spouse (rather than put in the Decedent's B Trust), the value of the surviving spouse's share of the estate would *increase*. In most cases, the surviving spouse's estate would then be valued at more than the $1 million federal estate tax exclusion. When the surviving spouse dies, federal estate tax would be due on the estate. The share of the estate originally attributed to the first to die would then have been subjected to federal estate tax on two occasions!

Although it is common practice to speak of a Living Trust as being an A Trust, a B Trust, or an A-B Trust, the terms are not really referring to separate Trusts, but merely to two divisions of the same Trust.

Note that Trusts A and B are not really separate Trusts. Although it is common practice to speak of a Living Trust as being an A Trust, a B Trust, or an A-B Trust, the terms are not really referring to separate Trusts, but merely to two divisions of the same Trust. The next chapter will give you a better understanding of the different forms of a Living Trust.

Comparison of Loving Will and Living Trust

What has the A-B Living Trust accomplished? Compare the amounts that Figure 6-9 shows remain for the heirs. The result is an additional $165,000 for the heirs!

The A-B form of the Living Trust has avoided $48,000 of probate costs on the first estate and $92,000 of probate costs on the second estate. The A-B form of the Living Trust has also avoided $25,000 of *unnecessary* federal estate taxes on the second estate. Moreover, although $165,000 is a substantial sum of money, it is inconsequential when compared with what has really been avoided—the agony of probate on the first to die and again on the second to die.

Appendix C presents comparisons for estates of the following sizes: $100,000, $200,000, $300,000, $400,000, $500,000, $600,000, $800,000, $1 million, $1.2 million, $1.5 million, and $2 million.

Married Couple with Estate Exceeding $2.5 Million

The following example illustrates a significant difference between a Loving Will and a Living Trust for a married couple's estate that exceeds $2.5 million, showing how an A-B-C Trust can be used to good advantage for such an estate. Any married couple with an estate exceeding $2.5 million should have an A-B-C Trust to avoid estate tax upon the death of the *first* spouse. We also recommend that a couple with a $1.5 million estate seriously consider an A-B-C Trust in order to anticipate the future effects of inflation.

With a Loving Will

When the first spouse dies (leaving only a Loving Will), the half of the estate attributable to the decedent would be subject to probate, as shown in Figure 6-10. The cost of probate would be 8 percent of $1,250,000, or $100,000! When the $1 million federal estate tax exclusion is deducted from the $1,250,000 estate being probated, a taxable estate of $250,000 would still exist if it were not for the Unlimited Marital Deduction provision, which auto-

matically allows the entire estate to pass to the surviving spouse without estate taxation.

Therefore, the estate would pay no federal estate tax and, presumably, no state inheritance tax upon the death of the first spouse. The net estate would be $1,150,000—the original estate of $1,250,000 minus the $100,000 of probate cost. This remaining estate would come down to the surviving spouse and, when added to the surviving spouse's $1,250,000 half of the original estate, would give the surviving spouse an estate valued at $2,400,000.

Upon the death of the surviving spouse, the entire remaining estate of $2,400,000 would be subject to probate, as shown next in Figure 6-10. At 8 percent, the cost of probate would be $192,000. Every penny beyond the surviving spouse's $1 million federal estate tax exclusion would be taxed. (Remember that passing the decedent's share of the estate to the surviving spouse effectively wastes the decedent's federal estate tax exclusion.) The estate tax on the balance of the estate ($2,208,000) would be $537,000, which would result in an estimated death cost (probate costs plus estate taxes) of $729,000! When this amount is deducted from the surviving spouse's estate of $2,400,000, only $1,671,000 of the original $2.5 million estate would be left for the heirs.

With a Living Trust

If the same married couple had an A-B Living Trust, the estate would again be divided in half upon the death of the first spouse. However, because the estate is in trust, there would be no cost of probate. The surviving spouse's half of the estate, $1,250,000, would pass down to Trust A (the survivor's Trust), and the deceased spouse's $1,250,000 could flow into Trust B (the decedent's Trust).

However, since the amount in Trust B exceeds the $1 million exclusion, an estate tax of $103,000 would be due on the excess $250,000, computed as follows:

Decedent's excess estate	$250,000
Less: Federal estate tax (40%)	($103,000)
Balance of decedent's estate	$147,000

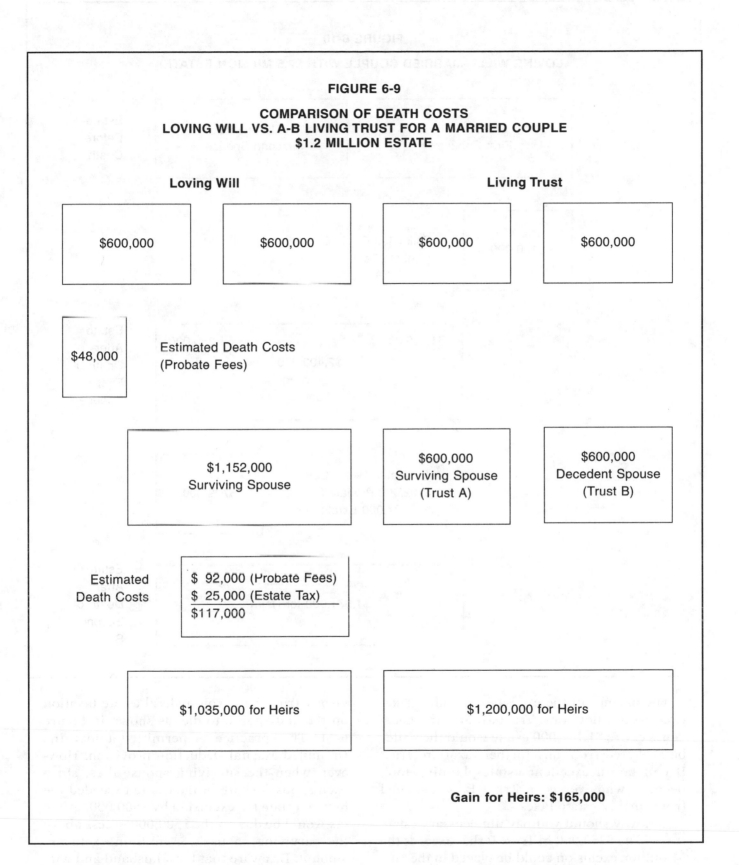

FIGURE 6-9

**COMPARISON OF DEATH COSTS
LOVING WILL VS. A-B LIVING TRUST FOR A MARRIED COUPLE
$1.2 MILLION ESTATE**

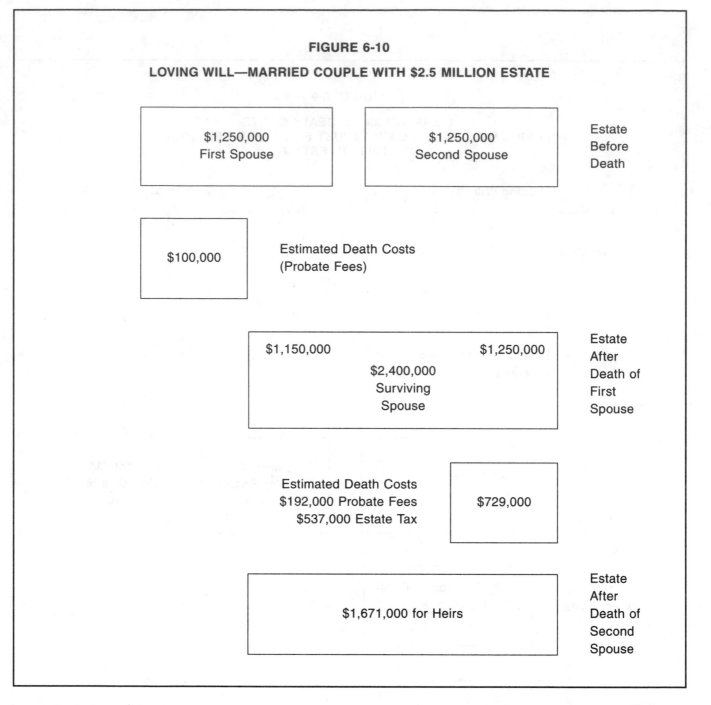

FIGURE 6-10

LOVING WILL—MARRIED COUPLE WITH $2.5 MILLION ESTATE

| $1,250,000 First Spouse | $1,250,000 Second Spouse | Estate Before Death |

$100,000   Estimated Death Costs (Probate Fees)

$1,150,000 $1,250,000   Estate After Death of First Spouse
$2,400,000
Surviving
Spouse

Estimated Death Costs
$192,000 Probate Fees $729,000
$537,000 Estate Tax

$1,671,000 for Heirs   Estate After Death of Second Spouse

The balance of the excess estate, after taxation, would flow into Trust B, and the decedent's entire $1,147,000 estate would thereafter be sheltered from any further taxation. Trust B can be an excellent estate-planning tool, because whatever is in Trust B is insulated from further estate taxes.

Yet, why should you pay unnecessary estate taxes? The $250,000 in Trust B that exceeds the $1 million exclusion could be placed in the Survivor's Trust A to avoid federal estate taxation on the first spouse to die, as shown in Figure 6-11. This practice is permitted under the Unlimited Marital Deduction provision. However, when the surviving spouse dies, since each spouse's share of the estate exceeded the federal estate tax exclusion by $500,000, estate tax would be due on the $500,000 excess above the surviving spouse's $1 million exclusion amount. Be aware that for a husband and wife

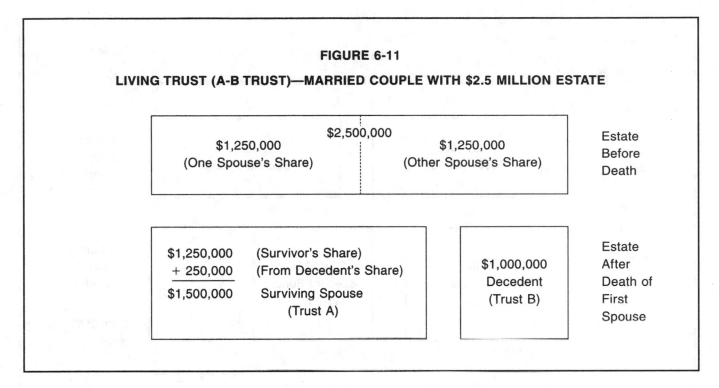

FIGURE 6-11

LIVING TRUST (A-B TRUST)—MARRIED COUPLE WITH $2.5 MILLION ESTATE

	$2,500,000		Estate Before Death
$1,250,000 (One Spouse's Share)		$1,250,000 (Other Spouse's Share)	

$1,250,000 (Survivor's Share)
+ 250,000 (From Decedent's Share)
——————
$1,500,000 Surviving Spouse (Trust A)

$1,000,000 Decedent (Trust B)

Estate After Death of First Spouse

who have been in previous marriages, a drawback to this approach is that the decedent's $250,000, once placed in the Survivor's A Trust, is now controlled by the survivor. The assets in the Survivor's A Trust are usually designated to be distributed to the survivor's heirs—thus potentially depriving the decedent's heirs of $250,000.

An even better approach, however, is to use the C Trust, also known as the Q-TIP Trust. (See Chapter 7 for an explanation of the Q-TIP Trust.)

If the couple have established an A-B-C Trust, the estate can defer paying estate taxes until the death of the surviving spouse, and they are assured that beneficiaries of the decedent spouse will ultimately receive their designated share. (The surviving spouse cannot change the beneficiaries or the allocation and distribution of assets to the heirs in the Q-TIP Trust.) Because the decedent has a federal estate tax exclusion of $1 million, only $1 million of the decedent's estate should be brought down into Trust B (to avoid payment of unnecessary estate taxes), and any excess (above $1 million) is placed in the C Trust.

Trust B is similar to a cup that holds only eight ounces: when you try to pour a quart of water into that eight-ounce cup, the balance will overflow. Here, the overflow (any amount greater than $1 million) would be subject to federal estate tax. With an A-B-C Trust, the overflow goes into the C Trust.

In this particular example, after deducting the $1 million federal estate tax exclusion from the decedent's $1,250,000 share of the estate, $250,000 would still remain. If the excess $250,000 is placed in a C Trust, as shown in Figure 6-12, no federal estate tax would be due—until the death of the second spouse.

Upon the death of the surviving spouse, there would be no probate, since all of the assets are in trust. Any estate tax would be computed on the assets *remaining* in Trust C *and* in Trust A. The tax is based not on what went into the Trust, but on what is *left* in the Trust, upon the death of the surviving spouse. The tax is not a deferred tax; it is simply a tax upon the assets remaining in Trust A and Trust C.

If the combined value of the assets in Trust A and Trust C were less than $1 million, no federal estate taxes would be due. In the illustration of the $2.5 million estate previously shown in Figure 6-12, Trust C contains $250,000, and Trust A contains $1,250,000, yielding a total

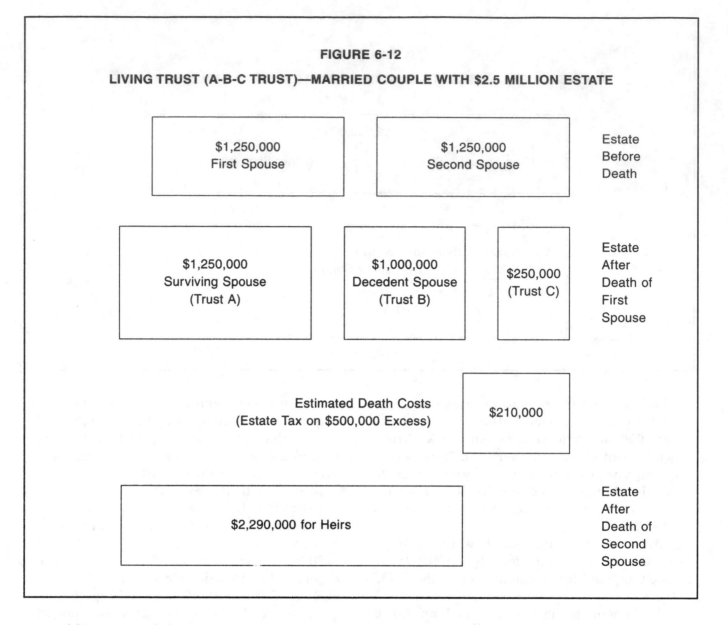

FIGURE 6-12

LIVING TRUST (A-B-C TRUST)—MARRIED COUPLE WITH $2.5 MILLION ESTATE

$1,250,000 First Spouse	$1,250,000 Second Spouse

Estate Before Death

$1,250,000 Surviving Spouse (Trust A)	$1,000,000 Decedent Spouse (Trust B)	$250,000 (Trust C)

Estate After Death of First Spouse

Estimated Death Costs
(Estate Tax on $500,000 Excess) $210,000

$2,290,000 for Heirs

Estate After Death of Second Spouse

taxable estate of $1,500,000. When the $1 million exclusion is subtracted from the $1,500,000 taxable portion of the estate, $500,000 would be subject to federal estate tax. The federal estate tax would therefore be $210,000. Deducting these taxes from the original estate of $2.5 million would leave $2,290,000 for the heirs.

By comparing the amounts remaining to the heirs in Figure 6-13, you can see that the heirs gain $619,000 from the use of an A-B-C Living Trust. The Living Trust has avoided $100,000 of probate cost on the first to die, has avoided $192,000 of probate cost on the second to die, and has reduced the bite of estate taxes by

$327,000. In addition, the agony of probate has been avoided twice—on the first and second spouses to die. Do not forget that the cost and length of the probate process are proportionate to the size of the estate.

Refer to Appendix D for comparisons of estates of the following sizes: $2.5 million, $3 million, $4 million, and $5 million.

COMPARISON OF A TESTAMENTARY TRUST WITH A LIVING TRUST

The Testamentary Trust is a Trust created *within a Will*—and takes effect only upon death. This type of Trust is only a half step in the right direction, because it is created upon

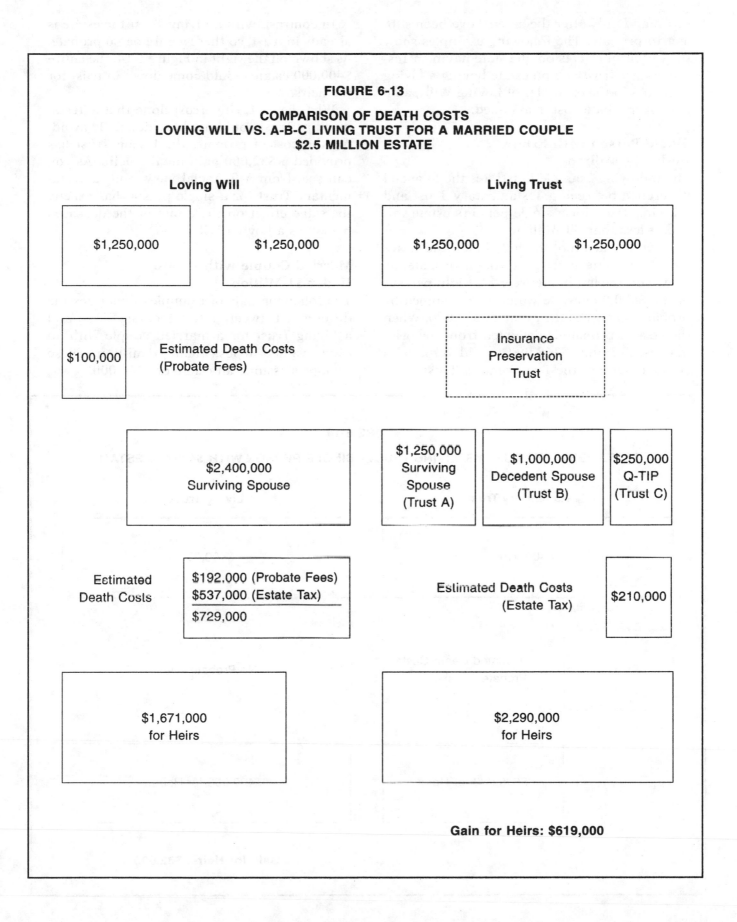

FIGURE 6-13

**COMPARISON OF DEATH COSTS
LOVING WILL VS. A-B-C LIVING TRUST FOR A MARRIED COUPLE
$2.5 MILLION ESTATE**

Loving Will

Living Trust

$1,250,000

$1,250,000

$1,250,000

$1,250,000

$100,000

Estimated Death Costs
(Probate Fees)

Insurance
Preservation
Trust

$2,400,000
Surviving Spouse

$1,250,000
Surviving
Spouse
(Trust A)

$1,000,000
Decedent Spouse
(Trust B)

$250,000
Q-TIP
(Trust C)

Estimated
Death Costs

$192,000 (Probate Fees)
$537,000 (Estate Tax)
—————————
$729,000

Estimated Death Costs
(Estate Tax)

$210,000

$1,671,000
for Heirs

$2,290,000
for Heirs

Gain for Heirs: $619,000

death and only after the assets have been subject to probate. The following examples show the different effects on an estate having a Testamentary Trust and an estate having a Living Trust. As in the examples of Loving Wills, an 8 percent probate cost is assumed.

Single Person with Estate Under $1 Million

The following example illustrates the financial difference between a Testamentary Trust and a Living Trust for a single person's estate valued at less than $1 million.

Upon the death of the individual, the entire $400,000 estate must go through probate, as shown on the left in Figure 6-14. Eight percent of the $400,000 estate would be consumed by probate—a cost to the estate of $32,000. When the cost of probate is deducted from the original estate, only $368,000 would remain to come down into the Testamentary Trust.

In contrast, with a Living Trust the estate is already in trust, so there would be no probate. As shown on the right in Figure 6-14, the entire $400,000 estate would come down in trust for the heirs.

What has a Living Trust done that a Testamentary Trust could not have done? By avoiding the cost of probate, the Living Trust has provided a $32,000 gain for the heirs. As you can see, from a financial viewpoint, a Testamentary Trust for a single person has exactly the same effect on the estate of the deceased person as a Loving Will.

Married Couple with Estate Under $1 Million

The following pair of examples illustrates the difference between a Testamentary Trust and a Living Trust for a married couple with an estate valued at less than $1 million. These examples assume an estate of $400,000.

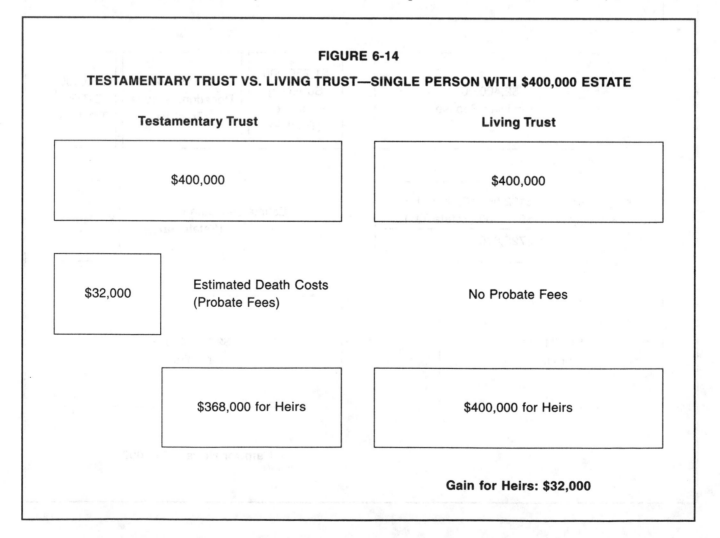

FIGURE 6-14

TESTAMENTARY TRUST VS. LIVING TRUST—SINGLE PERSON WITH $400,000 ESTATE

Testamentary Trust — Living Trust

$400,000 — $400,000

$32,000 — Estimated Death Costs (Probate Fees) — No Probate Fees

$368,000 for Heirs — $400,000 for Heirs

Gain for Heirs: $32,000

With a Testamentary Trust

For a couple with a Testamentary Trust, upon the death of the first spouse, the surviving spouse's half of the estate, $200,000, would come down directly to the surviving spouse (not in trust), as shown at the top of Figure 6-15.

The decedent's share of the estate would be subject to probate. An 8 percent probate fee on the $200,000 share of the estate would yield a probate cost of $16,000. After the probate cost is deducted from the original estate, $184,000 remains, which would then come down into the Testamentary Trust B. These funds are now insulated from further estate taxes, but the agony of probate was not avoided. The surviving spouse would end up with an overall estate of $384,000—the survivor's $200,000 original share of the estate and the $184,000 in Trust B.

Upon the death of the surviving spouse, the first decedent's half of the estate (the $184,000 in Trust B) would not be subject to probate or estate taxes; however, the second decedent's half of the estate would be subject to probate. The probate cost on the second decedent's $200,000 estate would be $16,000. When this amount is deducted from that spouse's estate and the remaining estate is combined with the $184,000 from the Decedent's Trust B, only $368,000 would be left for the heirs from the original $400,000 estate.

With a Living Trust

In contrast, with a Living Trust there would be no probate upon the death of a spouse, as shown in Figure 6-16, since the estate is already in trust. When the first spouse dies, the estate would be divided in half, and the surviving spouse's half of the estate, $200,000, would come down to the surviving spouse in Trust A. The decedent's half of the estate would come down to the Decedent's Trust B (without going through probate), where it would be insulated from further estate taxes.

Upon the death of the surviving spouse, since the entire estate is in trust, there would again be no probate. The entire $400,000 estate would come down in trust to the heirs.

Thus, a Living Trust avoids a $16,000 probate cost on the first to die and a $16,000 probate cost on the second to die—a total gain for the heirs of $32,000.

Appendix E contains additional comparative illustrations that examine the similarities and differences between a Testamentary Trust and a Living Trust for married couples with A-B Trusts. The illustrations present comparisons for estates of the following sizes: $400,000, $500,000, $600,000, $800,000, $1 million, $1.2 million, $1.5 million, and $2 million.

Married Couple with Estate Exceeding $2 Million

The final examples in this chapter illustrate the difference between a Testamentary Trust and a Living Trust for a married couple with an estate valued at more than $2 million. Here, the estate is valued at $2.5 million.

With a Testamentary Trust

If the couple's assets are held in a Testamentary Trust, upon the death of the first spouse, the surviving spouse's half of the estate, $1,250,000, would come down directly to the surviving spouse without going through probate, as shown in the upper portion of Figure 6-17. The decedent's half of the estate, however, would be subject to probate. An 8 percent probate fee for the decedent's $1,250,000 share of the estate would produce a probate cost of $100,000. After the probate cost is deducted from the original estate, $1,150,000 would be left to come down into trust.

When the decedent's federal estate tax exclusion of $1 million is deducted from the $1,150,000 remaining after probate, $150,000 of the estate would still be subject to federal estate tax. The excess $150,000 would be subject to a federal estate tax of $62,000! Together, the cost of probate and the estate tax would reduce the estate by $162,000. From the original $1,250,000 estate, only $1,088,000 would remain to be put in the decedent's Trust; the surviving spouse would have $162,000 less on which to live.

Upon the death of the surviving spouse, the first decedent's half of the estate (the $1,250,000 in Trust B) would not be subject to probate or estate taxes; however, the second decedent's half of the estate would be subject to probate, as shown in Figure 6-17. The probate cost on the $1,250,000 estate of the second spouse to die would also be $100,000. After

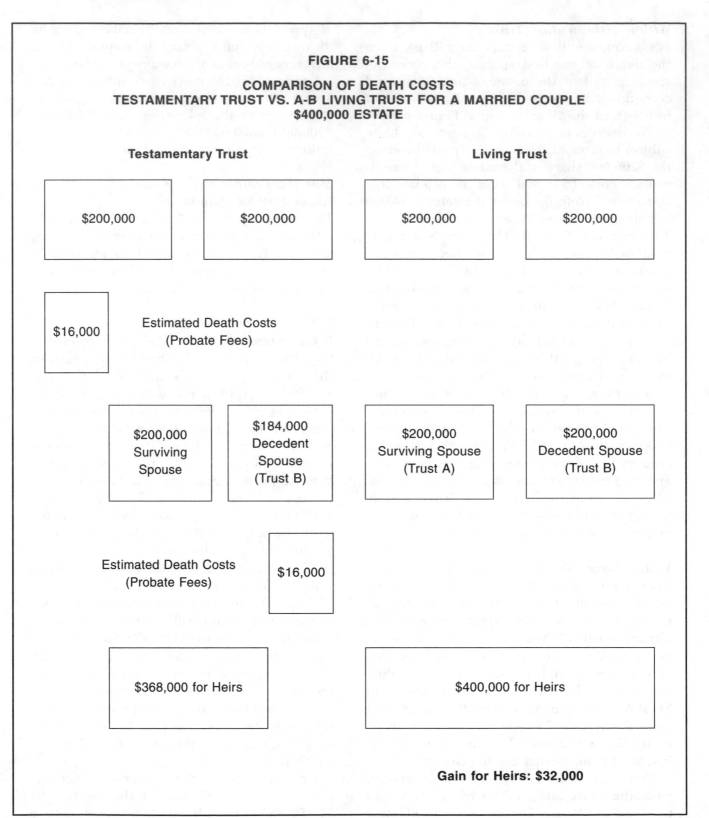

FIGURE 6-15

COMPARISON OF DEATH COSTS
TESTAMENTARY TRUST VS. A-B LIVING TRUST FOR A MARRIED COUPLE
$400,000 ESTATE

Testamentary Trust

Living Trust

$200,000

$200,000

$200,000

$200,000

$16,000

Estimated Death Costs
(Probate Fees)

$200,000
Surviving
Spouse

$184,000
Decedent
Spouse
(Trust B)

$200,000
Surviving Spouse
(Trust A)

$200,000
Decedent Spouse
(Trust B)

Estimated Death Costs
(Probate Fees)

$16,000

$368,000 for Heirs

$400,000 for Heirs

Gain for Heirs: $32,000

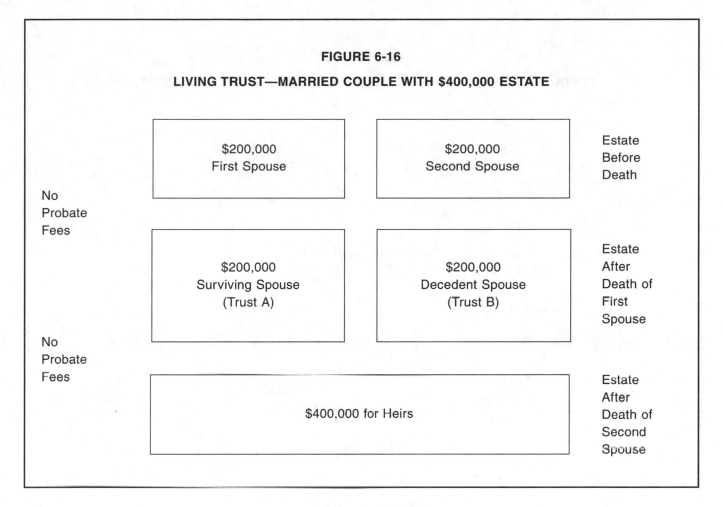

FIGURE 6-16

LIVING TRUST—MARRIED COUPLE WITH $400,000 ESTATE

No Probate Fees

$200,000 First Spouse | $200,000 Second Spouse | Estate Before Death

$200,000 Surviving Spouse (Trust A) | $200,000 Decedent Spouse (Trust B) | Estate After Death of First Spouse

No Probate Fees

$400,000 for Heirs | Estate After Death of Second Spouse

the probate cost is deducted from the original value of the estate, only $1,150,000 would be left—and some of that would be subject to federal estate tax. Deducting the second decedent's $1 million federal estate tax exclusion from the remaining value of the estate leaves a balance of $1,150,000 subject to federal estate tax. The estate tax on the $1,150,000 excess would be $62,000. Thus, the probate fee and the estate tax on the second spouse's estate would further reduce the estate by $162,000. From the original $2.5 million estate, only $2,176,000 would be left to come down to the heirs—a loss of $324,000.

With a Living Trust
In contrast, with the Living Trust, since the estate is already in trust, there would be no probate when either spouse dies. As Figure 6-18 shows, when the first spouse dies, the estate would be divided in half, and the surviving spouse's $1,250,000 half of the estate

would come down to the surviving spouse in Trust A. To avoid unnecessary estate taxation, only $1 million of the decedent's estate would be placed in the B Trust; the $250,000 excess would be placed in the C Trust.

The $1 million part of the decedent's estate in Trust B would be insulated from further estate taxes, because it would be offset by the $1 million exclusion. Trust B not only preserved the decedent's federal estate tax exclusion but also insulated the assets in Trust B from any further estate taxes.

Upon the death of the surviving spouse, since everything is in trust, there would be no probate. Estate taxes would be due on the total value of whatever assets remain in Trust C and in Trust A. In Figure 6-18, the $250,000 in Trust C and $1,250,000 in Trust A yield a total taxable estate of $1,500,000. Deducting the $1 million federal estate tax exclusion of the surviving spouse leaves $500,000 subject to federal estate tax. The estate tax on $500,000

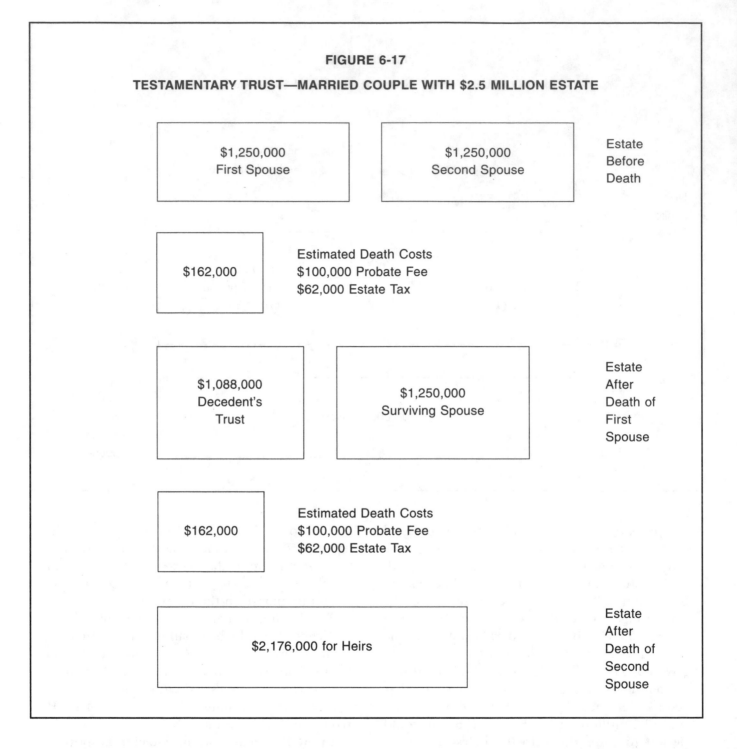

FIGURE 6-17

TESTAMENTARY TRUST—MARRIED COUPLE WITH $2.5 MILLION ESTATE

$1,250,000
First Spouse

$1,250,000
Second Spouse

Estate Before Death

$162,000

Estimated Death Costs
$100,000 Probate Fee
$62,000 Estate Tax

$1,088,000
Decedent's Trust

$1,250,000
Surviving Spouse

Estate After Death of First Spouse

$162,000

Estimated Death Costs
$100,000 Probate Fee
$62,000 Estate Tax

$2,176,000 for Heirs

Estate After Death of Second Spouse

would be $210,000. When the $210,000 of estate taxes is deducted from the original estate of $2.5 million, a total estate of $2,290,000 would be left for the heirs.

What has been done with the Living Trust that could not be done with a Testamentary Trust? Figure 6-19 summarizes the differences between the two types of Trusts. The Living Trust has avoided probate costs of $100,000 on the first to die, as well as payment of $62,000 of unnecessary estate taxes. A probate cost of $100,000 has also been avoided on the second to die. Comparing the two different estates left to the heirs shows that the Living Trust provides the heirs with a total gain of $114,000.

In addition, with the A-B-C form of the Living Trust, the entire estate has been preserved

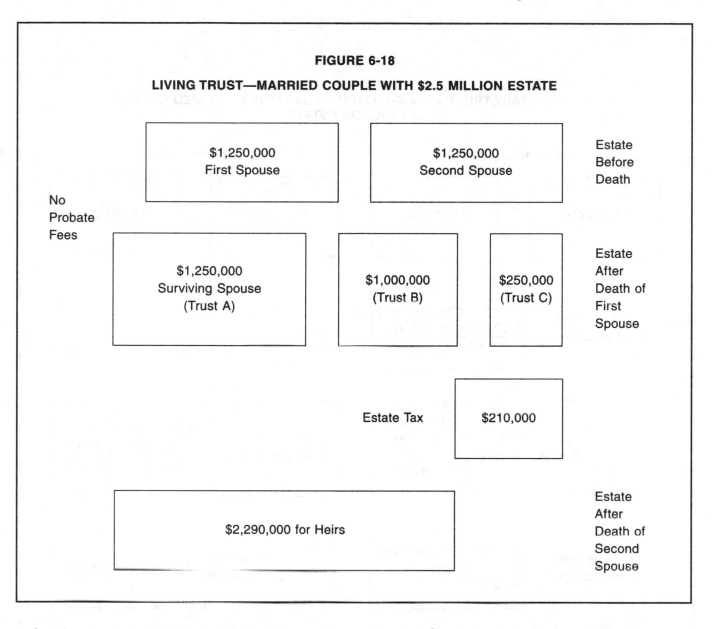

FIGURE 6-18

LIVING TRUST—MARRIED COUPLE WITH $2.5 MILLION ESTATE

No Probate Fees

| $1,250,000 First Spouse | $1,250,000 Second Spouse | Estate Before Death |

| $1,250,000 Surviving Spouse (Trust A) | $1,000,000 (Trust B) | $250,000 (Trust C) | Estate After Death of First Spouse |

Estate Tax — $210,000

$2,290,000 for Heirs — Estate After Death of Second Spouse

for the surviving spouse and the decedent's heirs—an essential advantage. The Testamentary Trust rarely, if ever, contains a C Trust. For estates in excess of $2 million, this lack of a C Trust means that the beneficiaries of the first spouse to die may not necessarily receive their designated share if the excess over $1 million in the decedent's estate is placed in the Survivor's A Trust rather than in a C Trust. (The surviving spouse may change the beneficiaries and the method of allocation and distribution of assets for the heirs of the Survivor's A Trust; however, the surviving spouse is restricted from making such changes to the assets in the Decedent's B Trust and in the C Trust.)

Appendix F contains additional comparative illustrations that examine the similarities and the differences of a Testamentary Trust and a Living Trust for married couples with A-B-C Trusts. The illustrations present comparisons for estates of $2.5 million and $5 million.

If you are astute enough to realize that estate planning is important to you and your heirs, recognize that what you really should have is a Living Trust, *not* a Testamentary Trust. The Testamentary Trust is rightfully referred to as the "Attorney's Retirement Plan." The attorney gets his or her fee for writing the Trust, and then gets a probate fee on top of it. If you are going to have a Trust, have a Living Trust. The economics speak for themselves.

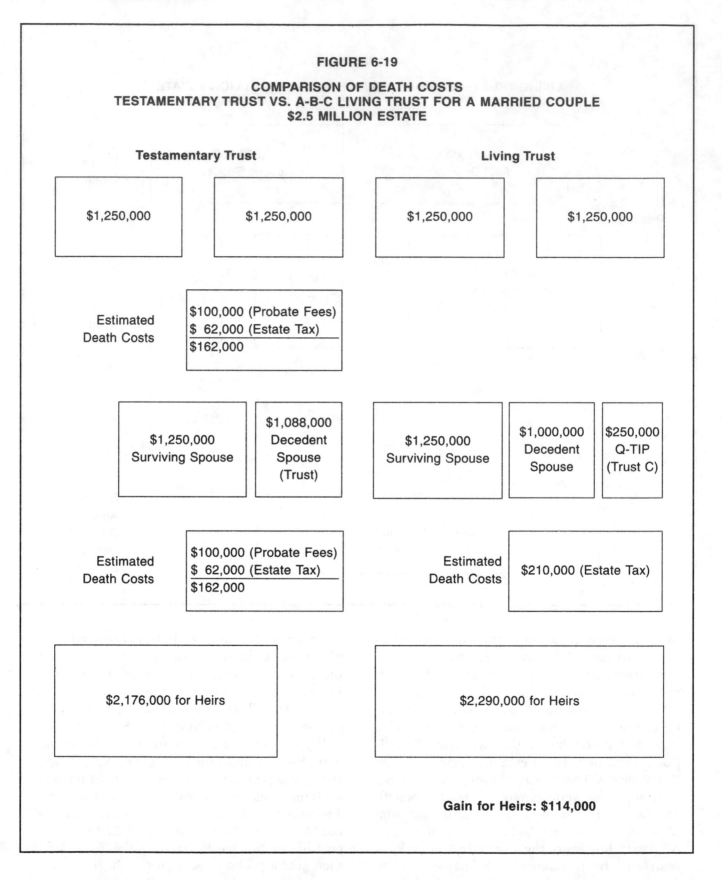

FIGURE 6-19

COMPARISON OF DEATH COSTS
TESTAMENTARY TRUST VS. A-B-C LIVING TRUST FOR A MARRIED COUPLE
$2.5 MILLION ESTATE

Testamentary Trust   **Living Trust**

| $1,250,000 | $1,250,000 | | $1,250,000 | $1,250,000 |

Estimated
Death Costs
$100,000 (Probate Fees)
$ 62,000 (Estate Tax)
$162,000

| $1,250,000 Surviving Spouse | $1,088,000 Decedent Spouse (Trust) | | $1,250,000 Surviving Spouse | $1,000,000 Decedent Spouse | $250,000 Q-TIP (Trust C) |

Estimated
Death Costs
$100,000 (Probate Fees)
$ 62,000 (Estate Tax)
$162,000

Estimated
Death Costs $210,000 (Estate Tax)

$2,176,000 for Heirs $2,290,000 for Heirs

Gain for Heirs: $114,000

7

Understanding the Living Trust

By now, you should be well aware of several important reasons for putting your estate in a Living Trust. Yet two common misconceptions about the Living Trust tend to become stumbling blocks for people learning about it and turn into exaggerated fears that prevent people from taking the necessary steps to create their own Living Trusts. People fear that they will lose control of their assets (after the assets are placed in the Trust) and that the surviving spouse will lose control over the assets in the Decedent's Trust B.

Even though the Living Trust is unknown to most people, the Trust does not need to be difficult to understand or use. This chapter illustrates the various advantages of Living Trusts and describes how each advantage would best apply to your particular situation. When you complete this chapter, you should be comfortable with the concept of the Living Trust and recognize that it is an outstanding solution for almost all estate-planning situations.

A BETTER WAY TO HOLD ASSETS

If you are like most people, you have done a reasonable job of putting your assets together and building your estate. You most likely own a home, some stocks and bonds, a savings account, and life insurance, and you probably participate in a pension plan. The problem is that, upon your death (whether you are married or single), your assets must go through probate, which is both costly and time-consuming. Fortunately, there is a better way—and that is for both husband and wife (if you are married) or just you (if you are single) to create and fund a Living Trust in which you are the trustee or trustees of your own Trust. (The roles of the trustee, surviving trustee, and successor trustee as well as the trustor, settlor, and beneficiary will be explained in Chapter 8.)

How the Living Trust Works

What, you may ask, does a Living Trust do for me? From the legal viewpoint of settling an estate, having a Living Trust means that you do not hold title to anything; since your assets are inside the Trust, the Trust holds title to everything. However, even though you have relinquished *ownership* of your assets, you still retain *control* of those same assets. As the trustee of your Trust, you continue to have the same power to buy, sell, transfer, borrow, and do whatever you wish with "your" assets. Your control of those assets is no different on the day after you put them into the Trust than on the day before you put them into the Trust.

If you are seriously concerned about retaining control of your assets, remember this concept: The only way you can truly retain control of your assets within your family is by placing all of your assets in a Living Trust—now. On the other hand, if you don't, you or your family will eventually *lose control* of your assets to the probate court for one to two years, upon your death or your spouse's death!

Even though you relinquish ownership *of your assets when you transfer them into your Trust, you still retain total* control *over those assets.*

The significance of your not "owning" anything becomes very important when you ultimately die. Upon your death, since you have nothing in title in your own name (because your assets are in the Trust), there is nothing to probate. If you are married, the surviving spouse typically becomes the surviving trustee and, as such, continues to have the same power to buy, sell, transfer, or do whatever is desired with those assets.

Upon the death of the surviving spouse, the same situation applies as before. Since no assets were in the name of the deceased, there is nothing to probate. In the Trust document, you would identify whom you want to act as the successor trustee or successor trustees. The successor trustee is the person who will take charge of the Trust upon the death of the original trustee(s). It is recommended that you stipulate one or more of your adult children, close family members, or close friends as successor trustees. That person, or persons, will immediately step in, upon the death of the surviving trustee, and have the same power to buy, sell, or transfer those assets and, more important, to use them and to distribute them as you would have wanted them used or distributed.

The Living Trust is just as important for a single person as for a married couple.

Even though our firm has prepared a few Living Trusts where the parents and a child or children are the joint creators and administrators, this situation is rare. Usually parents and children have entirely different objectives, and therefore the parents and children should each have their own separate Trusts.

The Trust works in the same manner for a single person as for a married couple. A Living Trust is meaningful for *all* individuals, regardless of whether they are single, widowed, married, or even two single persons living together. The Living Trust has just as much importance for a single person—especially for widows and widowers—as it does for a married person. (Chapter 4 explained why 90 percent of the estates of widows and widowers above age 60 would go through probate.)

All Assets Must Be in the Trust—Except Qualified Plan Assets

For a Trust to be effective in avoiding probate and minimizing taxation, all of the assets must be placed in the Trust, as symbolized in Figure 7-1. The one exception is Qualified Plan assets, specifically an IRA, a Keogh, a qualified annuity, and a 401(k) plan. This exception is discussed further in Chapter 14. Unfortunately, all too often today, Living Trusts are drawn up but not funded with the assets (the assets have not been placed in the Trust, as shown in Figure 7-2). In such cases, the Living Trust acts as a Testamentary Trust; since there are no assets in the Trust, the estate must go through the probate process upon the death of the first spouse before the assets can pour into the Trust.

Another important point to remember is that, as in a Testamentary Trust or a Loving Will, an unfunded Trust is readily challengeable. If you created a Trust and then did not transfer title to your assets into the Trust, your heirs could someday claim that circumstances have changed since the Trust's creation and that, if you were now present, you would wish to change the distribution of your Trust.

Simple vs. Complex Trust

All too often, people think that the number of assets they own determines the complexity of

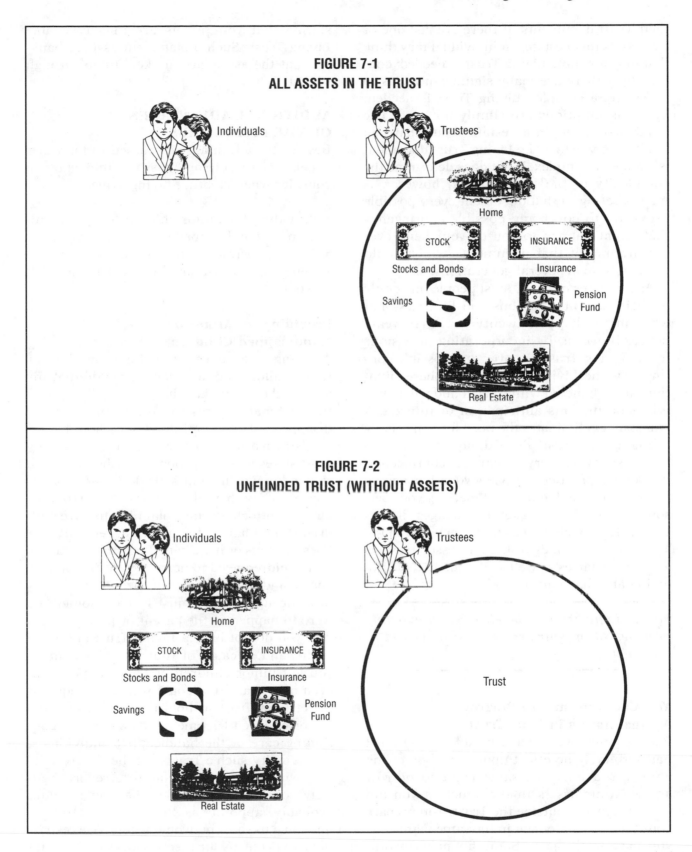

FIGURE 7-1
ALL ASSETS IN THE TRUST

Individuals

Trustees

Home

STOCK

Stocks and Bonds

INSURANCE

Insurance

Savings

Pension Fund

Real Estate

FIGURE 7-2
UNFUNDED TRUST (WITHOUT ASSETS)

Individuals

Trustees

Home

STOCK

Stocks and Bonds

INSURANCE

Insurance

Savings

Pension Fund

Real Estate

Trust

their Trust documents. If there are just one or two assets in an estate, an individual may think that only a simple Living Trust is needed; conversely, if there are many significant assets in an estate, a complex Living Trust is needed. These assumptions are simply not true. The number of assets in an estate should have no relation to whether the Living Trust document is simple or complex. What does determine the complexity of the Living Trust, however, is incorporating in that document every possible provision to cover any possible contingency that might happen to you or your heirs over the lifetime of that document—which could ultimately span several generations.

As creatures of habit, most people think only of their current situations and lifestyles—not what might happen twenty or thirty years hence. However, by incorporating provisions in the Living Trust to cover any possible contingency, the Living Trust allows these situations to be handled with ease, if and when they might occur. This anticipation of future circumstances eliminates the need for continually changing the Trust. Even though a good Living Trust covers every imaginable contingency, it is a good practice to review your Trust every five years to see that it is still meeting your personal goals and to make any changes, if necessary. The specific areas to be reviewed in the Trust are the names of the successor trustees and beneficiaries as well as the method of allocation and distribution.

For a Living Trust to be effective in avoiding probate, all of your assets must be placed in the Trust.

You Can Continue to Borrow Against Assets in Your Trust

Placing your assets in a revocable Living Trust has absolutely no effect upon your borrowing ability. You have the same right to borrow against your assets in the Trust as you did when they were outside the Trust. You prepare your financial statement in the same manner as you have in the past. Some financial institutions, however, would like to see a footnote stating that your assets are in a revocable Living Trust. Such a statement assures bankers that the assets are unlikely to go through probate.

ADDITIONAL ADVANTAGES OF THE LIVING TRUST

Besides the advantages discussed so far, other benefits of the Living Trust are important to consider when creating Living Trusts:

- Providing for minor children or grandchildren, or handicapped children of any age
- Assuring privacy of the estate
- Being able to use an A-B Trust for a small estate

Providing for Minor or Handicapped Children

A Living Trust is essential for providing for minor children or handicapped children of any age, in the event that the parents die prematurely. Small estates too often just seem to disappear—to be consumed somehow by administrative fees. The measurement used by most states to avoid probate is either an estate ranging in worth from $10,000 to $100,000 or any estate with real property. Nevertheless, anyone with children or planning to have children should have a Living Trust, regardless of the size of his or her estate. Remember, parents with children need to name a guardian of *their* choice and then provide for the children's welfare through a Trust, just in case something were to happen to the parent or parents.

If you do not have a Living Trust and were to die, and, because of your untimely demise, you left minor children or handicapped children of any age, the court would be required to set up a Trust to hold the assets until the minor children become adults or for the continuing care of the handicapped individuals. By necessity, such a Trust must be very restrictive, with the trustee required to report regularly to the court. Since the court would probably appoint as trustee an attorney unknown to you, you would want these restrictions to protect your assets. However, it would be much better to create your own Trust to provide for your children or grandchildren in the manner you would want and to name a trustee you know and trust.

If you have a Living Trust, you have already created that entity—and, more important, you have spelled out how you want your funds used. No court in the land can truly guess your particular personal desires for the care and upbringing of your children or grandchildren.

Assuring Privacy of the Estate

The Living Trust is not registered anywhere and is a confidential document. The only people who have a right to see the Trust document are the trustee(s) and, eventually, the successor trustee(s). Not even the beneficiaries have a right to see the document! This confidentiality is much in contrast to the way a Will is handled. Privacy, consequently, is one of the key advantages of a Living Trust.

Occasionally an adult child of a decedent calls me with the concern that his or her stepmother or stepfather is misusing the decedent's share of the funds. I will point out to this individual that the appropriate recourse available is to hire an attorney, who will then appeal to the probate court (the court that has jurisdiction over Trusts) and ask that the court review the trustee's use of the funds. The judge can then ask to see the Trust, review what that particular spouse has done with the decedent's funds, and, being satisfied or dissatisfied, so advise the child. In most states, neither the child nor the child's attorney has the right to see the Trust. Furthermore, my experience has been that abuse of a Trust is negligible, and my advice to most individuals is that to pursue such a course of legal action is a waste of time and energy. As of this writing, our clients have never done so.

Using an A-B Trust for a Small Estate

Another important advantage of having a Living Trust is that the A-B Trust form should be used for a small estate. Although most CPAs think of an A-B Trust as applying only when an estate exceeds $1 million, there are two sound reasons for using an A-B Trust for a small estate:

- The Decedent's Trust B becomes irrevocable upon death.
- No estate tax is due if the estate is eventually valued at more than $1 million.

Each reason has varying degrees of importance, depending on the individual circumstances of the estate.

Irrevocability of Decedent's Trust B

One of the primary reasons for using an A-B Trust for a small estate (one valued at less than $1 million) is to ensure that the assets attributed to the first to die eventually flow down to the decedent's heirs. Upon the death of a spouse with an A-B Trust, the decedent's share of the estate becomes irrevocable. Thus, each spouse can be assured that at least "his or her share" of the assets will go to his or her heirs as desired.

Upon the death of a spouse, his or her share of the estate will flow down into the Decedent's Trust B. Typically, the assets in Trust B are there for the use of the surviving spouse for as long as he or she lives; however, upon the death of the surviving spouse, those assets will go to the individuals specified by the original spouse. Although the surviving spouse has the right to use those funds, a major limitation specified in the Trust is that the surviving spouse *may not change* the beneficiaries of the B Trust.

Preservation of Both Estate Tax Exclusions

The second reason for using an A-B Trust for a small estate is to preserve the federal estate tax exclusions of both spouses. As an estate grows in value, an A-B Trust ensures that, as long as the value of the estate remains below $2 million (two federal estate tax exclusions), no estate tax will be due.

For example, as shown in Figure 7-3, a $500,000 estate in an A Trust would pay no estate tax upon the death of the first spouse. However, as the $500,000 estate grows, if only by inflation, its value could exceed the federal estate tax exclusion. Every dollar thereafter will be taxed! For the surviving spouse's estate of $500,000, 7 percent growth would double the estate in ten years, as shown at the bottom

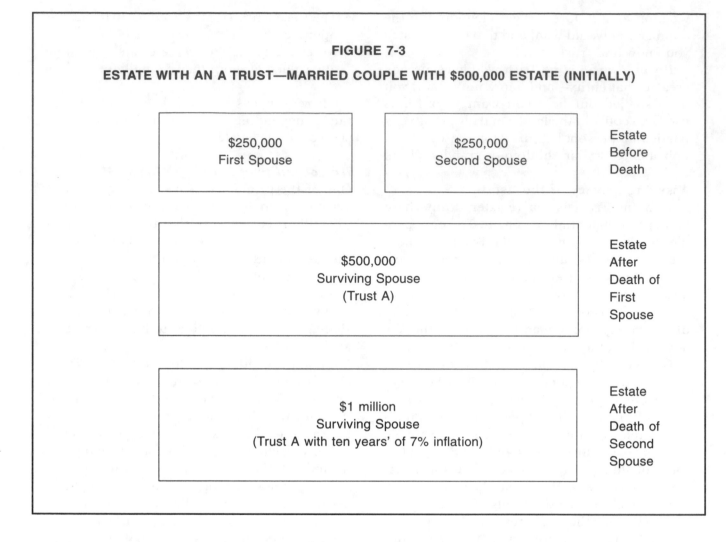

FIGURE 7-3

ESTATE WITH AN A TRUST—MARRIED COUPLE WITH $500,000 ESTATE (INITIALLY)

$250,000 First Spouse	$250,000 Second Spouse	Estate Before Death

$500,000
Surviving Spouse
(Trust A)

Estate After Death of First Spouse

$1 million
Surviving Spouse
(Trust A with ten years' of 7% inflation)

Estate After Death of Second Spouse

of Figure 7-3. Then, when the surviving spouse dies, the estate would be subject to federal estate taxes.

The A-B Trust can prevent these unnecessary taxes. If the surviving spouse had an A-B Trust already in place, there would be substantial room for growth in the surviving spouse's A Trust (from $250,000 to $1 million). Furthermore, the assets expected to appreciate in value (such as a house or stock) could be placed in the B Trust to insulate the growth from future taxation. Whatever is in the B Trust is sheltered from future estate taxes, as shown in Figure 7-4. How to use a Decedent's Trust B as an estate-planning tool to shelter growing assets will be discussed further in Chapter 14.

As these examples show, a couple with an estate valued at less than $1 million would most likely want to use an A-B Trust instead of a simple A Trust. Therefore, I now always recommend an A-B Trust for a husband and wife, even if they only have a modest estate. I ask the couple whether the pair expects at least one of them to be alive in ten years, and the answer is almost always "yes." In that short period of time, an estate can be expected to double in value—by inflation alone.

RIGHTS OF THE SURVIVING SPOUSE

One of the greatest fears of a married couple considering an A-B Living Trust is that the surviving spouse will somehow lose control of the assets in the Decedent's Trust B. I wish to dispel those fears. The rights of the surviving spouse to Trust B may, for good reasons, be restricted. However, most A-B Trusts for married couples name the surviving spouse as both

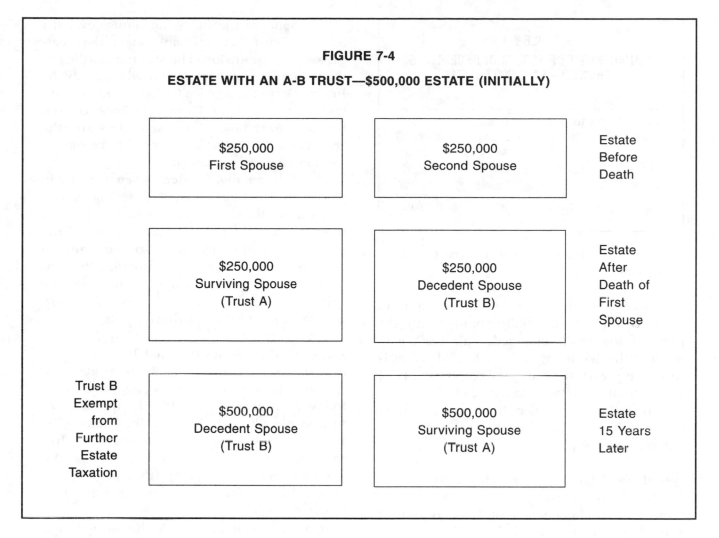

FIGURE 7-4

ESTATE WITH AN A-B TRUST—$500,000 ESTATE (INITIALLY)

$250,000 First Spouse	$250,000 Second Spouse	Estate Before Death
$250,000 Surviving Spouse (Trust A)	$250,000 Decedent Spouse (Trust B)	Estate After Death of First Spouse
$500,000 Decedent Spouse (Trust B)	$500,000 Surviving Spouse (Trust A)	Estate 15 Years Later

Trust B Exempt from Further Estate Taxation

surviving trustee and beneficiary of the Decedent's Trust B. Thus, the surviving spouse controls the assets in the Decedent's Trust B.

If the surviving spouse is named as surviving trustee, he or she maintains full control of the assets in the Decedent's B Trust.

Rights as Surviving Trustee

As the surviving trustee, the surviving spouse continues to retain the same power to buy, sell, transfer, and borrow against the assets in Trusts A and B in exactly the same manner as before the demise of his or her spouse. How can the trustee's right to buy, sell, and transfer the assets in the Decedent's B Trust be reconciled with the trustee's fiduciary responsibility to the heirs of Trust B? Let's consider an example.

Assume that the decedent's half of the estate ($400,000) is in the B Trust. Today, the assets include a house worth $100,000, stock valued at $100,000, bonds worth $50,000, certificates of deposit with a value of $100,000, and savings of $50,000, as shown in the left-hand column of Table 7-1.

During the next year, the trustee decides that it is more appropriate to sell the house. Of the $100,000 proceeds from the sale of the house, $50,000 is added to the stock, and the other $50,000 is added to savings. The trustee further decides to transfer $50,000 from CDs to savings. Assuming no growth, the B Trust will then have $150,000 of stock, $50,000 in bonds, $50,000 in CDs, and $150,000 in sav-

TABLE 7-1
MANAGEMENT OF ASSETS IN DECEDENT'S TRUST B—$400,000 ESTATE

Today		Next Year	
House	$ 100,000	House	-0-
Stocks	100,000	Stocks	$ 150,000
Bonds	50,000	Bonds	50,000
CDs	100,000	CDs	50,000
Savings	50,000	Savings	150,000
Total	$ 400,000	Total	$ 400,000

ings—for a total amount in Trust B of $400,000.

Notice that the total value of the assets in Trust B did not materially change; only the form of the assets changed. This change in form of the assets in the Decedent's B Trust is in keeping with the fiduciary responsibility of the surviving trustee. The trustee has the right to buy, sell, and transfer these assets without restriction, as long as the investments are considered "prudent."

Beneficial Rights of Surviving Spouse

In most Living Trusts, the surviving spouse is named as the beneficiary of Trust B and, as such, has three beneficial rights:

- The right to all of the income of Trust B.
- The right to use any or all of the principal in Trust B as is necessary to maintain the same standard of living, including any medical needs.
- The right to spend, each year, $5,000 or 5 percent of the assets in Trust B, whichever is greater, for any reason, regardless of how frivolous. This right is not cumulative; the right must be used during the year, or it is lost.

These three rights, in effect, give the surviving spouse the right to use the funds in Trust B without restriction.

In effect, the surviving spouse has the right to use the funds in Trust B effectively without restriction.

The rights of the surviving spouse over the assets in Trust B are probably one of the greatest areas of confusion. The specific wording in the Living Trust document is used to satisfy the Internal Revenue Service Code in order to insulate the assets in the Decedent's Trust B from further estate taxes. To best understand the restrictions on Trust B, you need to recognize the source of any challenge.

The children, if any, listed as beneficiaries in the Living Trust are only contingent beneficiaries; that is, the children are beneficiaries only if they are still living when the surviving spouse dies *and* if any assets are remaining in trust to pass on to the heirs. However, the contingent beneficiaries do have rights, and the surviving spouse, as trustee, has a fiduciary responsibility to protect those rights.

Abuse of the Rights to Trust B

An excellent example of a potential abuse of the fiduciary responsibility is illustrated in the following scenario involving the marriage of two people who have had previous marriages. Each spouse has children from his or her former marriage, and each brings substantial sums of separate property (that is, property attained before this marriage) into the new marriage.

It is the husband and wife's intent that their assets remain in place for the benefit of the surviving spouse. However, upon the death of the surviving spouse, each spouse's share of the estate shall pass to his or her own children, as shown in Figure 7-5.

If one of the spouses were to die and the surviving spouse were to take $200,000 from the Decedent's Trust B and lose the funds gambling in Las Vegas, this action would clearly be an abuse of the fiduciary responsibility of the surviving trustee.

Another example of fiduciary abuse is shown in Figure 7-6. If the surviving spouse had removed $200,000 from Trust B and added it to the Survivor's Trust A, so that the additional assets would eventually pass to the children of the surviving spouse (instead of to the decedent's children), that act also would be considered to be an abuse of fiduciary responsibility.

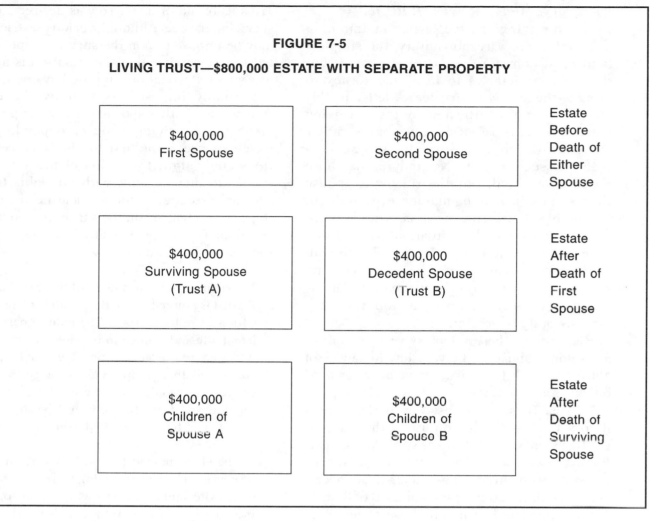

FIGURE 7-5

LIVING TRUST—$800,000 ESTATE WITH SEPARATE PROPERTY

$400,000 First Spouse	$400,000 Second Spouse	Estate Before Death of Either Spouse
$400,000 Surviving Spouse (Trust A)	$400,000 Decedent Spouse (Trust B)	Estate After Death of First Spouse
$400,000 Children of Spouse A	$400,000 Children of Spouse B	Estate After Death of Surviving Spouse

FIGURE 7-6

EXAMPLE OF FIDUCIARY ABUSE TO DECEDENT'S TRUST

Decedent's Trust B		Survivor's Trust A
$ 400,000		$ 400,000
(200,000)	Fiduciary Abuse	200,000
$ 200,000		$ 600,000

Yet who would object? The Internal Revenue Service? No! As far as the Internal Revenue Service is concerned, if the surviving spouse removes the funds from Trust B and places them into Trust A, the IRS will jump with glee. The reason is simple: The funds in Trust B are insulated from further estate tax. However, when the funds are moved from Trust B into Trust A, they will once again be subject to federal estate tax upon the death of the surviving spouse! Therefore, any funds removed from Trust B should be used up by the surviving spouse.

However, if assets are removed from Trust B and placed in Trust A, the contingent beneficiaries of the Decedent's Trust B (the decedent's children) could object—for their rights to these assets are being abused. The children are contingent beneficiaries because their rights to the assets of Trust B (upon the death of the surviving spouse) are contingent upon assets still being in Trust B and the beneficiaries still being alive. The surviving spouse, as surviving trustee, has a fiduciary responsibility to preserve these funds within the rights specified in the Trust for the contingent beneficiaries.

Solution to Abuse of Trust B Rights

If the surviving trustee is not maintaining proper fiduciary responsibility, the simplest (and most common) recourse is for the contingent beneficiaries to hire an attorney to oversee the surviving trustee. A letter to this effect, from the attorney to the surviving trustee, usually rectifies any abuses rather quickly. Invariably, the surviving spouse overreacts to such a letter. Not only is the abuse readily corrected, but the surviving spouse then stands in fear of making even normal, acceptable Trust transactions. On the rare occasion where such a situation arises, I find it necessary to do everything possible to convince the surviving spouse to calm down and simply to continue to act as trustee without any further concern—as long as the fiduciary responsibility is not abused.

Historically, these fiduciary responsibilities are seldom abused. The very few instances of abuse of which I am aware have been resolved quickly and easily.

If Trust B assets are used properly, there is no practical restriction on use of the assets in the Decedent's Trust B by the surviving spouse. For example, the beneficial right of the surviving spouse to invade the principal (as necessary to maintain the same "standard of living") is not considered to be an abuse of fiduciary responsibility. Who determines what is the standard of living? The surviving trustee. Who is the surviving trustee? The surviving spouse. Thus, the surviving spouse has substantial latitude in using funds in the Decedent's Trust B, but again the latitude must not be abusive. In effect, the surviving spouse has the right to use the funds in Trust B almost *without* restriction.

Could the Trust B assets be entirely consumed for medical needs? Yes, most definitely. If, for example, the surviving spouse contracted cancer and incurred enormous medical bills, all of the assets in Trust B could be consumed to meet those medical expenses. That is as it should be and as the decedent spouse would have wanted.

Latitude in Setting Powers of Trust B

In effect, the creators of the Trust have the latitude to make the powers of the Decedent's B Trust as broad or as narrow as desired for the surviving trustee. Although various restrictions may be imposed upon the surviving spouse as trustee, remember that the situation is a two-way street. Restrictions imposed by one spouse are usually imposed as well by the other spouse—and either spouse could end up as the restricted surviving spouse, depending on which spouse is the first to die. Such restrictions could limit the rights of the surviving spouse to income only, with no rights to the residual assets even for medical needs; could impose a co-trustee on the surviving spouse; or could distribute some or all of the assets upon the death of the first spouse.

The right to limit the powers of the Decedent's B Trust is pointed out in the example of a man with a $1 million estate. The man remarried late in life and wanted to provide for his wife if he were to predecease her. However, he was concerned that, if his wife were given the chance, she would "spend everything within thirty days." Unfortunately, as I became acquainted with his wife, I had to agree with his assessment!

The client named his eldest son from his former marriage as surviving trustee, instead of his wife, and limited his wife's rights to the income from Trust B. At the very least, 10 percent of $1 million would provide $100,000 income per year—a rather nice lifetime income for a spouse who had entered into the marriage with only $100,000 of her own assets.

Limits on Revocability

The A and B divisions of the A-B Trust are both revocable as long as both spouses are alive. However, upon the death of one spouse, the Decedent's B Trust becomes irrevocable. The difference between a revocable and an irrevocable Trust is changeability. A revocable Trust may be changed (amended) or terminated (revoked) as long as the settlor (the person who puts the assets into the Trust) lives. A Trust may be revoked or terminated simply by removing the assets from the name of the Trust. Upon the death of the first spouse, the B Trust becomes neither changeable nor terminable. On the other hand, the A Trust, the survivor's Trust, remains revocable during the life of the surviving spouse.

When the surviving spouse is also the surviving trustee and beneficiary of the B Trust, the only significant features that become unchangeable upon the death of the first spouse are the beneficiaries (who are named as future recipients of the assets in the B Trust) and the time, method, and percentage of distribution to the beneficiaries.

Absolute Right to Assets in Trust A

The surviving spouse's absolute right to the assets in Trust A includes being able to remove those assets from Trust A or to amend in any way the provisions in Trust A, including the naming of beneficiaries or changing the time, method, and percentage of distribution to the beneficiaries. Thus, the surviving spouse may change the heirs of Trust A (the survivor's Trust) but *not* of Trust B (the decedent's Trust) or of Trust C.

Typically, the only things the surviving spouse cannot do are to change the beneficiaries of Trust B; change the time, method, and percentage of distribution from Trust B; or jeopardize the rights of the beneficiaries by an unauthorized removal of funds from Trust B.

OTHER COMMON CONCERNS ABOUT LIVING TRUSTS

Many people who are interested in the Living Trust have concerns about this little-known entity for holding their assets. The common concerns expressed by client after client include questions regarding the size of estate needed to have a Living Trust, whether a Living Trust is revocable or not, how a Living Trust can be changed or amended, what effect a Living Trust has on income tax, whether a Living Trust must be registered, whether a Living Trust can protect an estate from lawsuits, how a Living Trust can be terminated, what effect a divorce has on a Living Trust, and the cost of a Living Trust in relation to the cost of a Will.

Size of Estate Needed

It has been my experience that everyone should have a Living Trust—regardless of the size of the estate. The probate codes in most states encompass almost all estates; unless people take appropriate estate-planning measures (placing their assets in a Living Trust), they will end up giving away part of their hard-earned estates by paying unnecessary probate fees. If a person is young and his or her estate has not grown sufficiently, most likely the estate will increase in value if given enough time.

Even smaller estates should consider the numerous advantages of the Living Trust, as shown in the following example.

Luke's entire estate was worth only $20,000. Luke died; then only six months later his wife also died. Probate of this small estate was handled by a reputable legal firm. However, the probate cost was an amazing $9,000! This outrageous fee left only $11,000 of Luke's small estate for the heirs.

Everyone who reviewed this sad case concurred that, if Luke had only had a Living Trust, there would have been little or no administrative cost. Even though $9,000 may not be a lot of money to some people, in this case it represented almost half of the estate— money that was desperately needed by the heirs.

Our study of probate in Washington state (see the Preface) shocked even the experts by showing that *the greatest impact of probate cost was on the smaller estates* (those valued at $100,000 or less)—precisely the estates that could *least afford it!* Consequently, don't make the sad mistake of thinking (or letting someone else convince you) that your estate is too small for a Living Trust.

You may modify or revoke your Living Trust whenever you wish.

Revocability of Trust

The Living Trust is revocable, which means that the creators of the Trust may modify it or revoke it at any time they so choose. It is a plan—a plan to manage your estate—and any plan should be subject to change to meet the varying needs of you or your family. As has been mentioned earlier, upon the death of one or both creators of the Trust, part or all of the Trust becomes irrevocable—and that, too, is as it should be.

An irrevocable Trust is seldom recommended for the body of the estate. The exceptions to that statement are the use of the Insurance Preservation Trust, the Spousal and Family Support Trust, the Gift Trust, and the Family Limited Partnership. Each of these special types of Trusts will be explained in Chapter 12.

Amendments and Changes

Unlike a Will (which requires formal change because of the past history of abuse), the Living Trust is readily changeable, either formally or informally. Formal changes are called amendments and are accomplished by having legal counsel formalize the changes to the Trust. Informal changes to a Living Trust can be made by the creators themselves, simply by striking out or adding a section, in pen, and then initialing such changes. This informal type of change should stand up in any court. However, as soon after making the change as possible, you should seek formalization of the change through appropriate legal counsel to ensure that the change is consistent throughout the entire Trust document.

The ready changeability afforded to people having Living Trusts is often used to handle unexpected situations.

An excellent example is that of a couple who had a modest estate and three grown children. One of the sons was killed in an industrial accident, leaving behind a wife and a baby. The company responsible for the accident settled the case by awarding $1 million to the survivors (the wife and the baby). Since the wife and child were now provided for financially, the clients decided to change their Living Trust to leave their modest estate to their remaining two children.

In formulating the change, legal counsel pointed out that a similar change should be incorporated to pass the couple's personal effects to their surviving two children—a desired change that might otherwise have been overlooked without the benefit of legal counsel reviewing the changes.

Effect on Income Taxes

The Internal Revenue Service's interpretation of the Living Trust states that the Living Trust "has no effect upon income taxes." With a Living Trust, all income still flows to the individual, who will continue to report all income, as in the past, on the U.S. Individual Income Tax Return (Form 1040)—whether the individual is a single person, married and filing a joint return, or filing as head of household.

Even though an individual has a Living Trust, he or she continues to use his or her social security number, as in the past, when filing the Form 1040 personal income tax return and reporting any income received from assets in the Trust. Later, on the death of the first spouse, the surviving spouse will use his or her social security number to identify any taxable income from assets in the Trust.

By far, the simplest way to avoid unnecessary correspondence with the IRS is to retain your assets under the social security number corresponding to your normal Form 1040 individual tax return. Thus, use your social security number as the Trust Identification Number if you are single; if you are married, use the husband's social security number. (In today's liberated society, however, the social security number used could just as well be the social security number of the wife.)

In 1981, Congress legislated that Form 1041 (the Trust tax return form) would no longer be required for a revocable Living Trust. If you are ever requested (because of a mistake on the part of the IRS) to file a Form 1041 for your revocable Living Trust, simply advise the IRS that your Trust is a "Grantor" Trust and that you are not required to file a Form 1041 as called out in Section 1.671-3(a)(1) of the IRS regulations.

About 1 percent of our clients each year receive a letter demanding to know why they have not filed a 1041 Trust tax return for their revocable Trust. There seems to be no rhyme or reason for this random selection, nor is there any basis for such a request. The inquiry stems from our firm having originally ordered the IRS Trust Identification Number as a service for our clients.

Some years ago, a former president of an insurance company received such an IRS demand. Being reasonably knowledgeable and astute, he answered the IRS inquiry in writing. His experience was similar to writing to a computer. After a whole series of letters and senseless responses, he sent the entire series of correspondence to our office in a plea for help.

In all of his well-written letters, the man had failed to use the magic words *Grantor Trust*. You see, the IRS recognizes the Living Trust as a Grantor Trust; until the right term is used, it is similar to talking to a brick wall. Recognizing that the IRS demand for 1041 Trust tax returns will continue in the future, our firm provides our clients with a letter of instructions for response, as shown in Figure 7-7.

Only the lower portion of the illustration needs to be duplicated, completed, and returned to the IRS. That action should be the end of the IRS inquiry—until possibly next year.

Registration of Revocable Living Trusts

There are eight states that specify that a Living Trust must be registered. In those states that require registration of the Trust, registration may be waived if the Trust language specifically states that "the Trust need not be registered." Including this language in the Trust eliminates the requirement to register a Trust in those eight states (or any of the other forty-two states).

Effect of a Living Trust on Lawsuits

Unfortunately, a Living Trust will not act as a legal barrier against lawsuits. Assets in a revocable Living Trust are just as subject to lawsuits as if they were outside the Trust—since you still control those assets, and you definitely don't want to give up control of your assets

unless you absolutely must. (The subject of giving up control of your assets is discussed in the Catastrophic Illness Trust section of Chapter 11.)

FDIC Insurance Coverage

Monetary assets in a revocable Living Trust placed in a bank may be protected by Federal Deposit Insurance Corporation (FDIC) insurance coverage at each bank in the amount of $100,000 per settlor times the number of settlor's children. However, in order to qualify for FDIC insurance coverage, the beneficiaries must be specifically named in the Living Trust, not just identified as a class.

The formula to use in arriving at the amount of FDIC insurance coverage available at each bank is: *number of settlors then living times number of qualifying beneficiaries then living times $100,000 equals the total amount of the deposit that is insured.*

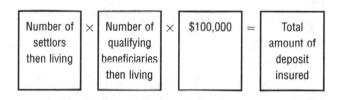

Let's assume, for example, that two settlors (a husband and a wife) have a Living Trust for themselves and their four children. While both husband and wife are living, the amount that could be insured in any one bank would be $800,000:

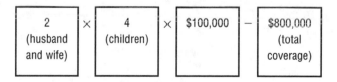

This formula will continue to apply upon the death of a spouse with an A-B Trust. However, with only a simple married A Trust, the insurance coverage would drop to $400,000 upon the death of a spouse:

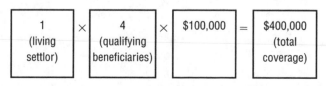

FIGURE 7-7
INSTRUCTIONS FOR HANDLING IRS REQUEST

What to Do If the IRS Asks for a Trust Tax Return

Fewer than 1 percent of our clients receive a request from the Internal Revenue Service for a tax return for their Living Trust. Another kind of trust might be required to file Form 1041, which is the proper tax return for a trust. However, the estate-planning trust that is revocable need not file such a return.

For federal income tax purposes, the Living Trust is called a "Grantor Trust," and this term should be used with the IRS if they raise any questions. For IRS purposes, this tells them that the trust is solely for estate-planning purposes and that the income tax due on income from assets or transactions on the trust assets will be reported on your Form 1040 just as if you owned those assets without the trust.

Letter to Be Sent to IRS If a Request for a Return Is Received

Internal Revenue Service   Date _____

Re: Tax Return for Living Trust
Re: IRS Employer Identification # _____

To Whom It May Concern:
We have received a request for a tax return for the estate-planning revocable trust ("Grantor Trust") we have had prepared for us. This trust is revocable during our lifetimes, and we are the beneficiaries of the trust as well as the trustees. Our understanding is that all income and expenses relative to assets or transactions on the assets held by the trust must be reported on our individual Form 1040 just as if we owned those assets without the trust. This we have done.

It is further our understanding that we should not prepare a return for this kind of trust separate from our Form 1040 and ask you to correct your records accordingly. [Regs. Sec. 1.671-3 (a) (1)].

Very truly yours,

_____

_____

Social Security #

_____

Since there are some contingencies that might arise, it is always advisable to check with your local bank to be certain that you do not violate them. (Refer to FDIC Insurance Regulations 12 C.F.R. and 330.8.) Be aware that it is easy to unintentionally forfeit the FDIC insurance coverage. For example, if your estate were to go through probate and the executor were authorized to use any funds to pay the debts of the estate, the beneficiaries would be considered "contingent beneficiaries" under the rule and, therefore, would no longer be "qualifying beneficiaries."

The FDIC has revised its regulations to specifically include Living Trusts. These revised regulations are readily available on the FDIC website. The new regulations confirm what I had written here in my 1997 update. Two paragraphs are of particular interest:

> Funds owned by an individual and deposited in a revocable trust account . . . evidencing an intention that on his death the funds shall belong to his spouse, child, or grandchild shall be insured up to $100,000 in the aggregate as to each such named beneficiary, separately from any other accounts of the owner.
>
> If the account records disclose an agency, trustee, or other custodial relationship, the details of the relationship and the beneficial interest of the owner(s) of the funds must be ascertainable from bank records or the depositor's records maintained in good faith and in the regular course of business.

Termination of the Trust
The Living Trust will typically terminate when the assets are distributed from the Trust (because an unfunded Trust simply ceases to exist). No court action by a trustee is necessary.

Nevertheless, in order to satisfy the IRS Code, a revocable Living Trust must specify a termination at some point in time. This concept is referred to as the "law of perpetuity." Unless otherwise specifically stated in the Trust document, the IRS can create a scenario whereby the Trust theoretically could continue indefinitely—and the Decedent's Trust B would then lose its insulation from further taxation.

Specifically, the law of perpetuity says that, upon the death of both creators of the Trust, a snapshot in time is effectively taken that identifies every potential heir then living—such as the creators' children, grandchildren, great-grandchildren, and any fetuses, as well as aunts, uncles, nieces, and nephews. The Trust must cease twenty-one years after the death of every one of those heirs. Frankly, such a lengthy time period is beyond the scope of most people's imaginations, and I have yet to find a client who really cares about his or her Living Trust being terminated—possibly as far in the future as eighty to one hundred years or more.

Effect of Divorce on a Living Trust
Unfortunately, if a married couple divorces, a Living Trust cannot in all practicality be cut in half. Therefore, one individual usually retains the Trust, and the other individual must revoke his or her interest in the Trust. The party who retains the Trust will retain his or her assets in the name of the Trust, and the other party will remove his or her assets from the Trust and will revoke his or her interest in the Trust. Such an action is accomplished by executing a "Disclaimer of Trust Interest" form as shown in Figure 7-8.

Cost of a Trust vs. a Will
Although a Will is initially less expensive to draw (create) than a Living Trust, the average individual will modify his or her Will four times during his or her lifetime, which ultimately becomes more costly than a Living Trust. In addition, by saving the cost of probate, a Living Trust ultimately saves an estate many times its original cost, by eliminating probate fees and eliminating or reducing estate taxes.

Joint vs. Separate Trusts in Separate Property States
There has long been an issue with attorneys asserting that joint Trusts (our A-B and A-B-C Trusts) are invalid in separate property states. They contend that a separate Trust is required for both husband and wife in a separate property state.

FIGURE 7-8
DISCLAIMER OF TRUST INTEREST

Disclaimer of Trust Interest
(Probate Code Section 280 et seq.)

To Whom It May Concern:

Effective this date, I hereby disclaim my interest in the revocable Living Trust known as "_____ Family Trust, dated August 18, 1993, _____ and _____ Trustors, and _____ and _____ and/or Trustees."

The Trust was originally created by _____ and _____ , and I disclaim each and every interest I may have therein.

I resign as Trustee of the Trust, and I disclaim and revoke my interest as Trustor, Settlor, and Beneficiary. I relinquish all my rights to the remaining Settlor, _____ .

I have withdrawn all assets which I placed into the Trust as a Settlor, and I have legal title to them at this time as an individual free of trust. I have no claim on any further Trust assets.

This disclaimer is executed and delivered with the intent to comply with the provisions of the Probate Code Sections and to be bound thereby.

_____   _____
Date   Trustee

I first encountered this argument in about 1989, when I was asked to go to Steamboat Springs, Colorado, to give seminars on our joint A-B and A-B-C Trusts. As it turned out, my presentation served a far more fundamental purpose than simply educating my audience about the merits of a good Living Trust. While Steamboat Springs is noted for its marvelous skiing in the winter, it is also the home of very successful farmers. Prior to my engagement there, two attorneys had come from Florida and were trying to sell the farmers on separate Living Trusts, costing $12,000 each, or $24,000 for a couple. I recognized it immediately as a scam and so informed my audience. I assumed that would be the end of it.

To my dismay, I learned that the concept of separate Trusts for each spouse has been per-petrated from Florida up through the Middle West. I have fought it for years. I concluded that attorneys were using the argument to write two Trusts instead of one and therefore charge more money.

Whenever I would give seminars in Florida, the first comment was always, "But our attorney told us that we had to have separate Trusts." I would give a logical response, and then the same person would ask, "But what do we do with the deed to our home?" Separate Trusts are a nightmare to administer while you are living, because you must record each asset, or part thereof, in each separate Trust. On the other hand, they are easy to settle when a spouse dies, because the assets have already been allocated to the separate Trusts. Nevertheless, the question still stands, "What do we do with the deed to our home?" because the attorney didn't know how to solve this problem and simply ignored it.

Attorneys are cautious, as they should be. If they hear one attorney say that they must use separate Trusts for husband and wife in separate property states, they tend to pick up on it. I often think of these attorneys as sheep following the one shepherd, rather than independently looking up the tax code and applying the appropriate theory. We have provided more than sixty thousand Living Trusts, and settled more than ten thousand Living Trusts without any problem. More than half of these Living Trusts are in separate property states. Regardless, that is not sufficient evidence for some attorneys. Recently, one attorney said that I had become the laughing stock in his circle because I continued to advocate joint A-B and A-B-C Trusts in separate property states.

In an effort to solve this problem, we hired one of the most prestigious estate-planning law firms and asked the firm to request a Private Letter Ruling on the subject from the IRS. That work is still in progress. In the interim, the IRS issued a Private Letter Ruling that clearly establishes that joint A-B and A-B-C Living Trusts are appropriate in separate property states. This is Private Letter Ruling 200101021 and can be found in Appendix K. Admittedly, an IRS Private Letter Ruling applies only to the particular party who requested it, but such rulings are generally considered the opinion of the IRS and as such are used as a standard guide to follow. I hope this issue is now closed.

Once and for all, the question of the viability of joint (A-B and A-B-C) Living Trusts in separate property states is resolved.

HISTORY OF THE LIVING TRUST

One of the most frequently asked questions is "When did we get this new concept, the Living Trust?" Surprise! The Living Trust is not really a new concept; it comes from English common law, which is the very basis for the legal system in the United States. The concept of a Trust existed long before this nation was conceived; the origins of a Trust go as far back as A.D. 800,

to the days of the Roman Empire. In fact, a Trust became the preferred method of holding property in Europe during the Middle Ages.

Adopted from Roman Law

The English people adopted the Trust from Roman law as early as the twelfth century to preserve their property from the many abuses under the crown. For example, a landowner was obligated to provide relief, or money, to help supplement the lord of the land for numerous causes (such as the marriage of the lord's daughter or the knighting of the lord's son). In addition, the king imposed nearly 100 forms of tax. The landowner was prohibited from selling his land or dividing the land among his children or grandchildren. If the landowner were convicted of a crime, he forfeited all he owned to the lord or king, leaving his family destitute.

Accusing a peasant of a crime was a very common means of acquiring the peasant's land and, in the end, was quite profitable for the landlord. The peasants soon found that the Trust provided a means to protect their lands from this wrongful acquisition by the noble of the land.

The practice of holding title to land in a Trust eventually became commonplace. The Trust permitted one party (the trustee) to hold the property for the benefit of the owner and eventually to pass this property to the owner's children. Over the years (and following continued abuse by the crown), passing title of land to a Trust became an ordinary practice.

Survived Challenge

By 1535, the king and his nobles challenged the legality of the Trust and attempted to prohibit its use with the "Statute of Uses." The king and his nobles considered the Trust to be evil, because it permitted privacy of transfer, legal avoidance of unreasonable taxes and regulations, preservation of the estate of convicted criminals and, most important, loss of revenue to the king and his lords.

The challenge to the Trust fell upon the common law judges of England in the chancery court, the highest court in the land. The judges, who had absolute jurisdiction over legal estates, upheld the validity of the Trust concept. Within the next five years, the Statute of Uses was effectively abandoned—and the Trust was securely embedded as part of English common law, having survived the formidable challenge by the king and his nobles.

Brought to America with Colonists

The colonists brought the Trust to America, where Patrick Henry is given the first recorded credit for drafting a Trust on this continent. In 1765, he wrote a Trust for Robert Morris, governor of the colony of Virginia. Thus, the Trust was written more than two decades before the adoption of the U.S. Constitution.

Historically, the Living Trust has been used by people of great wealth, such as the late President John F. Kennedy, William Waldorf Astor, John D. Rockefeller, H. L. Hunt (the Texas oil billionaire), and J. Paul Getty. Until very recently, very few people in the United States had Living Trusts; however, as people are becoming more sophisticated, more and more of them are adopting the Living Trust as a way to preserve their estates and avoid the unnecessary agony of probate.

Will Congress Take It Away?

Most people are afraid that Congress will take away the Living Trust. However, if the English king and his nobles failed in their attack on the Trust in the sixteenth century, then you should have little fear that Congress will deprive Americans of such an established institution as the Living Trust. The Living Trust is not a tax shelter, but rather it is the only means by which married couples can fully utilize the federal estate tax equivalent exemptions given to them by Congress. Reportedly, fewer than 1 percent of the people in the United States have discovered the value of the Living Trust and have taken advantage of its many benefits.

On the other hand, great legal minds occasionally figure out a loophole and then, in a manner of speaking, take a horse (the Living Trust), add a hump, and call it a camel. The Clifford Trust, which will be discussed later in this chapter, is such a creature. The Clifford Trust was created to shelter income taxes and prevailed for some twelve to fourteen years until 1986, when Congress effectively lopped off the hump, returning the camel to the horse—the Living Trust, the basic legal instrument.

Many senators and representatives in Congress have Living Trusts. When Congress enacts estate tax reform, it does so with the assumption that everyone should have a Living Trust. An example of such legislation is the Economic Recovery Tax Act of 1981, which provided today's $600,000 federal estate tax equivalent exemption. For both husband and wife to use and preserve their exemptions, they must have an A-B Trust.

Two hundred years ago, representatives from the thirteen founding states met to form one of the finest documents ever created—the U.S. Constitution. Specifically, the Constitution was created to form a central government to represent the people, and the Constitution granted certain rights to the federal government. The rights that were not specified in the Constitution (and, therefore, not relinquished by the states to the federal government) were retained by the states and are now often referred to as states' rights. Since such rights were fundamental to English law, they were therefore adopted as law when this nation was formed.

One of those states' rights is the right of a state to create a legal entity, such as a corporation or a Trust. Such a legal entity, once created, is equally recognized by all of the other forty-nine states. The right to create a legal entity is sacrosanct to the states, and it would be inconceivable to think that the federal government might trespass in this area. After 1,200 years of use and legal testing, the Living Trust is basically the same entity as its predecessor from English times. I can foresee little or no chance of Congress infringing upon this document.

THE LIVING TRUST AS A LEGAL ENTITY

The Living Trust is a legal entity created by the state to hold title to assets. It has been used to enable an individual or a family to hold title to assets so that the assets can eventually pass to the heirs without the intervention of any further legal process.

It may help you understand the concept of a Living Trust to compare a Trust to a corporation, as they both have the same basic characteristics. Both are legal entities created by the state. A Trust and a corporation are both entities that a person can neither touch, taste, nor smell. Regardless of which state creates the Trust or corporation, all other states recognize and accept the Trust or corporation that has been created.

A corporation has initial founders; a Trust has a creator (trustor). Stockholders place money in the corporation; settlors place their assets in the Trust. Corporate officers are authorized to buy, sell, and transfer the corporate assets; trustees (the administrators) are authorized to do likewise with the Trust assets.

If you were to form a corporation, you could take your assets and place them inside the corporation. As owner of a corporation, you do not own the assets; instead, the assets are owned by the corporation. However, if you were also the corporate officer or officers, you would have the power to buy, sell, transfer, and borrow against those assets without restriction. In a Living Trust, the income flows through to the creators and is reported, as before, on the regular Form 1040 tax return used by individuals. A corporation has an indefinite life, but a Living Trust must eventually cease and the assets be distributed to the beneficiaries. However, the significant difference between a corporation and a Trust is that a corporation has red tape and taxes—whereas a Trust has neither.

As long as the creators (trustors) of the Trust are living and competent, the Living Trust is revocable. Assets may be placed in the Trust or removed from it as desired. In fact, whether the assets are in the Trust or outside it does not change control of the assets one iota.

The Living Trust is known by many names: Living Trust, Revocable Trust, Changeable Trust, Inter Vivos Trust (which means Living Trust in Latin), Family Trust, and Grantor Trust. This last name is the Internal Revenue Service designation for a Living Trust. All these names refer to the *same* Trust.

In fact, in my early days, I used to advise my clients that they should have an "Inter Vivos Trust." Those words were impressive to my clients. (They did not know what I was talking about, but it sounded good.) Today I go out of my way to try to make the Trust sound simple and therefore use the term *Living Trust*. I choose this term to be consistent and to emphasize that the Living Trust, properly funded, lives with you and is therefore basically unchallengeable.

Two Other Trust Forms

Two other forms of Trusts are sometimes confused with the Living Trust: the Constitutional Family Trust and the Clifford Trust. However, these Trusts are not Living Trusts, nor are they different names for the Living Trust.

Constitutional Family Trust

The Living Trust should not be confused with the Constitutional Family Trust, sometimes improperly referred to as the Family Trust. The Constitutional Family Trust is specifically forbidden by the Internal Revenue Code and was a very poor legal attempt to create an irrevocable Trust that would circumvent the payment of income taxes. Unfortunately, the people who fell prey to this unwise use of a Trust ultimately suffered dire consequences; the IRS eventually collected unpaid income taxes and levied stiff penalties.

Occasionally, I encounter someone who needs a Living Trust but shies away from it because of a previous disastrous experience with the Constitutional Family Trust. One client's uncle, a judge in a midwestern state, wrote, "Don't get involved with that notorious Living Trust, because it was disallowed by the IRS." It is tragic that an incompetent abuse of a Trust form can reflect unfavorably upon such an outstanding estate-planning tool as the Living Trust.

Clifford Trust

The Living Trust should also not be confused with the Clifford Trust, which is a special form of Trust that *temporarily* transfers only the beneficial interest (the right to receive the income). This type of Trust typically names the children of the person who created the Trust as the beneficial interest parties. They have the right to all of the income from the assets in the Trust during the lifetime of the Trust (formerly ten years and one day).

The Clifford Trust was designed for a Dr. Clifford in San Francisco, who had a high income through his medical practice and owned several apartments. Through good legal research, his counsel created the Clifford Trust, whereby, for at least ten years and one day, the apartments were placed in trust, with the income going to Dr. Clifford's children and being taxed at the children's tax rate. The Trust allowed Dr. Clifford to retain control over the apartments; after ten years and a day, the apartments (and all their income) returned to Dr. Clifford. The Trust also specified that, if Dr. Clifford died during the ten-year period of the Trust, the apartments would be included in his estate.

Since then, the Clifford Trust has been used quite successfully by many high-income people to shift income to their children without giving up either the asset or the control of it. Even though the Clifford Trust was effectively eliminated with the 1986 tax code, because of its temporary income transfer, this Trust can still be created if you are willing to have the Trust run for thirty-two years! This type of Trust, running for the longer period of time, is still legal under the 1986 tax code.

For special situations in which it may be advisable to transfer appreciating assets to your children, the Gift Trust or the Family Limited Partnership is recommended. (The Gift Trust and the Family Limited Partnership will be more fully explained in Chapter 12.)

Trust Applicability

Unlike a Will, the Living Trust is applicable from state to state. Since the basis of the Trust is English common law, a Trust is also recognized in Canada, England, and all commonwealth nations. Although most European and South American countries use civil law, the Trust is recognized in these countries as well. With clients all over the world today, our experience has been that, by and large, most nations recognize the Living Trust.

The 1961 Hague Convention (which went into effect for the United States in October 1981) abolished the procedures requiring foreign governments to legalize documents of other nations. In effect, the convention decreed that documents notarized as public documents in a particular country would be recognized as valid documents by the other countries (where both countries are signatories to the Hague Convention).

In contrast, since probate varies from state to state and since Wills have a history of abuse, the required legal content of Wills varies from state to state. Someone who has a Will and moves from one state to another should have his or her Will reviewed by legal counsel in the new state and probably redrawn to comply with local state law. A Will accompanying a Living Trust (known as a Pour-Over Will) is a supplementary document to be used only as a contingency if assets were inadvertently left outside the Trust. Therefore, it is not absolutely essential to conform this document to local state law.

Universal Trust

While a Living Trust is legally valid in all fifty states, it is not necessarily *applicable* in all states. Many states have their own peculiar legal differences that must be addressed if your Living Trust is to be truly applicable in a particular state. For instance, if you have an attorney draw up your Living Trust in one state, and you then inform the attorney that you own property in another state as well, you will be advised to contact an attorney in that state to have your Living Trust reviewed and to transfer that property into your Trust.

The difference between an ordinary Living Trust and a "universal" Living Trust is scope. A universal Living Trust is more comprehensive and inclusive, addressing more real-life situations with individual state statutes. A universal Living Trust is essential if you own property in more than one state; if you live in two or more states—such as "snowbirds" who live in the North in the summer and the South in the winter; or if you ultimately move to another state.

Texas and Florida provide an excellent example of state differences. They have specific homestead rights that, if not included in your Living Trust, would be lost. In such cases having a universal Living Trust can be very important.

PROPER FORMS OF THE LIVING TRUST

The Living Trust document can take one of four basic forms: an A Trust, an A-B Trust, an A-B-C Trust, and a Partner A-A Trust. The form that best suits your particular situation depends on your marital status, the net worth of your estate, and the potential distribution you desire for your heirs.

A Trust

The A Trust can be used for single persons or married couples. As you learned earlier in the chapter, a husband and wife should always consider an A-B Trust, rather than only an A Trust, even if an A-B Trust is not financially needed for the size of their particular estate.

The A Trust must always be used when only one person is involved, such as an unmarried or a widowed person. For estates valued at less than $1 million, the entire estate will flow down to the heirs, since there will be no probate fees or estate taxes to pay. However, for estates valued at more than $1 million, estate taxes will be due.

The A Trust may also be used for a married or unmarried couple whose estate is valued at much less than $1 million, although this practice is not recommended. The entire estate will flow down to the surviving spouse, since there will be no probate fees and—because the estate is small—no estate taxes.

A-B Trust

The A-B Trust is used when two individuals are involved in the Trust, whether they are married or unmarried. The A-B Trust should be considered by every couple, and absolutely by any couple whose estate exceeds $1 million. Upon the death of one individual, half of the assets will flow down into the B (or decedent's) Trust, and the other half of the assets will flow down to the survivor in the A (or survivor's) Trust. Thus, the entire estate will remain available to be used by the surviving spouse.

Unmarried A-B Trust

A typical couple, man and woman, living together and desiring a mutual Trust will utilize the so-called Married A-B Trust. While it speaks of each person as a "spouse," if they never married, and one or both died, this terminology would not make any difference. They just couldn't use the Maximum Marital Deduction provision which is designed solely for married couples. When an unmarried couple comes in for a Trust, they are bonding, and most probably will marry eventually. When they do marry, their Trust is already in place. The only change they will need will be to amend the allocation and distribution section to provide for future children.

In the past several years, more and more unmarried couples find the term "spouse" objectionable. They far prefer the term "partner." In response, we at The Estate Plan, in effect, sterilized the Married A-B Trust by replacing the term "spouse" with "partner"and necessarily deleted the Maximum Marital Deduction provision. Thus, we have a ready-made Unmarried A-B Trust. Eventually, if the parties do get married, they will need to have their Trust amended to unsterilize it. The cost for the Unmarried A-B Trust should be the same as for a Married A-B Trust.

A-B-C Trust

The A-B-C Trust is used for a married couple whose estate exceeds $2 million (two federal estate tax equivalent exemptions). This form of Trust is used to assure that beneficiaries of the decedent spouse will ultimately receive their designated share of the estate. Of the decedent's portion of the estate, $1 million will flow down into the Decedent's B Trust, and the excess will flow into the C Trust. Even though this excess could pass tax free into the Survivor's A Trust under the Unlimited Marital Deduction provision, a much better approach is to use the C Trust, thus protecting the ultimate beneficiaries (since the surviving spouse may not change the beneficiaries or allocation and distribution of Trust C).

The C Trust is also known as a Q-TIP Trust. "Q-TIP" stands for *Qualified Terminal Interest*

Property, which means that, to qualify for this right, the surviving spouse must have a right to all of the income, a right that must be granted for the life of the surviving spouse. The income right may not be terminated, in a certain number of years or during the life of the surviving spouse. (For example, ownership based on the contingency that the surviving spouse not remarry would void the Q-TIP provision.) For the Trust to qualify, the surviving spouse need *not* be given the right to use the principal. In other words, the asset is preserved for the heirs, but the spouse may use any income derived from the asset (such as rental income from an apartment).

Occasionally, a situation arises where, for example, a couple have married, each spouse has children by a previous marriage, and both spouses have accumulated substantial estates prior to their new marriage. If one spouse (for example, the husband) desired that a large share of his estate pass directly to *his* children upon his death, his assets would not qualify for inclusion in the Q-TIP Trust, since the surviving spouse would not have the right to the income from these assets. Therefore, the husband's excess assets would be subject to federal estate taxes upon his death.

The husband may pass the assets directly from the B Trust to his heirs without those assets being subject to further federal estate taxation, leaving the excess assets in the C Trust for the use of his surviving spouse.

The C Trust is expandable. The surviving spouse may pass any amount in excess of $1 million to the C Trust (whether the amount is $150,000, $1.5 million, or $15 million) and thereby defer any assessment of estate taxes until the death of the surviving spouse.

When to Use the C Trust

The surviving spouse can elect to defer paying any estate taxes upon the death of the first spouse as a means of preserving the estate.

An example of such a situation involves Richard and Joan Hogan, who had an estate of approximately $2.5 million. Upon Richard's death, his estate would come down to Joan without paying any estate taxes:

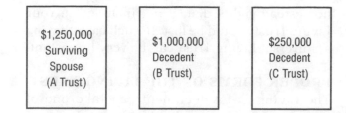

Upon the death of Joan (the surviving spouse), the portion of the estate in the B Trust would be insulated from federal estate taxes. Therefore, federal estate tax would be computed on the value of whatever amount is left in Trust C ($250,000) and in Trust A ($1,250,000), a total of $1.5 million. When the surviving spouse's exclusion ($1 million) is deducted, the remaining $500,000 would be subject to federal estate tax. The federal estate tax due would therefore be $210,000:

Trust C	$ 250,000
Trust A	$ 1,250,000
Subtotal	$ 1,500,000
Less: Surviving spouse's exclusion	($ 1,000,000)
Taxable estate	$ 500,000
Federal estate tax	$ 210,000

Do Not Underestimate the Importance of the C Trust

If a married couple has an estate of $1 million or more, I recommend a C Trust (Q-TIP Trust) *now*. Most estates of that size will reach $1.2 million within two years just by normal inflation and growth. All too often, I see estates of this size or larger that have only an A-B Trust. And all too often, I hear "Living Trust Specialists" saying that you don't need a C Trust. Their concept is that any excess of the decedent spouse's estate over the $1 million federal estate tax exemption can pour back over into the surviving spouse's A Trust. They don't know what they are talking about.

This can be illustrated by the example of Richard and Joan Hogan's estate of $3 million. They have only an A-B Trust. Richard dies. We split the estate in half, giving Joan her marital share of $1.5 million, which we place in the surviving spouse's A Trust. We utilize Richard's $1 million federal estate tax exclusion by placing that amount into the decedent's B Trust. This leaves $1 million, which we now pour back over into the survivor's A Trust. The end result would look like this:

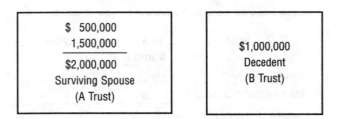

$500,000
1,500,000
———
$2,000,000
Surviving Spouse
(A Trust)

$1,000,000
Decedent
(B Trust)

This approach, of taking the decedent's remaining $500,000 and placing it in the survivor's A Trust, creates a multitude of potentially serious problems:

- They have no protection against an inadvertent generation skip. (See Chapter 12.)
- The survivor loses creditor protection on the decedent's $500,000. This applies equally to frivolous lawsuits.
- The survivor loses the early creditor protection on the decedent's $500,000 provided in many states by the Notice to Creditors. (See Chapter 2.)
- The survivor may ignore the decedent spouse's plan and change the beneficiaries as well as their allocations and distributions.
- If the survivor remarries, the decedent's $500,000 could easily be commingled with the assets of the new spouse and eventually reallocated or dissipated.
- The decedent loses the right to place part, or all, of an IRA in the C Trust which gives the wife lifetime benefits but assures that, following the surviving spouse's death, the IRA will pass to the desired heirs.
- If the surviving spouse becomes extravagant or wasteful, there is no protection for the decedent's $500,000.
- They lose the option, albeit one infrequently used, to give the surviving spouse a testamentary power of appointment. (This would be utilized if the decedent spouse had wanted to authorize the surviving spouse to increase or decrease the inheritance for a certain child who has yet to turn around and get on the straight and narrow path.)

Thus, the additional cost of the C Trust far outweighs the disadvantages.

Reverse Q-TIP Provision
The reverse Q-TIP provision should be included in the Q-TIP, or C Trust. We have discussed how each of us has a right to a $1 million federal estate tax exclusion. In Chapter 12, "Estate Preservation and Tax-Saving Documents," we will discuss how each of us also has a right to a $1 million Generation-Skipping Tax exemption. A generation skip is any bequest (other than your annual $10,000 exemption) to anyone other than your wife or children who is at least thirty-seven and a half years younger than you, such as your grandchildren. The penalty for such a skip is at the onerous 55 percent tax rate. Both of your rights, the $1 million federal estate tax exclusion and the $1 million Generation-Skipping Tax exemption, can be protected with a properly drawn reverse Q-TIP. Without the reverse Q-TIP provision, many estates lose a good portion of one or both of these exemptions. We include this provision in all of our C Trusts.

You Must File a Form 706
You must file an IRS Form 706 within nine months of the date of death of the first spouse in order to elect the Q-TIP Trust. Fail to so file and you lose your right to the Q-TIP Trust, with the result that all assets that would have been placed in this Trust are now subject to federal estate taxes.

When Not to Use the C Trust
Occasionally, however, a situation may arise where use of the C Trust may not be financially beneficial to the estate. If, in the earlier example of Richard and Joan Hogan, Joan had cancer and knew that she had only a short time to live, paying the estate taxes on the excess amount in Trust B would preserve more of the estate.

Joan chose to forgo using the C Trust and instead elected to pay the federal estate taxes on her husband's taxable share of the estate

($250,000) upon his death. The estate would therefore be distributed only into the **A** and **B** portions of the Trust:

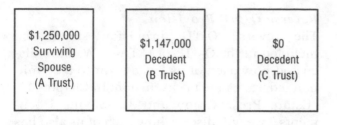

| $1,250,000 Surviving Spouse (A Trust) | $1,147,000 Decedent (B Trust) | $0 Decedent (C Trust) |

Computation of the federal estate tax would be as shown here:

Decedent's share of estate	$ 1,250,000
Less: Decedent's exclusion	($ 1,000,000)
Taxable estate	$ 250,000
Federal estate tax	$ 103,000
Decedent's original estate	$ 1,250,000
Less: Estate tax	($ 103,000)
Net estate	$ 1,147,000

After payment of estate taxes of $103,000 (on the $250,000 taxable portion of Richard's estate), the $147,000 remaining after taxes may now be added to the $1 million already placed in the Decedent's **B** Trust. The entire $1,147,000 would then be insulated from further estate taxes. Upon Joan's death, only the $1,250,000 in the Survivor's **A** Trust would be subject to federal estate taxes. Joan's federal estate tax computations would appear as follows:

Survivor's share of estate	$ 1,250,000
Less: Survivor's exclusion	($ 1,000,000)
Taxable estate	$ 250,000
Survivor's original estate	$1,250,000
Less: Estate tax (39%)	($ 103,000)
Net estate	$ 1,147,000
Plus: Decedent's estate from Trust B	$ 1,147,000
Total estate for the heirs	$ 2,294,000

The following computations show how Joan benefited the heirs by paying taxes on the excess amount in Trust B rather than putting the excess in Trust C:

	Using C Trust	Not Using C Trust
Total estate	$ 2,500,000	$ 2,500,000
Tax on decedent's estate	-0-	($ 103,000)
Balance of estate for surviving spouse	$ 2,500,000	$ 2,397,000
Tax on survivor's estate	($ 210,000)	($ 103,000)
Residual estate to heirs	$ 2,290,000	$ 2,294,000
Additional gain for heirs		$ 4,000

In effect, by not using the **C** Trust and instead paying the federal government $103,000 in estate taxes upon the death of the first spouse, Joan saved the estate $4,000 in additional federal estate taxes. (On the other hand, if Joan had retained the $103,000 and invested it in a tax-free entity paying 6 percent or in a taxable entity paying 9 percent, she would have earned back the $10,000 by the end of the year—and *still* retained the funds for future income.)

The amount of tax saved will increase for larger estates, but the principle is the same. However, generally speaking, dollars in hand today are more valuable than money saved tomorrow.

Following a seminar some time ago, a young man came up to me and rather pompously announced that he knew about the Q-TIP Trust and knew that it was better to pay the decedent's estate tax up front. My response to the young man was that, if the surviving spouse knows he or she will die within only a few months of the decedent spouse, then paying tax on the decedent's share of the estate may have merit. However, as a practical matter, the intent of most people is to preserve as much of the estate as possible for the survivor. After settling hundreds of estates, I have found only this one estate where it was appropriate to recommend paying taxes on the decedent's estate following the death of the decedent, rather than waiting until the death of the surviving spouse. The Q-TIP Trust is an ideal estate-planning tool and a protection for the surviving spouse, as well as for the decedent's ultimate beneficiaries.

Q-DOT Trust

The "Q-DOT Trust" *(Qualified Domestic Trust)* is a variation of the Q-TIP Trust that must be used (along with the Q-TIP Trust) when one spouse is a non-citizen of the United States. The new provision was instituted by Congress in 1988. The Q-DOT Trust requires that if the surviving spouse is a non-citizen of the United States, the trustee (or co-trustee) must be a citizen of the United States in order for the Q-TIP Trust to *qualify* as a vehicle for deferring estate tax. This trustee-citizenship requirement is now included in all of our Q-TIP Trusts, which means that our Q-TIP Trusts are automatically Q-DOT Trusts as well.

There is sensible logic to this provision requiring citizenship of the trustee:

> Let's suppose that a surviving spouse (who is not a United States citizen) elected to utilize the Q-TIP Trust and placed $400,000 therein, thereby deferring estate tax payments of about $168,000. Now, let's further suppose that this surviving spouse then decided to return to his or her country of origin. Upon the death of this surviving spouse, Uncle Sam would have no way of collecting the deferred tax of approximately $168,000.

Therefore, Congress now requires that if the non-citizen surviving spouse chooses to elect the Q-TIP Trust and defer the payment of such estate taxes, then the trustee (or co-trustee) must be a citizen of the United States. This citizen trustee (or co-trustee) has the responsibility to ultimately ensure that the appropriate tax is paid upon the death of the surviving spouse. As a result, with this provision, the Q-TIP Trust now qualifies as a Q-DOT Trust.

The important point to remember about the Q-DOT Trust is that the choice of appointing a citizen trustee (or co-trustee) and electing to use the Q-DOT Trust or of paying the estate taxes (in lieu of having the Q-DOT Trust) need not be made until the death of the first spouse. (The first spouse may not die until ten to twenty or more years in the future, and many things can change in that intervening period.) For now, you simply need to be aware of your *future* choices. The citizenship requirement for the trustee (or co-trustee) need apply only to the Q-DOT Trust; there is no restriction on the citizenship of the trustees for the A and B Trusts.

The Non-Citizen Use of an A-B-C Trust

An A-B-C Trust is a necessity when one or both spouses are non-citizens. A non-citizen spouse cannot utilize the Unlimited Marital Deduction and, therefore, cannot receive a decedent spouse's assets tax-free. This drawback emphasizes the need for an A-B-C Living Trust, in which the assets do not pass to the non-citizen spouse but instead remain in trust for the absolute use of the non-citizen spouse. Contrast this situation to the taxable impact that would be created by using a Will, which would pass the decedent's assets to a non-citizen spouse and thereupon be taxed.

Remember that a *resident* non-citizen is entitled to use the $1 million federal estate tax exclusion (as discussed previously in Chapter 5). However, as pointed out in the previous section, certain requirements for the Q-DOT Trust must be met (for example, the trustee or the co-trustee must be a citizen). Also, as mentioned earlier, a non-citizen does not qualify for the Maximum Marital Deduction.

Partner A-A Trust

The Partner A-A Trust was developed as the ideal estate-planning tool for same-sex couples. This would include two brothers or two sisters, or two friends, as well as gay or lesbian couples. Like the Unmarried A-B Trust, the Partner A-A Trust is also "sterilized" using the term *partner*. It is designed to accommodate separate goals and objectives for beneficiaries and the allocation and distribution of each partner. The individuals may own separate property, which is identified as such, and likewise may own assets together. In most instances, even though the individuals may have common interests, they usually have separate objectives when it comes to the ultimate disposition of their property. The Partner A-A Trust is predominantly two single A Trusts blended together, and this combination works quite well in such circumstances.

With the growing awareness of the needs of non-heterosexual couples, there is a demand for an estate-planning vehicle that will protect their property interests. The Partner A-A Trust was specifically tailored to meet this need.

POUR-OVER WILL

The Living Trust becomes, in effect, your Will and specifically spells out to whom, when, and how your assets are to be distributed—and does so with far greater latitude than a standard Will. Nevertheless, another document, known as the "Pour-Over Will," is needed to accompany the Living Trust. The Pour-Over Will transfers into the Living Trust assets that have been inadvertently left outside. The Pour-Over Will simply says, in effect, that if you forgot to place an asset into your Living Trust, it is your intent (upon your death) that such assets "pour over" into your Trust. As a client said so well, "It's similar to a P.S. to a letter." The Pour-Over Will is therefore a useful catchall and should be included in every Living Trust.

Assets passing into the Living Trust through a Pour-Over Will must, however, first go through probate. Ideally, you have done your job—have placed all your assets in trust—and will never have to use this pour-over feature. After all, one of the prime purposes of the Living Trust is to avoid probate! Unfortunately, not all people take full advantage of this feature.

Several years ago, for example, clients who had established a Living Trust to avoid probate learned that they had been named executors of the estate of the husband's brother, Bob Anderson. Wanting to avoid probate on his estate, the clients brought Bob in to establish his own Living Trust. Thereafter, they helped Bob transfer all of his assets into the Trust— that is, all but one asset. For some unknown reason, no matter how hard they tried, Bob resisted transferring one stock certificate into the Trust. At the most, it would have taken less than an hour to go to the bank, have his signature guaranteed, and forward the stock papers to the transfer agent.

Bob died six months later. His brother and sister-in-law, as trustees, sold his condominium within sixty days, liquidated his assets, and distributed them. The clients took care of all the assets—except the one stock certificate, which represented 5,000 shares of American Express stock, then worth $350,000. This single certificate had to go through twelve months of agonizing probate—and cost $8,500 in probate fees. As executors of Bob's estate, his brother and sister-in-law would be the first to say, "Don't leave *any* assets outside your Trust."

Provisions of the Pour-Over Will

A Pour-Over Will is a rather simple legal document that consists of five provisions:

- It identifies the individual by name.
- It revokes any prior Wills and related codicils.
- It pours into the Living Trust any personal or household effects left outside the Trust.
- It pours into the Trust any real assets left outside the Trust (but unfortunately, *after* probate).
- It names the executor and provides the necessary authority to take assets left outside the Trust through probate.

Identification of the Individual

The Pour-Over Will states your name. If you are married, the Pour-Over Will states that fact and names your spouse. All children (whether by this or any previous marriages) are each named. Often, a husband or wife who has married a spouse with children from a previous marriage feels close to these children and wishes to name them as his or her children and heirs, even though they are not formally adopted. This action is quite acceptable and common.

If a female child changes her name because of marriage or divorce, you do not need to change your Pour-Over Will or amend your Trust. Once identified as your child, that child remains identified as your child regardless of a name change.

If you wish to disinherit a child, this fact should be stated both in your Pour-Over Will and in your Living Trust. This action will protect your estate from any potential future challenge by an excluded child on the basis that he or she was overlooked or forgotten.

Revocation of Prior Wills and Codicils
The Pour-Over Will revokes any prior Wills or codicils (changes to a Will) you may have made. I am often asked whether a person who creates a Living Trust needs to notify the attorney who drew up his or her Will. My answer is no. Even though such a response does a minor disservice to the attorney, who will continue to retain that now-revoked document in his or her files, the attorney all too often takes such news ungraciously and tries to convince the client that he or she has done a stupid thing by creating a Living Trust and says, "Probate really isn't that much."

Pouring of Personal Effects into the Trust
Personal and household effects, including future acquisitions, should be transferred into the Trust by a document called Assignment of Furniture, Furnishings, and Personal Effects (explained in Chapter 13). The Pour-Over Will simply restates that, if some personal or household effects were somehow left outside the Trust, they are to pour over into the Living Trust.

Pouring of Real Assets into the Trust
The Pour-Over Will specifies that, upon your death, any real assets held outside the Trust are to pour over into the Trust. Real assets would include checking accounts, savings accounts, money market funds, certificates of deposit, Treasury bills, stocks, bonds, mutual funds, limited partnerships, notes due to you,

real estate, trust deeds, and business interests (such as a sole proprietorship, a partnership, or a corporation). Unfortunately, if these real assets exceed the probate criteria, they must go through probate first, and this task is the executor's job.

Naming of Executor and Granting of Authority
The Pour-Over Will names the executor and provides the executor with the authority to take any assets left outside the Trust through the probate process. If assets that have been left outside your Living Trust exceed the probate criteria, they must be taken through probate by the executor. Once the probate process is completed, the assets will pour over into the Living Trust to be utilized or distributed as you have specified in your Living Trust.

Typically, the surviving spouse should be named to serve as the executor; upon the death of the surviving spouse, the successor trustee should be named to serve as the executor. However, unlike the successor trustees (who may consist of several co-trustees), only one person should be appointed to serve as executor. That person should reside within the state where probate will occur because of the numerous court appearances and document signatures that are required.

Even though the Pour-Over Will often names the guardian for minor children, a far more appropriate way of naming a guardian is through an entirely separate document, titled Appointment of Guardian, which will be described in Chapter 11.

Potential Uses of the Pour-Over Will
Although one of the prime reasons for a Living Trust is to avoid probate, two potential uses of the Pour-Over Will still remain, even with all of the assets properly transferred to the Trust. If an individual were killed in an automobile accident, for example, there could potentially be proceeds from a wrongful death suit (which would become part of the decedent's estate).

Another situation would be individuals with great wealth and therefore potential exposure to liability suits, such as real estate developers, doctors, or contractors. In a situation of this nature, it may be advisable to probate a specific sum of money for the sole purpose of cutting off future claims at the conclusion of the probate process. For example, following the announcement that Bing Crosby had a Living Trust, $1 million was probated in Mr. Crosby's estate, specifically to terminate any future suits. Not only had Mr. Crosby accumulated a large estate, but also his holdings were quite diverse—and he was a famous person.

In today's litigious society, such circumstances can give rise to any type of suit, regardless of its merits. Suits go through the civil courts, which are extremely crowded today, may take up to five years just to get to court, and may cost anywhere from $50,000 to $200,000 in legal fees. Therefore, whenever there is a potential for any type of suit, it is far more beneficial to have such claims heard in the probate court, whether or not the claim is groundless. Unlike the civil court, the probate court will typically hear the claim within four months of death, and it is far more inclined to discharge the claim or to carefully examine its merits and to settle it on the basis of the true merits of the claim, rather than on the emotional whims of a jury (as would be the case with a civil trial).

To settle potential suits via the probate process, an executor must be named and then authorized to act on behalf of the deceased person. Once the claims have been expeditiously settled in the probate court, the remaining assets would then pour over into the Trust and be used or distributed as specified in the Trust.

A MOST VERSATILE DOCUMENT

Even though the concept of the Living Trust is new to most people, it stands as a pillar of the democratic system.

It is important to recognize that it is not just the Living Trust that matters, but rather it is the *entire process* of establishing and funding a Living Trust that really counts. The process ensures that the assets are transferred into the Trust and that the estate is organized. A Living Trust becomes your plan, and, as any plan should be, it is readily changeable (and revocable). In addition, a properly drawn and funded Living Trust is unchallengeable.

After working with the Living Trust for more than twenty-five years, helping to create the documents and settle the estates, I firmly believe that the Living Trust is one of the most versatile and remarkable documents available.

8

Parties to the Trust

Individuals often serve many functions simultaneously. A man may be a husband, father, engineer, and church leader; a woman may be a wife, mother, teacher, and community leader. Each role is distinct and important. Similarly, when you have a Living Trust, you will generally serve as the trustor, the settlor, the trustee, and the beneficiary. Two other roles, distinct from the Trust but related to it, are the roles of the executor and the guardian. Since many of the legal terms associated with Living Trusts are not commonly understood, this chapter explains each of the terms identifying the parties to the Trust.

TRUSTOR

The *trustor* is the individual or individuals who create the Living Trust. These individuals will be asked to sign as trustors (that is, the *creators* of the Trust). Having created the Trust, the trustors have nothing further to do unless they wish to make a change to their Trust. The trustors will also be asked to sign any future amendments to the Trust.

SETTLOR

The *settlor* (who is almost always the same individual or individuals as the trustors) is the individual or individuals who place the assets inside the Trust. As such, settlors have *absolute* power over those assets, with the freedom to do as they wish with the assets until their death. As you learned in Chapter 7, the settlors may buy, sell, borrow against, and transfer the assets. The settlors also have the power to amend or revoke the Trust and to name the heirs.

If the settlors are husband and wife, the surviving spouse inherits the power to buy, sell, transfer, borrow against, and distribute the assets. However, the right to amend the Decedent's Trust B or to name the heirs and method of distribution of the Decedent's Trust B dies with the decedent settlor. The surviving settlor retains *absolute power* over the assets in the Survivor's Trust A, since they are the survivor's assets. The right to make any changes to Trusts A, B, or C dies with the surviving settlor. The entire Trust then becomes irrevocable; the successor trustee may make no alterations whatsoever, and must thereafter abide by the specific directions of the Trust.

The settlor is sometimes referred to as the *grantor*, which is simply the Internal Revenue Service name for the settlor. Grantor Trust is the IRS name for a Living Trust.

TRUSTEE

The *trustee* is the individual or individuals who handle the administration of the Trust. When a Trust is first created, the trustees are usually the same individuals as the trustors and settlors of the Trust. For a married couple, usually husband and wife both act as trustees.

You have presumably managed your assets reasonably well, and this management should continue after you have created a Living Trust. Therefore, once your Trust is created, you will now step in as trustee of the Trust assets—with the same freedom and power to buy, sell, borrow against, or transfer the Trust assets as you had before creating a Living Trust. The management of your assets remains the same, and there are no different books to maintain because you have a Living Trust.

The trustee is not required to be a resident of the state in which the Trust is formed or settled. In fact, it is quite common for trustees to reside in other states or even outside the country.

Surviving Trustee

The *surviving trustee* is the individual who continues to manage the Trust after one of the original trustees has died. Upon the death of one spouse, the surviving spouse should become the surviving trustee, having the same freedom as before to manage the assets in the Trust. Typically, the surviving spouse also retains the right to change the successor trustee (the individual who will take over the administration of the Trust when the surviving spouse dies).

Historically, the wife was considered unsophisticated in financial matters, and a financial institution was usually named to serve as co-trustee with the wife. This attitude is a throwback to the promotion of the Living Trust by banking institutions during the 1920s. In today's society, it is recommended that the wife be named as surviving trustee as long as she is competent. If the wife feels the need, she may still hire (and fire at her discretion) good financial counsel. Of course, the same recommendations apply if the husband is the surviving spouse.

A good example of a financial institution being hired to manage Trust assets is that of Mrs. Adams, whose husband had been with a major bank for some thirty years. In drawing up their Trust, the pair's natural inclination was to name the bank as trustee or at least as a co-trustee with the wife. At my urging, they named the wife as sole surviving trustee. When Mr. Adams died some twelve months later, Mrs. Adams, as the surviving trustee, hired the bank to manage the Trust assets.

Within six months, however, Mrs. Adams was so frustrated with the bank's poor management that she moved her account to another financial institution. Nine years later, this financially unsophisticated widow has done very well—by demanding good service of the financial institution. Demanding good service was something she could do *only* as the sole surviving trustee.

Successor Trustee

A *successor trustee* also must be named to succeed you as the manager of the Trust assets upon your death or incompetence (if you are single) or upon the death or incompetence of both spouses (if you are married). This individual or individuals will step into your shoes upon your death or incompetence without requiring any court proceedings or legal action. The successor trustee will immediately have the same powers that you as trustee had to buy, sell, borrow against, and transfer the Trust assets. An even more important function for the successor trustee is to use or distribute the assets as you have instructed in your Living Trust. However, a successor trustee may not in any way change the Trust (since he or she was not the creator of the Trust). As a good practice, I recommend that you ask those individuals you desire to name as your successor trustee or trustees whether they are willing to serve as successor trustees.

A successor trustee, however, does have the freedom to manage the assets in the estate, but must do so in a prudent manner. For example, just as you might do, the successor trustee may take a first or second mortgage on real estate to improve the property or acquire other property in the name of the Trust. To borrow against an asset has to do with Trust management, not with asset distribution. The successor trustee may not borrow against assets in trust for the benefit of a beneficiary (rather than for the benefit of the Trust), unless you have so specified in your beneficial instructions, as described in the next chapter. For example, it could be appropriate for a successor trustee to borrow against Trust assets, rather than liquidate the assets, to pay for medical bills of minor children who are beneficiaries.

As you become aged and possibly infirm, though still competent, you may wish to relinquish the administration of your assets to the successor trustee or successor trustees. You may do so by a simple statement in writing to that effect. However, as long as you are competent, you retain the right to resume the role as trustee or to replace the successor trustee. This prerogative is your absolute right as the settlor. Since you created the Trust, you have full control over it.

The successor trustee's job of administering a Trust takes little effort. Location of residence therefore need not be a factor in naming successor trustees. From time to time, decisions must be made and papers signed in order to buy, sell, transfer, or distribute assets within the Trust. Such decisions usually can be made fairly easily from one or many locations.

For example, four children might be acting as successor trustees of a Trust. One of the children may live in San Francisco, another in Chicago, another in New York, and the other child in Miami. It is possible for the four trustees, by telephone, to agree to sell a particular piece of real estate and to authorize one of the trustees to take the appropriate action. Then, as would be the case in almost all real estate transactions, a real estate agent would be appointed, a buyer eventually found, and the real estate sold.

However, before escrow could close, the deed must be signed by all four trustees. The signature process would be accomplished by having, for example, the trustee in San Francisco sign the deed, forward it to Chicago, on to New York, and then to Miami for signatures. The trustee in Miami would then return the deed to San Francisco. The entire process should take no more than one to two weeks, depending upon the vagaries of the postal system.

The predominant characteristic of the successor trustee is *trust*. Thus, you should consider selecting your adult child or children, close family members, or close friends to serve as the successor trustee or successor trustees.

Fiduciary Capacity

The successor trustee serves in a *fiduciary capacity*. This means that, in all financial matters relating to the Trust, the trustee must act with prudence and strictly in accordance with the Trust instructions. The successor trustees have no protection for acting irresponsibly or contrary to the instructions of the Trust. *Not even bankruptcy* is an excuse.

I often cite the situation of three children named as successor trustees and also as beneficiaries. Each child was to receive $50,000 outright upon the death of the surviving parent and another $50,000 five years later.

One child was involved in a business venture that needed $100,000, and he coerced his two siblings into giving him not only the $50,000 legally due him, but also the $50,000 that was not due for another five years. The business venture failed, and the son who received the extra share of money returned to his siblings and advised them that, since they were all at fault in violating their fiduciary responsibilities, he wanted his $50,000 in five years when due—from *their* share. The child was correct, and he would most likely get his money.

Recognizing these consequences, anyone serving as successor trustee should respond to such a request by saying, "Brother, I love you, but . . ."

More than One Successor Trustee

If you are wondering who watches over the trustee, one way to alleviate your concerns is to appoint as trustee someone you trust. You can also obtain security in numbers by appointing two or more trustees. Multiple trustees tend to monitor each other, so it is less likely that one of the trustees will do something that is not in the best interest of the estate.

If more than one successor trustee is named, all successor trustees must act *in concert* as co-trustees. Any action on behalf of the Trust will require the agreement and signature of each successor co-trustee.

> The concept of compromise and joint agreement can be illustrated by the example of three children who are serving as successor trustees and have different investment concepts. The first child wants to be safe and place the funds under the mattress. The second child wants to double the money overnight on a "high-flyer." The third child wants to place the assets in the bank in certificates of deposit. Since the children must all agree, the funds are obviously not going under the mattress or into a high-flyer. The three must compromise and come up with a middle-of-the-road decision, which is in keeping with the fiduciary responsibilities of the trustees.

We usually require the successor trustees to act in concert, as this provides a greater degree of security, but you may elect to permit the successor trustees to act by majority rule. I strongly recommend against selecting majority rule because this approach begs conflict between the trustees, who tend to battle over who will side with each other.

> A wealthy couple desired to have their seven sons serve together as successor trustees. The couple admitted that their sons did not get along well with each other, and the pair suggested that their Trust be drawn so as to permit a majority opinion of successor trustees to prevail. Unfortunately, such an arrangement is not usually advisable; co-trustees should be required to *all* agree before there can be any decision. Even under these chal-

lenging circumstances, it is amazing to watch successor co-trustees compromise and ultimately reach the best decision for all concerned.

Clients frequently ask, "May we name all our children as successor trustees, so as not to hurt anyone?" The answer, of course, is yes. Unlike the committee that started out to design a horse and ended up with a camel, several trustees invariably make unified decisions that are in the best interest of the Trust.

Legal Age to Serve as Trustee

An individual must be of legal age (eighteen in most states) to serve as a trustee. One husband and wife felt that their only child, aged sixteen, was mature enough to be named successor trustee if something happened to them. In this situation, it was recommended that the father's sister be named as alternate successor trustee and that the sixteen-year-old son be named as the successor trustee. Then, if the parents died while the son were still a minor (less than eighteen years old), the father's sister, as alternate successor trustee, would serve as trustee until the son's eighteenth birthday. At that time, the son would step in as the successor trustee with all of the trustee powers his parents had possessed before him.

Recently, a husband and wife asked if they could name their children, ages five and seven, as successor trustees with an adult named as the alternate successor trustee. I suggested that the children were a little young for such responsibility and that the parents should wait until the children reached the age of fifteen or sixteen to see how well they were maturing.

Conflict Among Successor Trustees or Beneficiaries

Many people wonder what would happen in the event of unresolved conflict, such as sibling rivalry, where there are two or more successor trustees, or if there were a conflict between beneficiaries and/or trustees. In such rare situations, the Living Trusts written by our firm specify that a conflict shall be resolved by arbitration—a process that is swift, reasonable, and relatively inexpensive. As an added protection, a provision in the Living Trusts drawn up for our clients stipulates that there will be one arbitrator per individual, plus an independent arbitrator, if appropriate.

If there is an unresolved conflict, the named arbitration association will provide, upon request, its rules of arbitration and identify its nearest local office. When the local office is contacted, it will supply a list of arbitrators (typically five to ten people); each conflicting party then may choose his or her arbitrator. An arbitrator is simply a businessperson who serves as an impartial decision maker to resolve disputes. Conflict is typically emotional, and the arbitrator will take a businesslike approach. The arbitrator will simply look at the issues, eliminating the emotions, and will make a decision that is fair and in the best interests of all parties concerned.

You may appoint multiple successor trustees—for example, all of your children.

In the fifteen years since our firm has begun including this provision for resolving conflicts in the Living Trusts drawn up for our clients, I am not aware of any Trust that has gone to arbitration. People often operate on emotions; they will play the game as long as they can. However, when people recognize that they can no longer play their game, but must go to arbitration where their emotions will be set aside, they stop playing and proceed to work out a compromise.

Right to Elect Successor Trustee

If, for some reason, a successor trustee is not living or is no longer able to serve as trustee and no other successor trustees are named in the Trust, a good Living Trust will provide for just such a contingency. In a well-written Living Trust, the primary beneficiaries should be authorized to elect one or more successor trustees if there is no named successor trustee who is competent and still living.

BENEFICIARIES

The beneficiary—or beneficiaries, since there is often more than one—receives the benefits (i.e., the assets) of the Trust. There are three types of beneficiaries—the *primary* beneficiary, the *contingent* beneficiary, and the *remainder* beneficiary. Each of these types of beneficiaries plays a role in the Living Trust.

Because of our Will mentality, we tend to think of the beneficiaries as being our children, since we would have named them as beneficiaries in our Will. However, it is important to realize the difference between a Will and a Living Trust. A Will does not become effective until someone dies, whereas a Living Trust becomes effective the moment it is created (when it is signed by the creators, the document is notarized, and the assets are placed inside the Living Trust).

Primary Beneficiaries

Many people overlook the fact that, typically, the husband and wife are the initial beneficiaries of their own Trust. When a Living Trust is first created, the husband and wife (or the man or woman, if the Trust is for a single party) are designated as the Trust "beneficiaries." These individuals have a beneficial interest in the Trust assets and enjoy the income and principal from the assets in the Trust and are therefore known as the *primary* beneficiaries.

Upon the demise of a spouse, the surviving spouse usually becomes the remaining primary beneficiary of the Living Trust.

Contingent Beneficiaries

Any future beneficiary designations other than the trustors, usually the children, made by the husband and wife—or by the single man or woman—are considered to be *contingent* beneficiaries. As long as the husband and wife, or the individual, are still living and competent, they can change the beneficiary designations at any time; thus, these contingent beneficiaries may be changed or even deleted as long as the person or persons who created the Trust are living and competent.

With a couple in a second marriage, it is common for the husband and wife to name different contingent beneficiaries (usually each spouse's own children from a previous marriage). Thus, while both spouses are still living, the spouses are the primary beneficiaries of their Living Trust, and the children of both spouses are considered to be contingent bene-ficiaries of the Trust, since the beneficiary des-ignations can be changed at any time, as long as the husband and wife remain alive and competent.

Remember, though, that the creators (trustors/settlors) have the ability to alter the beneficiary designations of *their* share of the as-sets in whatever way they may so desire. In a good Living Trust, each of the trustors, or sett-lors, has the power to separately designate the contingent beneficiaries of his or her share of the Trust assets, as well as to specify *when* the contingent beneficiaries are to receive the assets.

For example, assume that a husband and wife who created a Living Trust are both in their second marriage and that the husband brought separate property into this marriage. The husband desires that upon his death, the joint marital assets remain in trust for the ben-efit of his surviving spouse but that his sepa-rate property be given to his children. This arrangement can be easily specified in the Liv-ing Trust.

In most cases, for couples who have not remarried, all of the assets are retained in trust, and the surviving spouse becomes the surviving *primary* beneficiary. Keep in mind that it is only after a trustor dies that the named heirs of the trustor truly become bene-ficiaries of the Living Trust—not before then.

Remainder Beneficiaries

A remainder beneficiary is an individual who is *irrevocably* named as the beneficiary of a Liv-ing Trust. A beneficiary designation becomes irrevocable when the person making such des-ignations dies or becomes incompetent; the named beneficiary then becomes a *remainder* beneficiary. A surviving spouse cannot change the beneficiary designations or allocations of the decedent spouse.

Typically, the importance of the remainder beneficiaries comes into play only when the husband and wife name different beneficiaries. While the husband and wife are living, they are the primary beneficiaries of their Living Trust, and they can change the *contingent* benefi-ciaries of their Living Trust at any time they desire. A similar scenario applies for a

single individual who has a Living Trust; he or she need not be concerned about providing any information to contingent beneficiaries, because the beneficiary designations can be changed at any time while the original trustor is still alive and competent.

Recall that when the first spouse dies, the B sub-trust (and C sub-trust, if it exists) becomes irrevocable; the surviving spouse cannot change it. Therefore, when the first spouse dies, any beneficiary designations made by that spouse are no longer "contingent"; instead, these *contingent* beneficiaries become irrevo-cable *remainder* beneficiaries of the B sub-trust (and/or C sub-trust). However, even after the first spouse has died, the beneficiaries named by the surviving spouse are still *contingent* ben-eficiaries for the second spouse's A sub-trust, since the surviving spouse may still change the beneficiary designations as long as he or she is alive and competent.

Let's assume that a husband and wife, in their first marriage, have two children and that each spouse has named both children as ben-eficiaries. As long as both spouses are still liv-ing, the children are considered to be *contingent* beneficiaries. When the first spouse dies, the beneficiaries named by the first spouse now become *remainder* beneficiaries (an irrev-ocable designation) of the decedent's B sub-trust (and/or C sub-trust), but these same children continue to be *contingent* beneficia-ries of the survivor's A sub-trust. Thus, at the same time, the children can be both remain-der beneficiaries and contingent beneficiaries. When the second spouse dies, the children become remainder beneficiaries of the second spouse's A sub-trust as well.

The significance of the remainder benefi-ciary comes into play when one spouse dies (where there is a Married A-B Living Trust or A-B-C Living Trust), leaving the surviving spouse as sole trustee and *primary* beneficiary. In this instance, the surviving spouse is the pri-mary beneficiary of the survivor's A sub-trust (his or her own Trust) and need not be con-cerned with the *contingent* beneficiaries of the A sub-trust, because the surviving spouse can change the beneficiaries of the A sub-trust at any time.

The situation is very different, however, for the decedent's B sub-trust and/or C sub-trust, since the Living Trust provisions (and beneficiary designations) become irrevocable upon the death of the first spouse—and the *contingent* beneficiaries become the *remainder* beneficiaries. The remainder beneficiaries of the decedent's B sub-trust now become very important. The surviving spouse, acting as trustee, must recognize that these remainder beneficiaries will ultimately be the recipients of the residual (the assets remaining in the B sub-trust and/or C sub-trust)—and their rights *cannot be altered*.

Since the rights of the remainder beneficiaries cannot be altered, they must be protected. If the remainder beneficiaries are the joint children of both spouses, there should be no concern. However, in the case of a second marriage, with children from each spouse, the surviving spouse (acting as surviving trustee) needs to follow the rules very carefully.

> Let's briefly explore the case in which a husband has two children from his former marriage, and his wife also has two children from her former marriage. The husband dies, leaving his share of the assets in trust for the benefit of his surviving spouse.
>
> Under these circumstances, the surviving spouse needs to judiciously recognize the ultimate rights of the husband's children. The surviving spouse must clearly understand and govern her actions according to the knowledge that if she abuses her rights as trustee and abridges the rights of the husband's children, she could ultimately end up in grave legal difficulty with the husband's children.

The remainder beneficiaries have a common-law right to know that their ultimate share of assets is being diligently protected. (This does not deny the surviving spouse the right to use all of the assets if necessary to retain the same style of living as when both spouses were alive.) It does mean that the surviving spouse, as the surviving trustee, has a common-law responsibility to annually advise the remainder beneficiaries of the status of the assets in the irrevocable portions of the Living Trust. Since a Form 1041 must be filed with the IRS each year, a copy of this form sent to the remainder beneficiaries should suffice.

The next chapter explains the allocation and distribution of the Trust assets to the beneficiaries upon the death of the settlor or settlors.

FINANCIAL INSTITUTION AS PARTY TO A TRUST

A financial institution may sometimes be named to serve in one of several capacities with a Living Trust, including as administrator, as co-trustee, as successor trustee, or as custodian of the Trust.

Financial Institution as Administrator

In the early 1920s, the banking industry seized upon the Living Trust and the Testamentary Trust as the ideal vehicles by which to obtain control of money. The idea of the Trust was promoted extensively, particularly to people who had money but were not necessarily sophisticated in financial or legal matters. In almost any bank lobby today, you will find numerous brochures promoting the advantages of the Trust and emphasizing the opportunity to have the bank manage your funds "as trustees." Even though there are numerous advantages to the Living Trust, management by a financial institution is not necessarily one of them.

Before the 1976 Tax Reform Act, many attorneys had a ready answer for clients who were venturesome enough to consider a Living Trust. The attorneys would simply ask their clients, "Do you know that a financial institution must be trustee and will charge you 1 percent of your assets *annually* as a management fee?" That statement is simply not true, but the question frightened many people away from creating Living Trusts—and eventually allowed the attorneys to extract fat probate fees from the estates of their clients.

As trustee, you or your surviving spouse always has the option to hire a financial institution for help in managing your estate.

Financial institutions are readily available to manage your estate—for a fee—if you so desire, but that fact has nothing to do with the need for a Living Trust. Most people want to manage their own assets. Therefore, when people create a Living Trust, they usually want to continue to manage their own assets as trustees. If you desire financial assistance, you always have the option to hire—and fire, as you see fit—any financial institution to act in your behalf.

The freedom to hire and fire a financial institution is also available to a surviving spouse. In the past, it was common practice to designate a financial institution as trustee or as co-trustee with a surviving spouse. In the last decade, however, as the Living Trust has been used more extensively, people have become more sophisticated. It is now recommended that the surviving spouse serve as sole surviving trustee—without being bound to a financial institution.

A sophisticated investor with a large portfolio of stocks and bonds did not want to saddle his wife with the responsibility of managing his extensive portfolio upon his death. The husband was very knowledgeable in buying and selling stocks and simply didn't want to burden his wife with an unfamiliar task. The husband was inclined to appoint a financial institution as surviving trustee upon his death instead of his wife.

It was suggested to the husband that he name his wife as surviving trustee and allow her to hire and fire, if necessary, a financial institution if she saw fit to do so. The husband concurred. This practice makes sound financial sense.

With the same reasoning, it is recommended that the adult children, close family members, or close friends, in lieu of a financial institution, be considered as successor trustees upon the death of both parents. The successor trustees can readily turn to a financial institution for financial assistance, if necessary.

Historically, banks have been far too conservative—and not necessarily astute—managers of Trusts. Typically, upon becoming a trustee, most banks liquidate all of the securities in an estate and then invest the assets in banking vehicles (such as certificates of deposit, Treasury bills, and bank stock). Appeals from the surviving beneficiaries for changes, regardless of how reasonable, usually fall upon deaf ears. Keep in mind that financial institutions tend to manage *your* assets to *their* best advantage—and not necessarily with your best interests in mind.

I remember a client's $1 million portfolio that was managed by a major bank. The husband, who had been a doctor, had died and left his share of the estate in trust for his surviving wife, with the bank as trustee. All of the wise investments in stocks and bonds had long been liquidated. The bank statement showed current earnings of only 3.1 percent—before the trustee fee was deducted. To add insult to injury, the surviving wife was receiving only $2,400 *quarterly* from a $1 million Trust, because the bank had invested for growth rather than for the income so badly needed by this eighty-two-year-old widow!

In my earlier years, I was more vocal in our estate-planning seminars about the abuse of banks as trustees.

Following one such seminar, an attendee came in to create his Trust and complimented me for "telling it like it is." The man said that he now owned several banks but had started his career in the trust department of a bank. He related that in his earlier years he had watched many Trust beneficiaries come into the trust department and plead for more money (that is, request a better return of income) from the Trust investments. The man confided that the bank officials were overly solicitous and offered to do everything possible, and the beneficiary would depart feeling much better and satisfied. However, once the beneficiary was outside the bank, the bank officials would break into hysterics, as if to say, "There goes another sucker."

Admittedly, great change is now taking place in the banking industry, and many banks and financial institutions are installing good financial managers. However, a trusted family member or close friend acting as successor trustee always has the option to select one of these financial institutions to manage the assets, if needed.

In a situation in which a couple has no trusted family members or close friends, a financial institution is the logical successor trustee for any minor children. In addition, if adult children are considered irresponsible, a logical choice for a successor trustee may well be a financial institution.

For the extremely few people who feel the need for a financial institution as trustee, there are many companies that perform reputably. Unfortunately, locating these companies requires extensive research. As a suggestion for consideration, our firm has been very pleased with the performance of one of the oldest Trust services in the country—Trust Services of America, Inc. This company was originally the respected Title Insurance and Trust Company, which was acquired by Northern Trust of California, an equally respected Trust services firm that is continuing the tradition of service established by the original company. The company is now known as Northern Trust of California, N.A. (9744 Wilshire Boulevard, Suite 445, Beverly Hills, California 90212).

Financial Institution as Co-Trustee
A more stringent alternative for administering the Trust would be to appoint a financial institution as co-trustee. The other trustees could be authorized to replace the financial institution co-trustee when appropriate.

Financial Institution as Successor Trustee
A financial institution should be named as successor trustee *only* as a last resort. In only about one in five hundred Trusts has it been appropriate to recommend a financial institution.

There are two situations in which a financial institution should be named as successor trustee. The first situation is where husband and wife have immigrated to this country, have minor children, and have neither relatives nor friends in this country who could provide for their minor children. The second situation is one in which an only child is handicapped and there are no family members to be responsible for the child. In each of these situations, naming a financial institution as successor trustee is the obvious solution.

Financial Institution as Custodian
Naming a financial institution to serve as custodian is another alternative to the management of a Trust. The *custodian* maintains the necessary records and provides regular reports to the beneficiaries. Although the trustee maintains control, the custodian would quickly identify any fiduciary abuses and might suggest appropriate action. The custodian need not be in your local area.

POSITIONS OUTSIDE THE TRUST
Although not an integral part of a Living Trust, two other key positions should be considered as part of *any* estate planning: executor and guardian. It is hoped that neither position ever has to be used. Nevertheless, it is essential that an executor be named and that a guardian be named for any minor children or handicapped individuals

Executor
The *executor* should not be confused with the trustee. The successor trustee is responsible for all assets *within* the Trust; the executor (who is named in the Pour-Over Will) is the administrator for all assets that have been left *outside* the Trust. The executor is necessary in case any probate action is required to settle the estate. The executor would take through probate any assets that were inadvertently left outside the Trust. After the probate process has been completed, the executor would then pour the probated assets over into the Trust. Of course, if you have properly placed all your assets within the Living Trust, no probate action will be necessary.

Only one person should be named as your executor.

Since probate is a time-consuming and frustrating experience that requires numerous legal signatures and occasional court appearances, it is preferable to name an executor who resides in the state where the probate will be conducted. Unlike successor trustees, however, the executor should be only one person.

An executor should always be named, just to take care of any unforeseen contingency. If you are married, your spouse should be named as executor; after the death of the surviving spouse, one of the successor trustees should be named as executor. Although you may name several of your children as successor trustees of the Trust, only one of them should be designated to handle this chore, preferably the child living nearest to the probate court.

Guardian

A *guardian* or guardians should always be named for minor children in case the parents should die before their children reach the age of eighteen. It is also important to appoint a guardian if you have handicapped children, regardless of their ages. The guardian and the successor trustee may be, and often are, different people.

Probably one of the most difficult decisions with which you will ever be confronted is whom to name as the guardian of your children. Any judge in the land would say, "Please, don't put this burden upon me." A more detailed discussion of the guardian appears in Chapter 11.

AN ORGANIZED SOLUTION

As with your various roles in life, you will hold numerous roles with a Living Trust. The positions of trustor and settlor cease upon your death. The positions of trustee and beneficiary will eventually pass to others. As you age, management of the Trust may become too burdensome, and you may wish to pass that function over to those whom you trust. With the Living Trust, you may easily relinquish your role as trustee, thus allowing your children to take over the administration of the Trust. Upon incompetency or death, administration of the Trust passes to the successor trustee. Upon the death of the settlor (if single) or both settlors (if married), the beneficial interest in the Trust passes to the individuals (such as children) you have named as beneficiaries.

In addition, you should name an executor to handle any unexpected probate, and you must name a guardian for minor or handicapped children. Designating trusted individuals for the various positions in your Living Trust will protect you and give you peace of mind.

9

Allocation and Distribution of Assets

Upon your death (if you are single) or upon the death of both husband and wife (if you are married), the successor trustee needs to know how you wish your assets to be allocated and then distributed, or whether you wish the assets to be held in the Trust for future growth and/or income.

If you have a Living Trust, your assets need not all be distributed outright; your choices for allocation and distribution are unlimited.

All too often, clients have what I call the "Will syndrome"—the understanding that, upon death, all of the assets in an estate must be distributed outright at the conclusion of the probate process. This distribution of all assets is true for a Will, because there is no legal entity left in which to hold the assets. If you have a Living Trust, however, the assets need not be distributed. In fact, when you have a Living Trust, the methods of allocating and distributing the assets are unlimited! When you are creating a Trust, you are opening horizons you never before imagined.

Over the years, our firm has accumulated a library of over fifteen hundred different allocations and distributions for the Living Trust! One of the outstanding features of the Living Trust is that it offers you enormous flexibility in planning for the eventual disposition of your assets. Not only do you have infinite choices, but you also have the opportunity to select the approach that best suits your desires and the maturity of your heirs.

The area of allocation and distribution of assets is probably the most difficult part of creating a Living Trust for the average individual. However, even though many clients have said they have for years been unable to determine what to do, by sharing my experience with these clients, I have in every case been able to show them how to solve their estate-planning problems and eventually come up with appropriate solutions for allocation and distribution of the assets in their estates.

In fact, Living Trusts should be designed to be consumer friendly. The allocation and distribution section of your Living Trust should be written in such a way that your desires will be met, without change, for years to come.

> As an example, a young woman, pregnant with her first child, asked whether we could write a Trust now to include her unborn child. I assured her that we could, because our Trusts use a class designation to name the parents' children as beneficiaries, thus automatically including any future unborn children without having to explicitly name each one.

ALLOCATION OF TRUST ASSETS

One of the first requirements is to determine how you wish your assets to be allocated among your heirs. Do you have specific bequests for specific individuals? How do you want your assets eventually shared with your children or other family members?

Specifically Named Beneficiaries for Special Bequests

Grandchildren, parents, aunts and uncles, and nieces and nephews are often named for specific amounts of distribution or income. To compensate for inflation, bequests should be specified as a percentage of your estate, rather than as fixed amounts. Determine the amount of the bequest, determine its current percentage of the estate, and then specify the bequest as that percentage. For example, a $10,000 bequest in a $200,000 estate would be stated as 5 percent.

In most cases, bequests should be specified as a percentage of your estate.

It is also quite acceptable, if desired, to specify a bequest as "5 percent or $10,000, whichever is greater." Then, for example, if ten years have elapsed and the estate has doubled in value, the 5 percent would be worth $20,000. On the other hand, a $10,000 bequest today could shrink in purchasing value to only $5,000 in ten years.

Small bequests of $500 to $1,000, however, should be listed as amounts only, ignoring the percentage approach. The reason is that these are minor gifts, where it is really the thought

that counts. After all, a $500 gift from a $500,000 estate would only be 0.1 percent.

Equal vs. Unequal Allocation

Several times each week, couples come into our office and, with some embarrassment, tell us that they desire unequal allocation of their assets to their children. The couples are convinced that they are the only ones who have ever considered this type of allocation. However, unequal allocation is far more common than you might believe. Almost one-fourth of our clients choose unequal allocation—and for very good reasons, as you will see in the following representative examples.

> Herb and Marge Allen have two children. The son is a very successful doctor and will probably earn far more than his parents. The daughter is married to a teacher and has seven children. The daughter and her husband will probably never have a farthing to their name. Therefore, the Allens' allocation heavily favored their daughter.
>
> Jim and Louise Harmon have four grown children. Since one of the Harmons' children is mentally retarded, the parents chose to have their assets remain in trust to provide for the mentally retarded child as long as he lives. Only after the retarded child dies will the Harmons' remaining estate be equally divided and distributed to their three other children.
>
> Kurt and Lisa Crowther have a son and daughter, but Kurt chose to disown their daughter. I advised Lisa that, with the A-B Trust, she could do anything she wanted with "her" half of the estate—even offset her husband's decision (by allocating her half of the estate to her daughter). In tears, she chose to allocate her half equally to the son and daughter.
>
> Steve and Betty Hutton have three children. The Huttons chose equal allocation of their estate to their three children—until the youngest child was killed in a work-related accident. Although the deceased son left a wife and child, his company's $1 million settlement provided more than enough for their needs. Therefore, the Huttons amended their Trust to

exclude their deceased son and their beloved grandson.

John has two grown children, a son and a daughter. As a divorcé, he is very aware of the battle over money that can ensue as a result of a divorce. He is concerned that his daughter's marriage is shaky. I recommended that he specify in his Trust that the trustee was to distribute no assets to his daughter until she had a Living Trust in place with *Separate Property Agreements*. John even went further, authorizing the trustee to pay for these documents. The distribution would then flow into his daughter and her husband's Living Trust as the daughter's separate property.

In contrast, Harry and Joan faced the same dilemma with their daughter whose marriage was shaky. They offered to pay for a Living Trust with Separate Property Agreements for their daughter and her husband *now*—in anticipation of the daughter's future inheritance. The daughter's husband refused the Living Trust in hopes of gaining access to his wife's future inheritance. This was solved by creating a Living Trust with Separate Property Agreement for the daughter only. Harry and Joan eventually passed away, and the daughter's share of the inheritance was carefully transferred to *her* Living Trust as her separate property. Shortly thereafter, the daughter and her husband decided to divorce. Because of this preplanning, the daughter's inheritance was fully protected from the husband's access.

Philip and Joan have no children, but Joan is four months pregnant. They want to create a Living Trust now that would provide for their expectant child. The answer is simple. We created what is called a class allocation; that is, the primary beneficiary is to be their issue (children), with assets equally allocated. This class approach applies to the expectant child as well as to all future children. In the interim period of pregnancy before the child is born, if anything were to happen to both of them, Philip named his siblings as contingent beneficiaries, and Joan named her parents as contingent beneficiaries.

Edna, a widow, was concerned that her two children, although fully employed, would not have enough money to retire. Edna decided to specify that her inheritance go to her two children equally, but not until each son either retired or attained age 65.

Jack and Julia have three children. Two of the children are employed and married, but they are concerned about their son Michael, who is on drugs. They fear that any money distributed to Michael would go directly into drugs and exacerbate the situation. We decided to withhold Michael's share of inheritance until he was drug-free. They directed the trustee to test Michael for drugs each year at random. If he fails the test, his inheritance is withheld in trust until he becomes drug-free. Also, they authorized the trustee to pay for Michael's drug rehabilitation if he so desired. Such money would be paid directly to the rehabilitation center—not to Michael.

Anthony and Maria are determined that their four children graduate from college. They specified that while their inheritance could be used for their education, no distribution was to be made to a child until such child graduated from a four-year accredited college or university.

George and Harriet have a married son. They love their son, but they are extremely upset with his wife, Helen. Helen refused to bear children, so they adopted two children. George and Harriet want their estate to go to their son, but if he were to predecease them, George and Harriet want to disinherit Helen as well as the two adopted grandchildren. We named their son the primary beneficiary, and if he were not living, half the inheritance would go to a named nephew, and the other half would go to their favorite charity, the American Heart Association.

DISTRIBUTION OF TRUST ASSETS

If you have minor children, it is advisable, but not required, to specify in your Trust that all assets remain in trust until the youngest child attains the age of twenty-one. This restriction is meant as a protection, since there can be innumerable unexpected needs for minor children (e.g., serious injury or a costly illness). If such an incident were to befall one of your children, you would probably want all of your assets available to provide for the care of that child. When all of the assets are in Trust, they are available for such use. This same restriction would apply to any share for minor children of a deceased child (your grandchildren).

Of the numerous approaches to distribution of Trust assets, the three most common methods of distribution are outright, at a specific age, and deferred distribution.

Outright Distribution

Outright distribution is often used as the form of distribution for adults. This method does not imply, however, that the assets must be distributed *immediately* following the death of the settlor or settlors. The concept of an asset being held in trust rather than distributed is a frequent concern of clients when they have substantial real estate holdings. The assets are *available* for distribution, but the successor trustees (who are also often the beneficiaries) have the discretion to delay distribution, or sale of the assets, until they deem it appropriate—for years, if necessary. For example, high interest rates may offer a poor market for real estate sales. It may be more prudent to lease the property for the next few years and to then ultimately sell the property in a more favorable market—only then distributing the proceeds of the sale to the beneficiaries.

Outright distribution means that the assets are available for distribution; distribution may be delayed if, for example, market conditions are unfavorable.

If you believe that your children are fully mature, you might decide to distribute your assets to them outright (all at one time). However, this practice is generally discouraged.

Whenever possible, the trustee should distribute in kind, rather than liquidate the assets and distribute cash. For example, real estate can be distributed by simply rewriting the deed in the name of the beneficiary or beneficiaries. Undivided interest, discussed in Chapter 4, can be written on the deed for distribution to more than one beneficiary. Securities, such as stocks, bonds, and mutual funds, can be rewritten in the name of the individual beneficiary.

Distribution at a Specific Age

Distribution at a specific age is another form of distribution for minors (children below the age of eighteen). Distribution should not be made at an age less than twenty-three. Delaying any distribution until age twenty-three gets the child, or children, through college and then adds a year or two for good measure—for the sake of maturity. However, many parents are so satisfied with their children's maturity and good judgment that they have named them to receive a distribution at the age of eighteen.

If the settlors died when their children were older than the ages specified for distribution, the children would receive their distributions outright (that is, they would receive the entire amount all at one time).

Deferred Distribution

The most common type of distribution specified by clients is deferred distribution. With deferred distribution, the assets are not distributed to the heirs at the time of death; instead, distribution is delayed for a specific number of years or until the heir reaches a specified age. A deferred distribution may be made outright at a specified age or portioned to the heir as he or she attains different ages.

The most frequently specified form of deferred distribution is a partial distribution when the heir attains a specified age.

Examples

Heir receives ⅓ of his or her share at age 25.	Heir receives ½ of his or her share at age 25.
Heir receives ⅓ of his or her share at age 30.	Heir receives ½ of his or her share at age 30.
Heir receives ⅓ of his or her share at age 35.	

Another form of deferred distribution is where the distribution is made in increments, following the death of the settlor or settlors.

Examples

Heir receives ⅓ of his or her share outright.

Heir receives ⅓ of his or her share in 5 years.

Heir receives ⅓ of his or her share in 10 years.

Heir receives ½ of his or her share outright.

Heir receives ½ of his or her share in 5 years.

If the surviving settlor dies after the children have already reached any of the ages specified for partial distributions, the children would receive outright those portions to which they were then entitled. Any remaining distributions would be made when the children reach the ages specified for those distributions.

For example, assume that a child is to receive a deferred distribution as one-third at age twenty-five, one-third at age thirty, and one-third at age thirty-five. If the surviving settlor dies when the child is thirty-two years old, the child will receive two-thirds of the distribution outright (the distributions specified for ages twenty-five and thirty); the remaining one-third would be distributed when the child attains the age of thirty-five.

Children of any age mature with time. Consequently, with a partial distribution at specified ages or time periods, if an heir receives a distribution and spends the entire amount (often frivolously), the heir later gets a second chance and is much less inclined to unwisely waste the inheritance. The deferred distribution method of one-half at age twenty-five and one-half at age thirty is used frequently with estates valued at less than $300,000.

A most tragic incident illustrates how important deferred distribution can be.

A nineteen-year-old woman was attending UCLA; she was in the middle of her junior year and was getting straight A's. Her parents were killed in an automobile accident, and she received $400,000 in one lump sum. She thereupon left school, took friends with her, and went on a European spree. She bought automobiles for her friends, and they all had a magnificent time—for two years. At the end of those two years, the money was gone.

How different the young woman's situation could have been if, instead, she had received one-third of her inheritance outright, another one-third in five years, and the final one-third in ten years. She could have squandered the first third, but she would have learned a valuable lesson and presumably would have handled the other two distributions quite differently.

As an investment adviser, all too often I see people of every age who receive money and, on the advice and good intentions of others, invest unwisely and lose it all. Through experience, I have become a very strong advocate of the deferred distribution method. For our own children, my wife and I have selected the distribution to be one-third at age twenty-five, another one-third at age thirty, and the final one-third at age thirty-five. If our children attain the age of thirty-five before we pass away, our family Trust further states that the children will receive *no more* than one-third outright, one-third in five years, and one-third in ten years.

Far too often, I have had clients say, "Our son (or daughter) at age forty-five is still immature; we wish to choose one-third at age fifty, one-third at age fifty-five, and one-third at age sixty." Why not? It is *your* plan, and *you* specify the desired type of distribution. Nothing in the plan is set in concrete. As long as the settlors live, they can change that plan—even daily, if they wish.

Income vs. Distribution
In many instances, it is deemed more advisable to bequeath to heirs the *income* derived

from assets in the estate, rather than directly giving the heirs the asset as a distribution. It is quite proper to bequeath only the income.

You might decide that one (or more) of your children is very immature and possibly also a spendthrift. In such a situation, it may be far more appropriate to retain the assets in the Trust and to provide "income only" to one or more of your children. If you choose to provide income only, you should authorize the trustee to meet a variety of emergency needs—whether for general care, medical care, educational assistance, or necessary professional services.

Income, or a combination of income and distribution, may be more preferable in large estates—particularly estates with substantial real estate holdings. Often, families that have accumulated substantial real estate desire to retain these holdings to provide future income for their children. The Living Trust provides this option; the successor trustees (often the same individuals as the beneficiaries) have the right to buy, sell, borrow against, and transfer these assets, as conditions dictate for investment purposes.

Under circumstances where most of the estate is held in trust and provides only income to the beneficiaries, it is often recommended that you specify at least *some* asset distribution. Alternatively, the successor trustees could be authorized to make a reasonable loan to each child—for example, to help each child purchase his or her home or begin a business.

Varying Distribution Methods for Each Child

You may select a different method of distribution for each child. If you believe one child is extremely mature, you may feel that it is appropriate to distribute the assets to that child outright. Another child may seem totally immature (or may be involved with drugs or alcohol), so that it seems far more appropriate to retain your assets in trust and to distribute only the income from the assets (but also authorizing the trustee to provide for unexpected and extraordinary circumstances). A third child, although still immature, may be progressing nicely, so it may be appropriate to distribute assets to that child as a deferred distribution

of one-third outright, one-third in five years, and one-third in ten years.

Not only may the distribution vary per individual, it may also vary for each asset where appropriate. For example, if one child has dependents and another has administrative skills, the parents might distribute their home to the first child and their business to the second child. However, this form of distribution is the exception.

PROVISIONS FOR SPECIAL SITUATIONS

Certain provisions in the area of allocation and distribution of assets take care of special situations, such as handling a deceased child's share of the estate and excluding the surviving spouse of a deceased child, deducting gifts and loans to children, providing for children with special needs, and disinheriting children.

Deceased Child's Share

If one (or more) of your children fails to survive you, that child's share of your estate will typically pass to the children of your deceased child (that is, your grandchildren). For the sake of illustration, let's look at some different situations relating to the inheritance of assets.

> Tom and Martha Hurst have two children, Susan and Jeff. Each child is to share equally in the assets of the estate. Both children are married and have two children each.
> Upon the death of Tom and Martha Hurst, their assets are to pass one-half to Susan and one-half to Jeff, as shown in Figure 9-1.

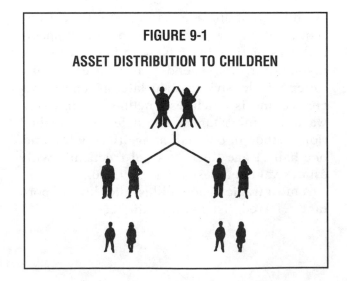

FIGURE 9-1

ASSET DISTRIBUTION TO CHILDREN

If Susan were not living upon the death of her mother and father, her share would pass equally to her two children, bypassing her husband, as depicted in Figure 9-2. If Jeff also were not living upon the death of his mother and father, his share would pass to his two children, bypassing his wife, in the same manner.

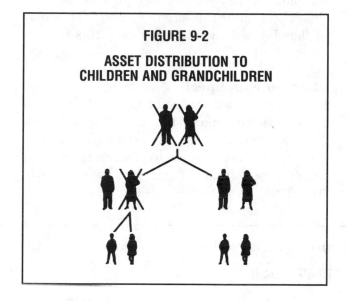

FIGURE 9-2

ASSET DISTRIBUTION TO CHILDREN AND GRANDCHILDREN

If Susan and her two children were not living when Tom and Martha Hurst died, Susan's share would pass to her brother Jeff, bypassing Susan's husband, as shown in Figure 9-3.

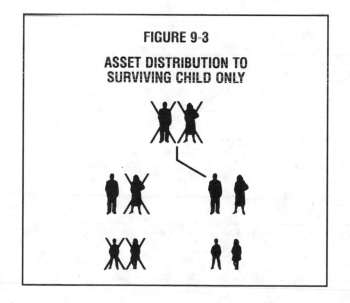

FIGURE 9-3

ASSET DISTRIBUTION TO SURVIVING CHILD ONLY

Note that, in these examples, the spouse is out. Neither Susan's husband nor Jeff's wife

received *anything*! Excluding the spouse is, as strange as it may seem, the standard method of distribution—that is, distribution is typically along blood lines or adoption. Historically, human nature has chosen the approach of excluding the surviving spouse of a deceased child.

The surviving spouse of a deceased child does not *need* to be excluded from distribution; your Living Trust may include the spouse. However, in all my experience with the Living Trust, I am aware of only two such alterations to the usual pattern: one family left $10,000 to a daughter-in-law; another family left only $1,000—and in both instances, their estates exceeded $1 million! This method of distribution is done by choice only.

A related concern is what will happen to the parents' assets if their children were to someday get divorced. There are several solutions to this dilemma.

One solution is for the parents to leave their assets in trust, with their children receiving income only. The assets held in the parents' Trust would not be considered the children's property and thus would not be subject to being divided between the divorcing parties.

A second solution is for the parents to leave their assets in trust and have them distributed in five-year increments. The assumption is that the longer the children are married, the more apt they are to remain so.

A third solution is for the married children to have their own Living Trusts with Separate Property Agreements (described later in chapter). More and more frequently, parents are coming to our office to create Living Trusts for their children. One reason is that these parents want to ensure that any "parental assets" passed on to their children will be designated as separate property—and thereby be preserved if something were to happen to a child's marriage.

For example, a father created a Living Trust for each of his four children, who were in their early to middle twenties. One child was married, and two more got married before the end of the year. In each case, the father had already distributed between $200,000 and $300,000 to his children; the father wanted to make sure that these funds *remained* as his children's separate property.

If there is a divorce, the community property is typically divided in half, whereas the separate property remains with the individual to whom the separate property belongs. Where there are children from the marriage and the children remain with the mother, the mother's separate property will almost always remain as hers. However, the court has the right to reach over into the father's separate property to make it available to provide for the children—since the children are the first concern of the court.

Gifts and Loans

Frequently, our clients make gifts or loans to one or more children. An example could be to help a child make a down payment on a home.

The parents may desire that, upon their death, these gifts or loans be considered part of the overall estate and be deducted from that child's share of his or her eventual distribution of the estate. To make this process simple, each of our Living Trusts includes a special form, shown in Figure 9-4. This form, which we call Schedule A, provides a convenient place where the parents may itemize any gifts or loans to their children (if they are to be considered part of the child's distribution). Use of this form is optional.

Children with Special Needs

If you have a handicapped child, a Living Trust is an absolute necessity! Creating a Living Trust is one of the most vital steps that you can take to protect the future interests of your handicapped child. In contrast, having a Will (or no Will at all) spells disaster.

FIGURE 9-4

SCHEDULE A—GIFTS AND LOANS

Gift	Recipient	Amount	Date	Trustor's Initials
G	Mary	$ 10,000	1/10/87	
L	Robert	15,000	2/15/88	

G — Gift
L — Loan

Supporting a child who is mentally or physically handicapped can be a very costly experience. In many situations, the individuals may qualify for government benefits or assistance, such as Supplemental Security Income (SSI) or Medicare, which is often crucial to the survival of the individual.

If a handicapped individual is named as a beneficiary of a Living Trust and has been receiving government assistance, dire consequences can occur when the handicapped individual finally receives his or her inheritance. Upon the death of both settlors (if married) or upon the death of the settlor (if single), one of two things will happen: Either the benefits will immediately cease (and this situation could be incredibly costly to the survivors), or the government agency can (and usually does) step in and grab the entire inheritance!

I remember the case of a young woman who was physically paralyzed from the waist down and confined to a wheelchair. She was originally given a life expectancy of fourteen years by her doctors. However, she was a determined youngster and eventually put herself through college and was able to obtain employment as a counselor at a school for handicapped children.

She didn't earn much money, but with her SSI assistance, government medical benefits, and an opportunity to live with her grandmother, she lived quite nicely. Most important, however, was that her mental outlook was outstanding. The young woman's father died when she was ten years old and left funds in trust to be distributed to her at age twenty-one. Both the young lady and her grandmother looked forward to the day when those funds would become available.

However, once the daughter reached the age of twenty-one, the government agency stepped in and took possession of her *entire inheritance of $100,000!*

As incredible as this callous act may seem, government agencies have the right to seize the inheritance because government funds have previously been expended on behalf of the handicapped child. Therefore, mentally or physically handicapped children should be excluded from directly receiving either assets (as a distribution) or income.

Instead, the successor trustee should be authorized and directed to provide for such a child's welfare. Thus, the trustee can directly pay rent, board, education, medical and psychiatric care, transportation, and entertainment—without making any *direct payment* to the child. In this way, the SSI payments are not jeopardized.

Disinheriting a Child

Occasionally, parents wish to disinherit a child; they can do so very simply with a Living Trust. Any child who is to be disinherited is specifically identified as being *excluded as a beneficiary* in both the Pour-Over Will and the Living Trust.

It is very important, however, to avoid any implication that a child was forgotten. By naming the "excluded" children in the Pour-Over Will and the Living Trust, you clearly indicate that the children were not forgotten (since both of these documents are signed on the same day).

A father came to me with an interesting dilemma. Following World War II, he had fathered one child in Germany and possibly a second child, both out of wedlock. He did not want either of these children coming forth at some later date to claim an inheritance.

This dilemma was resolved simply by naming his three children born of wedlock as his children in his Living Trust and in his Pour-Over Will. The children born out of wedlock were identified as *excluded as beneficiaries* in both the Pour-Over Will and the Living Trust.

If a son, for example, marries a woman who has two children from a former marriage, those children are not heirs by either blood or adoption. The son may, if he so desires, eventually adopt those children, whereby they would be included under the adoption provision. However, if the son does not adopt the children, they are *not* included as heirs under the Living Trust document—unless the Trust specifically states that the children are to be included as heirs.

Occasionally, a client has a child or children with one spouse, then remarries and has children in the second marriage. For some reason, the client may hold great anger toward one or more of the children of the first marriage, or the individual may not have seen or heard from them in decades. It is painful for the individual to confront the topic of the children by the first marriage, but the subject must be addressed. However, all children of this and any previous marriages *must* be named in the Pour-Over Will and Living Trust.

IMPORTANT DEFINITIONS

The Trust, being a legal document, is fraught with legal terminology. Unfortunately, the use of legal language is necessary in order to make the document one that legally establishes the Living Trust and then makes it unchallengeable by dissident heirs. Therefore, it is helpful if you understand some key definitions that will directly apply to the way your assets may someday be distributed.

Blood or Adopted

The Trust usually defines your children as *blood* or *adopted* and specifically includes, by definition, legally adopted children. Although people usually recognize children adopted by themselves, or by their children, as comparable to their blood issue, occasionally a client asks that the words pertaining to adoption be deleted.

> One example is a mother who was most disconcerted that her daughter-in-law refused to bear children but was willing to adopt them. The mother directed us to strike out the words pertaining to adopted children. She wanted to make it very clear that, if her daughter-in-law were willing to bear children, they would be included as heirs, but any adopted children would be excluded from the estate.

Issue

The term *issue* refers to your children, your children's children, your children's children's children, and so on, by blood—in other words, your biological children and their offspring. The term *issue* can also refer to your children and/or their offspring by adoption, if so defined in the Trust.

Per Stirpes

Per stirpes is a Latin term. By legal definition, the term refers to your children downward (your children, grandchildren, great-grandchildren, and so on).

All too often, I hear the argument that "I have no children or grandchildren, and, therefore, I want to eliminate the *per stirpes* provision." However, even if an individual has no descendants, this provision still has validity. For example, if a childless couple were to leave their estate to brothers or sisters (or friends) who have minor children or grandchildren, then the *per stirpes* provision would apply to them (the heirs). It is better for the provision to be included in your Trust (even though you may think it inapplicable), rather than for it to not be there if it is ever needed.

Intestate Succession

If there are no surviving heirs downward (*per stirpes*), then distribution will be by *intestate succession*. Your assets will be distributed to relatives "upward and outward." Specifically, any distribution would first be to father and mother (if living); otherwise, distribution would be to brothers and sisters. If neither mother, father, brothers, nor sisters were living, then distribution would be to aunts and uncles, nieces and nephews, and then to cousins. If none of those relatives were living, then distribution would be made to charity.

The specific pattern of succession for distribution of an estate and the related percentages are spelled out in the probate code of each state. Figure 9-5 illustrates the general succession of heirs when an intestate distribution is to be made.

> One of the most prominent examples of probate distribution by intestate succession is the case of Howard Hughes, where one or more cousins may eventually become the recipients of his vast estate.

With a Living Trust, of course, you can have the pattern of distribution that *you* want.

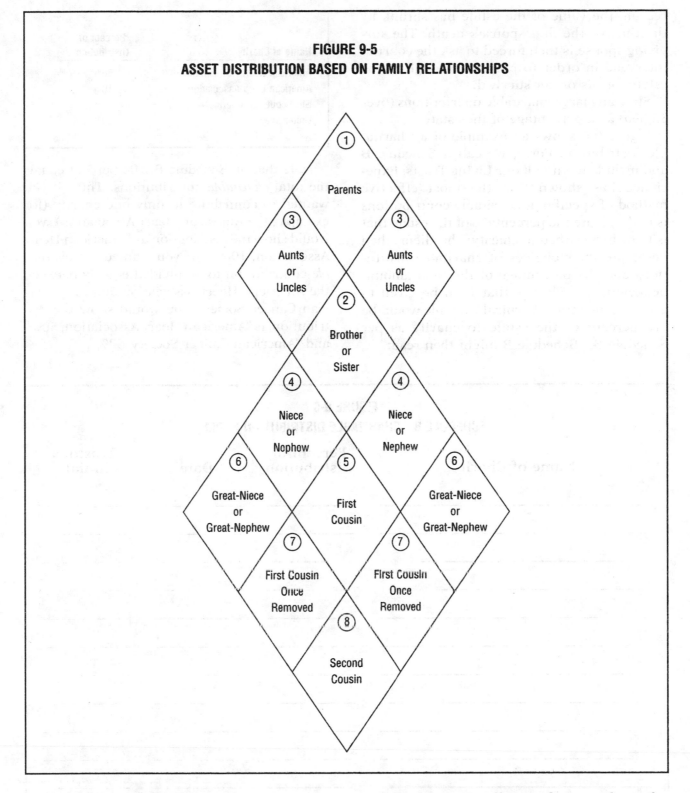

FIGURE 9-5
ASSET DISTRIBUTION BASED ON FAMILY RELATIONSHIPS

CHARITABLE DISTRIBUTIONS

Charitable distributions should always be stated as a percentage of the estate—never as a dollar amount. All too often, settlors of a large estate have designated a specific sum to charity, only to find that, for some unexpected reason, the value of the estate has shrunk by the time of the first spouse's death. The surviving spouse is then forced to ask the court to intervene in order to preserve enough of the estate for his or her survival.

State any large charitable distributions (over $5,000) as a percentage of the estate.

Figure 9-6 shows an example of a Charitable Distribution Form; we call it Schedule B and include it with all our Living Trusts. Experience has shown that the most effective method of specifying charitable contributions is to designate the percentage of the estate that is to be bequeathed to charity. The clients then designate their choices of charitable institutions and the percentage of the total amount bequeathed to charity that is to be given to each organization. A typical example would be "10 percent of the estate to charity as per Schedule B." Schedule B might then read:

Name of Charity	Percent of Distribution
American Heart Association	50%
American Lung Association	10%
Girl Scouts of America	10%
United Way	30%

Note that, in Schedule B, 100 percent equals the total *charitable* contributions. Thus, if you wanted to contribute to only one charity (for example, the American Heart Association), you would show the distribution as "American Heart Association, 100%." If you wanted the *charitable* contribution to be divided equally between the American Heart Association and the American Cancer Society, you would show the distribution as "American Heart Association, 50%" and "American Cancer Society, 50%."

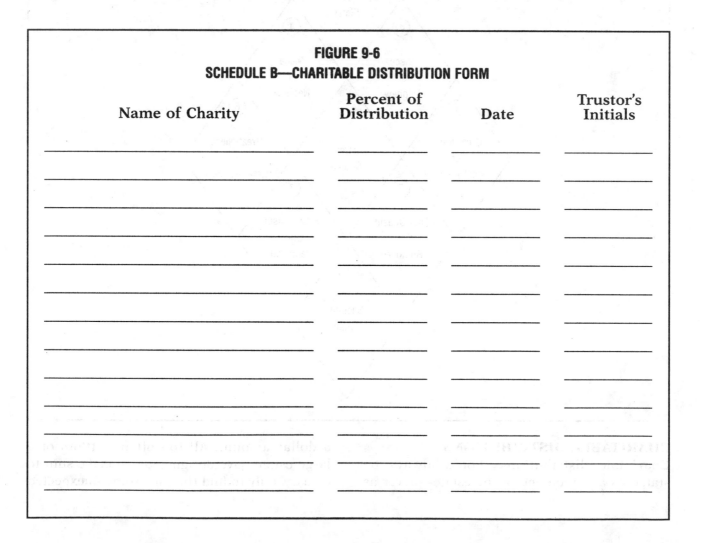

FIGURE 9-6
SCHEDULE B—CHARITABLE DISTRIBUTION FORM

Name of Charity	Percent of Distribution	Date	Trustor's Initials

The charities and percentages bequeathed to each organization may be changed with the simple stroke of a pen. Interestingly, although clients usually know how much they wish to leave to charity (the percentage of their estate), the hardest decision seems to be to which charities to give donations and how much to bequeath. The simplest way to solve the problem is for the Trust to state the percentage of the estate that is to benefit charity, and for Schedule B to be used to permit the client to make and change the specific details later—as often as is desired.

If no living heirs survive you, distribution of your estate will be made to qualified charitable institutions, as indicated in Schedule B. If you have not named any charitable organizations, the court will act for you. However, Schedule B allows you the opportunity to easily specify a favorite charity ahead of time.

State any large charitable distributions (over $5,000) as a percentage of the estate.

SEPARATE PROPERTY AGREEMENTS

Separate Property Agreements are documents that list any assets that, by definition, are the separate property of each spouse (that is, property received by one spouse as a gift or inheritance or property obtained before marriage). This list of separate property is attached to, and becomes an integral part of, the Living Trust. Since a Trust is simply a contract between two parties (an implied agreement between the trustor and the beneficiaries), if the parties agree to identify certain assets as separate property, the assets are so identified.

The effect of a Separate Property Agreement is that separate property assets placed in the Trust will retain their characteristic as separate property, even though they will take on the name of the Trust. In simple terms, this situation means that the assets separately belonging to each spouse may be brought together for the enjoyment of both spouses. Upon the death of one spouse, the assets *remain* in the Trust to provide for the surviving spouse. However, on the death of the surviving spouse, the separate property will go to the heirs specified by the spouse who owned the property.

Assets held as separate property are often commingled as the marriage progresses. For instance, you may enter into marriage and then receive an inheritance of stock, which you later decide to invest in your home for expansion or upgrading. Before you know it, this asset has become a part of the marriage property as a whole; the money received from the stock has lost its identity as separate property. However, with Separate Property Agreements included as part of your Living Trust, that property may easily be identified as separate property and be treated as such.

Use of Separate Property Agreements

The use of Separate Property Agreements can be best explained with an example.

Assume that a married couple have an estate valued at $400,000. Of this estate, the husband has separate property with a value of $200,000, the wife has separate property worth $100,000, and together the husband and wife have accumulated common or marital property with a value of $100,000.

If the husband is the first to die, the common or marital property would be divided in half, as shown in Figure 9-7. One-half of the property would come down to the Decedent's Trust B as the husband's share, and the other half would come down to the Survivor's Trust A as the wife's share. The husband's separate property would come down to his side of the Trust (the B Trust), and the wife's separate property would come down to her side of the trust (the A trust). Thus, the Decedent's Trust B would contain the husband's $200,000 of separate property, plus $50,000 of common or marital property, for a total of $250,000. The Survivor's Trust A would contain the wife's $100,000 of separate property, plus her $50,000 share of common or marital property, for a total of $150,000.

The husband, if he had so desired, could have distributed all or part of his share upon his death and left nothing in Trust B. However, in this example, the entire $250,000 may be used by the surviving spouse for as long as she lives. Upon her death, the assets in Trust B would be distributed to the heirs specified by the husband, and the assets in Trust A would be distributed to the heirs specified by the wife.

Separate Property Agreements are commonly used when a husband and wife have each been married before, and both have children by their former marriages. When the two people married, they brought their previously acquired assets together so that together they might enjoy a higher standard of living. The couple desires that, upon the death of one of them, the surviving spouse could continue to enjoy that same standard of living. However, upon the death of the surviving spouse, each partner in the marriage desires that his or her share of the estate will pass on to the children of his or her former marriage.

As mentioned previously in this chapter, the finest way I know to ensure that distributions made to your married children will remain their separate property is to have each of your children create a Living Trust with his or her spouse. In these situations, I normally recom-

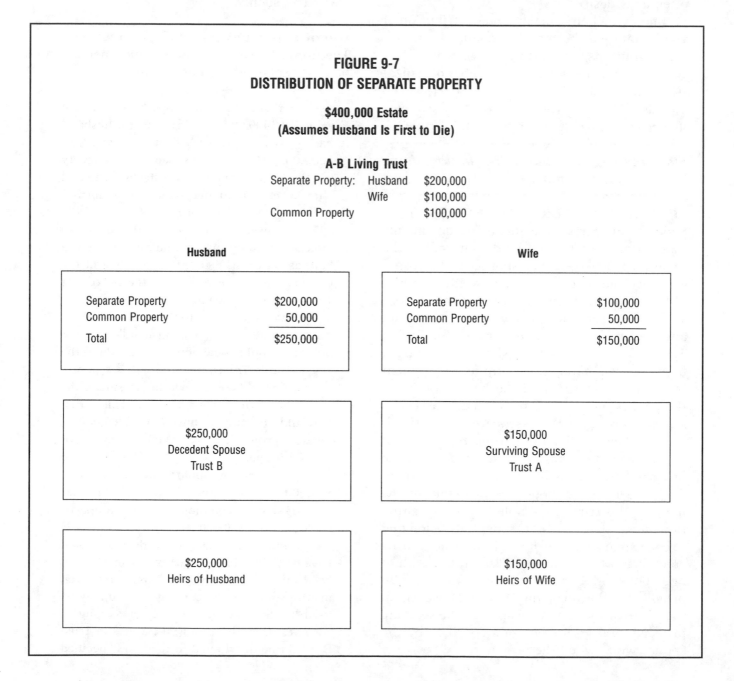

FIGURE 9-7
DISTRIBUTION OF SEPARATE PROPERTY

$400,000 Estate
(Assumes Husband Is First to Die)

A-B Living Trust

Separate Property:	Husband	$200,000
	Wife	$100,000
Common Property		$100,000

Husband

Separate Property	$200,000
Common Property	50,000
Total	$250,000

Wife

Separate Property	$100,000
Common Property	50,000
Total	$150,000

$250,000
Decedent Spouse
Trust B

$150,000
Surviving Spouse
Trust A

$250,000
Heirs of Husband

$150,000
Heirs of Wife

mend an A-B Trust, which clearly establishes that the beneficiary of each part (the Decedent's B Trust and the Survivor's A Trust) will be so recognized. Each spouse will then specify his or her separate property in Separate Property Agreements, which accompany their Living Trust. When these assets are then placed into the Trust, they will retain their characteristic as separate property.

The separate property may eventually be commingled with the other assets of the couple. However, as long as the trail is reasonably maintained (preferably with notes written directly on the Separate Property Agreement within the Trust), that property will remain separate property. If that child were to die, his or her assets would typically pass to the Decedent's Trust B to be used by the surviving spouse as long as the surviving spouse lives. However, upon the death of the surviving spouse, those assets would go to the heirs of the first to die. In the early part of the marriage, before the children arrive, the designated heirs may be a brother or sister; as children are born, they usually become the heirs. In case of a divorce, the divorce court will usually recognize a Separate Property Agreement.

Separate Property Agreements vs. Prenuptial Agreements

Separate Property Agreements have resolved many marriage conflicts. In contrast, the well-known divorce attorney Marvin Mitchelson states that 90 percent of his clients who have prenuptial agreements end up in divorce. A prenuptial agreement says in effect, "What is mine before marriage is not yours." My experience with thousands of clients supports the observation of Marvin Mitchelson. Prenuptial agreements are nothing more than a burr under the saddle; instead, I fervently recommend Separate Property Agreements where they are appropriate.

THE BEST SOLUTION

The most versatile part of the Living Trust is the section titled "Allocation and Distribution of Trust Assets." Once you understand that there are no limitations to how you may allocate and distribute your assets in a Living Trust, you realize that there are endless potential options for how you may pass your assets to your heirs. Every family, as well as each family member, is different. The Living Trust allows you to design the best solution for everyone.

—————————10—————————
Separating the Good from the Bad

Since *The Living Trust* was first published, I now realize that I have unintentionally opened Pandora's box. My good intentions of describing the advantages of a good Living Trust have, in too many instances, done a disservice to many individuals who then purchased a Living Trust, but who were victimized by unscrupulous and unqualified individuals and institutions that sold them an inadequate Living Trust.

It is now more important than ever to be able to discern a good Trust from a bad Trust. This chapter contains information that is more important *today* than it was when this book was first published!

A WORD OF CAUTION

The Living Trust is a popular item today, and it seems that almost everyone in the legal and financial professions is getting into the act. Unfortunately, the growing popularity of the Living Trust is also the root cause of innumerable scams being perpetrated on the unsuspecting public by insurance agents, financial advisers, and especially by a horde of inexpe-

rienced attorneys. More than ever before, you need to be wary—and to know the difference between a good and a bad Living Trust.

Unless you, the public, learn to tell the difference, the Living Trust (an outstanding solution to the abusive probate system) will be curtailed, simply because of the many schemes and abuses being foisted on innocent citizens who want Living Trusts.

As I travel around the nation giving Living Trust seminars, I continually have people come up to me and say, "We read your book, took your advice, and got a Living Trust. However, after listening to you, we realize that the Trust we purchased is terribly inadequate." Can you imagine how that makes me feel? I have worked diligently to write an easy-to-understand book that would be of great benefit to individuals and families—only to learn that my efforts have resulted in the wasteful expenditure of people's money for worthless documents. Heed my words: There is an enormous difference between a good Living Trust and a poorly written one—and the end result is either peace of mind or disaster.

To understand just how serious the abuse of the Living Trust has become, let me share with you some real-life examples:

In a recent seminar, a husband and wife told me how they had spent the last ten years running in and out of court as trustees of an inadequate Living Trust. They were forced to seek (from the court) powers that had not been anticipated by the author of their Trust, but which they needed to operate within the Trust. In addition, they often had to seek court solutions to numerous unexpected contingencies that had not been foreseen by the author of the document.

These frustrating proceedings never should have happened—and wouldn't with a *good* Living Trust.

I recently received a letter from a widow who was terribly disturbed about her Living Trust dilemma and wanted me to share her horrible experience with others. Here is her story.

The woman had been happily married to her husband for thirty-nine years. Since the husband, who handled all of their financial affairs, had suffered from cancer for the past eight years, he sought to protect his wife after he was gone. The couple attended a Living Trust seminar that was given by a young attorney who had graduated from law school just two years before. She drew up the couple's Trust in 1987.

Two years later, when the husband was in the last stages of cancer, he asked this same attorney to draw up an amendment to the couple's Trust. The young attorney offered to make the changes for $1,500. The husband agreed, and he and his wife dutifully signed the amendment. Unfortunately, the husband, preoccupied with his illness, was not fully alert in reviewing the amendment and relied to a great extent on the integrity of the attorney.

The husband died just two months later, and the widow received a bill for the amendment. However, instead of the bill being the agreed-upon $1,500, it was now $8,000. The widow refused to pay, but was sued by the attorney for $16,000—and the widow was eventually forced to pay.

To make matters even worse, the widow also learned that the attorney had unethically slipped an additional (but unexpected) paragraph into the amendment, naming the young attorney as the surviving trustee—and the attorney took over control of the widow's estate! The widow was eventually able to extract control of the estate from the attorney, but, in the end, it cost the widow enormous heartache, distress, and ultimately $45,000 in the process.

Unfortunately, such instances of blatant abuse by unethical attorneys are becoming far too common. Another way in which attorneys and institutions are preying on the unsuspecting public is by charging exorbitant and unwarranted fees to settle an estate in a Living Trust. (This issue will be addressed in Chapter 15.)

LEARN THE FACTS

In recent years, the general population has become increasingly aware that there is an alternative to the evils of probate—the Living Trust. Unfortunately, this popularity has given rise to a proliferation of Trusts, many of which are not worth the paper on which they are written. In effect, more and more unqualified attorneys, as well as insurance agents and financial advisers, are passing themselves off as experts and are exploiting the general public with poorly written Living Trusts. People are being constantly bombarded with newspaper, radio, and television ads from various attorneys and firms inviting the public to seminars on the Living Trust as a means of generating revenue. Regrettably, few attorneys today have the experience needed to write an adequate Living Trust.

Far too many attorneys, inexperienced in the details of writing Trusts, fail to refer clients to more knowledgeable counsel. All too often, I now see many attorneys promoting themselves as having "twenty years of experience in Wills and Living Trusts." Unfortunately, when you dissect such claims, they usually break down to mean nineteen and a half years of experience with Wills but only six months of exposure to Living Trusts. Unlike the medical profession, which recognizes today's need to specialize, the legal profession has not yet been able to accept this concept of specialization. No one can be an expert in every area of the complex field of law, but most attorneys are unwilling to acknowledge the absolute need for specialization or to admit their own inexperience in a particular area.

More than fifteen years ago, I was appalled to recognize how many attorneys were presenting "factual conclusions" to prospective clients in areas in which the attorneys had little knowledge. I finally took my concern to a very respected attorney, who gave me a very simple reason, which still rings in my ears: "The attorney is afraid to refer a client to another attorney more knowledgeable in a particular area for fear he will lose that client." In comparison, how would you like to have your family physician perform open-heart surgery on members of your family? Yet a similar situation is just what is happening all too frequently with your attorney with respect to Living Trusts. With the legal fraternity suddenly waking up to the need for Living Trusts, every attorney seems to be an expert—but most of them lack even the most rudimentary knowledge or experience needed to prepare an adequate Trust.

This lack of knowledge by attorneys is tragic, because these individuals do a great disservice to their profession. There are many very qualified, knowledgeable, and experienced estate-planning attorneys who will do an outstanding job in their specialty and will provide you with an outstanding Living Trust. This chapter is intended to provide you with the knowledge that you need in order to screen the "pretenders" from the true experts.

The legal profession seems to be at an interesting crossroads. Experienced, knowledgeable estate-planning attorneys are accustomed to writing Trusts only for wealthy clients. How, then, do these experienced attorneys use their talents and expertise to create a Trust that is economically feasible for the average individual? On the other hand, inexperienced attorneys naively write Trusts that, when subjected to various tests and legal challenges, fall *far short* of expected results.

WHAT TO AVOID

In 1985, I was asked to speak on the use of the Living Trust at the national FBI convention. Afterward, I was deluged by the members attending the seminar, asking for the Living Trust. Unfortunately, I had opened Pandora's box. These people lived all over the nation, were about to return to their homes, and desired Living Trusts! How could they obtain good Living Trusts—without being exploited? I tried to give the members some guidelines on selecting competent legal counsel and obtaining a comprehensive Living Trust. However, I have anguished over that situation in the intervening years since the convention; the more I see of today's Trusts (many written by attorneys who are unfamiliar with the Living Trust), the more concerned I become.

Trusts written by most attorneys suffer from a variety of shortcomings. Some of the Trusts are lengthy documents but still do not encompass all possible contingencies, and most of them are very disorganized; most Trusts are poorly understood by the clients on whose behalf they were written; more often than not, there is a lack of communication between the client and the attorney; and most Trusts are thin and therefore incomplete (that is, they do not cover many very important contingencies).

To further exacerbate the problem, most attorneys promoting Living Trusts do not know how to settle an estate when an individual dies; and those attorneys who *do* know how to settle an estate charge 1 percent to 3 percent of the gross estate—an outrageous price.

Unfortunately, the price of a Trust is also not indicative of the quality of the Trust. Be very aware that the quality of a Trust is of utmost importance, since a poorly written Trust can be a nightmare!

Lengthy and Disorganized Trusts

All too frequently, an attorney turns to his or her legal Trust reference manual and identifies those paragraphs that he or she feels should be included in the Trust. As a result, the Trust has neither organization nor pattern. To review the document adequately, the client or any financial institution must read it from cover to cover.

Now that the Living Trust has become such a sought-after item, inexperienced attorneys are moving into this field by offering someone else's prototype Trust or a standard document that is produced by many of the computer programs offered today. (This tactic is similar to performing heart surgery after reading a "how-to" book.) Everyone's needs are different, and no "boilerplate" Trust document can properly serve a wide range of people.

Trust in "Legalese"

Besides usually being disorganized, Trusts are typically written in "legalese" (language that is peculiar to the legal profession). Trusts are usually written with little thought for the client's understanding. The result is that few, if any, individuals understand their Trusts; therefore, the Trusts do not work for the individuals. In effect, the Trusts are not being properly utilized.

A husband and wife came to me with a draft of their Living Trust, drawn for them by an attorney who had been referred to them by a friend. The two were badly frustrated; they had paid $1,500 for the draft of their Trust, but no matter how they tried, they could not understand it—and they were highly educated. The husband had received his master's degree from Stanford University, and the wife had obtained her master's degree from Bryn Mawr College.

Legally, the couple's Trust was quite adequate. However, for the clients, the Trust was most *inadequate*. The document contained no organization, no subtitles, and no summary of the contents of the Trust. The couple had heard about our program and asked us to prepare a Living Trust for them. The frustrated husband and wife were willing to scrap their existing Living Trust draft and forgo the $1,500 they had already spent—in order to have a Living Trust that they could understand.

I appeal to every attorney who is fortunate enough to be knowledgeable of the Living Trust: Write the document in such a manner that the client will understand it—or provide a supplemental means of communication, such as a summary written in simple language!

Lack of Communication Between Client and Attorney

Even when the Trust document is well drawn, communication between the client and attorney often leaves much to be desired. The attorney may understand the Trust, but he or she is seldom able to simplify the concept or explain it so that the client understands it.

Many years ago, I would often describe and illustrate the Living Trust—ultimately convincing a client that he or she should have one—only to take him or her to an attorney and then watch the client walk away from the office shaking his or her head, as if to say, "I am now more confused than ever." I also remember going into the home of two clients—several months after the husband and wife agreed to have the attorney draw their Trust—only to see the unexecuted draft of their Trust still sitting in the living room. The couple explained that they did not understand the Trust; not only were they unable to get a satisfactory (or understandable) answer from the attorney, but they were billed as much as $200 per telephone call! Such an unpleasant experience can turn *anyone* off.

Even an individual of average intelligence who is not necessarily schooled in legal matters can understand the Trust and how it works—and with minimal effort on the part of the attorney drawing up the Trust—*if* the Trust is organized and the client is provided with a brief summary written in simple language.

Thin Trusts

A quick rule of thumb to use in determining if a Trust is comprehensive or not is to see whether the document is a "thin Trust" or a "thick Trust." A good Living Trust must necessarily be a rather thick document if it is going to adequately handle the many contingencies that may occur during the lifetimes of the creators. Two of the primary purposes of a Living Trust are to give the trustee or trustees the greatest latitude in which to operate (that is, to provide for all necessary powers) and to satisfy the specific requirements of the Internal Revenue Service.

Provision for All Contingencies

Our experience in doing thousands of Trusts has been that "Murphy's law" ("If anything can go wrong, it will") continues to prevail. Therefore, it is important to incorporate into every Living Trust all the provisions that are needed to encompass every imaginable contingency. Most of the contingencies will never happen to the majority of our clients, but sooner or later a client will be well served by a particular provision. Only a very few of these contingencies are predictable, but it is always better to be prepared. Since our Living Trust is based on drawing thousands of Trusts, as each new situation arises for a particular client, the "new" provision is added to all of our Trusts.

An example of the unexpected happening is the situation of Dr. and Mrs. Campbell. Dr. Campbell was a renowned oral surgeon who lectured worldwide and was deeply in love with his bride of fifty years. Since the couple had no children, they named Dr. Campbell's secretary of some twenty-five years' association to become the successor trustee.

I had numerous occasions to come in contact with this couple in the ensuing years, and it was always a delight to be in their presence, because the love between the two of them simply radiated. Unfortunately, Mrs. Campbell contracted Alzheimer's disease, and Dr. Campbell was genuinely concerned that his wife would outlive him, even though her mental abilities would be severely impaired. The doctor was satisfied that his trusted secretary would see that his wife was adequately cared for at all times. However, Mrs. Campbell ended up dying before her husband.

Six months later, after his wife's death, Dr. Campbell was waltzed off to the altar by another woman. I'm certain that he approached this marriage with rose-colored glasses, assuming that all women were similar to his beloved first wife. Tragically, this idealism was not to be upheld. In the ensuing months, I watched him turn into a very unhappy person.

Seven months later, Dr. Campbell came into our office to make some adjustments to the distributions within his Trust. After we reviewed his Trust, a few modifications were made, and Dr. Campbell was then satisfied that his Trust accomplished everything he wanted it to do. Only then did Dr. Campbell express his concern that his prostate cancer had not been controlled as the doctors had originally believed. Only a month later, Dr. Campbell was in the hospital, and he passed away shortly thereafter.

Upon his death, the new Mrs. Campbell made it known to everyone in the hospital, and to everyone in general, that "no little secretary was going to be the successor trustee of his Trust" and furthermore that she was going to break it. Mrs. Campbell had two brothers who were attorneys, and she simply considered that she was above the law.

Realizing that trouble lay ahead, I asked to see Mrs. Campbell a week after the funeral; I expressed my sympathy for her loss and then tactfully reviewed her deceased husband's desires for the distribution of his assets—which he had *reconfirmed* just a month earlier. I hoped that this meeting would clarify any misunderstanding on Mrs. Campbell's part and therefore stop any problems before they began.

However, Mrs. Campbell was not to be deterred. With the assistance of her attorney brothers, she proceeded to attack the Trust. The only time that our firm has ever had to go into court was when our legal counsel asked that the secretary be confirmed as the successor trustee. Six weeks later, the secretary was confirmed by the court as the successor trustee. Our legal counsel then advised the widow's brothers of the court action. Since the attorneys were still determined to attack the Trust, our firm once again found it necessary to go to court to request a formal court order—which was granted.

After the second court order was granted, the widow and her brothers realized that the integrity of the Trust document could not be assailed, and they finally backed away.

The power of the Living Trust had again been witnessed, but unfortunately under circumstances I never would have anticipated. I cite this case as an ideal example of "Murphy's law."

Another example of the perils of a "thin" Trust is the recent experience of a couple who came to our office after attending one of our seminars. The couple asked me to review and comment on a Living Trust they had acquired in 1983. The entire Trust document was five pages long, double-spaced. I pointed out to the couple that the outline alone of our Living Trust was thicker than their entire Trust. After reading the couple's Trust, I was appalled! Our legal counsel confirmed that the Trust was the worst Trust document that had ever come to our attention.

These innocent people understood the need to avoid probate, had gone to an attorney for a Living Trust, and had paid good money for their Trust documents, but they were now worse off than if they had done nothing. Their totally inadequate Trust was quickly replaced with our Living Trust. Seeing the couple's needless expense and frustration only reconfirmed my dedication to completing this book—so that everyone can differentiate between a good Trust and a poor Trust.

These examples show why a good Living Trust should be drawn to cover the lifetimes of the creators and possibly the lifetimes of the heirs. Frequently, people look at a Living Trust document only in light of how the document might apply to them at that particular moment in time; when they do so, they readily recognize many features that do not apply to their present situation. However, a good Living Trust should anticipate every contingent event that may conceivably be possible for the next ten, twenty, thirty, or forty years—in this generation as well as the next generation. Such a comprehensive Trust document comes only from an experienced attorney who has had many years of practice in drawing up Living Trusts. Unfortunately, these experienced individuals are as hard to find as a needle in a haystack!

Provision of Broad Powers to the Creators

When you create a Living Trust, whether as husband and wife or as a single individual, you want the broadest powers possible. The Living Trust permits this great breadth of power under the legal authorization that two parties are entering into a contract with each other. These two parties would be husband and wife, if you are married, or implied between you and your beneficiaries, if you are single. The scope of this extensive latitude is best illustrated later in this chapter in the outline of Trust provisions that should be included in all Living Trust documents.

Provision of Broad Powers to Successor Trustees

Although the powers of a trustee appointed by a probate court are defined under the state's probate code, such powers are necessarily far too restrictive. In contrast, however, a Living Trust provides the opportunity to specify the powers of the trustee. Those powers may be made as broad as each client wants them—thus creating a manageable document that allows the successor trustees to provide for the heirs in the manner deemed most appropriate by the creators of the Trust.

If, for example, minor children were orphaned and no Living Trust were in effect to provide for their well-being, the court would be required to appoint a guardian and to set up a Trust to hold the assets of the estate. Under these circumstances, the powers of the guardian and the trustee will be very restrictive, and the court should supervise their actions.

However, if an appropriate Living Trust has been drawn up, a trustee (or trustees) and a guardian (or guardians) who are *trusted* by the creators will have been named. In this situation, since the named persons are trusted individuals, it is reasonable to give them far broader powers. In the long run, this action will be far more beneficial to the heirs.

Price Is No Indicator

During a six-month period in 1977, three clients came to me and acknowledged that they needed Living Trusts. Each client was the president of a small corporation and desired to ask his or her own corporate legal counsel, whom each had known for years, to draw up the Trust. In each case, I was asked to review the Trusts drawn up by their personal corporate legal counsels, and I naively agreed.

Although the situation for each individual was different and each attorney was different, the Trust documents were astonishingly identical. All these documents were given to me for review within a period of weeks—and I was shocked! Not one of the Trusts was worth the paper on which it was written. To cross-check my conclusion, I took the three Trust documents to legal counsel I knew was expert in Trusts; this experienced counsel quickly came to the same opinion—that the Trusts were not properly written—and put this fact in writing to each of the clients. I had learned a sad lesson, which also became the impetus for the writing of this book.

Unfortunately, price is no measurement of a well-written Trust. In the preceding example, the clients were charged three to five times more than the price of a perfect (properly written) Trust that could be obtained from *experienced* and *knowledgeable* counsel. The clients had apparently been charged for all of the attorney's time—including the attorney's learning process (all of the time spent researching the provisions that should be included) for the attorney's first attempt at a Living Trust.

In today's enterprising Living Trust market, Living Trusts are advertised at every price imaginable. However, if you want to avoid probate and preserve your estate, you must "do it right" and get a *good* Living Trust with the appropriate documents. Remember: Anything less than a *good* Living Trust will eventually be a nightmare for you and/or your heirs.

Do-It-Yourself Living Trusts

The print and broadcast media are being saturated with advertisements for do-it-yourself Living Trusts ranging in price from $19.95 and up. Please—don't waste your money! The subject of Living Trusts is just too complex an area to "play with," and far too much of your estate is at stake to risk such an unwise move.

Some years ago, I was working with a retired gentleman to prepare his Living Trust. I gave him our workbook to take home to complete during the ensuing week. Having extra time on his hands, the gentleman went to the library, copied forms from a book of do-it-yourself Living Trusts, and completed them. He had no intention of actually utilizing those forms; instead, he merely filled them out in an effort to be helpful.

At the end of the week, the gentleman proudly brought all the forms to me. As I reviewed them, I was astonished to note that not one form would have been acceptable for the man's Living Trust. Even though this man was an educated and perceptive individual and had done his best to help expedite the Trust process, his efforts only served to point out the inadequacies of fill-in-the-blank forms.

Two Separate Trusts for a Married Couple

It has become standard procedure throughout the Midwest and some eastern states to write two separate Trusts for a married couple. The logic seems to be that this method is the only way to preserve both $1 million federal estate tax exclusions; however, creating two Trusts for one estate just creates an administrative nightmare for the spouses. When I first heard of this approach, I was convinced that it was simply an attempt by attorneys to get more money for their Trusts (two Trusts cost more than one). Later, however, I discovered that this common practice of writing two Trusts was really a case of the attorneys acting like sheep—all of them following a leader and assuming that the leader is correct. The fact is, however, that these attorneys are simply years behind the tax law.

After conversing with some of the most prestigious Living Trust masters and then exhaustively researching the tax codes and legal articles, our legal staff has concluded that there is no legal requirement for the two-trust concept—drawing two Living Trusts for a married couple in order to preserve both $1 million federal estate tax exclusions.

There is a belief floating around that the A-B Trust is applicable in community property states but not in separate property states, that somehow we can preserve both spouses' $1 million federal estate tax exclusions in a community property state with an A-B Trust, but we can't do so in a separate property state. This is nonsense. We are talking about federal law, not state law. There has never been a case where the IRS has denied both federal estate tax exemptions in a good A-B Living Trust because of residence in a separate property state.

I am appalled at the enormous amount of misinformation about Living Trusts that is being spewed forth by the legal profession. Much of it is by ignorance (they don't teach Living Trusts as a basic course in law school), much of it is intentional disinformation to steer you into the probate process, and the balance is just pure greed (an attorney gets twice as much money for two Trusts as for one). Also, an A-B Trust is quite complex and difficult to draft to satisfy the IRS requirements; a single Trust is much simpler to draft. And so you end up with two separate Trusts—and an administrative nightmare. This question is now formally resolved with the issuance of a Private Letter Ruling. See "Joint vs. Separate Trusts in Separate Property States" in Chapter 7.

SELECTING A COMPETENT LIVING TRUST PROVIDER

Everyone needs a Living Trust—and each person is faced with the same problem of finding the right estate plan provider. Even with my experience as an estate planner and licensed/registered investment adviser, I would be afraid to draw up my own Trust. I know the advantages of a good Trust—*and* the dire consequences of a poor one! Your Trust, to be effective, *must* be drawn by a knowledgeable, experienced estate-planning attorney.

To obtain an effective Living Trust, you must have it drawn by a knowledgeable, experienced estate-planning attorney.

Thus, in your quest for a Living Trust, the most important thing to look for is an estate plan provider who has the right experience and will provide some important services. Some words about our own company should give you a flavor of what you need.

The Estate Plan

In recognizing many years ago the problems of finding a well-written Living Trust, an associate and I formed a corporation called The Estate Plan to provide Living Trusts for our clients. Because of our continuing dissatisfaction with the caliber of Trusts being written, we learned that if you are going to do it right, you must do it yourself. I have worked diligently to incorporate into the Living Trust every experience we or our clients have ever encountered, so that our future clients will never be subjected to the same problems.

The Estate Plan has evolved into the National Estate Plan (doing business as The Estate Plan) and is now a nationwide organization with more than four hundred advisers in most of the fifty states. Our in-house legal counselors have some of the most brilliant legal minds in the industry. In addition, more than one hundred associate attorneys continually review our documents, offer constructive input, and keep us abreast of changes in local and state laws. Many of our thousands of clients have also offered their own constructive suggestions for making our Living Trusts even better. However, the true measure of the soundness of any Living Trust is whether or not it works. Our firm has "settled" thousands of Living Trusts without incident, and, thus, we know by experience that our Living Trusts work.

We take special pride in our ability to communicate the concept of the Living Trust and the associated documents to our clients. Our clients really *do* understand their Living Trusts, as well as how to make their Trusts work for them as living and readily changeable instruments for passing their assets on to their heirs.

Our firm regularly assists several generations of one family. Our customers continue to refer our services to their families and friends, because they are assured that our program *works*. Our customers have experienced, first-hand, The Estate Plan's dedication to creating the finest Living Trusts for the nation's families and individuals.

A good Living Trust is truly the result of years of experience and dealing with every problem imaginable. Only through years of *actual* experience (and not just contemplative thought) can someone write a Living Trust that contains provisions to handle every possible contingency.

In an effort to protect our Living Trust documents against future alteration or substitution, our Trust and all accompanying documents are printed on special paper imprinted with our logo—a feather with the words *The Estate Plan* superimposed on it. Thus, although the document is signed only on the last or signature page, if anyone—other than the creator or creators—were to fraudulently attempt to alter a line or lines or to substitute a page, the alteration or substitution would be obvious. Remember: *You*, and only you, may amend your own document anytime you wish (as discussed in Chapter 7).

Our Living Trust document is the result of more than twenty-five years of working together with legal counsel to cover every imaginable contingency. I have yet to find an instance in which our Living Trust has not worked perfectly. I am often asked about the downside of having a Living Trust, but I have yet to find one disadvantage in having a *properly written* Living Trust.

Experienced Legal Counsel

A well-written and comprehensive Trust document comes about only through extensive experience. Therefore, one of the first questions I would ask any attorney being considered for drawing up a Living Trust is: "How long have you been creating Living Trusts?" The number

of years the attorney has been creating Living Trusts gives you a measure of the attorney's experience. The legal counsel you select should have drawn up many hundreds of Living Trusts.

In a recent, rather important meeting on Living Trusts, I had the opportunity to discuss the creation of Living Trusts with three very prominent Trust attorneys, two of whom are noted professors. As professors, they made it very clear that they cannot really "teach" students in law school about Living Trusts. Law school classes get involved in the esoterics of such complex legal subjects as the doctrine of merger or the law of perpetuity, but they cannot teach the substantial practical experience that is needed to draw up a *good* Living Trust.

The most important point to remember is: A law degree does not a Living Trust expert make.

The legal counsel you select should have drawn up and settled hundreds of Living Trusts.

The next question I would ask is: "How many Living Trusts have you settled?" (The Estate Plan has settled thousands of Trusts.) I would follow that question by asking, "What do you charge to settle the estate?" What you really want to know is whether the attorney has had much experience in settling the estates, whether his or her Trusts settle without problems, and, in effect, whether the attorney stands behind the Trust. It is our experience that, if your Trust is properly drawn and your estate is well organized, the basic process of settling your estate should take less than an hour! The subject of settling an estate in a Living Trust will be discussed in greater detail in Chapter 15.

A client and her husband had executed a Trust with a well-known Beverly Hills firm in 1978. The husband died in 1982, and the widow went back to the firm to settle the estate. After attending meetings and spending many dollars, the woman still did not have her assets identified as being distributed in either the Survivor's A Trust or the Decedent's B Trust. No matter how hard she tried, the widow could not get the legal firm to respond to her requests. Eventually she was told, in so many words, to "go away."

In 1986, the woman went to another legal firm to get her assets properly distributed into the A and B Trusts. She was again told that she needed certain *unnecessary* papers drawn up and was given substantial bills for professional services rendered. However, even then, no assets were identified as being distributed to either the A Trust or the B Trust. She was finally referred to our office, and her assets were easily apportioned between the Survivor's A Trust and the Decedent's B Trust—in less than one hour!

Although both of the firms in the previous example were willing to draw Living Trusts and to charge substantial fees for their Trusts, I believe that neither of the firms understood how to settle the Trust. I do not wish to disparage the many fine, outstanding, legitimate, and experienced estate-planning attorneys who are doing excellent jobs. Unfortunately, the American Bar Association says that fewer than 1 percent of the legal fraternity understand the Living Trust—and my experience forces me to agree.

In addition to drawing up an extensive and all-encompassing Living Trust and the several related legal documents, any attorney or firm offering to draw up your Living Trust should also provide you with at least the following basic services:

- A simple, clear, English summary of the Trust
- Copies of transfer letters to assure that every asset gets properly placed into your Trust
- An agreement to advise you of future tax changes
- An agreement to periodically update your Trust at a reasonable cost
- A simple but methodical means to organize your estate for rapid settlement

Clear Summary of Trust

A Living Trust, by its very nature as a legal document, is written in legalese. No matter how hard I have tried, as long as I have worked with legal counsel, I have never been able to get a Trust written in a way that is totally understandable by a client. However, it is essential that the client be able to understand his or her own Trust. Therefore, legal counsel should provide the client with a summary in clear, concise, and simple English, which will allow the client to understand the Trust and how it works.

Because the Living Trust document must be written in legalese, it should come with a summary in plain English.

Every client is different. Some clients are interested only in a vague understanding of the concept, and other clients want to know the smallest details of every provision. Many people simply accept the Trust at face value but want to know that the necessary information is correct. The detail-oriented person may want to cross the *t* and dot the *i* and, therefore, may want to know how the Trust works in detail. A general understanding of the documents and the key provisions enables every client to establish a "comfort level." Without this comfort level, the Trust documents effectively cease to function for the client.

Our clients are provided with an additional five-page, simple mini-summary of their Trusts and ancillary documents. After the computer compiles all of the legal documents, the computer searches through the documents and generates a summary of the pertinent Trust and ancillary document information:

- Page 1 identifies the personal data. This information would include such items as your name and social security number, your spouse's name, children's names, parents' names and dates of birth, and so on.
- Pages 2 and 3 identify whom you have named where. This information includes such key individuals as trustee, surviving trustee, successor trustee(s), executor, dur-

able power of attorney, alternates, and the particular individuals named in your ancillary documents. (Ancillary documents will be explained in the next chapter.)

- Pages 4 and 5 identify the particular paragraphs that have been personalized to make the Trust documents meet *your* particular needs.

Thus, in five to ten minutes, you can be assured that all of the information in your legal documents is correct.

Transfer Letters

For your Living Trust to be effective, all of your assets must be transferred into the Living Trust. Without this transfer of assets, you effectively have only a Testamentary Trust—which means that your assets must go through probate upon your death, and only *after* the probate process will the remainder of your assets then pass into your Trust. Appropriate transfer letters should be provided to each client who creates a Living Trust, so that he or she may readily transfer his or her assets into the Trust. In Chapter 14, you will learn more about how to accomplish this very important action.

Notification of Future Tax Changes

You should have an agreement with the firm that draws your Trust that the firm will advise you of any future tax changes. Any related changes to your Trust should be made at a reasonable cost. Unfortunately, Congress gets around to changing the estate tax laws about every five years. Most people readily become aware of the income tax changes, but too few people are aware of the *estate* tax changes, usually made in different years. Unless clients have some means of notification, their Trusts may eventually become noncompliant with the IRS Code because of a new tax change of which they are unaware. I believe that it is the responsibility of every legal counsel who draws up Living Trusts to notify his or her clients of any estate tax change and to offer to make related changes to the Trust for a reasonable fee. Of course, you must also do your part; you must make certain that the author of your Trust is

promptly notified of any change of address. (If we can't find you, it's difficult to notify you.)

All of our Trusts have been cataloged inside our computer system. Whenever there is a major estate tax change (and if it is of *benefit* to our clients), the computer searches all of our Trusts and provisions and then identifies which Trusts would be subject to that particular tax change. The computer prints out the names and addresses of the affected clients, and each client is advised in writing that his or her Trust should be updated because of the tax change.

Because the computer processing is done en masse for all of our clients, the Trusts of all clients should remain current. A reasonable fee for typical tax-related changes to the Trust would be about $200, depending upon the extent of the tax change. This service is almost as important as the Living Trust itself.

Periodic Trust Updates

You should review the size of your estate at least every three years to determine if you should move from an A-B Trust to an A-B-C Trust. Has your estate, business, or insurance increased to the point that you should add an Insurance Preservation Trust, or any of the other estate planning vehicles that can be used to minimize the impact of estate taxes?

You should also review your Trust periodically for any personal changes that have occurred in your life and to see that your Trust still meets your objectives. A personal review of your Trust is suggested at least every five years—or sooner, if there is a significant change in your family status. Changes you may wish to make might include a change of a successor trustee, a change of a beneficiary, or a change in the method of allocation or distribution. These personal changes to your Trust, too, should be provided at a reasonable cost.

In contrast, all too often legal counsel charges $500 or more for a standard upgrade to a Trust! As ironic as this situation may seem, such an apparently exorbitant charge is frequently justified—because, when the Trust was drawn, it lacked organization, and therefore it is necessary for legal counsel to go through the entire Trust in order to identify which areas need to be updated! As you can see, it does not have to be that way.

If changes to your Trust are too expensive, your Trust eventually becomes outdated and ineffective, because you are unlikely to change it. Assume, for example, that an individual has had a Trust for five or six years and visits the attorney's office to ask him or her to review and update it—and following such updates, the client receives a bill for $500. The average person would probably be far less inclined to ever go back again. If this situation happens to you, your Trust has just stopped working for you!

Organization of Your Estate

As important as the Living Trust is, organization of your estate is equally important. Without an organized estate, the surviving spouse and/or children crawl around on hands and knees and turn drawers upside down, looking for missing documents. After the loss of a loved one, clients frequently search for documents that they "know exactly where they are," only to be unable to find them. After repeatedly seeing client after client spend hour after hour searching for documents that "have to be here someplace," I knew that there just had to be a better way. Thus, the Estate Plan Binder was created for our clients—to provide them with a simple and orderly way to organize their estates (and to keep them organized), as well as to put everything needed to settle an estate in one place. The Estate Plan Binder will be described and illustrated in Chapter 13.

With a Living Trust and an organized estate, the key elements of the estate can be settled in less than an hour. However, it takes both: the Living Trust *and* organization.

STRUCTURE OF A GOOD LIVING TRUST

Even though the organization and structure of a good Living Trust will vary from attorney to attorney, a well-written Living Trust requires a multitude of carefully worded provisions, so that the Trust can accommodate your changing circumstances without needing to be legally modified. Whenever possible, the Trust should be universal; that is, applicable in all fifty states, for you may eventually own

property in or even move to another state. There are certain nuances that are peculiar to some individual states (for example, see "Residence as homestead—State of Florida" and "Residence as homestead—State of Texas" in Table 10-1), and a well-written Trust will incorporate appropriate language that addresses each of the different nuances. Our Living Trust now contains many new provisions that have been added since this book was first published—to address these nuances, to keep the Trust up-to-date with the tax law, and to cover additional contingent situations. One of our A-B-C Living Trusts covers approximately sixty pages of legal language! The rest of this chapter will identify the more than 150 provisions that should be included in *every* Living Trust. This information should help you distinguish the good Trusts (and attorneys) from the bad ones.

Even though some of these Trust provisions may not apply at this particular moment in your life, any of the provisions could apply *someday*—and that is why they are included.

> An extreme example, but a true situation, was Harry Strom, who had no children and objected to the provisions for minor children. I persuaded him, however, to leave the provision in his Trust—just in case. Years later, when Harry died, his assets were divided between his brother and his sister. Since his brother had predeceased him and left minor nephews, the provision for minors in Harry's Living Trust was then essential.

Remember: Look not to today, but to what might happen tomorrow. Your Trust is designed for the future, and at some time any one of these provisions may be a necessity. Having a well-written Living Trust prepares you for the unknown or unexpected contingencies that may arise in the future.

However your Trust is organized, it should contain all of the provisions listed in Table 10-1.

The necessary provisions are listed in Table 10-1 by type of Trust: single person's A Trust, married couple's A Trust, married couple's A-B Trust, married couple's A-B-C Trust, unmarried couple's A-B Trust, and Partner A-A Trust. (The unmarried couple's A-B Trust is used by two individuals of opposite gender who are living together and retaining their assets for joint use but who are keeping their assets legally separate. The Partner A-A Trust is for two individuals of the same gender.) The "bullets" or dots within each column indicate *necessary* provisions for the particular type of Trust.

If you use the table as an outline of your criteria for a Living Trust, a knowledgeable, experienced estate-planning attorney will acknowledge that these provisions are a part of his or her Trust, whereas an inexperienced attorney will decline to draw the Trust. The time an inexperienced attorney would have to spend researching all the provisions would make the cost of the Trust prohibitive. It would take the average attorney 1,500 to 1,600 hours to create such a document from scratch! If he or she has not already created such a vehicle through years of experience, the attorney certainly cannot afford to begin now—and still provide you with a Living Trust at reasonable cost.

Therefore, you should use the outline in this chapter to demand that your Trust include these necessary provisions. Beware of the attorney who tries to pooh-pooh some or all of the provisions as unnecessary. After settling thousands of estates, I can testify to the necessity of every provision.

Although other Trusts may be organized in different ways, any well-drawn Trust should include every one of the provisions described in the outline. If a Trust does *not* include all of these provisions, then I believe that you are being shortchanged.

The list of provisions in Table 10-1 is probably one of the most important sections of this book. It is not placed here to read, but rather to glance through and recognize the number and types of provisions you should have in your Living Trust. More important, this outline is placed here to be used as a tool to enable you to differentiate a good Living Trust from a poor one—and thus be able to screen out the inexperienced attorneys.

CAVEAT EMPTOR ("LET THE BUYER BEWARE")

It is my intent to convince all people that they ought to have Living Trusts. The advantages of a well-written Living Trust are innumerable, and there are no disadvantages. On the other hand, I fully recognize the danger of sending you out into the cold at the mercy of those members of the legal fraternity who, when you say, "I want a Living Trust," will respond by saying, "OK, I'll draw it for you"—without having years of experience in this delicate area of legal technicalities. More than ever, the caution *caveat emptor* ("Let the buyer beware") applies in this situation. If you are offered a Trust that is not all-inclusive or that is not well organized, then quickly look elsewhere.

Almost daily I see advertisements of free seminars on the Living Trust. The information offered at these seminars may be worthwhile, but the abuses unfortunately are many:

- One firm tells you that an appraisal of real estate is necessary to transfer your property into the Trust. The firm just happens to be affiliated with a company that will do the appraisal for $250 per property! (No appraisal is *ever* necessary to transfer property into your Living Trust.)
- Another law firm offers *free* client follow-up interviews after its seminar. However, if you do not sign up for the firm's Living Trust, you are billed for "professional services rendered"!
- Some firms charge a fee of 1 percent to 3 percent of your *total* estate to settle your estate. Other firms charge you as much as one-third to one-half of what it would have cost if you had gone through probate! (If the Living Trust process is done correctly from the very beginning, very little should be involved in settling the estate, and—in the typical estate—you certainly don't need the assistance of legal counsel.)

A poorly written Trust can be worse than no Trust at all. Upon the death of a spouse (if a married couple have an A-B Trust), the decedent's half of the Trust becomes irrevocable; if a single person (with an A Trust) dies, the

TABLE 10-1
NECESSARY PROVISIONS FOR A GOOD LIVING TRUST

	Single	Married A Trust	Married A-B Trust	Married A-B-C Trust	Unmarried A-B Trust	Partner A-A Trust
Creation of the Trust						
Name of Trust	•	•	•	•	•	•
Notice of arbitration	•	•	•	•	•	•
Parties to the Trust	•	•	•	•	•	•
Heirs at Law	•	•	•	•	•	•
Trustee authority to act independently		•	•	•	•	•
Tax treatment of revocable Grantor Trust	•	•	•	•	•	•
Use of IRS employer tax identification number	•	•	•	•	•	•
Trust Property						
Property transferred to the Trust	•	•	•	•	•	
Commonly owned property		•	•	•	•[1]	•
Separate property		•	•	•	•	
Residence as homestead—State of Florida	•	•	•	•	•	•
Residence as homestead—State of Texas	•	•	•	•	•	•
Successor Trustee						
Surviving trustee		•	•	•	•	•
Successor trustee	•	•	•	•	•	•
No bond requirement	•	•	•	•	•	•
Successor trustees must act together	•	•	•	•	•	•
Resolution of conflict	•	•	•	•	•	•
No-contest clause	•	•	•	•	•	•
Litigation by arbitration	•	•	•	•	•	•
Discharge or resignation of trustee	•	•	•	•	•[2]	•
Trustee compensation	•	•	•	•	•	•
Competency clause	•	•	•	•	•	•
Trustor Powers						
Trustor retains absolute right as trustee	•	•	•	•	•	•
Description of powers	•	•	•	•	•	•
Gifts treated as revocation	•	•	•	•	•	•

	Single	Married			Unmarried A-B Trust	Partner A-A Trust
		A Trust	A-B Trust	A-B-C Trust		
Trustee Powers						
Discretionary powers of trustee	•	•	•	•	•	•
Needs of surviving spouse	•	•	•	•	•	•
After death of surviving spouse		•	•	•	•	•
Encourage thrift	•	•	•	•	•	•
Discourage extravagance	•	•	•	•	•	•
Trustee as the beneficiary of a qualified plan or account	•	•	•	•	•	•
Commonly owned property		•	•	•	•[1]	•
Separate property		•	•	•	•	
Incompetency	•	•	•	•	•	•
Specific trustee powers	•	•	•	•	•	•
Securities authorization	•	•	•	•	•	•
Sub-Chapter S	•	•	•	•	•	•
Precious metals and limited partnerships	•	•	•	•	•	•
Stock of professional corporation	•	•	•	•	•	•
Trust investments	•	•	•	•	•	•
Marital deduction election		•	•	•		
Payment to minor/disabled individual	•	•	•	•	•	•
Reimbursement of guardian's expenses	•	•	•	•	•	•
Occupancy of residence	•	•	•	•	•	•
Discretionary dissolution of Trust	•	•	•	•	•	•
Valuation of assets	•	•	•	•	•	•
Application to court	•	•	•	•	•	•
Life insurance provisions	•	•	•	•	•	•
Policy owner's rights	•	•	•	•	•	•
Trustee held harmless as custodian	•	•	•	•	•	•
Canceling a policy	•	•	•	•	•	•
Policy options	•	•	•	•	•	•
Insurance payment discharge	•	•	•	•	•	•
Suing an insurance company	•	•	•	•	•	•
Limitation on change of beneficiary	•	•	•	•	•	•
Payment of Death Costs						
Discretionary powers of trustee to pay death costs	•	•	•	•	•	•
Specific provisions for settling estate			•[3]	•[3]	•[3]	
Written statement as evidence	•	•	•	•	•	•
Flower bonds	•	•	•	•	•	•

(continued)

TABLE 10-1 (continued)
NECESSARY PROVISIONS FOR A GOOD LIVING TRUST

	Single	Married A Trust	Married A-B Trust	Married A-B-C Trust	Unmarried A-B Trust	Partner A-A Trust
Death of a Trustor						
Division of shares			•	•	•	
General Power of Appointment⁴		•	•	•	•	•
Survivor's Trust A			•	•	•	
Decedent's marital share			•	•		
Unlimited marital deduction		•	•	•		
Disclaimer of interest		•	•	•	•	
Division of "marital share"			•	•		
Equivalent exemption to B			•	•		
Marital deduction to C (Q-TIP)				•		
IRAs to A or C (Q-TIP)		•	•	•		
Decedent's Trust B			•	•	•	
Decedent's Trust C				•		
Use of Trust A and B—simultaneous death			•		•	
Survivor's Trust A						
Right to revoke		•			•	
Right to income		•	•	•	•	
Right to principal		•	•	•	•	
Right to withdraw principal		•	•	•	•	
Control of assets		•	•	•	•	
Right to change beneficiary		•	•	•	•	
Distribution of residual of Trust A and survivor's GST		•	•	•	•	
Distribution of residual of Trust A		•	•	•	•	
Decedent's Trust B						
Payment of income			•	•	•	
Payment of principal			•	•	•	
Other payments			•	•		
Control of assets			•	•	•	
Qualified terminable interest			•	•		
Distribution of residual of Trust B			•	•	•	
Decedent's Trust C (Q-TIP)						
Payment of income				•		
Payment of principal				•		
Other payments				•		
Control of assets				•		
Qualified terminable interest				•		

		Married				
	Single	A Trust	A-B Trust	A-B-C Trust	Unmarried A-B Trust	Partner A-A Trust
Reverse Q-TIP (GST only)				•		
Qualified domestic Trust (Q-DOT Trust)				•		
Distribution of residual of Trust C				•		
Generation-Skipping Trust (GST)						
Allocation to Trust A	•	•	•	•	•	•
Allocation to Trusts B and C (Q-TIP)			•	•	•	
Allocation of trustor's exemption to GST	•	•	•	•	•	•
Alter GST exemption if changed by law	•	•	•	•	•	•
Allocation of income to children	•	•	•	•	•	•
Allocation upon death of children	•	•	•	•	•	•
Distribution of GST	•	•	•	•	•	•
Termination of GST	•	•	•	•	•	•
Allocation and Distribution of Trust Assets						
Upon the death of trustor	•	•	•	•	•	•
Debt payment power of appointment (only by special order)			•	•		
Upon the death of the first trustor			•	•	•	
Upon the death of both trustors		•	•	•	•	
Personal property distribution	•	•	•	•	•	•
Retention of Trust assets	•	•	•	•	•	•
Support and education	•	•	•	•	•	•
Extraordinary distribution	•	•	•	•	•	•
Gifts or loans	•	•	•	•	•	•
Disabled beneficiaries	•	•	•	•	•	•
Court determination	•	•	•	•	•	•
Competency clause	•	•	•	•	•	•
Interest of incompetent beneficiaries	•	•	•	•	•	•
No discretionary rights	•	•	•	•	•	•
A Trust						
Support and education	•	•	•	•	•	•
Beneficiary becomes eligible for government benefits	•	•	•	•	•	•
Unused principal	•	•	•	•	•	•
Enrichment benefits	•	•	•	•	•	•
Disabled beneficiary may be reinstated	•	•	•	•	•	•
Primary beneficiaries	•	•	•	•	•	•
Special bequests	•	•	•	•	•	•
Allocation of Trust assets	•	•	•	•	•	•
Distribution of Trust assets	•	•	•	•	•	•
Per stirpes	•	•	•	•	•	•

(continued)

TABLE 10-1 (continued)
NECESSARY PROVISIONS FOR A GOOD LIVING TRUST

	Single	Married A Trust	Married A-B Trust	Married A-B-C Trust	Unmarried A-B Trust	Partner A-A Trust
Intestate succession	•	•	•	•	•	•
Exclusion	•	•	•	•	•	•
Charity	•	•	•	•	•	•
Property exposed to environmental hazards	•	•	•	•	•	•
The Tax Act Reconciliation						
Estate tax	•	•	•	•	•	•
Estate tax rate	•	•	•	•	•	•
Gift tax	•	•	•	•	•	•
Generation-skipping transfer tax rules	•	•	•	•	•	•
Act of 2001	•	•	•	•	•	•
Severing of trusts holding property having an inclusion ratio of greater than zero	•	•	•	•	•	•
Modification of certain valuation rules	•	•	•	•	•	•
Substantial compliance	•	•	•	•	•	•
Repeal of the generation-skipping tax	•	•	•	•	•	•
Changes, alterations, modifications, revocations, or revisions	•	•	•	•	•	•
Stepped-up valuation	•	•	•	•	•	•
Non-residents who are not U.S. citizens	•	•	•	•	•	•
Inflationary adjustments	•	•	•	•	•	•
Trustee authority	•	•	•	•	•	•
Changes, alterations, modifications, revocations, or recisions	•	•	•	•	•	•
State death tax credit (will be reduced)	•	•	•	•	•	•
General Provisions						
Intention to avoid probate	•	•	•	•	•	•
Trustee can use probate process	•	•	•	•	•	•
Annual accounting	•	•	•	•	•	•
Partial invalidity	•	•	•	•	•	•
Headings	•	•	•	•	•	•
Counterparts	•	•	•	•	•	•
Spendthrift provisions	•	•	•	•	•	•
Last illness and funeral expense	•	•	•	•	•	•
Glossary of Terms						
Trustee	•	•	•	•	•	•
Child or children	•	•	•	•	•	•

	Single	Married A Trust	Married A-B Trust	Married A-B-C Trust	Unmarried A-B Trust	Partner A-A Trust
Internal Revenue Code terminology	•	•	•	•	•[1]	•
Commonly owned property		•	•	•	•	•
Creation and Dissolution of Trust						
Situs of Trust	•	•	•	•	•	•
Situs as state of execution	•	•	•	•	•	•
Situs can be changed	•	•	•	•	•	•
Law of the situs controls	•	•	•	•	•	•
Trust exempted from registration	•	•	•	•	•	•
Recordation of Trust provisions	•	•	•	•	•	•
Termination of Trust	•	•	•	•	•	•
Rule against perpetuities clause	•	•	•	•	•	•
Ultimate termination	•	•	•	•	•	•
Assets go to income beneficiaries	•	•	•	•	•	•
Agreement between parties	•	•	•	•	•[1]	•
Schedule A						
Gifts and loans	•	•	•	•	•	•
Schedule B						
Charitable distributions	•	•	•	•	•	•
Letter of intent/declaration of gift			•	•	•	•
Separate Property Addendum		•	•	•	•[1]	

[1] The wording is specifically altered to reflect two unmarried single persons as the settlors.

[2] Under the unmarried A-B Trust, the right of the surviving settlor to replace the named successor trustee of the Decedent's B Trust has been specifically deleted.

[3] The wording is specifically altered to apply to the appropriate Trust: married A-B, married A-B-C, or unmarried A-B.

[4] To be used with discretion.

entire Trust becomes irrevocable. In these cases, a poorly drawn Trust can become a restrictive nightmare for the surviving spouse or successor trustee and beneficiaries.

As long as the clients are living, it does not matter what a Living Trust says, because it can always be changed or revoked. However, upon the death of the client, these poorly written Trusts are going to end up in probate court, with petitions being presented to revise or clarify the Trust wording. (Even though the main advantage of a Living Trust is to *avoid* probate, a Trust falls under the legal jurisdiction of the probate code; any need for clarification of a Trust therefore must be handled in the probate courts.)

A poorly drawn Trust can even become a nightmare while the creator is living. Fortunately, the Trust is still revocable at that time.

In spite of the abuses and the perils of a poorly written Trust, everyone *needs* a Living Trust. There are many reputable, knowledgeable, and experienced estate-planning attorneys throughout the United States. Unfortunately, there are far too many attorneys who purport to be experts but are exploiting the public. Remember the warning: "Let the buyer beware."

It is my hope that, by presenting the many details in this chapter, I have given you the necessary tools to make the appropriate decisions.

If an attorney agrees to incorporate the provisions in this chapter into a Living Trust, then you have reason to believe that he or she is reasonably knowledgeable.

I hope that this chapter has given you the proper groundwork and equipped you with the basic knowledge—*and cautions*—to seek out and select a competent professional to draw up your next step in sound financial planning—*your* Living Trust document.

---------- 11 ----------

Ancillary Documents

There are a number of other legal documents (each considered to be a separate legal entity) that are not legally required parts of the Living Trust but which should be included in or with the Trust to provide for future contingencies. These ancillary documents are so important that, with two minor exceptions, they are included automatically with our Living Trust with no additional fee. The ancillary documents that should be included with every Living Trust are:

- Living Will
- Durable Power of Attorney for Health Care
- Durable General Power of Attorney
- Competency Clause
- Assignment of Furniture, Furnishings, and Personal Effects
- Appointment of Guardian
- Appointment of Conservator
- Anatomical Gift

LIVING WILL

With modern technology, the Living Will is becoming more and more important as a protection for you and your loved ones. The term *Living Will* refers to what many people know as the "Right-to-Die Clause." This document says in effect that, if your life is being sustained *solely* by artificial means, it is your desire—a decision made when you were competent—that the plug be pulled. By making this election *before* the onset of major medical problems, you may thereafter tell the doctors and hospitals that you want to die with dignity—and not be subjected to being kept alive by a machine. (It is estimated that on average Americans spend more on the cost of medical care during the last few days of life than they do for medical care during their entire lives.)

People often say, "Well, that's all well and good, but I know that the doctors and/or hospitals will not abide by such a document." In the past several years, the courts and the medical profession have *slowly* come to the realization that each person *does* have a right to decide about his or her "quality of life." Only recently have several court decisions finally begun to uphold an individual's right to die.

Congress recently enacted legislation requiring all medical institutions—specifically hospitals and nursing homes—to advise an individual entering such an institution of his or her right to a Living Will. This legislation has created great concern among the administrators of these institutions, because they feel—rightly so—that such a time is absolutely inappropriate to be discussing the merits of a Living Will. I sincerely concur; I believe it is far more appropriate for you to take the time, while you are currently healthy, to review the merits of the Living Will and to make your decision *now*—without the pressure of a serious illness to distract you.

> For example, seven years ago when I was in Minneapolis giving seminars, I suddenly found myself in the hospital facing double-bypass heart surgery. This situation was totally unexpected, but immediate action was vitally necessary. What a traumatic experience that situation could have been, had I not already created my Living Will. Facing the immediate necessity of major heart surgery, my anxiety level was extremely high—*not* the time for me to calmly make important decisions that might affect my life. When the hospital staff asked me whether I had a Living Will, it was with great relief, and a feeling of calm, that I was able to say "yes," and everything proceeded smoothly from there.

From personal experience, I can assure you that facing heart surgery was *not* the time to spend discussing the merits of a Living Will. The time to do it is now, when you are not faced with that type of pressure.

Prior to Congress' recent legislation, however, very few doctors and hospitals would honor a Living Will. The following examples (which include factual names and cases that have been widely published in the media) will provide you with some interesting insight.

The case of William F. Bartling is a good example involving an individual's right to die and points out the typical position of many hospitals.

> In 1984, William F. Bartling, age seventy, entered the Glendale Adventist Medical Center, suffering from five potentially fatal diseases, and he was placed on an artificial life-support system. Subsequently, Mr.

Bartling asked that the artificial life-support system be disconnected. The doctors and the hospital refused—saying that they felt that "in their 'Christian, pro-life-oriented hospital' [the] doctors see 'disconnecting a life-support system in a case such as this inconsistent with the healing orientation of physicians.'"

William Bartling and his wife then sued the medical center and five doctors. The court found in favor of the doctors and the hospital. Mr. Bartling consequently remained connected to the artificial life-support equipment until he eventually died—five months later.

The day before Mr. Bartling died, his case was appealed. The appeals court found in his favor, but this decision was rendered two months after he died. Part of the judge's decision is significant enough to quote here: "The right of a competent adult patient to refuse medical treatment is a constitutionally guaranteed right, which must not be abridged. Bartling's right to refuse unwanted medical treatment outweighed the hospital's and his doctors' concerns about the preservation of life and the maintenance of the medical profession's ethics. Adults have the right to control their own medical care, 'including the decision to have life-sustaining procedures withheld or withdrawn in instances of terminal condition.'"

In effect, the court ruled that a terminally ill patient has the right to determine the *quality* of his or her own life. (On the following day, every doctor and medical institution in the state of California was aware of the *Bartling* decision.)

Another notable case involving an individual's right to die is that of Paul Brophy. His case was aired on the television program "20/20" in 1985.

> Paul Brophy was forty-five years old when an artery in his brain burst. Mr. Brophy underwent twelve hours of surgery, and sixteen hours later had a massive stroke. He never again regained consciousness. As months passed, Mr. Brophy's condition did not change. No machines were keeping him alive;

he breathed on his own. However, a feeding tube had been surgically implanted in his stomach to keep him alive.

After two years, his wife met with her family; the family decided that there was no chance of recovery and that Mr. Brophy should be taken off the feeding-support system. Being Irish Catholic, the family consulted its church leaders and was eventually directed to the Reverend John Paris, the church's ethicist located in Washington, D.C. Father Paris stated, "We have a medical intervention, and it is not really working, and so we are going to stop it. Removing the feeding tubes from patients is done regularly. I consult in medical ethics in several hospitals, and I myself have signed consult sheets stating that I believe that it was appropriate to have feeding tubes removed, and they were removed and those patients died."

Mrs. Brophy asked that the feeding tube be removed, but the hospital refused. With the approval of her family and of the church, Mrs. Brophy filed suit, but the judge ruled against withdrawing life support. His reason: Paul Brophy, in the judge's opinion, was not *terminally* ill; he was not a person about to die almost at any moment.

The decision was appealed, and in September 1986, the Massachusetts appeals court finally ordered that the feeding tube be removed. Eight days later, after removal of the feeding tube, Paul Brophy died.

Another famous "quality of life" case is that of Elizabeth Bouvia, a twenty-eight-year-old quadriplegic, whose tragic case received wide media attention several years ago.

Miss Bouvia had been stricken with cerebral palsy since birth and also suffered from progressive arthritis. She asked the court to order the hospital to stop force-feeding her by inserting a permanent tube through her nose into her stomach. The court upheld the involuntary use of the feeding tube; yet in 1986, in a unanimous opinion, the California appeals court stated that Miss Bouvia had the right to refuse medical treatment—even if the treatment were life-sustaining.

Most people will remember the landmark case of Karen Ann Quinlan, which was also widely reported by the media.

Miss Quinlan lapsed into a coma, apparently after ingesting a mixture of alcohol and barbiturates at a party. Her mother and father fought a yearlong court battle to have their comatose daughter removed from a respirator. In 1975, the New Jersey Supreme Court ruled unanimously in favor of her parents. After being removed from the respirator, Karen Ann Quinlan astounded the medical profession by continuing to live another nine years, until she died at the age of thirty-one.

The day that the Quinlans' daughter died was a sad day for the mother and father. However, all people have reason to thank this mother and father for their courage—because they began the legal process that has eventually made the medical and legal professions aware that each individual should have the right to determine his or her own quality of life.

Legality of the Living Will

There is no longer any question today that the Living Will is a legally accepted document. Each person has the right to determine his or her own quality of life. The U.S. Supreme Court confirmed our constitutional "right to die" on June 25, 1990, thanks to the courage and determination of the parents of Nancy Cruzan.

After nearly suffocating in an automobile accident at age twenty-six, Nancy Cruzan lay unconscious in a "persistent vegetative state" for the next six years. Like thousands of other patients in similar condition, she had no awareness of herself or her surroundings—and no hope of recovery. Yet, she was given a normal life expectancy. Her care at a state rehabilitation hospital cost about $130,000 a year.

Nancy had been a very vivacious, active young woman, who would have died the night of the accident if not for medical intervention. Her family knew that she would not have wanted to live in a vegetative state and sought "to set her free" by stopping her tube feedings. The family's request was ultimately rejected by the Missouri State Supreme Court because Nancy had not made her wishes known in writing. Finally, in a landmark decision, the U.S. Supreme Court ruled that if Nancy "had made her wishes known," she could have been removed from life support—including the removal of the feeding tube.

Even though Nancy had not made such desires known in writing, the stage was set for the family to return to the Missouri court, where a sympathetic judge listened to Nancy's friends and relatives testify to what they knew were Nancy's wishes. The judge eventually allowed Nancy to be set free.

A legal precedent has now been established. However, remember that, to benefit from the U.S. Supreme Court's landmark decision, your desires must first be expressed in writing.

Shortly after the U.S. Supreme Court's decision, the *New York Times* wrote, "The court found that people who make their wishes known do have a 'liberty interest' in being free of unwanted medical care. [It] has given a strong constitutional underpinning for living wills. . . ." The key to this decision is the phrase *"who make their wishes known."* If you fail to make your wishes known *ahead of time*, you lose the right-to-die privilege. Therefore, you should exercise your privilege now, by creating a Living Will—so that it is in place and can take effect in the event that it might someday be required. Without a Living Will, your family is helpless to end your coma or suffering. Remember, however, that the decision *must* be made before the onset of a terminal condition and while the individual is fully competent and not under mental duress.

The typical state-approved Living Will states:

If I should have an incurable and irreversible condition that will result in my death within a relatively short time without the administration of life-sustaining treatment or that has produced an irreversible coma or persistent vegetative state, and I am no longer able to make decisions regarding my medical treatment, I direct my physician to withhold or withdraw treatment, including artificially administered nutrition and hydration, that only prolongs the process of dying or the irreversible coma or persistent vegetative state and is not necessary for my comfort or to alleviate pain.

We have come a long way in a few short years to be able to *withdraw nutrition and hydration.* Don't lose this hard-fought right by apathy (i.e., by not taking the action to create your Living Will—*now*).

I had an interesting conversation with the sister superior of a nursing home. The sister, who had spent years serving in a hospice in Ireland, opened my eyes when she told me that if an individual is placed on artificial life support, the body tends to go through painful trauma, as opposed to allowing life to take its normal course. In other words, artificial life support may well result in painful continuation of life.

Even though none of us looks forward to death, let's not intentionally make it agonizing for our survivors by failing to exercise our right to a Living Will while we are competent.

There is no question today that the Living Will is a legally accepted document.

Remember that if you have a Living Will (the Right-to-Die Clause), you have an absolute right—supported by the U.S. Supreme Court—to determine *your own* quality of life.

The conflict over the legality of the Living Will arises from two opposing forces: the right-to-death force and the right-to-life force. The right-to-death force has successfully created the Living Will (the Right-to-Die Clause), which allows a terminally ill individual to determine his or her own destiny. In contrast, the right-to-life force does recognize an individual's right to determine his or her quality of life but takes the position that, if an individual has not exercised the right to put into effect the Living Will *while competent*, then the individual does not have the right to determine his or her own destiny once he or she becomes terminally ill. The right-to-life group further takes the position that, if an individual is in the hospital and under intense medication, he or she is no longer competent to exercise that right (if not previously done while competent). In addition, they believe that *no one else* has the right to act on behalf of the terminally ill person.

Some states have enacted laws stating that an individual may not execute a Living Will within five days of being notified that he or she is terminally ill. The states are saying, in effect, that such notification causes undue stress and influence; therefore, the individual is not truly competent to execute the Living Will.

The right-to-die group and right-to-life group are both extremely strong and active forces in America today. I do not take issue with either group, but I *do* strongly believe that everyone ought to have the Living Will (the Right-to-Die Clause) signed and available. In the past few years, many clients have used their Living Wills when they have been diagnosed as terminally ill with cancer.

Importance of the Living Will
A poignant story will emphasize the importance of having a Living Will.

One of my clients wrote to me to say that her aunt, who had terminal cancer, had entered Cedars-Sinai Medical Center, a prominent hospital in southern California. The aunt went in for surgery and then wished to return home to die in familiar surroundings.

Following surgery, the hospital directed that the aunt be placed on life-support equipment. The aunt's niece advised the hospital of her aunt's wishes, but was somewhat brusquely shunted aside—the hospital was determined to put the aunt on life-support equipment. However, the niece stood her ground, held up her aunt's Living Will, and said, "You will not place my aunt on life-support equipment." Seeing the executed copy of the aunt's Living Will, the hospital yielded to the niece's demand.

The key point of this example is that the medical profession is still re-evaluating and re-educating itself about how to cope with terminally ill patients. With the Living Will, *you* have the right to make your own decision. There may be times when you or your family may be intimidated by doctors or hospitals, but hold your ground and recognize that the medical profession knows, as you now know, that the Living Will has been upheld by the highest court.

Your Right to Act
The Living Will is not an *order* to act, it is simply your *right* to act. Clients sometimes worry that, if one of them has the Living Will and something happens (and he or she gets close to the edge of dying), the doctor is immediately going to pull the plug, even though there still might be a slight chance for the individual to recover. This worry is unfounded. The Living Will is available to be used—but *only you* or your family decides *when* it should be used.

Only you or your family decides when your Living Will is to be used.

After years of abuse, the Living Will has finally come into its own and is recognized and accepted nationwide. The problem today is that when there is an emergency, doctors and hospitals will put someone on life support if they lack the proper legal documentation at the time, the Living Will (or Durable Power of Attorney for Health Care, in some states). This is a serious problem today, because once someone is put on life support, it is a difficult struggle to get him or her off of it.

There is a simple solution: give a copy of your Living Will (or Durable Power of Attorney for Health Care, as applicable) to your doctors, and take it to the hospital when you enter for elective surgery. I suggest also having a copy readily available to you, or your immediate family, in the event of an emergency. As long as your doctor and hospital know your wishes in advance—they will abide by them.

As long as your doctor and hospital know your wishes in advance—they will abide by them.

The Doctor-Patient Relationship

Occasionally, a client will comment, "When mother was in that condition, her doctor let her go without putting her on an artificial life-support system; therefore, I don't see any need for the Living Will." When my own grandmother died at ninety-seven years of age, her doctor suggested that we keep her as comfortable as possible but quietly let her go. However, this doctor had been her doctor and mine for over twenty years, and we knew each other extremely well. Unfortunately, because people in the United States today have become a transient society, people change doctors regularly. The formerly close relationship between a person's family and the family doctor has nearly become history. The result is a strained doctor-patient relationship.

Some years ago, two doctors were subjected to the rigors of a murder trial because of actions they took on behalf of their patient (and with the agreement of the patient's spouse). Even though the doctors were eventually found innocent, the agony of having to go through a murder trial was more than anyone would want to face.

As I recall the circumstances, the husband had gone in for elective surgery. Something had gone wrong with the anesthesia, and, after the surgery, the husband was effectively brain-dead. The doctors so advised the wife and suggested that her husband be taken off the life-support system—and the wife concurred.

However, when the husband was taken off the life-support system, his life continued. The doctors then directed the nurse to remove the intravenous feeding tube, which was providing nourishment to the husband's body, but the nurse refused the doctor's request. Eventually, the intravenous feeding tube was removed, and the man died. At that point, the nurse told the wife that her husband would still be living if the doctors had not removed the feeding tube. Upon hearing this news, the wife filed a criminal complaint.

Under these circumstances, if I were a doctor, I, too, would require the Living Will before taking such life-or-death action on behalf of a patient.

As of this writing, all states recognize either the Living Will (forty-seven states) or a supplemental form, the Durable Power of Attorney for Health Care, which authorizes an individual to make these decisions for you. (Note: The Living Will currently is not recognized by the states of Massachusetts, Michigan, and New York.) We provide both documents, the Living Will and the Durable Power of Attorney for Health Care, because the Living Will has always been upheld by the courts whenever challenged, whereas the Durable Power of Attorney for Health Care has not been subjected to the same test. We still provide the Living Will even for those clients in Massachusetts, Michigan, and New York, because we anticipate that their legislatures will eventually adopt the Living Will. The U.S. Supreme Court has already set the appropriate precedent in the Nancy Cruzan case (discussed earlier). However, some states require the Living Will to be re-signed and redated (and preferably rewitnessed) every five years. This five-year re-signing of the Living Will has been required simply because the concept is new.

Eloquent Words

This discussion of the Right-to-Die Clause—one of the more important (but optional) provisions included with the Living Trust—is best concluded by sharing with you a significant letter, written by the late Sidney Hook, emeritus professor of philosophy at New York University, published in the *New York Times* in March 1987, and reprinted here with his permission:

A few short years ago, I lay at the point of death. A congestive heart failure was treated for diagnostic purposes by an angiogram that triggered a stroke. Violent and painful hiccups, uninterrupted for several days and nights, prevented the ingestion of food. My left side and one of my vocal cords became paralyzed. Some form of pleurisy set in, and I felt I was drowning in a sea of slime. At one point, my heart stopped beating; just as I lost consciousness, it was thumped back into action again. In one of my lucid intervals during those days of agony, I asked my physician to discontinue all life-supporting services or show me how to do it. He refused and predicted that someday I would appreciate the unwisdom of my request.

A month later, I was discharged from the hospital. In six months, I regained the use of my limbs, and although my voice still lacks its old resonance and carrying power, I no longer croak like a frog. There remain some minor disabilities, and I am restricted to a rigorous, low-sodium diet. I have resumed my writing and research.

My experience can be, and has been, cited as an argument against honoring requests of stricken patients to be gently eased out of their pain and life. I cannot agree. There are two main reasons. As an octogenarian, there is a reasonable likelihood that I may suffer another "cardiovascular accident" or worse. I may not even be in a position to ask for the surcease of pain. It seems to me that I have already paid my dues to death—indeed, although time has softened my memories, they are vivid enough to justify my saying that I suffered enough to warrant dying several times over. Why run the risk of more?

Secondly, I dread imposing on my family and friends another grim round of misery similar to the one my first attack occasioned.

My wife and children endured enough for one lifetime. I know that, for them, the long days and nights of waiting, the disruption of their professional duties and their own familial responsibilities counted for nothing in their anxiety for me. In their joy at my recovery, they have been forgotten. Nonetheless, to visit another prolonged spell of helpless suffering on them as my life ebbs away, or even worse, if I linger on into a comatose senility, seems altogether gratuitous.

But what, it may be asked, of the joy and satisfaction of living, of basking in the sunshine, listening to music, watching one's grandchildren grow into adolescence, following the news about the fate of freedom in a troubled world, playing with ideas, writing one's testament of wisdom and folly for posterity? Is not all that one endured, together with the risk of its recurrence, an acceptable price for the multiple satisfactions that are still open even to a person of advanced years?

Apparently those who cling to life no matter what think so. I do not.

The zest and intensity of these experiences are no longer what they used to be. I am not vain enough to delude myself that I can, in the few remaining years, make an important discovery useful for mankind or can lead a social movement or do anything that will be historically eventful, no less event-making. My autobiography, which describes a record of intellectual and political experiences of some historical value, already much too long, could be posthumously published. I have had my fill of joys and sorrows and am not greedy for more life. I have always thought that a test of whether one had found happiness in one's life is whether one would be willing to relive it— whether, if it were possible, one would accept the opportunity to be born again.

Having lived a full and relatively happy life, I would cheerfully accept the chance to be reborn, but certainly not to be reborn again as an infirm octogenarian. To some extent, my views reflect what I have seen happen to the aged and stricken who have been so unfortunate as to survive crippling paralysis. They suffer, and impose suffering on others, unable even to make a request that their torment be ended.

I am mindful, too, of the burdens placed upon the community, with its rapidly diminishing resources, to provide the adequate and costly services necessary to sustain the lives of those whose days and nights are spent on mattress graves of pain. A better use could be made of these resources to increase the opportunities and qualities of life for the young. I am not denying the moral obligation the community has to look after its disabled and aged. There are times, however, when an individual may find it pointless to insist on the fulfillment of a legal and moral right.

What is required is no great revolution in morals but an enlargement of imagination and an intelligent evaluation of alternative uses of community resources.

Long ago, Seneca observed that "the wise man will live as long as he ought, not as long as he can." One can envisage hypothetical circumstances in which one has a duty to prolong one's life despite its costs for the sake of others, but such circumstances are far removed from the ordinary prospects we are considering. If wisdom is rooted in knowledge of the alternatives of choice, it must be reliably informed of the state one is in and its likely outcome. Scientific medicine is not infallible, but it is the best we have. No rational person would forgo relief from prolonged agony merely on the chance that a miraculous cure might presently be at hand. Each one should be permitted to make his own choice—especially when no one else is harmed by it.

The responsibility for the decision, whether deemed wise or foolish, must be with the chooser.

With such eloquent words about the Living Will from the firsthand perspective of one who has been to the edge of life, need I say more?

DURABLE POWER OF ATTORNEY
The Durable Power of Attorney actually consists of two separate legal documents:

- Durable Power of Attorney for Health Care
- Durable General Power of Attorney

The Durable Power of Attorney was established by the states in recent years for the specific purpose of allowing you to name an individual to act for you when you become incapacitated. The Durable Power of Attorney gives the power to the individual whom you have specified to act for you *only* when you become incompetent; the document has no application whatsoever while you are competent. Remember, however, that you must create the Durable Power of Attorney while you are competent.

The person you name in your Durable Power of Attorney while you are competent can act for you only when you are incompetent.

In contrast, the more commonly known and used "power of attorney" gives the named individual the right to act on another's behalf only while the individual is competent. Many people think that if they extend their power of attorney to someone they trust, the assignment will apply when they become incompetent. This assumption is not so. When a person becomes incompetent or dies, the power of attorney given by that individual ceases. Remember, however, that you must create the Durable Power of Attorney while you are competent.

Most legal documents are uniform throughout the fifty states—but not the Durable Power of Attorney. Each state legislature seems to have adopted its own approach. As you move from state to state, your Durable Power of Attorney is one of those documents that should be reviewed to make sure that it complies with that particular state's legal requirements.

The Durable Power of Attorney for Health Care document provided to our clients also contains the Right-to-Die Clause. However, since the Right-to-Die Clause in the Durable Power of Attorney has never been tested in the courts, each client also receives the same provision in the form of a separate document, the "Living Will"—which has been successfully upheld in every state court where there has been a challenge, as well as in the U.S. Supreme Court. This duplication is part of our effort to design a Living Trust and accompanying documents that cover all eventualities.

Durable Power of Attorney for Health Care
The primary purpose of the Durable Power of Attorney for Health Care is to appoint someone to make health care decisions. This document specifically identifies whom you would want to make medical decisions for you if you were unable to do so yourself (for example, if

you were in a coma). This person is legally known as the "attorney-in-fact." The document authorizes that person to make such health care decisions for you.

For example, if you were involved in an automobile accident, were rushed to the hospital, were unconscious, and surgery were required, the hospital and the doctors would need an authorization to perform such surgery. Such authorization can only be provided by a person who *legally* holds the Durable Power of Attorney on your behalf.

The Durable Power of Attorney for Health Care is probably one of the most important documents an unmarried person could possibly have! Most people assume that their children have the right to sign an authorization for them in an emergency, but this assumption is simply not true. Your children do *not* have the authority to authorize the doctor or hospital to perform surgery or important life-saving acts on your behalf!

Some years ago, I did a Trust for an emergency room physician who made it very clear that everyone ought to have the Durable Power of Attorney for Health Care. The doctor lamented that, when people come into the emergency room with one of their family members, they do not realize that they do *not* have the authority to act for that family member if that individual is unconscious or incompetent. Of even greater surprise to most people is that parents *cannot* authorize emergency treatment for their legally adult children!

For a married person in most emergency situations, the spouse would be recognized as having the right to sign any medical release if the other spouse is unconscious or unable to sign those papers. The spouse would not normally be required to provide a Durable Power of Attorney for Health Care. On the other hand, it is also entirely possible that something could happen to the spouse.

Even though some people might consider the Durable Power of Attorney for Health Care to be less important for a married couple, this document is provided for all of our married clients for two specific reasons. First, realize

that the husband and wife could both be involved in an automobile accident. If, for example, one of the couple were killed and the other were rushed to the hospital unconscious, who could make the appropriate medical decisions? Second, and far more important, is the case where something could happen to one spouse, leaving the surviving spouse a widow or widower. It is highly unlikely in such a stressful time that the surviving spouse will suddenly remember that he or she needs the Durable Power of Attorney for Health Care. Therefore, wise planning dictates that everyone should have the Durable Power of Attorney for Health Care—at all times and regardless of his or her medical circumstances.

For a married couple, the spouse is typically named as the attorney-in-fact. Since something could happen to the spouse, it is suggested that you also name alternate individuals ("successor attorneys") whether you are married or single. The next in line can step in on your behalf if the primary attorney-in-fact should be unable to perform the function. The successor attorney would presumably be one of your adult children, close family members, or close friends.

In case something should happen to the attorney-in-fact, you should name a successor attorney-in-fact.

Occasionally, clients ask whether they can name two or three of their children to act together. Unfortunately, the states say that only one individual may act as the attorney-in-fact at any given time. It is possible to name more than one individual, but they would be named as first successor, second successor, third successor, and so on.

Durable General Power of Attorney

The Durable General Power of Attorney is the second Durable Power of Attorney document and identifies whom you would want to assume your Durable Power of Attorney—for matters *other* than health care decisions—if you should become incompetent. This document allows a spouse (or other such designated person) to act on behalf of an individual who becomes incapacitated. The individual appointed to act for the incapacitated person is called the "principal" or "attorney-in-fact."

The Durable General Power of Attorney is of secondary use only. The person named in your Durable General Power of Attorney has absolutely no access to your assets already in your Living Trust. The sole purpose for the Durable General Power of Attorney is to permit the designated person to transfer any assets inadvertently left outside your Trust into your Trust if you become incompetent. If you have done your job and have all of your assets in your Trust, then this Durable Power of Attorney document is meaningless. One particularly beneficial use of the Durable General Power of Attorney is that it can be a powerful instrument in creating or completing a Living Trust for someone who suddenly becomes incompetent.

We find that it is prudent to name one of the successor trustees of your Living Trust as your Durable General Power of Attorney. More and more, financial institutions are being overly cautious when someone is declared incompetent. While some institutions may not be familiar with the Living Trust, they are familiar with the Durable General Power of Attorney. If your successor trustee has been named as your Durable General Power of Attorney, he or she will have absolute power to carry out your wishes in the event of incompetency. Likewise, if you have named more than one successor trustee, you should include the other successor trustees as alternates to the Durable General Power of Attorney.

The following example (returning once again to using fictitious names, but real-life experiences, of my clients) points out the usefulness of the Durable General Power of Attorney.

Some years ago, Shirley Drake called me to say that her husband had just had a stroke and was in the hospital in a coma. I said, "Shirley, did you get everything into the Trust?" She responded, "Bob got everything into the Trust except the Treasury bills; he just never got around to getting those transferred."

Since I knew that the Drakes had the Durable General Power of Attorney, I then told her that I would bring the appropriate transfer papers and immediately meet her at the hospital, outside the intensive care unit. Then I took Shirley and the transfer papers directly to the bank. With the Durable General Power of Attorney and the transfer papers, Shirley had the Treasury notes transferred into the name of the Trust.

By putting all of the Treasury bills into their Living Trust, the Drakes avoided my greatest nightmare—a client going through probate. Bob died only five days later.

If the Durable General Power of Attorney document had not been available for Bob Drake, then the Treasury bills could *not* have been transferred into the Drakes' Living Trust—and nothing could have been legally done. This situation does not occur often. When it does, however, the Durable General Power of Attorney document can be *extremely* important.

Only one person at a time can be named as having your Durable General Power of Attorney.

Our firm has recently discovered another very vital use for the Durable General Power of Attorney: The person holding such power can create a Living Trust for you, if you are incompetent.

Recently, a retired admiral's wife used the Durable General Power of Attorney in a most effective way. The admiral and his wife had begun their Living Trust process, but they had not yet gotten to the final stage of signing the documents.

The admiral, who swam eight miles daily and appeared to be in excellent health, and his wife went to Arkansas, so that he could participate in a national swim meet. However, in the midst of the swim meet, the admiral suffered a massive heart attack and was rushed to a local hospital, where he was immediately placed on life support.

At the wife's request, we rushed the now-completed Trust documents to her in Arkansas. The admiral's wife signed them for herself, and, having her husband's Durable General Power of Attorney, she signed the documents on his behalf as well. Signing of the documents was completed by noon; the hospital took the admiral off life support shortly afterward, and he passed away by 1:30 P.M.

You never know when the Durable General Power of Attorney may be a most helpful document.

COMPETENCY CLAUSE

If an individual were to become incompetent—for example, as the result of an accident, a stroke, or senility—management of the individual's assets must continue. Someone would still need to be able to buy, sell, or transfer the assets and to write the monthly checks. Without the Competency Clause, a member of the family would eventually be forced to go into the courts and suffer through the rather degrading process of establishing incompetency. However, with the Competency Clause, the legal process is very much simplified. In our Living Trust, we specify that the attending physician, plus a doctor of his or her choice, may simply write a letter to the effect that you are no longer competent—thus, making the Competency Clause a universal provision that applies in every state. Then whomever you have designated to act on your behalf would have the power to carry on for you.

The Competency Clause applies only to indisputable situations.

The Competency Clause is an extremely important document. All too often, however, clients hesitate to incorporate this provision into their Trusts because they are concerned that someone might "take advantage" of it. However, rest assured that this provision is for a black-or-white (yes-or-no) area, not a gray (maybe) area. The only time the doctors are going to be involved is when the case is very clear (usually if you are in a coma or are clearly senile). The doctors are not going to be involved in a borderline medical decision or a family dispute over a questionable condition. Thus, the Competency Clause works *for* your protection.

Robert Sinclair's mother-in-law called him one day and asked him to rush up to meet her in a small town some forty miles away. Upon his arrival, Mr. Sinclair was informed that his mother-in-law had lost control of all her funds, and he was handed a two-page legal form. The last paragraph of the form stated, "This woman has been making poor investments, has been losing money, and in order to preserve her assets, I ask that I be appointed her conservator." The legal document was signed by an attorney who had befriended the woman. The court had approved the request, and the attorney had taken control of her assets. In actuality, the woman had not made any poor investments; she had, as a matter of fact, more than doubled her estate since her husband had passed away some ten years before. Regardless, the court granted the attorney's request, and the attorney had control of the woman's assets.

Steps were taken in the courts to have control returned to the woman, but the process took over six months and incurred substantial legal costs—as well as the fees extracted by the attorney who had made himself conservator of her estate.

If, in contrast, the woman had done as her daughter had been urging for the past two years—and had created a Living Trust—she would have named her daughter as the logical successor trustee. If, under these circumstances, an attorney were foolish enough to ask a court to determine that the woman was incompetent, then the daughter would take over as successor trustee—not some little-known attorney. Obviously, no attorney is going to waste time under such circumstances. Had the woman followed her daughter's advice, she would have saved herself substantial grief and expense.

The Competency Clause can be a protection against unscrupulous people attempting to exploit elderly and often infirm individuals. With the Competency Clause, *you* control who is to look after your estate if you become incompetent.

What Can Happen Without It

An excellent example of the need for the Competency Clause happened some years ago when a client who had initially elected to exclude the provision called to tell me of the following dilemma.

The client and his wife had sold their home, escrow had closed, and they had received a check for $125,000. The time was a Friday afternoon, and the client wanted to put the money to work. The client took the check to the bank, endorsed it, and handed it to the teller. The teller explained that the check also needed the signature of the client's wife. The client explained that his wife had suffered a stroke a week earlier and could not sign the check—and, in fact, was dying. The bank teller sympathized with my client, but she explained that the bank could not accept the check without the signature of both parties.

At this point, the client called me in sheer frustration. I explained to the client that, if he had the Competency Clause, it would be a very simple matter to get a letter (from the appropriate two doctors) stating that his wife had suffered a stroke and was no longer competent. With the signed letter and the Trust document, the client could resubmit the check to the bank, and it would be accepted under the Competency Clause.

However, since the client lacked the Competency Clause, he had only two other options available to him. The client could go into the courts and be subjected to the process of establishing incompetency (which would take six to eight weeks); alternately, he could wait until his wife died (which the doctors said would probably take six to eight weeks). The client elected to wait until his wife died; however, he called me every other week complaining that he was losing $30 a day in interest. I could only commiserate with him.

Seven weeks later, the client's wife finally died. The following day, with the death certificate in hand, the client finally deposited the check in the bank.

If the client had included the Competency Clause in his Living Trust, none of the delay would have been necessary.

If You Regain Competency

All of the necessary protections are built into the Competency Clause. If you regain your competency, the doctors can certify your competency and reinstate you as before, simply by writing a letter. On the other hand, if you disagree with the decision of the doctors, you have the right to solicit legal recourse in the courts—that is, the right to have the court determine your competency.

CATASTROPHIC ILLNESS TRUST

Congress attempted to destroy the Catastrophic Illness Trust with the Kennedy-Kassenbaum Act of 1996. However, a few years later, the Kennedy-Kassenbaum Act of 1996 went down in flames as the attorney general concluded that it was unconstitutional. I believe that the Catastrophic Illness Trust can be vital to many families with a catastrophic illness.

A catastrophic illness is an illness that is onerously expensive in relation to the size of the estate. Not only can it take its toll on a person's health (and eventually be terminal), but it can also be financially devastating.

With the progress of modern medicine, life expectancy has substantially increased, and it is becoming more and more frequent for one spouse to suffer a catastrophic illness. For example, one of the most costly illnesses for elderly people is Alzheimer's disease, a condition that involves slow mental and physical deterioration, ultimately requiring institutionalized care that eventually exhausts most family estates and leaves the surviving spouse poverty stricken. The prospect of getting Alzheimer's disease increases with age. Today, 5 percent of people age sixty-five have the disease, and the occurrence increases to 10 percent by age eighty-five.

My experience bears this out. For the past twenty years, I have watched an average of four couples come into our offices each month trying desperately to save some of their hard-earned estates after learning that one of the spouses has Alzheimer's.

While ideally everyone should have long-term medical insurance to provide for such contingencies, this insurance is prohibitively expensive, and even unattainable, for far too many people. Granted, large estates can usually afford the cost of a catastrophic illness, but small estates can be totally consumed by the financial drain. For example, a medical bill of $400,000 may not be catastrophic to a $1 million estate, but it would be *devastating* to an estate worth $400,000. When a couple faces a catastrophic illness for one spouse, the other spouse can be left penniless. I believe this was a congressional oversight and one that must be addressed without delay.

One specific example of a very sad case I have worked with is that of a widow who was barely able to hold on to her home.

> The woman and her husband had worked hard over the years and had saved their golden nest egg for their retirement years together. Then, just as the husband turned fifty-four years old, he was laid off by his company so that it would not have to pay retirement or lifetime medical benefits (for which the husband would become eligible at age fifty-five). As a result, the husband had only one year of medical coverage following his dismissal.
>
> Shortly after the medical coverage ceased, the husband was diagnosed with cancer; over the next ten years, the couple's golden nest egg disappeared in medical expenses. When the husband finally died, he left his widow all but penniless, with only their house as her sole possession. Their lifelong dreams of a retirement together had vanished.

We have developed two types of Catastrophic Illness Trusts, the Family Catastrophic Trust and the Irrevocable Catastrophic Illness Trust. Most families will find that the Family Catastrophic Illness Trust will be appropriate. It is a revocable Trust in which the children are designated the trustees and their primary respon-sibility is to use the funds in this Trust to take care of Mother and Dad. This Trust, once put into effect, requires three years before it can act as a protection. On the other hand, if you don't trust your children, then you may choose the Irrevocable Catastrophic Illness Trust. You may name whomever you desire to be the trustee(s). However, once this Trust is put into effect, it requires five years before it can act as a protection.

ASSIGNMENT OF PERSONAL EFFECTS

Many people overlook the transfer of personal property into a Living Trust. However, because it is quite easy nowadays for the average couple to accumulate personal property whose value exceeds the probate limits, all of the Living Trusts drawn for our clients include a separate document titled "Assignment of Furniture, Furnishings, and Personal Effects." This document is used for items that typically do not have written title—such as personal and household effects (furniture, appliances, pictures, china, silverware, glass, books, jewelry, clothing, and so on). Historically, personal effects and household items have simply been left outside the Trust and passed to the surviving spouse; if there is no spouse, typically the assets are passed to the children. Depending on the state, the value of an estate that requires probate ranges from $10,000 to $100,000. Visualize, if you will, the following scenario.

> For simplicity, assume that a deceased individual's personal effects are worth $80,000. In most cases, this situation is not a real problem, because the assets are simply distributed "under the table" to the heirs (without reporting the assets to the attorney). However, assume that one child says, "I want all the books." The child is told, "No, you cannot have all the books; they will be divided equally." Unfortunately, this child knows a friend who knows an attorney. The child announces that he or she understands that, since the personal effects exceed the dollar amount subject to probate (and if the child is not given all the books), the child will blow the whistle and thereby cause *all* the personal effects to go through probate!

Given the choice of taking all of the personal effects through the onerous process of probate or giving the child the books, guess what alternative the heirs will choose. Obviously, the child gets all the books.

The language of our Living Trust is structured to avoid just such a situation. With the Transfer of Personal Property document, our clients transfer all of their personal effects into the Living Trust—that is, all of today's personal assets and all personal assets they may acquire in the future. *The personal effects are transferred without a detailed inventory.* Chapter 13 describes how you can use a Memorandum to identify any personal effects that you wish to pass to someone special.

APPOINTMENT OF GUARDIAN

In the past, the Appointment of Guardian provision was usually included as a part of the Pour-Over Will. However, our experience has taught us that it is far more effective to use a separate single-page document to identify the guardian. The Appointment of Guardian document is used for minor children and also applies to handicapped individuals regardless of age.

It is customary to name a guardian until children reach the age of twenty-one. Most states have established that a child legally becomes an adult at age eighteen and is, thereafter, no longer subject to the guardian. Even though a child who is eighteen years of age may walk away on his or her own, by naming a guardian you have identified to whom you would want the child to return for advice and counsel if both parents were no longer living.

A guardian should also be appointed for adult children who are mentally or physically handicapped. Designation of a guardian also allows the parents to identify whom they would want to care for their adult handicapped child if something happened to both parents.

The appointment of a guardian is a very important decision for any parent to make. As you go through life, you establish certain goals and objectives, and you find others with similar goals and objectives. These people may be close family members, or they may be close friends. As many of our clients have discovered, if you go to the person whom you would appoint as a guardian and tell him or her that you have a Living Trust that will provide for your children financially and that you hope that he or she would provide for your children morally, spiritually, and educationally if both parents die, such an approach has almost always been received favorably.

Many times, people name a brother and his wife, or a sister and her husband, as co-guardians. Stop for a moment and think what would happen if your brother or sister died or got divorced. Would you want the spouse to be a guardian? Be aware that such awkward situations are always possible. Before you make a decision, carefully think about the alternatives available to you. You may simply decide to name your brother or sister as guardian, for example.

If both parents die without having legally appointed a guardian for their surviving children, the courts must appoint a guardian without knowing the parents' desires.

If both parents die without having legally appointed a guardian for their surviving minor children, the courts must appoint a guardian—without the benefit of knowing the parents' desires and preferences. There is not a court in the land that would not say, "Please don't place this burden upon me." People think that such a situation will never happen to them. Most people tend to feel immortal. Unfortunately, in the past ten years, I have had two sets of very close friends killed in automobile accidents; in both instances, they left orphaned children. In each case, the guardian appointed by the court was unfortunately not the one the deceased parents would have selected—and the results have been tragic!

If you have grown children, *please* convey the following message to them: Every parent should name an appropriate guardian (or guardians) for their minor children. To do otherwise ultimately may seriously jeopardize their children's future, if something were to happen to the parents.

Alternate Guardian

If your children are eleven years of age or younger, you should always name an alternate guardian. With a guardian being responsible for your children until they reach the age of twenty-one, there are often just too many years to elapse until the child reaches twenty-one, or at least eighteen. During those intervening years, the guardian specified in your Appointment of Guardian document could die. When that situation happens, if you are still living, you usually do not suddenly remember that you must change your guardian document. If you are not living, who would select another guardian for your children? Thus, it is wise at any time to name an alternate guardian—and it is *essential* to do so when your children are eleven years old or younger.

Single-Page Document

The Appointment of Guardian document included with our Living Trusts has evolved into a single-page document, which allows the named guardian to be easily changed from time to time as your particular situation may dictate. The Appointment of Guardian form works extremely well when parents have divorced and remarried.

A common situation involves a mother with very young children who becomes divorced and then remarries. Many years may have passed, and her present husband (although not having adopted the children) has effectively become their father. The mother elects to name her present husband as the guardian of her children upon her death. Of course, the children's biological father has certain legal rights to these children if the mother dies. On the other hand, the court is always concerned with the best interests of the children, and guardian papers naming the mother's current husband (the acting father) as the guardian can carry much weight.

The guardian of your children and the trustee of your Trust need not be the same person; one is responsible for your children, and the other is responsible for your assets.

APPOINTMENT OF CONSERVATOR

The Appointment of Conservator document identifies the individual who is to be responsible for your *person* if you become incompetent. This document should not be confused with the Competency Clause, which authorizes the successor trustee to administer the *assets* of your estate if you become incompetent.

The conservator becomes responsible for ensuring your safety and well-being. For example, if you were to become afflicted with Alzheimer's disease, eventually the Competency Clause would be used to authorize your successor trustee to step in and manage your assets and finances. The conservator you name should be the person you would trust to place you in a nursing home if necessary—to provide you with the kindest and the finest care possible.

Historically, Living Trusts have been concerned with managing and distributing the assets of an estate. Sadly, however, more and more people are becoming incompetent because of Alzheimer's disease and other maladies of age. Under these circumstances (and without the appropriate provisions in a Living Trust), the family finds it necessary to go into court to be appointed conservator of the afflicted individual.

It is the aim of our Living Trusts and accompanying documents to make it as simple as possible for our clients to manage their estates (and, where possible, to avoid the court process). Of even greater importance to our clients, however, is their desire to be the ones to identify (while they are competent) whom they want to be responsible for their person if they should later become incompetent. Therefore, the Appointment of Conservator provision is included with all of our Living Trusts.

No one likes to think of the possibility of going to a nursing home. In fact, almost everyone abhors the aging process. Unfortunately, all too often I have witnessed the agony of the transition process from home to a nursing home—not only with my clients, but also with my own family. At least with the Appointment of Conservator provision, along with a Living Trust, an individual is able to name that person in whom he or she has the greatest trust.

ANATOMICAL GIFT

With the Anatomical Gift document, you gift your vital organs upon your death, allowing them to be used to save other people's lives or to provide sight to elderly people with glaucoma. In many states, you may accomplish the same thing by simply filling out a small form and attaching it to the back of your driver's license. However, because so many of our clients asked for the Anatomical Gift as a separate legal document, the Anatomical Gift document was included with our Living Trusts as a separate (but optional) legal document some ten years ago.

Shortly after we had drafted the Anatomical Gift document, a doctor came in with his wife to create a Living Trust. When the doctor saw the Anatomical Gift provision, he immediately complimented us for providing the document, and he then related the following personal incident.

When the doctor first met his wife, she had the anatomical gift card on the back of her driver's license, and he immediately made her remove it. As a doctor, he recognized the enormous need for vital organs. However, he stated that, when an individual is in that gray area between life and death, there is often a tendency on the part of the medical profession to want to take those vital organs prematurely. The doctor said, "I don't want anyone making that decision except myself."

The man made that statement as a husband, not as a doctor. I have since had three other medical personnel express the same view.

As a result of such experiences, the Anatomical Gift provision is recommended for those people who are kind and generous enough to want to give their vital organs to others upon their death. However, it is further recommended to our clients that they keep this legal document at home in the possession of their families—not on the back of their driver's licenses, where the decision to remove vital organs may be made by someone who has never seen the clients before. Our clients are advised that the ideal place to keep the Anatomical Gift document is inside the Estate Plan Binder (which will be described in Chapter 13).

Not for Everyone

The Anatomical Gift provision does not appeal to everyone. Therefore, as a matter of course, we ask our clients whether they are interested in it. About 20 percent of our clients respond very positively, about 20 percent respond negatively, and the rest of our clients simply have no opinion on the subject.

I am often asked at what age one is too old to donate organs. A recent news article reporting the accidental death of a sixty-five-year-old woman stated that, since her death, she was responsible for saving two lives and giving two other people the gift of sight. How nice it would be if more people would consider being so generous.

Cost of Removing and Transporting Vital Organs

Occasionally a client asks, "If I donate my vital organs, will my family be burdened with the cost of removing and transporting those organs?" The answer is no. If the family gives permission, the organs are harvested, and the bill goes to the hospital. The hospital has an arrangement with the federal government, which reimburses the hospital through Medicare.

SATISFYING EVERY CONTINGENCY

To recap, although not legally necessary, it is greatly to your benefit for your Living Trust to include several important ancillary documents as discussed in this chapter, such as the Living Will (the Right-to-Die Clause); the Durable Power of Attorney for Health Care; the Durable General Power of Attorney; the Competency Clause; the Assignment of Furniture, Furnishings, and Personal Effects (into your Living Trust); the Appointment of Guardian (for your minor and/or handicapped children, where appropriate); and the Appointment of Conservator. All of these documents are an essential part of a well-written Trust.

In addition to these essential documents, you may wish to add an Anatomical Gift document, which should be available at no cost.

These important ancillary documents, when included with your Living Trust, should satisfy every potential contingency—now and in the years to come.

——————————————————————— 12 ———————————————————————

Estate Preservation and Tax-Saving Documents

To shelter your hard-earned estate from unnecessary estate taxes, you should consider several other documents to supplement your Living Trust:

- Insurance Preservation Trust
- Spousal and Family Support Trust
- Gift Trust
- Generation-Skipping Trust
- Spousal Gift
- Family Limited Partnership
- Charitable Remainder Trust

The Insurance Preservation Trust is significant and common, and therefore a substantial part of this chapter will be devoted to it. The Spousal and Family Support Trust is designed to use life insurance for the support of a surviving spouse and family. The Gift Trust is an ideal vehicle to curb inflationary tax growth and simultaneously provide for the needs of your children and/or grandchildren. The Generation-Skipping Trust has great tax-saving applications for both single persons and married couples. The Spousal Gift has limited use;

however, it can be very important in specific situations. The Family Limited Partnership can protect your estate from lawsuits, as well as substantially reduce estate taxes. The Charitable Remainder Trust can be an incredibly powerful tool in reducing capital gains taxes, as well as in reducing or eliminating estate taxes for large estates. In fact, the Charitable Remainder Trust should be considered by any single person with an estate that exceeds $1 million and any married couple with an estate that exceeds $2 million.

Each of these documents has its own place in estate planning. Therefore, each should be considered in conjunction with creating a Living Trust.

LIFE INSURANCE

Before you can appreciate the Insurance Preservation Trust, you need a basic understanding of the concept of life insurance. Why should you have life insurance? Who should own the life insurance? Who should be its beneficiary? How much should you pay for it?

Purposes of Insurance

There are basically two prime purposes for insurance: to supplement your estate (and provide for your family in the event of your premature death) and to pay estate taxes if your estate exceeds the federal estate tax equivalent exemption.

Providing for Family

A person's primary estate-planning objective should be to build an estate that is sufficient to eventually provide for his or her needs. In the interim, if the assets are insufficient to meet the needs of the family, then the individual has a responsibility to insure against the loss of income by premature death.

When your family is young, particularly when you have children, the loss of the family provider can be disastrous.

Years ago, I walked into the hospital room of a dear friend who was dying of bone cancer. When I opened the door, his wife was with him and he was in tears, so I quickly withdrew. Some moments later, I was invited back into the room, and my friend told me that he was in tears because he knew that his cancer was terminal and that he had not provided adequate insurance for his wife and seven young children.

My friend died several months later. However, I watched in admiration as that mother of seven went back to school to get her master's degree—all the while struggling to raise her children on what little money was available.

The woman has done a magnificent job, but how different it could have been if her husband had left enough insurance to adequately provide for the family's well-being. This husband and father loved his family dearly and had provided for his family in all but one area.

Because life insurance is designed to protect against such a loss of income, insurance on children and unmarried individuals is a waste of money. When a couple gets married, the two people should consider life insurance on either or both of their lives, *especially* when they decide to have children.

Paying Estate Taxes

Ideally, as you build the value of your estate, you will have less need for insurance as a means of providing for the family welfare, and you can eventually replace it with the assets of your estate. Many individuals will eventually get to a crucial crossing point—that is, when their assets exceed the federal estate tax equivalent exemption described in Chapter 5 ($1 million for a single person and $2 million for a married couple). At this point, the need for life insurance again arises, because the cheapest way to pay estate taxes on the assets that exceed the exemption is with insurance. Although this use of insurance may seem strange to you, the reasoning will be explained in more detail later in this chapter.

In deciding whether your estate is large enough to need this benefit of insurance, remember that upon the death of an individual, life insurance becomes an *asset* of the estate. Thus, its value will be included as part of the estate for the purpose of determining estate taxes. Over 50 percent of the clients who come into my office are shocked to learn that life insurance is subject to federal estate taxes.

Estate Tax—Single Person	
Total estate (other assets plus insurance)	$1,200,000
Less: Federal estate tax exclusion	($1,000,000)
Taxable estate	$ 200,000
Federal estate tax	$ 82,000

If, for example, you are single, with assets of $800,000 and insurance of $400,000, your total estate on your death would be $1.2 million. Using the single person's federal estate tax exclusion of $1 million would leave a taxable estate of $200,000. The federal estate tax on the additional $200,000 would be approximately $82,000.

The cheapest way to pay estate taxes is with life insurance.

If you are married and have an estate of $1.8 million plus life insurance with a value of

$600,000, upon your death, your total estate would be $2.4 million. If you and your spouse have an A-B Trust, $2 million of the estate could be sheltered from federal estate taxes. However, $400,000 of your estate would still be subject to federal estate tax. The federal estate tax on the additional $400,000 would be approximately $162,000!

Estate Tax—Married Couple	
Total estate (other assets plus insurance)	$ 2,400,000
Less: Federal estate tax exclusion	($ 2,000,000)
Taxable estate	$ 400,000
Federal estate tax	$ 162,000

Who Should Own the Insurance

Today, the person who is being insured should be the owner of the life insurance policies. The reason is that most life insurance policies have little value until the individual dies, and then the value is considered a death benefit, which is specifically exempted from probate. Therefore, it is not necessary for the Living Trust to be the owner of the policy.

Instead, your Living Trust should *always* be named as the "beneficiary" (to receive the funds paid out by the insurance company) unless you have an Insurance Preservation Trust. The Living Trust could be the owner, but taking such an action requires additional paperwork, which would be meaningless, because the insurance policy does not attain its full value until the death of an individual. At that time, if the Living Trust is the *named beneficiary*, the payout funds will flow into the Trust.

Upon the death of an insured spouse, the insurance is considered to be owned by both husband and wife, because the premium is assumed to have been paid from joint funds. The payout will, therefore, flow half into the husband's estate and half into the wife's estate—which is preferable in order to gain the maximum tax benefits of an A-B Trust.

The Best Beneficiary: The Living Trust

All of our clients are advised that their Living Trusts should be the beneficiaries of their insurance policies unless they have an Insurance Preservation Trust. There are two reasons for this advice. First, of course, is to eliminate the possibility of any probate. The insurance payout will pass to the *named beneficiary* without having to go through probate—one of the benefits of a life insurance policy.

However, consider the following scenario.

Assume a husband and wife are driving down the highway and are involved in an automobile collision, and both the husband and wife are killed. The insurance money from the husband's policy would pass to the named beneficiary (presumably the wife's estate) probate-free, but the wife's estate must now go through probate before the insurance money can be passed to their children. Admittedly, some people could be sophisticated enough to have named *contingent* beneficiaries, but years of experience have shown that these people are definitely in the minority.

The second, and even greater, reason for making your Living Trust the beneficiary of your life insurance is that your insurance policy (as so many other documents) takes *precedence* over your Will—which, of course, should be your Living Trust.

If you don't have an Insurance Preservation Trust, the best beneficiary of your life insurance is your Living Trust.

As people go through life, they often (and many times without much thought) name beneficiaries of their assets in all forms, which take precedence over their Trusts or Wills. Examples of such assets are life insurance, Keogh plans, IRAs, pension plans, profit-sharing plans, 401(k) plans, property held in joint tenancy, and others—the list goes on and on. As the following example points out, the insurance money may not always be paid to the desired individuals.

Four years ago, some clients who already had a Trust of their own brought in their brother-in-law to create a Living Trust. After the Trust was drawn, the brother-in-law's condominium was transferred into the Trust. Within the next few days, the clients worked with the brother-in-law to get his other assets transferred into the Trust. However, they somehow overlooked his National Service Life Insurance policy (taken out during the waning days of World War II).

Having just drawn the brother-in-law's Living Trust, I knew exactly to whom he wanted to leave his assets. Since the man's wife had died and he didn't have children, he named specific family members to receive the assets of his estate. When he took out his National Service Life Insurance policy in 1945, he designated his wife as primary beneficiary and his two nephews as secondary, or contingent, beneficiaries.

Since the brother-in-law's wife had predeceased him by some five years, when he died, his $10,000 National Service Life Insurance policy was paid to his two nephews. The nephews had not been named in the brother-in-law's Trust, and they were not part of his currently desired heirs. In fact, there was reason to believe that the brother-in-law had not communicated with his nephews in over twenty-five years!

If the brother-in-law had named his Living Trust as the beneficiary, the proceeds from that $10,000 life insurance policy would have flowed into his Living Trust, and the insurance money would have then been distributed to the desired heirs as specified in the Trust.

Estate Taxation of Insurance

More than half of our clients are convinced, or have been told by someone else, that their life insurance is "tax-free." Unfortunately, although the income on life insurance has been exempt from income taxes, life insurance is—similar to any other asset of an estate—subject to federal estate taxes. Upon the death of an individual, an insurance company converts the deceased person's insurance policy into a check for a specific amount of money. That money is added to the individual's estate and becomes subject to estate taxes.

Life insurance benefits are not exempt from estate taxation.

Therefore, in analyzing your estate, you should compute your net worth and then add the value of any insurance carried on the husband and the wife. The reason for including the value of insurance of both husband and wife is that, if your estate planning is done properly, no estate taxes will be computed until the death of the second spouse; therefore, insurance on both spouses will ultimately be included in the estate computations.

An A-B Trust can be used to avoid unnecessary estate taxation on insurance. To see how, let's examine the difference between an A Trust and an A-B Trust on a $1.2 million estate.

Without an A-B Trust

If a husband and wife have $400,000 of insurance and $800,000 of other assets, they have a total estate of $1.2 million. With only an A Trust, the entire estate of $1.2 million would come down to the surviving spouse, as shown in Figure 12-1. Upon the death of the surviving spouse, since the surviving spouse has only one federal estate tax exclusion of $1 million,

---

FIGURE 12-1
ESTATE TAXATION OF $1.2 MILLION ESTATE WITH AN A TRUST

Other assets		$ 800,000
Insurance		400,000
Total estate		$1,200,000
Surviving Spouse A Trust		
Total estate	$1,200,000	$1,200,000
Less: Federal estate		
tax exclusion	($1,000,000)	
Taxable estate	$ 200,000	
Federal estate tax	$ 82,000	($ 82,000)
Estate passing to heirs		$1,118,000

the excess estate of $200,000 would be subject to federal estate tax. A federal estate tax of $82,000 would leave only $1,118,000 for the heirs.

With an A-B Trust

If the husband and wife have an A-B Trust, the estate tax picture would look much brighter, as shown in Figure 12-2. Upon the death of the first spouse, half of the estate ($600,000) would come down to the surviving spouse in the Survivor's A Trust, and the other half of the estate would come down to the Decedent's Trust B. Since the Decedent's Trust B is valued at less than $1 million, no federal estate tax would be due, and Trust B would then be insulated from further estate taxes. Upon the death of the surviving spouse, only the assets in the surviving spouse's Trust A could be considered for estate tax purposes. Since the surviving spouse also has an exclusion of $1 million, no federal estate tax would be due. The net result is that the *entire* $1.2 million in the original estate would pass down to the heirs.

FIGURE 12-2
ESTATE TAXATION OF $1.2 MILLION ESTATE WITH AN A-B TRUST

Other assets	$ 800,000
Insurance	400,000
Total estate	$1,200,000

Surviving Spouse A-B Trust

	Decedent's Trust B	Surviving Spouse's Trust A
Total estate	$ 600,000	$ 600,000
Less: Federal estate tax exclusion	($1,000,000)	($1,000,000)
Taxable estate	-0-	-0-
Federal estate tax	-0-	-0-
Estate passing to heirs		$1,200,000

How Much to Pay for Insurance

In most cases, if you have done proper estate planning and have a Living Trust, the estate taxes for a married couple need to be paid only when the second spouse dies. When life insurance is being used for the purpose of ultimately paying federal estate taxes, you should consider *joint and survivor life insurance*. This type of coverage provides insurance on both spouses, but is payable only upon the death of the second spouse—precisely when you need the insurance money to pay the estate taxes. This kind of insurance will cost only about half of what it would if the insurance were carried on the life of only one of the spouses.

INSURANCE PRESERVATION TRUST

The primary benefit of an Insurance Preservation Trust is that it enables you to place a life insurance policy (which is effectively valueless while you are living) inside the Insurance Preservation Trust, without any gift tax consequences. (Only the premium is considered to be a gift and usually can be excluded under the annual $10,000 gift exclusion rule.) The insurance takes on value only upon the death of the insured, at which time the insurance company will pay the face value of the insurance policy to the trustee of the Insurance Preservation Trust.

Unlike the Living Trust, an Insurance Preservation Trust is an *irrevocable* Trust, which means that it is unchangeable. Nevertheless, you effectively still maintain control over the Trust. Even though the trustee cannot cancel an insurance policy, you already know that, the moment you cease paying the policy premiums, the insurance company will cancel that policy. Thus, you can change insurance policies, if necessary.

It is important that you name your heirs—typically your children—as beneficiaries of your Insurance Preservation Trust. Do *not* name your Living Trust as a beneficiary. The IRS has recently sought out and disallowed Insurance Trusts in which the Living Trust has been named a beneficiary—under the premise that there is insufficient "arm's length" in this relationship.

Estate Tax Savings

The Insurance Preservation Trust should be the owner/beneficiary of your insurance policies. (If you have any cash value in your insurance policy, you should borrow it out before transferring the policy into the Insurance Preservation Trust.) Since the Insurance Preservation Trust is irrevocable and is the owner/beneficiary of the insurance, funds paid by the insurance company upon the death of the insured are effectively removed from your estate for estate tax purposes. Yet you may still use these funds to provide for your surviving spouse, to pass on to your children, and to pay estate taxes. Thus, the Insurance Preservation Trust gives you the best of both worlds.

Some examples will show how the Insurance Preservation Trust can save you unnecessary estate taxes.

Single Person

As you will recall from earlier in this chapter, the federal estate tax on a combined estate of $800,000 in assets and $400,000 of insurance is $82,000. Assume you have an Insurance Preservation Trust and place the $400,000 insurance policy in the Insurance Preservation Trust. Upon your death, the $400,000 life insurance will be excluded from your estate, as shown in Figure 12-3.

Married Couple

Although an A-B Living Trust can shelter an estate of a married couple where the net worth and insurance are valued at less than $2 million, when the total of all assets including insurance exceeds $2 million, an Insurance Preservation Trust is strongly recommended. Let's look at the different tax consequences of an estate of a married couple worth $2.5 million, first using an example of an A-B-C Trust without an Insurance Preservation Trust, and then using an example of an A-B Trust coupled with an Insurance Preservation Trust. In both examples, assume an estate of $2 million plus $500,000 of life insurance.

As you learned in earlier chapters, with a total estate valued at $2.5 million, the couple can benefit from using an A-B-C Trust. As

shown in Figure 12-4 and previously explained in Chapter 6, upon the death of one spouse, the surviving spouse can elect to defer paying any taxes. However, on the death of the second spouse, there will be $210,000 of unnecessary estate tax.

In contrast, let's see what happens to the same estate using an A-B Trust along with an Insurance Preservation Trust. Figure 12-5 shows that the combination of the two types of Trusts avoids any federal estate taxes.

The Insurance Preservation Trust is a separate Trust, so the insurance of $500,000 in the Insurance Preservation Trust is no longer considered to be an asset of the estate, but rather is considered an asset of the Insurance Preservation Trust. With no insurance in the estate per se, the entire value of the estate is therefore $2 million.

Upon the death of the surviving spouse, no estate taxes would be due. Trust B would then be insulated from further estate taxes. The proceeds from the insurance in the Insurance Preservation Trust would also eventually flow down to the heirs (after the second spouse

FIGURE 12-3 TAXATION OF SINGLE PERSON'S $1.2 MILLION ESTATE		
	Without Insurance Preservation Trust	With Insurance Preservation Trust
Other assets	$ 800,000	$ 800,000
Insurance	400,000	400,000
Total estate	$1,200,000	$1,200,000
Insurance Preservation Trust	-0-	($ 400,000)
Taxable estate	$1,200,000	$ 800,000
Less: Federal estate tax exclusion	($1,000,000)	($1,000,000)
Taxable excess	$ 200,000	-0-
Estate tax	$ 82,000	-0-

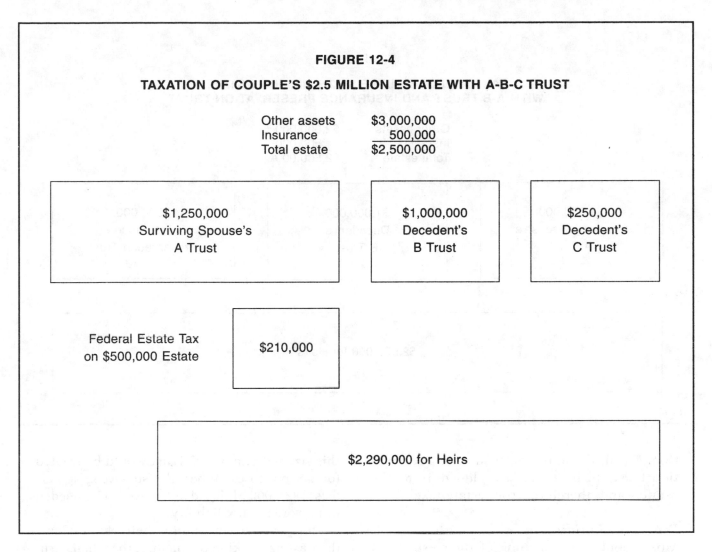

FIGURE 12-4

TAXATION OF COUPLE'S $2.5 MILLION ESTATE WITH A-B-C TRUST

Other assets	$3,000,000
Insurance	500,000
Total estate	$2,500,000

$1,250,000
Surviving Spouse's
A Trust

$1,000,000
Decedent's
B Trust

$250,000
Decedent's
C Trust

Federal Estate Tax
on $500,000 Estate

$210,000

$2,290,000 for Heirs

dies), without any estate tax being due. By creating an Insurance Preservation Trust, the couple in this example would have ultimately saved $210,000 of taxes—and therefore, the heirs would receive an "extra" $210,000.

As the example suggests, the significance of the Insurance Preservation Trust becomes more important as the amount of insurance becomes larger.

In most instances where people have estates valued in excess of $2 million, an A-B-C Trust should be recommended. However, if there is any insurance in the estate, the Insurance Preservation Trust is typically recommended. This recommendation holds true even when the amount of insurance is relatively small but the value of the estate is over $2 million.

For example, upon the death of both spouses, with only a $10,000 life insurance policy but an estate of $2 million in other assets, the federal estate tax would be $4,000 (a 41 percent tax rate). Wouldn't you rather spend only one-tenth of that amount today for an Insurance Preservation Trust—to save $4,000 in federal estate taxes upon the death of both spouses? Sound estate planning dictates that you should indeed do so.

The Cheapest Way to Pay Taxes

As mentioned earlier in the chapter, for people with large estates, the cheapest way to pay estate taxes is with insurance. There are three reasons for this fact. First, insurance provides liquidity. Second, insurance prevents liquida-

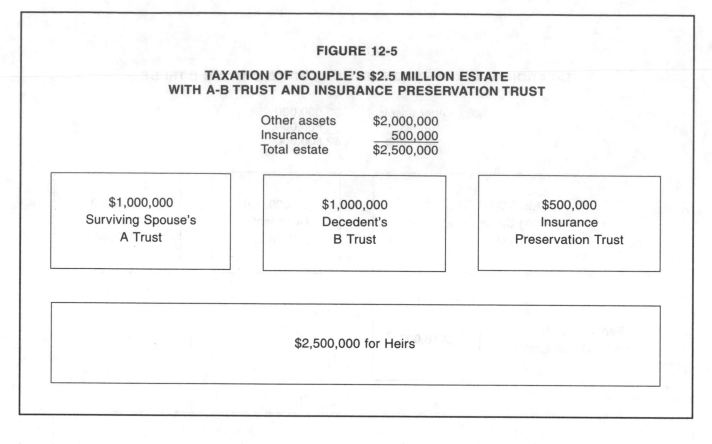

FIGURE 12-5

**TAXATION OF COUPLE'S $2.5 MILLION ESTATE
WITH A-B TRUST AND INSURANCE PRESERVATION TRUST**

Other assets	$2,000,000
Insurance	500,000
Total estate	$2,500,000

$1,000,000 Surviving Spouse's A Trust	$1,000,000 Decedent's B Trust	$500,000 Insurance Preservation Trust

$2,500,000 for Heirs

tion. Third, if you use an Insurance Preservation Trust, the insurance is excluded from your estate—and, therefore, from estate taxes.

Provides Liquidity

Most people tend to think of their estates as being akin to an orange; when they have to pay estate taxes, they neatly cut a proportionate slice from the orange, leaving the balance of the orange for the estate. Unfortunately, this simple analogy does not approximate what actually happens in the real world. People's estates are seldom very liquid, meaning that the assets of their estates cannot immediately be converted into ready cash. Therefore, the orange gets squeezed, and the juice comes out the bottom into a glass. The juice goes to pay taxes—leaving the beneficiaries with the pulp. In literal terms, the assets of the estate are sold for less than their actual worth in order to effect a quick sale and obtain the needed cash to pay the estate taxes.

On a $3 million estate for a married couple, for example, the federal estate taxes would be $435,000. Figure 12-6 shows how an estate of this size with an A-B-C Trust would be treated for tax purposes. When the surviving spouse dies, $435,000 of liquid assets would be needed to pay off the tax liability.

Most people who build their estates have their assets working for them, rather than earning simple interest in a savings account, so they typically do not have that large a sum of money in a liquid form. Insurance, in contrast, could provide the cash when it is most needed.

Prevents Liquidation

A related reason, and probably one of the most important, for using insurance to pay estate taxes is that failure to have adequate liquidity means that one or more of your assets must be liquidated (sold) in order to pay the estate taxes. An estate planner who knows the size of your estate can quickly estimate your estate taxes. (You can do so yourself by simply looking in Appendix A, B, C, or D for your particular estate and noting the estimated amount of estate taxes.)

Selling an asset to pay the estate taxes, however, is a much too simplistic description of the

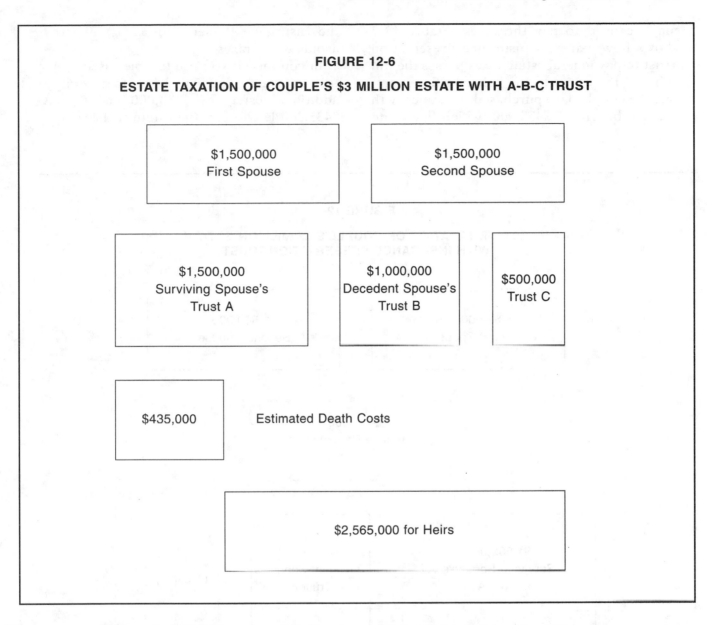

FIGURE 12-6

ESTATE TAXATION OF COUPLE'S $3 MILLION ESTATE WITH A-B-C TRUST

$1,500,000
First Spouse

$1,500,000
Second Spouse

$1,500,000
Surviving Spouse's
Trust A

$1,000,000
Decedent Spouse's
Trust B

$500,000
Trust C

$435,000　　Estimated Death Costs

$2,565,000 for Heirs

process. Sadly, the real world does not work that way. A more realistic scenario is that the survivor goes to an attorney, and, eight months later, the attorney notifies the survivor that he or she must come up with $435,000 in the next thirty days, because the taxes must be paid within nine months from the date of death. If he or she had known eight months earlier that it would be necessary to come up with $435,000, the survivor would have had a more realistic opportunity of raising those funds.

When you have only thirty days to liquidate assets, you are seldom able to sell the assets at full value. Such forced sales usually generate a return of only about ten cents on the dollar! I

used to know businessmen who made their living buying businesses from estates for ten cents on the dollar. The businessmen admitted that their objectives were to buy assets as cheaply as they could from estates that were forced to liquidate in order to pay estate taxes. I call these people vultures, but that is also the real world.

Excludes Insurance from Estate Taxes

The third reason to pay estate taxes with insurance money is that the Insurance Preservation Trust excludes the insurance from estate taxes, as described earlier in the chapter. Therefore, the entire amount of the insurance proceeds may be used to pay the taxes. Figure 12-7 shows how using an Insurance Preservation Trust to pay federal estate taxes passes the full value of the estate to the heirs. In this example, the couple have purchased insurance with a death benefit of $435,000, which flows into the Insurance Preservation Trust, where it avoids estate taxes.

In contrast, if you use taxable assets to pay the estate taxes, you would have to generate an additional estate of $853,000 just to have $435,000 left to pay the estate tax! From the

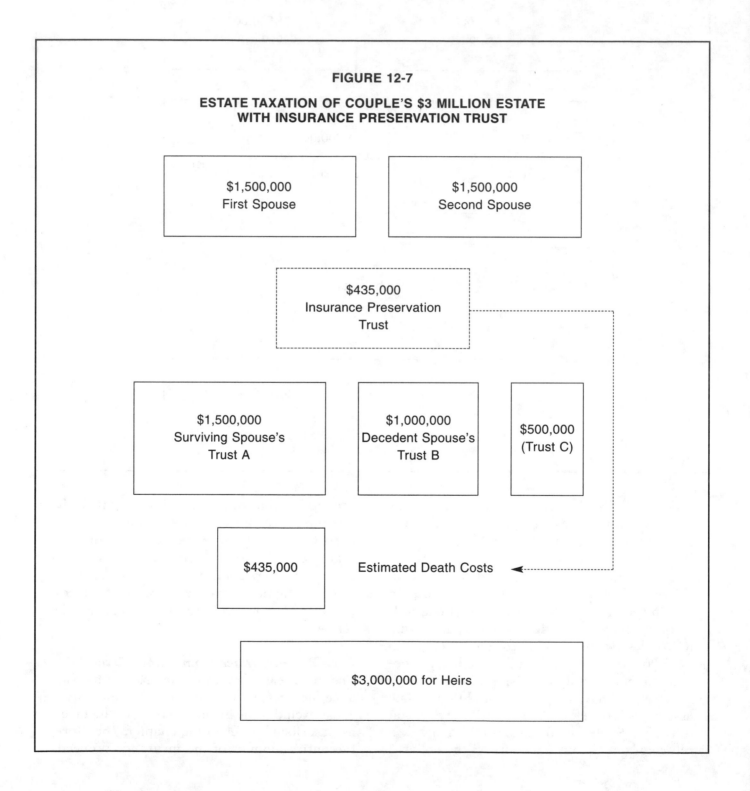

FIGURE 12-7

ESTATE TAXATION OF COUPLE'S $3 MILLION ESTATE WITH INSURANCE PRESERVATION TRUST

original $853,000, 49 percent, or $418,000, would be paid in taxes, leaving $435,000 to pay the estate taxes.

Additional estate to pay taxes	$ 853,000
Federal estate tax (49%)	(418,000)
Available funds to pay estate taxes	$ 435,000

The arithmetic indicates that it is much cheaper to pay estate taxes with insurance. However, to avoid the extra taxation, the insurance must be in an Insurance Preservation Trust.

Even though the Insurance Preservation Trust was designed originally to hold insurance solely to pay estate taxes, it can be used to provide for the wife and children upon the early demise of the husband. The following example shows how good planning and an Insurance Preservation Trust can avoid the adverse tax consequences of such "generosity."

An insurance executive who had built an estate with a net worth of $500,000 had taken out life insurance in the amount of $2 million—so that, if he were to die prematurely, there would be sufficient funds to provide for his wife and four children. This amount of insurance was an unusually large insurance policy in relation to the size of the estate, but the executive felt that the amount was appropriate to provide the standard of living he desired for his family.

The family's net worth plus the large amount of insurance—an estate with a value of $2.5 million—exceeded the $2 million that could be sheltered from federal estate taxes with an A-B Trust. Therefore, it was recommended to the executive that he should have an Insurance Preservation Trust (along with his Living Trust), in order to avoid having to pay unnecessary federal estate taxes.

Features of the Insurance Preservation Trust

As the previous pages have shown, there are economic advantages to having an Insurance Preservation Trust for estates with significant amounts of insurance. The Insurance Preservation Trust should be the owner/beneficiary of your life insurance policies.

Note that the trustors (the creators) of the Insurance Preservation Trust *cannot* also be trustees of the Insurance Preservation Trust. Therefore, another member of the family, one or more of the adult children, close family members, or close friends should be named as the trustee or trustees.

A separate bank account should be set up to pay the premiums for the insurance in the Insurance Preservation Trust. In order to protect the Insurance Preservation Trust from challenge by the Internal Revenue Service, you should utilize your $10,000 annual gift exclusion by making gifts to your children (heirs). Gifts to your children through a Trust for insurance premium payments are an exception to the rule and do not require the filing of the United States Short Form Gift Tax Return (Form 709-A) with the IRS unless the gift exceeds the annual $10,000 exclusion. (This practice assumes the use of the Crummey provision, which provides a thirty-day open gift window for the named Insurance Preservation Trust heirs.)

Make such gifts by depositing the "gifted" funds in a separate bank account and then advise your children in writing that you have made such a gift to them. Legally, the children may then withdraw their share and do as they like with the money, but obviously it is in their best interest not to do so. These "gifted" funds should be used to pay for the insurance premiums. If necessary, you may also make such gifts for insurance premiums to your grandchildren, as long as they are named as contingent beneficiaries of the Insurance Preservation Trust.

In the past several years, *single-premium* whole life insurance and *single-premium* universal life insurance have become investment vehicles used to take advantage of the tax benefit of deferred income. Because these two vehicles are investments per se, they would not normally be placed inside the Insurance Preservation Trust. You do not want to create a gift or lose the right to your funds. Instead, you would designate your Living Trust as the beneficiary of these types of insurance policies.

Company group insurance policies are considered to be "owned" by the insured. The only right the insured has over his or her insurance policy is the right to change the beneficiary. The IRS says that, as long as the insured has that right, the person has what is called the "incidence of ownership"; upon the death of the insured person, that insurance policy will be included in the deceased person's estate for estate tax purposes. Therefore, on company group insurance, be certain that you specifically transfer the "right to change the beneficiary" as well as transfer the beneficiary to the Insurance Preservation Trust.

The main provisions of The Estate Plan's Insurance Preservation Trust are:

- To supplement the surviving spouse's estate, if necessary
- To pass to the heirs the Trust funds that are exempt from estate taxation

Our Insurance Preservation Trust is designed to provide the surviving spouse with the right to borrow against the insurance, if his or her own estate were to substantially diminish. Why, you may ask, should someone borrow against his or her life insurance? The answer is: "for sound estate planning." If, for instance, the surviving spouse needed to withdraw $100,000 from the Insurance Preservation Trust, the spouse would be increasing his or her estate by $100,000—but, by signing a note back to the Insurance Preservation Trust indicating that $100,000 was borrowed from the Trust, the surviving spouse creates a comparable liability. Therefore, the transaction has not increased the survivor's estate for estate tax purposes.

Protection for Estate Taxes

Ten months following the death of the second spouse, or the individual if single, the monies from the insurance in the Insurance Preservation Trust pour over to the heirs without being subject to federal estate taxation. Since the insurance was never owned by the trustors

(creators of the Trust), the insurance will not be considered to be an asset of the trustor's estate (for purposes of estate and inheritance taxes). The funds will therefore pass to the heirs without being subject to federal estate taxes.

We withhold the insurance monies in the Insurance Preservation Trust to be assured that they will be used to pay federal estate taxes and not squandered by the heirs in the interim period. Federal estate taxes are due nine months following the date of death of the second spouse (or an individual, if single). These taxes are so onerous that most heirs don't expect such an enormous bite out of the estate. If these monies are distributed to the heirs early, there is a tendency to spend the cash and then be deficient when the federal estate taxes suddenly become due. At the nine-month period, a paper transaction transfers a share of their inheritance comparable to the federal estate tax from the Living Trust into the Insurance Preservation Trust, in exchange for the monies, and the federal estate tax is paid. One month later, the assets transferred to the Insurance Preservation Trust flow down to the beneficiaries. This provides an excellent safeguard.

Applicability of Insurance Preservation Trust

As a general rule, in considering whether an Insurance Preservation Trust applies to your particular estate, keep in mind the following guidelines:

- If the assets of your estate, including the value of insurance, will not be subject to federal estate tax—for example, if the total value of your estate is less than $600,000 (if single) or is less than $1.2 million (if married)—your Living Trust should be named the beneficiary of your insurance policies.
- If the assets of your estate plus the value of any insurance exceed the federal estate tax equivalent exemption, then the Insurance Preservation Trust should be used as part of your estate planning—to avoid estate taxes on the insurance proceeds.

SPOUSAL AND FAMILY SUPPORT TRUST

The Spousal and Family Support Trust was created to utilize insurance to provide for the surviving spouse and children without generating a federal estate tax problem. While providing for the surviving spouse and children is a common motivation for purchasing life insurance, despite its advantages, a traditional Insurance Preservation Trust is not adequate to provide for family needs per se. To remedy this situation, The Estate Plan designed a new Trust known as the "Spousal and Family Support Trust." This trust is devised expressly to hold a single life insurance policy on one spouse (typically the husband) to provide for the needs of the other surviving spouse (typically the wife). The trustee is explicitly directed to provide for the needs of the trustor's spouse (typically the wife) above all else, but the trustee is also authorized to use the assets of the Trust for the benefit of the couple's children.

Consider the example in which the husband is the primary wage earner, and the couple has accumulated $1.2 million in assets but lacks adequate liquidity. In order to provide for his spouse in the event of his premature death, the husband purchases a $500,000 life insurance policy on his life. Both spouses are concerned about estate taxes, but the husband wants to ensure that his wife and children will have access to the insurance proceeds to provide for their welfare. The Spousal and Family Support Trust will readily satisfy this couple's desires by removing the insurance from their estate and yet ensure that the trustee shall provide for the wife's needs, for her lifetime, and also for the needs of the children as required.

This type of Trust is more complex to administer than a traditional Insurance Preservation Trust. It is clear from the language of the Trust that it is drafted primarily to benefit a surviving spouse. The children are also clearly identified as beneficiaries of the Trust in order to resolve an IRS problem. In several rulings, the IRS has suggested that if a surviving spouse is the sole beneficiary of an Insurance Preserva-

tion Trust during the spouse's lifetime, the IRS will closely examine the document in an attempt to include the Trust assets in the spouse's estate for federal estate taxation.

One Spouse Is Trustor, the Other Spouse Is Beneficiary

It is essential to understand that one spouse creates this Trust to benefit the other spouse. In other words, either the husband creates this Trust to benefit the wife, or the wife creates the Trust to benefit the husband. One Trust cannot be used to simply provide for the benefit of either surviving spouse. If each spouse desires to purchase life insurance to provide benefits for the other spouse, and a Trust is desired or appropriate, each spouse must create his or her own Trust. We would then have two separate Trusts, with the husband the trustor of one Trust and the wife its beneficiary, and the wife the trustor of the other Trust and the husband its beneficiary.

Split Gifts

The language of the Trust provides the option for the couple to make "split gifts." Split gifts are gifts made by each spouse that utilize both of their annual gift tax exclusions. This is particularly helpful when the premiums of the insurance policy exceed the trustor's available gift tax exclusion ($10,000 per beneficiary per year). By splitting gifts, the husband in the previous example may transfer up to $20,000 to the Trust per beneficiary each year. However, an often forgotten prerequisite for gift splitting is that the gift must not be made to the donor's spouse. When gifts are made to an irrevocable Trust in which the spouse is one of the beneficiaries, the trustee must allocate the gift to separately identifiable beneficiaries—for example, the children—in order for the gift to qualify for the annual exclusion.

The gifts must clearly be made to someone other than the surviving spouse. Thus, gift splitting is available only for Trusts granting withdrawal powers for that specific gift to beneficiaries other than the surviving spouse. This makes the other beneficiaries' interests separately identifiable for the purpose of gift split-

FIGURE 12-8

FORM 709-A GIFT TAX RETURN

Form **709-A**	**United States Short Form Gift Tax Return**	OMB No. 1545-0021
(Rev. July 1993)	(For "Privacy Act" notice, see the Form 1040 instructions)	Expires 5-31-96
Department of the Treasury Internal Revenue Service	Calendar year 19 <u>97</u>	

1 Donor's first name and middle initial	2 Donor's last name	3 Donor's social security number
JOHNATHON E.	DOE	123-45-6789

4 Address (number, street, and apartment number)	5 Legal residence (domicile)
123 MAIN STREET SOUTHWEST	U.S.A.

6 City, state, and ZIP code	7 Citizenship
ANYTOWN, NEVADA 89506	U.S.A.

8 Did you file any gift tax returns for prior periods? .... ☐ Yes ☒ No

If "Yes," state when and where earlier returns were filed ▶

9 Name of consenting spouse	10 Consenting spouse's social security number
MARY J. DOE	234-56-7891

Note: *Do not use this form to report gifts of closely held stock. Instead, use Form 709.*

List of Gifts

(a) Donee's name and address and description of gift	(b) Donor's adjusted basis of gift	(c) Date of gift	(d) Value at date of gift
JOHN E. DOE, JR. 123 MAIN STREET SOUTHWEST ANYTOWN, NEVADA 89506	$10000	1/1/97	$10000
SUZANNE E. DOE 123 MAIN STREET SOUTHWEST ANYTOWN, NEVADA 89506	$10000	1/1/97	$10000

Consent

I consent to have the gifts made by my spouse to third parties during the calendar year considered as made one-half by each of us.

Consenting spouse's signature ▶ _____ Date ▶ _____

Under penalties of perjury, I declare that I have examined this return, and to the best of my knowledge and belief it is true, correct, and complete. Declaration of preparer (other than donor) is based on all information of which preparer has any knowledge.

Donor's signature ▶ _____ Date ▶ _____

Preparer's signature (other than donor's) ▶ _____ Date ▶ _____

Preparer's address (other than donor's) ▶ _____

For Paperwork Reduction Act Notice, see the instructions on the reverse side of this form.   Form **709-A** (Rev. 7-93)

ting. It is not permissible to use the spouse as a withdrawal beneficiary in a gift splitting situation.

When spouses split a gift, they must timely file a simple federal gift tax return (Form 709-A; see Figure 12-8). Failure to file Form 709-A when gifts are made to the Spousal and Family Support Trust that exceed $20,000 per year per donee will result in the insurance proceeds being included in the surviving spouse's gross estate and/or gift taxes being due when the gift is made.

Special Requirement for Community Property States

In community property states each spouse is considered to own 50 percent of the assets of the marital estate. This imposes a further requirement on the use of this Trust. One of two options must be used to avoid inclusion of the Trust assets in the estate of the surviving spouse. The simplest approach is to file a gift tax return (Form 709-A) making an election to treat all gifts to the Trust as split gifts. The other option is to have each spouse open a separate bank account. Then each spouse must equally allocate a sufficient amount of money to each bank account to cover the insurance premium (e.g., the gifts to be made by the trustor spouse to the Trust). Once the money has been placed in the separate bank accounts, the funds are identified as gifted by that spouse to the children and/or grandchildren. The same would be true for the second spouse.

GIFT TRUST

The Gift Trust is one of the finest vehicles available to skim off the inflationary growth of your estate and at the same time provide for the needs of your children and/or grandchildren.

Annually Gift Away Inflationary Growth

The Gift Trust is an ideal vehicle to absorb the impact of inflation on estates that will be subject to federal estate taxes—estates of single persons greater than $1 million (one federal estate tax exclusion) and estates of married couples utilizing the A-B-C Living Trust that are greater than $2 million (two federal estate tax exclusions).

It is almost inevitable that any estate will increase in size, even if due only to the effects of inflation. I chuckle with amusement at an individual who says, "I'm going to spend it all." Tell me when you are going to die, and I'll tell you what to spend. Since we cannot foretell the future, we typically become more cautious as we become older. We want to make sure that there will always be enough money in our old age. Therefore, our estate continues to grow—and so does our potential federal estate tax liability. However, the good news is that now there is a simple solution to that inflation problem: the Gift Trust.

For illustration purposes, let's assume an annual inflation rate of 7 percent and a married couple who have an estate worth $2 million. Inflation alone will double the estate in ten years. Consequently, Uncle Sam will eventually receive $981,000 of inflationary increase.

However, there is a way to avoid such an unnecessary tax bite. Each person can annually gift up to $10,000 to as many people (i.e., children or grandchildren) as he or she desires. Gifting is an annual privilege, but it must be used or the privilege is lost. Let's assume, for example, that a married couple have one child and two grandchildren. The husband can gift, through the Gift Trust, $10,000 to the child and each grandchild, for a total of $30,000. The wife can do likewise, gifting another $30,000, thus giving the couple an annual gift total of $60,000 that is now exempt from taxation and does not affect either of the couple's $1 million federal estate tax exclusions. For consequences of inflationary estate taxes, or the benefit of gifting, see Figure 12-9.

Designate Each Gift Separately

Using the Gift Trust, you can designate each gift separately, each and every year. Each year, you can designate whom you want as the beneficiary of each gift, as well as when and how the gift is to be used. For instance, you may wish to allocate more to one child than to another (but not exceeding the $10,000 annual exclusion per person); you may specify that a child's gift is to be used for the down payment on a home in five years; you may specify that a grandchild's gift is to be held for education

FIGURE 12-9
INFLATIONARY GROWTH OF AN ESTATE OF $2 MILLION

	No Gifting	$60,000 Annual Gifting
Estate	$2,000,000	$2,000,000
Estate inflation at 7% for 10 years	$4,000,000	
Estate inflation at 7% for 10 years when gifting $60,000 a year to a Gift Trust		$3,115,000
Size of taxable estate in 10 years	$4,000,000	$3,115,000
Estate tax	$1,415,000	$ 981,000
Net estate after taxes	$2,585,000	$2,134,000
Inflation of $60,000 annual gift at 7% for 20 years		$ 885,000
Net estate to heirs plus Gift Trust		$3,019,000
Net gain using a Gift Trust with $60,000 annual gifts		$ 434,000

and any remaining balance is to be distributed to the grandchild at age twenty-five; or you may specify any such combination. The beauty of the Gift Trust is its absolute flexibility.

Gifting to Children and Grandchildren

The Gift Trust is an excellent method to gift assets to one's children or grandchildren for their future education and general benefit. The 1986 tax code had a major impact on this type of Trust. The tax code now attributes the income of a Gift Trust to the parents while the children are under the age of fourteen. Initially, many financial advisers saw this tax interpretation as the demise of this type of Trust. However, more and more people are now discovering that an excellent use of the Gift Trust is to invest in growth, rather than income-producing, assets.

The Benefit of Gifting Appreciating Assets

An alternative use of the Gift Trust is to transfer an appreciating asset (such as real estate) into a Gift Trust for the future benefit of the children and/or grandchildren. Effectively, you remove an appreciating asset from your own personal estate, and all future growth of the

asset will be in the estate of your children and/or grandchildren.

Assume that a dynamic investor, a young man about forty-three years old with four children, has a net worth of about $1 million—all of which is invested in real estate. This individual expects to double his net worth in the next year and to continue growing his estate in that fashion.

The investor decides that it would be most appropriate to gift the $1 million of real estate holdings to his four children in a Gift Trust. Based on the investor's expectations, the $1 million of real estate will grow by appreciation to many millions of dollars in the coming years. Even though there may be some income to be realized, the major gain will be in unrealized appreciation that will be attributable to the Gift Trust. All of the real estate holdings (the growth assets) will be in the Gift Trust and will eventually pass on to the children without being subject to federal estate taxes on the investor's estate.

Many years from now, when the investor and his wife pass on, that real estate will not be in their estate; it will instead be in the children's estate and will be there without having been subject to federal estate taxes. Admittedly, the investor and his wife will have given up $1 million of their $1.2 million federal estate tax equivalent exemption in that gift. However, that $1 million of real estate could now be worth four or five times the value of the initial gift. In this situation, using a Gift Trust would be very good estate planning.

$1 Million Lifetime Gift

An alternative method of gifting part of your estate is the one-time lifetime gift of $1 million. If you are single, you can gift up to $1 million; if you are married (with an A-B Trust), you and your spouse can gift up to a total of $2 million. However, be aware that once you exceed this amount, you must then pay gift tax, and the gift tax is the same as the estate tax! In fact, the estate tax code is known as the Gift and Estate Tax Code.

Do not be under the misapprehension that, if you make such a one-time gift from your estate, you have reduced the value of your estate for estate tax purposes. IRS Form 706, Federal Estate Tax form, requires the trustee of your estate to identify your estate and also to identify *all gifts* (other than the $10,000 excluded gifts) that have been made from your estate since December 31, 1976. The IRS adds these gifts from your estate back into your estate for the purpose of determining the value of your estate.

For example, if you have an estate of $2 million and have made gifts of $800,000, upon the death of both spouses, your taxable estate will be $2.8 million. With an A-B Trust, you and your spouse have a federal estate tax exclusion of $2 million, which is applied against the value of your estate. Therefore, your net taxable estate will be $2.8 million. As you can see, gifting in this form does not reduce your estate for estate tax purposes. However, gifting $800,000 and placing it in a Gift Trust shifts the growth of the assets to the children. Ten years later, that $800,000 could be worth $1.6 million, assuming an annual growth rate of 7 percent. The growth would be in the children's estate and not in yours. Thus, today, more and more people with large estates are finding that the Gift Trust has considerable application in estate planning. (See the following example.)

Estate	$2,000,000
Gifts since December 31, 1976	800,000
Taxable estate	$2,000,000
Less: Federal estate tax exclusion	($2,000,000)
Estate subject to federal estate tax	$ 800,000

Gifting Forfeits Stepped-Up Valuation

When you make a gift to your children or grandchildren, you pass on to them your cost basis for that gift. Therefore, the children or grandchildren do not get stepped-up valuation on the gifted assets upon your death.

For example, assume that today you gift $200,000 worth of real estate to your children, and twenty years later when you die that real estate is worth $1 million. The children own the real estate (it is not in your estate); if they decide to sell it, they have a taxable gain of

$800,000. This gain will be taxed at only 20 percent, and expect Congress to lower the capital gains tax rate in the future.

If, however, the children had received the real estate as part of their inheritance upon your death, the cost basis to the children would be market value at the date of death ($1 million, not the original cost of $200,000). Thus, if the children decide to sell the real estate, their taxable gain would be zero, but the estate would be subject to federal estate tax ranging from 41 percent to 49 percent. The lower capital gains tax rate is always preferable.

The concept of stepped-up valuation was explained in detail in Chapter 4.

Husband and Wife Cannot Be Trustees of the Gift Trust

As with the Insurance Preservation Trust, the IRS is beginning to scrutinize Gift Trusts. Therefore, to be protected, the ones giving the gift—that is, mother and father—must be at "arm's length." To be at "arm's length" means that mother and father must not be the trustees of the Gift Trust. Fail to abide by this rule, and the IRS can attribute the gifts back to your estate.

For single persons with estates valued at more than $1 million, and for married couples with estates valued at more than $2 million, the Gift Trust provides a wise estate-planning option that minimizes federal estate taxes by absorbing the impact of inflation—while providing for the needs of your children and grandchildren.

GENERATION SKIP

Congress has decreed that a "generation skip" takes place when estate assets pass to anyone—other than the trustor's spouse or children—who is more than thirty-seven and one-half years younger than the trustors. Theoretically, if assets are left to someone (other than the spouse or children) more than thirty-seven and one-half years younger, such an action circumvents the federal estate tax. Thus, in most cases, if you leave your assets to your grandchildren instead of your children, you bypass any federal estate tax on those assets—estate tax that would be imposed on those same assets if they were left to your children. Therefore, Congress has imposed the maximum estate tax rate of 55 percent on such a generation skip. This consumptive 55 percent generation-skipping tax is imposed after the federal estate tax has been assessed. This makes the generation-skipping tax a very aggressive and consumptive tax.

Inadvertent Generation Skip

Congress has finally found some mercy in its soul and has repealed the inadvertent generation skip. Formerly, if you left assets to your children and a child died before such distribution, and those assets inadvertently passed to the deceased child's own child or children (your grandchild or grandchildren), this would be considered an inadvertent skip and would be subject to the 55 percent generation-skipping tax. Fortunately, this is no longer the case. If your child dies, and his or her share of the estate inadvertently passes to that child's own child or children, these assets will not be considered an inadvertent skip. In the event of your child's death, your grandchild or grandchildren from that child step into the shoes of your deceased child.

Generation-Skipping Exemption

When Congress established the generation-skipping tax, it granted each of us a $1 million generation-skipping exemption. As with the federal estate tax exclusion, if you don't take appropriate and wise estate-planning steps, you can lose all or part of it. If you have a Will and you die, typically all of your assets flow to your surviving spouse—which means you're effectively throwing away the decedent's $1 million generation-skipping exemption.

Generation-Skipping Trust

A Generation-Skipping Trust protects the $1 million generation-skipping exemption for an individual and for each spouse in the case of a married couple. A Generation-Skipping Trust also permits the children of a trustor to disclaim their interest in their parents' estate in favor of their own children and yet retain their right to any Trust income for life.

For example, let's assume a $2 million estate of a mother and father who pass away and leave their estate to their only child, a son. The son is married, has two children, and has already accumulated his own estate of $2 million. The son's estate is already subject to a 49 percent tax rate on the value that exceeds two federal estate tax exclusions of $1 million each, or a total of $2 million.

If the son were to "accept" his parents' estate, this addition to his own estate of $2 million would be subject to a tax rate ranging from 41 to 49 percent. However, by disclaiming his interest in the principal of his parents' estate, the son can have the best of both worlds. The son would retain the right to use the income from his parents' $2 million estate for his entire lifetime, and upon the son's death, his parents' estate would pass to his children (his parents' grandchildren) free of any federal estate tax. However, the portion of the estate that "skips" the children and passes to the grandchildren would be considered a generation skip.

The Generation-Skipping Trust performs another important service: it enables you to specify which assets are exempt (i.e., which assets are included in the generation-skipping exemption) and which assets are not exempt. Each individual has a $1 million generation-skipping exemption that may be claimed. All future growth of exempt assets continues to be free of any further estate tax liability, whereas the value of nonexempt assets is included in the surviving spouse's estate when determining federal estate tax liability for the second spouse to die.

To illustrate, let's assume that the same trustors had an estate of $3 million and a Generation-Skipping Trust. Let's further assume that the estate assets were to remain in trust for a specified period—until the death of the son—and then be distributed to the grandchildren.

The Generation-Skipping Trust permits you to identify which assets are exempt (i.e., fall within the $1 million exemption allowed for each of the trustors). The generation-skipping tax is theoretically imposed when the assets are distributed to the grandchildren; if the assets appreciate over time, then the generation-skipping tax increases proportionately. However, by designating which of the assets are to be exempt, you can directly affect the ultimate amount of taxation.

For example, let's assume that the estate consists of $2 million of real estate that has a good chance of appreciating over the years, as well as $1 million in certificates of deposit (CDs) that only produce income but whose value never appreciates, as illustrated in Figure 12-10. Simple logic tells us that it is the real estate, worth $2 million, that should be declared exempt.

Years later, when the estate is to be distributed to the grandchildren, the real estate has appreciated to $4 million, but the value of the CDs has remained at $1 million. Since the real estate was initially declared exempt, the generation-skipping tax would be imposed only on the $1 million in CDs, which now represents a smaller portion of the total estate value, as illustrated in Figure 12.11.

Remember, however, that without a Generation-Skipping Trust, no specific assets would be considered exempt. Therefore, the total estate—which has now appreciated to $5 million—would be included for allocating the generation-skipping tax. Thus, the $5 million estate would be prorated using the ratio (as of the date of death) of the originally exempt portion of the estate ($2 million, which represents two-thirds of the estate) to the nonexempt portion ($1 million, one-third of the original estate). If the appreciated estate value of $5 million were subjected to the consumptive generation-skipping tax, two-thirds of the appreciated value of the estate ($3.3 million) would be exempt from the generation-skipping tax, and one-third of the appreciated estate ($1.65 million) would be nonexempt (i.e., subject to the generation-skipping tax).

In summary, without the Generation-Skipping Trust, which allows you to allocate specific assets instead of a percentage of the estate, you would be faced with a generation-skipping tax on $1.65 million of the appreciated estate value, instead of on only $1 million, as shown in figure 12.12.

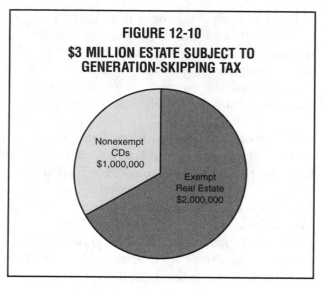

FIGURE 12-10
$3 MILLION ESTATE SUBJECT TO GENERATION-SKIPPING TAX

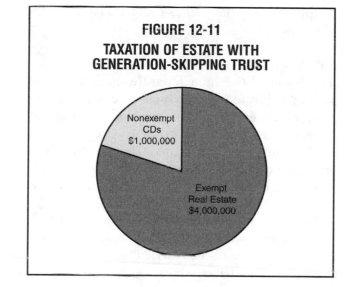

FIGURE 12-11
TAXATION OF ESTATE WITH GENERATION-SKIPPING TRUST

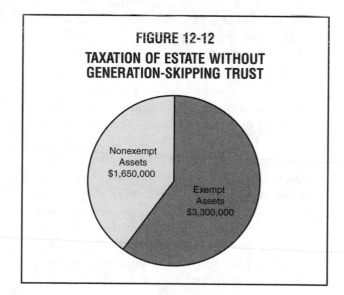

FIGURE 12-12
TAXATION OF ESTATE WITHOUT GENERATION-SKIPPING TRUST

Even though the generation-skipping tax is theoretically computed when the assets are distributed to the grandchildren, in practice, the tax is computed (and must be paid) following the death of the trustors, regardless of when the grandchildren actually receive the funds.

A Powerful Estate-Planning Tool

The Generation-Skipping Trust, which provides you with three simple principles to help unravel a very complex topic, has great merit for estates that are eventually going to be subject to paying federal estate taxes. The Generation-Skipping Trust is just one of the many estate tax-planning concepts that should be considered for larger estates. (Although the case of a married couple was illustrated, the Generation-Skipping Trust has just as much merit for a single person.)

SPOUSAL GIFT

The Spousal Gift is a separate document that allows a spouse with a large estate to gift a portion of that estate to the other spouse, who has a very small estate, in order to use both federal estate tax exemptions. This document is infrequently used. However, the Spousal Gift can have great significance in certain estates.

For example, an heiress to a large fortune held substantial stock in a publicly traded corporation. She had been married for many years to a police officer who was retired on disability. The couple were obviously quite happily married and had been so for many years.

The wife's assets were in the millions, whereas the husband's assets were in the thousands. If the husband were the first to die, although he would have a $1 million federal estate tax exclusion, he would have very little estate to exempt it against. The wife would not be able to use the benefit of any of her husband's federal estate tax equivalent exemption to ultimately reduce the estate taxes that would be assessed on her large estate. The solution was for the wife to make a spousal gift to her husband of $1 million, thereby reducing her estate by that amount but also enabling full use of her husband's federal estate tax exclusion.

To allow you to better understand the tax-saving advantages of a Spousal Gift (in situations that warrant it), Figure 12-13 illustrates this example with numbers and shows the effect before gifting and the effect after gifting. Assume an estate with a value of $2 million. Notice that, by prudent use of the Spousal Gift, the wife was able to effect a tax savings of $435,000 on her estate!

The Spousal Gift can also be an excellent vehicle for one spouse to annually gift $100,000 to a non-citizen spouse in order to eventually utilize the non-citizen's $1 million federal estate tax exclusion, as discussed in Chapter 5.

FAMILY LIMITED PARTNERSHIP

The Family Limited Partnership (FLP) is one of the most oversold yet least understood of all estate-planning vehicles. Most oversold, because when marketed it is frequently offered as a solution to every estate planning need. Least understood because it is not marketed

---

FIGURE 12-13
TAX ADVANTAGES OF SPOUSAL GIFT

Before Gifting

	Husband's Estate	Wife's Estate
Net worth	-0-	$2,000,000
Less: Federal estate tax exclusion	($1,000,000)	($1,000,000)
Taxable estate	-0-	$1,000,000
Federal estate tax	-0-	$ 435,000

After Gifting

	Husband's Estate	Wife's Estate
Net worth	$1,400,000	$1,400,000
Less: Federal estate tax exclusion	($1,000,000)	($1,000,000)
Taxable estate	-0-	-0-
Federal estate tax	-0-	-0-
Tax savings		$ 435,000

properly. When used properly, it can be one of your most valuable tools for protecting your assets from frivolous lawsuits and confiscatory estate and inheritance taxes. The FLP offers a host of features for an older generation to pass along assets to a younger generation, as well as an excellent method to protect assets from lawsuits.

How the Family Limited Partnership Works

One of the great features of the Family Limited Partnership is the ability to give away your assets and still retain control. The lifetime $1 million federal estate tax exclusion discussed throughout the book is known as a federal estate exclusion and *gift* tax exemption, which means that while everyone has a $1 million lifetime exclusion from federal estate taxes you also have the right to use this exemption during your lifetime as a one-time tax exempt gift—but you can only use it once. Let's assume a couple are married and have four children (their ages are somewhat academic) and an estate of $3 million, consisting of a home, a small business, and a vacation condo that they rent out. Upon properly creating a Family Limited Partnership, they decide to transfer all of their assets to their four children. They use

their $2 million lifetime federal estate tax exclusion to transfer this amount to the children in the FLP and retain, for the time being, the remaining $1 million.

The father and mother will be the general partners of the FLP. As such they will have absolute control of the partnership and all of the assets therein. The children will each be limited partners. As limited partners, they are merely entitled to their shares; they will have no say in the management of the partnership or any ownership interest in the partnership assets. The initial transaction is shown in the example below.

The father and mother each own 17 percent of the partnership, and each of the four children owns 17 percent of the partnership. However, the ownership and control of the assets have not been segregated; rather, each individual owns a percentage of the limited partnership, which in turn owns the assets. The general partners (father and mother) retain control of the partnership and the assets. The father and mother may now use their annual $10,000 excluded gift to transfer the balance of their estate to their children. (Everyone has a right to gift $10,000 per year, per person, without incurring taxes.) Since each parent can give away a total of $40,000

$3 MILLION ESTATE PLACED IN A FAMILY LIMITED PARTNERSHIP

| General Partner Father $500,000 17% | General Partner Mother $500,000 17% |

| Limited Partner Child A $500,000 17% | Limited Partner Child B $500,000 17% | Limited Partner Child C $500,000 17% | Limited Partner Child D $500,000 17% |

a year ($10,000 to each of their four children per year), it would take the parents twelve years to complete the gifting, assuming no inflation. But in the end father and mother, as general partners, each need to retain 1 percent of the assets if they wish to retain control of the Family Limited Partnership. The completed transaction ten years later would look like the example below.

The father and mother could have accomplished the same thing by initially gifting $500,000 to each child and then loaning each of them the remaining $235,000. They could then forgive $20,000 of the debt each year ($10,000 from father and $10,000 from mother to each child annually). This would resolve the issue of inflation.

How to Avoid Frivolous Lawsuits

The partners (both general and limited) of a Family Limited Partnership must report their proportionate shares of partnership income (or loss) each year. The partnership itself does not pay taxes (it is considered a "pass-through entity" in that it passes its income and loss through to the partners) but does report any income (or loss) annually to the IRS on Form 1065 and attaches Schedule K-1 to show which partner receives how much income (or loss). This is an information form only. Each partner must report his or her proportionate share of partnership income (or loss) to the IRS on an individual Form 1040 and must pay the tax thereon as an individual. However, there is no requirement for a limited partnership to ever distribute income. This is the key to lawsuit protection. While typically a Family Limited Partnership will pay out just enough income to the family members to pay any additional tax burden, there is no such requirement. This is done solely at the discretion of the general partners (father and mother).

Like most of us, the father and mother are concerned about the possibility of facing a frivolous lawsuit by someone hoping to "get rich quick" at their expense. A Family Limited Partnership offers a beautiful and nearly impregnable barrier to this threat. Suppose a trespasser, attempting to break into the parents' home, were attacked by the family dog and sued the parents and won (don't laugh; this has actually happened). Their assets are all "owned" by the FLP. As a result, the trespasser does not get title to the assets but rather is

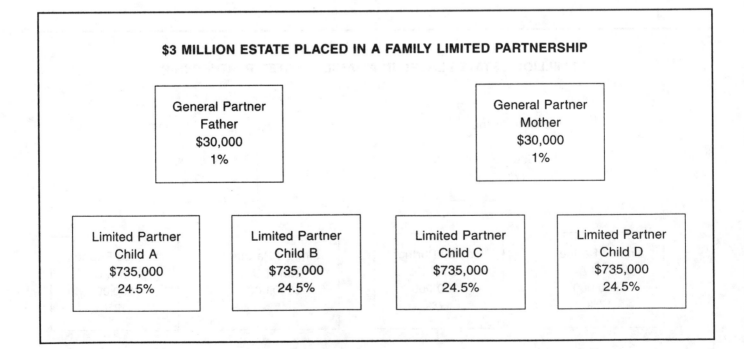

$3 MILLION ESTATE PLACED IN A FAMILY LIMITED PARTNERSHIP

General Partner
Father
$30,000
1%

General Partner
Mother
$30,000
1%

Limited Partner
Child A
$735,000
24.5%

Limited Partner
Child B
$735,000
24.5%

Limited Partner
Child C
$735,000
24.5%

Limited Partner
Child D
$735,000
24.5%

given a "charging order" against the mother and father's partnership interests. A judgment creditor, such as our trespasser, with a charging order does not own the partnership interests, become a partner, have any rights in the partnership assets, or have the ability to participate in management. Instead, the creditor is merely entitled to a proportional share of any distributions actually made by the partnership and is forced to pay income taxes on partnership income, even if there are no distributions of partnership income. This is known as a tax on "phantom (undistributed) income." Over time, the creditor will want out as the tax bills keep rising and there is no sign of the partnership ever making any distributions. As a result, creditors with a charging order typically settle for much less than the amount of their judgment.

But consider the possibilities for a moment. Assume the home in which the mother and father live has a low cost basis of $35,000 and a fair market value of $500,000. If the general partners were to sell the home, the creditor would have to report their share of the capital gains on his individual 1040. If the creditor had a charging order over a large percentage of the partnership, it is possible to force the creditor into bankruptcy. The possibilities for a devious general partner are endless. A smart attorney, learning that the defendant's assets are in a Family Limited Partnership, would stop the suit at once. An unknowing attorney would go forward with the suit, and end up with a very unhappy client. It works beautifully.

While the Family Limited Partnership offers a strong barrier to frivolous lawsuits, I have come to the conclusion that the sure defense against the frivolous lawsuit is the Offshore Trust. I have discussed this at length in Chapter 3, "The Million-Dollar Lawsuit, or What Price Integrity?"

How to Reduce the Size of Your Estate Tax with an FLP

The Family Limited Partnership is also an ideal vehicle to dramatically reduce the value of your estate for federal estate tax purposes due to the concept of discounting. To illustrate, let's assume the same family circumstances as in the previous example: married couple with four children (again, the children's ages are academic). But let's assume the couple have an estate of $4 million, which consists of a home, a vacation condo, some stocks and bonds, and their own business. Again, they are going to create a Family Limited Partnership and gift their estate to their children, but with a major difference. They are going to find a very good appraiser who understands the concept of discounting and will value the assets and then *discount* them.

Typically, we are looking at two major discounts: a *minority interest discount* and a *marketability discount*. A *minority interest discount* reflects the fact that the limited partners have no ability to control the partnership. A limited partner cannot influence management, acquire control of the partnership, force a liquidation of the partnership, or control the investment and use of partnership assets. This minority interest discount also reflects the fact that each child holds only a partial share of a home, a vacation condo, and a closed (personally owned) business. The *marketability discount* is based on the fact that no ready or established market exists for closely held business interests. This discount reflects the fact that it is equally difficult to get anyone to buy an asset over which they will never have any control. The combined discounts vary from 20 percent to as high as 90 percent. The amount of the discount depends on the surrounding facts and the type of assets. For instance, stocks and bonds are usually readily negotiable, as is cash, which leads to a much lower total discount. For simplicity, we will assume that the value of the stocks and bonds is negligible and the total discount for all the assets is 50 percent. The discount is taken at the time the assets are transferred into the Family Limited Partnership. Once the discount is calculated, the parents may gift the partnership interests to their children. The transfer to the FLP, creating a 50 percent discount, would reduce the value of the estate from $4 million to $2 million and would look like this:

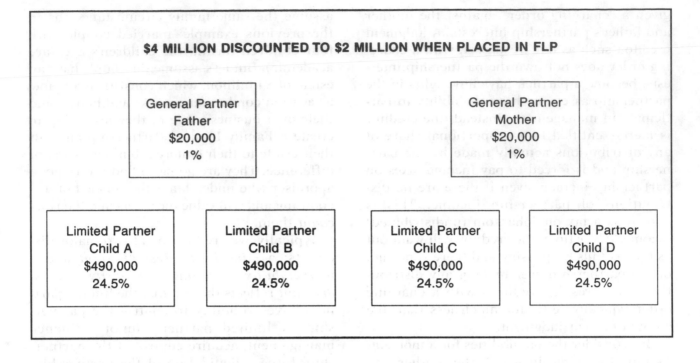

$4 MILLION DISCOUNTED TO $2 MILLION WHEN PLACED IN FLP

The estate tax comparisons to using an FLP would look like this:

	Living Trust	Family Limited Partnership Discounted Value
Estate of father and mother	$4,000,000	$4,000,000
Value of total estate after discounting to FLP		$2,000,000
Value of father's and mother's estate after discounting to FLP		$ 40,000
Federal estate tax exclusion	$2,000,000	$ 40,000
Taxable estate	$2,000,000	-0-
Less federal estate taxes	(980,000)	-0-
Net estate after federal estate taxes	$3,020,000*	$ 40,000
Recap		
Parent's share of partnership passing to children (without discounting) ($40,000 × 2)		$ 80,000
Less: Federal estate taxes		-0-
Parent's share of partnership passing to children (without discounting)	-0-	$ 80,000
Children's value of partnership (without discounting) ($1,960,000 × 2)	-0-	$2,920,000
Net to children	$3,020,000	$4,000,000
Difference		$980,000

*The father and mother gave up $1,960,000 lifetime federal estate tax exclusion when they initially gifted their partnership interest to their children. They still retain a $40,000 exclusion, which together with their $1,960,000 gift totals $1 million—equal to their total exclusion.

Father was probably an important individual, or keyman, in the business and therefore we could also take a *keyman discount* (which applies to partnerships, corporations, and sole proprietorships), further reducing the estate tax liability.

Good Estate Tax Planning
The Family Limited Partnership can be a vital approach to keeping a business going after the loss of the founders, thanks to discounting and the ability to get the next generation involved without giving them unfettered control. This concept equally applies to a single person or to a surviving father or mother. We call this good estate tax planning.

A Family Limited Partnership must be accompanied by a good Living Trust. Your trust will take care of non-partnership assets as well as your partnership interests when you pass on. It may also be advisable to create an irrevocable trust to hold and manage a minor child's limited partnership interests. This is especially important if you are contemplating dissolving the partnership prior to the child's attaining the age of majority.

Disadvantages
The single disadvantage to Family Limited Partnerships is the initial cost of the partnership and a good appraiser, and thereafter the annual accounting cost to produce the IRS Schedule K-1 and a Form 1065 information return for the partnership. That's a very small price to pay for an accountant and an appraiser to save, in this case, $1 million or more—and even more important—to save the business.

Personal Experience
My wife and I created a Family Limited Partnership some years ago and transferred key assets into it. We each retained a 1 percent interest and acted as general partners. And then, after a few years, we gave up our 1 percent interests and resigned as general partners. We named our two oldest sons as general partners. Initially, they had divergent opinions, but they quickly resolved their differences and now run a very smooth and cohesive partnership

for the benefit of all our children. It has given my wife and me the opportunity to work with these young men as they operate a microcosm of what they will eventually inherit when we step out of the picture.

CHARITABLE REMAINDER TRUST
The Charitable Remainder Trust is one of the best-kept secrets in the area of estate planning. I know of no greater tool to protect an estate or a business than the Charitable Remainder Trust, an instrument that is especially ideal for handling highly appreciated property, such as stock, real estate, or a family-owned business.

The real potential of the Charitable Remainder Trust can be seen in the sale of a family business. There are several financial strategies to taking maximum advantage of the benefits of a Charitable Remainder Trust, and we will cover these tactics, step by step. Although there are numerous variations of the Charitable Remainder Trust, I believe the most practical version is the Charitable Remainder Unitrust, which is presented in this section.

The only easily understood way to describe the advantageous use of the Charitable Remainder Trust is to break down the subject into small pieces. Let's look at two methods of estate planning where a family-owned business is the major asset—first, without using a Charitable Remainder Trust, and second, taking advantage of the Charitable Remainder Trust.

Let's assume that a married couple have children and an estate of $10 million (consisting solely of a family-owned business) that is in an A-B-C Living Trust. Let's further assume that, similar to most privately held businesses, there is little or no cost basis; thus, if the business were to be sold, a 100 percent taxable gain would result.

What Happens Without a Charitable Remainder Trust
Let's first look at what happens to the net estate ultimately inherited by the children when a Charitable Remainder Trust is not used.

While the husband and wife are living, the business is sold for $10 million and (without any cost basis) realizes a fully taxable gain on appreciation of the entire $10 million. Considering capital gains taxes of 20 percent will yield a tax bite of $2 million. When the taxes are deducted from the original sale of $10 million, $8 million is left for investment. At an interest rate of 8 percent, the investment would produce an annual income of $640,000—not too objectionable, but we could do better by using a Charitable Remainder Trust, as you will see.

Upon the death of both spouses (assuming an A-B-C Living Trust), the two federal estate tax exclusions ($1 million each for husband and wife) are deducted from the net estate of $8 million, leaving a taxable estate of $6 million. The federal estate tax rate on this amount is 49 percent (a tax of $2,395,000), leaving a net estate of only $5.6 million.

Sale of business	$10,000,000
Less: Federal and state taxes (49%)	($ 2,000,000)
Net amount (for investment)	$ 8,000,000
Less: Federal estate tax (49%)	($ 2,395,000)
Net estate	$ 5,605,000

The children receive a total inheritance of $5.6 million—only 56 percent of the original amount of the estate. Uncle Sam and the state have gobbled up $4,395,000 for taxes!

What Happens with a Charitable Remainder Trust

If, instead of using the tax-hungry approach above, a Charitable Remainder Trust with a Replacement Trust were utilized, the outcome for the children would be significantly better.

Let's assume that instead of subjecting the $10 million business to federal and state income taxes, and then to federal estate taxes, the business is placed in a Charitable Remainder Trust, with the husband and wife as income beneficiaries. The husband and wife also select the charities to which they desire the business to eventually pass on the death of the second spouse. In addition, they also select a fixed income that they desire to receive for the rest of their lives, typically somewhere between 5 percent and 10 percent of the total assets in the Charitable Remainder Trust. This approach assumes that the business is generating a 5 percent to 10 percent return, which is a dividend considered to be tax-free inside this type of Trust. (Even though there are numerous other approaches to allocating income, I prefer the simple fixed-income approach.)

To place the business into the Charitable Remainder Trust, two competent CPA firms must carefully value the business and be prepared to defend such valuation to the IRS—not a difficult task, but essential. Then, when the business is sold, since it is technically in a charitable environment, the tax impact on the $10 million would be zero! By investing the $10 million at 8 percent interest, an annual income of $800,000 would be realized—a nice improvement.

At this point, by placing the business in the Charitable Remainder Trust, federal and state income taxes (on the sale of the business) have been eliminated, federal estate taxes have been eliminated, a nice income has been provided for the husband and wife, and one or more charities have been made expectantly happy. However, in so doing, one large problem has been created—the couple's children have been deprived of what could have been a $5.6 million inheritance for them.

The Replacement Trust

To solve the problem of depriving the children of their inheritance, let's consider another money-saving solution—a Replacement Trust. A Replacement Trust is created and funded with a $10 million *joint and survivor life insurance policy* on the lives of the husband and wife, payable to the Replacement Trust upon the death of the second spouse. (Joint and survivor life insurance was previously described in the insurance section of this chapter.) The children are named as the beneficiaries of the Replacement Trust, which is a simple Insurance Preservation Trust.

Upon the death of the second spouse, the assets in the Charitable Remainder Trust flow down to the designated charities, as described previously. The joint and survivor life insurance policy now pays $10 million to the Replacement Trust—and thereupon flows down to the children.

Now everyone should be happy, but, unfortunately, this solution has created another problem—the $10 million insurance policy has a costly premium that must somehow be paid.

The Charitable Contribution Tax Deduction

As you might have expected, there is also a solution to the problem of paying the costly insurance premiums. When the husband and wife made their $10 million contribution to the Charitable Remainder Trust, they received a charitable tax deduction at that time (just as if they had made the gift outright to charity)—and that tax deduction may be used to reduce their income tax.

The tax deduction for the $10 million must be computed using the IRS tax tables and is dependent upon two factors: the ages of the income beneficiaries (in this case, husband and wife) to determine their life expectancies, and the percentage of income selected for payment to the income beneficiaries. Obviously, the older the income beneficiaries, the greater will be the tax deduction. This tax deduction may be deducted from income up to 50 percent, unless the contributed assets were highly appreciated (and then the deduction is limited to 30 percent).

If such a large deduction is more than the couple could use in one year, the unused balance of the deduction can be carried forward for the next five years to be used in subsequent tax years. However, if such an arrangement still provides more deduction than the couple can utilize over the next six years, the pair could, over time (every sixth year), make incremental contributions of the business into the Charitable Remainder Trust.

What about paying the insurance premium? It's simple: The tax savings is used to pay the joint and survivor life insurance premium. Thus, Uncle Sam essentially pays for the premium to replace the assets contributed to the Charitable Remainder Trust. If highly appreci-

ated property, such as stock or real estate, were contributed to the Charitable Remainder Trust, once the assets were in the Charitable Remainder Trust, the property could be sold with zero tax consequences—thus giving the income beneficiaries the best income possible.

Therefore, although the steps are a little complicated, you can see that, as shown in Figure 12-14, upon the death of the second spouse the children end up with an inheritance of $10 million instead of $5.6 million—a dramatic difference, and it works!

What If You Want to Keep the Business?

Yes, there is a way to take advantage of the charitable contribution and still effectively keep your business in the family. If you do not want to sell the business, but want to keep it in the family instead, you still follow the steps

---

FIGURE 12-14
ADVANTAGES OF A CHARITABLE REMAINDER TRUST (CRT)

	Without CRT	With CRT
Business value	$10,000,000	$10,000,000
Charitable Remainder Trust		
Less: Contribution to CRT		($10,000,000)
Net estate		-0-
Business Sold—Zero Cost Basis		
Less: Capital gains tax (20%)	($ 2,000,000)	-0-
Balance for investment	$ 8,000,000	$10,000,000
Inheritance to Children		
Net worth	$ 8,000,000	-0-
Taxable estate	$ 8,000,000	
Less: Estate tax (49%)	($ 2,395,000)	
Net estate	$ 5,600,000	-0-
Plus: Replacement trust (insurance)	-0-	$ 10,000,000
Estate to children	$ 5,600,000	$ 10,000,000
Income to Parents		
Balance for investment	$ 8,000,000	$10,000,000
Income at 8%	$ 640,000	$ 800,000

previously described—of valuing the business and placing it in the Charitable Remainder Trust. However, in this case, since it is a business and the husband and wife must remain at "arm's length," they must relinquish the trusteeship of the Charitable Remainder Trust to someone else. It is suggested that you name one or more of your family's adult children, close family members, or close friends as trustee or trustees. This "arm's-length" trustee requirement applies only to a business. In all other cases, the husband and wife can be named as both beneficiaries and trustees.

You may ask, "Does a charity really want to inherit a business, or would it rather receive the money?" Usually "money" is the answer. Therefore, the trustees of the Replacement Trust (for example, the children) go to the specified charities and enter into a "Buy-Sell Agreement" with the charities. This agreement states that when both spouses die and the business eventually passes to the charities, the children will "buy back" the business from the charities—by using the insurance dollars from the Replacement Trust. Yes, this arrangement also works well.

Select Multiple Charities

The one absolute requirement for the Charitable Remainder Trust is that you select one or more *IRS-qualified* charities. Be very aware that if you select only one charity and it fails to retain its qualification, then your Charitable Remainder Trust will be disallowed in its entirety by the IRS. For instance, if you had chosen PTL (Praise The Lord ministry) as the only specified charity for your Charitable Remainder Trust, your Trust would today be disqualified! It has been my experience that our clients are primarily interested in the preservation of their assets, and one of the best services the adviser can provide is to recommend one or more qualified charities.

I find the Charitable Remainder Trust to be one of the most exciting estate-planning tools available. I have tried to give you a glimpse of what can be done with it, but the horizon is unlimited. It's just one more arrow in a large quiver of estate-planning strategies available to those individuals who are willing to explore. Please understand that Congress fully endorses the Charitable Remainder Trust, because, without charitable contributions from the private sector, most charities would die. At the same time, Congress is turning itself away from charitable giving and relying more and more upon the private sector for support to charities.

Never before has our nation been confronted with a greater need for large charitable contributions from the private sector than it is today. Our government can do just so much before its resources are strained to the limit. Charity—in enormous amounts—must then come to the rescue. As you can see, the Charitable Remainder Trust can be one of the most advantageous ways to make substantial charitable gifts.

ESTATE PRESERVATION AND TAX-SAVING POTENTIAL

While the Living Trust is essential to avoid unnecessary estate taxes, several other estate planning tools will be extremely important to preserve your estate. These tools are the Insurance Preservation Trust, the Spousal and Family Support Trust, the Gift Trust, the Generation-Skipping Trust, the Spousal Gift, the Family Limited Partnership, and the Charitable Remainder Trust. Of these estate planning tools, the most widely used by far is the Insurance Preservation Trust. The Spousal and Family Support Trust provides income to the surviving spouse and family. The Gift Trust is a necessity to control the inflationary tax impact on an estate while providing for the future of your children or grandchildren. The Generation-Skipping Trust is absolutely essential to reduce the impact of the Generation-Skipping Tax, particularly for your grandchildren. The Spousal Gift has a very limited use. The Family Limited Partnership will provide protection against lawsuits as well as substantially reduce estate taxes. The Charitable Remainder Trust can relieve capital gains taxes on highly appreciated assets as well as reduce or eliminate estate taxes.

13

Organizing Your Estate

There are two crucial, and equally important, elements in settling an estate: having a Living Trust and having an organized estate. The Living Trust avoids the agonizing probate process and unnecessary estate taxes; an organized estate facilitates a quick settlement and identifies what assets exist and where they are located.

THE PUZZLE OF SETTLING AN ESTATE

For most people, the biggest problem involved in settling an estate of a loved one is just being able to find all of the pieces. Even spouses do not always keep track of what the other spouse is accumulating. For example, many widows do not really know all of the stocks and bonds their husbands have purchased or all the pension benefits their husbands have earned over many years. Further, many people find it difficult to talk about such things, because they relate to the eventual death of a loved one—a very unpleasant thought for most people.

Losing a loved one—especially a spouse—is a traumatic experience. People in mourning can think only of the loss and not of the many details that must be resolved to settle the estate. Unfortunately, at such a time, very few people can confidently go to one source and know that they will find all the puzzle pieces required to settle an estate.

The Estate—What and Where

What do you do when someone you love is dying—and then dies? Most people's natural reaction is to become mentally paralyzed. After more than twenty years of experience with clients and beginning with my own personal experience of my father's death thirty years ago, I realized the need for a "what-to-do" sequence.

How large is the estate, and where are the assets? Where is the deed to the house? Where are the checking and savings accounts and certificates of deposit? (The banks love to retain unclaimed accounts.) Who was your last stockbroker, and where are all those U.S. Government savings bonds?

People know where their important papers are—until they go to retrieve them. I have watched both spouses, even in the most organized families, search high and low for missing documents. Imagine the problem if one spouse were removed. Similarly, trying to step in and assemble the estate of a single person is a nightmare.

Even if you cannot locate a missing document, it is easy enough to order a replacement. One of the most common missing documents is the grant deed (ownership papers) to your home. Everyone who has purchased a home received a grant deed and typically meant to put it in a safe-deposit box. However, so often when someone ultimately looks in the safe-deposit box, the grant deed is not there. Instead, the person finds only the title insurance policy or a reconveyance (release of lien when the mortgage has been paid in full). How easy it is *now* to write to the county recorder's office for a copy of your grant deed; do not wait until you are under the stress of the loss of a loved one.

Years ago, a client was trying to go through the probate process for his father. The mother and father had lived in New York and worked as domestic help. When the parents reached retirement age, being of the old school, they informed their only son that they were moving west to live with him. The son knew that his parents had no money, so he purchased a small home for them nearby. The father soon died, and the mother was rapidly deteriorating with cancer, so the son moved his mother into his own home.

Months later, as the son was going through the probate process for his father, he literally stumbled onto a stack of stock certificates. The son learned that, as his parents worked, they would take their meager savings and buy one or two shares of blue-chip stocks and hide them away. The buying of stock had begun in the early 1930s, and now the stock certificates totaled $300,000. What a shock for a son who thought his parents were penniless!

Then the mother died. When the son was finally about to close probate on his father's estate, he cleaned out his parents' home prior to selling it. As the son removed the paper that lined the bottom of a drawer, he came upon yet another stock certificate. Neither the son nor the local stockbrokers had ever heard of the company; however, detailed research revealed that the company held oil rights in West Germany, and the stock certificate was then worth $400,000. What a pleasant discovery. Unfortunately, probate on the father's estate, which was about to close, now had to be reopened. By the end of the probate process, this newfound fortune had all but vanished as the price of oil spiraled downward.

One client died of a stroke while driving home, and his wallet was stolen. (I think he owned every credit card produced.) You can imagine the urgency of trying to reconstruct, and cancel, those cards before massive charges were illegally made—and at a time of great stress.

How about those insurance policies? Many people have small insurance policies that their parents took out for them years ago or that they purchased themselves when they were first married. The policies are paid up but have been shoved away in a drawer someplace. Did you know that you do not need the actual insurance policy to collect the insurance money? However, you *do* need to know to what insurance company the claim should be submitted. In addition, do not forget "accident policies," which are often purchased through credit card companies or ordered through the local newspaper.

Have you identified all of your retirement plans? Retirement plans would include your IRAs, Keogh plans, annuities, pension plans, and profit-sharing plans, as well as many other programs such as stock or savings plans in which you may be involved. Adding them all together could make the difference between decent survival or severe hardship.

Do you have any business agreements such as a buy-sell agreement (an agreement to buy back your company interest at a predetermined price) or deferred compensation (income earned but not yet paid)? These agreements, too, are assets of the estate.

How about all those legal documents you worked so hard to put together: Living Trust, Amendments, Pour-Over Will, Durable Power of Attorney for Health Care, Durable General Power of Attorney, Appointment of Conservator, Living Will (Right-to-Die Clause), Gift of Vital Organs, Abstract, Insurance Trust, and Appointment of Guardian? These important documents are *essential*; they will be needed at the greatest moments of stress. Are they readily at your fingertips? Do you really *know* where they are?

Who are your advisers? These people are the individuals your spouse or children can turn to for assistance and would include such key people as successor trustee(s), special friends or relatives, guardian, financial adviser, and CPA. How can you reach them? Do you have readily at hand the current addresses and telephone numbers of these key people?

Do you have personal property you would like to leave to a son or daughter or to a special friend? How do you simply and easily identify the item and who is to receive it? Would you like to be able to add to this list periodically? One of my greatest regrets was that my father did not identify something personal—and meaningful between the two of us—to be left to me. Do not make the same mistake.

There Must Be an Easier Way

My first experience in settling the estate of a loved one came when my own father died in 1966. He was a very private person, and he was the only one who knew anything about his estate. (Does this scenario sound familiar?) When my father passed away, I was confronted with an impossible task. Figuratively speaking, I had to piece together a jigsaw puzzle.

I started with a three-ring binder with dividers. As I discovered an asset, I categorized it. Slowly, agonizingly, and tediously, I assembled the pieces of my father's estate. The search was similar to looking for needles in a haystack. Did my father have other accounts in banks unknown to me? I will never know.

It took me three months to assemble my father's estate. I believe that I eventually found most of the estate, but I will never really be certain. This trying experience was the birth of what is now referred to as the "Estate Plan Binder"—a simple means to *organize* your estate.

Without organization, you have a nightmare; however, with organization, you create an orderly process for your surviving spouse, children, or other heirs. The orderly process allows the survivors to quickly identify your assets, legal documents, and distribution desires and then to settle your affairs—and then get back to living their own lives.

I have a magnificent wife and four lovely children; they are my life. When my time comes, I want it to be as easy as possible on my family. Most people feel the same way about their own families. So that you, too, will not have to leave a jumble of jigsaw pieces as your legacy to your family, I offer you the fruits of my experience and the means by which you can organize your estate—the Estate Plan Binder.

By organizing your estate now, you can save your heirs the arduous task of assembling your estate after your death.

After my clients complete their estate-planning process, I watch them walk away from the office holding the Estate Plan Binder, with their Living Trust inside it, as if it were a precious possession. The clients act as if a great weight has just been lifted from their shoulders. Many clients express their appreciation for giving them peace of mind. The Estate Plan Binder offers you that same peace of mind.

Time and again, I have seen the Estate Plan Binder in action and know how vitally important it was to the survivor. I settle approximately one estate a week, and I could recite innumerable stories of how the binder saved a survivor. The following true story illustrates the binder's importance.

Some years ago, a couple came in to our office to draw up a Living Trust. The husband was a CPA. As a result, the necessary documents were quickly put together, and the couple's assets were transferred into the Trust.

The husband died two years later. Five days later, his wife, Nancy, came into our office with the Estate Plan Binder under her left arm and a stack of checkbooks, passbooks, and trust deeds in her right hand. Nancy laid the documents on the table, and said, "Henry, I am embarrassed to tell you that I don't understand numbers; I never have. My husband always took care of that. I have no idea of what I have." I simply added together the balances shown in the passbooks, checkbooks, and trust deeds. The total came to $350,000. I said, "Nancy, you have an estate of $350,000."

I then proceeded to go through the Estate Plan Binder, and, when I came to the section entitled "Financial Statement," I found that, as a CPA, Nancy's husband had computed their net worth as of December 31; the financial statement showed a net worth of $550,000. I said, "Nancy, you are missing $200,000. Where would it be?" She said, "Henry, I wouldn't have the slightest idea where to begin!"

I again went to the Estate Plan Binder and turned to the two sections titled "Savings and Investment Documents" and "Real Estate Documents." Nancy and her husband had done as I had instructed them when their Living Trust was first created, and they had placed copies of all their assets in these sections of the binder. I checked off the various documents Nancy had placed on the table against the copies filed in the binder. When that comparison was completed, I took little yellow tabs and marked each page that had not been checked off. The page identified the name of the financial institution, its address, the account name, and the account number. I said, "Nancy, I want you to take this binder and, during the next week, go to each of these financial institutions and get a current financial statement of the assets in that institution."

Nancy returned a week later with the current financial statements from each institution. I added them all up—and they totaled $200,000. The missing $200,000 had been found! Right there, the Estate Plan Binder had more than done its job. Similar situations have been repeated time and again.

THE ESTATE PLAN BINDER

The remainder of this chapter is devoted to a description of the Estate Plan Binder. Use this information as a basis for organizing your estate as you work with your own estate-planning professional.

The Estate Plan Binder organizes your estate and takes the survivor step by step through the settlement process. The binder itself is an 8½-by-11-inch three-ring binder with large rings and twenty-four tabbed dividers. The dividers label the following sections:

- Letter with Special Administrative Instructions
- Durable Power of Attorney
- Conservator
- Living Will and Anatomical Gift
- Final Instructions
- Personal Data
- Advisers
- Trust Certification
- Living Trust
- Amendments
- Abstract
- Assignment of Personal Effects
- Estate Preservation Documents
- Guardian
- Insurance Preservation Trust
- Pour-Over Will and Codicils
- Financial Statement
- Asset Distribution by Trust
- Savings and Investment Documents
- Retirement Programs
- Real Estate Documents
- Insurance Policies
- Business Agreements and Documents
- "Living Trust Times"

Letter with Special Administrative Instructions

When a Living Trust is executed, our clients are provided with an extensive letter of instructions, which specifically covers what they are to do to transfer all their assets into the Trust and thereafter to implement the Trust while they are living. All clients are also provided with special administrative instructions advising them what to do if the IRS asks for a Trust tax return and also telling them what to do when they are sent a form to reinstate their homeowner's property exemption.

Durable Power of Attorney

Two separate Durable Power of Attorney documents go in this section. The Durable Power of Attorney for Health Care identifies whom you would want to make medical decisions for you if you were unable to do so yourself. The Durable General Power of Attorney enables the designated individual to pass any assets inadvertently left outside the Trust into your Living Trust if you become incompetent. Be forewarned that the Durable Power of Attorney ceases upon your death.

Conservator

This section contains the Appointment of Conservator document, in which you identify whom you would want to be responsible for your *person* if you were to become incompetent.

Living Will and Anatomical Gift

If you have elected the Anatomical Gift document (Gift of Vital Organs), this document is placed on top. Following the Anatomical Gift document, if any, this section also contains the Living Will (the Right-to-Die Clause).

Final Instructions

In this section are three pages of instructions identifying the steps that need to be followed upon the death of a spouse or a parent. This information is included because experience has shown that, upon the death of a spouse or parent, the surviving spouse and/or children are often mentally paralyzed.

When our clients first receive their Estate Plan Binder, we recommend that they go through this section and complete the right-hand side of those final instructions, as shown in Figure 13-1.

Beginning with the middle of the second page, the final instructions identify the steps that will need to be accomplished to settle the estate. Since, to a great extent, everything needed has already been done by putting the assets in the Living Trust, there is little to do following the death of a spouse, both spouses, or a parent. My experience has been that I can usually go through this section of the Estate Plan Binder with a client (or a surviving family member) in less than an hour, as detailed in Chapter 15.

Not long ago, one of my clients asked me if I knew how to identify where a safe-deposit box might be if I were given a key. I must admit that I did not have a ready answer. The client went on to tell me that, when her husband died, he left behind over a dozen keys to safe-deposit boxes—and three years later, the widow still did not have the slightest idea where to look!

In the final instructions section, identify the number of safe-deposit boxes you have and where they are located, and also mention where the keys are located.

At the bottom of the third page of final instructions is a special area where clients may designate any special instructions they desire to be carried out upon their death.

The final instructions provide a page on which you should list all of your credit cards. The simplest way to make this list is to lay down eight cards at a time on a copy machine and photocopy them. The page is then simply inserted into the Estate Plan Binder. You may also want to write on the page the telephone number to call if the card is ever lost or stolen. This page (or pages) now becomes an excellent record of all of your credit cards in case your wallet is stolen or somehow lost.

Personal Data

The section of the Estate Plan Binder titled "Personal Data" should include copies (not the originals) of military papers (particularly discharge papers), vital papers of personal interest, and vehicle registration certificates.

Divorce papers can be particularly sensitive, but it is very important that they be included. On numerous occasions, a previous spouse has submitted a claim to the estate—claiming that there had never been any divorce. The divorce papers filed in the Estate Plan Binder can be your protection against such false claims.

For a simple and complete record of your credit cards, make photocopies of the cards, and next to each card write the number to call if the card is lost or stolen.

Military papers are the honorable discharge papers you may have received years ago and then filed away and forgotten. If the husband is the first to die, which is so often the case, the funeral home will ask the wife whether her husband served in the military. If the answer is yes, the Veterans Administration will apply $150 toward the cost of the funeral expenses

FIGURE 13-1
FINAL INSTRUCTIONS

Carl Sandburg said, *"There is no agony in the world greater than decision."* Now is the time to resolve *together* some of these essential decisions.

	Name	**Telephone No.**
Check as Accomplished		
_____ Doctor		
_____ Religious representative		
_____ Hospital for anatomical gifts		
_____ Funeral home		
Place and manner of interment		
_____ Immediate family		
_____ Close friends		
_____ Business associates		
_____ Notify out-of-town friends and relatives		
_____ Notify Successor Trustee		
_____ Notify Insurance Trustee (if you have Insurance Preservation Trust)		
_____ Notify company Personnel Department		

IMPORTANT TASKS

_____ Review "Personal Data" in Estate Plan
Binder for Death Certificate accuracy

_____ Make funeral arrangements

_____ If a veteran, take military papers to
funeral home*

_____ Order 12 Death Certificates through
funeral home

_____ Determine if a memorial is to be suggested
in lieu of flowers

_____ Prepare and deliver notice to newspaper
(include date, time, and place of funeral)

_____ Advise Social Security (if receiving or
eligible for benefits)

_____ Check safe-deposit box for special
instructions or messages

Box # _____ Location _____

Key location

Individual(s) authorized to open box

_____ Notify advisers (see Figure 13-2, "Advisers
Page")

_____ Meet with your Adviser on _____ to:

(Month)　　　　　(Year)　　　　　(Time)

_____ Review Trust instructions

Note: Another executed copy of your Trust and Will is located at:

_____ Review Estate Plan Binder.

_____ Notify life insurance companies—include copy of Death Certificate.

_____ Ensure that all assets are within the Trust ("Savings and Investment Documents," "Real Estate Documents," "Insurance Policies," and "Business Agreements and Documents") and, if not, which assets must be probated.

_____ Review size of estate (see "Financial Statement").

_____ Determine if the estate is subject to federal inheritance taxes. Do forms need to be filed and taxes paid?

Keep an accurate record of last illness and funeral costs.

_____ Review business agreements for action, disposition, and benefits (see "Business Agreements and Documents").

_____ Obtain written valuation of real assets (includes stock market quotation—at date of death, and six (6) months later to determine best valuation).

_____ Review credit cards—determine if they should be changed or cancelled. (See attached Credit Card List.)

_____ Distribute personal effects, as per Will, and special Memorandum (see Figure 13-3, "Memorandum"). Make special estate distributions if called for.

*Veterans Administration will provide $150 toward funeral expense, headstone marker, and an American flag, if desired.

(continued)

FIGURE 13-1 (continued)
FINAL INSTRUCTIONS

_____ If assets are to be distributed or retained in Trust for heirs: Determine which assets, and real estate, should be distributed, sold, or converted to income. (Determine debts outstanding to be paid prior to distribution of estate.)

_____ Identify which assets are to be placed in the A Trust and the B Trust and/or the C Trust.

_____ Review investments to see if they meet objectives of income, growth, and security. Determine if some assets should be reinvested to provide adequate income as well as appropriate growth for hedge against inflation. Review assets at least annually to determine if assets should be reinvested for best growth/income and if assets should be shifted between A, B, and/or C Trusts to preserve anticipated appreciation.

_____ If any part, or all, of the Trust becomes irrevocable, order an IRS Employee Identification Number. Use form W-9 or its appropriate alternate form as specified by IRS Regulations.

_____ It may be appropriate to change the identification number on your Trust assets: Substitute surviving spouse's social security number or IRS Employee Identification Number. See Trust section "Trust Identification Number." Use form W-9 or its appropriate alternate form as specified by IRS Regulations.

_____ If any part, or all, of the Trust becomes irrevocable, and assets are retained therein, file form 1041 Trust tax return annually for the irrevocable part of the Trust.

_____ Provide Notice to Creditors, if applicable. See "Notice to Creditors—A New Concept."

If a spouse survives:

_____ Continue to maintain income tax records—you will usually file a joint return in the year of the loss of spouse.

SPECIAL INSTRUCTIONS

If the decedent was living alone:

_____ Remove important documents and valuables to a safe location.

_____ Notify utility companies and landlord.

_____ Advise post office where to send mail.

Other _____

_____

_____

_____

_____

_____

_____

We strongly urge you to take this opportunity to leave a tape-recorded message to loved ones to be sealed until your death.

as well as provide an American flag. At such a traumatic moment as this one, how does the grieving widow know where to look for those important military papers? The Estate Plan Binder is the logical choice for keeping copies of *all* of your important documents.

Thanks to the computer, our clients are now provided with a personal data sheet in this section of the Estate Plan Binder. This one-page data sheet lists all of the pertinent personal information of the clients, including the names of the husband's and wife's parents (and maiden names of the mothers) and the cities and states (or countries) of their birth.

When my mother-in-law passed away, I did not want to burden my wife, so I went down to the funeral home to answer the necessary questions. I was embarrassed when the funeral director asked me the questions, because of all the people who should have been prepared, I should have been. But I was not. I had not brought the necessary information with me. When I was asked for the name of my mother-in-law's father (and where he was born) and her mother's name (and where she was born), I just did not know. I had to tell them I would return later with that information. How silly I felt!

The personal data sheet provides all such information—needed at the time when you are least mentally able to supply it. You might ask why the state wants to know where the mother and father were born. The answer is that someone, somewhere, does a census of migration—tracking how people move from country to country and from state to state.

My real excitement comes from being able to provide the heirs with information that allows them to begin tracing their roots. Most of our children are Americanized and give little thought today to their origin. As this personal data information is included with our Trusts, I am delightfully surprised to see how many of our clients (or their parents) came from countries far and wide to eventually become a part of this great nation. One day your children are going to seek their roots, and the personal data page may be their beginning.

Advisers

In the next section of the binder, you list your special friends and relatives, successor trustees, guardians, financial planners or advisers, attorneys, and CPA, along with their names, addresses, and telephone numbers. Since these individuals change from time to time, it is suggested that you enter the information on this page with a pencil, so that you can easily and clearly keep your Estate Plan Binder up-to-date. Figure 13-2 shows a sample of the Advisers page included in the binder.

Trust Certification

The Estate Plan Binder contains several Trust Certification forms that simply verify that your Living Trust is current. We now provide this section because certification is being requested more and more frequently by financial institutions.

The Trust Certification needs to include the names of the current trustees and the dates of any amendments. The financial institution must know if the trust presented is complete. The trustees must sign the Trust Certification; it does not need to be notarized.

Living Trust

This section of the Estate Plan Binder is where the original copy of your Living Trust document should reside. It may be an A Trust, an A-B Trust, an A-B-C Trust, or a Partner A-A Trust.

Amendment

From time to time, there may be changes to your Living Trust; these changes are called amendments. The amendments may be personal changes (such as a change of beneficiary, a change of method of distribution, or a change of successor trustee), or they may be tax changes as a result of tax laws passed by Congress that could be of benefit to your estate planning.

As mentioned earlier, all of our Trusts have been codified (arranged systematically) in the computer. Whenever there is a major tax change, the computer prints out the name and address of each client who would be affected.

FIGURE 13-2
ADVISERS PAGE

We suggest that you complete this section in pencil so that changes can be made as necessary.

	Name	Address	Telephone No.
Successor Trustee*	_____	_____	_____
Special relatives or friends	_____	_____	_____
	_____	_____	_____
	_____	_____	_____
	_____	_____	_____
	_____	_____	_____
	_____	_____	_____
Guardian	_____	_____	_____
Financial	_____	_____	_____
Attorney	_____	_____	_____
CPA	_____	_____	_____

*Other than husband, wife, or client.

The service of reviewing *all* of our Trusts for applicable tax law changes is as important to our clients as are the Living Trust and the Estate Plan Binder themselves.

Abstract
The abstract is a three-page legal summary of your Living Trust. However, the abstract does *not* identify the allocation or distribution of assets upon your death. The abstract is simply a legal summary of the Trust, which identifies the key issues.

From time to time, a financial institution may ask to see a copy of your Trust. You need only loan the institution a copy of this abstract; in most cases, the abstract will be sufficient. Occasionally, however, a financial institution may ask to see a complete copy of your Living

Trust, rather than just the abstract. Do not be concerned if an institution insists on seeing your entire Trust—simply loan it a copy of your Living Trust. By and large, an institution only wants to see the first page, the signature page, and the trustee powers. The institution wants to make sure that your Trust is a valid document and that you have the necessary authority to perform certain actions. In the case of a mortgage, the mortgage company wants to make sure that there is no provision in the Trust that would stand between the institution and the right to foreclose on your home if you were unable to make the required mortgage payments.

Assignment of Personal Effects

This section includes the document entitled "Assignment of Furniture, Furnishings, and Personal Effects," which assigns these untitled assets into your Living Trust *without having to inventory any of the personal effects*. This document includes any personal effects that you presently have as well as any future acquisitions.

Following the "Assignment" document is the "Memorandum." In the Trust document, under the section "Allocation and Distribution of Trust Assets," the Trust specifically requests the trustee to abide by any "Memorandum." Almost everyone has certain personal effects that he or she wants to leave to a son, daughter, or close personal friend. The Memorandum included as part of the Estate Plan Binder provides a form, as shown in Figure 13-3, that can be used to describe the personal property and to identify to whom you want to leave it.

If you really stop and observe your children or, better yet, simply ask them, you will no doubt find that each child has at least one or two items that he or she would want because of a personal attachment. How nice it is to be able to write, in the "Memorandum" section of the Estate Plan Binder, a simple description of that property and to whom you would like it to be given.

I remember, as a child, spending rare moments with my father each September when we went dove hunting. He loaned me his double-barreled twenty-gauge shotgun. It wasn't a fancy shotgun by my father's standards. In fact, when my father died many years later, he had many very expensive shotguns, and some even had gold triggers.

However, that double-barreled shotgun in some way was a bond between my father and me. Today, the thought of shooting a bird or animal is repugnant to me, so that shotgun would be worthless to me. Still, because of the link it represented between my father and me, I would give my eyeteeth to have it.

Sadly, my favorite shotgun was sold along with the rest of my father's expensive gun collection. I don't think that is what my father would have wanted; however, he wasn't around anymore, and he hadn't put anything in writing.

The Estate Plan Binder is a workbook. The binder does not belong in a safe-deposit box; it belongs at home, on a shelf, or in a drawer, where it is readily available. When you wake up in the middle of the night and suddenly remember that your oldest son indicated that he would someday like to have a particular painting, make a note of it. When you get up in the morning, take out the Estate Plan Binder, open it to the Memorandum section, write down a simple description of the picture, and enter the son's name.

Keep the Estate Plan Binder in a place where it is readily available to you to review or amend.

Estate Preservation Documents

If you have a Spousal and Family Support Trust, Gift Trust, Generation-Skipping Trust, Spousal Gift, Family Limited Partnership, or Charitable Remainder Trust, it will be placed in the Estate Plan Binder behind a divider labeled "Estate Preservation Documents."

Guardian

If you have named a guardian for your minor children (or a handicapped child), the Appointment of Guardian document would be placed in the Estate Plan Binder behind a divider labeled "Guardian."

FIGURE 13-3
MEMORANDUM

DESIRED DISTRIBUTION OF PERSONAL PROPERTY

Certain of my personal effects have special meaning. I desire that upon my death these items be given to those herein indicated.

Description of Personal Property   **Desired Recipient and Relationship**

_____   _____

_____   _____

_____   _____

_____   _____

_____   _____

_____   _____

_____   _____

_____   _____

                                                    _____
                                                    Signed

_____   _____

_____   _____

_____   _____

_____   _____

_____   _____

_____   _____

_____   _____

_____   _____

                                                    _____
                                                    Signed

Insurance Preservation Trust

If you have an Insurance Preservation Trust, it will be placed in the Estate Plan Binder behind a divider labeled "Insurance Preservation Trust."

Pour-Over Will and Codicils

The Pour-Over Will simply says that, if you forgot to put an asset into your Trust, it is your intention upon your death that the forgotten asset should "pour over" into your Living Trust. Unfortunately, if the asset is not in your Trust at the time of your death, the asset must first go through probate if its value exceeds the probate limits.

The executor is the person responsible for shepherding any of your forgotten assets through the probate process. The Pour-Over Will identifies the executor and gives the executor the power to take those assets through probate. Once the probate process is complete, the executor is then empowered to pour over what is left of those assets into the Trust.

If you have done your job, no assets are left outside your Trust; therefore, the Pour-Over Will should never have to be used.

A codicil is simply a change to your Pour-Over Will.

Financial Statement

Included in the Financial Statement section of the Estate Plan Binder is a very simple form for our clients to complete, which provides them with a summary of their financial net worth. Net worth is discussed in greater detail in Chapter 16. Our clients are instructed, when filling out this form, to round the figures to the nearest thousand dollars and to fill out the form in pencil. It is further suggested that the clients review and update this form yearly. The form in the Estate Plan Binder is simple and, if kept up-to-date, simplifies determining whether a Federal Estate Tax Return (Form 706) needs to be filed and, thus, whether any federal estate taxes need to be paid. (The federal estate tax return will be discussed more fully in Chapter 15.)

Asset Distribution by Trust

The "Asset Distribution by Trust" section identifies, upon the death of a spouse, which assets go into the Survivor's A Trust, which assets go into the Decedent's B Trust, and, where appropriate, which assets go into the C (or Q-TIP) Trust. This section of the Estate Plan Binder also includes simple forms that are used as aids to settling the estate of a client with a Living Trust. Figure 13-4 is an example of the form used for distribution into the A Trust. Similar forms with different titles are used for the B and C Trusts. Once the assets are divided and identified on these forms, nothing else needs to be done.

Generally, the appreciating assets should be placed in the B Trust, because this Trust will be insulated from any further estate taxes. On the other hand, when the desired objectives of the estate are discussed with a surviving spouse, the placement of assets in the A, B, or C portion of the Trust may be quite different for each situation.

Of almost equal importance is the inclusion in this section of the Estate Plan Binder of forms that provide the trustee with a simple means of transferring assets back and forth, as necessary, among the A, B, and C Trusts. Figure 13-5 shows an example of the transfer form included in the Estate Plan Binder for the use of our clients. These forms will be explained in greater detail in Chapter 15.

When a client first receives the Estate Plan Binder, we usually postpone discussing the area of asset distribution. There are so many advantages to the Living Trust for people while they are living, and there is so much information to learn and retain, that a detailed discussion of this particular area is deferred until the death of a spouse or parent—at which time all of the advantages of estate planning with a Living Trust are individually discussed with each client.

Savings and Investment Documents

This section of the Estate Plan Binder should include *copies* of any forms that provide the pertinent information (such as name and address of an institution, your account number, and so on) for all of your checking accounts, savings accounts, company and credit union savings accounts, money market funds, certificates of deposit, Treasury bills, stocks, bonds, mutual funds, and notes due.

FIGURE 13-4
TRUST FORM FOR SETTLING AN ESTATE
Trust A

Asset Description	Valuation		
	Amount	Date	Source*
_____	_____	_____	_____
_____	_____	_____	_____
_____	_____	_____	_____
_____	_____	_____	_____
_____	_____	_____	_____
_____	_____	_____	_____
_____	_____	_____	_____
_____	_____	_____	_____
_____	_____	_____	_____
_____	_____	_____	_____
_____	_____	_____	_____
_____	_____	_____	_____
_____	_____	_____	_____

Date: _____   Signature of Trustee: _____

*Source of valuation.

© The Estate Plan, 1984

FIGURE 13-5
ASSET TRANSFER FORM

Asset Description	Amount	Valuation Date	Source*	Transfer From Trust	Transfer To Trust	Trustee Signature	Date

*Source of valuation.

To provide an accurate picture of your estate, however, you should also include copies of documents that identify your liabilities—such as home mortgage, bank loans, credit union loans, and personal loans.

Since this section of the Estate Plan Binder should contain only *copies* of the original documents, it is also important to note where all of the originals may be found (such as in a bank safe-deposit box, a filing cabinet in your den, or wherever the documents are kept).

I am often asked, "How do I make a copy of my checking account?" The answer is simple: Just lay one of your checks down on the surface of a copy machine and make a copy of the check—which immediately makes a record of the name of the bank, the bank's address, the name under which the account is listed, and the account number. It is a simple trail to follow when the need eventually arises. The amount of money in the account is immaterial at this time.

To make a record of your checking account, simply photocopy a check; for your savings accounts, copy the inside cover of each passbook.

The pertinent information for your savings accounts is recorded in the same manner. Simply make a copy of the inside cover of each passbook. For stocks and bonds held in a "street account" by your broker, the quarterly statement of your brokerage account is sufficient. Similarly, the value of each of these accounts is immaterial at this time.

The term *street account* is used by stockbrokers to indicate an account where you allow the stockbroker to hold your stocks at the brokerage firm. The broker/dealer holds your stocks and bonds in the firm's name (otherwise referred to as the "street name"), and the dealer can easily and quickly buy, sell, and transfer those assets—either upon your authority or at the discretion of the broker/dealer if you have given the firm power of attorney. A copy of a quarterly statement is sufficient.

For stocks and bonds held in your name, if you have possession of the certificates, you should also make a copy of every stock and every bond. If these documents should ever happen to be lost, the copy could be used to re-establish your rightful ownership.

> Years ago, a newly widowed woman called me with a problem. The widow said that her husband was so well organized that she always knew where everything was—but, for some unknown reason, she could not find the Treasury notes. I simply said to the widow, "Bring in your Estate Plan Binder." I knew that there was a copy of each Treasury note in the binder; with copies of the original Treasury notes, the widow could then have new Treasury notes issued.

Retirement Programs

The "Retirement Programs" section of the Estate Plan Binder should include copies of your retirement programs with "beneficial interests"—such as your IRAs, Keogh plans, SEPs, pension plans, profit-sharing plans, annuities, tax-sheltered annuities, 401(k) plans, ESOPs, and any deferred-compensation plans. "Beneficial interest" means investments that (upon the death of the primary individual) will continue to provide a benefit to the surviving spouse or children or heirs. For example, a husband may have a retirement plan option to receive a lower pension while he is living in order that the widow may continue to receive the same payment until her death.

Real Estate Documents

The section of the binder labeled "Real Estate Documents" should contain copies (definitely *not* the original documents) of grant deeds and any first and second trust deeds due you; time-share documents should also be included here. You may also wish to include copies of any mortgages you owe, but doing so is optional. Remember, the asset is the important item to record in the binder; the liability will always follow the asset. If you have homesteaded your home, include a copy of the homestead papers.

Insurance Policies

The Insurance Policies section of the Estate Plan Binder should include copies of the *face page* of your insurance policies for any life insurance, accident insurance, disability insurance, and medical insurance policies in force. All too often, people think of an insurance policy for some reason as being sacred. All you really need in the binder is a copy of the face page of the insurance policy, which identifies the name of the insurance company, the name of the insured, the policy number, and the face value of the policy.

If the insurance policy is lost, you can always contact the insurance company, and the policy can be replaced. Unfortunately, there are hundreds of insurance companies, and therefore you *must* know the name of the insurance company that issued the policy. It is surprising how many people have small insurance policies given to them by their parents or acquired early in a marriage. These policies, although not worth much today, are still valuable and usually have been stuck away in a corner and forgotten. How much more effective to have copies of *all* of your insurance policies in this section of the binder.

Business Agreements and Documents
The last section of the Estate Plan Binder should contain copies of any corporate stock certificates (of privately held corporations), partnership agreements, buy-sell agreements, and stock-redemption agreements.

SETTLING AN ESTATE IN LESS THAN AN HOUR
When the Living Trust has been executed by and explained to clients, and copies of all the client's documents have been placed in the Estate Plan Binder, I close the binder and hand it to the wife or husband or to the single client (if unmarried) with these words: "It is our experience with this binder—with the Living Trust—that we can settle the key elements of your estate in less than one hour—and that certainly beats two years of probate." In every instance, the clients react as though the world has just been lifted off their shoulders; they leave our offices smiling and with peace of mind.

In working with thousands of clients, it has been my experience that when a husband and wife (or a surviving parent and child) get

together, they can ultimately find all of their assets. Everyone "knows" where his or her assets are located—until he or she goes to look for them! However, with each other's assistance, members of a family are ultimately able to put together a complete record of their assets.

One couple were incredibly organized. The couple came into our office to execute a Living Trust, bringing a metal box that contained every legal document or asset title in envelopes (filed alphabetically). As the couple took each title or deed from its envelope, the document was photocopied. However, when the husband and wife were supposedly finishing copying all of the documents, I watched them in amazement as they went back and searched through everything—looking for the "pink slip" (the title of legal ownership) for one of their automobiles.

Finally, after they had undergone an exhaustive ten-minute search, a light dawned on the husband. Sheepishly, he reached into his pocket and took out his wallet. From one of the wallet's recesses, the husband pulled out a small piece of paper that had been folded into a half-inch square. The husband laid down the folded piece of paper on the table, unfolded it, pressed out the wrinkles, and said with a sheepish grin, "Here it is!"

If the husband had died, how would anyone have ever found that document? This scene is another of the many examples of how two people—when given the chance to work together—can reconstruct their assets.

A natural question is what will happen if the Estate Plan Binder and Living Trust are somehow destroyed. At The Estate Plan, we execute two complete sets of the Living Trust and all ancillary legal documents for each client. One complete set goes into the Estate Plan Binder, which is given to the client, and the other complete set should be placed in the client's safe-deposit box (or a comparable safe place). Then, if anything were to happen to the client's binder, between the legal documents and the legal titles of assets that are presumably held in the client's safe-deposit box, it should be possible to reconstitute the Estate Plan Binder with all legal and supporting documents within about two days. You can benefit by setting up this kind of arrangement with your own adviser.

Even though your successor trustee does not need to *see* your Trust, know the *size* of your estate, or *see* the Estate Plan Binder while you are living, you should tell your successor trustee where to find your Estate Plan Binder upon your death!

One day when I was in my mother's apartment, she asked me to go into the den and get her Estate Plan Binder, so that we could make a change to it. Fifteen minutes later, I came from the den and asked her where she had hidden it. "Oh, I forgot to tell you—it's in the bottom drawer of the dresser, at the very bottom of the drawer." I wondered how I would have ever found that binder if something had happened to her.

The Estate Plan Binder is a workbook—*it belongs at home*. However, please let your successor trustee know where to find it!

14

Funding Your Trust for Life

All too often, attorneys create Trusts but then do not have the clients' assets transferred into the Trusts. Instead, the attorneys simply list the assets in "schedules" attached to the Living Trust—Schedule A (assets) and Schedule B (life insurance). Typically, attorneys also write the clients a letter advising them to open a bank account for $50 in the name of the Trust in order to "fund the Trust." Theoretically, these actions release the attorneys from any further liability, because an unfunded Trust is no Trust at all.

However, the client's assets are not actually recorded in the name of the Trust, and—as you learned in Chapter 7—this situation means that the Trust is legally nothing more than a Testamentary Trust. On the death of a spouse, the assets must still go through probate before they will pass into the Trust! Such situations happen all too frequently, because of a lack of proper communication between the client and the attorney.

In many cases, the lawyer has even told the client that listing the assets in Schedules A and B transfers them into the Trust. However, this information is absolutely false! The primary purpose of Schedules A and B in many Trusts drawn up by inexperienced attorneys is to identify the client's assets in Schedule A and the client's insurance policies in Schedule B—but the schedules serve no legal purpose.

Listing your assets in a Schedule A or B merely identifies them; it does not transfer them into your Trust.

Many attorneys get their clients from insurance agents and financial planners. "Professional courtesy" often means scratching each other's back. Thus, the attorney, having received a referral from an insurance agent, can look at the amount of insurance carried by the client and suggest to the client that he or she should have more insurance—and who better to provide that insurance than the insurance agent who brought the client to the attorney? Such back-scratching is called third-party influence. The same situation would be true for assets (instead of insurance) when a financial planner provides the referral.

In 1979, I took a client to an attorney to draw up a Trust for his mother, who was dying of cancer. The attorney elected "not to bother" the mother with signatures needed to transfer each asset into the Trust and instead chose only to list the assets in a Schedule A. I reminded the attorney that only listing the assets in Schedule A would *not*, in fact, transfer them into the Trust; however, the attorney was not about to listen to me and told me in no uncertain terms that *he* was the attorney and that he knew the law.

Six months later, the mother died. Then the troubles began, as the client discovered that, indeed, the assets were *not* legally in the Trust.

To assist the client, I went to the secretary of state, who advised me that the assets listed on Schedule A were not inside the Trust. I pleaded that it was very definitely the woman's intent to have the assets placed inside the Trust. However, my pleading was fruitless; I was told that the assets definitely must go through probate. To my understanding, the assets were still going through probate twelve years later!

Listing assets and insurance in Schedules A and B for a Trust is absolutely meaningless. Furthermore, if you list your assets in your Trust, you must thereafter amend your Trust each time you change one of the assets—an unnecessary and wasteful cost. (In fact, such schedules are not included in our Living Trust, expressly to avoid such situations.) Instead, you need to transfer the title of all your assets into your Trust. This chapter explains how to do so.

PROTECT YOUR ASSET TRANSFERS

Before making any transfers into your Living Trust, a married couple should sign a "Letter of Intent/Declaration of Gift." This will assure that your assets, when transferred, will retain their desired status. Your Letter of Intent/Declaration of Gift should read something comparable to these words: "By transferring assets to this Trust, I intend to give my spouse a 50 percent interest in all property transferred to this Trust unless otherwise expressly provided for."

This requirement applies to both community property states and separate property states.

WHAT TO TRANSFER INTO YOUR TRUST

As a general rule, you should leave *nothing* outside your Trust. However, only your assets (such as a house, stocks, bonds, savings accounts, and so on) need to be transferred into the name of your Living Trust. Liabilities (such as any debts you owe) and general insurance policies (such as house and automobile insurance) are not transferred into the name of the Trust.

All of your assets should be transferred into your Living Trust.

After years of creating thousands of Living Trusts in every state (and in every situation imaginable), I now recommend that you put *everything* in your Trust—including checking accounts, automobiles, and safe-deposit boxes. (If you have any doubt about such a recommendation, look again at Table 2-1 in Chapter 2, where you will see that thirty-nine states and the District of Columbia probate *every dollar* of your estate that exceeds just $30,000.) Remember that assets outside the Trust are subject to the agonizing probate process. Fortunately, as you will see, transferring your assets into your Living Trust is really quite simple.

Checking Accounts

In the past, I recommended that checking accounts be left outside the Living Trust because I knew that some people would succumb to the demands of a bank teller who insisted that they place the name of their Living Trust on their checks—which eventually would cause them problems. Please understand that *the name of your Trust need not be placed on your checks*, even though your checking account is recorded in the name of your Living Trust. However, I now accede to the wise counsel of one bank officer who offered an obvious but elusive suggestion: Don't go to the teller; go to an officer of the bank. Ask him or her to record your checking account in the name of your Living Trust, but insist that your checks still read the same as they did before being placed in your Trust. This practice gives you the best of both worlds: You get your checking account in your Living Trust (and thus avoid the possibility of probate), and you also avoid the hassle of having to justify to unknowing clerks why checks are written in the name of your Living Trust. We provide our clients with letters of transfer to make this transfer process very simple.

Be aware of the awkward situation that can occur if the name of your Living Trust is printed on your checks:

You go to the bank and ask the teller to transfer your checking account into the name of the Trust. The teller informs you that you must now get new checks showing the Trust name. Is the teller right? Absolutely not. However, since you don't know any better, you order the new checks.

Several weeks later, you pick up your checks, and you stop on your way home at your favorite department store to pick up some shoes, which you had ordered. You give one of your new checks to the sales clerk, who looks at the check and says, "Oh, I'm sorry, I can't cash this check, because it's in the name of a Trust." You are then sent upstairs to the credit manager, where, after a half hour of frustration and no further satisfaction, you take out your credit card and charge the shoes.

Continuing on your way home, you stop by your favorite grocery store; it's seven o'clock at night, and the lines are long. You finally get up to the front of the line and hand another clerk your new check. The clerk responds, "I cannot accept this check, because it is in the name of a Trust." In frustration, you finally reach into your wallet and dig through your pockets to come up with enough money to pay for the groceries.

After you have experienced this frustration, you can't wait to get home to call me—to find out just what kind of a mess I created for you. Were any of the clerks right? Absolutely not! Yet is such a situation actually going to happen? Yes, over and over again.

As this example shows, you don't want to put the name of your Living Trust on your checks—*and you don't have to do so*. However, be sure to have the bank record your checking account in the name of your Living Trust.

Series EE U.S. Government Savings Bonds
You need to take your Series EE Bonds to your local bank and ask them to transfer the bonds for you. They have the appropriate forms and will do this as a service for you. There will be no change in your interest rate or maturity date. Fail to transfer your Series EE Bonds, and your heirs will ultimately find it necessary to go through an arduous process with the Federal Reserve Bank.

Motor Vehicles
As is true with checking accounts, I now recommend that you also place motor vehicles in your Living Trust. If you own an expensive automobile, more than one moderately priced vehicle, or a motor home, it is in your best interest to record those vehicles in the name of the Trust. The transfer process is very simple and involves only a simple trip to your local department of motor vehicles. More important, you will avoid any future question of whether the value of your estate exceeds the limit that would require probate. We provide our clients with letters of transfer that make this process very simple.

One exception is the state of Florida, which will charge $125 to record your automobile in your Living Trust. Wait until you replace your automobile, and then have it recorded in your Living Trust.

In some states, mobile homes were once registered as motor vehicles but are now registered in a different department. For example, all new mobile homes purchased in California must register with the Department of Housing and Community Development. Under these circumstances, a mobile home should definitely be in the name of the Living Trust.

Airplanes
All American aircraft are registered with the Federal Aviation Administration (FAA)—the

state is not involved. You need to assign your airplane to your Living Trust by completing FAA form 1511, attach your certificate of registration, and forward both form and certification to the FAA at DOT/OST/OAA, P-56, 400; 7th St. SW, Room 6401, Washington, D.C. 20590.

Boats

If your boat is registered with the state, contact your appropriate state agency and acquire their transfer form. Complete the form and submit it, with your boat registration certificate, to your state agency. If, instead, your boat has a Certificate of Documentation issued by the Coast Guard, you need to contact the Coast Guard to request their transfer forms.

TRANSFERRING SAFE-DEPOSIT BOXES

To be on the safe side, you should put your safe-deposit boxes in the name of the Trust. To transfer your safe-deposit boxes into your Trust, you simply go to the bank and have the bank representative rewrite your file card for the safe-deposit boxes in the name of your Trust.

TRANSFERRING DEEDS

Transferring real estate deeds into your Living Trust is the one area of funding your Trust that should *not* be a do-it-yourself project! Only attorneys should transfer deeds, unless you specialize in this particular area (that is, you are a real estate agent or escrow agent). The cost of transferring deeds should be nominal (less than $100), but the importance of making the transfer legally proper cannot be overemphasized. An improper and possibly ineffective transfer of real estate deeds can be disastrous!

As you learned in Chapter 5, transferring the deed to your house, for example, into your Living Trust will not affect your right to borrow against your house or to refinance it. If the deed is properly transferred, the transfer will not accelerate your mortgage (cause it to become due, as if you had sold your home).

We now recommend that it is a good practice to notify your mortgage company that you have a Living Trust and have placed your home

therein. Most mortgage companies now understand the importance of a Living Trust and further recognize that it does not affect their interest in your home as collateral to your loan.

Figure 14-1 shows a typical deed for property held in joint tenancy by a husband and wife. Figure 14-2 shows how the same deed would look when ownership of the property has been transferred into the name of the Living Trust.

Effect on Tax Base of Property

Some years ago, California voters approved Proposition 13, which rolled back the property tax base and permitted it to be increased at a maximum rate of only 2 percent per year. Many states have followed California's lead in rolling back property taxes and limiting future increases. If you live in such a state, placing your assets in a Living Trust will have no effect whatsoever on your favorable property tax base.

Putting your home in your Living Trust will not cause your property taxes to increase.

In California, four months after Proposition 13 was passed, the state legislature quickly addressed the problem of transferring real estate into a Living Trust and, by legislation, made it very clear that transferring property into such a Trust would have no effect on the tax base of real estate (that is, the assessed valuation used to assess property tax). In simple terms, your property taxes will *not* increase when you place your home in a Living Trust. California voters also passed Proposition 58, which allows assets to pass from parents to children or from children to parents with no effect upon the tax base of the asset.

Clients also wonder what happens when a widow remarries and wishes to put her home in a Trust created with her new husband, which effectively transfers ownership of the home. Proposition 13 and its counterparts in other states typically provide that, when a surviving or divorced spouse remarries, his or her part of the interest in the property may pass to the new spouse without being subject to

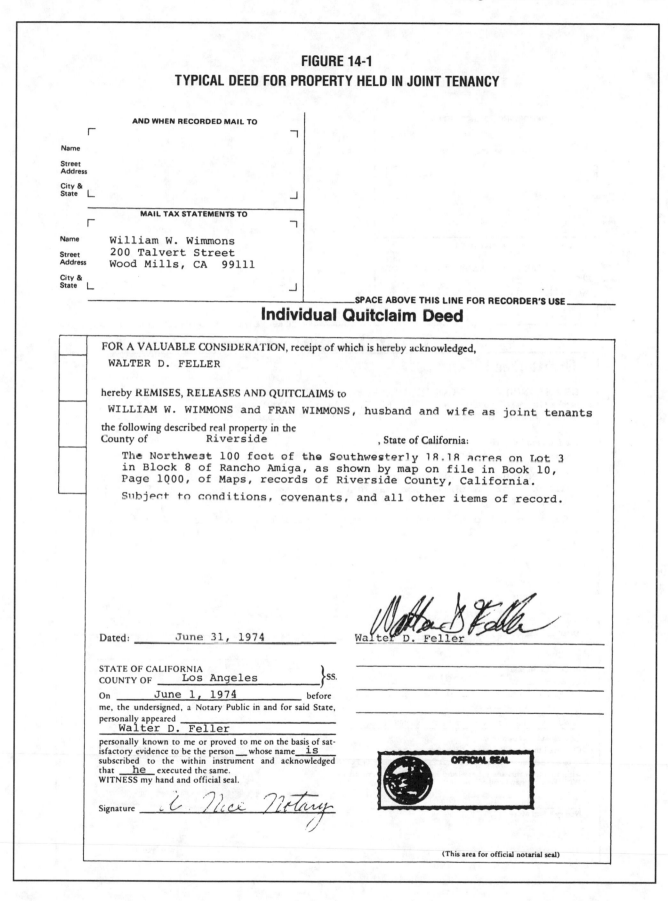

FIGURE 14-1
TYPICAL DEED FOR PROPERTY HELD IN JOINT TENANCY

AND WHEN RECORDED MAIL TO

Name

Street
Address

City &
State

MAIL TAX STATEMENTS TO

Name   William W. Wimmons

Street   200 Talvert Street
Address   Wood Mills, CA 99111

City &
State

SPACE ABOVE THIS LINE FOR RECORDER'S USE

Individual Quitclaim Deed

FOR A VALUABLE CONSIDERATION, receipt of which is hereby acknowledged,

WALTER D. FELLER

hereby REMISES, RELEASES AND QUITCLAIMS to

WILLIAM W. WIMMONS and FRAN WIMMONS, husband and wife as joint tenants

the following described real property in the
County of   Riverside   , State of California:

The Northwest 100 feet of the Southwesterly 18.18 acres on Lot 3
in Block 8 of Rancho Amiga, as shown by map on file in Book 10,
Page 1000, of Maps, records of Riverside County, California.

Subject to conditions, covenants, and all other items of record.

Dated: June 31, 1974   Walter D. Feller

STATE OF CALIFORNIA
COUNTY OF   Los Angeles   }SS.

On   June 1, 1974   before
me, the undersigned, a Notary Public in and for said State,
personally appeared
Walter D. Feller

personally known to me or proved to me on the basis of satisfactory evidence to be the person __ whose name is
subscribed to the within instrument and acknowledged
that   he   executed the same.
WITNESS my hand and official seal.

Signature

OFFICIAL SEAL

(This area for official notarial seal)

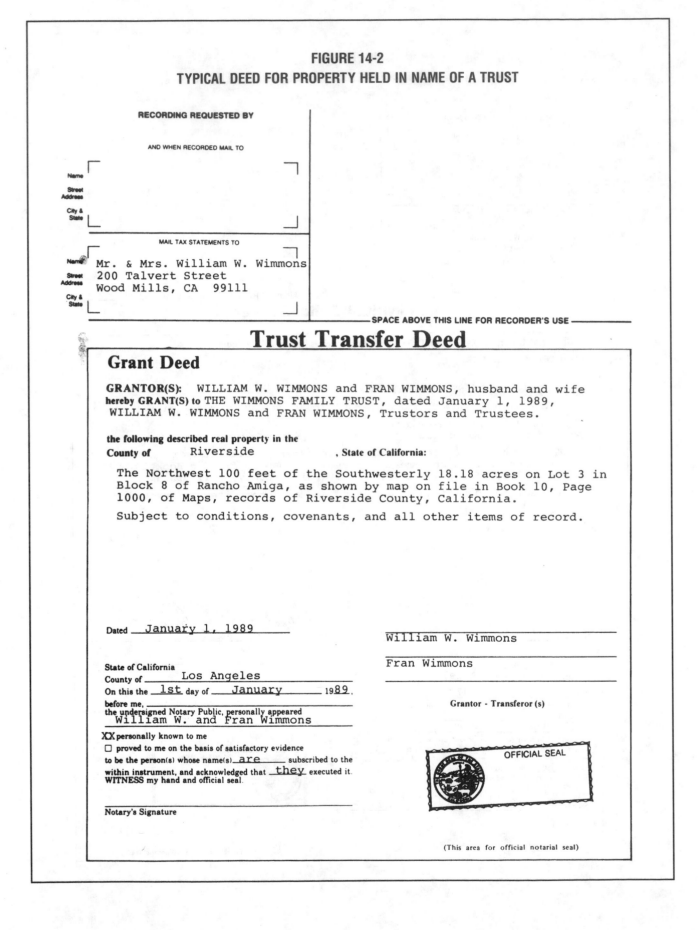

FIGURE 14-2
TYPICAL DEED FOR PROPERTY HELD IN NAME OF A TRUST

RECORDING REQUESTED BY

AND WHEN RECORDED MAIL TO

Name

Street Address

City & State

MAIL TAX STATEMENTS TO

Name   Mr. & Mrs. William W. Wimmons
Street Address   200 Talvert Street
City & State   Wood Mills, CA 99111

——— SPACE ABOVE THIS LINE FOR RECORDER'S USE ———

Trust Transfer Deed

Grant Deed

GRANTOR(S): WILLIAM W. WIMMONS and FRAN WIMMONS, husband and wife
hereby **GRANT(S) to** THE WIMMONS FAMILY TRUST, dated January 1, 1989,
WILLIAM W. WIMMONS and FRAN WIMMONS, Trustors and Trustees.

the following described real property in the
County of   Riverside   , State of California:

The Northwest 100 feet of the Southwesterly 18.18 acres on Lot 3 in
Block 8 of Rancho Amiga, as shown by map on file in Book 10, Page
1000, of Maps, records of Riverside County, California.

Subject to conditions, covenants, and all other items of record.

Dated __January 1, 1989__

State of California
County of _____Los Angeles_____
On this the __1st__ day of __January__ 19__89__,
before me, _____
the undersigned Notary Public, personally appeared
      William W. and Fran Wimmons

XX personally known to me
☐ proved to me on the basis of satisfactory evidence
to be the person(s) whose name(s) __are__ subscribed to the
within instrument, and acknowledged that __they__ executed it.
WITNESS my hand and official seal.

_____
Notary's Signature

William W. Wimmons

Fran Wimmons

Grantor - Transferor (s)

OFFICIAL SEAL

(This area for official notarial seal)

reappraisal and potentially higher property taxes.

A similar concern arises when parents and children share ownership of real estate. In today's extremely high-cost housing market, it is becoming more and more common for grown children to need their parents to join them as co-owners when they purchase property, because the children's income is insufficient to satisfy the mortgage requirements. In such cases, the parents may remove their names from the title to the home and allow the children to put the home in a Living Trust without any impact upon the tax base. However, under such circumstances, it is necessary to specify (on an accompanying form, which is attached to the real estate deed) the reason that the parents' names were on the title—specifically, to allow the children to be able to qualify for the mortgage.

Effect on Homeowner's Insurance

Transferring the grant deed of your real estate into your Living Trust will have no effect upon your homeowner's insurance.

> Many years ago, I received a distress call from one of our clients, a widow, who said she had been turned down by two insurance companies for insurance on her home because it was in a Living Trust. Rather than call her agent, I called the head of the legal department of both her insurance companies. Both gentlemen assured me that their agents were wrong and offered to call my client and rectify the situation. Later that afternoon, I received a call from the grateful widow, who told me that not only had the parties called, but that she had ended up with her homeowner's insurance at a lower rate than had previously been quoted.

Effect of "Due-on-Sale" Clause

Transferring the grant deed of your real estate into the Living Trust has no effect upon the "due-on-sale" clause in your mortgage. However, we do suggest, if you live in the Midwest or the East, that it might be appropriate to advise your mortgage company that you are transferring your deed into a Grantor Trust (simply another name for a Living Trust) because these companies are not as familiar with the Living Trust. Please recognize that the key word is "Grantor" Trust—which means that you continue to control your assets even though you have technically transferred them into the name of the Trust.

$250,000 Exemption on Home

When you transfer your assets into a Living Trust, you do not affect in any way the $250,000 exemption on your home. This exemption is available to those who are age fifty-five and above and who have lived in their home for at least three years. The only caution that I would offer is that if your home is placed in the Decedent's B Trust, you will want to transfer it from the B Trust to the A Trust at least two years prior to the sale of the house. If the house were to remain in the B Trust, the surviving spouse would lose the $250,000 exemption on the home.

Effect on Property Tax Exemptions and Homesteading

The homeowner's property tax exemption is a state exemption, which in some states is limited to veterans only and in other states is made available to all homeowners. Placing the deed to your home in a Living Trust has absolutely no effect upon the state tax exemption, except in Pennsylvania, Florida, and Texas. Great care should be taken in transferring real estate into a Living Trust in these three states.

The Homestead Act is a federal law that protects your home from creditors if the equity in your home is less than allowed and you file bankruptcy. As part of good financial planning, everyone should consider recording his or her home under the federal Homestead Act with the county recorder's office. Placing your home in a Living Trust has no effect upon the protections offered by the federal Homestead Act.

If, when you first transfer your home into your Living Trust, the county assessor sends you a letter indicating that your homeowner's property tax exemption has been terminated, you can re-establish your exemption. The attorney who prepared your Living Trust should be able to advise you on this matter.

The Grant Deed

When you transfer your home into the Trust, give your legal expert a copy of your grant deed for the property. If the grant deed says, "See Exhibit A Attached," then you must also provide the attached exhibit, since it is considered to be part of the deed.

Some clients mistakenly believe that they do not have a grant deed, because they have not yet paid off the mortgage. However, in most states, when you buy real estate, you are given a grant deed, which gives you ownership to the property. In some states, title to the property may be known as a land grant or land lease, but, under any name, this document gives title to the property.

If you are unable to locate the grant deed—as often happens with our clients—you may easily acquire a copy by calling the county recorder's office. Someone there will tell you how to request a copy of the grant deed. You will have to request it in writing and pay a nominal fee.

Transferring When an Owner Is Not a Family Member

If you have property in a state with legislation similar to California's Proposition 13, be very careful about recording real estate in the name of your Trust when you are transferring all of the property into the Trust and one of the owners is *not* a family member. Under Proposition 13, if property ownership is passed to a non-related party, this transfer of ownership is not an exempt transaction (family transfer) and would therefore trigger reappraisal of the property to the current market value.

An unmarried couple owned a home in joint tenancy. When the woman decided to create a Living Trust, the man volunteered to transfer his entire interest in the property to her. Therefore, the deed to the property was written in the name of her Trust. However, the deed was *not* recorded, because doing so would cause the interest in the property given to the woman to be reappraised. When a deed is notarized it is legally placed in the Trust; it is not necessary to record it with the county recorder. When real estate is transferred to another person and recorded with the county, it is reappraised, and the property taxes are increased accordingly.

TRANSFERRING TRUST DEEDS

If you have lent money to people, using their home as collateral, and have taken back a first or second trust deed, the trust deed is an asset to you. It is another individual's obligation to pay you money. Usually the value of trust deeds is high enough that this asset would cause your estate to go through the probate process; therefore, trust deeds should *always* be in the name of your Trust.

To transfer a trust deed (a legal document), you must have the trust deed redrawn by an attorney or real estate specialist and recorded with the county recorder's office in the name of your Trust. A trust deed should always be recorded, because it is your protection to ensure that the property against which you hold a lien may not be sold until the debtor has repaid the money owed to you.

TRANSFERRING TIME-SHARES

Today, more and more people have invested in time-share property, in which they typically own a piece of property for one or more weeks of the year. Time-share ownership is, in fact, ownership in real estate; therefore, title to the property should be transferred into the name of your Trust. Again, the title should be redrawn in the name of your Trust and then recorded with the county recorder's office.

TRANSFERRING A BUSINESS INTEREST

If you own part or all of a business in the form of stock that is publicly traded over the counter or on one of the stock exchanges, the company's transfer agent should change the ownership of your stock to the name of the Trust. This action can usually be done through your company's personnel office or treasurer.

If your business interest is in a privately owned corporation, it may be easily transferred by voiding your existing stock certificates and reissuing new stock certificates in the name of the Trust. Blank stock certificates are typically found in your corporate minutes book.

I often hear that if a business is placed in a Living Trust, operation of the business will be severely restricted. However, such a statement is very much in error. A partnership or sole proprietorship usually perishes quickly after the death of a principal. The only recourse for the survivors is to sell quickly—an impossible feat during the probate process, but a quick and easy solution if the business is in a Living Trust. To transfer a partnership interest or sole proprietorship, an attorney should draw a legal Bill of Sale/Letter of Transfer, which describes the business and transfers it into your Trust. A typical Bill of Sale/Letter of Transfer for transferring a business into a Living Trust is shown in Figure 14-3.

UNUSUAL TRANSFERS

If you own shares in a limited partnership, ask the general partners to transfer your interest into your Trust. On rare occasions, a general partner responds that it cannot transfer your limited partnership into the Trust. What the general partner is really saying is that it doesn't know how to do the transfer. Legal counsel can resolve this dilemma by creating a Bill of Sale/Letter of Transfer for your limited partnership interest.

The same approach would apply to any other assets that the agents will not readily transfer, as well as to expensive artworks or an extensive collection of antiques. This approach would also apply to patents and copyrights.

TRANSFERRING GENERAL ASSETS

General assets include savings accounts, money market accounts, certificates of deposit, Treasury bills, Ginnie Maes, credit union accounts, stocks, bonds, mutual funds, limited partnerships, and notes due. All these general assets can be transferred into your Trust with simple letters of transfer at no cost.

Real Assets Other than
Real Estate and Securities

To transfer each general asset into your Living Trust, you need only write the name and address of the financial institution as well as the particular asset and account number on the letter of transfer. We advise our clients to use one letter per financial institution. If you have more than one account at a particular financial institution, you would simply list each of the accounts on the same letter. The letter states that the specified assets are to be transferred into the name of the Living Trust (the full name of which is included as part of the letter).

The letter of transfer also specifies that the identification number of the Trust will be the social security number of the trustee. For reasons pointed out in earlier chapters, if an individual is single, his or her social security number should be used as the Trust Identification Number. If individuals are married, the husband's social security number should be typically used, but it is appropriate to use either the husband's or the wife's number. The individuals then sign the transfer letter in two places—as the transferors (they are the ones who are transferring the assets) and as the transferees (they are the ones who are receiving the assets on behalf of the Trust).

We provide each of our clients with six letters of transfer. If clients need additional copies, they can simply photocopy one of the original letters; the photocopies usually are just as acceptable as the originals.

You should mail or hand-deliver these letters of transfer to the various institutions that have your accounts. In many cases, a financial institution has its own form, which it requires you to sign. If so, your letter of transfer simply causes the institution to send you its form (which it typically fills out for you); you then need only sign the institution's special form, have your signature witnessed or notarized, and then return the form to the institution holding your account. When you send a letter of transfer to a financial institution and the necessary paperwork has been completed (either your transfer letter or the signing of the institution's own transfer form), the institution should acknowledge that it has made the requested transfer.

Stocks and Bonds

The easiest way to transfer stocks and bonds into your Trust is to take them to your stockbroker and ask the brokerage firm to transfer

FIGURE 14-3
TYPICAL BILL OF SALE/LETTER OF TRANSFER

BILL OF SALE
OF
"DOE'S DRY CLEANERS"

We, John J. Doe and Jane J. Doe (Assignors herein), do hereby sell, transfer and assign, without consideration, to "**The Doe Family Trust dated December 24, 1973, John J. Doe and Jane J. Doe, Trustors and/or Trustees,**" all right, title and interest which we have in our business, which we operate under the name "Doe's Dry Cleaners" at 9012 N. Smutz Rd., Westerfield, IL 60606, together with all of the assets of the business, their uses and profits. This business has a Federal Tax Identification Number of 67-0912873. This Assignment includes all furnishings, fixtures, appliances, inventory and supplies of the business, the lease on the premises where the business is located, all insurance owned in connection with the business, and all bank accounts, and accounts receivable connected with the business.

IN WITNESS WHEREOF, we have signed this assignment on September 24, 1996.

ASSIGNORS:

_____

John J. Doe   Jane J. Doe

             (STATE OF ILLINOIS
ss. (
             (COUNTY OF WASHINGTON

On September 24, 1996, before me, a Notary Public, personally appeared John J. Doe and Jane J. Doe, personally known to me (or proved to me on the basis of satisfactory evidence) to be the persons whose names are subscribed to this instrument, and acknowledged that they executed it.

(NOTARY SEAL)

_____
NOTARY PUBLIC
My Commission Expires: _____

them for you. The firm may want to charge you for such a transfer; however, since you most likely have bought your stocks and bonds in the past from this particular brokerage house, the firm should be more than happy to make your stock transfers free of charge (if it would like your continued business).

If you do not have a stockbroker, or have one who wants to charge you for transferring your security or securities, the nationwide firm of Charles Schwab has offered to transfer your securities into your Living Trust, as a service, at no fee. However, if you choose to make the transfer yourself, you will need to send your stocks or bonds to the transfer agent, whose name is typically listed on the stocks and bonds. When you send stock certificates to a transfer agent, you should do so by using an Irrevocable Stock or Bond Power, such as the one shown in Figure 14-4. You must sign this Irrevocable Stock or Bond Power in *exactly* the same manner as the stock or bond has been registered. You must have your signature guaranteed—which may be done only by a stock brokerage firm with a seat on any stock exchange or by any bank. Unfortunately, a savings and loan institution may not guarantee your signature on such a form.

Your stocks or bonds are nonnegotiable as long as they are unsigned. Once signed, your stock or bond certificates are now negotiable by anyone! For your protection, send the *unsigned* stocks or bonds in one letter and the Irrevocable Stock or Bond Power in a separate letter. Thus, only when both envelopes arrive at the destination can the two be put together, at which time the stock and bond certificates will be negotiable. An alternative solution is to name the transferring brokerage firm as the designated power of attorney.

Your letter of transfer for the stocks or bonds should be sent to the transfer agent along with the other paperwork.

Many people have accumulated stocks and bonds over a long period. Even though the people bought only small quantities at any one time, they fail to realize how the value of their stock and bond portfolio may have increased to a sizable amount.

A widower once came to our office to do a Living Trust and transferred all of his assets into the Trust, with one exception—a single stock certificate for 5,000 shares of IBM stock. It would have taken the man less than an hour to drive down to the bank, have his signature guaranteed, and then send that stock certificate forward to be transferred into the name of his Trust, but he never got around to it. The man died six months later.

Since the rest of the man's estate was in his Living Trust, most of his estate was settled immediately. Within two months thereafter, all of the assets, including his house, had been sold, and the assets were distributed to his heirs. In contrast, that single piece of paper not in the Trust was then worth $500,000 and had to go through probate. The process took one full year and cost more than $10,000! The man's family learned—the hard way—about the agony of probate. How much simpler it would have been had the man transferred that stock certificate into the name of his Living Trust.

TRANSFERRING INSURANCE, ANNUITIES, AND RETIREMENT ASSETS

Your Trust should be the beneficiary of all of your life insurance and non-qualified annuity policies. This is no longer true of Qualified Plan assets, specifically an IRA, a Keogh, a qualified annuity, and a 401(k) plan. Qualified Plan assets are a different kind of animal and are discussed at length further on. Specifically, the beneficiary of Qualified Plan assets is usually the spouse, and thereafter you may wish to consider a Qualified/IRA Trust.

When you name your Living Trust as the beneficiary of your insurance policies, this will take precedence over any Will or Trust. For example, if you have named your spouse as the beneficiary of your life insurance policy, and you and your spouse happen to be killed simultaneously, the insurance policy will pass (in the legal sense) without probate to your spouse, but then must go through probate to pass on to your children. Although some people are smart enough to name contingent beneficiaries (such as their children), most people have not

---

FIGURE 14-4
TYPICAL IRREVOCABLE STOCK OR BOND POWER FORM

FOR VALUE RECEIVED, the undersigned does (do) hereby sell, assign and transfer to

_____

_____ | _____
                                                (Social Security or Taxpayer Identifying No.)

IF STOCK, COMPLETE THIS PORTION { _____ shares of the _____ stock of _____

represented by Certificate (s) No (s)_____inclusive,

standing in the name of the undersigned on the books of said Company.

IF BONDS, COMPLETE THIS PORTION { _____ bonds of _____

in the principal amount of $_____, No (s)_____ inclusive,

standing in the name of the undersigned on the books of said Company.

The undersigned does (do) hereby irrevocably constitute and appoint_____

_____attorney to transfer the said stock or bond (s), as the case may

be, on the books of said Company, with full power of substitution in the premises.

Dated_____

X _____

X _____
   (Person(s) Executing This Power Sign(s) Here)

OFF	Account No.	T

93-0163

---

bothered to do so. Contingent beneficiaries would be the recipients of the insurance (without probate) upon the simultaneous death of both husband and wife.

To transfer assets with a beneficiary—such as life insurance—our clients use a beneficiary letter of transfer. The beneficiary letter of transfer is similar to the general asset letter of transfer. The transfer should be without cost.

Life Insurance

For transferring life insurance policies into the Trust, for either single or married persons, the letter states, "The beneficiary should now read," followed by the name of the Trust and the creator's social security number.

For each asset with a named beneficiary, you simply write in the name and address of the institution, such as an insurance company, as well as the policy or account number. If you have more than one policy or account with that company, you would list the numbers for all policies or accounts with that particular company. We suggest to our clients that they send only one letter of transfer to each company.

You must sign the letters twice—once as the transferors (the individuals who are transferring the assets) and again as the transferees (the individuals who are receiving the assets on behalf of the Trust). We provide our clients six copies of the transfer letter for their use in transferring their beneficial interests into their Living Trust.

Upon receipt of your letter of transfer, an insurance company almost always will send back to you its own form (which it has usually filled out) to be signed by you and then witnessed. Each insurance company does a beneficiary change in its own way.

Single-Premium Life Insurance

Unlike ordinary life insurance policies, single-premium life insurance is an investment vehicle under the insurance company umbrella. Single-premium insurance policies can be either single-premium whole life insurance or single-premium universal life insurance. With this investment vehicle, you make a single investment (such as $100,000), and, because of the income tax-favored basis of insurance, the growth—as well as the income from the investment—can be tax deferred.

The single-premium life insurance policy also is life insurance; it pays a death benefit. Depending upon the age of the insured individual when the single premium is paid, the death benefit will vary from six times the amount of the investment (for someone around the age of forty) to twice the amount of the investment (for someone around the age of sixty). Since these insurance policies have a death benefit, your Living Trust should be named as beneficiary, using the beneficiary letter of transfer.

Annuities

As another type of insurance company investment, annuities have designated beneficiaries. You should use the beneficiary letter of transfer to name your Living Trust as the contingent beneficiary of all annuities.

Typically, your spouse will be the primary beneficiary, and your Living Trust will be the contingent beneficiary. This applies to non-qualified annuities. Qualified annuities are addressed in the following paragraphs.

Qualified Plan Assets

Qualified Plan assets are an IRA, a Keogh, a qualified annuity, and a 401(k) plan. These plans should *not* be placed in your Living Trust. In 1997, when I was writing *How to Settle Your Living Trust*, I addressed this issue with a number of experts. The IRS continued to change the rules at its own whim—not based

on the laws passed by Congress and formalized by the Treasury Department. We agreed that we could modify the Living Trust to satisfy the IRS at the time, but we recognized that the IRS would continue to change the rules as they applied to the Living Trust. Sure enough, the IRS rules changed twice during the next several months. We thus concluded that we needed a separate Trust designed just for Qualified Plans. In response, we developed the IRA/Qualified Plan Trust and the Roth IRA Trust.

The beauty of these Qualified Trusts is that they become excellent recipient vehicles for Qualified Plans, allow you to control the beneficial interest, and at the same time maximize your federal estate tax exclusion. Ideally, the spouse is the primary beneficiary, and the Qualified Trust is the contingent beneficiary. This gives the surviving spouse the greatest latitude in preserving the Trust assets. The surviving spouse may disclaim part or all of the Qualified Plan in favor of the Qualified Trust. This is explained in detail in *How to Settle Your Living Trust*.

What you need to understand at this juncture is that you do *not* name your Living Trust as a beneficiary of your Qualified Plan. We have developed the IRA/Qualified Plan Trust and the Roth IRA Trust as the ideal estate-planning vehicles.

The IRA Will vs. Qualified Plan Trusts

Today, my greatest concern in this regard is that since a Living Trust is no longer an appropriate beneficiary of your IRA and other Qualified Plans, an alternative, called an IRA Will, is being offered. The IRA Will pays directly to the beneficiaries and as such incurs a number of shortcomings. Since the IRA Will pays the IRA directly to the beneficiary, there is no method to control the IRA expenditure. A recent study reports that most inherited IRAs are spent within fourteen months. The IRA Will does not provide for minors, fails to provide creditor protection for the beneficiary, and does not protect the IRA if a beneficiary gets a divorce.

In contrast, our Qualified/IRA Trust protects the IRA funds from irrational spending by specifying the annual amount to be distributed. It is designed to care for minors and provide appropriate funds for their needs. (Remember that while your child may be a named beneficiary, if something were to happen to him or her, the beneficiary would most likely be your grandchild, who could be a minor.) It provides creditor protection for the beneficiaries, protects the IRA in the event the beneficiary is involved in a divorce, and equally important, offers sophisticated estate tax planning.

IRAs

Individual retirement accounts have serious tax implications, for both income and estate taxes. Because of this, you should review your options with a competent financial adviser. As a general rule, if you are married, you will want to name your spouse as the primary beneficiary. Like all of your other assets, your IRA will be included in your estate for estate tax purposes. When you step out of the picture, the entire IRA will be included in the beneficiary's side of the estate. Eventually, this can create a serious estate tax problem. If your estate is sizeable, you should seriously consider a Qualified/IRA Trust as the contingent beneficiary.

As an example, assume an estate of $2 million that consists of a home and assets worth $1 million and an IRA worth $1 million. If the husband dies, the allocation of assets would look like this:

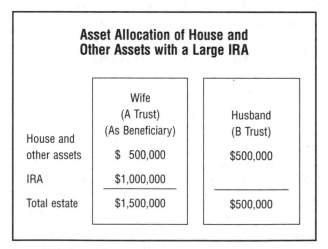

Asset Allocation of House and Other Assets with a Large IRA

	Wife (A Trust) (As Beneficiary)	Husband (B Trust)
House and other assets	$ 500,000	$500,000
IRA	$1,000,000	
Total estate	$1,500,000	$500,000

In this example, the Decedent's B Trust is obviously underutilized (short of the $1 million federal estate tax exclusion).

Proper estate planning could have averted this situation. If this couple had previously adopted the Qualified/IRA Trust, the surviving spouse could disclaim an amount of the IRA to fully utilize the decedent's federal estate tax exclusion of $1 million. Since the surviving spouse is typically the beneficiary of the Qualified/IRA Trust, he or she still has the right to the assets in the Qualified/IRA Trust. This approach offers the best of both worlds and is illustrated in the following example:

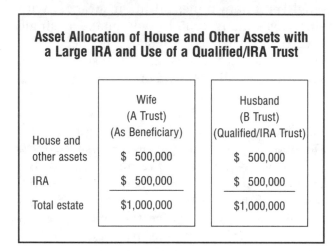

Asset Allocation of House and Other Assets with a Large IRA and Use of a Qualified/IRA Trust

	Wife (A Trust) (As Beneficiary)	Husband (B Trust) (Qualified/IRA Trust)
House and other assets	$ 500,000	$ 500,000
IRA	$ 500,000	$ 500,000
Total estate	$1,000,000	$1,000,000

If you live in a community property state, you should consider signing a Community Property Recognition Agreement. This will give the surviving beneficial spouse the power to place up to half of the IRA in the Qualified/IRA Trust. The surviving spouse, as beneficiary of the Qualified/IRA Trust, retains the right to the IRA income. See the discussions of community property states in Chapters 4 and 6.

If you live in a separate property state, you should consider signing a General Power of Appointment. This will give the surviving beneficial spouse the power to place half, or more, of the IRA in the Qualified/IRA Trust to attain maximum funding of the decedent's $1 million federal estate tax exclusion. Again, the surviving spouse, as beneficiary of the Qualified/IRA Trust, retains the right to the IRA income. See the discussions of separate property states in Chapters 4 and 6.

If you are in a second marriage, and you would like the income of your IRA to pass to your surviving spouse and thereafter to your own children or the beneficiaries of your choice, you should consider naming your Qualified/IRA Trust as the primary beneficiary of your IRA.

If you are single, name your heirs as primary beneficiaries. However, if you want to utilize the benefits of the Qualified/IRA Trust and control the amount and period of distributions, you will want to adopt the Qualified/IRA Trust and name it as the primary beneficiary of your IRA or other Qualified Plans.

Title "ownership" of the IRA must remain vested in you. Never transfer title of your IRA to your Qualified/IRA Trust (or to your Living Trust). Doing so would immediately trigger income taxation as a distribution. Transfer only the beneficiary—as indicated here, or as advised by your financial adviser.

Pension Plans

If your pension plan is substantial, you should consider a Qualified/IRA Trust and name it as the contingent (or, in some cases primary) beneficiary of your pension plan. This is particularly true if your pension plan has a death benefit or if payments from the plan will continue to other than your surviving spouse after his or her death. The personnel department of a corporation may be reluctant to transfer the contingent (or primary) beneficiary to your Qualified/IRA Trust. Do not be concerned. Simply insist that the personnel department make the appropriate transfer.

A Word of Caution

Remember to make sure that you are transferring only the beneficial interest in these assets, not ownership. Most financial institutions understand that a transfer of beneficial interest is not a change in ownership and will help you to avoid mistakes in this area. However, sometimes even financial institutions are not as knowledgeable as you would expect.

Some years ago, a client called me and said she had a $45,000 Keogh in a no-load mutual fund. The woman had called the sales office in Boston and asked the firm to change her beneficiary designation into the name of her Trust. The woman then sent a copy of her beneficial letter of transfer to the mutual fund company. Three months later, the woman received IRS Form 1099 (used to indicate the receipt of income), showing that she had received $45,000 of taxable income!

The woman called the sales department; after numerous fruitless attempts to get the erroneous "distribution of income" rectified, she eventually called me for assistance. I thereupon called the salesman, who rather abruptly made it very clear that he had followed the woman's instructions and had transferred her "ownership" into her Living Trust. From the IRS viewpoint, this action had distributed the Keogh outright to the woman— and that is *not* what she wanted!

I didn't make any headway with the salesman either, so I asked to speak to his manager. It took me three minutes of discussion with the manager to clarify the situation. The manager said he would rectify the problem immediately but asked that I please verify our conversation in writing. I did so, and the woman's problem was quickly resolved.

MOVING FROM STATE TO STATE

If you move from state to state, your Living Trust is still valid, but there are probably some changes that you should consider incorporating into it. You should find out whether there are any particular legal nuances specific to the new state that you would want to be included in your Trust. (For example, in Florida and Texas you would want a special provision for homesteading your property. In New York you would want to consider the preferability of utilizing co-trustees instead of a single trustee.) It is also important to review the Durable Powers of Attorney (both the Durable Power of Attorney for Health Care and the Durable General Power of Attorney) and the Living Will to ascertain that the legal language complies with the laws of the new state.

As pointed out in Chapter 4, assets classified as *community property* have substantial tax advantages. If you move from a separate property state to a community property state, it is extremely important that you consider changing the status of your property to community property in order to utilize full stepped-up valuation upon the death of a spouse.

FIGURE 14-5
DECLARATION OF COMMUNITY PROPERTY

DECLARATION OF COMMUNITY PROPERTY

As part of our estate plan, we have established a Revocable Living Trust. We have transferred separate property into the Trust. We are now residents of the State of Washington, and we desire that all our property held in the Trust be our community property.

In consideration of our continuing marital relationship and mutual love and affection, I, John J. Doe, and I, Jane J. Doe, do each individually, and together, declare that all of our property held in our Revocable Living Trust, **"The Doe Family Trust dated December 24, 1973, John J. Doe and Jane J. Doe, Trustors and/or Trustees,"** is our Community Property, subject to the laws governing community property ownership. We intend this Declaration to be effective as to all property in the Trust on the date of this Declaration and as to all property which we may in the future add to the Trust. We further declare that any property which we intend to be the separate property of either spouse shall be so designated by writing in the Trust documents, or in the manner in which title is held in the Trust.

It is our intent to enter into this Declaration as husband and wife, contracting with each other regarding our property. We jointly and severally indemnify, and hold harmless from any liability all persons acting in reliance upon this Declaration.

IN WITNESS WHEREOF, the parties have hereto executed this Declaration of Community Property.

Date: September 24, 1997

_____   _____
John J. Doe   Jane J. Doe

        (STATE OF WASHINGTON
ss.   (
        (COUNTY OF WINDSOR

On September 24, 1997, before me, the undersigned, a Notary Public in and for said State, personally appeared John J. Doe and Jane J. Doe, personally known to me or proved to me on the basis of satisfactory evidence to be the persons whose names are subscribed to the within instrument and acknowledged that they executed the same.

WITNESS my hand and official seal.

                                                    (NOTARY SEAL)

_____
NOTARY PUBLIC
Residing at: Castle Rock, Washington

My Commission Expires: _____

One of the problems with people coming from separate property states to community property states and wanting to convert their assets to community property is that an attorney will give the people everything *except* the proper document. The attorney too often will prepare an innocuous amendment, do an abstract, or provide some other equally meaningless document and then collect a substantial fee. You should, in fact, receive a letter of agreement for a married couple, where the husband and wife convert their separate property to community property in the Living Trust. This conversion can be done quite simply by executing a Declaration of Community Property amendment, as shown in Figure 14-5.

TRANSFER ALL YOUR ASSETS

I cannot emphasize strongly enough the importance of transferring all of your assets into your Trust. *All* of your assets (particularly your house) should be transferred into your Trust. If you create a Living Trust but fail to fund it with your assets, you will not have a working Living Trust (with all of its intended benefits), but only a Testamentary Trust, which is a very costly mistake indeed.

Remember, the greatest benefit of the Living Trust is to avoid probate. As a general rule, if you follow the recommendations made in this book, your estate will avoid probate, regardless of the probate laws of the state where you are living. However, the probate laws vary from state to state, so it is worthwhile to check with an attorney who is knowledgeable about the laws of your state. It is true nationwide that you avoid probate only by getting *all* of your assets properly transferred into your Living Trust.

15

Settling the Estate

Settling an estate is an area of concern for every client. Since certain actions are legally required with probate, clients assume that certain things must legally be done with a Living Trust. However, as you will see in this chapter, aside from the usual steps that need to be taken upon the death of any individual, settling an estate in a Living Trust is really quite easy—and can usually be done by the surviving trustee or successor trustee(s) without any legal intervention by an attorney.

As a result of some attorneys charging unnecessarily exorbitant settlement fees, an increasing number of concerned clients are now seeking some form of written guarantee for estate settlement costs rather than an open-ended settlement fee based on the value of the estate. Therefore, our firm has elected, upon request, to provide our clients with a written guarantee to assist in the settling of the estate for a reasonable fixed fee. Providing this fixed-fee guarantee when requested makes clients feel more secure about avoiding a possible excessive settlement in the future. (Income tax returns would still be prepared by the client's own tax preparer. If federal estate tax or state inheritance tax is due, clients may prefer to use their own accountants.)

If all of your assets are in a *good* Living Trust and if the estate is organized with the Estate Plan Binder, settling the key issues of the estate typically takes less than an hour and costs almost nothing. I use the term *settling* rather loosely, because there is not really anything to settle, per se. However, a number of things must be done.

If all your assets are in a good Living Trust and your estate is well organized, settling your estate should take less than an hour.

HOW TO SETTLE YOUR LIVING TRUST

As the years passed since the first publication of this book in 1989, I watched the legal fraternity take advantage of individuals who came to them to settle a Living Trust. Frequently, the Trusts were taken through an administrative procedure that parallels the probate procedure. In other cases, the lawyers tried to learn how to settle a Living Trust at the time and expense of the client. Sometimes, they simply used this opportunity to charge unbelievable fees. It is my experience that an attorney will charge at least 5 percent of the estate for settling it in a Living Trust.

Having written *The Living Trust*, which has influenced so many people to adopt a Living Trust, I felt a moral obligation to write the next book, *How to Settle Your Living Trust*. This latter book was published in 1999. I hope that you will also acquire *How to Settle Your Living Trust*. My goal is not to sell books, but rather to guide your family through the settlement steps. From it, you'll learn the basic steps that any family member can follow, and then the book becomes a reference manual designed to cover each and every situation.

I hope that you will also acquire How to Settle Your Living Trust. *My goal is not to sell books, but rather to guide your family through the settlement steps.*

The intent of this chapter is to show you how easy it really is to settle an estate in a good Living Trust. Be aware that we make our company and advisers available to help settle any Living Trusts produced by our company, The Estate Plan.

CHECK "FINAL INSTRUCTIONS" SECTION OF THE ESTATE PLAN BINDER

Immediately upon the death of a loved one, the survivor should notify certain people, in order to set in motion the many steps that must be taken. The basic steps that should be followed upon the death of an individual are delineated in the "Final Instructions" section of the Estate Plan Binder:

- Make important telephone calls.
- Review personal data summary (in Estate Plan Binder).
- Make funeral arrangements, including memorial or flowers and funeral notice.
- Notify other people.
- Check the safe-deposit box and checking accounts.
- Make an appointment to meet with your primary adviser.

The death of a loved one is always a traumatic time for the survivors, and the death of a spouse is almost always mentally paralyzing to the surviving spouse. Many people get totally confused and literally do not know what to do first. Fortunately, the "Final Instructions" pages of the Estate Plan Binder help to guide the survivors in the steps that are necessary to begin the process of settling the estate of the deceased.

Review Personal Data

Review the "Personal Data" section in the Estate Plan Binder to ascertain the accuracy of information that will be needed for completing the death certificate. This section was described in Chapter 13.

Information for Death Certificate

Have you ever looked at a death certificate? You will find that it is probably one of the best sources of misinformation available, because the surviving family members often have no idea of the correct information.

The information required on a death certificate is so much easier to gather and record when you and your spouse are both still living.

The information contained in the "Personal Data" section of the Estate Plan Binder is required on most death certificates. That information is so much easier to gather and record in the binder while you and your spouse are both still living. When our clients first begin to fill out the "Personal Data" section, they often guess at where their mothers or fathers were born and then call back days later when they have had a chance to find the correct information. How nice it is to be able to correct the data now, instead of guessing later—at a time of emotional upset and bereavement.

Military Papers

Copies of military discharge papers are filed in the "Personal Data" section of the Estate Plan Binder. If an individual who served in the armed forces dies, the Veterans Administration will provide a small contribution toward funeral expenses and an American flag, if desired. How nice it is to easily be able to put your fingers on copies of the required military separation papers.

In the process of making funeral arrangements, you will need to take the military separation papers to the funeral home. These papers are needed to show proof that the deceased person was a veteran of military service.

Order Death Certificates

Order at least twelve death certificates. A separate death certificate will be needed for each insurance policy and each real asset (real estate, stocks, bonds, and so on) that you desire to ultimately sell or transfer. A simple copy of the death certificate is *not* sufficient; it must be a certified copy, obtained from the county recorder's office. Unfortunately, certified copies of the death certificate are seldom available until about ten days after the death of an individual. However, you can usually obtain one or two copies of the death certificate for immediate use directly from the funeral home. With a copy of the Living Trust and a certified copy of the death certificate, the surviving trustee or successor trustee then has exactly the same power to manage the estate as the deceased individual had while living.

Check Safe-Deposit Box and Checking Accounts

The death of a spouse can drastically limit the surviving spouse's ability to gain access to funds needed for daily subsistence.

In 1971, on a Friday afternoon, I was called to a local hospital and advised that one of my dearest friends had just passed away as the result of bone cancer. Upon arriving at the hospital, I told my friend's grieving widow to immediately go to the bank and clear out their checking account and safe-deposit box. What a horrible thing to have to say to a grieving widow! However, in those days, the banks read the obituary columns in the newspapers and immediately locked up the safe-deposit boxes and the checking accounts of deceased individuals.

I erroneously thought that this primitive practice no longer exists, but, I am sorry to say, it still does in some states. Therefore, as a general rule, make certain that both your checking account and your safe-deposit box are transferred into the name of your Living Trust.

You should look in the safe-deposit box for two reasons. First, the deceased may have left a message or a statement of posthumous desires that should be carried out by the survivors. The second, and more important, reason to look in the safe-deposit box is to inventory the contents to be sure that all of the valuable assets (such as real estate deeds and stocks and bonds) are in the name of the Trust.

Because only *cash* is acceptable for settling the funeral expenses, you should confirm the amount of readily available funds in the checking account of the deceased person and make arrangements to have access to the checking account funds.

As good business practice, it is worthwhile to put your safe-deposit box in the name of your Living Trust. With the Trust document and a death certificate in hand, the bank should readily give the successor trustee access to the safe-deposit box. In your estate-planning process, do not forget to let your successor trustee know where your safe-deposit box is located, as well as the location of the key to the safe-deposit box.

Make an Appointment with Your Primary Adviser

The next step is to make an appointment to meet with your primary adviser. The actual settlement process—involving the estate and financial affairs—will begin at the meeting with this person.

We use the term *your primary adviser* in a broad sense, because he or she is the person with whom *you* may choose to counsel. He or she may be from any of several different backgrounds, be it legal, financial, or accounting, or simply a family member or a close friend. No particular discipline is required—the primary adviser is your choice.

THE SETTLEMENT PROCESS

If you have done your estate planning properly—if you have all of your assets in a *good* Living Trust—your survivors have nothing to do from a legal standpoint. They do *not* have to change your Trust or change title to any of your assets. The one exception would be, upon the death of a single individual or the *second* spouse (if married), when the estate is large enough to be subject to federal or state taxation.

Although I make it a point to be readily available to help our clients settle an estate, some clients worry about what will happen if The Estate Plan might not be available. Even without our services the surviving spouse or adult children should be able to settle the estate without difficulty—*if* it has been organized. The surviving trustee or successor trustee needs only a copy of the death certificate and a copy of the Living Trust to allow him or her to take whatever action is necessary on behalf of the Trust.

In contrast, consider the following scenario: The survivor goes to an attorney and is told that a special document needs to be drawn. The "special document" drawn up by the attorney may be a simple statement to the effect that the surviving spouse is the surviving trustee, or it may be an abstract (which is simply a legal summary of the Trust) or some other innocuous document that has little or no legal meaning but establishes the basis for the attorney to charge a legal fee. The document is unnecessary, and the legal fee usually ranges from $250 to $500. Even though the document is legally unnecessary, the minor expense certainly beats two years of probate and a cost of 8 percent to 10 percent of the gross estate!

For example, about a year ago, a widow made an appointment to discuss her estate shortly after the death of her husband. Two days later, the widow called and said that it wouldn't be necessary for her to come, because she had found a local attorney who would draw up a legal document stating that she was now the surviving trustee. The widow probably paid the attorney $250 to $500 for this unnecessary document. (However, she did save herself a forty-mile trip to our office.)

Unfortunately, similar stories are repeated much too frequently. However, today I have a far greater concern: Most clients, and most attorneys, do not know how to properly settle an estate that is in a Living Trust. This unfortunate situation is best illustrated by the following story.

In 1978, a couple went to a rather large legal firm in Beverly Hills to draw up a Living Trust. The husband died four years later. The widow immediately returned to the same legal firm to have her Living Trust settled.

The widow was astute enough to realize that she had an A-B Trust and that the assets somehow needed to be divided between these two parts of the Trust. At that time, inheritance taxes were due upon the husband's death. The legal firm computed the value of the estate, estimated the taxes, and then filed the appropriate papers; however, the firm then stopped.

Although the widow had been billed extensively for the firm's legal services, she recognized that she still didn't have the required division of her assets into the Decedent's B Trust and the Survivor's A Trust. She continued to call the firm until it finally told her to go away.

Still concerned about the lack of distribution of assets, the widow contacted a different legal firm in 1986. The firm produced a rather immature legal summary of the Trust and charged the widow a hefty fee for its services, but still did not distribute her assets! The widow persisted, calling the firm for clarification and action; the firm responded by billing her $200 for each telephone call!

In utter frustration, the widow gave up. Later she was referred to our office. Based upon the 1982 state inheritance tax return filed on behalf of her husband, we reconstructed the estate and made a reasonable distribution of the assets into the A and B Trusts. Even though distributing the assets was not difficult, I believe that neither legal firm knew how to do it!

Unfortunately, situations such as this one seem to be surfacing more and more frequently.

Because only a few people—even among the professionals—really know how to settle an estate in a Living Trust, the major thrust of this part of the chapter will be to take you, step by step, through the Living Trust "settlement process." Even though nothing needs to be done legally to your Trust or in changing title to the assets in your estate, your survivor needs to take a number of steps in order to put your accounts in order and to ensure that he or she will enjoy the appropriate tax benefits your Living Trust provides.

The following steps should be followed by your primary adviser to settle an estate in a Living Trust:

- Review the Trust instructions in the Estate Plan Binder and in the Living Trust document.
- Notify life insurance companies.
- Ensure that all assets are inside the Trust.
- Review the size of the estate.
- File an income tax return.
- Obtain a written valuation of assets.
- Review business agreements.
- Review credit cards.
- Distribute personal effects.
- Review allocation and distribution of assets.

Review the Estate Plan Binder and Trust Document

The importance of the Estate Plan Binder, which was discussed in detail in Chapter 13, is especially apparent during the process of estate settlement. By organizing the estate, the binder prevents a guessing game upon the death of a settlor. The Estate Plan Binder allows the survivor the privilege of *settling* the estate in minutes (or possibly an hour), rather than trying to piece together the assets in the estate over several months.

After you have done the preliminary review of the Estate Plan Binder as described previously in this chapter, you and your primary adviser should then specifically look at the following sections:

- The actual Trust (specifically, the section titled "Successor Trustee" and the section titled "Allocation and Distribution")
- The "Amendment" section for any changes to the Trust

- The Memorandum for any specific desired distribution of personal property
- The Financial Statement to determine whether the net worth is reasonably current and whether the estate may be subject to federal estate taxes or state inheritance taxes
- The "Business Agreements and Documents" section to determine whether there are any partnerships, buy-sell agreements, or stock-redemption agreements

Review the Living Trust document, which is found in the "Trust" section of the Estate Plan Binder. Specifically check the section in the Trust on Successor Trustee for authority in administering the Trust, as well as the "Allocation and Distribution" section to find out the desires of the deceased person.

If the successor trustee is the surviving spouse, I make a special point of showing him or her the Trust language that states that he or she has exactly the same power to administer the Trust as before the death of the spouse. Now that only one of the original trustees is still living, it is *most important* to be sure that the Trust names competent successor trustees to assume responsibility for the Trust upon the eventual death of the second spouse.

The "Allocation and Distribution" section should be reviewed to determine whether any of the decedent's assets are to be immediately distributed, rather than remaining in trust for the benefit of the surviving spouse.

Remember, if you cannot find the original Living Trust and Will(s), a duplicate executed copy should be obtainable from your safe-deposit box. The Estate Plan provides duplicate documents to all its clients; whoever draws your Trust should provide you with comparable protection.

Notify Life Insurance Companies

Your adviser should check to be sure that each of the life insurance companies has been notified of the death of the insured. Each insurance company will require a certified copy of the death certificate. In the Estate Plan Binder, copies of the face pages of any insurance policies would be listed behind the divider tab entitled "Insurance Policies."

Ensure Assets Are Within the Trust

Your adviser should help you ensure that all of the assets are within the Trust. In the Estate Plan Binder, evidence of ownership of these assets will be found in the sections entitled "Savings and Investment Documents," "Real Estate Documents," and "Business Agreements and Documents." Remember to check the safe-deposit box, just in case an expensive personal asset is not recorded in the name of the Trust.

If any asset is not in the Trust and the value of all assets outside the Trust exceeds the value established by the particular state for probate, then the assets outside the Trust must go through probate. If everything is in the Trust, the surviving trustee or successor trustee steps in immediately and—with the Trust and a death certificate—has identically the same power to buy, sell, or transfer any of the assets as did the individual who placed those assets into the Trust.

Review Size of Estate

The adviser should check the information in the "Financial Statement" section of the Estate Plan Binder; ideally, the financial statement has been updated within the last twelve months. The adviser should also review the last year's federal and state income tax returns, and determine whether any gifts were reported on IRS Form 709. All this information determines whether the estate is subject to federal estate taxes and state inheritance taxes. If so, the adviser should ascertain which forms need to be filed and how much tax needs to be paid.

As you learned in Chapter 6, with proper estate planning, there need not be *any* estate taxes to pay upon the death of the first spouse, regardless of the size of the estate. However, if estate taxes are due, a Form 706 (Federal Estate Tax form) must be filed, and any taxes due must be paid within nine months of death. We suggest that an accountant complete and file this Form 706 for you. There are options available under the tax code for extending estate tax payments over a period of ten years, but for most estates, the taxes do not qualify for the extension. (If, upon the death of a spouse, taxes would be payable but can be deferred because of the Unlimited Marital Deduction, such deferral still must be reported to the IRS on Form 706.)

Many states have conformed to the federal estate tax code to the extent that, if no federal estate tax is due on an estate, then no state inheritance tax is due. For further information about state taxes refer to Chapter 5, "Estate and Inheritance Taxes." Since each state is different, the particular state laws for inheritance taxes need to be checked at the time of death. (You may wish to review Table 5-6 in that chapter, which lists the states that have an inheritance tax.) Recognize that states that have a pickup tax will most likely change their inheritance tax laws in order to account for the federal state death tax credit being phased out. This is also discussed at length in Chapter 5.

File Income Tax Return

Upon the death of a spouse, the adviser should explain that the surviving spouse has a right to file a joint income tax return (Form 1040, as had been done while the spouse was alive) for the year in which his or her spouse died. The surviving spouse should keep an accurate record of the decedent's last medical and funeral expenses, because the medical expenses can be deducted from the survivor's taxable income, and the funeral expenses can be deducted for estate tax purposes.

The surviving spouse should use his or her social security number to identify all of the assets in the Trust, including the assets in the Survivor's A Trust as well as the assets in the Decedent's B Trust. The reason for reporting the assets in this manner is that it enables the trustee to transfer assets back and forth between the A Trust and the B Trust (and the C Trust, where applicable). The IRS Trust Identification Number is used to identify the assets upon the death of a single settlor or upon the death of the second spouse.

A surviving spouse acting as the surviving trustee will typically pay out all the income from the Trust to himself or herself and continue to report the Trust income on his or her personal Form 1040 income tax return.

Upon Death of First Spouse

If a couple have an A-B Trust, upon the death of a spouse, one-half of the Trust (the Decedent's B Trust) becomes irrevocable. A Form 1041 tax return should then be filed, but only for the decedent's irrevocable B Trust. This form must be filed each year until no assets remain in the B Trust.

If you have an A-B-C Trust, upon the death of the first spouse, the surviving spouse needs to file a Form 706 to elect the Q-TIP (C Trust). This is an information return only, but it must be filed within nine months of the date of death; otherwise, you lose the right to utilize the C Trust.

If any part of the Living Trust becomes irrevocable, request a Trust Identification Number (referred to by the IRS as an EIN—Employee Identification Number). Use form W-9.

I must emphasize that only one Trust Identification Number is necessary for any Living Trust. This rule applies to the A-B and A-B-C Trusts as well. I hear that attorneys are advising their clients that they need a separate EIN for each sub-trust— A, B, and C. This is absolutely fallacious.

The IRS Trust Identification Number will be used on the Form 1041 tax return. The Form 1041 and the accompanying Schedule K-1 are the only places where the special Trust ID number will be used during the life of the surviving spouse.

All of the income in Trust B is usually paid to the surviving spouse. However, since the surviving spouse is still a settlor of the Trust, the net effect is paying all of the income to oneself. Therefore, on Form 1041, the surviving spouse would subtract from the income of Trust B an income distribution deduction in the same amount.

Since the amount paid out from the Trust (the decedent's share) is the same as the amount received (income), the taxable income is zero! Thus, it is easy to see that the Form 1041 tax return on the decedent's half of an A-B Trust is simply an information return. The surviving trustee would continue to report any income received from the Trust on his or her regular Form 1040 tax return, as was done before the spouse's death.

To show you how simple the Form 1041 Trust Tax Return really can be, Figure 15-1 depicts a sample Form 1041. All of the income received by the Trust was paid out to the surviving trustee, and therefore the taxable balance is zero. Note that Form 1041 indicates that a Schedule K-1 must be attached to the return, to show who received the distribution from the Trust. A sample of Schedule K-1, "Beneficiary's Share of Income, Deductions, Credits, Etc.," is shown in Figure 15-2. Note that the Form 1041 and Schedule K-1 forms both require the taxpayer to include the Trust Identification Number (shown on the form as the Employer Identification Number).

To prevent confusion at the IRS office that receives Form 1041, we recommend to our clients that they include a short letter that reminds the IRS that all of the distributions from the Trust are being reported on individual Form 1040 returns. Figure 15-3 shows a sample of the letter that should accompany the Form 1041 and Schedule K-1.

Upon Death of Both Spouses or a Single Person

Upon the death of both spouses or a single person, the entire Living Trust becomes irrevocable. Depending upon the distribution instructions, income may or may not be retained in the Trust. In either case, however, the successor trustees of the Trust must then file a Form 1041 income tax return. For example, if the Trust were providing for minor chil-

---

Computation of Decedent's Trust B

Income: Interest and dividends	$50,000	Decedent's half of the income of the Trust
Deductions: Distribution	($50,000)	Amount paid to survivor and reported on survivor's Form 1040 tax return
Balance: Taxable income	-0-	

FIGURE 15-1

FORM 1041 TAX RETURN

Form **1041**	Department of the Treasury—Internal Revenue Service **U.S. Income Tax Return for Estates and Trusts**	**2001**	

For calendar year 2001 or fiscal year beginning _____ , 2001, and ending _____ , 20 ____   OMB No. 1545-0092

A Type of entity:
- ☐ Decedent's estate
- ☒ Simple trust
- ☐ Complex trust
- ☐ Grantor type trust
- ☐ Bankruptcy estate–Ch. 7
- ☐ Bankruptcy estate–Ch. 11
- ☐ Pooled income fund

B Number of Schedules K-1 attached (see instructions) ▶

Name of estate or trust (If a grantor type trust, see page 10 of the instructions.)

The Smith Family Trust

Name and title of fiduciary
Mary Ann Smith

Number, street, and room or suite no. (If a P.O. box, see page 10 of the instructions.)
1571 Oak Street

City or town, state, and ZIP code
Santa Barbara, CA 91382

C Employer identification number
95: 4632475

D Date entity created
August 18, 1988

E Nonexempt charitable and split-interest trusts, check applicable boxes (see page 11 of the instructions):
- ☐ Described in section 4947(a)(1)
- ☐ Not a private foundation
- ☐ Described in section 4947(a)(2)

F Check applicable boxes: ☒ Initial return ☐ Final return ☐ Amended return ☐ Change in fiduciary's name ☐ Change in fiduciary's address

G Pooled mortgage account (see page 12 of the instructions): ☐ Bought ☐ Sold Date: _____

Income

1	Interest income	**1**	3,210
2	Ordinary dividends	**2**	109
3	Business income or (loss) (attach Schedule C or C-EZ (Form 1040))	**3**	
4	Capital gain or (loss) (attach Schedule D (Form 1041))	**4**	
5	Rents, royalties, partnerships, other estates and trusts, etc. (attach Schedule E (Form 1040))	**5**	
6	Farm income or (loss) (attach Schedule F (Form 1040))	**6**	
7	Ordinary gain or (loss) (attach Form 4797)	**7**	
8	Other income. List type and amount _____	**8**	
9	**Total income.** Combine lines 1 through 8 ▶	**9**	3,319

Deductions

10	Interest. Check if Form 4952 is attached ▶ ☐	**10**	
11	Taxes	**11**	
12	Fiduciary fees	**12**	
13	Charitable deduction (from Schedule A, line 7)	**13**	
14	Attorney, accountant, and return preparer fees	**14**	
15a	Other deductions **not** subject to the 2% floor (attach schedule)	**15a**	
b	Allowable miscellaneous itemized deductions subject to the 2% floor	**15b**	
16	**Total.** Add lines 10 through 15b	**16**	
17	Adjusted total income or (loss). Subtract line 16 from line 9. Enter here and on Schedule B, line 1 ▶	**17**	3,319
18	Income distribution deduction (from Schedule B, line 15) (attach Schedules K-1 (Form 1041))	**18**	3,319
19	Estate tax deduction (including certain generation-skipping taxes) (attach computation)	**19**	
20	Exemption	**20**	
21	**Total deductions.** Add lines 18 through 20 ▶	**21**	3,319

Tax and Payments

22	Taxable income. Subtract line 21 from line 17. If a loss, see page 17 of the instructions	**22**	0
23	**Total tax** (from Schedule G, line 7)	**23**	
24	**Payments: a** 2001 estimated tax payments and amount applied from 2000 return	**24a**	
b	Estimated tax payments allocated to beneficiaries (from Form 1041-T)	**24b**	
c	Subtract line 24b from line 24a	**24c**	
d	Tax paid with extension of time to file: ☐ Form 2758 ☐ Form 8736 ☐ Form 8800	**24d**	
e	Federal income tax withheld. If any is from Form(s) 1099, check ▶ ☐	**24e**	
	Other payments: **f** Form 2439 _____ ; **g** Form 4136 _____ ; Total ▶	**24h**	
25	**Total payments.** Add lines 24c through 24e, and 24h ▶	**25**	
26	Estimated tax penalty (see page 17 of the instructions)	**26**	
27	**Tax due.** If line 25 is smaller than the total of lines 23 and 26, enter amount owed	**27**	
28	**Overpayment.** If line 25 is larger than the total of lines 23 and 26, enter amount overpaid	**28**	
29	Amount of line 28 to be: **a** Credited to 2002 estimated tax ▶ _____ ; **b** Refunded ▶	**29**	

Sign Here ▶

Under penalties of perjury, I declare that I have examined this return, including accompanying schedules and statements, and to the best of my knowledge and belief, it is true, correct, and complete. Declaration of preparer (other than taxpayer) is based on all information of which preparer has any knowledge.

Signature of fiduciary or officer representing fiduciary	Date	▶ EIN of fiduciary if a financial institution	May the IRS discuss this return with the preparer shown below (see page 7)? ☐ Yes ☐ No

Paid Preparer's Use Only

Preparer's signature ▶	Date	Check if self-employed ☒	Preparer's SSN or PTIN 527-60-3524
Firm's name (or yours if self-employed), address, and ZIP code ▶	KENNETH N. CRAIG PO 6697 INCLINE VLG, NV 89450	EIN 99÷0293089 Phone no. (775) 832-7080	

For Paperwork Reduction Act Notice, see the separate instructions.   Cat. No. 11370H   Form **1041** (2001)

Form 1041 (2001) — Page **2**

Schedule A — Charitable Deduction. Do not complete for a simple trust or a pooled income fund.

1	Amounts paid or permanently set aside for charitable purposes from gross income (see page 18)	1	
2	Tax-exempt income allocable to charitable contributions (see page 18 of the instructions)	2	
3	Subtract line 2 from line 1	3	
4	Capital gains for the tax year allocated to corpus and paid or permanently set aside for charitable purposes	4	
5	Add lines 3 and 4	5	
6	Section 1202 exclusion allocable to capital gains paid or permanently set aside for charitable purposes (see page 18 of the instructions)	6	
7	**Charitable deduction.** Subtract line 6 from line 5. Enter here and on page 1, line 13	7	

Schedule B — Income Distribution Deduction

1	Adjusted total income (see page 18 of the instructions)	1	3,319
2	Adjusted tax-exempt interest	2	
3	Total net gain from Schedule D (Form 1041), line 16, column (1) (see page 19 of the instructions)	3	
4	Enter amount from Schedule A, line 4 (reduced by any allocable section 1202 exclusion)	4	
5	Capital gains for the tax year included on Schedule A, line 1 (see page 19 of the instructions)	5	
6	Enter any gain from page 1, line 4, as a negative number. If page 1, line 4, is a loss, enter the loss as a positive number	6	
7	**Distributable net income (DNI).** Combine lines 1 through 6. If zero or less, enter -0-	7	3,319
8	If a complex trust, enter accounting income for the tax year as determined under the governing instrument and applicable local law	8	
9	Income required to be distributed currently	9	3,319
10	Other amounts paid, credited, or otherwise required to be distributed	10	
11	Total distributions. Add lines 9 and 10. If greater than line 8, see page 19 of the instructions	11	3,319
12	Enter the amount of tax-exempt income included on line 11	12	
13	Tentative income distribution deduction. Subtract line 12 from line 11	13	3,319
14	Tentative income distribution deduction. Subtract line 2 from line 7. If zero or less, enter -0-	14	3,319
15	**Income distribution deduction.** Enter the smaller of line 13 or line 14 here and on page 1, line 18	15	3,319

Schedule G — Tax Computation (see page 20 of the instructions)

1	Tax: a ☐ Tax rate schedule or ☐ Schedule D (Form 1041)	1a	
	b Tax on lump-sum distributions (attach Form 4972)	1b	
	c Alternative minimum tax (from Schedule I, line 39)	1c	
	d **Total.** Add lines 1a through 1c	1d	
2a	Foreign tax credit (attach Form 1116)	2a	
b	Other nonbusiness credits (attach schedule)	2b	
c	General business credit. Enter here and check which forms are attached: ☐ Form 3800 ☐ Forms (specify) ▶	2c	
d	Credit for prior year minimum tax (attach Form 8801)	2d	
3	**Total credits.** Add lines 2a through 2d ▶	3	
4	Subtract line 3 from line 1d. If zero or less, enter -0-	4	
5	Recapture taxes. Check if from: ☐ Form 4255 ☐ Form 8611	5	
6	Household employment taxes. Attach Schedule H (Form 1040)	6	
7	**Total tax.** Add lines 4 through 6. Enter here and on page 1, line 23 ▶	7	

Other Information

		Yes	No
1	Did the estate or trust receive tax-exempt income? If "Yes," attach a computation of the allocation of expenses Enter the amount of tax-exempt interest income and exempt-interest dividends ▶ $		X
2	Did the estate or trust receive all or any part of the earnings (salary, wages, and other compensation) of any individual by reason of a contract assignment or similar arrangement?		X
3	At any time during calendar year 2001, did the estate or trust have an interest in or a signature or other authority over a bank, securities, or other financial account in a foreign country? See page 21 of the instructions for exceptions and filing requirements for Form TD F 90-22.1. If "Yes," enter the name of the foreign country ▶		X
4	During the tax year, did the estate or trust receive a distribution from, or was it the grantor of, or transferor to, a foreign trust? If "Yes," the estate or trust may have to file Form 3520. See page 21 of the instructions		X
5	Did the estate or trust receive, or pay, any qualified residence interest on seller-provided financing? If "Yes," see page 21 for required attachment		X
6	If this is an estate or a complex trust making the section 663(b) election, check here (see page 21) ▶ ☐		
7	To make a section 643(e)(3) election, attach Schedule D (Form 1041), and check here (see page 21) ▶ ☐		
8	If the decedent's estate has been open for more than 2 years, attach an explanation for the delay in closing the estate, and check here ▶ ☐		
9	Are any present or future trust beneficiaries skip persons? See page 21 of the instructions		X

Form **1041** (2001)

(continued)

FIGURE 15-1 (continued)
FORM 1041 TAX RETURN

Form 1041 (2001)   Page **3**

Schedule I   **Alternative Minimum Tax** (see pages 21 through 27 of the instructions)

Part I—Estate's or Trust's Share of Alternative Minimum Taxable Income

1	Adjusted total income or (loss) (from page 1, line 17)	**1**	3,319
2	Net operating loss deduction. Enter as a positive amount	**2**	
3	Add lines 1 and 2	**3**	3,319
4	**Adjustments and tax preference items:**		

a	Interest	**4a**		
b	Taxes	**4b**		
c	Miscellaneous itemized deductions (from page 1, line 15b)	**4c**		
d	Refund of taxes	**4d**	(	)
e	Depreciation of property placed in service after 1986	**4e**		
f	Circulation and research and experimental expenditures	**4f**		
g	Mining exploration and development costs	**4g**		
h	Long-term contracts entered into after February 28, 1986	**4h**		
i	Amortization of pollution control facilities	**4i**		
j	Installment sales of certain property	**4j**		
k	Adjusted gain or loss (including incentive stock options)	**4k**		
l	Certain loss limitations	**4l**		
m	Tax shelter farm activities	**4m**		
n	Passive activities	**4n**		
o	Beneficiaries of other trusts or decedent's estates	**4o**		
p	Tax-exempt interest from specified private activity bonds	**4p**		
q	Depletion	**4q**		
r	Accelerated depreciation of real property placed in service before 1987	**4r**		
s	Accelerated depreciation of leased personal property placed in service before 1987	**4s**		
t	Intangible drilling costs	**4t**		
u	Other adjustments	**4u**		

5	Combine lines 4a through 4u	**5**	
6	Add lines 3 and 5	**6**	3,319
7	Alternative tax net operating loss deduction (see page 25 of the instructions for limitations)	**7**	
8	Adjusted alternative minimum taxable income. Subtract line 7 from line 6	**8**	3,319
	Note: *Complete Part II below before going to line 9.*		
9	Income distribution deduction from line 27 below	**9** 3,319	
10	Estate tax deduction (from page 1, line 19)	**10**	
11	Add lines 9 and 10	**11**	3,319
12	Estate's or trust's share of alternative minimum taxable income. Subtract line 11 from line 8	**12**	0

If line 12 is:

- $22,500 or less, stop here and enter -0- on Schedule G, line 1c. The estate or trust is not liable for the alternative minimum tax.
- Over $22,500, but less than $165,000, go to line 28.
- $165,000 or more, enter the amount from line 12 on line 34 and go to line 35.

Part II—Income Distribution Deduction on a Minimum Tax Basis

13	Adjusted alternative minimum taxable income (see page 25 of the instructions)	**13**	3,319
14	Adjusted tax-exempt interest (other than amounts included on line 4p)	**14**	
15	Total net gain from Schedule D (Form 1041), line 16, column (1). If a loss, enter -0-	**15**	
16	Capital gains for the tax year allocated to corpus and paid or permanently set aside for charitable purposes (from Schedule A, line 4)	**16**	
17	Capital gains paid or permanently set aside for charitable purposes from gross income (see page 26 of the instructions)	**17**	
18	Capital gains computed on a minimum tax basis included on line 8	**18** (	)
19	Capital losses computed on a minimum tax basis included on line 8. Enter as a positive amount	**19**	
20	Distributable net alternative minimum taxable income (DNAMTI). Combine lines 13 through 19. If zero or less, enter -0-	**20**	3,319
21	Income required to be distributed currently (from Schedule B, line 9)	**21**	3,319
22	Other amounts paid, credited, or otherwise required to be distributed (from Schedule B, line 10)	**22**	
23	Total distributions. Add lines 21 and 22	**23**	3,319
24	Tax-exempt income included on line 23 (other than amounts included on line 4p)	**24**	
25	Tentative income distribution deduction on a minimum tax basis. Subtract line 24 from line 23	**25**	3,319
26	Tentative income distribution deduction on a minimum tax basis. Subtract line 14 from line 20. If zero or less, enter -0-	**26**	3,319
27	**Income distribution deduction on a minimum tax basis.** Enter the smaller of line 25 or line 26. Enter here and on line 9	**27**	3,319

Form **1041** (2001)

Form 1041 (2001)   Page **4**

Part III—Alternative Minimum Tax

28	Exemption amount			**28**	$22,500
29	Enter the amount from line 12	**29**	0		
30	Phase-out of exemption amount	**30**	$75,000		
31	Subtract line 30 from line 29. If zero or less, enter -0-	**31**			
32	Multiply line 31 by 25% (.25)			**32**	0
33	Subtract line 32 from line 28. If zero or less, enter -0-			**33**	22,500
34	Subtract line 33 from line 29			**34**	0

35 Go to Part IV of Schedule I to figure line 35 if the estate or trust has a gain on lines 15c and 16 of column (2) of Schedule D (Form 1041) (as refigured for the AMT, if necessary). **All others: If line 34 is—**

- $175,000 or less, multiply line 34 by 26% (.26).
- Over $175,000, multiply line 34 by 28% (.28) and subtract $3,500 from the result . . .   **35**   0

36	Alternative minimum foreign tax credit (see page 26 of instructions)	**36**	
37	Tentative minimum tax. Subtract line 36 from line 35	**37**	0
38	Enter the tax from Schedule G, line 1a (minus any foreign tax credit from Schedule G, line 2a)	**38**	
39	**Alternative minimum tax.** Subtract line 38 from line 37. If zero or less, enter -0-. Enter here and on Schedule G, line 1c	**39**	0

Part IV—Line 35 Computation Using Maximum Capital Gains Rates

Caution: *If the estate or trust **did not** complete Part V of Schedule D (Form 1041), see page 27 of the instructions before completing this part.*

40	Enter the amount from line 34	**40**	
41	Enter the amount from Schedule D (Form 1041), line 21, or line 9 of the Schedule D Tax Worksheet, whichever applies (as refigured for AMT, if necessary)	**41**	
42	Enter the amount from Schedule D (Form 1041), line 15b, column (2) (as refigured for AMT, if necessary)	**42**	
43	Add lines 41 and 42. If zero or less, enter -0-	**43**	
44	Enter the amount from Schedule D (Form 1041), line 21, or line 4 of the Schedule D Tax Worksheet, whichever applies (as refigured for AMT, if necessary)	**44**	
45	Enter the **smaller** of line 43 or line 44	**45**	
46	Subtract line 45 from line 40. If zero or less, enter -0-	**46**	
47	If line 46 is $175,000 or less, multiply line 46 by 26% (.26). Otherwise, multiply line 46 by 28% (.28) and subtract $3,500 from the result . . . . ▶	**47**	
48	Enter the amount from Schedule D (Form 1041), line 20, or line 16 of the Schedule D Tax Worksheet (as figured for the regular tax) . . .	**48**	
49	Enter the **smallest** of line 40, line 41, or line 48	**49**	
50	Enter the estate's or trust's allocable portion of qualified 5-year gain, if any, from Schedule D (Form 1041) line 27 (as refigured for the AMT, if necessary)	**50**	
51	Enter the smaller of line 49 or line 50	**51**	
52	Multiply line 51 by 8% (.08) . . . . ▶	**52**	
53	Subtract line 51 from line 49	**53**	
54	Multiply line 53 by 10% (.10) . . . . ▶	**54**	
55	Enter the **smaller** of line 40 or line 41	**55**	
56	Enter the amount from line 49	**56**	
57	Subtract line 56 from line 55. If zero or less, enter -0-	**57**	
58	Multiply line 57 by 20% (.20) . . . . ▶	**58**	
59	Enter the amount from line 40	**59**	
60	Add lines 46, 49, and 57	**60**	
61	Subtract line 60 from line 59	**61**	
62	Multiply line 61 by 25% (.25) . . . . ▶	**62**	
63	Add lines 47, 52, 54, 58, and 62	**63**	
64	If line 40 is $175,000 or less, multiply line 40 by 26% (.26). Otherwise, multiply line 40 by 28% (.28) and subtract $3,500 from the result	**64**	
65	Enter the **smaller** of line 63 or line 64 here and on line 35 . . . . ▶	**65**	

Form **1041** (2001)

FIGURE 15-2
SCHEDULE K-1 (ATTACHMENT TO FORM 1041)

SCHEDULE K-1 (Form 1041)	**Beneficiary's Share of Income, Deductions, Credits, etc.**	OMB No. 1545-0092
Department of the Treasury Internal Revenue Service	for the calendar year 2001, or fiscal year beginning .... , 2001, ending .... , 20 .... ▶ Complete a separate Schedule K-1 for each beneficiary.	**2001**

Name of trust or decedent's estate THE SMITH FAMILY TRUST	☐ Amended K-1 ☐ Final K-1

Beneficiary's identifying number ▶ 541-38-3210	Estate's or trust's EIN ▶ 95-4632475
Beneficiary's name, address, and ZIP code MARY ANN SMITH 1571 OAK STREET SANTA BARBARA, CA 91382	Fiduciary's name, address, and ZIP code MARY ANN SMITH, TRUSTEE 1571 OAK STREET SANTA BARBARA, CA 91382

(a) Allocable share item		(b) Amount	(c) Calendar year 2001 Form 1040 filers enter the amounts in column (b) on:
1	Interest.	1	3,210	Schedule B, Part I, line 1
2	Ordinary dividends.	2	109	Schedule B, Part II, line 5
3	Net short-term capital gain	3		Schedule D, line 5
4	Net long-term capital gain: a Total for year	4a		Schedule D, line 12, column (f)
b	28% rate gain	4b		Schedule D, line 12, column (g)
c	Qualified 5-year gain	4c		Line 4 of the worksheet for Schedule D, line 29
d	Unrecaptured section 1250 gain	4d		Line 11 of the worksheet for Schedule D, line 19
5a	Annuities, royalties, and other nonpassive income before directly apportioned deductions	5a		Schedule E, Part III, column (f)
b	Depreciation	5b		Include on the applicable line of the appropriate tax form
c	Depletion	5c		
d	Amortization	5d		
6a	Trade or business, rental real estate, and other rental income before directly apportioned deductions (see instructions)	6a		Schedule E, Part III
b	Depreciation	6b		Include on the applicable line of the appropriate tax form
c	Depletion	6c		
d	Amortization	6d		
7	Income for minimum tax purposes	7		
8	Income for regular tax purposes (add lines 1, 2, 3, 4a, 5a, and 6a)	8	3,319	
9	Adjustment for minimum tax purposes (subtract line 8 from line 7)	9	-3,319	Form 6251, line 12
10	Estate tax deduction (including certain generation-skipping transfer taxes)	10		Schedule A, line 27
11	Foreign taxes.	11		Form 1040, line 43 or Schedule A, line 8
12	Adjustments and tax preference items (itemize):			
a	Accelerated depreciation	12a		Include on the applicable line of Form 6251
b	Depletion	12b		
c	Amortization	12c		
d	Exclusion items	12d		2002 Form 8801
13	Deductions in the final year of trust or decedent's estate:			
a	Excess deductions on termination (see instructions)	13a		Schedule A, line 22
b	Short-term capital loss carryover	13b	( )	Schedule D, line 5
c	Long-term capital loss carryover	13c	( )	Schedule D, line 12, columns (f) and (g)
d	Net operating loss (NOL) carryover for regular tax purposes	13d	( )	Form 1040, line 21
e	NOL carryover for minimum tax purposes	13e		See the instructions for Form 6251, line 20
f	....	13f		Include on the applicable line of the appropriate tax form
g	....	13g		
14	Other (itemize):			
a	Payments of estimated taxes credited to you	14a		Form 1040, line 60
b	Tax-exempt interest	14b		Form 1040, line 8b
c	....	14c		
d	....	14d		
e	....	14e		Include on the applicable line of the appropriate tax form
f	....	14f		
g	....	14g		
h	....	14h		

For Paperwork Reduction Act Notice, see the Instructions for Form 1041.   Cat. No. 11380D   **Schedule K-1 (Form 1041) 2001**

FIGURE 15-3
LETTER TO ACCOMPANY FORM 1041

Internal Revenue Service   Re: 1041 Tax Return
                                                 Accompanying K-1

Dear IRS Agent:

   The attached 1041 Trust Tax Return and accompanying K-1 are submitted for information only. This tax information was submitted on various 1099s and is reported under my social security number _____
on my 1040 Tax Return.

                     Sincerely,

                     _____

---

dren, possibly only a portion of the Trust income would be distributed to the children. The children would be responsible for reporting the income they received from the Trust on their own individual income tax returns, and the Trust would be responsible for paying taxes on any income that was retained in the Trust.

Any assets retained in trust must use the special IRS Trust ID number. The practice of using the Trust ID number after the death of the settlors is logical, because the social security numbers belonging to the settlors cease upon their deaths.

In our Trust, we require that the successor trustee make an annual accounting to the beneficiaries. This accounting is done easily by providing the beneficiaries with a copy of the 1041 Trust income tax return. No other accounting is necessary. Obviously, the surviving spouse need not account to the beneficiaries since typically the surviving spouse is the beneficiary.

Payment of Taxes
Needless to say, if the Trust has retained income and is required to pay federal income taxes, then presumably a state income tax return must also be filed, and any taxes due must be paid.

On the other hand, if all of the income is paid out from the Trust, then the recipients of the income will report such income on their own Form 1040 returns and pay any taxes due. The Trust must still file a Form 1041 Trust tax return. However, as previously mentioned, if all the Trust income is paid out, then the Trust has no taxable income to report on Form 1041.

The income tax statement is usually filed by the executor, who is named in the Pour-Over Will and is typically the same person as the surviving trustee or successor trustee.

Income Retained in the Trust
It may be very disadvantageous to retain income in the Trust. The 1986 tax code eliminated the income tax advantages of retaining income in the decedent's irrevocable half of the Trust and having it act as a separate tax entity, but Congress continues to change the tax laws. The Omnibus Budget Revenue Reconciliation Act of 1993 raised the income tax rate on estates and trusts to 39.6 percent (on all income over $7,500). This simply reinforces our recommendation that, since the 1986 Tax Code, it is far more advantageous, taxwise, to pass Trust (irrevocable) income to the surviving spouse and heirs. Therefore, your CPA should review the pros and cons of whether to use the irrevocable Trust as a separate tax

entity. It is interesting to note that this new 39.6 percent tax rate also applies to estates—that is, estates going through probate. We have the option to avoid this high tax rate with a Living Trust, but we would have no such option if our estate is tied up in probate litigation.

Obtain Written Valuation of Assets

The adviser should explain that one of the most important functions to be completed upon the death of an individual who has a Living Trust is to establish written valuation of all of the assets in the Trust. It is absolutely necessary to obtain written valuation of all real estate and securities to determine a new cost basis for these assets and to take advantage of stepped-up valuation, thus minimizing the taxable gain when the assets are eventually sold.

The adviser should describe why and how to get stepped-up valuation. Upon the death of a settlor, it is essential to establish a written valuation of each asset, for it provides a valid and documented justification of the asset's current market value for determining stepped-up valuation (see Chapter 4).

Real Estate

The simplest way to establish current market value for real estate is to call two real estate agents from separate firms. Tell them you are always interested in the possibility of selling your real estate and ask them to estimate the value for which you should be able to sell your property (preferably on the high side when no estate taxes are due). Ask the agents to give these figures to you in writing and to back up their valuations with selling prices of recent sales of comparable real estate. On the death of the last settlor, if the estate is subject to estate taxes, you may desire to seek a valuation on the low side. In general, however, you should never ask for either over- or undervaluation of the real estate.

If the valuations from the two real estate agents are fairly close together, take the average of the two estimates for the value of your real estate. If the two estimates are far apart, ask an agent from yet another company for another valuation of your real estate.

It is important to put these written valuations in your Estate Plan Binder (or somewhere else safe and accessible), so that you can use them to substantiate your new stepped-up cost basis to the IRS, possibly years later when you decide to sell your real estate. You must be able to prove your cost basis in writing.

For example, assume that a husband and wife buy a home for $50,000. The couple have their home in a Living Trust in a community property state. Years later, when the market value of the home is $200,000, the husband dies. Because the surviving spouse inherits the house at current market value at the time of death, the *new* cost basis is $200,000.

Five years later, the surviving spouse sells the home for $350,000—a gain of only $150,000. However, the surviving spouse must have established the new cost basis in writing at the time the first spouse died. Failure to have done this might make it difficult or impossible to justify the new cost basis to the IRS, which would dearly love to restore the valuation to the *original* cost basis.

The same principle of establishing written proof of current market valuation at date of death applies to any real estate and to any survivor, whether a surviving spouse or children. Note that your children also get stepped-up valuation as their cost basis of assets in the Survivor's A Trust upon the death of the surviving spouse.

Securities

Establishing the current market value of stocks and bonds is very simple—just look in the newspaper. The stock and bond quotations in the newspaper on or near the date of death are sufficient. Simply put the stock quotation page from the newspaper in the Estate Plan Binder, but be sure that the entire page with the newspaper's dateline is included, so that the date of the quotation is recorded for future use.

Alternatively, your stockbroker can give you the actual stock and bond prices on the date of death. Most brokers will provide these figures to you in writing if you ask them to do so. In many cases, a monthly statement of account from a brokerage firm will include the value as of the date of the statement. Remember, the market value of the stocks and bonds at date of death becomes the new cost basis, which will be used to compute any taxable gain when the assets are eventually sold.

Review Business Agreements

Your adviser should review business agreements for action, dispositions, and benefits. Copies of any corporate stock certificates, partnership agreements, buy-sell agreements, and stock-redemption agreements are found in the "Business Agreements and Documents" section of the Estate Plan Binder.

Any businesses must be valued *very* carefully and wisely. You should hire at least two, and possibly three, certified public accounting firms to value your business. Since most privately held businesses have a minimal cost basis, stepped-up valuation can become extremely important. However, you must establish a sound and justifiable basis to satisfy the Internal Revenue Service!

Assume that a husband and wife have built a corporation that is worth $1 million and that they developed the business from almost nothing, so their cost basis was minimal. When the parents finally die, their children inherit the business. The children wisely hire appraisers to value the business, whose value is established at $1 million. Two years later, the children have the opportunity to sell the business for $1.5 million, and they do so.

If the children have established a sound valuation upon the death of their parents and upon the sale of the business, the children will have a capital gain of only $500,000. Failure to establish a sound valuation at the time of the parents' death, however, would cause the children to have a gain of $1.5 million—quite a difference in taxes!

When you have an interest in a business of substantial value, you should be aware that a number of estate-planning tools can be used to freeze or establish the value of the business and, if desirable, to shift the gain to your children. The various alternatives should be pursued with a knowledgeable estate-planning attorney.

The IRS has some fourteen different methods by which to compute corporate valuation, and, upon your death, the IRS will always strive to come up with the highest valuation for your business. For valuation purposes, the IRS looks at a business the day *before* an individual dies, not the day after. For example:

A surgeon has no clients except patients referred to him by other doctors, and he earns $300,000 a year. The surgeon's assets are his hands. The IRS will typically value his business at two years of earnings, or $600,000—the day before the surgeon dies. In reality, the day after the surgeon dies, his business is worth nothing.

Assume that the doctor died leaving a spouse and an appropriate estate plan. Since, under these circumstances, there will be no estate taxes upon the death of the first spouse, the value of the business at date of death is not really of concern. Assume that the surviving spouse is able to collect her husband's business receivables of $50,000, which she places in a certificate of deposit. Upon the death of the surviving spouse, the only remaining business item of value is the CD ($50,000 plus interest).

Thus, where there is an interest in a privately held business, a proper estate plan is essential. While you are living, you can usually do something about determining a proper valuation for your business. Failure to do so, however, may have a tragic result.

Review Credit Cards

The next step to take in settling an estate is to review the credit cards that were issued to the deceased individual and to determine whether they should be destroyed. Cards that should definitely be destroyed are those issued only in the name of the deceased or for business use only.

As a matter of practice, you should always have a list of your credit cards readily available for the surviving trustee or successor trustee. Chapter 13 describes the easiest way to keep and maintain such records.

Distribute Personal Effects

At this time, it is appropriate to distribute personal effects as specified in any special Memorandum. Any special estate distributions should also be made, if specified. Your adviser should help you begin this step by checking the section titled "Memorandum" in the Estate Plan Binder. Our Living Trusts, in the section on personal effects, specifically refer to the Memorandum and request the surviving trustee or successor trustee to abide by any Memorandum that may have been specified by the decedent.

The "Memorandum" section in the Estate Plan Binder provides a place where clients can specify the desired distribution of their personal property. Occasionally, a client meticulously identifies almost every item to go to a particular child or to a brother, sister, mother, or father. However, most people are not quite this efficient.

Review Allocation and Distribution

If assets are to be distributed or retained in trust for the heirs, your adviser should help you determine which assets and real estate should be distributed, sold, or converted to income. Remember, though, to first determine any outstanding debts or taxes that must be paid before the estate is distributed.

The importance of the allocation and distribution aspects of settling an estate cannot be overemphasized. The "Allocation and Distribution" section of the Trust should be reviewed carefully. Even if only one spouse has died, the decedent may have left specific instructions as to certain assets that are to be distributed outright upon his or her death. Since the trustee should be given the choice of distributing in cash or in kind (by the language in the Trust), the trustee preferably should distribute the assets outright, rather than selling them and then distributing cash.

The "Allocation and Distribution" section of the Trust should be carefully reviewed even if only one spouse has died.

If the decedent is single or the surviving spouse, then the allocation and distribution of the assets in the estate must conform to the "Allocation and Distribution" section of the Trust. Again, it is always preferable to distribute the assets, where appropriate, rather than simply selling the assets and then distributing cash. On the other hand, to be perfectly fair to all heirs, it is often difficult to divide assets equally, so it may be necessary to sell some assets and then distribute equal dollar amounts in cash to each heir.

Trustees Not Liable for Trust Debts

If there are insufficient assets to meet the debts of the Trust, the trustee is not liable for those debts. In such circumstances, the trustee would simply file bankruptcy for the Trust estate.

Assets/Losses Should Be Transferred to the Beneficiaries

Assets may be valued at the date of death or six months later. If the assets (such as a home or securities) lose value after valuation, the trustee should distribute such assets directly to the beneficiaries, who can sell the assets and utilize the loss on their tax returns. Unfortunately, if the assets instead are sold while in the Trust and the resultant cash is distributed to the heirs, the tax loss is lost.

For example, years ago I had a client whose father died and left his home to his son. A bank was handling the estate, and, as time progressed, the home fell in value. I advised the son to direct the bank not to sell the home, because, if the home were sold while in trust, the depreciation in value would be lost. Instead, the home was distributed to the son, who then sold the home and took advantage of the loss in value on his personal income tax.

FINAL ISSUES

After the survivor has met with the primary adviser, he or she still has several months within which to take care of some important issues: making sure assets are most advantageously placed into the various Trusts, reviewing the way these assets are invested, and filing Form 706 for estate taxes, if required.

Asset Placement into
A Trust, B Trust, and C Trust

People who have only an A Trust do not need to worry about allocating their assets, because the assets will continue to remain in the A Trust. However, people who have an A-B Trust or an A-B-C Trust need to be concerned about allocating assets among the A Trust, the B Trust, and, where applicable, the C Trust.

The decedent's share of community and separate property should be identified and placed in the Decedent's B Trust, with any excess over $600,000 placed in the C Trust, if available. (As described in Chapter 6, there is occasionally an exception to this rule.) The surviving spouse's share of community property and separate property should then be identified and placed in the Survivor's A Trust.

The decedent's assets consist of the decedent's separate property and the *value* of the decedent's share of the community or common property. One-half of the asset value of the community or common property must flow into Trust B (and Trust C, if applicable). Most people think that, if they own a home, the decedent owns half of the house and the surviving spouse owns the other half of the house—and, therefore, they need to put one-half of the house into Trust A and the other half into Trust B. However, this belief is not true. You may put the entire house into either Trust A or Trust B, as long as you put an equal value of assets into the other Trust. If you think of the dollar value of the house, instead of the house itself, as what is being placed in the Decedent's Trust B, then apportionment of assets into the A and B Trusts is much easier to understand.

With an A-B Trust, the value of the common assets must be apportioned equally between the A and B Trusts, not the assets themselves.

The procedure for placing assets in the A, B, and C Trusts is really very simple. To place an asset in an A, B, or C Trust, the trustee merely needs to describe the asset, the valuation amount, the date on which the valuation was made, and the source of valuation. This description can be made on a form such as the one shown in Figure 15-4, which lists the assets placed in the A Trust. The forms for Trusts B and C are the same except for their titles. The trustee should date and sign these forms.

We call this the *ledger method*. I know that some attorneys scoff and discard this method as inappropriate because they haven't found it in an IRS publication. However, they need only to understand the principle of accounting for the assets by sub-trusts to recognize how appropriate—and simple—it is. It works, and it meets all of the IRS requirements. (I view these comments with the same mentality that I had when I answered a letter by an individual who said he had read my book *How to Settle Your Living Trust* and was told by his attorney that what I had to say on a particular subject was wrong. The attorney said that I must be wrong because he couldn't find it in the state probate code. I wrote back that the appropriate source for a federal issue is the IRS tax code—not the state probate code. Need I say more!)

Thereafter, the trustee may totally ignore this distribution of assets among the A, B, and C Trusts, other than to annually report the income on the Form 1041 Trust tax return, as mentioned before. The trustee must also abide by the rules for the use of those assets, as described in the Trust under the provisions of the B and C Trusts.

As you learned in Chapter 7, growth assets typically are placed in the Decedent's B Trust, since these assets will henceforth be insulated from further estate taxes. Nevertheless, each surviving spouse has his or her own set of objectives.

You should be aware in transferring assets into the Decedent's B Trust that although these assets will avoid any estate tax in the future, they will not get stepped-up valuation upon the death of the surviving spouse. Thus, before you make the decision on which assets to place in the A and B Trusts, you need to have good estate-planning advice.

An example of somewhat unusual placement of assets in the B Trust involved a widow who was quite angry at the daughter of her deceased husband.

The daughter, who was from a former marriage of her father, had apparently been extremely unkind to her father, right up to and

FIGURE 15-4
FORM FOR ASSET DISTRIBUTION BY TRUST

Asset Description	Valuation		
	Amount	Date	Source*
Real estate at 1571 Oak St., Santa Barbara, California	$400,000	8-1-96	Real estate valuation
Bank of America Certificate of Deposit #364382	$200,000	8-6-96	Statement

Date: 8-6-97   Signature of Trustee: *Mary Ann Smith*

*Source of valuation

including the last days of his life. The father had left 20 percent of his share of the assets in his Decedent's Trust B to his daughter, upon the eventual death of his spouse.

The widow felt that even 20 percent was too much of an inheritance for the daughter. The widow made it very clear that the assets placed in Trust B were to have *no* growth. Further, the widow would annually take *all* the income from the B Trust and would also exercise her frivolous right to $5,000 or 5 percent (whichever was greater) once a year. The widow intended to see that the daughter got no more than was absolutely essential under the terms of the Trust.

One of the most important features of the Living Trust is the right of the trustee to trans-

fer assets between the survivor's portion of the Trust and the decedent's part of the Trust (that is, from the A Trust to the B Trust or from the B Trust to the A Trust—and to the C Trust, if included). Figure 15-5, which illustrates typical asset transfers among parts of a Living Trust, shows that the process is quite easy. You need only describe the asset, the amount of valuation, the date of valuation, and the source of valuation. Then you show from which Trust the asset is being taken and to which Trust the asset is being transferred. The transfers would then be signed and dated by the trustee.

Assume an estate of $800,000, an A-B Trust, and the death of a husband. Assume also that the estate consists of $400,000 in real estate and $400,000 in stock. If the stock market is

FIGURE 15-5
ASSET TRANSFER—TRUST TO TRUST

| Asset Description | Valuation | | | Transfer | | Trustee Signature | Date |
	Amount	Date	Source*	From Trust	To Trust		
Stock Brokerage Account #1764397 Merrill Lynch	$400,000	8-1-95	Statement from Broker	B	A	Mary Ann Smith	8-6-95
Real estate at 1571 Oak St. Santa Barbara, California	$400,000	8-6-96	Real estate valuation	A	B	Mary Ann Smith	8-6-95

*Source of valuation

expected to rise substantially in the next year and real estate is expected to remain relatively static, the stock should be placed in the Decedent's B Trust, and the real estate should be placed in the Survivor's A Trust.

VALUE AT DATE OF DEATH

Assets	Decedent's Trust B	Survivor's Trust A
Stock	$400,000	
Real estate		$400,000

Assume that after a year has passed the stock is worth $600,000, and the real estate is still worth $400,000. Now you believe that the stock market has reached its high and that the real estate will begin to grow. Since it is quite permissible to transfer *dollar for dollar* between the decedent's and survivor's Trusts, $400,000 of the stock would be transferred into the A Trust. In exchange, the $400,000 of real estate would be transferred into the B Trust. The B Trust would then have $400,000 of real estate plus $200,000 of stock; the A Trust would have $400,000 of stock.

ONE YEAR LATER

Assets	Decedent's Trust B	Survivor's Trust A
Stock	$600,000	
Real estate		$400,000

AFTER TRANSFER

Assets	Decedent's Trust B	Survivor's Trust A
Stock	$200,000	$400,000
Real estate	$400,000	

After another year has passed, the real estate has grown from $400,000 to $600,000. As a result, there is now $800,000 in the B Trust ($600,000 of real estate and $200,000 of stock), and there is still $400,000 in the Survivor's A Trust. Remember, whatever is in the B Trust is insulated from further estate taxes. If the surviving spouse were now to die, the estate tax would be zero.

TWO YEARS LATER

Assets	Decedent's Trust B	Survivor's Trust A
Stock	$200,000	$400,000
Real estate	$600,000	
Total	$800,000	$400,000

All of the transfers in the above example could be made with the Asset Transfer form shown in Figure 15-5.

Few, if any, of our clients transfer their assets from A, B, or C. The exception is if the surviving spouse placed the home in Decedent's B or C Trust and now decides to sell the home and utilize the $250,000 exemption. (This is a personal exemption, not a Trust exemption.) Therefore, the home must be transferred from the B or C Trust to the Survivor's A Trust. Such transfer must be a dollar-for-dollar exchange of assets. (See Figure 15-5.) Following the transfer, the home may be sold out of the Survivor's A Trust and the $250,000 exemption will qual-

ify. Capital gains must be realized on any gain made over the original stepped-up valuation when the home was placed in the B Trust.

Since there are many different approaches to placing assets in the various Trusts, you have a most versatile vehicle in the Living Trust. More important, however, the Living Trust is an outstanding estate-planning tool upon the death of a spouse.

Review Investments and Investment Objectives

Review the investments in the Trust to see whether they meet the objectives of income, growth, and security. Determine whether some assets should be reinvested to provide adequate income as well as appropriate growth for a hedge against inflation. The assets should be reviewed at least annually to determine whether they should be reinvested for the best balance between growth and income and whether assets should be shifted among the A, B, and C Trusts to preserve anticipated appreciation.

Upon the death of an individual, it makes sense to review the types of investments in the estate to see whether they still correspond with the objectives of the survivors. This review is particularly necessary when the survivor is a spouse, a minor child, or a handicapped individual of any age. Typically, upon the death of a spouse or parent, the family income is reduced substantially. It may be far more appropriate to sell assets that were invested for growth and to replace them with income-producing assets.

On the other hand, if both parents are deceased, the beneficiaries of the Trust are the children, and the children are to receive the assets with an outright distribution, then the simplest way to distribute the assets is just to change title to the assets. However, if the assets are to be retained in trust for a period of time, it may be more appropriate to leave the assets invested for growth.

It also may be appropriate to change the identification number on your Trust assets. The surviving spouse's social security number should be used. If there is no surviving spouse, then the IRS Trust ID Number (Employee Identification Number) should be used. This number should have been recorded in the Estate Plan Binder. IRS Form W-9, or its appropriate alternate form as specified by IRS regulations, should be used to change the tax number for each asset. This form may be obtained from any financial institution.

As mentioned earlier, if part or all of the Living Trust becomes irrevocable and assets are retained in the Trust, it will be necessary to annually file a Form 1041 Trust tax return for the irrevocable part of the Trust.

File Federal Estate Tax Form 706

The Federal Estate Tax Form 706 is one of the more complicated tax forms and should be avoided if at all possible. This form consists of eighteen pages of various forms, schedules, and instructions! The basic Form 706 consists of three very complex pages of information needed by the IRS; it is followed by Schedules A through P. Figure 15-6 shows the front page of this form. Remember, the Form 706, "United States Estate Tax Return," is one IRS form with which you *do not* want to get involved!

The only redeeming feature of Form 706 is that it need only be submitted if there are federal estate taxes to pay or defer. (If you have an A-B-C Trust, you can defer any taxes due until the death of the second spouse, but Form 706 must still be filed after the death of the first spouse.) If no taxes are owed, no Form 706 is necessary. If any federal estate taxes are due, the Form 706 must be filed within nine months, and any taxes due must also be paid within nine months. With proper estate planning, Form 706 need not be filed for a single person's estate of less than $1 million or for a married couple's jointly owned estate of less than $2 million. As you have seen, good estate planning can raise these limits substantially.

NOTHING ELSE TO DO

If you have done your homework—you have a Living Trust and an organized estate—settling the estate should take only a matter of minutes and not drag on for years. If any cost is involved, it should be minimal—and not consume 6 percent to 10 percent of the gross estate. Much of the hour we spend settling an estate is devoted to convincing the survivor that there really is nothing else to do.

About six years ago, a husband and wife attended one of our seminars and then came into our office to draw up a Trust. As they completed the Trust, the husband told me that, as a retired FBI agent, he received a monthly newsletter from an individual in Washington who, in effect, continued to tell them to "get their houses in order." The former FBI agent said to me, "You've done it. You've created that process. Would you be willing to come down to Los Angeles and attend our monthly luncheon and present your seminar?" I told him that I would be delighted. Within the month, I had received an invitation and accepted.

Seventy-seven FBI agents, active and retired, attended my presentation. Recognizing that most FBI agents are either attorneys or CPAs, I did not quite know what reaction to expect to my seminar on the Living Trust. In retrospect, however, I regret not having a tape recorder to capture the comments at the conclusion of the seminar.

In particular, I remember one man who stood up and said, "I have been a federal referee for the past two years. My responsibility has been to investigate estates being stripped by attorneys. By the time we complete our investigations, the estates are typically stripped bone dry. The Living Trust and the program presented here today are the one means of preventing that from happening."

So often, I have received a call from a client telling me that her husband is dying in the hospital. There is little that I can do except to extend my sympathy. However, the individual is really calling from fear—fear of the unknown. The woman is calling to find out if settling an estate is really as easy as we told her when we created the Trust. The answer is that settling an estate in a Living Trust really *is* that easy.

FIGURE 15-6

FORM 706 ESTATE TAX RETURN

Form **706**	**United States Estate (and Generation-Skipping Transfer) Tax Return**	
(Rev. November 2001)	Estate of a citizen or resident of the United States (see separate instructions).	OMB No. 1545-0015
Department of the Treasury Internal Revenue Service	To be filed for decedents dying after December 31, 2000, and before January 1, 2002. For Paperwork Reduction Act Notice, see page 25 of the separate instructions.	

Part 1.—Decedent and Executor

1a Decedent's first name and middle initial (and maiden name, if any)	1b Decedent's last name	2 Decedent's Social Security No.
3a Legal residence (domicile) at time of death (county, state, and ZIP code, or foreign country)	3b Year domicile established	4 Date of birth	5 Date of death

6a Name of executor (see page 4 of the instructions)

6b Executor's address (number and street including apartment or suite no. or rural route; city, town, or post office; state; and ZIP code)

6c Executor's social security number (see page 4 of the instructions)

7a Name and location of court where will was probated or estate administered

7b Case number

8 If decedent died testate, check here ▶ ☐ and attach a certified copy of the will. 9 If Form 4768 is attached, check here ▶ ☐

10 If Schedule R-1 is attached, check here ▶ ☐

Part 2.—Tax Computation

1	Total gross estate less exclusion (from Part 5, Recapitulation, page 3, item 12)	1
2	Total allowable deductions (from Part 5, Recapitulation, page 3, item 23)	2
3	Taxable estate (subtract line 2 from line 1)	3
4	Adjusted taxable gifts (total taxable gifts (within the meaning of section 2503) made by the decedent after December 31, 1976, other than gifts that are includible in decedent's gross estate (section 2001(b)))	4
5	Add lines 3 and 4	5
6	Tentative tax on the amount on line 5 from Table A on page 12 of the instructions	6
7a	If line 5 exceeds $10,000,000, enter the lesser of line 5 or $17,184,000. If line 5 is $10,000,000 or less, skip lines 7a and 7b and enter -0- on line 7c . . . [7a]	
b	Subtract $10,000,000 from line 7a . . . . [7b]	
c	Enter 5% (.05) of line 7b	7c
8	Total tentative tax (add lines 6 and 7c)	8
9	Total gift tax payable with respect to gifts made by the decedent after December 31, 1976. Include gift taxes by the decedent's spouse for such spouse's share of split gifts (section 2513) only if the decedent was the donor of these gifts and they are includible in the decedent's gross estate (see instructions)	9
10	Gross estate tax (subtract line 9 from line 8)	10
11	Maximum unified credit (applicable credit amount) against estate tax . [11]	
12	Adjustment to unified credit (applicable credit amount). (This adjustment may not exceed $6,000. See page 4 of the instructions.) . . . . [12]	
13	Allowable unified credit (applicable credit amount) (subtract line 12 from line 11)	13
14	Subtract line 13 from line 10 (but do not enter less than zero)	14
15	Credit for state death taxes. Do not enter more than line 14. Figure the credit by using the amount on line 3 less $60,000. See Table B in the instructions and **attach credit evidence** (see instructions) .	15
16	Subtract line 15 from line 14	16
17	Credit for Federal gift taxes on pre-1977 gifts (section 2012) (attach computation) [17]	
18	Credit for foreign death taxes (from Schedule(s) P. (Attach Form(s) 706-CE.) [18]	
19	Credit for tax on prior transfers (from Schedule Q) . . . . . . [19]	
20	Total (add lines 17, 18, and 19)	20
21	Net estate tax (subtract line 20 from line 16)	21
22	Generation-skipping transfer taxes (from Schedule R, Part 2, line 10)	22
23	Total transfer taxes (add lines 21 and 22)	23
24	Prior payments. Explain in an attached statement . . . . . . [24]	
25	United States Treasury bonds redeemed in payment of estate tax . [25]	
26	Total (add lines 24 and 25)	26
27	Balance due (or overpayment) (subtract line 26 from line 23)	27

Under penalties of perjury, I declare that I have examined this return, including accompanying schedules and statements, and to the best of my knowledge and belief, it is true, correct, and complete. Declaration of preparer other than the executor is based on all information of which preparer has any knowledge.

Signature(s) of executor(s)   Date

Signature of preparer other than executor   Address (and ZIP code)   Date

Cat. No. 20548R

16

Determining Your Net Worth

All too often, I see a very good Trust that is, unfortunately, inappropriate for the client. The attorney who wrote the Trust failed to ask the proper questions to establish the necessary client picture before writing the Trust. To properly identify the type of Living Trust and the provisions that are best suited to clients and their individual circumstances, it is essential to establish not only the size of the estate (the net worth), but also the different types and sizes of assets that make up the estate.

FACT GATHERING

Fact gathering is essential to creating the right type of Living Trust and its accompanying provisions. When clients come to our office with their minds already made up that they want a Living Trust, it is sometimes tempting to skip the important process of establishing a client profile. For example, a couple will say, "We're convinced; we know we want the Living Trust. We've got our papers, and we are ready to write the check." Under these circumstances, it is difficult to back off and to start from the very beginning—the fact-gathering process—but it is a most necessary step.

I typically begin a session with a new client by saying something similar to the following: "Like a doctor, before I can diagnose your financial health, I need to know the symptoms. Therefore, I need to ask you some personal questions and then some financial questions." On a rare occasion—possibly one in a thousand—I encounter a client who does not want to reveal his or her financial information. When that situation arises, I simply stop the fact-gathering process and explain to the clients (most often a husband and wife) that, unless I can gather the appropriate information, I cannot do an adequate job in helping them design their Trust. If the clients are unwilling to cooperate at that point, I nicely terminate our meeting, because I cannot in good conscience do anything more for them. I can only hope that someday the clients will find someone in whom they can confide—before it is too late.

Clients wonder what information they need to bring to our office when they are ready to create their Living Trust. My standard answer is, "Simply yourselves." To do a proper financial analysis, you need no preparation—only to respond to a series of simple financial questions. (However, I would suggest that for convenience you bring in copies of any deeds and property tax bills.) When working with new clients, I am most concerned with putting them at ease while also getting the job done. It is more important to ask them simple questions and to get the clients responding. Then the financial answers can be gathered rather easily.

Most people are not financially detail-oriented and are unprepared to answer detailed financial questions. If the clients were asked to bring in a financial statement, most would end up putting off their appointment—either because they still have not gathered their financial data together or because they do not know enough about what a financial statement should contain. Most people dread dealing with finances, since it is too much like working with a budget or doing their taxes.

At the other extreme are clients who are extremely detailed, will bring in reams of paper, and are prepared to discuss each and every asset—down to the last penny. This detailed analysis can take an hour and a half or more and really is unnecessary. An adequate financial picture of a client's estate can be gathered within twenty minutes and will be accurate within 10 percent (more than adequate for what is required to establish the type of Trust and appropriate provisions).

It has been my experience that everyone knows the value of his or her estate or business at any time, if he or she is just asked the proper questions. Occasionally, a client goes home and meticulously rechecks the figures developed during our financial fact-finding interview. After thousands of similar interviews, I have yet to have a client come back and tell me that the paper-and-pencil valuation of his or her estate was off by more than 10 percent.

An adequate picture of a client's estate can be gathered within twenty minutes.

Even though our office has an expensive computer program that will allow our staff to do almost any type of sophisticated financial analysis, I still find that I can do the basic financial fact gathering for a new client more simply with just paper and pencil. I have been doing this fact gathering with thousands of clients over many, many years—and it works like a charm.

Every once in a while, a client will come into our office with his or her own computer printout or financial statement done on a home computer. I occasionally feel rather silly using my simple paper-and-pencil method, but I find that it always works. The questions in this chapter follow the same steps I take with my clients.

To develop an accurate financial picture of a client's estate, it is desirable to separate ordinary investments from retirement funds. To ensure that the various categories are kept separate, retirement investments are itemized first. Later questions address ordinary investments. The sequence of questions about cash accounts begins with the credit union and then continues with CDs, money market accounts, savings accounts, and finally checking accounts.

Most insurance has very little, if any, cash value and therefore is valueless when computing the net worth of your estate while you are alive. As described in Chapter 12, many clients benefit from placing their life insurance in an irrevocable Insurance Preservation Trust, which allows them to avoid paying estate taxes on their life insurance. In most cases, however, it is not advisable to take an investment vehicle (such as a single-premium whole life policy) and place it in an Insurance Preservation Trust. If you were to do so, you would have made a gift of this policy, which might eventually have undesirable tax consequences. Even more important, however, the tax-deferred income and the cash investment are no longer available to you. To prevent this situation from happening, you should identify these investments in an insurance vehicle for what they are—investments—and distinguish them from insurance per se.

DETERMINING YOUR NET WORTH

To determine your own net worth, use the questions on the following pages as a guide to "interview" yourself. To help you sort out your assets without duplication, the questions are in inverse order, beginning with your insurance and concluding with your savings.

If you are married and you wisely elect an A-B Trust, and if you have separate property and choose to have separate distributions or want to ensure that at least your share of common assets plus your separate property gets to your heirs as you have specified, then you should identify these assets as separate property. Once the financial analysis of your estate is completed, it is a simple matter to go back and add up the separate property of the husband and of the wife and the common property of both.

For this fact-gathering process, simply estimate to the nearest thousand dollars; you need only be accurate within 10 percent.

Since the same financial questions apply whether the client is single or married, the questions in this chapter are posed as if a husband and wife are being interviewed. If you are single, you can simply ignore the occasional question regarding the spouse.

For purposes of this financial fact-gathering process, you only need to provide estimates to the nearest thousand dollars, and you only need to be accurate within 10 percent.

Use the following format only as a guide, entering the necessary figures on your own separate notepad. The financial questions asked in this chapter serve simply as a format to help you go about identifying your net worth.

Insurance

The questions in this section about insurance are asked separately of the husband and wife. If you are single, you need only answer one set of questions.

Note that the cash value in an insurance policy is the amount of money you may borrow (take out) at any given point in time. For most insurance policies issued to the majority of people (e.g., $100,000 or less), the cash value is usually very low in comparison with the face value of the policy—thus, simply ignoring it will not materially affect your net worth (unless you have a policy with high face value).

Therefore, not including the policy's cash value amount will have minimal effect upon your net worth, unless you have a policy with high face value in which the cash value could be significant.

Do not include the value of any accidental death benefits. Your chance of dying by accident is about one in forty. In addition, do not include the accidental life insurance that you have taken out with your credit card or local newspaper, since these policies are also accident policies.

To the husband: How much life insurance do you have?

	Face Value	Cash Value
How much company group life insurance do you have?	$ _____	$ -0-
Do you have NSLI (National Service Life Insurance, also known as GI Insurance)? If so, how much?	$ _____	$ _____
What individual life insurance policies do you have? How much cash value do you have in these policies?	$ _____	$ _____
	$ _____	$ _____
Total Husband's Insurance	$ _____ (1)	$ _____ (2)

To the wife: How much life insurance do you have?

	Face Value	Cash Value
How much company group life insurance do you have?	$ _____	$ -0-
Do you have NSLI (National Service Life Insurance, also known as GI Insurance)? If so, how much?	$ _____	$ _____
What individual life insurance policies do you have? How much cash value do you have in these policies?	$ _____	$ _____
	$ _____	$ _____

Total Wife's Insurance $ _____ (3) $ _____ (4)

Total Insurance
Bring down totals (1), (2), (3), and (4)

Husband $ _____ (1) $ _____ (2)

Wife $ _____ (3) $ _____ (4)

Total Insurance of Both Spouses
Add together the amounts for husband and wife:
(1) + (3) = (G); (2) + (4) = (F) $ _____ (G) $ _____ (F)

Tax-Sheltered Investments

The following questions about various types of tax-deferred investments apply to husband and wife together. If you do not know what these plans are, you most likely do not have them, so do not worry about them.

IRAs

How much money do you have in IRAs? $ _____

Do you have an IRA rollover account? If so, how much is in it? $ _____

Keogh Plans

Do you have a Keogh plan? If so, how much is in it? $ _____

SEP Programs

Do you have a SEP (Simplified Employee Pension)? If so, how much is in it? $ _____

Pension Plans

Do you have a pension plan? If so, what is your vested interest (that is, money you may take out in the form of a lump sum)? How much could you take out if you left the company today? $ _____

Profit-Sharing Plans

Do you have a profit-sharing plan? If so, how much is in the plan? $ _____

Tax-Sheltered Annuities

Do you have a TSA (tax-sheltered annuity)? If so, how much is in the annuity? $ _____

401(k) Plans

Do you have a 401(k) (company savings) plan? If so, how much is in the plan? $ _____

Deferred-Compensation Plans

Do you have a deferred-compensation plan? If so, how much is in the plan? $ _____

Employee Stock Option Plans

Do you have an ESOP (employee stock option plan)? If so, how much is in the plan? $ _____

Total Tax-Sheltered Investments
Add together all of these tax-sheltered investments $ _____(E)

Fixed and Other Investments

Your fixed and other investments include your home, personal property, first and second trust deeds that you hold, limited partnerships, and business interests.

The primary concern with this part of the fact-gathering process is to identify any expensive possessions you may own. When I ask the question about personal property, I am really listening for one spouse to turn to the other and say, "What is that Picasso worth?" Specifically, you want to identify any valuable art objects or antiques you may have. Such valuable possessions should be separately inventoried and *separately transferred* into your Trust by Bill of Sale/Letter of Transfer. You should figure the value of your personal property as somewhere between the price at which you could buy it and the price at which you could sell it. If you have no objects of special value, it is common practice to value personal property (upon the death of both spouses) at $10,000. In almost all cases, this personal property is going to "disappear" into the homes of your children.

Home

What is the sales value of your home? That is, what could you sell your home for today? $ _____

Do you have a mortgage? If so, what is the unpaid balance?   ($ _____)

Net Value of the Home
Subtract the unpaid balance from the sales value $ _____

Personal Property

What is the value of your personal property—including furniture, furnishings, antiques, artworks, clothing, furs, jewelry, automobiles, recreational vehicles, hobbies, tools, and so on? (Estimate to the nearest $10,000.)   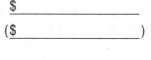 $ _____

First and Second Trust Deeds

List all first and second trust deeds you hold on someone else's property.

$ _____

$ _____

$ _____

Total First and Second Trust Deeds $ _____

Limited Partnerships

Do you have any limited partnerships? If so, what is the value? If you do not know today's value, enter what you paid for each partnership, in anticipation that you will at least get back your money.

$ _____

$ _____

$ _____

Total Value of Partnerships $ _____

Business Interests

Do you have an interest in a sole proprietorship, partnership, or corporation? What is the value of the business? Or, in other words, if someone were to place cash on the table, for what amount of money would you sell it? If you own only a partial interest in a business, then, after having valued the business, record only your share.

Total Value of Business Interests $ _____

In the early 1960s, I was a consultant with Cresap, McCormick, and Paget—one of the leading consulting firms in the nation. The company did a number of corporate valuations for merger acquisitions. As financial analysts, we went through a long, arduous (typically three-month) process to determine the corporate valuation.

Then one day I made an interesting discovery. I asked the owner, "If I placed cash on the table today, for what amount would you sell the company to me?" The owner's answer came within 10 percent of our company's three-month-long valuation.

I continued this practice for years, doing similar valuations (but for days, not for months) and then posed the same question to the owner. I consistently found that the owner would value the business within 10 percent of my detailed valuation. I learned by experience that everyone knows the value of his or her business at any given time, if asked the right question.

All too often, I get a response such as, "I really don't know what my business is worth."

To me, that response is just a form of modesty. I respond to such an answer by saying, "If I laid $5 million in cash on the table, would you sell the business to me?" If the answer is no, I offer a higher amount. However, if the answer is a quick yes, I quickly make a lower offer (for example, $3 million). If the owner's response is again a quick yes, I offer $1 million. If the response is then a thoughtful no, I try an offer in the area of $1.5 million. If the response is slow in coming forth (allowing time for thought) and then a yes, I have finally arrived at the proper value. This approach works every time. Whether I ask the questions or you ask them of yourself, the result should be the same.

However, heed a word of warning: Do not get caught in the trap of valuing your business for the IRS. Every business owner always has two valuations readily at hand: an amount for which he or she would sell the business and an amount at which he or she would value the business for IRS tax purposes. Do not play games, and do not fool yourself. The IRS will

Total Investments—Fixed and Other

Add the totals for your home, personal property, first and second trust deeds,
limited partnerships, and business interests. $ _____ (D)

---

value your business typically for a much larger amount than the amount for which you think you could sell it. Therefore, value your business realistically—for the price at which you think you could sell it. By doing so, you can identify the magnitude of your estate-planning needs, and then the appropriate type of Trust can be determined.

Real Estate Equity (Other than Home)

Now consider any real estate that you own other than your home. Each property should be listed separately, since the list identifies the number of deeds that must be specifically transferred into the name of your Living Trust.

It is important to know in what state each of your properties is located. This information should remind you that, if you hold property in different states—*and do not have ownership in the name of your Living Trust*—probate will be required in each of those states! For example, if you own a residence in California and a condominium in Utah, your residence would be probated in California, and your condominium would go through a separate probate process in Utah. As mentioned earlier in the book, absentee probate is an absolute nightmare! Furthermore, although you are considering only your equity in your real estate to determine your net worth, any probate fees would be based on the gross value (sales value) of your real estate.

Investments—Market Securities

Securities listed in this section should specifically exclude any assets already identified under the tax-sheltered category. Stock brokerage houses commonly shift your investments back and forth among stocks and bonds and their money market funds, and the ratio of investments varies from time to time. If your securities are handled in this manner, include the money market fund as part of your stocks and/or bonds.

What real estate do you own other than your home? How would you describe it, and where is it located (for example, commercial building, home, or land in Las Vegas, Nevada)? For what amount could you sell it? Do you have a mortgage? If so, how much do you still owe? You can easily compute the net value (your equity) by deducting your mortgage from the sales value.

Description of Property	Sales Value	Mortgage	Equity (Sales Value Less Mortgage)
	$	($)	$
	$	($)	$
	$	($)	$
	$	($)	$
Total Equity in Real Estate Other than Home		$ _____ (C)	

Stocks

How much money do you have invested in stocks (the purchase price)? $ _____

Do you have any stock on margin? If so, how much is on margin? (For example, if you bought $1,000 worth of stock and paid only $500, you owe the remaining $500—you would thus have 50 percent of the stock on margin.)   ($ _____)

Net Value of Stocks
Subtract margin figure from amount of stocks $ _____

Bonds

How much money do you have in bonds (municipal bonds, corporate bonds, government bonds, and Ginnie Maes)? $ _____

Mutual Funds

How much money do you have invested in mutual funds? $ _____

Annuities

How much money do you have invested in annuities? $ _____

Single-Premium Life Insurance

How much investment money do you have in single-premium whole life insurance or single-premium universal life? $ _____

Gold

What amount do you have invested in gold? $ _____

Silver

What amount do you have invested in silver? $ _____

Diamonds

What amount do you have invested in diamonds (investment-grade stones, not personal jewelry)? $ _____

Other Investments

What amounts do you have in other investments not previously mentioned?

Type of investment: _____ $ _____

Total Investments—Market Securities
Add together all of the investments in this section $ _____ (B)

Savings

The savings category includes any remaining assets. If these figures have already been included in any other area, they should not be included here.

Credit Union

How much money do you have in credit union accounts? $ _____

Government Securities

How much money do you have in Treasury bills or notes? $ _____

Savings Bonds

What is the face value of your savings bonds? $ _____

Certificates of Deposit

How much money do you have in certificates of deposits (CDs)? CDs are now referred to by many names, but typically they are investments tied up for periods of three months to several years that command a specific interest rate dependent on the investment time period. $ _____

Money Market Accounts

What funds do you have in money market accounts? $ _____

Savings Accounts

What funds do you have in regular (passbook) savings accounts? $ _____

Checking Accounts

What is the average amount of money in your checking accounts? $ _____

The balance in most people's checking accounts varies from a large amount at the beginning of the month to a small amount at the end. Simply guess at an average of your ending balance. (At this stage of the financial fact-gathering process, the amount of money in your checking accounts is usually inconsequential in relation to the rest of your estate.)

Total Savings

Add together all of the savings amounts $ _____ (A)

Summation of Your Net Worth

Now that you have answered the questions and have determined totals for your insurance, tax-sheltered investments, fixed and other investments, real estate equity (other than home), market securities investments, and savings, you are ready to find out your net worth. Your net worth is the sum of the amounts for the six previously discussed categories. Each of these category totals has been identified by a letter, from (A) to (F), in the right-hand margin. Bring each of these category totals down to the following blanks to find your net worth.

Total Savings	$ _____	(A)
Total Investments—Market Securities	$ _____	(B)
Total Equity in Real Estate Other than Home	$ _____	(C)
Total Investments—Fixed and Other	$ _____	(D)
Total Tax-Sheltered Investments	$ _____	(E)
Total Cash Value of Insurance	$ _____	(F)
Total Net Worth	$ _____	
Total Face Value of Life Insurance	$ _____	(G)

Total Net Worth and Life Insurance
Add together the preceding two figures $ _____

IDENTIFYING THE PROPER TYPE OF TRUST

The total net worth and life insurance amount is the primary figure you will use to determine whether you need an A Trust, an A-B Trust, an A-B-C Trust, and/or an Insurance Preservation Trust. Even though your financial analysis may indicate that you only need an A Trust, several other reasons why you may well want to select an A-B Trust are identified in Chapter 7.

As a general reminder from previous chapters, your choices (assuming moderate-sized estates) are as follows:

- Single person
  A Trust—Your only choice.

- Married couple
  A Trust—Suitable only if your estate is less than $1 million but not recommended.
  A-B Trust—Suitable for estates of less than $2 million.
  A-B-C Trust—Suitable for estates that exceed a value of $2 million. Taxes may be deferred until death of second spouse (regardless of value of estate).

- Unmarried couple
  Unmarried A-B Trust—Designed for an unmarried couple, typically living together. Trust is similar in form to a married A-B Trust.
  Partner A-A Trust—Specifically created for two individuals of the same gender. Trust is similar in form to two single A Trusts blended together. Each individual's estate

(if over $1 million) will ultimately be subject to estate taxes as a single person.

For a refresher on why the different types of Trusts are suitable for different-sized estates, you may want to review the examples in Chapter 7. For estates valued at more than $2 million, an Insurance Preservation Trust, a Spousal and Family Support Trust, a Generation-Skipping Trust, a Gift Trust, a Family Limited Partnership, and even a Charitable Remainder Trust may also be advisable.

A SIMPLE PROCESS

Valuing your estate can be simple and swift. Take my word for it—you do not need any papers in front of you. Simply go through the questionnaire presented in this chapter and answer the questions. It should take you no more than twenty minutes, and your valuation will be within 10 percent of the actual value; you do not need to be any closer. Recognize that the value of your estate will fluctuate during the year for any number of reasons, but you need not worry about such changes.

If you follow the simple process presented in this chapter, you can identify the type of Trust you need. In addition, if you decide now that you need only an A Trust or an A-B Trust, recognize that, at any future date, you can always update your Trust by amendment.

As an old adage says, "People don't eat a whole cow in one sitting; they just take one bite at a time." Similarly, as you build your estate, you should review and build your Living Trust a piece at a time.

17

Creating Your Estate Plan

Once you have decided to create your own Living Trust and have selected the type of Trust that is most appropriate for your estate, you have arrived at the stage where you are finally ready to create your estate plan. People seldom create the perfect plan on the first attempt. Yet, remember, your Living Trust is changeable—monthly, weekly, or even daily. Often, the most difficult part of developing a plan is to get started. The decisions you make now are not etched in stone. Therefore, begin your plan now, put it into effect, and then, as time goes on, modify it as necessary to meet your current goals. In the end, you will come up with the perfect solution—but you need to start now.

MAJOR DECISIONS

For many people, deciding to create a Living Trust is the easy part. To create a Trust that is tailored to the individual circumstances and needs of each client requires the client to make several important decisions:

- Whom to name as the trustees for your Trust
- Whom to name as the executor of your estate
- Whom to name as guardian or guardians, if you have minor or handicapped children

- To whom you want to leave your assets, in what proportion, and when you want your assets to be distributed
- Which ancillary documents are to be included with your Living Trust

These decisions are difficult, so do not make them in a hurried manner. Instead, give the various alternatives some thought and discussion, make some tentative decisions, and then sleep on them. It is particularly important for a married couple to discuss each potential decision jointly—so that their Living Trust will reflect their mutual desires, and not just the desires of either the husband or the wife.

These decisions are difficult, but once you make them, you will enjoy peace of mind.

Unfortunately, at about this time in the process of creating your estate plan, the dreaded disease called apathy sets in, and all of your best efforts cease. This situation often happens because many of the necessary decisions are difficult to make and many people find the subject to be somewhat unpleasant. However, you must make these decisions, or eventually the court will make them for you. Once you make the decisions, however, you will enjoy peace of mind.

Selection of Trustees

The trustee(s), co-trustees, and successor trustee(s) are responsible for administering the Living Trust. Whether you are married or single, the decisions you need to make are almost identical, although your selections will be based on different criteria. For guidance in making your decisions, refer to the information about trustees in Chapter 8.

Decisions for a Married Couple   ·

If you are married, you and your spouse need to identify the individuals who will administer your Trust while you are both living, after one of you passes away, and after both of you are gone. These people are the initial trustee or co-trustees, the surviving trustee, and the successor trustee.

Since you have most likely done a reasonably good job of managing your assets to this point in your life, you would presumably want to continue to do so; therefore, it is typical to name both husband and wife as trustees of their Living Trust. On rare occasions, where one spouse is not well and everything is being handled entirely by the other spouse, it would be appropriate to name only the active spouse as the trustee.

If one spouse dies, the surviving spouse is typically named as the surviving trustee. Occasionally, a client considers naming a child (or children) as co-trustee with the surviving spouse. However, only in rare situations would doing so be recommended.

> For example, a man who was dying of cancer named his daughter to serve as co-trustee with his wife upon his death. He was concerned about his wife's ability to manage the estate after his demise, because his wife's mental faculties were rapidly deteriorating.
>
> In another situation, a husband had built a very large estate in real estate. His daughter was very active in the management of the real estate, while his wife had little or no involvement. The husband therefore felt that it was appropriate to name his daughter as co-trustee with his wife upon his death.

As a last resort, you may wish to name a financial institution as surviving trustee, either in lieu of the spouse or as a co-trustee with the spouse. Before you do so, however, review the discussion of this alternative in Chapter 8.

One or more of your adult children, close family members, or close friends should be named as successor trustees to serve upon the death, incompetence, or resignation of the surviving spouse. Administration of your Living Trust is quite easy, and whether you name one child or four children as successor trustees is entirely academic. Clients most often name the child they consider most mature or name all of their children. Either approach works well. However, you must be aware that the minimum age to be a trustee is eighteen years old.

If you have named one successor trustee, you should consider naming one or more alternate successor trustees in case the named successor trustee is unable or unwilling to serve when the need finally arises. If you do not name an alternate successor trustee, your Trust should have within it a provision in which the primary beneficiaries would have the right to elect a successor trustee. Such a provision is included in all Living Trusts drawn up for our clients.

You may sometimes find it appropriate to name a financial institution as successor trustee; however, such action is recommended only as a last resort. Situations in which such an arrangement may be appropriate are described in Chapter 8.

Decisions for a Single Person

If you are a single person, you must make almost the same decisions regarding the administration of your Trust as are required of a married couple. You need to identify the initial trustee or co-trustee and the successor trustee. However, you cannot name a surviving trustee, because your Trust becomes irrevocable upon your death.

Assuming you have managed your assets reasonably well, you would presumably want to be the trustee of your own Trust.

Assuming that you have managed your assets reasonably well, you would presumably want to be the trustee of your own Trust.

One or more of your adult children, close family members, or close friends should be considered as successor trustees upon your death, incompetence, or resignation. The previous information about selecting a successor trustee for a married couple would also apply to a single individual.

Selection of Executor

After selecting your various trustees, you must select an executor to handle any of your assets that have been inadvertently left outside your Living Trust. The responsibilities and selection of an executor are described in Chapter 8. If you have all of your assets inside your Living Trust, there will be absolutely nothing for the executor to do.

For a Married Couple

Upon the death of a spouse, the surviving spouse is typically named as the executor. If the surviving spouse is not physically or mentally able to withstand the eventual appearances in court, it may be more appropriate to name one of the adult children, a close family member, or a close friend as executor.

Upon the death of both husband and wife, the successor trustee is normally the person who is named to be the executor. For guidelines in selecting this person, see Chapter 8.

For a Single Person

If you are a single person, you need to be concerned only about whom to name as the executor to handle your estate upon your demise. Upon the death of the settlor, the successor trustee is typically named as the executor.

Appointment of Guardian

If you have minor children or mentally or physically handicapped children, it is essential that you name a guardian (or guardians) for the children. Selection of a guardian is probably one of the most important—and one of the most difficult—decisions you can ever make. For some guidance, you may wish to review the information about appointment of a guardian in Chapter 11.

Naming an Alternate Guardian

If your children are eleven years of age or younger, it is strongly suggested that you name an alternate guardian. As mentioned earlier in the book, many years will pass before your children attain adulthood, and in the meantime your named guardian could die. When such an event occurs, you are not likely even to remember that your Appointment of Guardian document now needs to be changed. It is much better—for the ultimate protection of your children—to take a little more time now and thoughtfully select an alternate guardian.

Naming a Guardian for a Handicapped Child

If you have a handicapped child, you should review the discussion of this subject in Chapter 11. This critical decision of naming a guardian for a handicapped child should be made *only* after careful thought.

In recent years, many of our clients have drawn up guardianship papers for their adult handicapped children, who were once very bright contributors to society but who experimented with drugs and are now mentally incapacitated. This sad situation is one of the most frightening and insidious occurrences that has happened to our society, but the true-to-life consequences are little known to the general public. When my clients are drawing up Living Trusts, the subject of guardianship for an adult child who has been incapacitated because of drugs is one of the last issues to surface—and then it is almost as if the subject were an embarrassment to the sad parents. Appallingly, the number of such cases is large and seems to be growing without end.

Allocation and Distribution of Assets

Unlike a Will, the Living Trust gives each spouse an *independent* right to determine to whom he or she wants his or her assets distributed, in what proportion, and when. For a couple with an A-B Trust, upon the death of the first spouse, the Decedent's Trust B becomes irrevocable—and the named beneficiaries, the percentage of allocation, and the time of distribution for the decedent's share of the assets become cast in concrete. However, the surviving spouse may continue to change the allocation and distribution for his or her own share of the assets in the Survivor's A Trust.

> A mother and father were estranged from their only child. The couple left only 10 percent of their assets to the child, and the mother died shortly thereafter. During the ensuing years, the child re-established a close relationship with the father. When the father eventually came into our office to increase the portion of the estate going to the child, I simply asked him to tell me what percentage of the total estate he wanted to go to the child. We thereupon drew an amendment adjusting the Survivor's A Trust to meet the client's desire.

Allocation of Assets

If you have children, presumably you will want your assets to go to them upon the death of both you and your spouse (if you are married) or upon your death (if you are single). Obviously, you may make any number of special bequests to whomever you desire (such as to your grandchildren, brothers and sisters, relatives, friends, favorite charities, or church). Chapter 9 provides guidance in making these decisions.

Probably the most important decision that needs to be made at this juncture is whether you want to allocate your assets equally to your children or to allocate each child's share unequally. About one-fourth of our clients have very good reasons for allocating the assets to their children in other than equal proportions. Chapter 9 provides some examples to help you decide what is right for you.

When a husband and wife have been married before, have children from their former marriages, and have remarried, an A-B Trust is the logical choice for allocating assets fairly. The A-B Trust allows the spouses to combine their assets so that they may upgrade their standard of living. The A-B Trust also retains the combined assets so that the surviving spouse may maintain the same standard of living as when both spouses were alive. Upon the death of the surviving spouse, the A-B Trust can ensure that the assets in the Survivor's A Trust go to the children of the surviving spouse, and the assets in the Decedent's B Trust go to the children of the first spouse to die. Thus, the A-B Trust provides a simple, ideal way to solve what could be a complex situation. In fact, I have seen this particular solution restore harmony to many marriages that were under stress because of the issue of allocation and distribution.

Distribution of Assets

Once you have decided who is to get what portion of your estate, you need to decide *when* the specified distribution is to be made. Most people desire to distribute their estates to their children. As you may recall from Chapter 9, the most commonly used types of asset distribution are outright, at a specific age, income only, and deferred distribution. If you are unsure which arrangement would be best for your situation, you should review the material in Chapter 9.

Deferred distribution is the most common method of distribution selected by our clients, and I lean very heavily toward this type of distribution for two important reasons. First, all people mature with age. Second, if an individual gets a sum of money and wastes it, the individual gets a second chance. Some individuals need to learn by experience. Being a registered investment adviser, I have learned from observing many "mature" people that age is no guarantee of wisdom. All too often, people between fifty-five and sixty years old take their retirement money and invest it on well-intentioned advice, which has often been disastrous.

I feel so strongly about deferred distribution—and providing a second chance—that I have used deferred distribution in my own family's Living Trust for my children, specifying that distribution for each child will be one-third at age twenty-five, one-third at age thirty, and one-third at age thirty-five. However, at no time (regardless of the children's ages) will distribution be greater than one-third outright, one-third in five years, and one-third in ten years. Thus, if my wife and I were to die after our children had all attained the age of thirty-five, they would still receive their inheritances as deferred distributions.

Deferred distribution gives your heirs a chance to learn from experience.

Occasionally, however, a spouse desires to make an outright distribution of a particular asset or of a particular dollar amount to his or her children upon his or her death. Such a situation often occurs when the parents have been married before and have children from their former marriages. The situation is even more prevalent when there is a disparity of age between the parents.

For example, a husband had married a woman much younger than himself, and they had a young child. The husband was concerned that, because his wife was near in age to the children of his former marriage, if he were to leave all of the assets in trust for his surviving spouse, his own children from his first marriage would probably never benefit from his estate. The husband therefore decided to distribute his $50,000 retirement program to the children from his first marriage at the time of his death. Although I understood the husband's logic, I could foresee conflict over the distribution with his present wife.

I agreed that the husband should include such a distribution in the Trust, but I also suggested to the husband that he should take out $50,000 worth of life insurance on his life payable to the Trust, in order to offset the loss of the asset to his present wife. Buying the insurance policy would leave his current wife in the same financial position (that is, she would not be denied $50,000). The wife accepted the insurance alternative, but it was obvious that, without such a compromise, there would have been much future conflict at home.

If you still feel unsure about how you want to allocate and distribute your assets, please take some time to review the material in Chapter 9. That chapter explains some of the many possibilities and answers some frequently asked questions.

Selection of Ancillary Documents
The next step is to select which of the ancillary documents to include with your Living Trust. These documents are described in Chapter 11. The following documents should be considered:

- Living Will (Right-to-Die Clause)
- Durable Power of Attorney for Health Care
- Durable General Power of Attorney
- Competency Clause
- Catastrophic Illness Trust (not currently available)
- Assignment of Furniture, Furnishings, and Personal Effects
- Appointment of Guardian
- Appointment of Conservator
- Anatomical Gift
- Separate Property Agreements

Six documents I feel should be included with every Trust are the Living Will, the Durable Power of Attorney for Health Care, the Durable General Power of Attorney, the Competency Clause, the Conservator Provision, and the Catastrophic Illness Trust (not currently available). However, each document requires your *personal* decision and may require reflection and thought before you arrive at the decision that is right for you. Not everyone decides to include all of the documents, but each document offers desirable legal protections. For guidance in selecting these documents, refer to the discussion in Chapter 11.

YOUR FIRST VISIT FOR YOUR TRUST
Now that you have reviewed the critical questions that need to be answered and have made the decisions you believe are best for your particular situation, you are ready to seek out a qualified professional who is well versed in drawing up Living Trusts. Chapter 10 provides some guidelines for identifying a qualified adviser. If you would like some help with this difficult task, you may want to use the referral number given in Chapter 19.

When you make your first visit, you should take with you the necessary items of personal data (such as your parents' dates and places of birth); the names of the individuals whom you have chosen as trustees, executor, and guardian; and notes outlining the allocation and distribution of assets you desire for your heirs. In addition, take any real estate deeds, trust deeds, Separate Property Agreements, any business interest papers you have, and any Will of a deceased spouse.

Real Estate Deeds

You need to bring a copy of the grant deeds to real estate you own, because these deeds need to be transferred into the name of your Living Trust. Unless you are particularly knowledgeable in this area, you should have legal counsel prepare and file these documents. If you bring copies of these documents with you, the new deeds can be drawn up at the same time that your Living Trust is being drawn. The new deeds will be prepared and awaiting your signature and notarization when you return to sign the necessary Trust documents.

As a precautionary measure, you should include with each deed the Assessor Parcel Number (which you will find on your tax bill) and the address of the property. In addition, be sure to read the property description on the deed. If the description says "See Exhibit A attached," be sure that Exhibit A is attached to the deed.

Be sure to bring deeds for each of your real estate properties, including any time-share properties in which you have an economic interest.

Trust Deeds

If you hold any first or second trust deeds on other people's property, these trust deeds are an asset to you and must also be transferred into the name of your Living Trust. Therefore, take them with you on your first meeting.

Separate Property Agreements

You should also take along a list of any assets that are to be designated as separate property.

To refresh your memory about the formal and specific information required for each asset, review the section on Separate Property Agreements in Chapter 9.

Business Interest Papers

If you have any business interest in a partnership or sole proprietorship, take your business documents representing this interest. Ask for a Bill of Sale/Letter of Transfer so that your interest in the business can be transferred into the name of the Trust.

Wills

If you are a widow or widower, bring a copy of your deceased spouse's Will.

WISE ESTATE PLANNING

The most important thing you can do now is to gather together as much information as possible on potential trustees, executor, and guardians, and your desires for allocation and distribution of your assets and then jot down your thoughts. Then find a professional who has in-depth experience in working with people and creating Living Trusts. Such an individual can bring priceless experience to bear upon your particular problem.

You need not have *all* the answers before you take that most important first step—the creation of your Living Trust. You should begin now to lay out your agenda for wise estate planning. Remember, any plan is better than no plan at all. Once you have a plan, you have the ability to adjust it to meet your changing needs or circumstances. As you do so, you will eventually create the perfect plan for your individual situation.

Once you have executed your Living Trust, I must say, "Congratulations! You have now taken a giant step in the direction of wise estate planning."

18

Appropriate Costs of the Living Trust and Accompanying Documents

The Living Trust and its ancillary documents are probably the most important papers that you will ever sign. To a great extent, they will determine your peace of mind, as well as your future quality of life—and that of your heirs. A good Living Trust includes all of the appropriate and necessary ancillary documents needed to protect your interests and your estate in the future. When it is *your* Living Trust, it should be the best; anything less can lead to heartache, frustration, and tragedy.

This chapter presents appropriate costs of a Living Trust for a typical estate. Most of our clients have estates ranging in value from $200,000 to $2.5 million. For large estates, an exceptionally good estate-planning specialist has every right to charge fees far in excess of the fees mentioned here. The reason is that the estate-planning expert is bringing all of his or her skills to bear in an effort to preserve the client's estate. The estate-planning professional with extensive experience has developed skills that are well earned, and this person should be rightfully paid for his or her expertise.

In the first edition of this book, I urged the legal profession to provide a Living Trust that would be within financial reach of everyone.

Unfortunately, the answer has been a rash of very poorly written Trusts in which the quality of the documents is disastrous. I had unwittingly created a monster. My greatest concern today, as well as that of many state attorneys general, is the misrepresentation of Living Trusts that has become so prevalent by many unqualified attorneys, institutions, and firms preying on the unsuspecting public.

I must also warn you about the dangers of an "inexpensive" Trust. Occasionally a client says, "I know of an attorney who will prepare a Trust for $250 or $350 or $550." Be careful; you get exactly what you pay for. Remember, a poorly written Living Trust can be just as disastrous as not having a Trust at all!

PRICE STRUCTURE

Keep these comments in mind as you review the price structure for the Living Trust and its accompanying documents. Table 18-1 lists suggested fees for the basic forms of the Living Trust and the ancillary documents.

Amendments

With the sophisticated computer equipment, programs, and techniques used in our office, a

TABLE 18-1
THE ESTATE PLAN FEE SCHEDULE

Revocable Living Trusts	Suggested Retail
Single or Married A Trust	$1,395–$1,695
Married/Unmarried A-B Trust	$1,695–$1,895
Married A-B-C Trust	$1,995–$2,195
Partner A-A Trust	$1,895–$2,195
Single A Q-Tip Trust	$1,495–$1,695

Ancillary documents for the state the Living Trust is drawn for are included at no charge.

Special Estate-Preservation Vehicles	
Community Property Recognition Agreement	$ 200
Insurance Preservation Trust	$ 600–$ 800
Spousal Support Preservation Trust	$ 700–$ 900
Irrevocable Catastrophic Illness Trust	$ 300–$ 500
Family Catastrophic Illness Trust	$ 300–$ 500
Gift Trust	$ 600–$ 800
Generation-Skipping Trust	$ 750–$ 950
IRA Q-TIP[1] Trust or IRA/Qualified Plan Trust	$ 800–$1,000
Roth IRA Trust/Single Roth	$ 800–$1,000
Family Limited Partnership	$2,000–$2,400
Charitable Remainder Trust (includes Preservation Trust)	$2,000–$2,500

Special Processing	
Expedite (3 days to final; no draft)	$150
Priority (3 days to draft; 3 days to final)	$150

Amendments	
Partial Amendment	
Standard (1 section—i.e., Successor Trustee)	$200–$250
Complex (more than 1 section—i.e., ST & A&D)	$300–$350
Full Amendment (to replace an Estate Plan Trust)	$750–$800
(full revocable Living Trust package)	
Tax Change Amendment	$400

Ancillary Documents (additions/changes or stand-alone)	
Living Will	$ 50–$ 60
DPOA—Assets	$ 50–$ 60
DPOA—Health Care	$ 50–$ 60
Nomination of Conservator/Guardian	$ 50–$ 60
Pour-Over Will	$ 50–$ 60

Assignment of Personal Property	$ 50–$ 60
Appointment of Guardian for Minor or Handicapped Person	$ 50–$ 60
Abstract (set of 3)	$ 50–$ 60
Transfer Letters	$ 50–$ 60
Anatomical Gift	$ 50–$ 60
Ancillary Document Package	$150–$200
(includes the Living Will, DPOA—Assets, DPOA—Health Care, and Nomination of Conservator/Guardian)	
Miscellaneous	
Reprint of Draft Documents	$35
Reprint of Final Documents	$60
Reprint of Page	$1 per page ($25 minimum)
Living Trust Additions	
Bill of Sale/Letter of Transfer	$ 60
Separate Property Agreement	$200
Spousal Gift	$100

[1] Includes Community Property Recognition Agreement in community property states

typical simple amendment—such as a change of beneficiary, a change of successor trustee, or a change in the allocation or method of distribution—can be made for a cost of about $200. Such a fee structure assumes that the firm making the amendment is the same as the firm that drew the original Trust document.

For each Living Trust created for our clients, all of the client information and Trust data are computerized. Therefore, it is a simple task to call up the client data and, by asking for an amendment, immediately have everything on the computer screen, except the appropriate paragraph that needs to be added to or changed in the client's Living Trust. Since almost all of the clauses and provisions have been standardized in our Living Trusts, the proper paragraph formats are already contained in our computer library.

You should review your Trust at least once every five years to make sure that it is continuing to meet your personal desires. With such a small fee to make a standard change, clients rarely hesitate to make necessary changes to their Trusts, so their Trusts continue to work for them. Many years of experience have proven that, if the cost of amendments is excessive, clients will not keep their Trusts up-to-date with their personal desires.

Tax-Change Updates

Congress seems to change the estate tax laws about every five years. Depending upon the extent to which each tax change affects the Trust, our clients are charged only about $200 for such an amendment—such a fee is quite reasonable. Providing notice of tax changes is a special service that is necessary to ensure that all clients' Trusts will continue to work for them regardless of the whims of Congress.

The Estate Plan codifies your Trust and will notify you of any tax change that affects your Trust. When there is a major tax change, the computer in our office searches all of the Trusts and associated provisions drawn up for our clients. The computer identifies which Trusts will be subject to a particular tax change and prints out the name and address of each client who is affected. (However, our clients must remember to keep us apprised of any address changes.) The clients are then informed that they should have their Trusts amended to take advantage of the particular tax change. Thus, because The Estate Plan's Living Trusts have been logically organized, it is relatively easy to print a standard tax-change amendment, which simply needs to be signed and notarized by each client who needs the change.

Transfer of Deeds

Since legal accuracy is crucial in transferring grant deeds and trust deeds into the name of a Living Trust, any firm offering to create your Living Trust should, as a service, rewrite your deeds. An appropriate fee would be charged for each deed, depending on whether the property is located inside or outside your state of residence, and would pertain to grant deeds, first and second trust deeds, and time-share deeds.

A deed is a formal, legal document. Therefore, transferring a deed into the name of your Living Trust is *not* a do-it-yourself project. Before a deed can be recorded, it must meet all of the legal requirements, which vary from county to county and from state to state. Of even greater importance, however, is that if the deed is not drawn properly, filing the deed may trigger reappraisal of your property in certain states, which will ultimately result in higher taxes! Over the years, I have seen too many do-it-yourself deed transfers go awry—with disastrous results—to be able to recommend such an approach to clients. The few dollars saved are usually spent many times over in time and anguish—and often at the additional expense of an unnecessary tax increase on the property involved.

Annual Upkeep

If you have a well-written Trust, which covers every contingency, and if all of your assets are placed in the Trust, an annual upkeep fee is unnecessary. Many clients seem to be concerned about continued upkeep fees, possibly because they have heard of firms that make such an annual charge. Since no annual accounting or administration needs to be performed, there is simply no ethical reason for charging an annual fee.

Clients are encouraged to call for answers to any Trust-related or estate-planning questions or for help in resolving any problems that might arise. Such a service is provided to clients with our Trust without charge, since most questions are easily answered and most problems easily resolved. Every once in a while, a client tells me that, for every telephone call made to an attorney, he or she was billed $200! Such charges for Living Trust questions are entirely unnecessary. Years of experience and modern computer technology have shown us that a new era is dawning—offering outstanding Living Trusts and related appropriate services to clients at reasonable rates.

If you have a well-written Living Trust, a fee for annual upkeep should be unnecessary.

On the other hand, occasionally a client does abuse his or her privilege related to this service. One client brought *twelve pages* of bequests to our office to be included in his Living Trust! Courtesy and consideration should be a two-way street. Under such circumstances, a client should understand that extra services, above and beyond the ordinary, can willingly be accommodated—but for an appropriate additional fee.

Settlement Fee

If you have a *good* Living Trust, an organized estate, and a knowledgeable professional adviser serving you, the fee to settle your estate should be fixed and reasonable. I have already addressed my deep concern for what is happening in this industry. Living Trusts are being sold like used automobiles, but when it comes time to settle the estate, either the seller does not know how to settle the estate or else charges an exorbitant fee! I know of many law firms that charge 1 to 3 percent of the *total* estate to settle an estate in a Living Trust; another law firm charges *one-third* of what it would otherwise cost to take the same estate through probate! Such fees are outrageous!

Since many concerned people are now seeking a commitment of a reasonable settlement fee—rather than a potentially unlimited settlement fee based on the value of the estate—our firm will provide our clients, on request, with a guarantee to settle their estates for a reasonable fixed fee. Providing a written settlement-fee guarantee to a client who requests it seems to provide peace of mind now to that client from being charged an excessive settlement fee in the future.

However, keep in mind that where estate tax needs to be paid (and the Federal Estate Tax Form 706 needs to be filed), the client will likely need the assistance of a knowledgeable CPA.

HIDDEN COSTS

There should be *no* hidden costs, fees, charges, or administrative expenses related to creating a Living Trust!

I am appalled by one particular law firm that advertises extensively and presents seminars to generate clients. The firm tells its clients how much the Trust will cost (not too different from the fees listed in Table 18-1). However, as the firm progresses with the client's new Trust, "hidden" fees start to appear. For example, the firm suddenly advises its client that all property needs to be appraised before it can be placed in the Trust—and the firm "just happens" to have an appraiser whom it recommends. The appraisal fee is $250 per property!

For the life of me, I cannot figure out why, with a properly written Living Trust, you would need to appraise property to place it into the Trust—for any other reason than to generate additional (unjustified) fees.

CLIENT COOPERATION

The prices mentioned in this chapter are realistic only if each client cooperates. Working with most clients is absolutely delightful, but a few people unfortunately take advantage of the relaxed, friendly, low-key approach our firm endeavors to use with them. Abuses, although usually caused by only a very few individuals, can eventually make the Living Trust more expensive for everyone. Consequently, in an effort to keep the cost within

reach of everyone, the following suggestions are offered:

Read this book—and understand the Living Trust and its desirable provisions.

Determine the size of your estate—and decide whether you should have an A Trust, an A-B Trust, or an A-B-C Trust. In addition, try to anticipate beforehand whether you should include any tax-saving provisions.

Make your key decisions. Before meeting with the adviser to draw up your Living Trust, give some serious thought to those difficult-to-make decisions:

- Selection of successor trustee(s)
- Selection of executor
- Selection of guardian (where appropriate)
- Selection of beneficiaries
- Desired allocation of Trust assets
- Desired distribution of Trust assets

Keep your appointments—particularly the appointment at which you will sign your Trust documents (referred to as the execution of your Trust), when the Trust becomes a legal entity. Occasionally, a client will call at the last moment to reschedule an appointment to execute the Trust. Since the Trust documents must be specifically dated, the documents must then be reprinted if you change your Trust execution appointment at the last minute. It costs our firm $60 to replace those documents. After too many abuses related to last-minute rescheduling, our firm has finally found it necessary to pass the added cost on to the client who reschedules his or her appointment at the last minute.

Photocopy your personal documents—ahead of time, whenever possible. On the day that you will be signing your new Trust, you should bring copies of such documents as your checkbook and savings account passbooks; stocks, bonds, and mutual funds; life insurance policies; grant deeds for real estate; first and second trust deeds; and titles to other such valuable assets. If you are unable to photocopy your own documents, you should come into the office at least a half-hour ahead of your scheduled appointment, so that the documents can be copied before your appointment. The process of executing your Living Trust typically takes about one hour, but that time does not include the time needed to copy your personal documents.

If you bring copies of your documents at the time you execute your Trust, the job is finished. Too many people execute their Trusts and then never get around to organizing their estates with the Estate Plan Binder or transferring all of their assets into their Trusts. By bringing copies of your documents with you, you ensure that everything can be handled at once. Nothing is overlooked or put off until tomorrow, when it is often forgotten.

If you will follow these simple courtesies, then the cost of the Living Trust can be kept reasonably low—ideally within reach of everyone.

IT CAN BE DONE

Admittedly, the comments made in this chapter have entered areas where angels fear to tread. On the other hand, thousands of happy and satisfied clients are proof that a well-written Living Trust, accompanied by the Estate Plan Binder (for organizing your estate) and a highly experienced organization (readily available and willing to answer questions, as well as to help settle your estate), produces the right formula for enlightening people about the superiority of the Living Trust.

19

Conclusion

Now that you have read *The Living Trust*, you have become acquainted with the many advantages of a Living Trust, and you have begun to think about how a Living Trust fits into your own situation. You also have been made aware of the many fallacies that are being perpetrated on the general public by Will and Probate attorneys. (Appendix I contains a comprehensive exposure of these fallacies, as well as an explanation of what is fallacy and what is fact.) You should now be able to determine what type of Trust will best suit your needs and the ancillary documents that are most appropriate for you. You should have some ideas about who should be the successor trustee and how to allocate and distribute your assets upon your death, or upon the death of you and your spouse. Finally, you should be able to differentiate between a good Trust and a poor one.

YOUR CHOICE

Now that you have become familiar with the Living Trust, the next step is up to you. You have three choices to make in establishing your estate plan:

- Do nothing.
- Find a competent professional on your own.
- Use a professional referral service.

If, after reading this book, you still think that probate is the better approach to settling your estate, the decision is certainly your prerogative. Everyone should be given the opportunity to go through the agonizing and frustrating process of probate—at least once.

Doing Nothing

Remember that, if you take the do-nothing approach (and such lack of action is an actual decision), you can at least take comfort in knowing that you will be doing the same thing as almost 80 percent of the adult population in the United States. If you do nothing, your state government already has a Will for you, and it is a very complicated legal document that may be very much to your and your family's detriment.

I hope, however, that you have wisely elected to preserve your estate. If you are like most people, your attitude may now be that "I have worked hard to build my estate, as meager or as large as it may be, and I would like to have a say in where it goes."

The choice is now yours. This book has shown you the good and the bad sides of passing on your estate to your heirs. Think a moment about what you would leave behind if—God forbid—you were to suddenly die tomorrow.

Remember the many benefits that accrue to you, your family, and your heirs when you have a well-written Living Trust and the accompanying documents *and* you have placed all your assets in the Trust.

Searching for a Competent Professional

If you have decided that the best solution for your estate plan is a Living Trust, then you may go in search of a qualified, experienced, and competent estate-planning professional.

In the first edition of this book, I recommended that with this book in hand (and the outline in Chapter 10), you would be armed with the information that should enable you to identify a qualified attorney who could draw up your Living Trust document. However, as I have traveled throughout the nation these past several years giving more than three thousand seminars, innumerable individuals have said, "I read your book and got a Living Trust, but, after attending your seminar, I am suddenly aware that I have a very inadequate Trust."

Even with this book as guidance, many of our readers are still falling prey to unqualified attorneys who claim to have twenty years of experience with Wills and Trusts, but who, in reality, often have nineteen and a half years of experience with Wills but only six months' experience with Living Trusts.

In today's world, there is a proliferation of inexperienced attorneys, and non-attorneys, who are drawing up poorly written Living Trusts and trying to meet the rapidly increasing demand for this simple solution to the agony of probate. In fact, there are even "do-it-yourself" kits and computer software programs for both professionals and the public. A crucial legal instrument such as the Living Trust is just too important for you (and your heirs) to leave to chance. An inadequate Trust,

with insufficient trustee powers and inappropriate contingency provisions, can be an absolute nightmare for you and your heirs. Don't take a chance, and don't waste your money. If you are going to get a Living Trust, do it *right*. Your Trust should incorporate *all* of the provisions identified in Table 10-1.

Using a Professional Referral Service

In the first edition of this book, we offered an attorney referral service to our readers. In the first six months after publication of the book, I was shocked to learn that 70 percent of the callers said, "I don't want an attorney!" What an incredible condemnation of the legal fraternity. I believe that much of this negativism arises because of the discredit created by the actions of Will and Probate attorneys. I work closely with the legal profession, and, though I criticize it regularly, I know many outstanding attorneys for whom I have the very highest respect and who bring great credit to their profession. I wish I could make the same statement about Will and Probate attorneys.

It seems that ever since my book came out in 1989, everyone is offering Living Trusts. They come in all sizes, shapes, and prices—and unfortunately, most of these Living Trusts are not worth the paper on which they are written. To be effective, a Living Trust must be a very comprehensive and sophisticated document. In an effort to be of service to our readers, The Estate Plan has established a nationwide network of more than 400 professional advisers and more than 100 attorneys. Our advisers have been carefully screened. Most are graduates of the Abts Institute for Estate Preservation personally taught by me and have attended many of our advanced courses and work closely with local legal counsel. These advisers come from a variety of backgrounds: financial planners, CPAs, accountants, insurance agents, and attorneys. Their specialty is estate planning, and they are particularly skilled at communicating complicated subjects in simple terms.

We are always looking for more advisers, but good professionals are hard to find. Our attorneys work directly with our advisers, or are advisers themselves. They keep us abreast of local activity in their state legislatures and new statutes, so that we can keep our documents current and applicable in all fifty states. This is particularly important when you own property in more than one state, live in two separate states—like "snowbirds," or ultimately move to another state.

Every professional is chosen especially to represent the client's interests. Specifically, legal counsel in each area must ascertain that the Living Trust, and all other estate preservation vehicles, are appropriate for the client, and that the subsequently created Living Trust and associated documents meet the client's needs. In some states, to satisfy state requirements, the adviser works directly for local legal counsel. Regardless, the documents are produced in our corporate offices and can be recognized by our blue feather logo preprinted on every page. This logo assures you of the finest quality.

Each professional is put through an extensive training program, so that when you sit down with the professional, you hear almost identically the same thing as if I had the opportunity to sit down with each of you. With this trained staff of professionals to meet with our clients, I am able to do what I consider to be of greatest service to the general public—regularly giving seminars throughout the country and carrying my message to the greatest number of people.

I am often asked, "Do The Estate Plan professionals have the twenty-five or more years of experience needed to create the Living Trust?" The answer is no. The professional doesn't need the twenty-five years of experience, because he or she doesn't create the Trust—that's done by The Estate Plan. The Estate Plan is the only national organization with more than twenty-five years of experience in producing Living Trusts nationwide. We continually benefit from the input of some of the finest legal minds in the country as well as the thousands of clients we have already served. Even though we take great pride in our current staff of professionals, we are always looking for more, so that we might be of greater service to our clients everywhere.

If you would like to be referred to one of The Estate Plan professionals in your area, call our toll-free number at (800) 350-1234.

As I have said many times in the past and will continue to say in the future, I am an ardent believer that one of the finest gifts one spouse can give another, or that parents can give their children, is the Living Trust.

Appendix A

Comparison of Death Costs: Loving Will vs. Living Trust for Single Person with A Trust

This appendix consists of illustrations that compare death costs for a single person who has a Loving Will with the costs for a single person who has a Living A Trust. The comparisons use the following sizes of estates:

- $100,000
- $200,000
- $300,000
- $400,000
- $500,000
- $600,000
- $800,000
- $1 million
- $1.2 million
- $1.5 million
- $2 million

Each illustration shows that having a Living Trust rather than a Loving Will provides benefits in the areas of probate, estate taxes, and gain for the heirs.

To use this appendix, find the illustration that most closely corresponds to the size of your own estate, and study the comparison of the two methods of holding assets. For a further explanation of the computations used in the illustrations, please refer to Chapter 6.

Note that all examples assume a probate cost of 8 percent and a federal estate tax exclusion of $1 million.

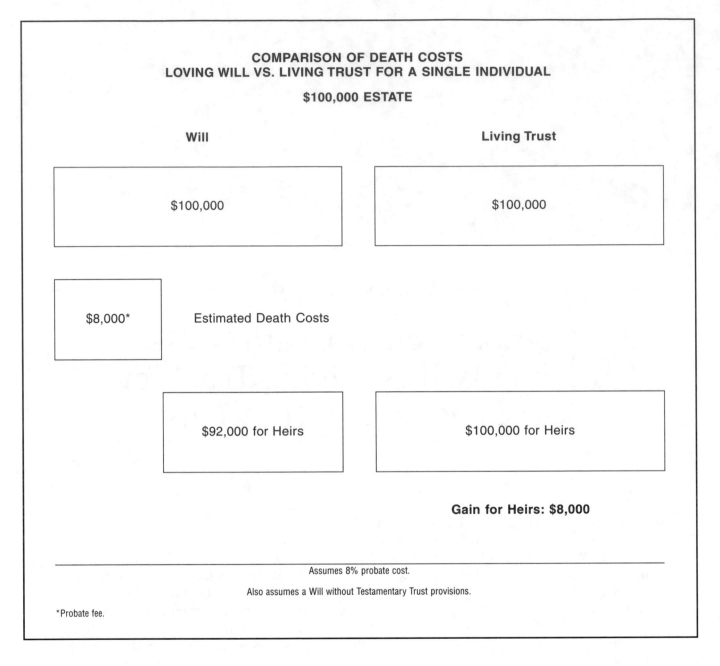

COMPARISON OF DEATH COSTS
LOVING WILL VS. LIVING TRUST FOR A SINGLE INDIVIDUAL

$100,000 ESTATE

Will	Living Trust
$100,000	$100,000

$8,000*   Estimated Death Costs

$92,000 for Heirs	$100,000 for Heirs

Gain for Heirs: $8,000

Assumes 8% probate cost.

Also assumes a Will without Testamentary Trust provisions.

*Probate fee.

COMPARISON OF DEATH COSTS
LOVING WILL VS. LIVING TRUST FOR A SINGLE INDIVIDUAL

$200,000 ESTATE

Will   **Living Trust**

$200,000 $200,000

$16,000*   Estimated Death Costs

$184,000 for Heirs $200,000 for Heirs

Gain for Heirs: $16,000

Assumes 8% probate cost.

Also assumes a Will without Testamentary Trust provisions.

*Probate fee.

COMPARISON OF DEATH COSTS
LOVING WILL VS. LIVING TRUST FOR A SINGLE INDIVIDUAL

$300,000 ESTATE

Will	Living Trust
$300,000	$300,000

$24,000*   Estimated Death Costs

$276,000 for Heirs	$300,000 for Heirs

Gain for Heirs: $24,000

Assumes 8% probate cost.

Also assumes a Will without Testamentary Trust provisions.

*Probate fee.

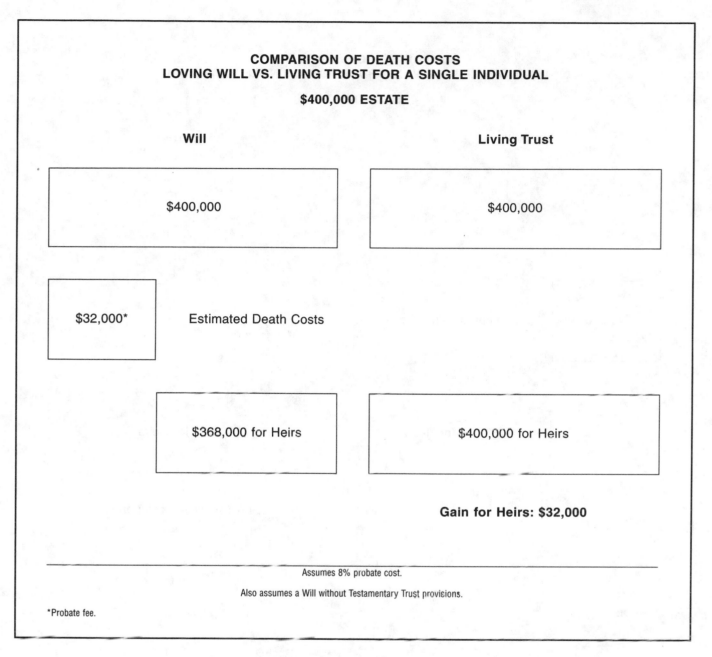

COMPARISON OF DEATH COSTS
LOVING WILL VS. LIVING TRUST FOR A SINGLE INDIVIDUAL

$400,000 ESTATE

Will   **Living Trust**

$400,000 $400,000

$32,000*   Estimated Death Costs

$368,000 for Heirs $400,000 for Heirs

Gain for Heirs: $32,000

Assumes 8% probate cost.

Also assumes a Will without Testamentary Trust provisions.

*Probate fee.

COMPARISON OF DEATH COSTS
LOVING WILL VS. LIVING TRUST FOR A SINGLE INDIVIDUAL

$500,000 ESTATE

Will	Living Trust
$500,000	$500,000

$40,000*	Estimated Death Costs	

$460,000 for Heirs	$500,000 for Heirs

Gain for Heirs: $40,000

Assumes 8% probate cost.

Also assumes a Will without Testamentary Trust provisions.

*Probate fee.

COMPARISON OF DEATH COSTS
LOVING WILL VS. LIVING TRUST FOR A SINGLE INDIVIDUAL

$600,000 ESTATE

Will

Living Trust

| $600,000 | $600,000 |

| $48,000* | Estimated Death Costs |

| $552,000 for Heirs | $600,000 for Heirs |

Gain for Heirs: $48,000

Assumes 8% probate cost.

Also assumes a Will without Testamentary Trust provisions

*Probate fee.

COMPARISON OF DEATH COSTS
LOVING WILL VS. LIVING TRUST FOR A SINGLE INDIVIDUAL

$800,000 ESTATE

Will	**Living Trust**
$800,000	$800,000

$64,000*	Estimated Death Costs

$736,000 for Heirs	$800,000 for Heirs

Gain for Heirs: $64,000

Assumes 8% probate cost.

Also assumes a Will without Testamentary Trust provisions.

*Probate fee.

COMPARISON OF DEATH COSTS
LOVING WILL VS. LIVING TRUST FOR A SINGLE INDIVIDUAL

$1 MILLION ESTATE

Will	**Living Trust**
$1,000,000	$1,000,000

$80,000*   Estimated Death Costs

$920,000 for Heirs	$1,000,000 for Heirs

Gain for Heirs: $80,000

Assumes 8% probate cost.

Also assumes a Will without Testamentary Trust provisions.

*Probate fee.

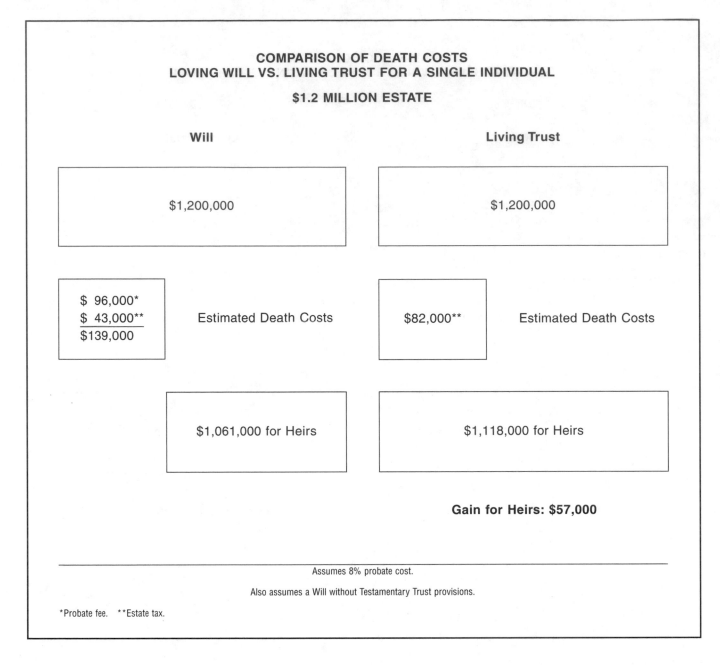

COMPARISON OF DEATH COSTS
LOVING WILL VS. LIVING TRUST FOR A SINGLE INDIVIDUAL

$1.2 MILLION ESTATE

Will	Living Trust
$1,200,000	$1,200,000

Will		Living Trust	
$ 96,000* $ 43,000** $139,000	Estimated Death Costs	$82,000**	Estimated Death Costs

Will	Living Trust
$1,061,000 for Heirs	$1,118,000 for Heirs

Gain for Heirs: $57,000

Assumes 8% probate cost.

Also assumes a Will without Testamentary Trust provisions.

*Probate fee.   **Estate tax.

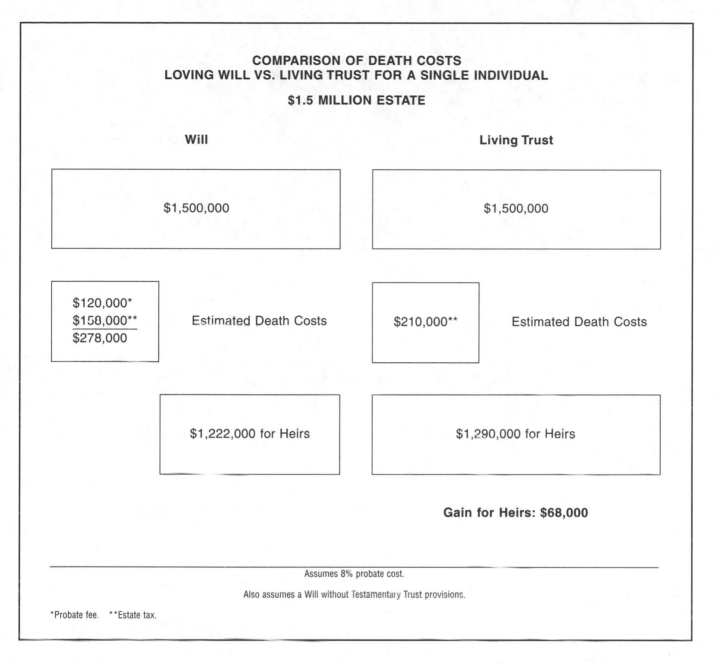

COMPARISON OF DEATH COSTS
LOVING WILL VS. LIVING TRUST FOR A SINGLE INDIVIDUAL

$1.5 MILLION ESTATE

Will   **Living Trust**

$1,500,000 $1,500,000

$120,000*
$150,000**   Estimated Death Costs $210,000**   Estimated Death Costs
$278,000

$1,222,000 for Heirs $1,290,000 for Heirs

Gain for Heirs: $68,000

Assumes 8% probate cost.

Also assumes a Will without Testamentary Trust provisions.

*Probate fee.   **Estate tax.

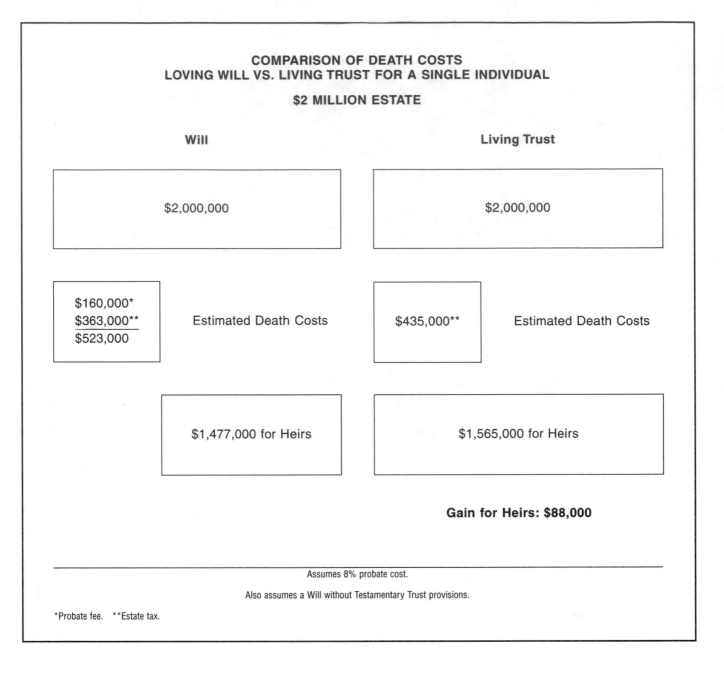

COMPARISON OF DEATH COSTS
LOVING WILL VS. LIVING TRUST FOR A SINGLE INDIVIDUAL

$2 MILLION ESTATE

Will	Living Trust
$2,000,000	$2,000,000

$160,000*
$363,000**
—————
$523,000   Estimated Death Costs

$435,000**   Estimated Death Costs

$1,477,000 for Heirs

$1,565,000 for Heirs

Gain for Heirs: $88,000

Assumes 8% probate cost.

Also assumes a Will without Testamentary Trust provisions.

*Probate fee.   **Estate tax.

Appendix B

Comparison of Death Costs: Loving Will vs. Living Trust for Married Couple with A Trust

This appendix consists of illustrations that compare death costs for a married couple who have a Loving Will with the costs for a couple who have a Living A Trust. The comparisons use the following sizes of estates:

- $100,000
- $200,000
- $300,000
- $400,000
- $500,000
- $600,000

Each illustration shows that having a Living Trust rather than a Loving Will provides benefits in the areas of probate, estate taxes, and gain for the heirs.

To use this appendix, find the illustration that most closely corresponds to the size of your own estate, and study the comparison of the two methods of holding assets. For a further explanation of the computations used in the illustrations, please refer to Chapter 6.

Note that all examples assume a probate cost of 8 percent and a federal estate tax exclusion of $1 million per person.

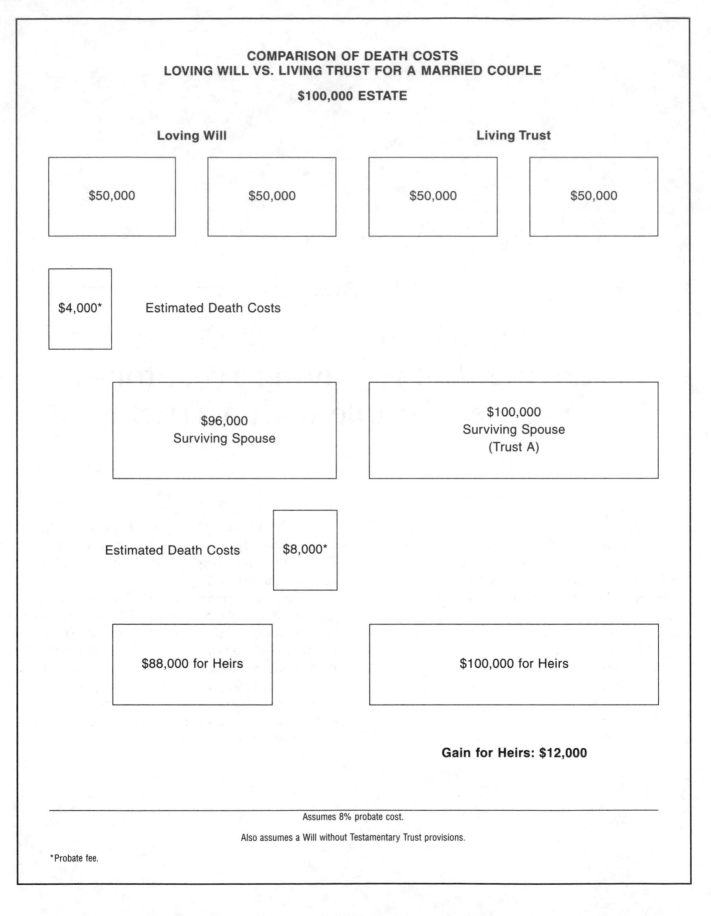

COMPARISON OF DEATH COSTS
LOVING WILL VS. LIVING TRUST FOR A MARRIED COUPLE

$100,000 ESTATE

Loving Will	Living Trust

$50,000 $50,000 $50,000 $50,000

$4,000*   Estimated Death Costs

$96,000
Surviving Spouse

$100,000
Surviving Spouse
(Trust A)

Estimated Death Costs $8,000*

$88,000 for Heirs

$100,000 for Heirs

Gain for Heirs: $12,000

Assumes 8% probate cost.

Also assumes a Will without Testamentary Trust provisions.

*Probate fee.

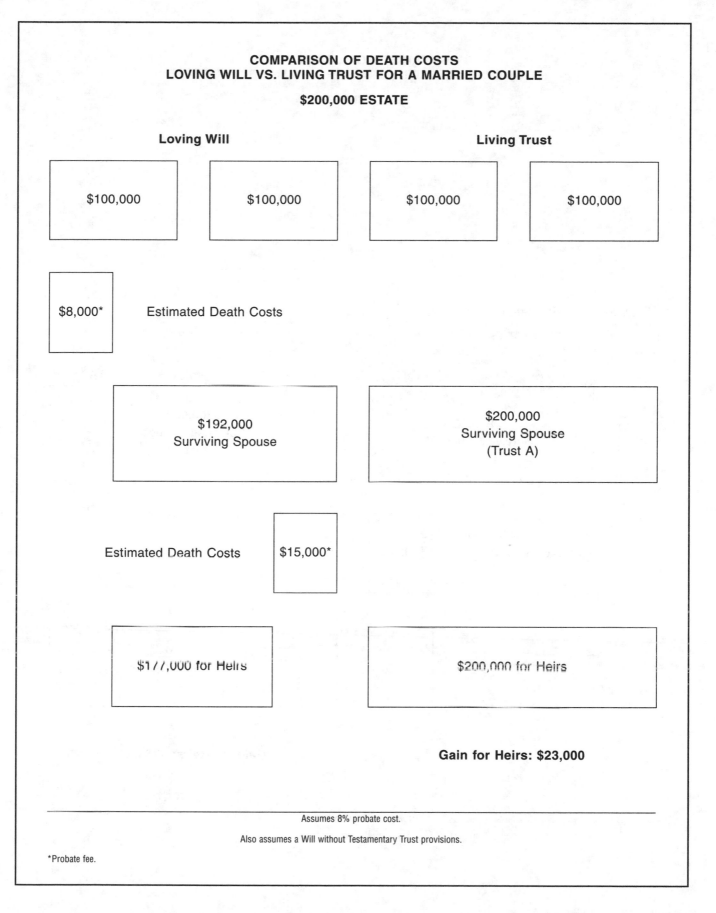

COMPARISON OF DEATH COSTS
LOVING WILL VS. LIVING TRUST FOR A MARRIED COUPLE

$200,000 ESTATE

Loving Will   **Living Trust**

| $100,000 | $100,000 | | $100,000 | $100,000 |

$8,000*   Estimated Death Costs

$192,000
Surviving Spouse

$200,000
Surviving Spouse
(Trust A)

Estimated Death Costs $15,000*

$177,000 for Heirs $200,000 for Heirs

Gain for Heirs: $23,000

Assumes 8% probate cost.

Also assumes a Will without Testamentary Trust provisions.

*Probate fee.

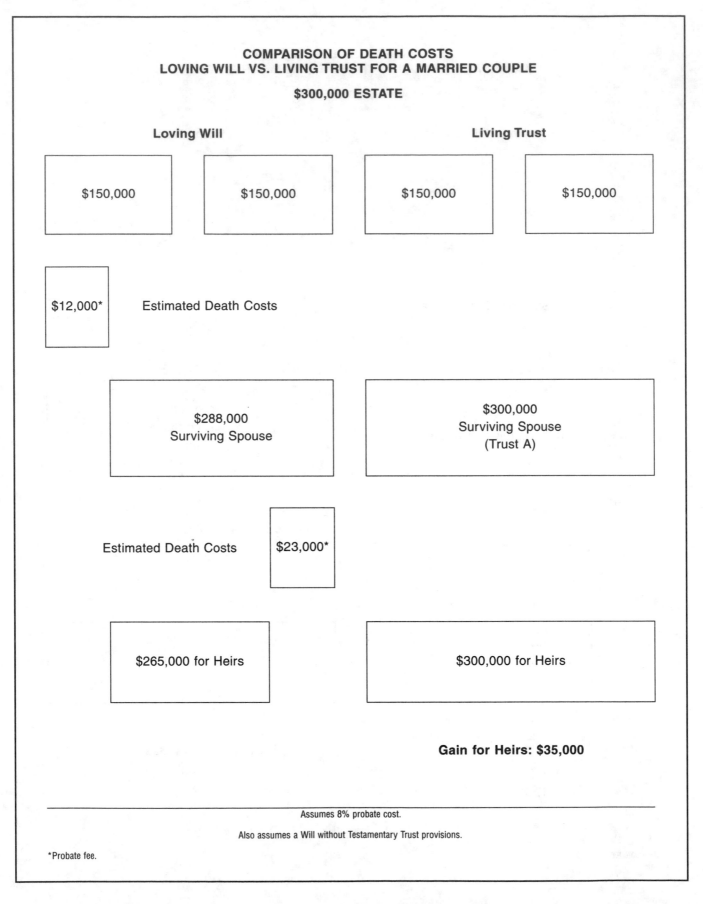

**COMPARISON OF DEATH COSTS
LOVING WILL VS. LIVING TRUST FOR A MARRIED COUPLE**

$300,000 ESTATE

Loving Will   **Living Trust**

$150,000 $150,000 $150,000 $150,000

$12,000*   Estimated Death Costs

$288,000
Surviving Spouse

$300,000
Surviving Spouse
(Trust A)

Estimated Death Costs $23,000*

$265,000 for Heirs

$300,000 for Heirs

Gain for Heirs: $35,000

Assumes 8% probate cost.

Also assumes a Will without Testamentary Trust provisions.

*Probate fee.

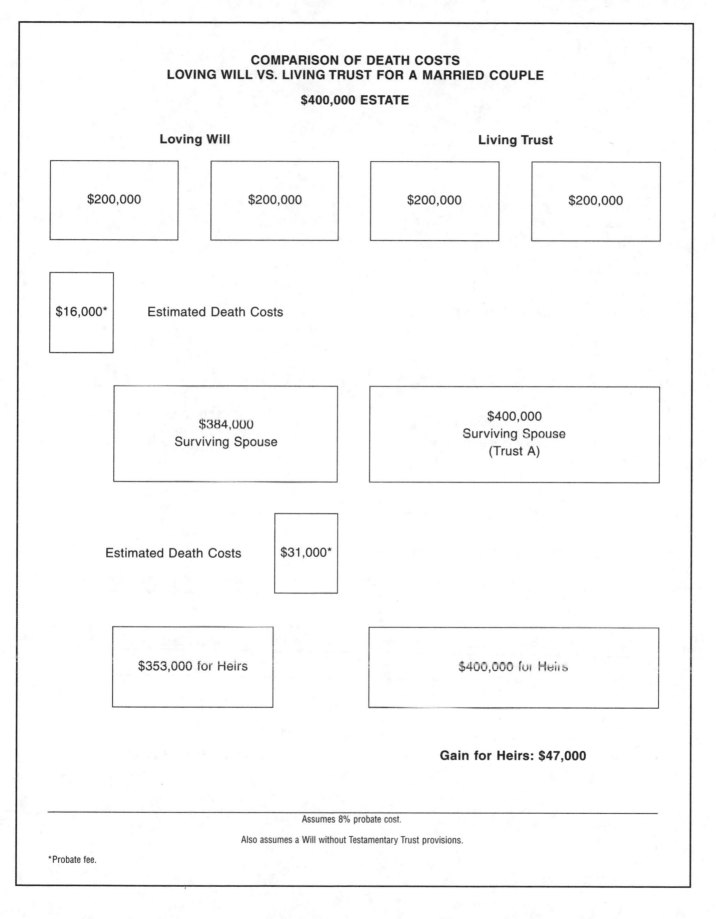

**COMPARISON OF DEATH COSTS
LOVING WILL VS. LIVING TRUST FOR A MARRIED COUPLE**

$400,000 ESTATE

Loving Will   **Living Trust**

$200,000 $200,000 $200,000 $200,000

$16,000*   Estimated Death Costs

$384,000
Surviving Spouse

$400,000
Surviving Spouse
(Trust A)

Estimated Death Costs $31,000*

$353,000 for Heirs

$400,000 for Heirs

Gain for Heirs: $47,000

Assumes 8% probate cost.

Also assumes a Will without Testamentary Trust provisions.

*Probate fee.

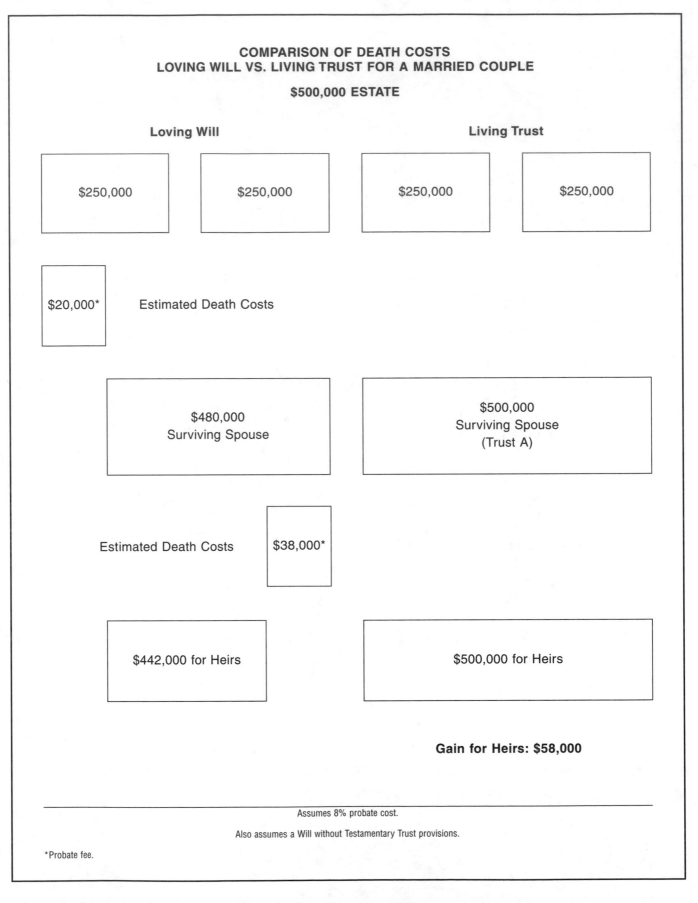

COMPARISON OF DEATH COSTS
LOVING WILL VS. LIVING TRUST FOR A MARRIED COUPLE

$500,000 ESTATE

Loving Will   **Living Trust**

| $250,000 | $250,000 | | $250,000 | $250,000 |

$20,000*   Estimated Death Costs

| $480,000 Surviving Spouse | | $500,000 Surviving Spouse (Trust A) |

Estimated Death Costs $38,000*

| $442,000 for Heirs | | $500,000 for Heirs |

Gain for Heirs: $58,000

Assumes 8% probate cost.

Also assumes a Will without Testamentary Trust provisions.

*Probate fee.

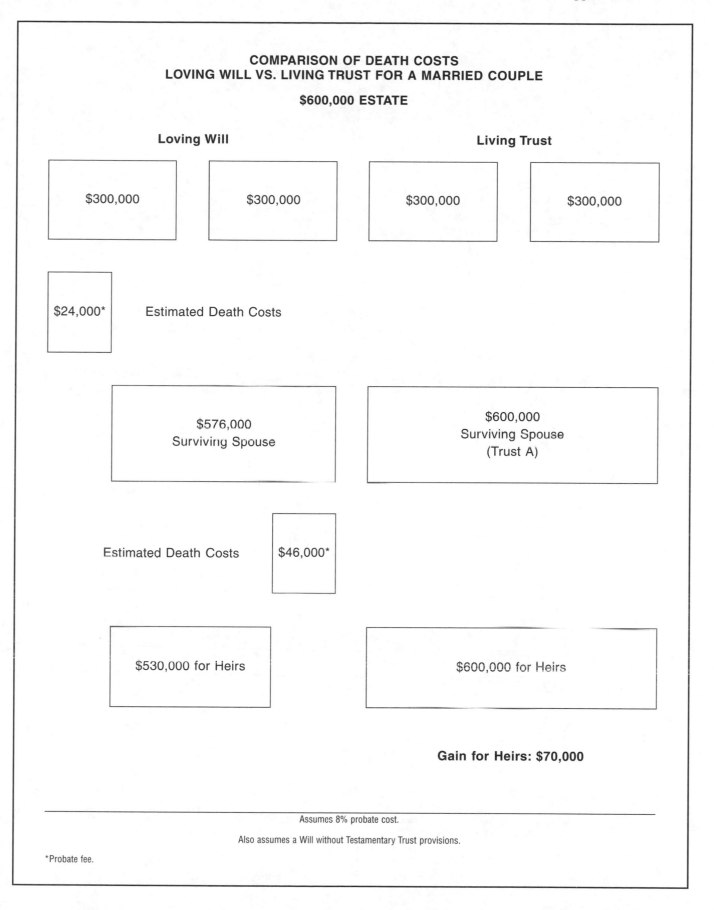

COMPARISON OF DEATH COSTS
LOVING WILL VS. LIVING TRUST FOR A MARRIED COUPLE

$600,000 ESTATE

Loving Will   **Living Trust**

$300,000 $300,000 $300,000 $300,000

$24,000*   Estimated Death Costs

$576,000
Surviving Spouse

$600,000
Surviving Spouse
(Trust A)

Estimated Death Costs $46,000*

$530,000 for Heirs $600,000 for Heirs

Gain for Heirs: $70,000

Assumes 8% probate cost.

Also assumes a Will without Testamentary Trust provisions.

*Probate fee.

Appendix C

Comparison of Death Costs: Loving Will vs. Living Trust for Married Couple with A-B Trust

This appendix illustrates death cost comparisons for a married couple who have a Loving Will with a couple who have a Living A-B Trust. The comparisons use these estates:

- $100,000
- $200,000
- $300,000
- $400,000
- $500,000
- $600,000
- $800,000
- $1 million
- $1.2 million
- $1.5 million
- $2 million

Each illustration shows that having a Living Trust rather than a Loving Will provides benefits in the areas of probate, estate taxes, and gain for the heirs.

To use this appendix, find the illustration that most closely corresponds to the size of your own estate, and study the comparison shown of the two methods of holding assets. For a further explanation of the computations used in the illustrations, please refer to Chapter 6.

Note that all examples assume a probate cost of 8 percent and a federal estate tax exclusion of $1 million per person.

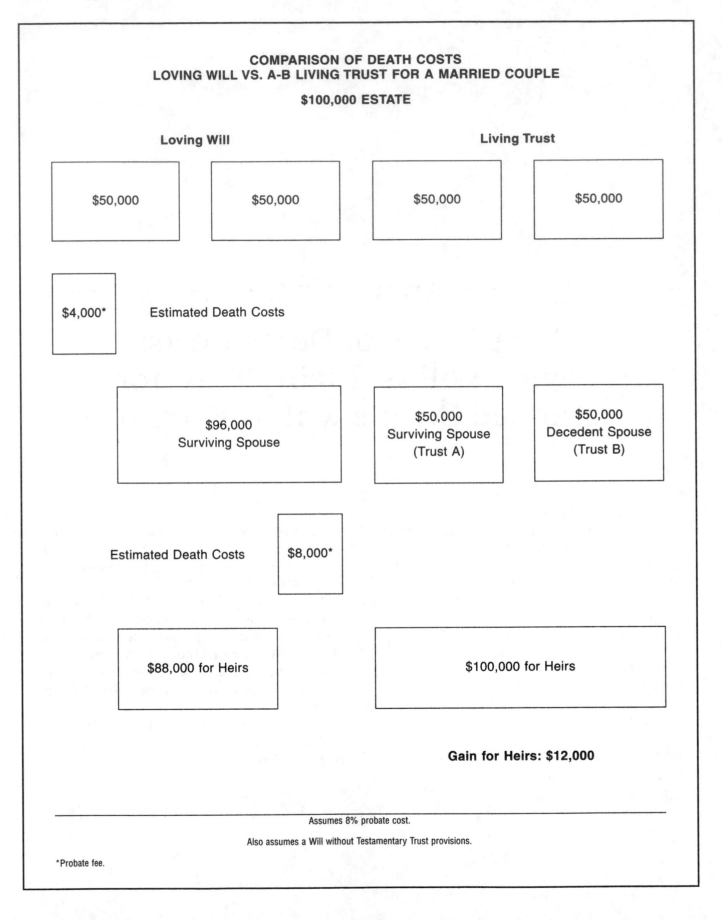

COMPARISON OF DEATH COSTS
LOVING WILL VS. A-B LIVING TRUST FOR A MARRIED COUPLE

$100,000 ESTATE

Loving Will

Living Trust

$50,000

$50,000

$50,000

$50,000

$4,000*   Estimated Death Costs

$96,000
Surviving Spouse

$50,000
Surviving Spouse
(Trust A)

$50,000
Decedent Spouse
(Trust B)

Estimated Death Costs $8,000*

$88,000 for Heirs

$100,000 for Heirs

Gain for Heirs: $12,000

Assumes 8% probate cost.

Also assumes a Will without Testamentary Trust provisions.

*Probate fee.

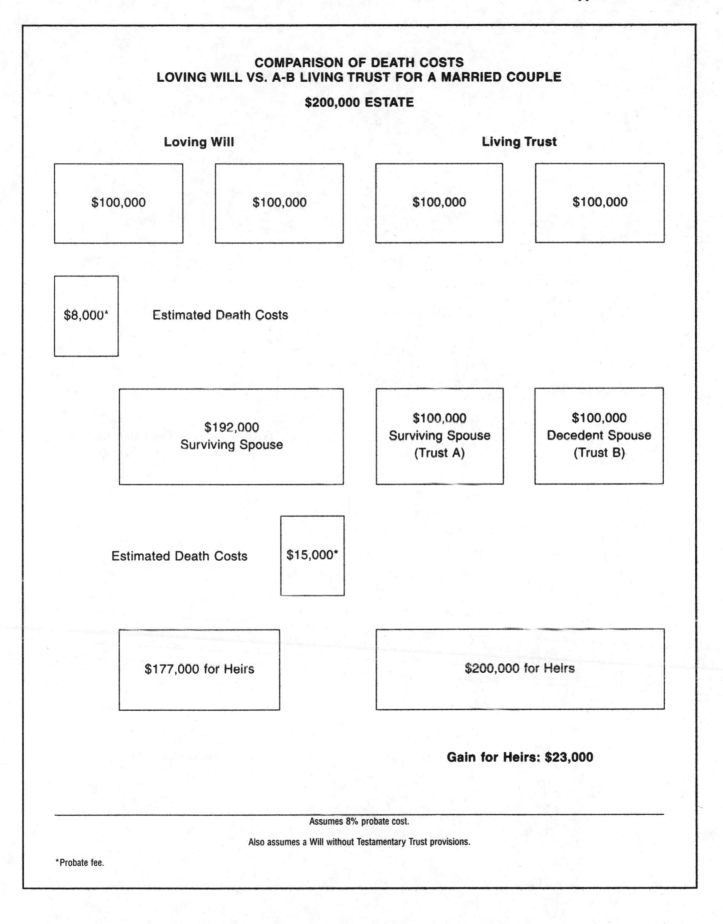

COMPARISON OF DEATH COSTS
LOVING WILL VS. A-B LIVING TRUST FOR A MARRIED COUPLE

$200,000 ESTATE

Loving Will   **Living Trust**

| $100,000 | $100,000 | $100,000 | $100,000 |

$8,000*   Estimated Death Costs

| $192,000 Surviving Spouse | $100,000 Surviving Spouse (Trust A) | $100,000 Decedent Spouse (Trust B) |

Estimated Death Costs $15,000*

| $177,000 for Heirs | $200,000 for Heirs |

Gain for Heirs: $23,000

Assumes 8% probate cost.

Also assumes a Will without Testamentary Trust provisions.

*Probate fee.

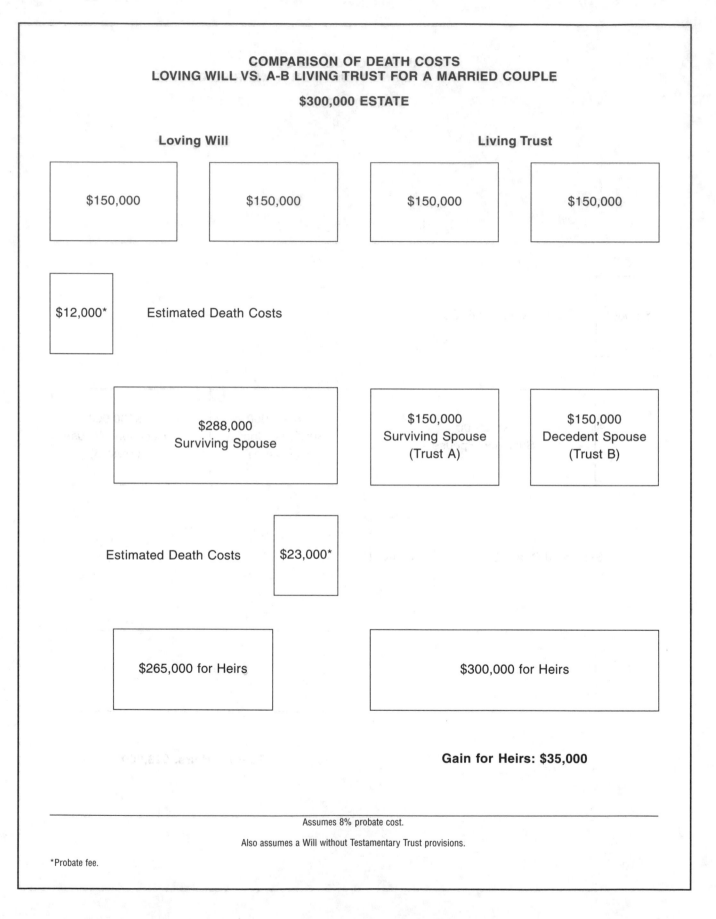

COMPARISON OF DEATH COSTS
LOVING WILL VS. A-B LIVING TRUST FOR A MARRIED COUPLE

$300,000 ESTATE

Loving Will   **Living Trust**

$150,000 $150,000 $150,000 $150,000

$12,000*   Estimated Death Costs

$288,000 $150,000 $150,000
Surviving Spouse   Surviving Spouse   Decedent Spouse
                            (Trust A)   (Trust B)

Estimated Death Costs $23,000*

$265,000 for Heirs $300,000 for Heirs

Gain for Heirs: $35,000

Assumes 8% probate cost.

Also assumes a Will without Testamentary Trust provisions.

*Probate fee.

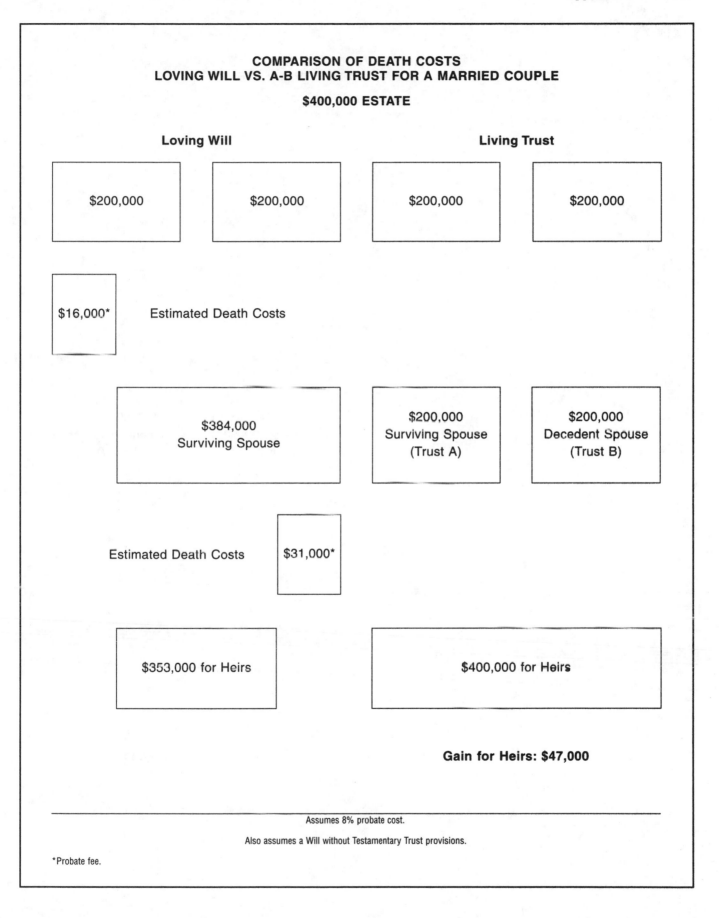

COMPARISON OF DEATH COSTS
LOVING WILL VS. A-B LIVING TRUST FOR A MARRIED COUPLE

$400,000 ESTATE

Loving Will   **Living Trust**

$200,000 $200,000 $200,000 $200,000

$16,000*   Estimated Death Costs

$384,000 $200,000 $200,000
Surviving Spouse   Surviving Spouse   Decedent Spouse
                   (Trust A)   (Trust B)

Estimated Death Costs $31,000*

$353,000 for Heirs $400,000 for Heirs

Gain for Heirs: $47,000

Assumes 8% probate cost.

Also assumes a Will without Testamentary Trust provisions.

*Probate fee.

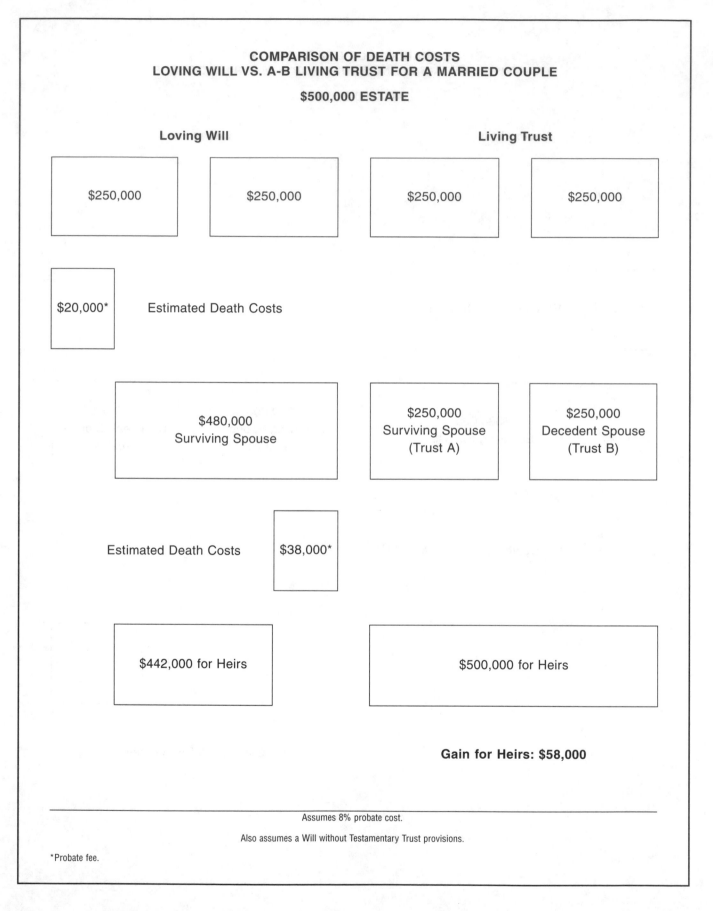

COMPARISON OF DEATH COSTS
LOVING WILL VS. A-B LIVING TRUST FOR A MARRIED COUPLE

$500,000 ESTATE

Loving Will   **Living Trust**

| $250,000 | $250,000 | $250,000 | $250,000 |

$20,000*   Estimated Death Costs

$480,000
Surviving Spouse

$250,000
Surviving Spouse
(Trust A)

$250,000
Decedent Spouse
(Trust B)

Estimated Death Costs $38,000*

$442,000 for Heirs

$500,000 for Heirs

Gain for Heirs: $58,000

Assumes 8% probate cost.

Also assumes a Will without Testamentary Trust provisions.

*Probate fee.

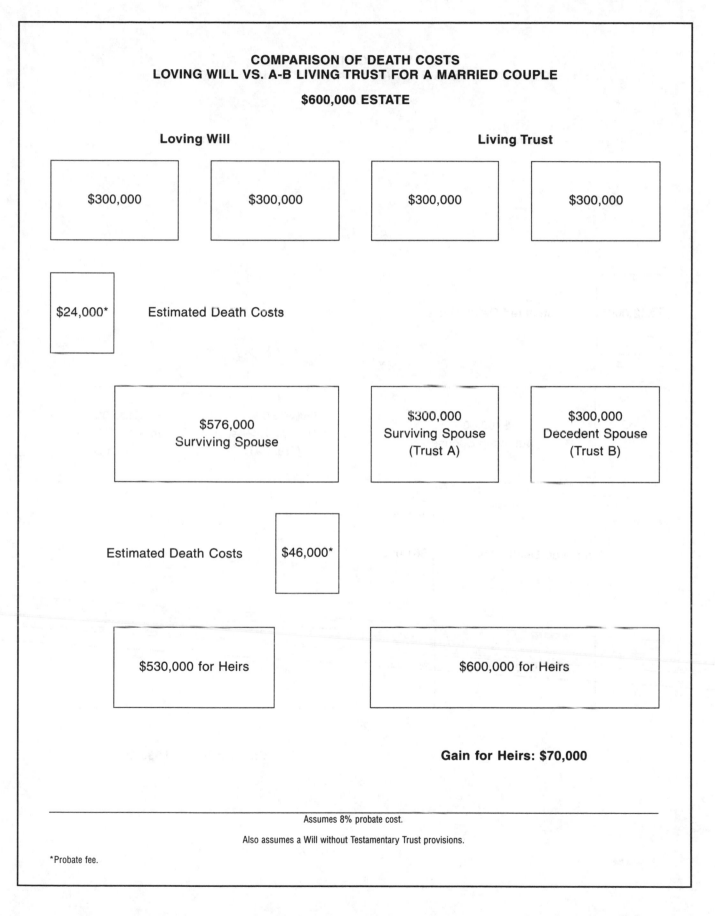

**COMPARISON OF DEATH COSTS
LOVING WILL VS. A-B LIVING TRUST FOR A MARRIED COUPLE**

$600,000 ESTATE

Loving Will   **Living Trust**

$300,000 $300,000 $300,000 $300,000

$24,000*   Estimated Death Costs

$576,000
Surviving Spouse

$300,000
Surviving Spouse
(Trust A)

$300,000
Decedent Spouse
(Trust B)

Estimated Death Costs $46,000*

$530,000 for Heirs $600,000 for Heirs

Gain for Heirs: $70,000

Assumes 8% probate cost.

Also assumes a Will without Testamentary Trust provisions.

*Probate fee.

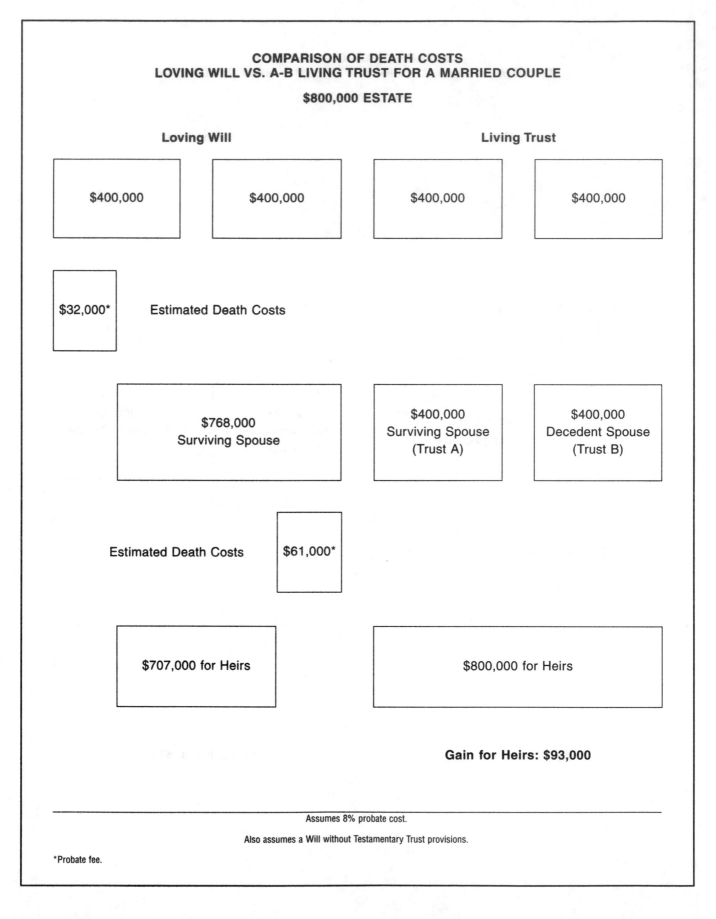

COMPARISON OF DEATH COSTS
LOVING WILL VS. A-B LIVING TRUST FOR A MARRIED COUPLE

$800,000 ESTATE

Loving Will	Living Trust

| $400,000 | $400,000 | $400,000 | $400,000 |

$32,000*   Estimated Death Costs

| $768,000 Surviving Spouse | $400,000 Surviving Spouse (Trust A) | $400,000 Decedent Spouse (Trust B) |

Estimated Death Costs $61,000*

| $707,000 for Heirs | $800,000 for Heirs |

Gain for Heirs: $93,000

Assumes 8% probate cost.

Also assumes a Will without Testamentary Trust provisions.

*Probate fee.

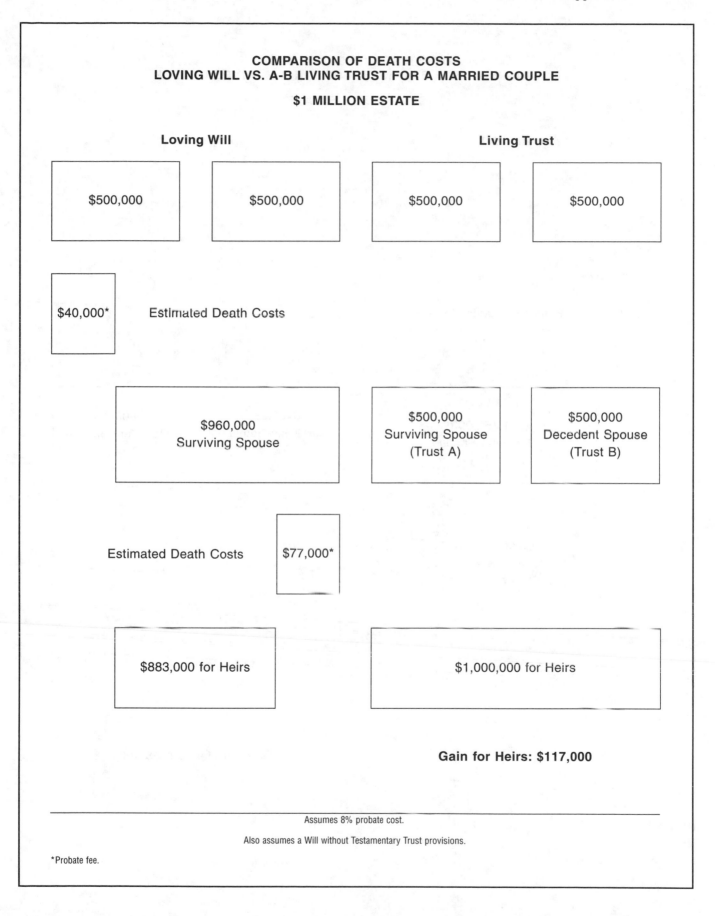

COMPARISON OF DEATH COSTS
LOVING WILL VS. A-B LIVING TRUST FOR A MARRIED COUPLE

$1 MILLION ESTATE

Loving Will   **Living Trust**

| $500,000 | $500,000 | | $500,000 | $500,000 |

$40,000*   Estimated Death Costs

| $960,000 Surviving Spouse | | $500,000 Surviving Spouse (Trust A) | $500,000 Decedent Spouse (Trust B) |

Estimated Death Costs $77,000*

$883,000 for Heirs $1,000,000 for Heirs

Gain for Heirs: $117,000

Assumes 8% probate cost.

Also assumes a Will without Testamentary Trust provisions.

*Probate fee.

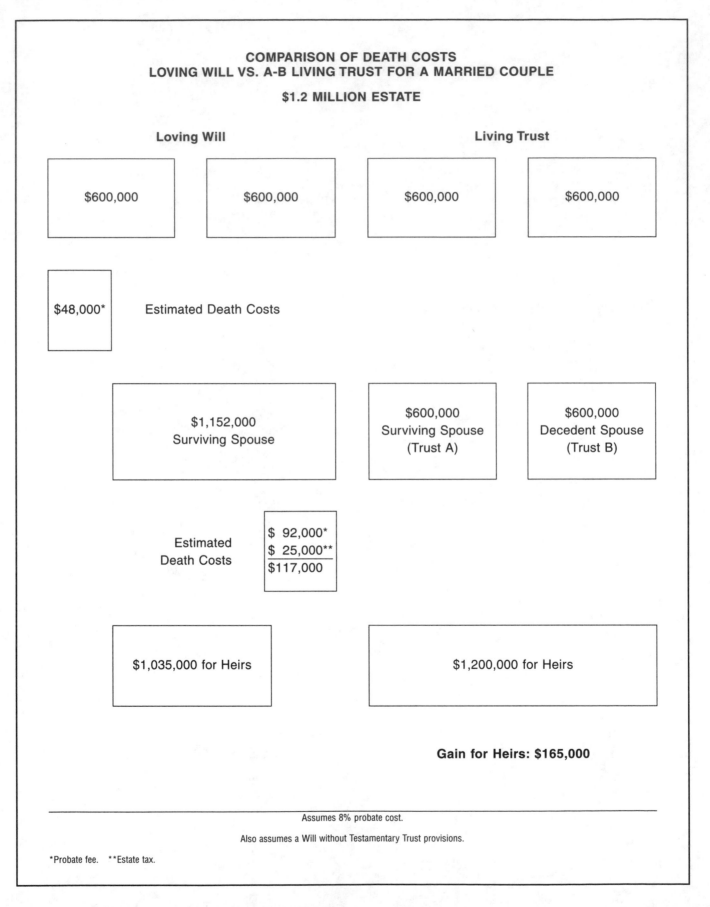

COMPARISON OF DEATH COSTS
LOVING WILL VS. A-B LIVING TRUST FOR A MARRIED COUPLE

$1.2 MILLION ESTATE

Loving Will   **Living Trust**

$600,000 $600,000 $600,000 $600,000

$48,000*   Estimated Death Costs

$1,152,000
Surviving Spouse

$600,000
Surviving Spouse
(Trust A)

$600,000
Decedent Spouse
(Trust B)

Estimated
Death Costs

$ 92,000*
$ 25,000**
$117,000

$1,035,000 for Heirs

$1,200,000 for Heirs

Gain for Heirs: $165,000

Assumes 8% probate cost.

Also assumes a Will without Testamentary Trust provisions.

*Probate fee.   **Estate tax.

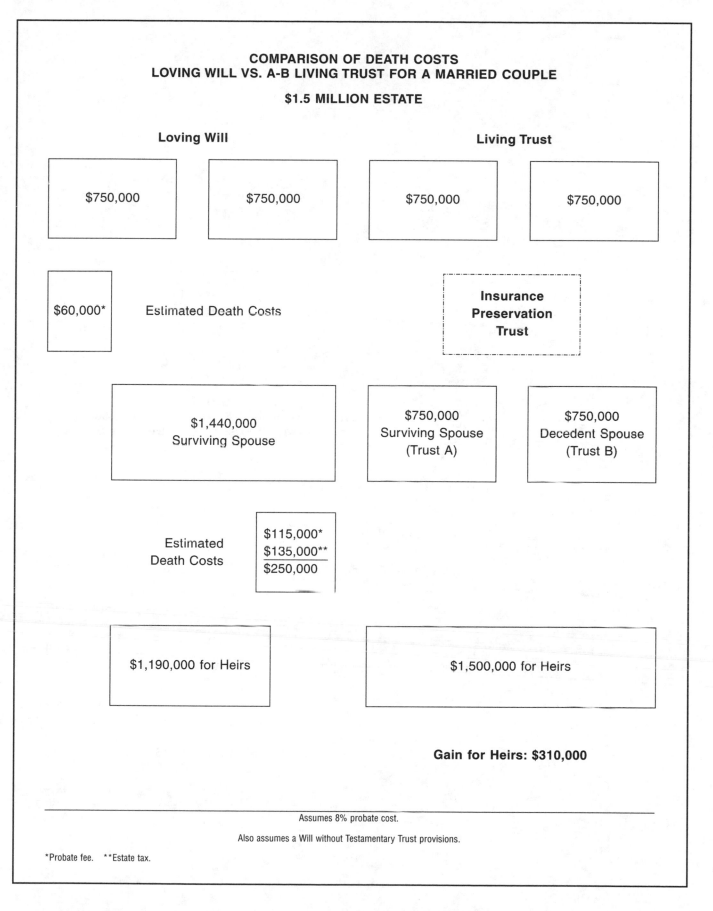

COMPARISON OF DEATH COSTS
LOVING WILL VS. A-B LIVING TRUST FOR A MARRIED COUPLE

$1.5 MILLION ESTATE

Loving Will   **Living Trust**

$750,000 $750,000 $750,000 $750,000

$60,000*   Estimated Death Costs   Insurance
                                               Preservation
                                                  Trust

$1,440,000 $750,000 $750,000
Surviving Spouse   Surviving Spouse   Decedent Spouse
                                    (Trust A)   (Trust B)

Estimated $115,000*
Death Costs $135,000**
                   $250,000

$1,190,000 for Heirs $1,500,000 for Heirs

Gain for Heirs: $310,000

Assumes 8% probate cost.

Also assumes a Will without Testamentary Trust provisions.

*Probate fee.   **Estate tax.

318   Appendix C

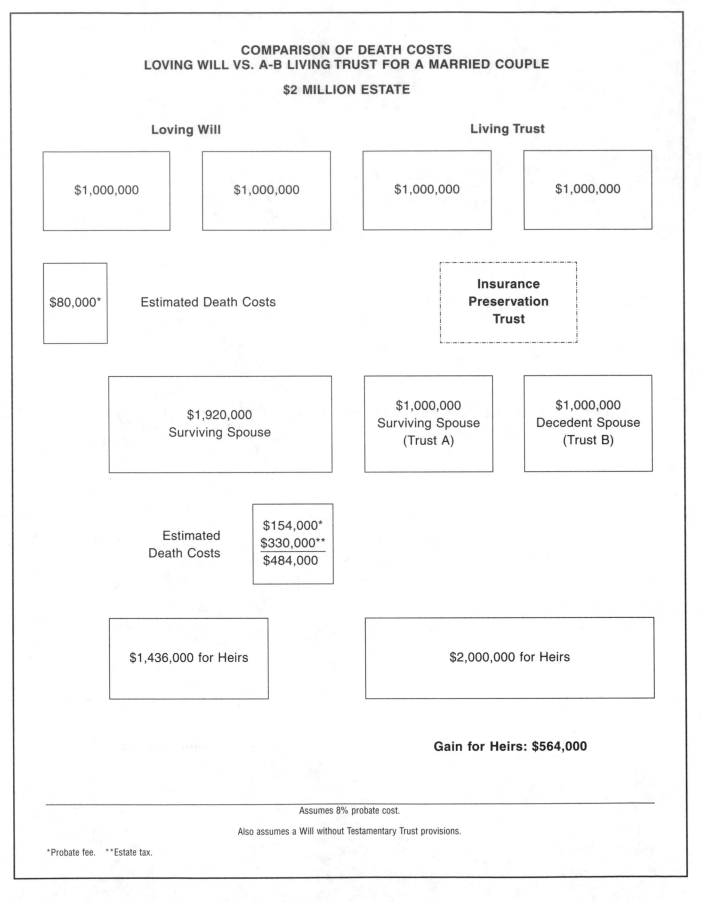

Appendix D

Comparison of Death Costs: Loving Will vs. Living Trust for Married Couple with A-B-C Trust

This appendix consists of illustrations that compare death costs for a married couple who have a Loving Will with the costs for a couple who have a Living A-B-C Trust. The comparisons use the following sizes of estates:

- $2.5 million
- $3 million
- $4 million
- $5 million

Each illustration shows that having a Living Trust rather than a Loving Will provides benefits in the areas of probate, estate taxes, and gain for the heirs.

To use this appendix, find the illustration that most closely corresponds to the size of your own estate, and study the comparison of the two methods of holding assets. For a further explanation of the computations used in the illustrations, please refer to Chapter 6.

Note that all examples assume a probate cost of 8 percent and a federal estate tax exclusion of $1 million per person.

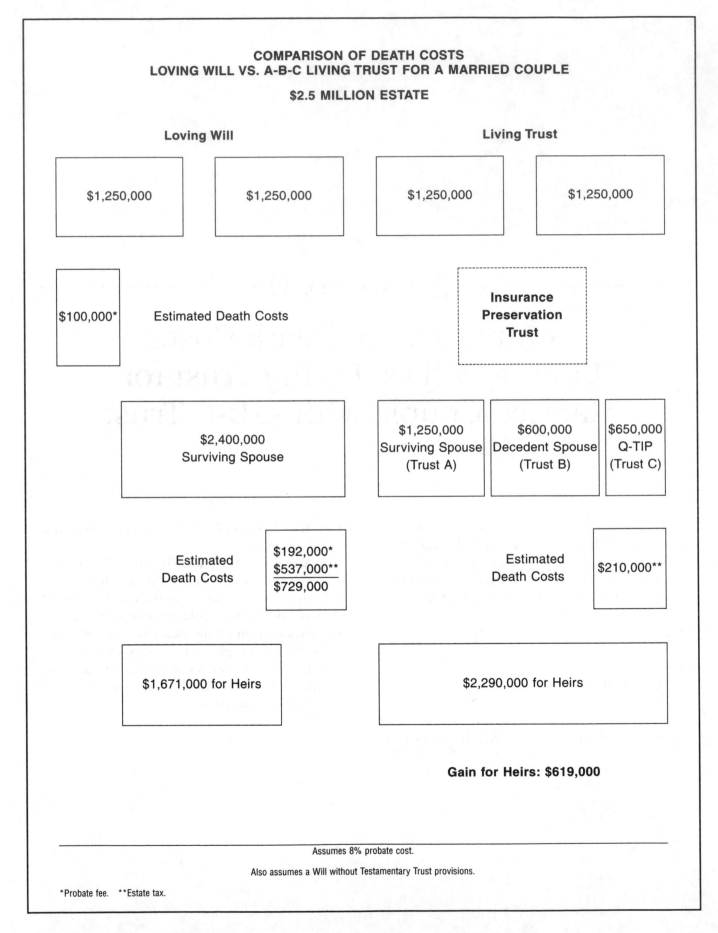

COMPARISON OF DEATH COSTS
LOVING WILL VS. A-B-C LIVING TRUST FOR A MARRIED COUPLE

$2.5 MILLION ESTATE

Loving Will

Living Trust

$1,250,000	$1,250,000

$1,250,000	$1,250,000

$100,000*   Estimated Death Costs

Insurance
Preservation
Trust

$2,400,000
Surviving Spouse

$1,250,000 Surviving Spouse (Trust A)	$600,000 Decedent Spouse (Trust B)	$650,000 Q-TIP (Trust C)

Estimated
Death Costs

$192,000*
$537,000**
$729,000

Estimated
Death Costs

$210,000**

$1,671,000 for Heirs

$2,290,000 for Heirs

Gain for Heirs: $619,000

Assumes 8% probate cost.

Also assumes a Will without Testamentary Trust provisions.

*Probate fee.   **Estate tax.

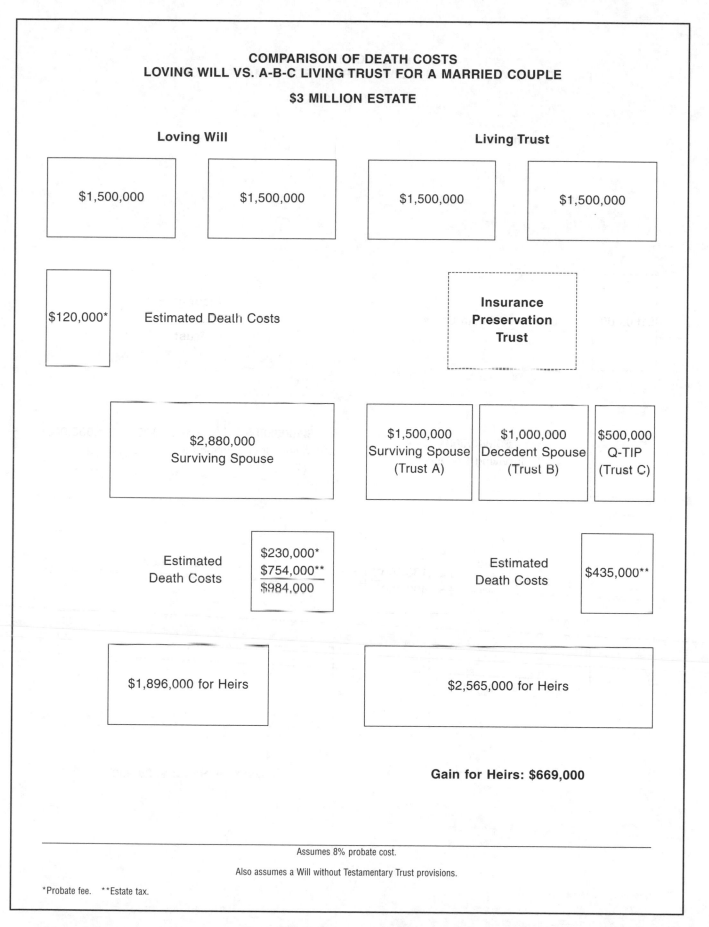

COMPARISON OF DEATH COSTS
LOVING WILL VS. A-B-C LIVING TRUST FOR A MARRIED COUPLE

$3 MILLION ESTATE

Loving Will

Living Trust

$1,500,000

$1,500,000

$1,500,000

$1,500,000

$120,000*   Estimated Death Costs

Insurance Preservation Trust

$2,880,000
Surviving Spouse

$1,500,000
Surviving Spouse
(Trust A)

$1,000,000
Decedent Spouse
(Trust B)

$500,000
Q-TIP
(Trust C)

Estimated
Death Costs

$230,000*
$754,000**
$984,000

Estimated
Death Costs

$435,000**

$1,896,000 for Heirs

$2,565,000 for Heirs

Gain for Heirs: $669,000

Assumes 8% probate cost.

Also assumes a Will without Testamentary Trust provisions.

*Probate fee.   **Estate tax.

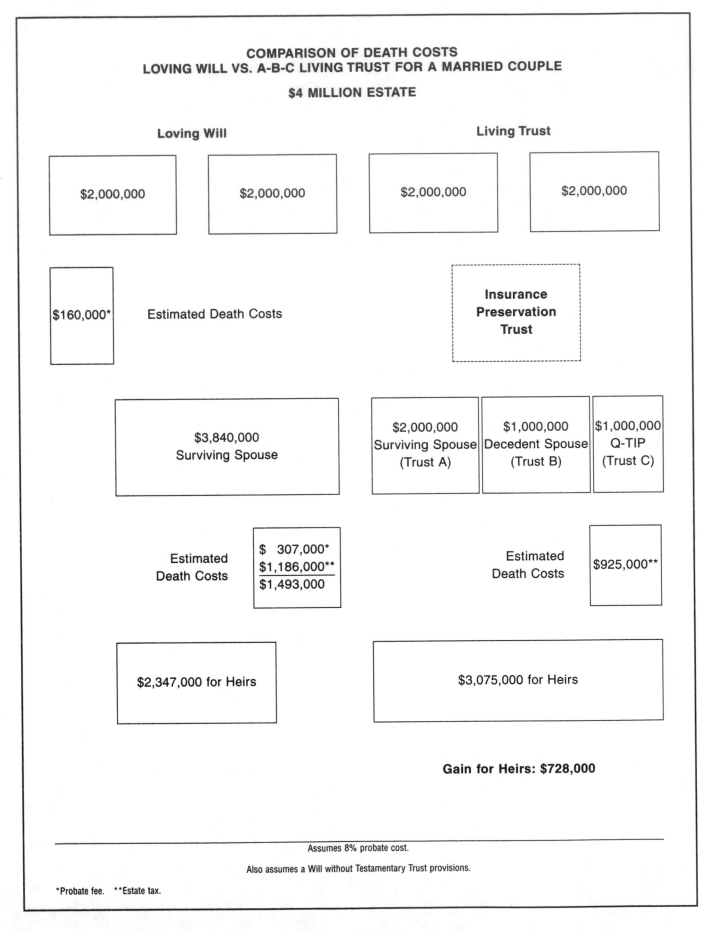

COMPARISON OF DEATH COSTS
LOVING WILL VS. A-B-C LIVING TRUST FOR A MARRIED COUPLE

$4 MILLION ESTATE

Loving Will

$2,000,000

$2,000,000

$160,000*   Estimated Death Costs

$3,840,000
Surviving Spouse

Estimated
Death Costs

$ 307,000*
$1,186,000**
$1,493,000

$2,347,000 for Heirs

Living Trust

$2,000,000

$2,000,000

Insurance
Preservation
Trust

$2,000,000
Surviving Spouse
(Trust A)

$1,000,000
Decedent Spouse
(Trust B)

$1,000,000
Q-TIP
(Trust C)

Estimated
Death Costs

$925,000**

$3,075,000 for Heirs

Gain for Heirs: $728,000

Assumes 8% probate cost.

Also assumes a Will without Testamentary Trust provisions.

*Probate fee.   **Estate tax.

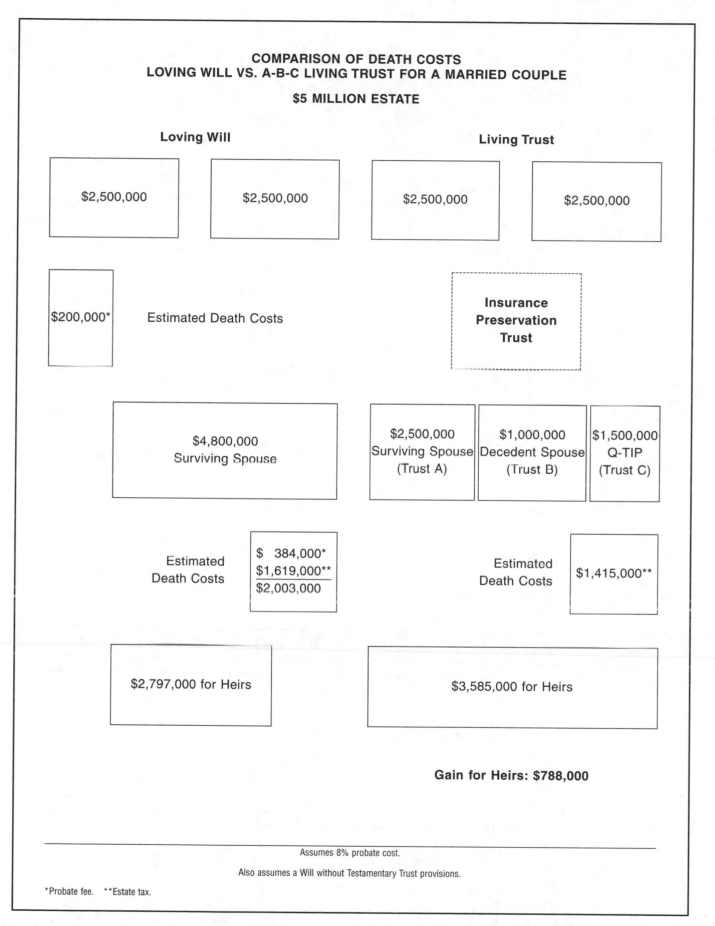

COMPARISON OF DEATH COSTS
LOVING WILL VS. A-B-C LIVING TRUST FOR A MARRIED COUPLE

$5 MILLION ESTATE

Loving Will   **Living Trust**

$2,500,000 $2,500,000 $2,500,000 $2,500,000

$200,000*   Estimated Death Costs   **Insurance Preservation Trust**

$4,800,000
Surviving Spouse

$2,500,000 $1,000,000 $1,500,000
Surviving Spouse   Decedent Spouse   Q-TIP
(Trust A)   (Trust B)   (Trust C)

Estimated Death Costs

$ 384,000*
$1,619,000**

$2,003,000

Estimated Death Costs $1,415,000**

$2,797,000 for Heirs $3,585,000 for Heirs

Gain for Heirs: $788,000

Assumes 8% probate cost.

Also assumes a Will without Testamentary Trust provisions.

*Probate fee.   **Estate tax.

Appendix E

Comparison of Death Costs: Testamentary Trust vs. Living Trust for Married Couple with A-B Trust

This appendix consists of illustrations that compare death costs for a married couple who have a Testamentary Trust with the costs for a couple who have a Living A-B Trust. The comparisons use the following sizes of estates:

- $400,000
- $500,000
- $600,000
- $800,000
- $1 million
- $1.2 million
- $1.5 million
- $2 million

Each illustration shows that having a Living Trust rather than a Testamentary Trust provides benefits in the areas of probate, estate taxes, and gain for the heirs.

To use this appendix, find the illustration that most closely corresponds to the size of your own estate, and study the comparison of the two methods of holding assets. For a further explanation of the computations used in the illustrations, please refer to Chapter 6.

Note that all examples assume a probate cost of 8 percent and a federal estate tax exclusion of $1 million per person.

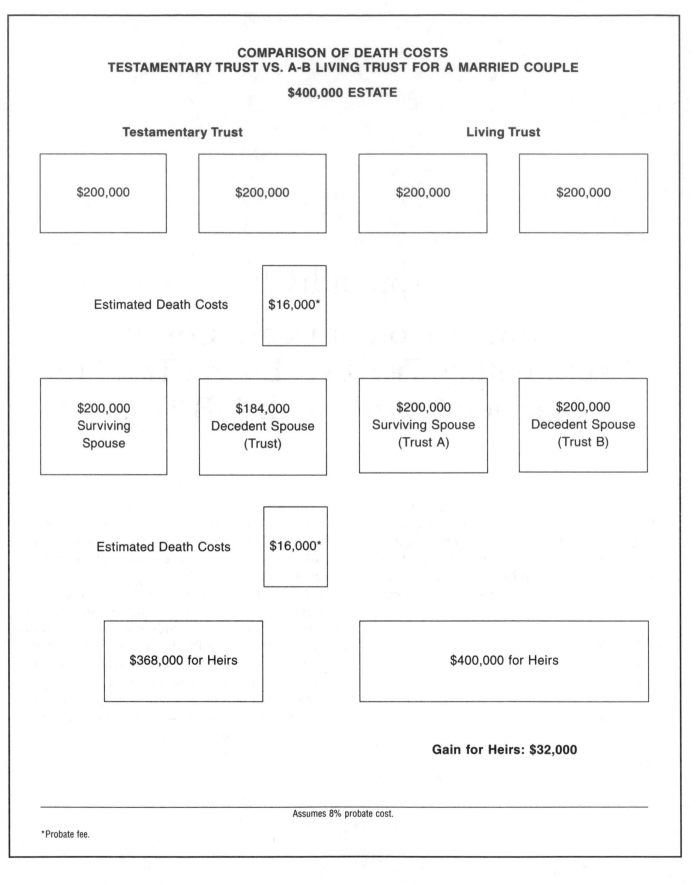

COMPARISON OF DEATH COSTS
TESTAMENTARY TRUST VS. A-B LIVING TRUST FOR A MARRIED COUPLE

$400,000 ESTATE

Testamentary Trust	Living Trust

$200,000	$200,000	$200,000	$200,000

Estimated Death Costs $16,000*

$200,000 Surviving Spouse	$184,000 Decedent Spouse (Trust)	$200,000 Surviving Spouse (Trust A)	$200,000 Decedent Spouse (Trust B)

Estimated Death Costs $16,000*

$368,000 for Heirs	$400,000 for Heirs

Gain for Heirs: $32,000

Assumes 8% probate cost.

*Probate fee.

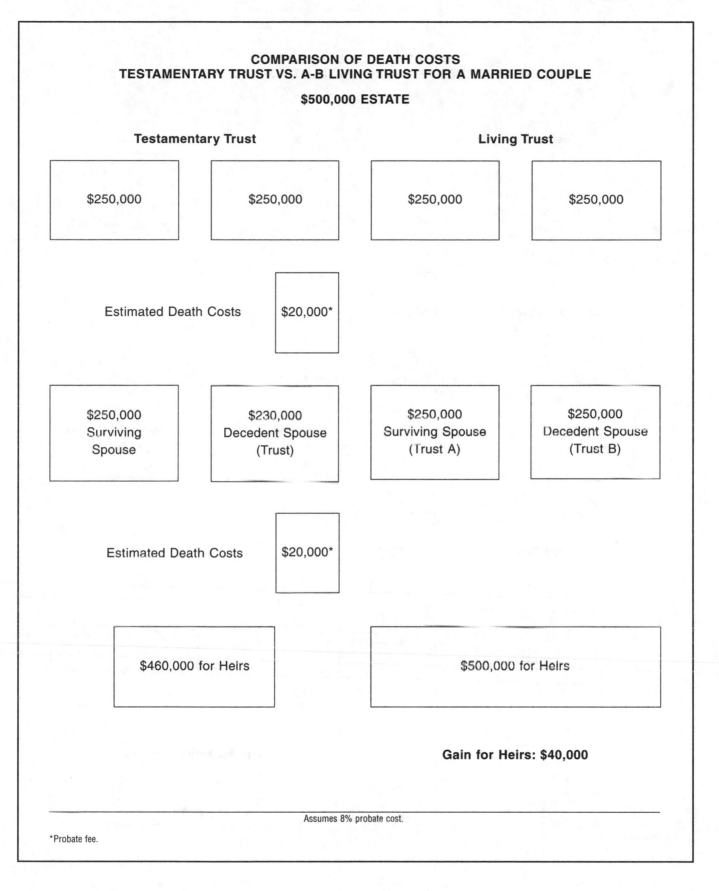

COMPARISON OF DEATH COSTS
TESTAMENTARY TRUST VS. A-B LIVING TRUST FOR A MARRIED COUPLE

$500,000 ESTATE

Testamentary Trust   **Living Trust**

$250,000 $250,000 $250,000 $250,000

Estimated Death Costs $20,000*

| $250,000 Surviving Spouse | $230,000 Decedent Spouse (Trust) | $250,000 Surviving Spouse (Trust A) | $250,000 Decedent Spouse (Trust B) |

Estimated Death Costs $20,000*

$460,000 for Heirs $500,000 for Heirs

Gain for Heirs: $40,000

Assumes 8% probate cost.

*Probate fee.

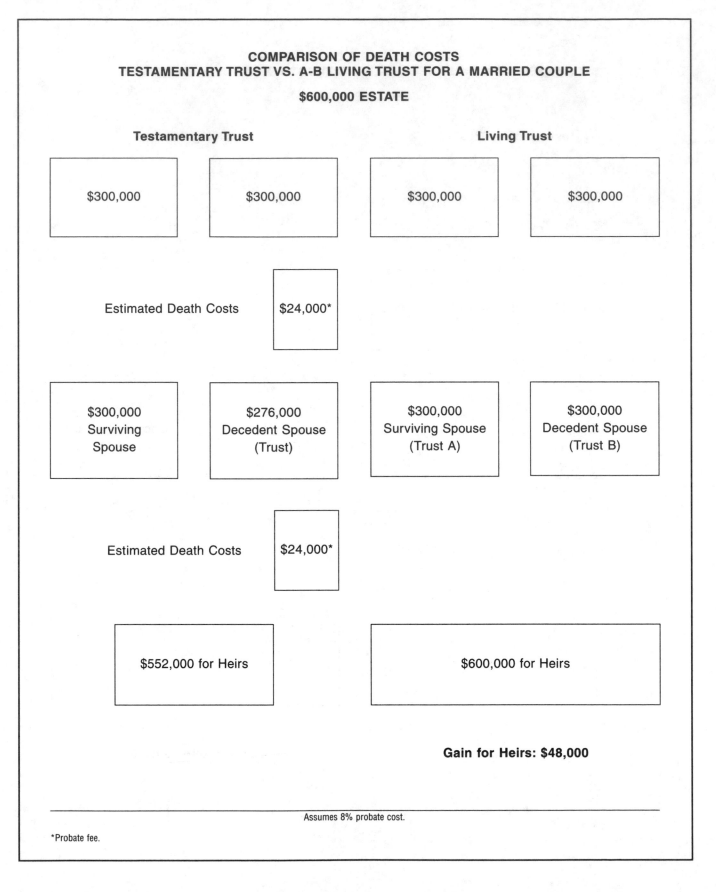

COMPARISON OF DEATH COSTS
TESTAMENTARY TRUST VS. A-B LIVING TRUST FOR A MARRIED COUPLE

$600,000 ESTATE

Testamentary Trust   **Living Trust**

| $300,000 | $300,000 | | $300,000 | $300,000 |

Estimated Death Costs $24,000*

| $300,000 Surviving Spouse | $276,000 Decedent Spouse (Trust) | | $300,000 Surviving Spouse (Trust A) | $300,000 Decedent Spouse (Trust B) |

Estimated Death Costs $24,000*

| $552,000 for Heirs | | $600,000 for Heirs |

Gain for Heirs: $48,000

Assumes 8% probate cost.

*Probate fee.

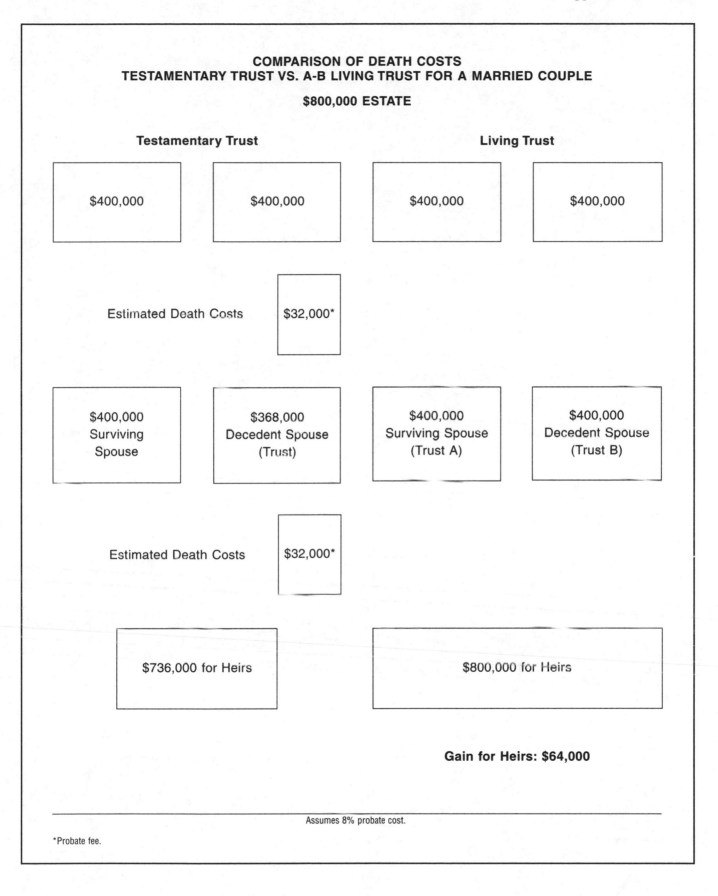

COMPARISON OF DEATH COSTS
TESTAMENTARY TRUST VS. A-B LIVING TRUST FOR A MARRIED COUPLE

$800,000 ESTATE

Testamentary Trust   **Living Trust**

| $400,000 | $400,000 | | $400,000 | $400,000 |

Estimated Death Costs $32,000*

| $400,000 Surviving Spouse | $368,000 Decedent Spouse (Trust) | | $400,000 Surviving Spouse (Trust A) | $400,000 Decedent Spouse (Trust B) |

Estimated Death Costs $32,000*

$736,000 for Heirs $800,000 for Heirs

Gain for Heirs: $64,000

Assumes 8% probate cost.

*Probate fee.

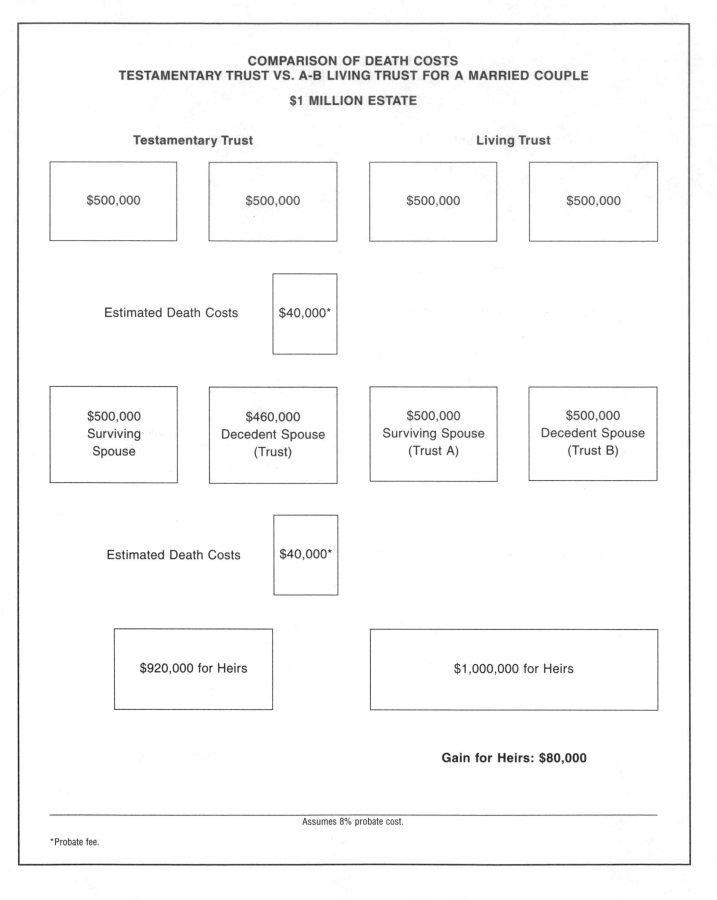

COMPARISON OF DEATH COSTS
TESTAMENTARY TRUST VS. A-B LIVING TRUST FOR A MARRIED COUPLE

$1 MILLION ESTATE

Testamentary Trust   **Living Trust**

| $500,000 | $500,000 | $500,000 | $500,000 |

Estimated Death Costs $40,000*

| $500,000 Surviving Spouse | $460,000 Decedent Spouse (Trust) | $500,000 Surviving Spouse (Trust A) | $500,000 Decedent Spouse (Trust B) |

Estimated Death Costs $40,000*

$920,000 for Heirs $1,000,000 for Heirs

Gain for Heirs: $80,000

Assumes 8% probate cost.

*Probate fee.

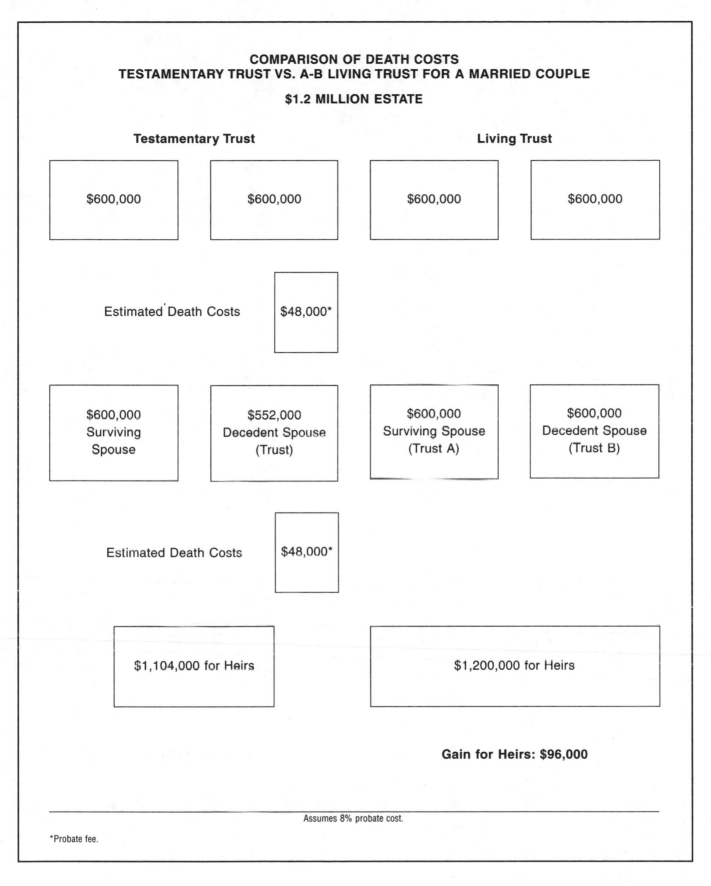

COMPARISON OF DEATH COSTS
TESTAMENTARY TRUST VS. A-B LIVING TRUST FOR A MARRIED COUPLE

$1.2 MILLION ESTATE

Testamentary Trust		Living Trust	
$600,000	$600,000	$600,000	$600,000

Estimated Death Costs $48,000*

$600,000 Surviving Spouse	$552,000 Decedent Spouse (Trust)	$600,000 Surviving Spouse (Trust A)	$600,000 Decedent Spouse (Trust B)

Estimated Death Costs $48,000*

$1,104,000 for Heirs	$1,200,000 for Heirs

Gain for Heirs: $96,000

Assumes 8% probate cost.

*Probate fee.

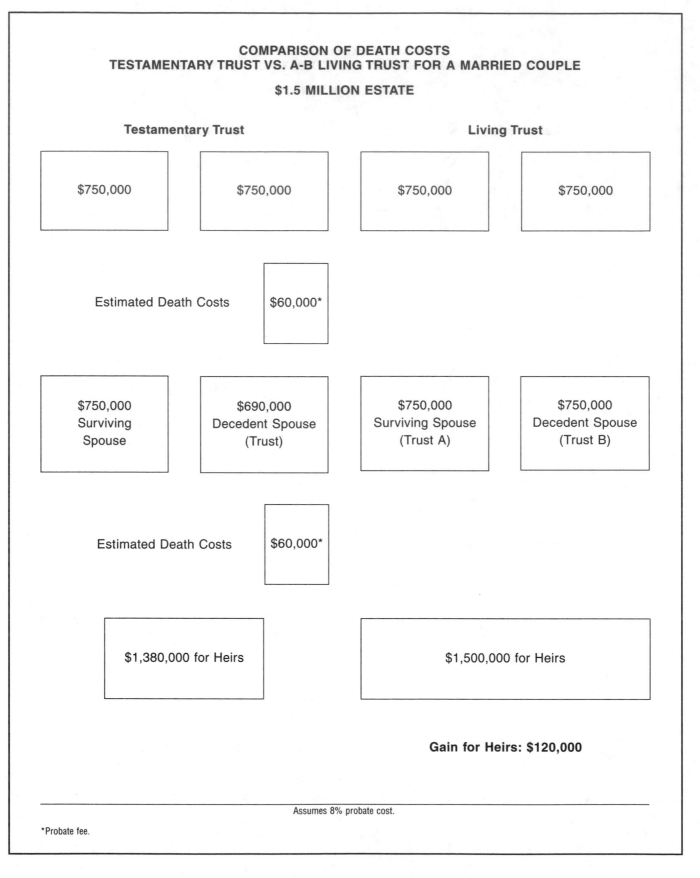

COMPARISON OF DEATH COSTS
TESTAMENTARY TRUST VS. A-B LIVING TRUST FOR A MARRIED COUPLE

$1.5 MILLION ESTATE

Testamentary Trust   **Living Trust**

| $750,000 | $750,000 | | $750,000 | $750,000 |

Estimated Death Costs $60,000*

| $750,000 Surviving Spouse | $690,000 Decedent Spouse (Trust) | | $750,000 Surviving Spouse (Trust A) | $750,000 Decedent Spouse (Trust B) |

Estimated Death Costs $60,000*

$1,380,000 for Heirs $1,500,000 for Heirs

Gain for Heirs: $120,000

Assumes 8% probate cost.

*Probate fee.

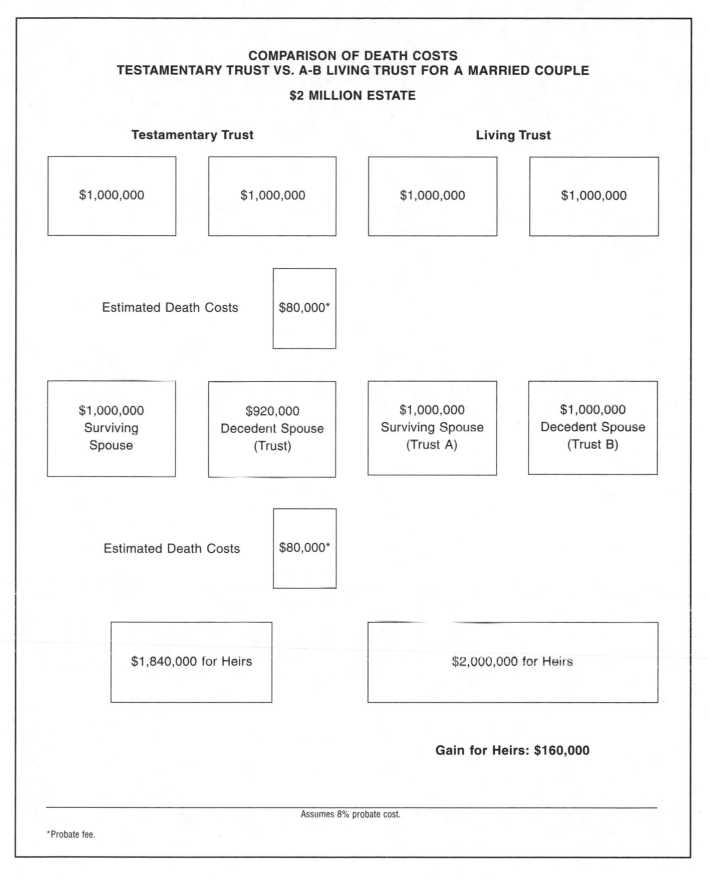

COMPARISON OF DEATH COSTS
TESTAMENTARY TRUST VS. A-B LIVING TRUST FOR A MARRIED COUPLE

$2 MILLION ESTATE

Testamentary Trust   **Living Trust**

$1,000,000 $1,000,000 $1,000,000 $1,000,000

Estimated Death Costs $80,000*

$1,000,000 $920,000 $1,000,000 $1,000,000
Surviving   Decedent Spouse   Surviving Spouse   Decedent Spouse
Spouse   (Trust)   (Trust A)   (Trust B)

Estimated Death Costs $80,000*

$1,840,000 for Heirs $2,000,000 for Heirs

Gain for Heirs: $160,000

Assumes 8% probate cost.

*Probate fee.

Appendix F

Comparison of Death Costs: Testamentary Trust vs. Living Trust for Married Couple with A-B-C Trust

This appendix consists of illustrations that compare death costs for a married couple who have a Testamentary Trust with the costs for a couple who have a Living A-B-C Trust. The comparisons use the following sizes of estates:

- $2.5 million
- $5 million

Each illustration shows that having a Living Trust rather than a Testamentary Trust pro- vides benefits in the areas of probate, estate taxes, and gain for the heirs.

To use this appendix, find the illustration that most closely corresponds to the size of your own estate, and study the comparison of the two methods of holding assets. For a fur- ther explanation of the computations used in the illustrations, please refer to Chapter 6.

Note that all examples assume a probate cost of 8 percent and a federal estate tax exclusion of $1 million per person.

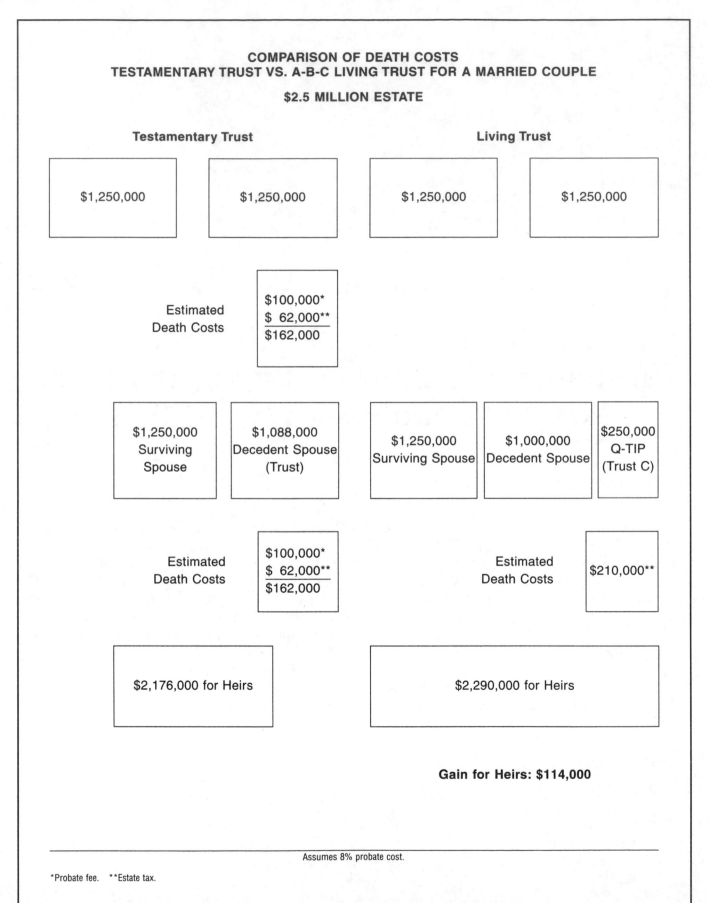

COMPARISON OF DEATH COSTS
TESTAMENTARY TRUST VS. A-B-C LIVING TRUST FOR A MARRIED COUPLE

$2.5 MILLION ESTATE

Testamentary Trust	Living Trust

$1,250,000 $1,250,000 $1,250,000 $1,250,000

Estimated Death Costs

$100,000*
$ 62,000**
$162,000

$1,250,000 Surviving Spouse $1,088,000 Decedent Spouse (Trust)

$1,250,000 Surviving Spouse $1,000,000 Decedent Spouse $250,000 Q-TIP (Trust C)

Estimated Death Costs

$100,000*
$ 62,000**
$162,000

Estimated Death Costs $210,000**

$2,176,000 for Heirs

$2,290,000 for Heirs

Gain for Heirs: $114,000

Assumes 8% probate cost.

*Probate fee.   **Estate tax.

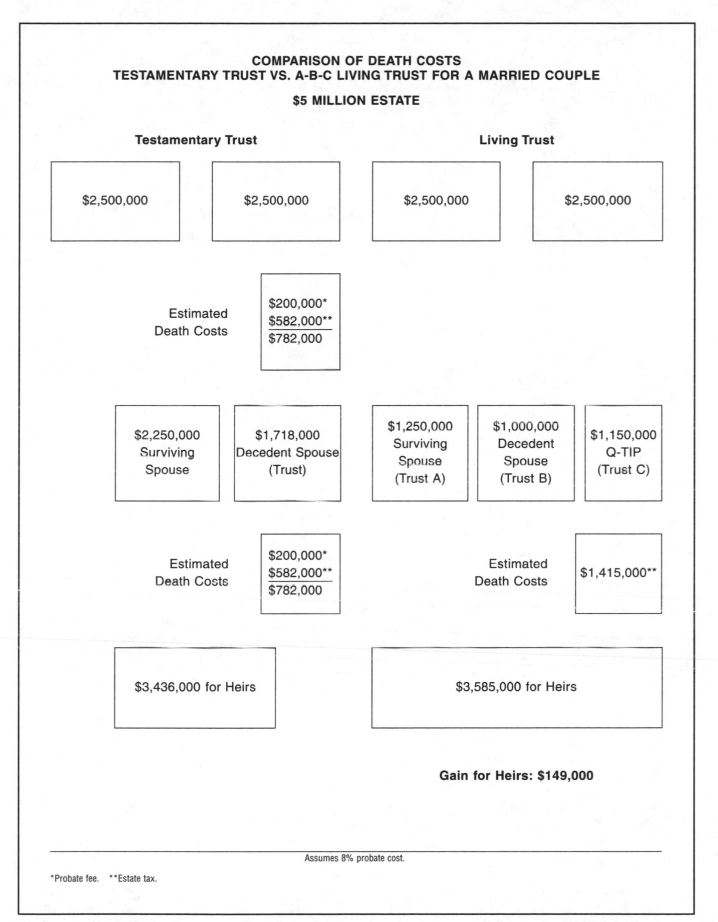

COMPARISON OF DEATH COSTS
TESTAMENTARY TRUST VS. A-B-C LIVING TRUST FOR A MARRIED COUPLE

$5 MILLION ESTATE

Testamentary Trust   **Living Trust**

| $2,500,000 | $2,500,000 | | $2,500,000 | $2,500,000 |

Estimated
Death Costs

$200,000*
$582,000**
—————
$782,000

| $2,250,000 Surviving Spouse | $1,718,000 Decedent Spouse (Trust) | | $1,250,000 Surviving Spouse (Trust A) | $1,000,000 Decedent Spouse (Trust B) | $1,150,000 Q-TIP (Trust C) |

Estimated
Death Costs

$200,000*
$582,000**
—————
$782,000

Estimated
Death Costs

$1,415,000**

$3,436,000 for Heirs $3,585,000 for Heirs

Gain for Heirs: $149,000

Assumes 8% probate cost.

*Probate fee.   **Estate tax.

Appendix G

Everything You Always Wanted to Know About the Living Trust—But Were Afraid to Ask

Today, more and more people are beginning to know a little bit about the Living Trust; however, an enormous amount of misinformation about the Living Trust is being disseminated. The American Bar Association says that less than 1 percent of the legal profession understands the Living Trust—and I heartily concur! As more and more people become aware of the agony of probate—and of the much better alternative of the Living Trust—the proliferation of Living Trusts has dramatically reduced the quality of the Trust documents being produced.

To correct the misperceptions and fears caused by misinformation, this chapter answers the questions that people most commonly ask about the Living Trust. The questions, along with their answers, are grouped into the following categories:

- Wills
- Probate
- Joint tenancy
- The Living Trust

- Beneficiaries
- Rights of the surviving spouse
- Amendments to the Living Trust
- Successor trustee
- Requirements
- Taxes
- Assets
- Perceived disadvantages

Although these questions have been answered in more detail in various parts of the book, they are presented here to provide a quick overview of the Living Trust. This compilation of questions and answers is not designed to be a summary of the book, but rather it is structured to go directly to the heart of the most common areas of misinformation and fear.

WILLS
Almost half of the people attending our seminars have been told by some misinformed person that, if they have a Will, their estates will avoid probate. Unfortunately, too many people

are unaware of the agony that awaits them. To paraphrase the instructions of a popular board game, "If you have a Will, you must go through probate, you shall not pass Go, and you shall not collect $200."

Q: *What happens if I don't have a Will?*
A: If you die without a Will, then the state automatically provides one for you; it is much more complex for your survivors, and the distribution of your assets may not be as you desired. (See Chapter 6.)

Q: *How is distribution different if I have a Living Trust rather than a Will?*
A: Most people have the "Will syndrome," which means that they believe that all of their assets must be distributed upon their death. Such a belief is correct for a Will, but not for a Living Trust. When you have a Will, once probate is completed, your assets must be immediately distributed outright, since there is no legal entity to hold your assets. However, with a Living Trust, the assets may remain in the Trust almost indefinitely, since the Trust is a legal entity and "lives on" after a person's death. (See Chapter 9.)

Q: *Why didn't my attorney tell me about the Living Trust?*
A: The best answer to this question is to repeat the words of an attorney (previously quoted in this book): "In most states, the only justification for not having a Trust is that the attorney will not get his probate fee." Remember that 8 percent to 10 percent of the gross estate is charged *each time* an individual dies—which is a lot of money! Many practicing attorneys today are not aware of the alternative to probate offered by the Living Trust. (See Chapter 7.)

Q: *Do I need to notify my attorney that I replaced my Will?*
A: There is no need to notify your attorney. When you execute your Trust (and specifically your Pour-Over Will), you revoke any former Wills. (See Chapter 7.)

PROBATE

Frequently, an individual will say, "My spouse died, and I never went through probate." Upon the death of a spouse, no one directs that you must go through probate. You do not have to go through probate—until you want to sell an asset that is held in the name of the deceased person. As long as you do not desire to sell anything, you do not need to go through probate. The purpose of probate is to establish clear title, and you must have clear title in order to sell an asset.

For example, assume that, seven years after the death of your spouse, you decide to sell your house. You list the house with a real estate broker, who finds a buyer, and you enter escrow. When escrow is ready to close, you are invited to come into the escrow office to sign over the deed. After you sign your name, the escrow officer says, "We also need to have the signature of your spouse." When you say, "My spouse died seven years ago," the words fall on deaf ears. Escrow immediately stops, the buyer for your home is gone—and you now have to go through probate. The same situation would be true with your stocks, bonds, and other assets.

Q: *My accountant tells me that, since my estate is worth less than $1 million, I don't need a Living Trust. Is this statement really true?*
A: The $1 million amount has *nothing* to do with probate. The $1 million amount is your federal estate tax exclusion. This means that, as long as your total estate is valued at less than $1 million, it will not be subject to federal estate tax.

In most states, if the value of your real estate exceeds $10,000 *or* if the amount of your total assets, including personal effects, exceeds $30,000 (in one state the figure is $100,000), your estate must go through probate—unless your estate is in a Living Trust. The greatest advantage of a Living Trust is that it avoids the agony of probate—as well as the unnecessary costs, frustration, and mental anguish that automatically accompany the probate process. (See Chapter 2.)

Q: *Is an attorney required to charge statutory fees for probate?*

A: Statutory fees are those fees established by the state legislature as the theoretical maximum. In most instances (even for the simplest of estates), it is commonplace to begin by charging the statutory fee as the standard fee. Thereafter, "extraordinary fees" are usually added on to the standard fee. Extraordinary fees are simply additional costs submitted by the attorney and approved by the court, usually without any discussion or examination for reasonableness. (See Chapter 2.)

Q: *How can attorneys justify their exorbitant probate fees?*

A: The fees charged by attorneys to take an estate through the probate process often cannot be justified. Many people call the practice just plain greed. The American Bar Association has strongly urged all fifty states to substantially revise their probate codes. However, all fifty states rejected this recommendation—and made virtually no changes to their probate codes. A few states made some modest adjustments and called the changes the "Revised Probate Code."

Today's probate system is unjustifiable. The entire process is running along unchecked, and it has become far too costly and bureaucratic. Eventually, enough people will adopt the Living Trust, and the state legislatures will be forced someday to revise the probate code to a reasonable procedure and a justifiable cost. Until then, your only solution is the Living Trust. (See Chapters 2 and 6.)

Q: *What happens to assets that are outside my Living Trust? Since they pour over into the Trust, must they go through probate?*

A: Any assets that are inadvertently (or intentionally) left outside your Living Trust—and whose value exceeds the probate limits of your particular state—must go through probate. The Pour-Over Will, which is provided for just such a contingency, identifies the executor and gives him or her the necessary power to take the assets through probate. Once the assets have gone through the long, onerous probate process, the assets can then be "poured over" into the Trust. (See Chapter 7.)

JOINT TENANCY

Q: *Can probate be avoided by the use of joint tenancy?*

A: Yes—and no. Joint tenancy can *delay* probate, but it cannot avoid probate altogether. The probate process (but not necessarily the cost) can be avoided only on the first to die if you hold your assets in joint tenancy (for example, between husband and wife) or, in some community property states, if you have executed a Community Property Agreement. However, when the second spouse finally dies, *all* of the assets in the estate must go through the probate process. Consequently, all that you have really accomplished with joint tenancy is to delay the inevitable—ultimately causing your heirs to go through the agonizing probate process. In addition, by holding assets in joint tenancy, you lose half of the stepped-up valuation when the first spouse dies. You have also forfeited one of your $1 million federal estate tax exclusions.

If you decide that the way to avoid probate is to go into joint tenancy with your children, any such assets in joint tenancy are subject to any lawsuits to which your children might be a party. The problems with holding property in joint tenancy are covered in detail in Chapter 4.

Q: *In a community property state, why isn't property that is held in joint tenancy treated as community property?*

A: In a community property state, husband and wife each have an *equal* interest in the assets acquired during their marriage. However, everyone has the right of free agency (that is, the right to take his or her assets from community property and place them into joint tenancy). In effect, such an action simply deprives those misinformed individuals of the right to get full stepped-up valuation upon the death of the first spouse. (See Chapter 4.)

Q: *Is there any problem with transferring assets held in joint tenancy into the Living Trust?*
A: Transferring assets held in joint tenancy into a Living Trust causes no problems. Once an asset held in joint tenancy is transferred into the Trust, it is automatically transferred from joint tenancy. (See Chapter 4.)

Q: *What would happen if I owned stock or real estate in joint tenancy with my children?*
A: The answer depends upon how your children acquired their interest in the asset. If the children received the asset by your gift, you should, in effect, take the gift back—and transfer the asset into the Living Trust in your name, so that, when that asset passes on to your children upon your death, the asset will receive full stepped-up valuation.

On the other hand, if the children paid for their share of the asset, then only your share should be transferred into the Living Trust. However, be aware of a pitfall of such an arrangement with your children. If your children were to die, their share of *your* assets (passed to your children) would then be subjected to the probate process—unless your children have their own Living Trusts. (See Chapter 4.)

THE LIVING TRUST

Q: *Where did this "new idea" of the Living Trust come from, and how long has the Living Trust been in existence?*
A: The Living Trust has been around for 1,200 years! The Living Trust dates back to A.D. 800 as Roman law, and was adopted by the English. The king and the nobles challenged the Living Trust in 1535 in the highest court (the Chancery Court)—and lost! The Living Trust was adopted by the United States when this nation was formed, using English law as the basis of the legal system. The first known Living Trust drawn in the United States was written by Patrick Henry. A more detailed discussion of the Living Trust is presented in Chapter 4.

Q: *When will Congress take away the Living Trust?*
A: Nearly half of my clients are concerned about whether Congress might take away the Living Trust and when that might happen. Almost every one of my clients feels that "Congress is out to get me." (If I were a congressman or a senator, I would be deeply concerned about this lack of confidence on the part of my constituents.)

Basically, Congress has little chance of ever taking away the Living Trust. Two hundred years ago, thirteen states met to form a federal government and, in so doing, created one of the finest documents in existence—the Constitution of the United States of America. In the process of creating this nation, the states relinquished to the federal government certain "states' rights," which are spelled out in the Constitution.

One of these states' rights that was not granted to the federal government and that is sacrosanct to the states is the right to create a "legal entity," such as a corporation or Trust. A corporation or a Trust created in one state is recognized by the other states. Congress has little chance of invading this area of states' rights. (See Chapter 7.)

Q. *Does my adviser need to be an attorney?*
A: No, but depending upon state law, the adviser must work either with, or under, an attorney to assure that the Living Trust is appropriate for you, and that the documents produced meet your needs. It's most vital that you know that whoever *produces* your documents is extremely knowledgeable and sophisticated. You are betting your estate on it. (See Chapter 19.)

Q. *Since a Living Trust is not registered, is private, and is not monitored or approved by any federal or state body, how do we know that the Trust is good, that it is legally acceptable, or whether it is worthless?*
A: You must be assured that your Living Trust has the more than 150 vital Living Trust provisions identified in Chapter 10, "Separating

the Good from the Bad." As with the preceding question, you are betting your estate on it.

Q. *How can I be assured that I have the Living Trust described in this book?*
A: See the answer to the previous question. A good Living Trust must contain the more than 150 provisions identified in Chapter 10. If you use The Estate Plan referral service identified in Chapter 19, and get an Estate Plan trust, you'll note that every page of The Estate Plan documents are printed on feather paper—high-quality paper, preprinted with a blue feather. This blue feather logo assures you of a Living Trust of the highest quality.

Q. *What is the importance of having a "universal" trust?*
A: A "universal" Living Trust is applicable in all fifty states. This is extremely important if you own real estate in more than one state, if you live part-time in two or more states—such as "snowbirds"—or if you ultimately move to another state. In each case, you know that your trust will meet the legal requirements of each and every state. (See Chapter 7.)

Q. *My attorney says that my wife and I should each have separate Trusts and that an A-B Trust (joint Trust) will not work in my state.*
A: This is nonsense. We are talking about federal law, not state law. There has never been a case in which the IRS has denied both federal estate tax exemptions in a good A-B Living Trust because of residence in a separate property state. I am appalled at the enormous amount of misinformation about Living Trusts that is being spewed forth by the legal profession. Much of it is by ignorance (they don't teach Living Trusts as a basic course in law school), much of it is intentional disinformation to steer you into the probate process, and the balance is just pure greed (an attorney gets twice as much money for two Trusts as for one). Also, an A-B Trust is quite complex and difficult to draft to satisfy the IRS requirements; a single Trust is much simpler to draft. And so you end up with two single Trusts—

and an administrative nightmare. (See Chapter 10.)

Q: *Is the Living Trust valid in all fifty states?*
A: Yes, the Living Trust is valid in each state and in all commonwealth nations—since the Trust came specifically from English law. The Living Trust should also be valid in most nations that have a civil code. With clients all over the world today, we have found that, by and large, most nations recognize the Living Trust. (See Chapter 7.)

Q: *Is a Living Trust that has been notarized in the United States recognized as a legal document in a foreign country?*
A: The 1961 Hague Convention (which went into effect for the United States in October 1981) abolished the requirements of having to have foreign governments legalize public documents of other nations. In effect, the convention decreed that documents notarized as public documents in a particular country would be recognized as valid documents by the other countries, where both countries are signatories to the Hague Convention. (See Chapter 7.)

Q: *What's the difference between a revocable and an irrevocable Trust?*
A: *Revocable* means "changeable." As long as your Trust is revocable, you can continue to change it whenever you desire. More significant, however, is that as long as your Trust is revocable, you continue to control your assets. Conversely, with an irrevocable Trust, you *give up control* of your assets. In most instances, you don't want to give up control of your assets—that is, unless you are faced with the choice of either giving up control of your assets or losing your assets entirely. Usually, this condition comes into play when you are faced with a catastrophic illness. In such a case, I'm sure that you would rather only give up *control* of your assets than lose them entirely. The Catastrophic Illness Trust can be either a revocable or an irrevocable Trust that enables your heirs to keep those assets (see Chapter 11).

Q: *How is a Living Trust named?*
A: The most appropriate way to name a Living Trust is as follows:

The Smith Family Trust, dated August 18, 1997, John J. Smith and Mary Ann Smith, Trustor(s) and/or Trustee(s).

Q: *Is the Living Trust formed by a state in the same manner as a corporation is formed?*
A: Each state has the right to create a legal entity—whether it is a corporation or a Trust. The difference between a corporation and a Trust is that a Trust has neither the red tape nor the taxation of a corporation. The Trust is a very simple legal entity to handle. (See Chapter 7.)

Q: *Where do I register my Living Trust?*
A: The Living Trust document does not have to be registered anywhere. In fact, on the death of the trustor (or trustors), the only person who has a right to see the Trust document is the successor trustee; no one else has a right to view the document—not even by court subpoena.

The name of the Living Trust is submitted only to the Internal Revenue Service, in order to request a Tax Identification Number for the Trust. Even this step is unnecessary when you first draw up your Trust; however, the number will be needed upon the death of a settlor. (See Chapter 7.)

Q: *How long does it take to establish a Living Trust?*
A: With the sophisticated technology available today, the time needed to establish a Living Trust is based upon the client, not the actual time required to create the document itself.

Usually, a client's first visit lasts for about an hour and a half, during which time the advantages of the Living Trust are discussed, as well as the type of Trust the client should have and the provisions that should be included in the Trust. During the first visit, the many options available to the client are also discussed and reviewed, and the important decisions that must be made are identified. Presumably, if you have read this book, you have already made

those critical decisions and are ready to proceed. A workbook will be completed in order to prepare the draft documents.

A client usually needs anywhere from two to three weeks to pull together copies of all of his or her assets—to be included in the Estate Plan Binder. During this same time period, draft documents of the Trust and the various associated legal documents are printed and then sent to the client—with summaries in plain English—so that the client has the opportunity to review the documents and to understand them.

The client then returns to sign the documents—which legally puts the new Living Trust into effect. From beginning to end, the process typically takes from four to six weeks. However, in urgent situations, the entire process—making the decisions and creating and signing all of the documents—has been completed in less than two days. (See Chapters 13 and 17.)

Q: *Can a Living Trust be contested in the same manner as a Will?*
A: Yes, anybody can sue a Trust. However, I have yet to learn of any properly drawn Living Trust that has been *successfully* contested. Because a Trust is a "living" document that can be changed as often as desired by the trustors, it is much more difficult for dissident heirs to successfully challenge than is a Will, which is usually written and then placed in a safe-deposit box and forgotten. With a Living Trust, you should have the Trust readily available to you, and you have the right to alter your Trust, right up to the date of your death—and the change will be upheld in court. In contrast, about one-third of the Wills that are contested are successfully challenged—and the Wills are overturned. (See Chapter 6.)

Q: *Can I have a Living Trust if I am unmarried?*
A: Most definitely. If you want to avoid probate, you should have a Living Trust whether you are married or not. (See Chapter 6.)

Q: *Can two unmarried people who are living together create a Living Trust?*
A: It is quite common to create an A-B Trust for an unmarried couple and to identify the

individuals' Separate Property Agreements. A Living Trust, with Separate Property Agreements, is particularly appropriate for an unmarried couple when the two individuals have purchased a house together. If the two parties were John Jones and Mary Brown, the Trust would typically be known as the "Jones/Brown Trust Agreement." (See Chapter 7.)

Q: *Can parents create a Living Trust with their children?*
A: Yes, such a Living Trust could be created, but such a situation is most unusual. Parents have their particular goals and objectives, and the children eventually have their own goals and objectives. Since parents and children who are establishing a Trust together must be co-trustees, parents and children both must have common objectives. Such Trusts have been done successfully on a few occasions, but this arrangement is not recommended. (See Chapter 4.)

Q: *Can a Living Trust continue on, generation after generation?*
A: A Living Trust can go on for several generations, but there is a time when the Trust must cease to exist. A Living Trust *must* dissolve at some point—but, with the law of perpetuity, the time can be decades away! Typically, the Trust will simply dissolve when all of the assets have been distributed from the Trust.

The law of perpetuity, on the other hand, states that, upon the death of the trustors, every potential heir then living is identified—including children and grandchildren as well as aunts, uncles, nieces, and nephews. Under the law of perpetuity, the Living Trust must cease twenty-one years after the death of the *last* of the potential heirs! I have yet to discover a client who finds the law of perpetuity to be of any concern. (See Chapter 9.)

Q: *Is an A-B Trust actually two different Trusts?*
A: An A-B Trust is one Trust while both spouses are living and even after a spouse dies. The terms *Trust A* and *Trust B* are used to differentiate between the decedent's share of the assets (Trust B) and the survivor's share of the

assets (Trust A). Only upon the death of the first spouse does the distinction between the A part of the A-B Trust and the B part have any significance. Other than the A and B parts, which are used to apportion assets, the Living Trust is a single entity. Assets identified as being in the B Trust are thereafter insulated from further estate taxes. (See Chapter 7.)

Q: *What is involved in "settling" an estate in a Living Trust?*
A: The word *settle* is used rather loosely, simply to mean that certain things need to be done upon the death of one or both settlors (creators of the Trust). These steps are identified in the Estate Plan Binder under "Final Instructions" and are also covered in more detail in Chapters 13 and 15.

With all of an estate's assets in a Living Trust, the survivor and/or heirs can best perform the tasks required to "settle" the estate themselves—when they fully understand the specific requirements that need to be satisfied.

Q: *How would a creditor make a claim against a Living Trust?*
A: Unlike probate, the death of the trustor does *not* trigger a requirement that any liability be satisfied. The liability is in the Trust and is still backed by the same assets. The creditor's position has not changed. A creditor may not accelerate the claim on the death of a settlor, but a creditor does have the right to have the originally agreed-upon contract fulfilled. (See Chapter 14.)

BENEFICIARIES
It is extremely important for anyone creating a Living Trust to understand that the creator of the Trust, along with all of his or her other rights, is also the beneficiary of that Trust. If a husband and wife create a Living Trust, they are also the beneficiaries of that Trust. Upon the death of the first spouse, the surviving spouse is the beneficiary of the Trust. The primary purpose of the Trust is to do whatever is necessary to provide for the surviving spouse—even if that means exhausting the entire estate in order to adequately provide and care for the surviving spouse.

Most people tend to think of their children as the beneficiaries. However, with a Living Trust, the children are *contingent* beneficiaries. Being a contingent beneficiary means that the children must fulfill two conditions in order to ultimately become beneficiaries. First, the children must be living upon the death of the trustors (the creators of the Trust). Second, there must be assets remaining in the Trust to be distributed to the beneficiaries. If either of these requirements is not met, the children are not considered to be beneficiaries. A more complete discussion of beneficiaries can be found in Chapter 8.

Q: *Can I leave all or part of my estate to an as-yet-unconceived child or grandchild?*
A: Yes, with a Living Trust, it is possible to leave assets to an individual who has not yet been conceived. For instance, a young couple get married and then desire to create a Living Trust. The couple have no children, but husband and wife do have separate property. In anticipation of future children, the husband and wife name their yet-to-be-conceived children as the primary beneficiaries. The language of the Trust states that, if there are no children living upon the death of the settlors, the assets of the estate will thereupon go to the contingent beneficiaries designated—typically to the settlors' brothers and sisters or parents.

In a similar manner, it is quite common to leave a specific amount or a specific percentage of your estate to each of your grandchildren. When you first draw up your Living Trust, you may have only one grandchild; however, as the years pass, you may eventually have many grandchildren. The language of the Trust provides for such a change in the number of grandchildren. (See Chapter 9.)

Q: *If my child dies before me, does his or her spouse become a beneficiary of that child's share of the estate?*
A: The answer is almost always a sound *no*. The deceased child's share of the estate passes on to the children of that child (your grandchildren), whether the children are by blood or adoption. If the deceased child has no children, then the deceased child's share of the estate would be redivided among your other remaining children.

However, your assets do *not* have to be distributed that way. You may leave all or part of your child's share (or whatever portion you desire) to your child's spouse. Most clients desire to pass their assets to those individuals who are related by blood or adoption but seldom by marriage. (See Chapter 9.)

Q: *How do I prevent my assets, destined for my son, from being acquired by his wife if they get divorced?*
A: There are several ways to avoid such an outcome. First of all, recognize that, if you distribute your assets to your son outright, the assets may well become commingled with the community assets of your son and his wife. Thereafter, the assets would be considered community assets in the event of a divorce. Several alternatives could be used to ensure that the assets distributed to your son *remain* as his assets.

First, you could leave all of your assets in trust, with only the income from the assets going to your son; the assets themselves would then pass on to your grandchildren upon your son's eventual death. Such assets in your Trust would never be subject to divorce claims of your son's wife.

Second, you could distribute the assets to your son as a deferred distribution—one-third outright, one-third in five years, and one-third in ten years. This practice assumes that the longer your son and his wife are married, the greater the possibility is that they will remain married.

The third, and most logical, approach would be for your son to have a Living Trust of his own. Then, upon receipt of those assets being distributed to him, he would establish them as separate property, under Separate Property Agreements within his own Trust. If there should eventually be a divorce, in most circumstances, the court would recognize these separate assets as distinctly belonging to the son. (See Chapter 11.)

Q: *What happens if my daughter divorces or remarries and changes her name?*

A: One of the nice aspects of a properly written Living Trust is that your daughter's name does not make any difference. In your Trust, you have identified your children in your Pour-Over Will as your children. No matter what name the children may go by in the future, they are still your children. You need not change any of the children's names in your Living Trust. (See Chapter 9.)

Q: *Can I make a gift to charity through my Living Trust?*

A: Yes, you may designate a charity to be the recipient of assets in your estate. The Living Trust that is drawn up for our clients includes a "Schedule B" where the client can simply indicate each charity and the percentage of distribution that is desired. (See Chapter 9.)

Q: *Can I use a Living Trust for my handicapped child?*

A: I believe that the *only* way by which you can adequately provide for your handicapped child is with a Living Trust! This special situation is provided in all Living Trusts drawn up for our clients. Specific language is used to ensure that the well-being of the handicapped individual is protected. The language of the provision will protect your handicapped child's share of the estate from being acquired by a federal agency and will also prevent jeopardizing the ability to receive government benefits that would otherwise be available to that handicapped child. (See Chapter 9.)

Q: *How do I exclude children as beneficiaries of my Living Trust?*

A: All of your children are identified in your Pour-Over Will—which clearly establishes, from a legal standpoint, that you have not overlooked anyone. Since the Living Trust is a contract, you simply exclude (in the allocation and distribution sections of the Trust) those children whom you do not want to be included as beneficiaries. You do *not* have to state in writing, "I leave this child one dollar and no more." (See Chapter 9.)

Q: *Can I provide for my pets in my Living Trust?*

A: Yes, a well-written Trust can provide for the continued care of your beloved pets after you are gone. It is suggested that you find someone whom you trust and then leave an incentive, whether it is money, the right to live in your home, or something to that effect, for that person to provide for your pets. However, I do not recommend that you select your favorite veterinarian and then leave him or her $20,000 to provide for your pet. All too often, when family or friends later inquire as to the whereabouts of the pet or pets, they are rebuffed. Where are the pets? Are they still alive?

One couple solved the problem of caring for their pet by suggesting that a young man down the street would be more than happy to take care of the dog for the rest of its life, giving this young neighbor a gift of $10,000 toward his education. (See Chapter 9.)

RIGHTS OF THE SURVIVING SPOUSE

A well-written Living Trust ensures that the surviving spouse continues to have almost all of the same rights as when both spouses were alive. Special provisions in the Trust assure that the surviving spouse cannot be deprived of the right to remain in the family home as long as he or she is still living.

However, clients often have the misperception that, when one of the spouses dies, the rights of the surviving spouse are drastically reduced. Remember that, even when both spouses are alive, the Living Trust allows either of the trustees to act independently on behalf of the Trust. Therefore, when one spouse dies, the other trustee can continue to act on behalf of the Trust.

Q: *What are the rights of the surviving spouse as trustee?*

A: As the surviving trustee, the surviving spouse continues to retain the same rights as before—the power (without restriction) to buy, sell, and transfer any or all of the assets in the Trust. However, the rights of the surviving trustee may be restricted by the settlors when they create their Living Trust or, thereafter, by amending the Trust while both settlors are still living. (See Chapters 7 and 8.)

Q: *What are the beneficial rights of the surviving spouse to the Decedent's Trust B?*
A: At every seminar, at least one attendee wants to know why the surviving spouse is entitled to only 5 percent or $5,000 of the Decedent's B Trust each year. All too often, people only seem to hear this particular right of the surviving spouse, while entirely missing the other rights—which are, by far, the most important!

The surviving spouse is the beneficiary of the Decedent's B Trust (and the Decedent's C Trust, where appropriate). The tax code specifically provides that the surviving spouse has three rights:

- The right to *all* of the income
- The right to all of the principal that is necessary to maintain the *same* standard of living as before the decedent passed away
- The right to $5,000 or 5 percent of the assets (in the B Trust only), whichever is greater, once a year—for any reason, regardless of how frivolous

These three rights in effect give the surviving spouse the right to use the funds in the Decedent's B and C Trusts without restriction. In fact, the only real restriction is "the right to use the principal to maintain the same standard of living." Who is responsible for determining the standard of living? Why, of course, the trustee is responsible for making that determination. Who is the trustee? Usually, the surviving spouse is the trustee. Therefore, there really is no restriction!

However, the one thing that the surviving spouse *cannot* do is to change the beneficiaries designated in the Decedent's B and C Trusts or to jeopardize the beneficiaries' rights to the assets in the Decedent's B and C Trusts. Such a restriction is very appropriate when a husband and wife have been married before and each have children from former marriages. Specifically, the surviving spouse may not reach into the B and/or C Trust, take out $200,000, go to Las Vegas, and then gamble away the money. The decedent's children have a right to say, "Mother, you effectively took that $200,000 from *your* side—the Survivor's A Trust." The surviving spouse also does not have the right to reach into the Decedent's B and C Trusts, take out funds, and move them to the A Trust—so that, upon the death of the surviving spouse, a greater share of the estate will go to the heirs of the surviving spouse. (See Chapter 7.)

Q: *What are the rights of the surviving spouse to the assets in Trust A?*
A: Since the assets in the Survivor's Trust A are the assets of the surviving spouse, the surviving spouse may do anything with these assets—including being able to remove the assets from the Trust entirely. (See Chapter 7.)

Q: *If the surviving spouse relinquishes the position of trustee, can he or she regain the position at a later time?*
A: The surviving spouse is always given the right to relinquish trusteeship; however, the surviving spouse retains the right to take back (reassume) the trusteeship, as well as to name a different successor trustee. (See Chapter 8.)

Q: *Can the surviving spouse change the successor trustee(s)?*
A: Unless the wording of the Trust is modified to exclude such a right, the surviving spouse may change the successor trustee or successor trustees at any time. (See Chapter 8.)

AMENDMENTS TO THE LIVING TRUST

A Living Trust is a *revocable* Trust, which means that the Trust may be changed whenever the clients desire. A change to the Trust is legally called an amendment. Typical changes to a Living Trust would be a change of a beneficiary, a change of a successor trustee, or a change to a different method of allocation and/or distribution. Those items are changes to your *plan*.

On the other hand, changes of assets—to buy, sell, or transfer an asset—are not "changes" to your Living Trust; these changes are actually the process of managing your assets. Simply tell your stockbroker that you want to sell a particular stock or that you want to buy some stock (and, by the way, put ownership in the name of the Trust). In a similar manner, if you buy a piece of real estate, simply have the deed recorded in the name of your Trust. Such changes of assets are *not* changes to your plan.

You may change your Living Trust as often as you want—even every day or every week. However, it is a good idea to review your Trust at least every five years and to formally amend your Trust for any changes you might have made in the interim.

A more detailed discussion of making changes to the Living Trust is presented in Chapter 7.

Q: *Is it difficult to change my Living Trust, and when would I want to make a change to my Living Trust?*
A: It is a simple matter to make an amendment to your Living Trust. Typically, there are two types of changes you would want to make to your Trust. One type of change involves making a change to your plan, such as a change of a beneficiary, a change of method of distribution, or a change of successor trustee. You should review your Trust every five years to see whether it needs this type of modification.

The second type of change involves amending your Trust to keep it current with estate tax laws authorized by Congress. If a particular tax change would benefit your estate, you would obviously want to incorporate such a change into your Trust. (See Chapter 18.)

Q: *Do I ever need to update my Living Trust?*
A: You should periodically review and update your Living Trust. As mentioned previously, you should review your Trust every five years. Circumstances change, and no one can really look ahead clearly for a time span of five years or more. (See Chapters 7 and 9.)

Q: *Can my successor trustee make changes to my Living Trust?*
A: Upon your death (if you are single), or upon the death of both husband and wife (if you are married), the right to change *any* part of that Living Trust ceases. The successor trustee may

not make any changes whatsoever in the Trust document. Instead, the successor trustee is under a fiduciary responsibility to fulfill every requirement spelled out in that Trust. (See Chapter 8.)

Q: *What happens to my Living Trust if I get divorced?*
A: Unfortunately, a Living Trust cannot, in all practicality, be cut in half. Therefore, one individual usually retains the Trust, and the other individual must revoke his or her interest in the Trust. The party who retains the Trust will retain his or her assets in the name of the Trust, and the other party will remove his or her assets from the Trust and revoke his or her interest in the Trust. Such an action is accomplished by executing a Disclaimer of Trust Interest form. (See Chapter 7.)

Q: *What happens to my Living Trust if I remarry one day?*
A: The answer to this question depends somewhat on the age of the individuals. If you are young and still building your estate, it would be most appropriate to include your new spouse in the existing Living Trust. It would also be appropriate to identify each individual's separate property by including Separate Property Agreements in the Trust. Using this approach, your new spouse would become trustor, settlor, trustee, and beneficiary.

If you are older and have, in essence, finished building your estate, it may be more appropriate to simply retain the Trust in its existing form and not to include your new spouse in the Trust. Such occurrences are quite common when an individual is in his or her seventies or eighties, is retired, and is a widow or widower. Since the original spouse has died, the B Trust is now irrevocable. Although the new spouse could be included within the Survivor's A Trust, it is much simpler just to retain the assets in the Trust, as is. In this situation, the new spouse should then have a separate Trust for his or her own assets.

When two older individuals have remarried and are living in the home previously occupied by one of them, another important aspect of the Trust comes to light. It is most important that the owner of the home in which both parties are residing make an appropriate amendment to his or her Trust to ensure that the surviving spouse is allowed to remain in that home during his or her lifetime. (See Chapter 11.)

Q: *How does the Living Trust dissolve, and is there any probate at that time?*
A: Once all of the assets are distributed from the Living Trust, the Trust is effectively dissolved. There will be no probate if all of the assets had been in the Living Trust. Once all the assets are removed from the Trust, you may put your Trust document up on a shelf or dispose of it in any manner. (See Chapter 7.)

Q: *Can I revoke my Living Trust?*
A: The creators of the Living Trust always reserve the right to revoke the Trust at any time. However, I have yet to learn of a valid reason to revoke a Trust. The easiest way to revoke an entire Living Trust, although such action is discouraged, is simply to transfer *all* of the assets from the Trust. (See Chapter 7.)

SUCCESSOR TRUSTEE
The successor trustee is the individual (or individuals) who assumes management of the Living Trust upon the death, incompetence, or resignation of the trustors (creators of the Trust).

The most logical parties for consideration as successor trustee or successor trustees are one or more of your adult children, close family members, or close friends. Only under the most unusual circumstances should a financial institution be considered as successor trustee.

Q: *Should my children read my Living Trust?*
A: It is not necessary for your children to read your Living Trust, and in many cases they would most likely be confused by it. However, it would certainly make sense to advise your children that you have a Living Trust. Depending upon how close you are to your children, you may want to apprise them of what you want to accomplish with your Living Trust, particularly where special circumstances are

involved (such as caring for a handicapped individual).

In most instances, however, I do not recommend to clients that they share the contents of their Living Trust with their children. Although such a recommendation may sound strange, there is valid logic behind it. When the contents of the Living Trust document are not shared with future heirs, the settlors feel much more at ease in altering the document at any time and for any reason—without feeling guilty or feeling a compunction to explain the reasons behind the changes to their Trust. A Living Trust is a document created to meet the needs of the *settlors*; the document belongs to them, to do with it as they see fit, and no one else really needs to know its contents.

However, always be sure to tell your successor trustee or successor trustees where your Estate Plan Binder and Living Trust documents are located, in the event that something happens to you. It would also be appropriate to inform the successor trustee of the name and address (or telephone number) of the firm that drew up your Trust documents, so that, if there were a fire or for some reason the Trust documents could not be located, the successor trustees would know where to get a duplicate copy of the Trust documents. (See Chapter 13.)

Q: *How old must a child be in order to be a successor trustee?*
A: The minimum age for a successor trustee is eighteen years. (See Chapter 8.)

Q: *How is the successor trustee forced to abide by the wishes of the creators of the Living Trust?*
A: To me, the greater part of the word *trustee* is *trust*. Consequently, a trustee should be someone whom you trust. Two or three children acting together as successor co-trustees can often be better than only one child, particularly when there is a question about the proper way to handle various aspects of the estate. Successor co-trustees tend to monitor each other. Every parent should have his or her children read the section of this book titled "Successor Trustee" in Chapter 8, so that each

of them understands his or her fiduciary responsibility as successor trustee.

Q: *Are the successor trustees personally liable for the debts of the Living Trust?*
A: The successor trustees are not responsible (liable) for debts attributable to the Living Trust. A creditor has a claim solely against the assets of the *Trust*—not against the trustees (assuming, of course, that the successor trustees have acted in good faith and have not abused their capacity as successor trustees). If, on the other hand, a successor trustee has illegally appropriated funds from the Trust, then a creditor would obviously have a right to those funds.

If the liabilities in the Living Trust exceed the value of the assets in the Trust, the successor trustees are *not* responsible for making good on those debts. (See Chapter 8.)

REQUIREMENTS

A frequent fear of many people concerns the "requirements" of the Living Trust; in other words, what restrictions would be placed on an individual or on the control of his or her assets if the assets were in a Living Trust? Frankly, your control over your assets does not change one iota, whether you have your assets inside or outside a Living Trust.

Q: *Is there a federal or state agency that watches over Living Trusts?*
A: No federal or state agency "watches over" the trustees of a Living Trust (either surviving trustees or successor trustees). In other words, Big Brother is *not* watching over you.

Q: *Are there any restrictions on how the surviving spouse can use the estate?*
A: Remember that a surviving spouse has the right to do anything he or she desires with the Survivor's A Trust, because that part of the Trust is solely under his or her personal direction. In addition, in an A-B Trust, the surviving spouse typically has the right to *all* of the income from the Decedent's B Trust, the right to the principal of the B Trust (as necessary to

maintain the same standard of living), and also the right of 5 percent of the assets in the B Trust or $5,000 (whichever is greater) once a year for any reason, regardless of how frivolous. The children, on the other hand, are specifically restricted to the provisions of the Trust, and they must adhere to the provisions without any alteration whatsoever. (See Chapter 7.)

TAXES

When an individual dies, two types of taxes suddenly make an appearance. The first type is the combination of federal estate tax and state inheritance tax. The second type, the yearly income tax, will also take its bite one more time. Under the concept of the federal estate tax, Uncle Sam says that he is in business with you; however, upon your death, he wants out, and he wants his interest right now. Congress has decreed, to everyone's benefit (at least at the present), that each person has a federal estate tax exclusion of $1 million.

As long as the total value of an estate is under $1 million, Uncle Sam will not get any estate taxes at all. If you are married and have done *proper* estate planning (have a Living Trust), Uncle Sam will not get any estate taxes upon the first spouse to die. However, once the federal estate tax exclusions have been exhausted ($1 million for a single person and $2 million for a married couple), Uncle Sam will eventually get his share. If you are single, the tax rate begins at 41 percent of every dollar beyond $1 million. If you are married, the tax rate begins at 41 percent of every dollar beyond $1 million. The tax rate rises to 49 percent at $2 million and then at 49 percent of everything after $2 million.

What is most important to emphasize, though, is that the tax is on the estate—not on the heirs. Strangely, although the states justify their inheritance tax based on the right of the assets to pass to the heirs, in fact, the tax is imposed upon the estate (and paid by the estate) *before* any distribution is made to the heirs. Once the taxes are paid, the assets pass to the heirs and are thereafter free of any estate taxes.

Income will continue to be paid, as earned, on investments. The Living Trust may pay the income to the heirs, and the heirs must include such income on their personal income tax returns. If the Trust is irrevocable, the Trust may retain the income in trust, and the trustee must then file a Trust income tax return, including any Trust income in the Trust tax return.

Q: *What is a Q-TIP Trust?*
A: The term *Q-TIP Trust* stands for "Qualified Terminal Interest Property" Trust, which is simply an extension of the Living Trust created to hold any part of the decedent's assets that exceed the $1 million limit (one federal estate tax exclusion) usually placed in the Decedent's Trust B.

Even though such a long name sounds imposing, the Q-TIP Trust (also referred to as a C Trust) allows taxes on a large estate to be deferred until both spouses have died. For example, if you are married, have an A-B-C Trust, and have an estate that exceeds $2 million, and if the surviving spouse has the right to the income of the assets in the Q-TIP Trust, then the surviving spouse has the right to elect to defer paying any taxes upon the death of the first spouse. The Q-TIP Trust specifically assures that the assets of the decedent spouse will go to the heirs as so specified. (See Chapter 6.)

Q: *What is the Unlimited Marital Deduction, and how does it differ from the federal estate tax equivalent exemption?*
A: In 1981, Congress created what is called the Unlimited Marital Deduction, which gives a spouse the right to gift all of his or her assets to his or her surviving spouse without any gift or estate tax impact.

Generally speaking, the Unlimited Marital Deduction applies to a husband and wife who do not have a Living Trust. One spouse can, in effect, gift all of his or her assets to the other spouse.

If a husband and wife are astute enough to have a Living Trust, the Unlimited Marital Deduction applies as well—but the provisions of a well-written Trust utilize the Decedent's B Trust and, where appropriate, the C Trust. This action preserves both $1 million federal estate tax exclusions and assures that the decedent's assets will eventually pass to the heirs as specified.

The Decedent's Trust B and the C Trust allow people to put their assets in trust and gift the income from those assets to the surviving spouse (as well as the rights to those assets for life, as described in Chapters 6 and 7), and no federal estate tax will be computed until the death of the second spouse.

The Unlimited Marital Deduction can be both a blessing and a disadvantage. For example, if you have a Loving Will (instead of a Living Trust) and an estate whose value exceeds $1 million, by passing all of your assets to the surviving spouse with the Unlimited Marital Deduction, you effectively throw away one of the federal estate tax exclusions. (This subject is more fully discussed in Chapter 6.)

Q: *What is the federal estate tax exclusion?*
A: The federal estate tax exclusion is comparable to exempting $1 million for *each* spouse from federal estate taxes. Thus, if you have a Loving Will and an estate that exceeds $1 million and if you pass the entire estate to your surviving spouse, you throw away one of your federal estate tax exclusions.

If, on the other hand, you have an A-B Trust, you preserve the federal estate tax exclusions of *both* spouses and, therefore, can have an estate valued at up to $2 million before any federal estate taxes must be paid. (See Chapter 6.)

Q: *How do I file an income tax return with a Living Trust?*
A: In 1981, Congress specifically mandated that a Trust tax return (Form 1041) should *not* be filed for a revocable Trust (that is, a Living Trust). However, upon the death of a spouse, the decedent's share (the B Trust) becomes irrevocable, and the surviving spouse must then file a Trust tax return.

With a Living Trust, the Trust tax return should be nothing more than an information return, because all of the income is usually paid out from the Decedent's Trust B to the surviving spouse. (See Chapter 7 for a more in-depth discussion of this subject.)

If you are single, your Living Trust becomes irrevocable upon your death. In the same manner, if you are married, the Trust becomes irrevocable upon the death of both husband and wife. If any assets are retained in trust, a Trust tax return must be filed each year. The tax return shows the income of the Decedent's Trust B and the income paid out. Any income that is retained in the Decedent's Trust B is taxable to the Trust. Therefore, you compute the taxes on the income and pay the taxes due, since the Trust is treated as a separate tax entity. (See Chapter 7.)

Q: *Can a Living Trust shelter my income from income taxes?*
A: A Living Trust does not in any way act as a tax shelter for income taxes. A revocable Trust is transparent, because the Internal Revenue Service says that, as long as the Trust is revocable, there is no impact upon income tax. You must continue to file your income tax return (the normal Form 1040 individual tax return) as you have in the past.

Upon the death of a spouse, the decedent's half of an A-B Trust becomes irrevocable and is thereafter treated as a special tax entity. Under current tax laws, filing a Trust tax return for the Decedent's B Trust provides no income tax advantage. (See Chapter 7.)

Q: *Will I lose any of my income tax deductions by placing my assets in a revocable Living Trust?*
A: No, tax deductions are *not* lost by placing your assets in a Living Trust. A Living Trust is transparent as far as income is concerned. A revocable Trust has absolutely no impact upon income taxes from either an income or expense viewpoint. With a Living Trust, you will continue to file your Form 1040 Individual Income Tax Return, as you have in the past. (See Chapter 7.)

Q: *Is the cost of a Living Trust tax deductible?*
A: Yes, the cost of creating a Living Trust is tax deductible. However, you must first subtract the cost of the Pour-Over Wills, which, though minimally priced, are *not* tax deductible. Innumerable tax cases have clearly established that the cost of a Living Trust for "estate tax planning" purposes is tax deductible. However, such a tax deduction comes under "Miscellaneous Expenses," and, because of the 1986 tax code, miscellaneous expenses must exceed 2 percent of your adjusted gross income in order to have any effect.

Q: *If I put my home in a Living Trust, can I still deduct my mortgage interest?*
A: Since a revocable Living Trust has no impact upon income taxes and since you are still in control of your assets, you will continue to file your income and expenses—including your mortgage interest—on your Form 1040 income tax return, as you have done in the past. (See Chapter 7.)

Q: *Do I place rental properties in my Living Trust, and, if so, how is the rent treated?*
A: Yes, you should put your rental properties into your Living Trust. The rental income will be recorded on your Form 1040, just as before, as will the depreciation expense on your rental real estate. (See Chapter 7.)

Q: *Will having a Living Trust affect my social security benefits?*
A: A Living Trust will have no impact on your social security benefits. Social security benefits are considered income, and the Living Trust has no effect upon income received. (See Chapter 7.)

ASSETS

When assets are transferred from an individual or individuals and placed in the name of the Living Trust, the process involves simply changing the title (ownership) of the asset to the name of the Trust. The individual who *controls* those assets has not changed at all. In other words, you retain the same control over your assets once they are in the Trust, in exactly the same manner as before you had placed the assets in the Trust.

Q: *Is it costly to transfer assets into the Living Trust?*

A: Except for real estate deeds, transferring assets into a Living Trust should have no cost. Legal counsel should transfer real estate deeds, unless you specialize in this particular area. The cost of transferring deeds should be nominal (less than $100). All other assets can be transferred by letter of transfer, and no fee should be charged. Stocks and bonds typically should be transferred by your stockbroker, as a service to you, without fee. Overall, the cost of transferring your assets into the Trust should be minimal. (See Chapter 14.)

Q: *Who transfers the assets into the Living Trust?*

A: With the exception of your grant deeds and trust deeds (which should be transferred by legal counsel), you can easily transfer the assets into the Trust yourself by using the appropriate transfer letters. (See Chapter 14.)

Q: *Can I transfer my assets from my Living Trust?*

A: The settlor is the individual who places the assets into the Trust, and this same individual (or individuals) has the absolute right to also transfer those assets from the Trust or do whatever is desired with those assets. (See Chapter 14.)

Q: *Can I sell my assets once they are in a Living Trust?*

A: You have exactly the same control over your assets—the right to buy, sell, or transfer the assets—when they are in the Trust as you did when the assets were outside the Trust. (See Chapter 8.)

Q: *What do I do with the cash I receive from the sale of my home, which is in my Living Trust?*

A: Until you are ready to make another investment, you should place the proceeds from the sale of your home in a savings account that is already in the name of the Living Trust. It is extremely important that you do *not* place such a large amount of money in a checking account—if it is outside your Living Trust. If you do so and you or your spouse dies, those funds in your checking account outside your Trust *must* go through probate! (See Chapter 14.)

Q: *How are assets acquired after my Living Trust is created?*

A: Acquiring assets after you have a Living Trust is done just as easily as before. Simply tell your real estate broker, stockbroker, or bank officer to record title to the asset in the name of your Living Trust. It really is that simple! (See Chapter 14.)

Q: *What should be inside my Living Trust?*

A: For your Living Trust to be effective, every asset must be inside your Trust. (See Chapter 14.)

Q: *Do I need to change ownership of my stocks and bonds?*

A: Absolutely! *All* of your assets must be recorded in the name of your Living Trust, in order to avoid probate. (See Chapter 14.)

Q: *Do I need to transfer ownership of stocks and bonds that are held in street name?*

A: Yes, stocks held in street name also should be transferred. Simply have your brokerage account changed to the name of your Living Trust. (See Chapter 14.)

Q: *Will my homeowner's policy be affected by the Living Trust, and do I need to notify my insurance company?*

A: Your homeowner's insurance policy will automatically follow the asset. Thus, your homeowner's insurance policy need not be placed in the name of your Living Trust, nor do you need to advise your insurance company of the change in ownership (that is, putting the house into the Trust). (See Chapter 14.)

Q: *Will I lose my $250,000 exemption on my home if it is in a revocable Living Trust?*

A: No, you will not lose your homeowner's exemption by placing your home in the name of the Living Trust. However, if you have an A-B Trust and a spouse dies—and you are planning to utilize this $250,000 exemption—it is recommended that you retain the house in the Survivor's A Trust rather than putting the home in the irrevocable Decedent's Trust B. (See Chapters 14 and 15.)

Q: *Should I transfer my mortgage into the Living Trust?*
A: Transferring your mortgage into the Living Trust is not necessary, because liabilities follow assets. You are transferring your assets, not the liabilities associated with those assets. (See Chapter 7.)

Q: *If I place my home in the Living Trust, will it affect my mortgage? Can the mortgage company "call" my mortgage?*
A: There is no effect on your mortgage when you place your home inside the Living Trust. Many clients are concerned about the change of ownership in their property when it is placed in the name of the Trust. Such a change of ownership does *not* trigger the "entire balance due and payable" clause in many mortgages—because the same individuals continue to maintain control of the real estate. (See Chapter 14.)

Q: *By placing my home inside the Living Trust, will I cause my home to be reappraised under California's Proposition 13 or similar property tax rollback provisions in other states?*
A: No, your home will not be reappraised by placing it in your Living Trust. Four months after Proposition 13 was passed, for example, the California state legislature specifically addressed the issue of reappraisal and legislated (by Constitutional article) that your real estate would not be reappraised under Proposition 13 if you place your home or other real estate into a revocable Living Trust. You also avoid reappraisal in other states that have similar property tax rollback provisions. (See Chapter 14.)

Q: *Do I have to value my assets as they go into the Living Trust?*
A: Valuation of your assets before putting them into a Living Trust is totally unnecessary. Such

an action would accomplish nothing useful or legally required. The only time you need to value your assets would be upon the death of one of the settlors, at which time the new valuation would be needed to substantiate stepped-up valuation. Obtaining a current valuation when a settlor dies is extremely important. (See Chapter 14.)

Q: *Should I record our cemetery plots in the name of the Living Trust?*
A: Cemetery plots do not need to be recorded in the name of the Living Trust. Such plots are not really considered to be real estate, in the true sense of the term. The value of cemetery plots is usually very small in relation to the overall value of the estate. (See Chapter 13.)

Q: *Should my personal effects be placed inside the Living Trust?*
A: Years of experience have shown that it is better to transfer your personal effects into the Living Trust. A document entitled "Assignment of Furniture, Furnishings, and Personal Effects," which is provided to all of our clients, is used to transfer all untitled assets (such as furniture, appliances, furnishings, antiques, artworks, china, silverware, glass, jewelry, books, wearing apparel, and so on) into the Trust without having to inventory them. By transferring all of the personal effects into the Trust, you eliminate any future conflict among the heirs. (See Chapter 11.)

Q: *Should I put my safe-deposit box in the name of my Living Trust?*
A: Yes, it is advisable to put your safe-deposit box in the name of the Living Trust. (See Chapter 14.)

Q: *Is there anything that I should not put into the Living Trust?*
A: Everything must go into the Trust, in order to avoid probate. (See Chapter 14.)

Q: *Should an expensive car go into the Living Trust?*
A: Any automobile of unusually high value should be recorded in the name of the Living

Trust. The motor vehicle department will make such a transfer for you. All you need to do is fill out a simple form. As a precautionary measure, you should record in the name of the Trust all of your vehicles. (See Chapter 14.)

Q: *Do I put recreational vehicles and boats into the Living Trust?*
A: Yes, such items should be put into the Living Trust, because they are usually of substantial value. Putting such items into the Trust acts as a precautionary measure against the possibility of probate. (See Chapter 14.)

Q: *Can I borrow against my assets in my Living Trust?*
A: Whether your assets are inside or outside your Trust, your ability to borrow money against them (that is, use the assets as collateral for a loan) is not affected in any way. (See Chapter 9.)

Q: *Can I pledge my Living Trust as collateral for a loan?*
A: Pledging your Living Trust as collateral for a loan does not satisfy lenders. You may pledge your assets, but not your Trust. Think about the question from the viewpoint of the lender: If you have control over your Living Trust and pledge your Living Trust as collateral, the lending institution has no assurance that you would not withdraw those assets from the Living Trust, leaving the lending institution with a Living Trust that contains no assets. (See Chapter 8.)

Q: *Should my life insurance policies be placed inside the Living Trust?*
A: Your Living Trust should be the beneficiary of all of your life insurance policies. By making your Trust the beneficiary of all policies, you will avoid probate, regardless of who may die simultaneously with the insured person. If your Trust is *not* the beneficiary of your life insurance policies (and you and the beneficiary die simultaneously), the insurance money must go through probate before the money can pass from the now-deceased beneficiary to any heirs.

It always makes good sense to name your Living Trust as the recipient of all of your ben-

eficial assets. Then, in the future, when you want to make any type of change, you need only change the Trust instrument, and not each of the policies. (See Chapter 14.)

Q: *Should I put IRAs and Keoghs inside the Living Trust?*
A: The Living Trust should be the *contingent beneficiary* of IRAs and Keoghs. The Living Trust should never be the *owner* of your IRAs or Keoghs, because that is comparable to an outright distribution. (See Chapter 14.)

Q: *What happens if one or both spouses have separate property?*
A: In the case where husband and/or wife have separate property, the spouses should use Separate Property Agreements when their assets are placed in the Living Trust. The separate property will go into the Trust in the Trust name, but the assets will retain the characteristics of separate property. (See Chapter 9.)

Q: *Is there any circumstance where I should keep any assets outside the Living Trust, so they can be probated?*
A: No. If it is ultimately deemed necessary to probate an asset or assets to discharge a creditor's claim, the trustee is authorized to remove such assets from trust and to process them through probate.

Even though the probate process may be long and arduous, the probate court looks at civil suits in a very different manner. The objective of the probate court is to dispatch any civil claim as swiftly as possible; settlement is typically completed within a four-month period and without a jury. In contrast, civil suits can be dragged through the courts for as long as five years. The one advantage of the probate court in such situations is that it effectively shortstops a potentially long civil suit. (See Chapter 7.)

Q: *Do I need to liquidate the Living Trust assets in order to distribute the assets?*
A: No, liquidation of the Living Trust assets is not required. Preferably, the assets will be distributed directly to the heirs, rather than selling the assets and then distributing the resultant cash. For example, a real estate deed

may be simply recorded in the name of one or more of the heirs (without their having to first sell the home or property). (See Chapter 9.)

PERCEIVED DISADVANTAGES

Q: *What are the disadvantages of a Living Trust?*
A: After more than twenty-five years of working with the Living Trust, I have yet to find a disadvantage to a *well-drawn* Living Trust that is accompanied by a well-designed estate-planning program. All too frequently, however, I see Trusts that ultimately become nightmares. In fact, one of the primary objectives of writing this book is to help people identify the characteristics of a good Living Trust.

The following statements address what some people *perceive* to be disadvantages of a Living Trust. Bear in mind that a well-written Trust (along with a good estate-planning program) should overcome or prevent the perceived disadvantages from becoming real.

The Living Trust document may be poorly written. This book should help you to identify the difference between a poorly drawn Trust and a well-written Trust. A poorly drawn Trust can be particularly disastrous upon the death of a trustor (settlor). In contrast, a well-drawn Trust, which includes the provisions outlined in Chapter 10, has absolutely no disadvantages. Indeed, such a Trust literally identifies and provides for every possible contingency.

The client does not understand the Living Trust. Unfortunately, attorneys are not necessarily good communicators. Thus, even the best estate-planning attorney may create an outstanding document but fail to convey an adequate understanding of the Trust to a client.

The assets are not placed in the Living Trust. All too often, Trusts are well written, but the assets have not been recorded in the name of the Trust. Recognize that a Living Trust that is not funded by having assets placed in the name of the Trust is nothing more than a Testamentary Trust—which does not avoid the probate process. For a Living Trust to be truly effective, all of the assets must be recorded in the Trust. Any grant deeds or trust deeds should be redrawn and recorded in the name of your Trust. Letters of transfer should be provided to enable you to transfer all of your assets into your Trust. (See Chapter 14.)

The Living Trust failed to meet the client's needs. Even the best estate-planning attorney often fails to do an in-depth client financial analysis; therefore, even though the attorney may draw an outstanding Living Trust, the Trust may lack adequate provisions to cover the individual circumstances of the client. For example, a Trust drawn for an estate that exceeds $2 million might not include a C Trust, or a Trust drawn for a client who has substantial amounts of insurance might not provide an Insurance Preservation Trust (in addition to the basic Living Trust).

If you have read this book, particularly Chapter 16, you should be able to identify for yourself the type of Trust and provisions that you should have. You need not rely on the judgment of others; you are now the master of your own destiny.

It costs $500 to $1,000 to update the Living Trust. Death and taxes are inevitable—and just as inevitable is the knowledge that Congress will change the estate tax laws about every five years. It should be the responsibility of the person or firm who drew up your Living Trust to notify you of any appropriate tax changes that would benefit your situation. Further, it is the responsibility of the same individual or firm to organize the Trust in such a manner that the Trust can be quickly reviewed and economically updated when the need arises.

When you have a Living Trust drawn up, you have the right to be assured that you will be notified of any necessary updates to your Trust, and that such updates will be reasonably priced, and to know, ahead of time, the cost of such updates. (See Chapter 18.)

A Living Trust can be expensive, ranging from $750 to $3,500 or more. With the sophisticated computer equipment now available, a good Living Trust can be made available to everyone and can be priced within a reasonable range. This area has been addressed directly in Chapter 18, which specifically identifies what a good Trust should cost when you utilize today's sophisticated computers.

Even though the Living Trust avoids probate, it is still quite costly to settle the estate. Most Living Trusts can be settled by the surviving spouse and/or heirs—without requiring the services of an attorney. Settling large estates may well require the services of an estate-planning attorney, but settling the average estate does *not* require the services of legal counsel. In fact, all too often, I see attorneys either charging unnecessary fees to "settle" an estate in a Living Trust or trying to settle an estate in a Living Trust when they do not have the slightest idea of what they are doing. (See Chapter 15.)

Financial institutions charge excessive fees for managing the assets in a Living Trust and generate very little return on investments. Although this is not always the case, it is certainly true that selecting a financial institution as your successor trustee is seldom a wise move. The ideal successor trustee(s) for your Living Trust should be your adult children, close family members, or close friends. For a more detailed description of who would best serve as the successor trustee, refer to Chapter 8.

──────────── Appendix H ────────────

American Association of Retired Persons (AARP) Study

The American Association of Retired Persons (AARP) commissioned a two-year study conducted by attorneys on probate titled *A Report on Probate: Consumer Perspectives and Concerns*. The AARP study, published in 1990, is one of the most comprehensive and perceptive analyses of the probate system done to date, and it deserves far more credit and publicity than have been given it.

This study produced some very convincing evidence that the probate process is inflicting undue strain and emotional and financial duress on the unsuspecting public. It also presented a strong message that consumers should be educated about the evils of probate and about simple alternatives to avoid it.

Sadly, after publishing this revealing study about probate practices, AARP did little to publicize the existence of this excellent document. Thus, thousands of retired people—those needing the advice the most—failed to learn about the horrors and financial consequences of the tactics being used by the Will and Probate attorneys.

The AARP study made a very significant comment about Wills versus Living Trusts:

> Generally, it costs more to set up a living trust than to draft a *will*. But the cost for drafting a trust can be less in the long run than the combined cost of an inexpensive *will* and the ensuing expense of probate. . . . Those who go to an attorney and merely ask for a *will* may get less, and pay more, than they bargained for.

EXTRACTS FROM THE AARP STUDY

The following paragraphs present important information contained in the AARP study.

The Purpose of Probate Is to Pay Creditors

The AARP Study quoted Professor John Langbein of the University of Chicago, who wrote in a *Harvard Law Review* article, "Many of the details of American probate procedure, as well as much of its larger structure, would not exist but for the need to identify and pay off creditors. These procedures are indispensable, but . . . only for the most exceptional cases. In general, creditors do not need or use probate."

The AARP study went on to say, "Langbein surveyed several retail companies and found that credit departments for major stores do not read legal newspapers for information about deceased debtors. One credit officer, reported Langbein, estimates that 95 percent of these outstanding debts are paid at the initiative of the survivors. The debts of the other 5 percent, usually involving unmarried persons, get paid after collections personnel inquire about the account."

Professor Langbein continues, "Even creditors who traditionally use probate are now beginning to question the system's usefulness. . . ." The AARP study stated, "Provided that family members can agree on how to divide the deceased person's property, and pay the deceased's debts, there is little need for probate."

Education Is Needed

The AARP study made some very strong recommendations that consumers be educated about the evils of probate and simple alternatives. Specifically, the study recommended that "aging organizations should provide information to older consumers about estate-planning issues, including (1) information about the procedural and cost problems of probate . . . [and] (2) information about alternatives to probate such as living trusts. . . ." The study also recommended that "state and local bar associations should require members of the probate bar, when drafting a will, to disclose the estimated cost of the eventual probate proceeding. . . . Clients should be informed of any percentages currently charged for probate and how this might affect the assets they intend to pass to survivors."

Probate Avoidance Is Common

The AARP document stated, "The use of alternative methods of succession, that is, of transferring property after death, appears to be growing. The popularity of living trusts, [and] joint tenancies, . . . give evidence that many people would rather side-step the cost, delay, and lack of privacy in probate court. These efforts to avoid probate appear to be warranted. The potential for unfair fees in an unnecessary proceeding is reason enough to seek alternatives."

The AARP study found that a startling 90 percent of all the estates of widows and widowers age 60 and above will go through probate. This practice is the obvious result of spouses holding property in joint tenancy (or, where applicable, in community property) with the survivor taking all. The two prime disadvantages of this approach are that the decedent spouse's $1 million federal estate tax equivalent exemption is thrown away, and even though probate can be avoided on the first to die, it cannot be avoided on the estate of the surviving spouse.

Probate Is a "Cash Cow" for Attorneys

The AARP study noted that "John McCabe, the Legislative Director for the National Conference of Commissioners on Uniform State Laws, once remarked, 'The probate process has been a cash cow for attorneys. Small law firms pay their basic office expenses with probate fees.' And one attorney sardonically notes that probate practice traditionally has been a 'guaranteed retirement annuity program' for attorneys. Small firms and solo practitioners in probate practice do more than pay the phone bills with these fees. They make a good living on them."

According to AARP, "Many attorneys in smaller firms have built lucrative practices handling probate for the modest estates of the middle class. Indeed, small firms dominate probate practice. In one state, the results . . . show that law firms with fewer than ten attorneys handled 80 percent of the probate cases, and nearly half of those went to solo practitioners. In another state, small firms handled fully 95 percent of probate cases."

Nationally, the AARP study projects the combined cost of attorney and personal representative fees to be nearly *$2 billion* annually. Attorney fees alone could constitute more than $1.5 billion of that amount. In addition, probate generates hundreds of millions more for bonding companies, appraisers, and probate courts themselves.

The *Will* Is the Attorney's Ticket to Probate

The AARP report found that "attorneys lay the groundwork for their probate practice by writing *wills*. Some use *wills* as a 'loss leader.' [They] write *wills* cheaply as a way to generate other business [specifically, future probate business]. . . . When the client later dies, the same attorney, or another member of the firm, probates the *will* at a fee high enough to recover any money lost on the earlier discount."

The American Association of Retired Persons study noted that ". . . the American Bar Association (ABA) identified two problems this practice ['loss leader' *wills*] creates for consumers. The first, the committee wrote, is that the practice of charging 'less than a reasonable fee [for drafting a *will*] may lower the quality of planning work done and thereby results in a disservice to the client.' Second, attorneys 'may be tempted to charge the estate a higher than appropriate fee to compensate for the bargain given on . . . the [will] drafting work.' Thus, consumers may not get a *will* that meets their estate planning needs, and in the end the attorney's fee could be excessive to compensate for the earlier bargain."

The AARP report stated that its "results are consistent with another study, in which 43 percent of the attorneys surveyed reported that their probate business derives from deceased persons for whom they wrote a *will*. The AARP document pointed out that ". . . the client who goes to a general practice lawyer for estate planning services may get a *will* because a *will* is what the attorney knows best, not because a *will* best suits the client. . . . [In fact], the attorney may never mention that living trusts exist." A case in point is a client who went to an attorney in the state of Washington and specifically

requested a Living Trust and, $1,800 later, received a *will*.

A Different Estate-Planning Option

The AARP study noted that "another issue related to the ABA committee's concern about low-quality estate-planning work is whether attorneys actively inform their clients about estate-planning options other than wills. The living, or inter vivos, trust can be a reasonably priced alternative to a will and it avoids probate altogether."

While Unnecessary, Probate Is Both Time-Consuming and Costly

As the AARP study put it, ". . . probate is costly and time consuming. Nationally, probate fees—for attorney and personal representative services alone—could cost $2 billion or more each year. . . ." In contrast, our studies indicate that a more realistic, current figure is $14 billion.

The AARP report analyzed three states—California, Wisconsin, and Delaware—as the most representative of the three different methods of charging probate fees nationwide. The study found that the average time in the probate process was one year and three months, and the average cost of probate consumed 5 to 10 percent of the gross estate. (Gross estate is the total value of your estate prior to any reduction for liabilities such as mortgages or loans.)

The AARP document stated that "In some cases, attorney's fees consume 20 percent or more of estate value. This is especially true of small estates. For the estates of the middle class, attorney and personal representative fees can deplete the assets by as much as 10 percent even in uncomplicated cases."

It further states, "Aside from the cost, probate is time consuming. With redundant reporting requirements, and flexible 'deadlines' that are often unenforced or ignored, probate frequently lasts more than a year. (In one state, probate requires notification to every possible heir by right of intestacy, regardless of what the will specifies: This is an incredibly unnecessary burden placed upon any estate.)"

The AARP report determined that "probate's procedures and protections, even with recent reforms, are inappropriate for all but the most exceptional cases. And, attorney's fees in connection with probate work are unreasonable."

Original Premise Confirmed

The AARP study convincingly affirms the initial premise of the first edition of *The Living Trust*—that probate is unnecessary! If the only function of probate is to pay creditors who aren't using the process in the first place, then probate is an obsolete system foisted upon an unwitting public for the sole purpose of lining attorneys' pockets—and $2 billion dollars annually in probate fees is a tempting gold mine for far too many attorneys. (We estimate that the Will and Probate attorney's fees are closer to $14 billion dollars annually.)

Appendix I

Fact vs. Fallacy: Misrepresentation by Will and Probate Attorneys

With more than $14 billion in probate fees being collected each year by the Will and Probate attorneys, many of them are now misrepresenting the advantage of a Living Trust—with the intent of making you believe that a Will is really a better means to handle the settlement of your estate. If these attorneys can create sufficient doubt in your mind about creating a Living Trust, they have won their battle. Why? The reason is simple: If you choose to create a Will, or choose to do nothing, *you lose*, and the attorneys siphon money from *your* estate that would otherwise go to *your* heirs.

YOUR RIGHT TO INTELLIGENT CHOICE IS BEING DENIED

All people should have the right to make their own informed decisions about whether they want to subject their heirs to the agonies and expense of probate or whether they want to create a Living Trust. Unfortunately, you are being disenfranchised by the attorneys. Your right to choose between a Will and a Living Trust is being systematically distorted by their presenting you with misstatements of the facts concerning the pros and cons of Wills versus Living Trusts.

The only way to avoid probate is to create a Living Trust and to then place all of your assets inside the Trust.

The Will and Probate attorneys are currently waging a very aggressive campaign of misinformation to purposely confuse you. With more than $14 billion at stake (yearly probate fees from all those people with Wills who have died), the attorneys are desperately trying to protect their vested interests—at the expense of the consumer—by writing misleading arti-

363

cles in every type of forum, including their own legal periodicals.

Many of the arguments against the Living Trust are similar to saying that you should not buy a car because it won't run unless you put gas in it! The concept of a Living Trust, although more than twelve hundred years old, is a new subject to most of the American public who are not involved in the legal profession. Because the concept of a Living Trust is a new and complex concept to most people, the average consumer is not able to understand, and then refute, the many misstatements that are continually being made about Living Trusts. The natural tendency of people who don't understand something is to simply ignore it—and that is just what the Will and Probate attorneys are hoping you will do.

The intent of this appendix is to respond to many of the fallacies (misstatements) that are being printed almost daily in an effort to convince you that a Will is better for you than a Living Trust. By carefully reading this appendix, you will be better informed about the less-than-whole truths being perpetrated by the Will and Probate attorneys, as well as the facts about the subject matter. Once you are informed, it is then up to you to make your own decision about which legal vehicle (a Will or a Living Trust) is better for your particular estate.

Remember: *You* must make the choice!

FACT VS. FALLACY

Now let's review, by major subject areas, the misrepresentations being made *for* Wills and *against* Living Trusts by the Will and Probate attorneys. In the following material, the **Fallacy** is the misleading or totally untrue statement being perpetrated on the unsuspecting public, and the **Fact** is my response from the vantage point of having more than twenty-five years of experience with well-written Living Trusts.

Tactic: You Need a Will

Many misleading statements are made, trying to convince the public that a Will is "still the way to go." There are several fallacies that are stated by attorneys to supposedly support the need for a Will, even though you may already have a Living Trust.

Fallacy: You can avoid probate with a good Will.
Fact: Wrong! The words *Will* and *Probate*, unfortunately, are synonymous. If you have a Will, you *will* go through probate!

Fallacy: With a Living Trust, you still need a Will. You will need it to handle unforeseen contingencies as well as to name a guardian for your minor children.
Fallacy: It will be necessary to have a Will in order to cover those assets that may *not* be transferred into Living Trusts. These assets excluded from the Trust will still be subject to probate.
Fallacy: A "pour-over" provision can drop any remaining assets into trust upon death.
Fact: Every well-written Living Trust includes a whole host of contingency provisions to be sure that your Trust works in all situations. Rather than include a guardian in the Pour-Over Will, it is simpler and more versatile to name a guardian by using a separate Appointment of Guardian document.

Every good Trust includes a Pour-Over Will, but remember that anything of significant value left outside the Trust *must* go through probate *before* it can be placed in the Trust.

Fallacy: Only a Will can appoint guardians for minor children.
Fact: Guardians of minor or handicapped children may be named in the Pour-Over Will of a Living Trust, or, as is often done in a well-written Trust, in a separate Appointment of Guardian document.

Tactic: Probate Is Not Objectionable

In their efforts to dissuade the public from getting Living Trusts, the Will and Probate attorneys continually barrage the printed media with articles purporting to give reasons why Wills and the resultant process of probate are "not really that bad." However, many of these arguments are either blatantly false or are very misleading, particularly to people who are not familiar with Living Trusts.

Fallacy: You cannot save money by placing your assets in a Living Trust. Probate fees as such are trifling: $1,000 or thereabouts, so any savings is minor.

Fallacy: In our state, we have an extremely simplified probate system, and, therefore, the expense of a Living Trust to avoid probate is absolutely unnecessary.

Fallacy: Since the new trend is for attorneys to charge by the hour rather than based on a percentage of the estate for probate fees, attorney fees may be negligible when compared with the value of the estate in probate proceedings not involving extraordinary problems.

Fact: These misleading arguments are all too common—and have absolutely no basis in fact. We initiated our own extensive study of probate in the state of Washington because of the state's claims of having a very simplified probate system and using an hourly fee system. Washington is typical of the many states claiming to have a simplified probate system. However, the study results directly contradicted the claims of the Washington attorneys. One example stands out in our probate study that clearly refutes these fallacious statements: The probate of a $10,000 estate incurred a probate fee of $7,400—wiping out nearly 75 percent of the estate!

Unfortunately, such outrageous probate fees are much too common.

Our study showed that in 80 percent of the cases examined, it would have been less expensive to have purchased a $1,500 Living Trust than to have paid the probate fees, which ranged from an average of 4 percent to 54 percent of the estate's value!

Fallacy: In spite of all of the hoopla you have heard, probate only takes one to three months or, at the most, six to seven months unless you leave a large estate and someone contests it.

Fallacy: In large estates (where a federal estate tax return is due), significant time may not be saved with a Living Trust, because trustees may not wish to distribute assets until estate tax returns have been filed.

Fact: These fallacies represent all-too-common arguments—with absolutely no basis in fact—used almost daily by the attorneys. The AARP study (see Appendix H) showed that the average time of probate was *588 days!* Our independent study of the state of Washington showed that the average time of probate varied from thirteen months to more than three and one-half years.

After doing more than forty thousand Trusts, I have yet to see a Living Trust successfully contested, although more than 30 percent of Wills are successfully contested.

A good (well-written) Living Trust gives the trustee the power to distribute assets almost immediately. With a Living Trust, an estate can be settled in a matter of hours instead of the usual year or more required with probate.

The beauty of a Living Trust is that complicated estates are simplified and resolved swiftly—which is in sharp contrast to probate, where complicated estates can be an absolute nightmare.

For those large estates that owe estate tax, the trustees will obviously retain the necessary assets to pay the estate taxes that are due (and must be paid) nine months after the date of death. Estate taxes can also be paid early. A nine-month waiting period is certainly less agonizing than the thirteen to forty-two months required by probate.

Tactic: You Can Avoid Probate Without a Living Trust

Occasionally, the Will and Probate attorneys get nervous about the primary advantage of a Living Trust being to avoid the agonies of probate, and they gamely put forth arguments as to how people can avoid probate—but without having a Living Trust.

Fallacy: If you and your spouse own assets jointly and you are planning to leave your assets to your spouse, there is no need for a Living Trust, since such assets do not pass through probate.

Fallacy: Don't create a Living Trust for cash-type estates; they can be separately arranged in joint tenancies.

Fallacy: You don't need a Living Trust, because you can avoid probate with joint tenancy or, where applicable, community property agreements.

Fallacy: There are a lot of assets that can be set up for distribution without probate, thus saving the expenses incident thereto. Assets such as U.S. saving bonds, stocks, bank accounts, time certificates, IRAs, life insurance, retirement benefits, credit union accounts, and the like can be held jointly or have particular beneficiaries designated, thus avoiding probate.

Fact: The AARP probate study revealed that the estates of 90 percent of all widows and widowers over the age of 60 went through probate. Why? The reason is because the people were caught up in (and believed) the false perception about joint tenancy being a favorable way to hold title to property. Yes, the estate can avoid probate on the *first* spouse to die, but *not* on the death of the surviving spouse!

However, there is a shred of truth in the statement made by Will and Probate attorneys to their clients about joint tenancy. If a husband and wife own their assets in joint tenancy, or, where applicable, have created a "community property agreement," upon the death of the first spouse, all the assets will pass to the surviving spouse without going through probate. However, when the second spouse dies, the entire estate must go through probate. There are other forms of ownership that can avoid probate, such as IRAs, life insurance policies, and so on, which pass by *beneficial interest* (i.e., to a named beneficiary).

Be aware, however, that by using joint tenancy or beneficial interest and passing all of an estate to the surviving spouse, one of the couple's $1 million federal estate tax exclusions is essentially "thrown away"—which can be a very costly mistake, indeed, as the assets continue to appreciate in the future.

Also be aware that if you hold your assets (particularly a house) in joint tenancy, the surviving spouse will only get stepped-up valuation on *one-half* of the assets. Don't be fooled. Joint tenancy is the worst of all worlds for your family. Think, for a moment, about what happens if both spouses are killed at the same time in an accident—then, joint tenancy doesn't mean a thing, and the *entire estate* must go through probate.

Remember, you may not have to go through probate for your estate, but your survivors will—being subject to countless hassles and delays, as well as forfeiting a substantial portion of the estate to pay unnecessary probate and attorney fees.

Tactic: A Living Trust Is Not Advisable

Along with repeated misstatements about why you need a Will, many attorneys also put forth a wealth of misleading information about the purported reasons why you don't need a Living Trust.

Fallacy: Living Trusts can be important tools, but they are not for everyone!

Fallacy: Your estate is not large enough to justify having a Living Trust!

Fallacy: For estates that have very little property, no formal probate may be required.

Fallacy: If the estate is very small, there are "summary" proceedings that move quickly and at low cost through the system.

Fallacy: Small estates not subject to federal inheritance taxes may not need trust protection. For some estates, a Will is simpler and more cost effective than a Living Trust.

Fallacy: Married couples can have over $2 million (because of the $1 million federal estate tax exclusion for each spouse) before they have to think about estate taxes.

Fallacy: A Living Trust may be appropriate for an elderly person who in time will not want to be burdened with business decisions. The individual can name several outside trustees to take control of things in due time.

Fact: The statements above (implying that a Living Trust is not for everyone) form the basis of insidious arguments put forth by the Will and Probate attorneys against having a Trust. Our probate study of Washington state showed that *the most severe impact of the cost of probate was on estates of $100,000 or less.*

Remember that real estate is almost always subject to probate. However, even such a simple asset as cash will be subject to probate if it exceeds the minimums identified in Table 2-1 (found in Chapter 2). The argument about using summary proceedings if your estate is small only applies to a very small percentage of estates. If you take a close look at Table 2-1, you will notice that *very few people escape probate*!

A Living Trust *is* particularly ideal for elderly people. It provides the means and designates the individual(s) who is to manage the estate if the settlor(s) becomes incompetent. (As always, I recommend that one or more of your adult children, close family, or close friends be designated as trustees. A financial institution is seldom the right choice.) A Living Trust is equally important for younger people, especially if they have children. It provides the vehicle to hold the estate for the benefit of the minor children.

The previous section of this appendix pointed out the pitfalls of losing stepped-up valuation and throwing away a federal estate tax exclusion—which can be very costly mistakes to estates with highly appreciated assets.

Fallacy: The purpose of today's probate court is to provide a method for the settlement of a person's final affairs.

Fallacy: While a Living Trust can avoid probate, sometimes it is not a good idea to avoid probate!

Fallacy: If you are worried about litigation or creditors, a Will and the probate process may be better able to protect your assets.

Fallacy: After your death, it is beneficial to have your property pass under your Will rather than through a Living Trust.

Fallacy: The probate courts provide safety nets for persons who do not have an updated Will. There are no such safety nets for a poorly prepared or out-of-date Trust.

Fallacy: In a Living Trust, a new trustee would be required to pay the debts of the grantor for up to ten years after his or her death. There is no statute of limitations in a Living Trust that would allow a quick settlement of the Trust.

Fact: Yes, a probate court will settle a person's final affairs. My contention is that the probate court is unnecessary, because a Living Trust does the same thing, but in a matter of hours or days—not months or years as is true with probate.

The argument that your estate should go through probate to avoid creditors' claims or lawsuits is basically meaningless. The AARP study indicated that less than 1 percent of estates are subject to the actions of challenging creditors or lawsuits. If a lawsuit were to arise, the trustee of a well-written Trust would be authorized to remove any assets from the Trust and run them through the probate process to dispose of such claims. Just recently, California established a simple system that allows a trustee to dispense with such potential claims by filing appropriate notice to creditors—without going through the probate process. Other states are reviewing California's legislation and are adopting a similar process.

Probate sales of homes are almost always a disaster for the survivors. Usually the home is put up for sale at the end of the probate process (and the home is often in poor repair by that time). Probate sales are often hurried, and most buyers know that the property can often be picked up at much less than the asking price—because the court or survivors want a quick sale. Such sales are not in the best interests of the survivors.

It is true that a Trust entity cannot directly take advantage of any loss realized on the sale of a depressed property. However, a knowledgeable trustee will distribute the house directly to the heirs (thus removing it from the Trust). When the heirs sell the house, they can then take full advantage of any tax benefits that may accrue.

A *well-written* Trust should not need to be legally updated to cover various contingent situations that may arise. However, if a Trust needs to be updated for some reason, the trustee has the right to petition the probate court (in the same manner as can an executor of an estate with an outdated Will).

To say that the successor trustee would be responsible to pay debts for up to ten years after the grantor's death is a totally misleading statement and is little more than a brazen scare tactic. Any debts of the estate are paid from estate funds, not from the trustee's funds. If there are insufficient funds to pay the debts of the estate, the trustee can then file bankruptcy for the estate.

Fallacy: The following are some of the key disadvantages of a Living Trust:

- reduced opportunities for tax planning
- extension of time in the settlement of your affairs
- reduced protection from the probate court
- probable increase in the ultimate costs of settlement of your estate

Fact: Each of these statements has little or no validity.

The Living Trust is highly versatile when it comes to tax planning—much more so than the average Will. For a married couple, an A-B Trust is the *only way* to preserve both $1 million federal estate tax exclusions. Even though the preservation of the tax exclusions can also be accomplished with a Testamentary Trust, the estate assets must first go through probate—thus incurring enormous and unnecessary probate expense—before the assets can be placed in the Trust.

A Living Trust can be settled almost immediately and needs no extension of time. In contrast, with the probate process,* your estate is tied up for one to two years and will thus require an extension of time to settle your affairs, which simply means more money extracted from your estate that would otherwise have gone to your heirs.

The only protection the probate court offers you is the relatively quick settlement of lawsuits, but the AARP study found that lawsuits happen in less than 1 percent of all probate cases. A well-written Living Trust gives the trustee the power to take an asset or assets through the probate court to settle such an issue, if it is ever necessary to do so.

The AARP study identified that the average cost of probate was 5 percent to 10 percent of the gross estate, while our Washington state probate study identified that the average cost of probate was 4 percent to a maximum of 54 percent of the gross estate. There is no basis for extensive settlement fees for an estate that is protected by a well-written Living Trust.

Fallacy: As with estate and income taxes, there is essentially no protection from creditors through the use of a Living Trust.

Fallacy: Your creditors and claimants have from one to four years to file against your Living Trust, whereas your claimants and creditors have *only four months* during a probate proceeding to file formal claims before they are *barred forever*.

Fact: These issues are discussed over and over again by Will and Probate attorneys. In contrast, however, the AARP study clearly established that less than 1 percent of estates are subject to lawsuits. Having now produced more than forty thousand Trusts and having settled thousands of estates, I have yet to see one Trust successfully challenged with a lawsuit—although Wills are successfully challenged all the time.

California legislation has already established a means for the trustee to very simply publish a notice to creditors, without going through the probate court, and thus force any lawsuits to the forefront within the four-month period. Many state legislatures are following California's lead and implementing similar legislation.

The term *creditor* implies those to whom someone owes money. Neither a Living Trust nor probate will release a person (or the person's estate) from the obligation of paying debts. In almost every case, when the bills come in, the surviving or successor trustee usually pays the bills without question.

The contention that a Living Trust will not protect you from creditors is really referring to potential lawsuits—which are very rare. A well-written Trust provides the trustee with the power to remove assets from the Trust and run them through probate in order to settle a lawsuit. The probate court can discharge such a lawsuit within a four-month period.

Fallacy: Use of a Living Trust can avoid court proceedings to establish a conservatorship, but it only handles your financial affairs. It does not provide for the care of your person if you become unable to make personal decisions as to your care.

Fact: It is true that a Living Trust is not a conservatorship. However, a separate Appointment of Conservator document should be provided as an ancillary document with every well-written Trust. A conservatorship document identifies whom you would want to be responsible for your person in the event that you become incompetent.

Tactic: You Lose Control of Your Assets with a Living Trust

Another scare tactic used by the Will and Probate attorneys is to instill the fear in people that they lose control of their assets if they are placed in a Living Trust. Hogwash!

Fallacy: You will lose control of your assets by placing them in a Living Trust.

Fallacy: The usual problem with most Living Trusts is the same as the problem with outright gifts. If our "wealth" is tied up in our home or our business, we are usually not in a position to part with it while we are alive.

Fact: The statements above are examples of the scare tactics being used to confuse people about Living Trusts. With a well-written Living Trust, you have the same control over your assets in the Trust as if you held them in your own name. In addition, upon your death, the surviving spouse typically *continues* to have that same control over the assets. Your "wealth" is in no way restricted, nor is your home or business. Conversely, remember that disgruntled heirs can easily (and often successfully do) contest a Will, but a well-written Living Trust has not yet been successfully challenged—even by experienced attorneys. With all of your assets in a Living Trust, *your family maintains control* of those assets at all times; whereas, if you have only a Will, control of your assets will be lost to the probate process and the courts.

Fallacy: An A-B Trust between husband and wife requires trust. If one mate or the other has footloose tendencies, turning money over to the surviving spouse may be unwise. This situation is particularly true of a client who is on his or her third marriage.

Fact: A well-written Living Trust gives you complete freedom to grant *or restrict* your assets to or from your surviving spouse. In most cases, a Trust gives the surviving spouse all of the freedom necessary to use the funds, as appropriate, without restriction. With a well-written Living Trust, you can be as generous or penurious as you desire.

For example, one of my clients was an elderly gentleman who had four children, had accumulated an estate worth more than $1 million, had been widowed, and then later remarried. Since his new wife was a spendthrift, the gentleman's Trust named his eldest son as the surviving trustee and, on the gentleman's death, would provide only income to his new wife (with the assets remaining in the Trust under the control of his eldest son). (The income from $1 million, at that time, was over $100,000 per year!)

Tactic: A Living Trust Is More Costly than a Will

With this statement, the Will and Probate attorneys are teasing (as well as misleading) you by mentioning only *part* of the total cost of a Will versus a Living Trust. While the initial fee for *just the creation* of a Will is often less expensive, the *overall end cost to the estate is ultimately much higher* with a Will than with a Living Trust! (In fact, many attorneys prepare Wills for little or *no* cost—simply to lock in the eventual probate fees that will result when the estate is probated.)

Another ploy used by the Will and Probate attorneys to discredit a Living Trust is to bring up the deductibility of various expenses relating to the creation of a Living Trust as opposed to the eventual deduction of the probate fees from an estate. (Even if you can eventually deduct the expenses siphoned from your estate by probate fees from taxes, your heirs are still not receiving the *full value* of your hard-earned estate!)

Fallacy: A Living Trust can cost as much as four or five times more to set up than a good Will with tax-saving provisions because all property must be transferred to your Trust *now*, and you pay for that *now*.

Fact: Yes, a *well-written* Living Trust is more expensive to create than a standard Will—because of its complexity. Not surprisingly, the AARP study found that the majority of Wills are written as "loss leaders" in order for the attorney to ultimately get the probate fees for that estate. The study also found that most of these loss-leader Wills are poorly drawn. Furthermore, when these estates eventually come up for probate, the attorneys feel that they can charge more for the probate proceedings—in order to make up for the discounted cost of the original Will!

In contrast, remember that a Living Trust avoids the probate process altogether—saving a significant amount of cost to the estate. The independent study of probate in Washington state revealed that in 80 percent of the cases studied the initial—and *only*—cost of the Living Trust would have been *far less* than the actual probate costs that were incurred by the estate. Some estates had about *half* of their value consumed by probate fees! My advice to you is: If you want to save your heirs a tremendous amount of grief and pass along *all* of your estate—then avoid probate at all costs.

The argument that a Living Trust will cost more than a good Will with tax-saving provisions is just not true. A Will with tax-saving provisions is really a Testamentary Trust. You can be sure that any time a client goes to an attorney with an estate large enough for tax-saving provisions, and the attorney recommends not a standard will but rather a Testamentary Trust, the client is going to pay dearly for that document. I can assure you that, historically, a Testamentary Trust (which is a Will with tax-saving provisions) costs many times more than a well-written revocable Living Trust. Remember that a Living Trust avoids probate as well as provides tax-saving provisions.

The transfer of your assets into a Living Trust should cost you *absolutely nothing* (except for the transfer of real estate deeds that need to be rewritten in the name of the Trust and recorded again with the county recorder's office). Reasonable fees for rewriting and recording your real estate deeds should be no more than $100 per deed. Be wary of those attorneys, institutions, or firms that want to charge you a percentage of your estate to transfer the assets into your Trust!

Fallacy: If the Living Trust is prepared for lifetime management of your property, its preparation is many times more expensive than the preparation of a Durable Power of Attorney.

Fact: The above statement is very misleading. Yes, a Durable Power of Attorney document is less expensive than a Living Trust, but the two legal documents have very different purposes. A well-written Living Trust will *include* a Durable Power of Attorney as one of its ancillary documents.

A Durable Power of Attorney applies *only* to the control of assets inadvertently left outside your Trust if you become incompetent (for example, with Alzheimer's disease), and its power ceases upon your death. The Durable Power of Attorney document has absolutely nothing to do with avoiding probate or preserving your $1 million federal estate tax exclusion.

Fallacy: The cost of a Living Trust is not even tax deductible, while all expenses of probate are tax deductible, either against the federal estate tax or against the income tax.

Fact: The above statement is basically false. The cost of creating a Living Trust can be deducted as tax/estate-planning expenses. There are more than fifty tax cases on record that support the basis for allowing the tax deduction for creating a Living Trust, whereas there is no deduction allowed for a Will. Remember that the cost of creating a Living Trust is *far less* than the expenses associated with probating an estate (even if the Will costs you nothing).

It should cost you *absolutely nothing* to terminate a Living Trust! (When all of the assets are removed from the Trust, it effectively ceases to exist—and you can simply place it among your memorabilia.)

Fallacy: In addition to the cost of drawing up the Living Trust, you will have to pay annual trustee fees.

Fallacy: A professional trustee or a bank or trust company, if named as a trustee, will probably charge an annual fee of 1 percent or more of the value of the Trust estate. If you live for three years or more and pay out those trust fees annually, there go the supposed savings of avoiding probate. Then, when you die, the successor trustee probably won't terminate the Trust and distribute the assets to your beneficiaries without more significant costs.

Fact: As always, I recommend that you and your spouse (if you are married) be the trustees of your Living Trust. The surviving spouse typically should be named as the surviving trustee, and upon the incompetency or death of the surviving spouse, one or more of your adult children, close family members, or close friends should be identified as the successor trustees. Usually, these individuals faithfully administer the Trust without even thinking of collecting trustee fees. Only in rare cases should you select a financial institution as trustee for your Trust. Yes, these institutions will charge a yearly fee, usually based on a percentage of the estate's value, to administer your estate.

Tactic: A Living Trust Does Not Avoid Income Taxes

Part of the smear campaign used by the Will and Probate attorneys attempts to exploit most people's aversion to paying taxes (for just about anything), as well as their fear of the Internal Revenue Service.

Fallacy: You cannot avoid income taxes with a Living Trust.

Fact: The above statement is ludicrous, because it attempts to mislead you—even though the statement is true! However, the statement is *very misleading*, because *a Living Trust has no impact whatsoever on income tax*. You must pay exactly the same income tax whether or not your assets are inside a Trust. (The most common way of avoiding income tax today is by investing in tax-free government bonds or annuities—and the favorable tax impact is the same with or without a Trust.) A Living Trust is not a vehicle to avoid paying income taxes. There is no way to avoid death and, with a large enough estate, eventually taxes.

Fallacy: Income tax treatments for probated estates are generally more favorable than for Living Trusts.

Fact: The IRS looks at a Living Trust as being absolutely transparent when it comes to income taxes. As long as you are alive and income flows to you, you continue to file your individual Form 1040 income tax return (using your own personal social security number) and pay the taxes due. When a spouse dies, the income typically continues to flow to the surviving spouse, who then files his or her individual Form 1040 (using his or her own social security number). After the death of the surviving spouse, any Trust income may flow directly to the beneficiaries, who then report the income on their personal Form 1040 and pay the taxes due. (This material is covered in Chapter 15.) However, if Trust income is retained in the Trust after the death of the surviving spouse (rather than distributed to the beneficiaries), the resultant tax is now 39.6 percent (over $7,500) as a result of the Omnibus Budget Revenue Reconciliation Act of 1993. Thus, it is far better to exercise your options and pay the trust income to the surviving spouse or heirs where it will be taxed at their substantially lower tax rates. In contrast, if the estate were tied up in probate litigation, the estate must pay the 39.6 percent tax rate (over $7,500) for the entire litigation period.

Fallacy: Preparation of income tax returns costs more with a Living Trust than with a Will.

Fact: During the lives of the spouses, including the life of the surviving spouse, there are no additional income tax forms to fill out, so the expense would be the same with or without a Trust. Only after the death of the surviving spouse (and if assets are retained in the Trust) must a Form 1041 Trust return be filed. (See Chapter 15 for a detailed description of just how easy it is to fill out Form 1041.)

Fallacy: Living Trusts are not vehicles for deducting personal expenses. In fact, some practitioners feel that clients with Living Trusts are more likely to be audited by the IRS (specifically to detect the deduction of personal items).

Fact: This statement is just another one of many that are used as scare tactics and have no basis in fact. You will not file an income tax return for a revocable Living Trust but will continue to file your personal Form 1040.

Fallacy: You do not save federal estate taxes by avoiding probate. Your federal estate tax will be the same whether you use a Trust or a Will.

Fact: The claim that a Living Trust will not save estate taxes is one of the most common attacks made by the Will and Probate attorneys. It is very misleading to imply that avoiding probate does not save estate taxes—since probate and estate taxes are two *entirely separate* subjects.

If you are single, it is true that a Living Trust will not save you estate taxes (because there is no surviving spouse to take advantage of the additional $1 million federal estate tax exclusion). On the other hand, if you are married, the only way that you can preserve the $1 million federal estate tax exclusions for *both* spouses (a total exclusion of $2 million) is with an A-B Living Trust.

What is so misleading about comparing a Living Trust with a "well-drawn Will" is that when most people think of a Will, they typically think of a "standard" Will—the type that is usually obtained from an attorney or in do-it-yourself form at a stationery store. Unless you are an attorney, you don't think of a "well-drawn Will" as being a Testamentary Trust.

An A-B Testamentary Trust (referred to by many attorneys as a "properly drawn Will") can avoid unnecessary estate taxes by utilizing an A-B Trust, but, unlike a Living Trust, the estate must go through the probate process for the decedent spouse's share when the first spouse dies and again go through probate for the surviving spouse's share upon the death of the surviving spouse. Once each spouse's share of the estate has gone through probate, it is then placed in trust and is not included in the estate of the other spouse. (Since the Testamentary Trust does not take effect until the death of an individual, it is technically a Will. It is also invariably an expensive document.) Conversely, an A-B Living Trust also preserves both $1 million federal estate tax exclusions as well as avoids probate altogether; no probate is required on the death of *either* the first spouse or the surviving spouse.

I am not aware of any way in which a Will (other than a Testamentary Trust) can be drafted to preserve a decedent spouse's $1 million federal estate tax exclusion (in order to save federal estate taxes).

Tactic: Asset Transfer into a Living Trust Is Costly and Complicated

The Will and Probate attorneys spend a lot of energy trying to convince you that the costs of a Living Trust are more burdensome than the costs associated with probate, or that transferring your assets into a Trust is complicated. Much of the information is untrue, and the rest is very misleading.

Fallacy: Transferring assets into your Living Trust can take time and can result in various additional costs. There will be costs and expenses to transfer titles and prepare deeds, bills of sale, letters to brokers, bank signature cards, stock transfers, and so on.

Fact: Here again, the attorneys are presenting "almost untrue" statements in their attempt to dissuade you from considering a Living Trust. The only cost involved in transferring your assets into your Living Trust should be rewriting and recording your real estate deed(s). This cost should range from about $80 to $100. All other assets (such as bank and credit union accounts, life insurance, and so on) should cost you nothing to transfer into your Living Trust. Also, there should be no cost to name your Living Trust as beneficiary for such assets as retirement accounts and pension funds, IRAs, and so on. We provide all our clients with transfer forms that make this process very simple.

For those of you who cannot get your broker to change the ownership name of your stocks and bonds without charging you a fee, the discount brokerage firm of Charles Schwab has offered, as a special service, to transfer your securities into your Living Trust at no cost.

Fallacy: A securities portfolio can go into a Living Trust, but not houses, cars, furniture, and the like, for which transfer would become incredibly complicated.
Fallacy: Retitling bank accounts, securities, and mutual funds can require hours of work and reams of forms that must be completed. Moreover, you will probably need your lawyer to retitle your house and any other real estate.
Fallacy: The revocable Living Trust can raise a variety of new problems regarding title insurance and Sub-Chapter S stock.
Fact: The statement that it is extremely difficult to place houses and cars in a Living Trust is totally absurd. Transferring these assets into your Trust is of utmost importance in protecting your estate and is easily done without very much time or effort.

Transferring your assets into a Living Trust does take some effort on your part, but the effort spent today is minuscule compared with the effort your survivors would otherwise expend in a lengthy probate. If you want to avoid probate, all of your assets should be placed in your Living Trust—including houses, additional real estate, cars, furniture, and the like.

For your home, your deed needs to be rewritten and recorded in the county recorder's office. Unless you are familiar with this process, knowledgeable legal counsel should do it. The typical charge should be about $80 to $100. Changing the legal ownership of your cars requires only a single trip to the department of motor vehicles. Furniture is transferred into your Trust by using a special letter that transfers all personal effects owned today (or added in the future) *without inventorying them*. Bank and credit union accounts usually take only a single trip to the financial institution, but remember to take your Trust document; most institutions want to be sure that you have the proper trustee powers to transfer those assets.

Title insurance companies will always accept a *good* Living Trust. Placing your home in a Living Trust will not affect your ability to get title insurance. Every *good* Living Trust should have a special provision authorizing the Living Trust to hold Sub-Chapter S stock.

Fallacy: A Living Trust will be worthless if you do not bother to transfer to it title to your real estate, stocks, mutual funds, bank accounts, and other property.
Fact: It is true that if you do not transfer all of your assets into your Living Trust, those assets remaining outside the Trust upon your death will go through probate. The transfer of assets does require some effort on your part, but remember that the effort is minuscule in relation to going through probate, and the ultimate cost savings to your estate is extremely beneficial!

Once you have placed your existing assets in your Trust, you only need to remember to place newly acquired *real assets* (such as a motor home, additional real estate, stocks and bonds, an inheritance, and so on) into the name of your Trust. (Real assets are those that have a title or deed associated with the ownership.) In most instances, the easiest way to put the new asset in your Trust is to record the title, deed, or ownership directly into the name of your Trust when the asset is purchased or acquired.

Tactic: Real Estate Held in a Trust Has Many Problems

Here again, the attorneys are using scare tactics—preying on people's fear of losing their home—to try to discourage people from getting Living Trusts. Many of the following fallacies contain snippets of truth, and most of the statements are extremely misleading—unless you understand the detailed facts.

Fallacy: Some insurance companies may not insure property owned by a Living Trust.
Fact: This argument is fallacious and definitely false. It is intended to plant a seed of doubt in your mind. A Living Trust will have no effect on your homeowner's insurance policy.

Fallacy: You cannot borrow against your assets if they are in a Living Trust.

Fallacy: You cannot refinance your home if it is in a Living Trust.

Fallacy: Some financial institutions may not provide a mortgage on property owned by a Living Trust because of the difficulty a lender might have in selling such a mortgage on the secondary market.

Fact: I must reiterate that with your assets in a Living Trust you maintain the same right to borrow against your assets whether they are in the Trust or outside the Trust. Your financial statement should look exactly the same. (Some institutions like to see a footnote stating that your assets are in a revocable Living Trust.)

I am not aware of any case in which a mortgage has been refused because real estate was in a revocable Living Trust. Citibank of New York announced that it will issue mortgages on real estate held in a Living Trust.

Yes, it is true that some lenders will ask you to take your house out of trust in order to refinance it, but this action is easily (and temporarily) accomplished with minimal effort. In the mid-1980s, banks were confronted with rapidly dropping interest rates and consumer demand for extensive refinancing. Because most Trusts are poorly organized and poorly written, the banks chose, in unison, to not read all the Trusts. (An attorney must read every paragraph to be certain that one of the paragraphs is not written in such a way that the bank could be restricted from foreclosing if the mortgage payments were not made.)

To circumvent this problem of poorly written Trusts, a bank or finance company will usually ask you to remove your real estate from trust in order to process the financing. Once the financing is completed, you then put your real estate right back in your Trust. We accomplish this process with a double deed: We create a deed placing the real estate in joint tenancy (or your name, if you are single) and also create a second deed placing the real estate back in your Living Trust. You sign (and have notarized) the deed removing the real estate from your Trust and then immediately sign (and have notarized) the second deed placing your real estate back in your Living Trust. It is the notarization that counts; thus, the later deed, though not recorded, will prevail in the event of a death. The first deed is recorded with the county recorder, removing the real estate from your Trust. Once your new financing is complete, you can then record the second deed, which places the real estate back in your Living Trust. This process is simple and works very well.

Fallacy: Due-on-sale clauses in real estate investments may be triggered by a transfer to a Living Trust.

Fact: This argument is a classic smoke screen. After creating thousands of Trusts, I have yet to see one due-on-sale clause in a mortgage triggered by placing a home in a Living Trust. However, you would be wise to notify your mortgage company that you are placing your real estate in a "Grantor" Trust—particularly in the Midwest and East, where finance companies are less familiar with Living Trusts.

Fallacy: Transferring real estate into a Living Trust may jeopardize the ability for homestead (unless provisions are provided in the Trust).

Fact: Yes, this statement is true, but notice the caveat—*unless special provision has been made in your Living Trust*! Without such a provision in your Trust, you cannot homestead your home in Florida or Texas. If you look at the provisions that should be included in a *good* Living Trust (Table 10-1 in Chapter 10), you will note that provisions are included for both of these states. Although you may not now be living in either of these states, it is possible that someday you may live there or have the opportunity to own some property there. In any event, a good Living Trust will provide for just such a contingency.

Tactic: With a Living Trust You Lose Certain Privileges

In their continuing efforts to discredit the Living Trust, the Will and Probate attorneys try to mislead the public by making less-than-truthful statements about not being able to place certain assets into a Living Trust or certain privileges being lost if you have a Trust.

Fallacy: It may be difficult for a trustee to operate a small business through a Living Trust; therefore, the major asset of a decedent may be required to be held outside a Living Trust.

Fact: I contend exactly the opposite. Most small businesses are dependent for survival on the owner, and if the owner dies the small business perishes very rapidly. If the small business is in a Living Trust, it can be sold immediately upon the death of the owner, offering a potential value to the heirs. However, if that small business is tied up in probate for two years, the sale value rapidly diminishes to zero.

For sole proprietorships and partnerships (few have written agreements), a special "Bill of Sale/Letter of Transfer" should be created specifically to transfer the business into the Living Trust. For small corporations, the stock is simply reissued in the name of the Trust. Other than placing title to the business into the Trust, everything else remains as is—including the business name, its "dba" (the name under which it is doing business), checking account, and borrowing capacity.

Fallacy: Individual retirement accounts and pensions should not be placed in a Living Trust, since they will cause immediate taxation on the amounts in the IRA or pension plan.

Fact: Yes, the statement is true, but read ahead—carefully. You should not place retirement accounts themselves into the Living Trust; instead, the Living Trust is named as the *beneficiary* of the retirement accounts—whether they are IRAs, Keoghs, pension plans, profit-sharing plans, ESOPs, PASOPs, deferred-compensation plans, or similar accounts. Carefully note the distinction between being an *owner* and being a *beneficiary*; the tax implications are very different for the two. (See Chapter 14 for specific details.)

Fallacy: Use of Living Trusts will cause the loss of the benefits from Section 1244 stock (original-issue stock) and statutory stock-option and stock-purchase plans.

Fact: The above statement is factually correct. However, you can create a "Bill of Sale/Letter of Transfer" document to transfer original-issue stock or stock options into the Living Trust—without affecting their status. (These "Bill of Sale/Letter of Transfer" documents should be placed in your safe-deposit box to show proper ownership, but they should *not* be returned to the company or broker issuing the stock.) If the stock has not yet been issued and the individual dies, the executor of the Pour-Over Will may execute the option and have the stock issued in the name of the Trust. (The executor and the trustee are typically the same person.)

Fallacy: Gifts made directly from a Living Trust, including gifts intended to qualify for the $10,000 annual exclusion, will be brought back into the grantor's (creator's) estate if gifts are made within three years of the grantor's death.

Fact: Even though the statement is true, it can easily be misread or misinterpreted. An individual, not a Trust, has the right to make gifts. Therefore, the asset to be gifted is simply removed from the Trust (so that *you*, not the Trust, own it), and then you make the gift as you normally would.

Under the tax code, only life insurance is subject to being included in the grantor's estate if it has been gifted within three years prior to the grantor's death. If you are utilizing an Insurance Preservation Trust, it is better to have the Insurance Preservation Trust buy the insurance outright on the individual, thus circumventing this recapture provision.

Fallacy: Persons dealing with the Trust (such as banks and insurance companies) may want to review the Living Trust to check on the trustee powers and duties.

Fallacy: There have been occasions when transfer agents (for stock), banks, or title companies have required successor trustees to produce copies of entire Trust agreements before they will recognize the successor trustee(s) or their powers, thereby defeating "privacy" and speed of transfer.

Fact: We provide our clients with an abstract, which is simply a three-page legal summary of their Living Trust, to show to financial institutions upon request. Occasionally, but not often, a financial institution would like to see more detail about your Trust, specifically the front page of your Trust (citing the trustors and trustees), the signature page of your Trust, and the pages listing the powers of the trustees. In a few instances, a financial institution may ask to see the entire Trust, but such cases are not common. The institutions respect the privacy of the documents, and complying with their request (loaning them a copy of your Trust for a few days) is a far cry from the probate process, which puts your entire Will and the contents of your estate on file for public viewing.

Tactic: A Living Trust Is Difficult to Manage

Next on the agenda for the attorneys is to present you with more scare tactics purporting how difficult it is to manage a Living Trust. (However, once you are familiar with Living Trusts, these fallacious arguments become amusing rather than alarming.)

Fallacy: It's inconvenient. Once the Living Trust is established, you must be sure that Trust books are maintained, and all assets must continue to be registered in the name of the Trust.

Fallacy: If you create a Living Trust, you must thereafter keep extensive records.

Fallacy: Trustees often fail to keep track of their assets.

Fact: Other than transferring title of your assets into your Living Trust, there is not one thing you must do with a Living Trust that you would not do without one. A Living Trust requires no more records, accounting, or paperwork than you would have maintained without the Trust. You will continue to file your 1040 income tax return as you always have in the past—and you will *not* file a tax return for your revocable Living Trust. I do recommend, however, that you maintain a copy of all real assets, deeds, stocks, bonds, savings accounts, and so on, so that your heirs will know what to look for and where to find them. It's easy to do, takes very little effort on your part, and is a blessing for your heirs after you pass on.

Fallacy: Each person who has a Living Trust must regularly prepare an updated inventory of the property and consider whether property should be added or removed.

Fact: This statement is utterly ridiculous. Imagine having to inventory your assets! All of us know that we should make an inventory—for possible use in case of a fire, but very few of us do. There is absolutely no advantage to describing your assets in your Living Trust and a severe disadvantage if you do.

In order to place your high-value assets in your Living Trust, you must actually change the title of each asset—recording the deed to your home, the legal ownership of your cars, and the ownership of all your stocks and bonds in the name of your Trust. This process is not a difficult or time-consuming job and is one which *must* be done to protect your assets.

Be very aware that simply listing your assets in your Trust does *not* legally place them in your Trust; however, such action does create the necessity to amend (change) your Trust regularly as you change your assets. This process of amending costs money and makes your attorney very happy and wealthy.

For personal effects such as furniture, fixtures, antiques, clothing, furs, and jewelry, we provide our clients with an "Assignment of Furniture, Furnishings and Personal Effects" document, which transfers all personal effects held now and acquired in the future *without inventorying them*.

Fallacy: A Living Trust must be registered with the state!

Fact: Technically, eight states require that you register your Living Trust. Interestingly, however, when these states were presented letters of registration for Living Trusts, they did not know what to do with them! The requirement to register the Trust may simply be waived, however, if the Trust language specifically states that "the Trust need not be registered." As strange as it may seem, in such cases, the Trust then does not have to be registered.

Fallacy: In separate property states (states other than community property states), a husband and wife must have separate single Trusts in order to retain their $1 million federal estate tax exclusions! (An A-B Trust will not qualify.)

Fact: It has become standard practice throughout the Midwest and some eastern states to write two separate Trusts for a married couple. The logic seems to be that this method is the only way to preserve both $1 million federal estate tax exclusions, except that it creates an administrative nightmare for the spouses. When I first heard of this practice, I was convinced that it was simply an attempt by lawyers to get more money: two Trusts cost more than one. Later, however, I discovered that the practice of writing two Trusts was so prevalent that the attorneys were like sheep following the leader, all assuming that the leader was correct.

After probing this matter and querying some of the most prestigious Living Trust masters, as well as exhaustively researching the field of legal literature, our legal staff has determined that there is *no basis* for drawing two Living Trusts for a married couple in order to preserve both $1 million federal estate tax exclusions.

Fallacy: If you become incompetent and are unable to be the trustee of your Living Trust, the successor trustee will be required to file separate income tax returns for the Trust in addition to your individual income tax returns. Many income tax preparers are not familiar with the fiduciary tax returns that must be filed.

Fact: If a person becomes incompetent, a 1040 income tax return must still be filed—and the IRS is rather hard-nosed about this rule. Since someone must file a tax return for the incompetent individual, it is logical that the successor trustee assumes this responsibility. A Trust tax return (Form 1041) is not required to be filed simply because a person is no longer competent. However, banks and financial institutions will usually file a Trust tax return as a matter of their accounting (and it also gives them something to do to earn their fees).

Tactic: Settlement of a Living Trust Can Be Costly, Difficult, and Disadvantageous

The Will and Probate attorneys expend a lot of energy trying to convince you that the costs of settling an estate in a Living Trust are more burdensome than the costs associated with probate. The Will and Probate attorneys continue their tactics of spreading untrue or misleading information by intentionally not mentioning the much higher ultimate cost to the estate of using the probate process.

Fallacy: Upon the death of a spouse, it is important that the assets be transferred and the Living Trust terminated!

Fact: This statement makes no sense at all! There is absolutely no need to transfer any assets upon the death of a spouse. Upon the death of the first spouse, the assets typically remain in the Living Trust (in the same Trust name) for the benefit of the surviving spouse. Upon the death of the second spouse, the successor trustee then usually administers or distributes assets as specified in the Trust.

Fallacy: It is very expensive to settle a Living Trust.

Fallacy: Even with a Living Trust, your heirs or the successor trustee will probably need to consult an attorney to perform almost all of the services that have to be performed in an estate. Filing of tax returns (income, inheritance, and estate taxes), transfers of property from the Trust, preparation of accounting, and general settlement of your affairs can be easier when legal advice is sought.

Fact: These statements are rife with misinformation. Settling an estate, when it is properly organized, can easily be done, in most cases, by the successor trustees themselves. Usually legal assistance is *not* required.

Unfortunately, many individuals and firms offering Living Trusts today do not know *how* to settle an estate—and that includes most attorneys. Those individuals or firms that do know what to do are charging an unconscionable rate of 1 percent to 3 percent of the *gross* estate in order to settle the estate! Many people, however, are now seeking fixed-fee settlement costs to protect themselves from settlement abuses in the future. Because of this concern, our firm, on request, will offer a written agreement to our clients to settle their estates for a nominal fixed fee. Even though our firm does not charge to settle the key issues of an estate, providing a request such as a fixed-settlement fee guarantee seems to provide clients with built-in protection from being charged an exorbitant settlement fee in the future.

Upon the death of the surviving spouse, income tax returns still need to be prepared by your tax preparer, and, if your estate exceeds $1 million (for a single person) or $2 million (for a married couple), a federal estate tax return (Form 706) must be filed. This form is so complex that a good accountant should fill it out, but in most cases it is not necessary to consult an attorney.

The only cost involved with eventually transferring assets from the Trust should be with real estate, where the deeds must be redrawn in the name of the new owner. The cost, as mentioned previously, should be no more than $80 to $100 per deed.

Fallacy: In a Living Trust, the trustee only has the powers that are granted in the Trust document. If the property must be sold to pay the debts or make the distribution, the trustee may sell the property if the Trust document gives him or her that power. If no such authority is granted to the trustee, he or she must petition the court for authority. It will take a minimum of twenty days to get that authority.

Fact: A *good* Living Trust provides all of the appropriate powers for the successor trustee, so that all necessary actions can be taken immediately (and *without* any court intervention), such as paying debts, selling assets if necessary, and distributing assets as specified. One of the advantages of a Living Trust is that asset sale and/or distribution is *not required* upon the death of either spouse. However, it is true that if you have a *poorly drawn* Living Trust, you may be frequently appealing to the courts to give you the necessary powers or to clarify unexpected contingent situations.

Fallacy: If no successor trustee is named or provided for in the Living Trust document, the beneficiaries of the Trust would have to petition the probate court to appoint a successor trustee. This process would typically take a minimum of twenty days.

Fact: Again, a *good* Living Trust will always provide for this common contingency. In addi-

tion, a well-written Trust specifies that if a successor trustee is unable to serve, the primary beneficiaries have the "right to elect the successor trustee," thus avoiding the need to turn to the courts.

Fallacy: The trustee of a Living Trust must be a resident of that particular state where the Trust is to be settled.

Fact: This statement is totally untrue! Not one of our fifty states requires that the trustee be a resident of the state.

Fallacy: Unless the Trust document requires an accounting by the trustee in a Living Trust, he or she may not have to account to the beneficiaries for his or her actions.

Fact: A *good* Living Trust requires that the successor trustee account annually to the beneficiaries. This task can be done by simply providing the beneficiaries with a copy of the annual Trust tax return (Form 1041). Obviously, the trustors (creators) need not account to each other, and the surviving trustee (surviving spouse) need not account to those people who will become beneficiaries on the surviving spouse's death, since the surviving spouse is the specified beneficiary as long as he or she is alive.

Fallacy: It is easier for a dishonest trustee to embezzle funds from a Living Trust than for a dishonest administrator to embezzle funds in probate, because the trustee has no court supervision.

Fact: The main part of the word *trustee* is TRUST—someone who can be trusted. The surviving spouse is typically recommended to be named as the surviving trustee (although you can also name someone else as a co-trustee with the surviving spouse or name someone other than the surviving spouse). It is recommended that you name as successor trustee one or more of your adult children, close family members, or close friends, or any combination thereof.

There is also security in numbers—naming more than one successor trustee, all of whom must act in concert on matters pertaining to the Trust. In settling thousands of estates and working with the successor trustees and beneficiaries, I have yet to discover one single incident of embezzlement.

Fallacy: The obligation to pay funeral expenses falls on the trustee of a Living Trust.

Fact: If you die, someone has to arrange for the funeral and then pay for it. The funeral industry is being rather finicky these days and asking for the money up front. This task is one of the first powers that the trustee should be authorized to perform—to see that you have a proper funeral and that your estate pays for it. If your estate lacks the funds for the funeral, such financing is *not an obligation* of the trustee. Presumably your family would come forward with the necessary funds.

Fallacy: The trustee of a Living Trust will be liable for any unpaid debts of the Living Trust if there are insufficient assets in the Trust.

Fact: The trustee pays the outstanding bills from the assets of the estate. If there are insufficient assets in the estate to meet the outstanding debts, the trustee is *not* personally liable for the debts. The trustee would simply declare the estate bankrupt.

Fallacy: If there are more debts than assets, the trustee must file bankruptcy in the federal bankruptcy court.

Fact: If, upon the death of the surviving spouse, there are more debts than assets with which to pay the outstanding bills, the trustee would file bankruptcy for the estate. However, there is a much less likely chance of this situation happening in a Living Trust than if the estate were to go through probate and be subject to those enormous probate costs—which are *always paid first*.

Fallacy: Living Trusts can introduce arcane headaches for people with real estate losses.

Fallacy: Losses on assets are disallowed when assets are distributed to beneficiaries of a Living Trust.

Fact: Here again, if you know *how to properly settle an estate*, these statements are little more than hot air. The assets may be valued at the date of death *or* six months later. If the assets lose value after such valuation, such as a home or securities, the trustee should distribute such assets directly to the beneficiaries rather than sell the asset while it is still in the Trust. If the assets are sold while inside the Trust and the resultant money is then distributed to the heirs, neither the Trust nor the beneficiaries can take advantage of any loss on the sale. If the assets are distributed directly to the beneficiaries (i.e., they receive the house, rather than the proceeds from selling the house), the beneficiaries can then sell the house and claim any loss on their personal tax returns.

Fallacy: You have the best opportunity of getting the best price for your real estate through the probate system. The reason is that your executor has the privilege of selling your property with court assistance, which requires that the property be *actively marketed for a reasonable period of time* in order to give it good market exposure.

Fact: This statement is blatantly false, even though it may sound plausible. Have you ever seen a home that is being sold under probate? Many of these sales are referred to as "estate sales"—where you have an opportunity of picking up a bargain. How do the grounds usually look after one or two years without care? Homes being sold under probate have often been neglected, have not been lived in for months or years, and often are offered at far below market value—just to get them sold and probate finished! In probate, most executors (as attorneys) do not want to rent the property for fear of a potential lawsuit from a tenant over an injury on the property. Of course, in most cases, the mortgage payments must still be met monthly—even if the house sits empty while probate lingers on and on.

If a home is in a Living Trust, you have the opportunity to sell it immediately or rent it, if you so desire, until the market improves. The successor trustees decide what is best for the Trust.

Fallacy: A deceased person's probate estate can elect to file a joint income tax return with the surviving spouse for the year of the death; this option is not available under a Living Trust.

Fact: Wrong! The surviving spouse certainly *does have the right* to file a joint tax return with the deceased spouse for the year of death. The trustee (who is usually the surviving spouse) simply passes the income to the surviving spouse, who files a joint income tax return at year's end. The surviving spouse would also file a simple Trust tax return (Form 1041). This form's first section identifies the income generated in the decedent's share of the Trust; the second section identifies the income paid out from the decedent's share of the Trust (which should be all of it), usually to the surviving spouse. The last section shows the net result—zero—a simple computation that takes all of two minutes.

Fallacy: A trustee of a Living Trust has no legal authority to file a final income tax return for the grantor (creator) or to make special elections that can save income taxes.

Fact: Be very careful of the misleading semantics in this statement. Rather than the trustee, the executor (who is named in the Pour-Over Will and *who is usually the same person*) has the power to file the final income tax return.

Fallacy: Estimated tax payments must be made by a Trust but are not required for the first two years of an estate.

Fact: Since a Living Trust can be settled almost immediately, the income taxes can be paid at the end of the year without any difficulty. In contrast, if an estate is tied up in probate for two years, the survivors do not know the final value of the estate or the taxable expenses and income. Thus, in probate, the survivors have two years to file income taxes. Remember, however, that the taxes still have to be paid, and, if they are late, there will be interest and penalties. Many assets under probate are sold very cheaply in order to quickly raise enough money to pay the taxes—even if probate is still not concluded. How much simpler it is (and very much less costly) to have a Living Trust.

Fallacy: While Living Trusts must file calendar-year tax returns, probate estates can file fiscal-year returns. The use of a fiscal year allows valuable tax deferral for estates.

Fact: Almost all individuals use calendar-year accounting (in which the year ends on December 31) as a matter of habit. Regardless of the year-end date used for tax purposes, your income taxes still must be paid. To delay paying income taxes only incurs interest and possible penalties. With a Living Trust, your affairs can be settled almost immediately, whereas if you are in probate, your affairs are tied up in limbo for one to two years. That's certainly not an advantage!

Fallacy: If people are disposed to fight over your assets, they can and will fight just as easily inside or outside probate.

Fact: Yes, this statement is true. The probate process often generates conflict, whereas the Living Trust is designed to eliminate conflict. More than ten years ago, we added the provision to our Living Trust that if there were a conflict between trustees and/or beneficiaries, it would be resolved through arbitration. Since then, we have yet to see a single conflict among successor trustees. I believe that most conflicts are emotional, and if the parties realize that they cannot resolve the problem themselves, an independent arbitrator will do so for them—unemotionally. It works. In contrast, remember that 30 percent of Wills end up in serious battles.

Fallacy: Your choice of plan will make no difference to your beneficiaries.

Fact: The choice of suffering through probate or having a well-written Living Trust is a family affair. Parents must remember that they may not have to go through probate, but unless they create a Living Trust, their children *will* suffer through the probate process. In going through probate, the children will forfeit a substantial share of their rightful portion of the estate to the probate attorneys. For example, my father did not have to go through probate—but I did for his estate. After helping a number of clients through the probate process, I assure you that I will never again go through probate for anyone; it is not worth the emotional stress.

Today, in more and more cases, adult children are paying for their parents' Living Trust. The children have learned that spending a little money now certainly beats the future alternative of the expense, time, and agony of probate.

Appendix J

Most Attorneys Are Not That Well Versed in the Living Trust

As discussed in Chapter 3, which addresses the "million-dollar lawsuit" launched against me and my company, I was amazed at the deposition of the attorney who was hired by the client to review our Trust. Despite his impressive credentials, his responses at the deposition seemed less than competent. The impression was of someone taking a test on a subject he had not studied and trying to bluff his way through by throwing out enough of the right words so that it might be construed that he was suitably knowledgeable.

Following are excerpts from that deposition, lightly edited for clarity.

Have you ever given any seminars that covered the area of joint Living Trusts as opposed to separate property Trusts?

No.

. . . How many Wills would you estimate you had drafted?

Hundreds.

. . . Living Trusts?

. . . Certainly be less than the Wills, but I would say a hundred . . . I use computer-assisted drafting . . . West product.

. . . In 1991, what were the benefits of Living Trusts over Wills, if any?

. . . Living Wills can be structured in virtually any manner you want them to be structured. They're contracts that can be structured almost on infinite possibilities . . . They had the benefit of creating a vehicle for the current administration of their assets in the event something happens to one or both of them, talking about a couple. They have the benefit in most states of sheltering, to some extent, what occurs regarding their assets—general public scrutiny. They're more private. In certain states, they have the benefit of sheltering some of the assets from certain tax aspects that would be attributable if they die within the time of their probate estate . . . inheritance taxes . . .

. . . Inheritance tax could be avoided?

With certain types of Living Trusts, yes.

. . . In 1991, what were the benefits of Wills over Living Trusts, if any?

One less document . . . simpler for the estate to administer . . . can't really think of any major benefits that couldn't be accomplished through a Trust.

. . . A Will would be simpler to administer than a Living Trust?

It would be one less document, one less entity that you could potentially not have to create . . . If you just had a simple power of a Will pouring over to a Trust and that Trust distributing the assets, that's just one more document it has to flow through.

. . . What were the factors that would cause a client to place their assets in trust versus not place their assets in trust?

The health of both parties; their ages; whether or not they have other people to assist them; whether or not they felt comfortable having things done through a power of attorney as opposed to a Trust.

. . . What advantages did Living Trusts have, if any, over Wills with respect to techniques used to save federal estate taxes?

Living Trusts . . . you obviously can remove assets from your estate for the use of irrevocable Trusts as a Life Insurance Trust. That obviously you can't do by a Will, because a Will only affects assets over which you have control. That's the primary area in which Living Trusts would have significant differences.

. . . Did revocable Living Trusts have any advantages over Wills with respect to tech-

niques used to save federal estate taxes?

Probably not.

Are there any advantages that revocable Living Trusts offer over Wills in respect to techniques used to save federal estate taxes?

Again, I feel like I'm taking a final in law school on Trusts and Wills. Right off the top of my head, I can't think of any.

What is your current understanding of the benefits and drawbacks of using joint Living Trusts?

Again, it depends upon whether or not the joint Trusts are structured as tenancy in common Trusts or joint and survivorship Trusts, whether or not they intend—whether or not in fact they create two separate Trusts that are administered under a single document in effect, which is what you frequently see in joint Living Trusts these days, where you try to keep the independence of the asset ownerships or restructuring the assets' ownerships.

. . . There were different kinds of joint Living Trusts?

. . . Trusts, like contracts, can be structured as variably as the imagination.

. . . Are you aware of any disadvantages of joint Living Trusts that are unique to joint Living Trusts as opposed to Trusts generically?

They create, if improperly structured particularly and even when properly structured—can give cause to confusion as to how the assets will be administered or treated—particularly if you attempt to maintain the survivorship character of those assets through some point in the Trust.

. . . Under some of these survivorship joint Living Trusts, the Trusts are crafted with a view toward using disclaimers at some point in the future?

. . . Yes. That would primarily involve real estate that was placed into them with parties that did not want to alter the real estate ownership . . . a Crummey Trust or Cristifoni Trust . . .

Is another name for a Crummey Trust an irrevocable Life Insurance Trust?

A Crummey Trust in my opinion is an irrevocable Life Insurance Trust with withdrawal powers or Crummey powers.

What is the purpose—or what was the purpose in 1991—of a Crummey Trust?

Pretty much the same as it is now. It's to permit the removal of an asset or the creation of an asset. For instance, if you had bought a life insurance policy, you would create the Trust to allow the trustee to buy the policy, which is probably in most cases the better way to do it if you're talking about buying insurance. But it creates the—for lack of a better word—the fiction that . . . the asset is out of the estate because of the withdrawal rights of the beneficiaries.

When you're creating a situation where you have an insurance policy that you know that the decedent is going to have to continue to fund, then if the decedent—or insured, I should say—continued to fund that Trust without withdrawal powers even though it's owned by a separate Trust independently, the Trust is pulled back into the estate because of that payment of that.

So, you create the fiction that instead of the insured paying the premium, the insured makes a gift to the Trust. The Trust, by offering premiums to the beneficiaries, having them have the right to withdrawal or not, revoke or withdraw it, the presumption is that they in effect give withdrawal and passed it back in and use that money to buy it and, therefore, created them, purchasing a premium with a gift that they made to the Trust, and permit the taxability of that insurance policy.

What was the consequence in 1991 of not handling the Crummey powers properly in the administration of the ILIT (irrevocable Life Insurance Trust) . . . of failing to give Crummey notices to demand beneficiaries?

Assuming the IRS ever asked for them. I've been involved in an awful lot of estates where

they've never asked . . . for the notices. But assuming they asked for them and you haven't given them withdrawals, then it's presumed they didn't. Well, actually, there's a fairly recent case, I believe, that puts some question upon whether or not that can even be waived.

But I think in 1991, probably the presumption would be that the asset would be pulled back into the decedent's estate—insured's estate.

Did it have any gift tax consequences if the Crummey powers were not properly administered?

Yes. It could potentially have gift tax provisions. That's why your Crummey powers had certain limitations on the withdrawal rights, to try to stay within those gift tax consequences, a formula for determining that situation. And that's why sometimes you had to go to alternative beneficiaries to make it work out—the use of grandchildren, for instance, that have withdrawal rights and really have no benefit in the Trust.

Are you familiar with the use of the phrase *wealth-replacement Trust* in referring to an ILIT performing a special function in an estate-planning design?

Yes, I've seen it before. And again, I think it's one of those kind of things that certain estate-planning gurus or hemi-cults use to try to sell a particular type of product.

All right.

I don't know that it has any specific legal relevance.

Does the phrase *wealth-replacement Trust* have any particular meaning to you as far as the function of an ILIT in a particular estate plan design?

Only in the sense that because of the fact that you are diminishing your estate by the payment of premiums, the insurance can take the place of that asset . . .

Before 1992, how many irrevocable Life Insurance Trusts would you estimate you drafted?

Not much better than speculation: thirty or forty, something in that neighborhood—thirty probably, tops.

. . . $400,000 death benefit, and the premium would be approximately $40,000 a year?

$40,000 a year . . . in ten years, you're going to pay as much as the thing is going to pay out.

. . . How would you determine whether the use of a CRAT (Charitable Remainder Annuity Trust) was appropriate for use by your clients?

Well, a lot depends upon their income tax bracket. If they don't get a fairly significant income tax deduction for it, unless they just want to create a situation where they want to give their kids or somebody else some money and have a particular charity they want to eventually benefit, they tend not to be as useful, because if you can't utilize the income tax deduction to a major, then you obviously—if you've got a beneficiary who . . . is paying no income taxes, it probably is not one of those kind of things you want to recommend. A lot depends . . . it's very factor-driven and whether or not your client has charitable tendencies . . . software produced by Probate Softwares . . .

Assuming that he asked you to help him decide whether to implement such a CRAT, what questions would you have asked him in order to help him make the decision?

His income bracket; the total size of his estate; whether or not he had close ties to particular charities; whether he was willing to give up that portion of the estate; whether he had any way to replace that portion of the estate; whether or not the annuity spun off to him would generate, potentially replace that.

What do you mean by that, the potential to replace that?

Well, let's say you pick up a term policy for the 10 percent, that $500,000 term policy; then it's renewable without an increase in premium: it may not be a bad bet. In that case, you're picking up $100,000 if he had that scenario. I think that would be a rare scenario.

. . . Assume that his marginal rate was 31 percent, his total estate was $1.6 million, he had relatively strong charitable ties, and he wanted to eliminate federal estate taxes, but he did not want to diminish the amount that his children would receive following his and his wife's death. What would you say to him about the use of a CRAT?

Again, whether or not he—how he's going to replace that $400,000 asset. And I'd probably want to have a CPA do an analysis of . . . all the tax benefits that that would create upon his estate, on his current income tax situation, to see how that benefit tied in with if he'd take a 10 percent return. Plus you take a substantial savings in your income taxes through a reduction in your income taxes. There may be some situations where between those things you might be able to offset that. That's basically it.

. . . The client might consider purchasing . . . life insurance, but there would be a question whether the premium would be a level premium or an increasing premium. Why would that be a consideration—whether it was level or increasing?

Well, obviously . . . with most term policies, they only hold the premium level for a certain number of years. And if you're paying out basically the total benefit that you're going to get from it to pick up that extra—in my scenario—$100,000 worth of benefit to your estate, if that premium increases 10 percent down the road, five years or ten years, and you end up living fifteen years, you've lost money.

In 1991, were distributions from CRATs to non-charitable beneficiaries—in other words, the annuity amount—subject to federal income tax?

I don't believe so, but I'm not positive off the top of my head.

What about under current law?

Again, I think the same thing is true, but I'm not positive.

Do you take time to explain the legal effect of the various estate-planning docu-

ments that you recommend your clients implement?

... Generally, the document program ... the preparation program I'm using creates a synopsis of those documents that also gives a more layman-friendly explanation of what they do ... ask them to read it and get back to me if they need questions ... testamentary capacity ...

I'm fifty-one; I have forgetfulness myself.

Do you believe that you are required not to participate in the unauthorized practice of law?

... The Will could be probated, and the documents were enforceable ... It is my belief that the documents are otherwise valid and appropriate under Maryland law. . . . They were enforceable under Maryland law.

In referring to your opinion letter, . . . what does the term Q-Tip, . . . and. . . Q-TIP treatment mean?

Well, Q-TIP is the qualified terminal interest property treatment, which is . . . an exception placed in by Congress to the terminal interest rule, which basically says that property that passes to a surviving spouse as terminal interest does not qualify for the marital deduction unless the appropriate official—in this case, the executor—elects to have it so treated upon the death of the decedent.

Does your opinion letter reference the ability of any of these documents to be probated under Maryland law?

If every asset owned by the plaintiff without exception was in the family Trust, then there would be nothing to probate.

I would like to direct your attention to page 4 of Exhibit 31. At the middle of the page the document provides—and I want you to follow along with me so you can verify, and you see the language I am talking about: Quote, joint property transferred to the trustee by the settlers shall be their joint property held in trust subject to the terms thereof as tenants by the entireties and treated as such. This property as invested and reinvested together with the rents,

issues, and profits therefrom, paren, herein referred to as the quote, joint estate, unquote, or the quote, joint property, unquote, shall retain its character as their joint or common property during the joint lifetimes of the settlers in spite of any change in the city of the trust, subject, however, to the provisions of this agreement, period, end of quote.

Do you see the language to which I'm referring, sir?

Yes.

Just hold your place on that document. I want to show you one other page out of this Exhibit 31. Turn to the back of the exhibit, to the page that bears the caption "Letter of Intent and Declaration of Gift." It is at the very back of the document. It probably is the last page of the exhibit. Have you found that page, sir?

Yes.

In 1991, when you read the language that I just pointed out to you, the language found on page 4 and the language contained on the page captioned "Letter of Intent and Declaration of Gift," did you have any concerns regarding the appropriateness of attempting to preserve the tenants-by-entireties character of the property held in the plaintiff's family trust.

In what respect? I mean, the ability to do so? . . .

The appropriateness of doing so.

In what respect? I'm not sure if I'm following your question.

Well, let me put it in—

It is not inappropriate to do so in the right case.

Didn't you testify earlier in this deposition that you could not think of an appropriate case in which a Trust maker would attempt to preserve the tenants-by-entirety character of Trust property?

I may have.

But you don't recall that?

I don't recall specifically, you know.

What is the right case in which to attempt to preserve the tenant-by-the-entirety character of property held in a Trust, in the XXX Trust?

It would not be, in my opinion, inappropriate to preserve it where that property was the property you're going to have pass to the surviving spouse.

. . . How does that affect the operation of the credit shelter Trust contained in the XXX family Trust?

It reduces the amount of property passing . . . It reduces it from the extent that it passes outside the Trust.

To the extent that all of the property held in the XXX family Trust was tenants-by-the-entirety property, how much property passed into Mrs. XXX's credit shelter Trust upon her death?

Whatever was in there? I'm sorry.

Assume that all of the property held in the XXX family Trust was tenancy-by-the-entireties property. Assume that Mrs. XXX dies. Does any money pass into Mrs. XXX's credit shelter Trust under those assumptions?

By way of disclaimer, whatever was disclaimed appropriately?

But only by disclaimer; correct?

Yes, that's correct.

Without the disclaimer, it is true, isn't it, that no property would pass into Mrs. XXX's credit shelter Trust.

If all was held in that Trust . . . unless I was using a disclaimer Trust . . . I know of nothing that makes it unenforceable.

. . . Page 17, discretional distribution of Trust . . . discretional dissolution of Trust . . . Page 20 . . . Does the language that you

read give the authority to the settlor to allocate federal and state taxes to the marital deduction Trust?**

It appears to.

. . . Page 23 . . . undiminished by any estate, inheritance, succession, death, or similar taxes . . . Does this parenthetical language suggest to you that the settlor of the Trust, the surviving settlor of the Trust, has authority to allocate taxes to Trusts B or C? . . . Can the settlor allocate taxes to the decedent's Trust?

. . . The language in B and C . . . notwithstanding the settlor's ability to allocate, B and C prohibit the diminution of those Trusts by those items. Correct.

. . . On page 23, with the language highlighted on page 20, which indicates that the surviving settlor shall allocate and charge the final costs of the death of the first settlor to Trust A . . . Doesn't that language on page 20 suggest the surviving settlor has authority to allocate federal and state taxes to Trust B and Trust C? . . .

Would you agree with me that the Trust language that I have highlighted is ambiguous in the sense that the language found on page 20 dictates a different answer than the language located on page 23? . . . Page 29 . . . what does the phrase *qualifying Trust* mean to you? . . . Is it your opinion that the language that I highlighted for you on pages 20 and 23 represents valid and appropriate language for use by the XXXs as you sit here today?

. . . To the extent that 20 is limited by 23, it certainly wasn't . . . the most artful method of drafting the document.

Did you consider . . . those two excerpts that I highlighted to be valid and appropriate?

. . . They aren't the most advantageous way of drafting—to say you can do A, B, or C, but you really can only do A.

. . . Did you consider the language that I highlighted to be valid?

. . . Whether or not that was the best language that could have been used, whether that language would hurt them or help them, again, was not what I was asked to do.

. . . Do you think that the language that I highlighted on pages 20 and 23 of Exhibit 31 are today valid and appropriate under Maryland law?

. . . I would not have used that language.

Appendix K
Private Letter Ruling

This Private Letter Ruling clearly establishes the position of the IRS on joint Trusts (A-B and A-B-C Trusts). The hope is that this ruling will put to rest those negative opinions offered by attorneys. If they still doubt this ruling, they should seek their own Private Letter Ruling, as we have.

Every Private Letter Ruling is destined for the party that requested it and is not binding upon the IRS for all other cases. At the same time, Private Letter Rulings are the voice of the IRS, and, therefore, it is standard practice to apply such voice to all similar cases.

This particular Trust, reviewed by the IRS, included the *general power of appointment*, which has advantages (both spouses' marital assets receive full Stepped-Up Valuation upon the death of the first spouse) and disadvantages (the deceased spouse can appoint part or all of the assets to one or more persons or entities as the deceased spouse may direct in the Will).

This is described at length in my book *How to Settle Your Living Trust*. It is a precaution of which anyone considering a general power of appointment must be aware. Nevertheless, this fact does not alter the importance of the A-B Living Trust or the significance of this ruling.

This Private Letter Ruling was issued at the beginning of 2001 and deals with the situation where spouses (in a separate property state) wish to create a joint Living Trust. If the husband and wife proposed to create a Trust to which they would transfer property they own as tenants in its entirety, the husband would be the initial trustee.

The benefits afforded by the Private Letter Ruling are fairly obvious. Primarily, it allows joint assets to be divided equally between the two taxable estates upon the death of the first spouse, without having to divide the property during their joint lifetimes. This would provide the ability to safely create a bypass trust (or

B Trust) without the risk of there being a deemed gift by the surviving spouse. In addition, similar to community property assets, all of the assets would obtain a new stepped-up basis upon the death of the first spouse.

PRIVATE LETTER RULING 200101021, 1/08/2001, IRC SEC(S). 2033; 2038; 2041; 2501; 2523

UIL No. 2033.00-00; 2038.00-00; 2041.03-00; 2501.00-00; 2523.00-00

Headnote

Reference(s): Code Sec. 2033; Code Sec. 2038; Code Sec. 2041; Code Sec. 2501; Code Sec. 2523

The Service has ruled that a trust for the benefit of a couple will be included in the estate of the first spouse to die and the surviving spouse will be treated as making a completed gift of his or her interest in the trust on the death of the first spouse.

Release Date: 1/5/2001
Date: October 2, 2000
Refer Reply To: CC:PSI:4—PLR-118834-99

PRIVATE LETTER RULING 200101021, 1/08/2001, IRC SEC(S). 2033; 2038; 2041; 2501; 2523

UIL No. 2033.00-00; 2038.00-00; 2041.03-00; 2501.00-00; 2523.00-00

Headnote

Reference(s): Code Sec. 2033; Code Sec. 2038; Code Sec. 2041; Code Sec. 2501; Code Sec. 2523

The Service has ruled that a trust for the benefit of a couple will be included in the estate of the first spouse to die and the surviving spouse will be treated as making a completed gift of his or her interest in the trust on the death of the first spouse.

Full Text

Release Date: 1/5/2001
  Date: October 2, 2000

Refer Reply To: CC: PSI:4—PLR-118834-99

This is in response to your letter dated November 24, 1999, and subsequent correspondence, requesting a ruling concerning the estate and gift tax consequences of the creation of a proposed trust (Trust) under Code Sections 2033, 2038, 2041, 2501, and 2511 of the Internal Revenue Code.

The facts and representations submitted are summarized as follows: Grantor A and Grantor B, who are husband and wife, propose to create a joint trust ("Trust"). Grantor A will be the initial trustee of Trust. The Grantors will fund Trust with assets that they own as tenants by the entireties having a value of approximately $x.

Under the terms of Trust, during the joint lives of the Grantors, the trustee may apply income and principal of Trust as the trustee deems advisable for the comfort, support, maintenance, health and general welfare of the Grantors. The trustee may also pay additional sums to either or both of the Grantors or to a third person for the benefit of either or both Grantors as Grantor A directs, or if he is not capable of this decision, then as Grantor B directs. While both Grantors are living, either one may terminate Trust by written notice to the other Grantor. If Trust is terminated, the trustee will deliver the trust property to the Grantors in both their names as tenants in common. Either Grantor may also amend the trust while both grantors are living by delivering to the other Grantor the amendment in writing at least 90 days before the effective date of the amendment.

Upon the death of the first Grantor to die, he or she possesses a testamentary general power of appointment, exercisable alone and in all events, to appoint part or all of the assets of Trust, free of trust, to such deceased Grantor's estate or to or for the benefit of one or more persons or entities, in such proportions, outright, in trust, or otherwise as the deceased Grantor may direct in his or her will.

If the first Grantor to die fails to fully exercise his or her testamentary general power of appointment, and providing the surviving Grantor survives the first Grantor to die by at least six months, an amount of Trust property sufficient to equal the largest amount that can pass free of federal estate tax by reason of the unified credit is to be transferred to an irrevocable Credit Shelter Trust. Any amount in excess of the amount needed to fully fund the Credit Shelter Trust that has not been appointed by the deceased Grantor will pass outright to the surviving Grantor.

The terms of the Credit Shelter Trust provide that during the life of the surviving Grantor, the trustee is to pay or apply for the benefit of the surviving Grantor any part of the income and/or principal of the trust as is reasonably necessary for the survivor's support and maintenance. The trustee shall also have the authority to pay or apply for the benefit of the joint descendants of the Grantors any portion of the income and/or principal of the trust, as the trustee deems necessary for such descendants' maintenance, support, and education. All distributions, however, shall be limited by an ascertainable standard relating to health, education, support, or maintenance. Upon the death of the surviving Grantor, he or she shall have a limited power to appoint the Credit Shelter Trust assets to any one or more of the class consisting of the Grantors' joint descendants. Any assets not so appointed are to be divided into equal shares so as to provide one share for each living child of both Grantors and one share for the surviving issue collectively, per stirpes, of a deceased child of both Grantors.

You have requested the following rulings:

1. The contribution of jointly held assets to Trust will not constitute a gift by either Grantor A or Grantor B.
2. Payments to or for the benefit of either Grantor during the term of Trust will not be considered a gift, or, if so, the gift will qualify for the gift tax marital deduction.
3. The value of the entire Trust will be includible in the gross estate of the first Grantor to die.
4. On the death of the first deceasing Grantor, the surviving Grantor will be treated as making a gift that qualifies for the marital deduction, to the deceasing Grantor, with respect to the portion of the Trust property that is attributable to the surviving Grantor's contributions to the Trust.
5. To the extent that the Credit Shelter Trust is funded, any portion of the funds that will pass to the trust that originated with the surviving Grantor will not constitute a gift by such Grantor.
6. Future payments from the Credit Shelter Trust to beneficiaries other than the Surviving Grantor will not constitute a gift from the surviving Grantor to those beneficiaries, and none of the assets attributable to the surviving Grantor held in the Credit Shelter Trust will be includible in his or her gross estate.

Section 2001(a) of the Internal Revenue Code imposes a tax on the transfer of the taxable estate of every decedent who is a citizen or resident of the United States.

Section 2033 provides that the gross estate shall include the value of all property to the extent of the interest therein of the decedent at the time of his death.

Section 2038(a) of the Code provides that the value of the gross estate includes the value of all property of which the decedent has at any time made a transfer (except where there has been a bona fide sale for adequate and full consideration in money or money's worth) by trust or otherwise where the enjoyment thereof was subject at the date of death to any change through the exercise of a power by the decedent to alter, amend, revoke, or terminate the interest in the property or where the decedent relinquished this power within the three year period ending on the date of the decedent's death.

Section 2041(a)(2) provides for the inclusion in the gross estate of any property to which the decedent possesses, at the time of his death, a general power of appointment created after October 21, 1942.

Section 2041(b)(1) provides that the term "general power of appointment" means a power that is exercisable in favor of the decedent, the decedent's estate, the decedent's creditors, or the creditors of the decedent's estate, except that a power to consume property for the benefit of the decedent that is limited by an ascertainable standard relating to health, education, support, or maintenance of the decedent is not deemed a general power of appointment.

Section 20.2041-1(b)(2) provides that the term power of appointment does not include powers reserved by the decedent to himself within the concepts of LJ sections 2036 to 2038.

Section 2501 imposes a tax for each calendar year on the transfer of property by gift during such calendar year by any individual, resident or nonresident.

Section 25.2511-2(b) provides that as to any property, or part therein, of which the donor has so parted with dominion and control as to leave in him no power to change its disposition, whether for his own benefit or for the benefit of another, the gift is complete. Section 25.2511-2(c) provides that a gift is incomplete in every instance in which a donor reserves the power to revest the beneficial title to the property to himself or herself.

Section 2523 provides that where a donor transfers during the calendar year by gift an interest in property to a donee who at the time of the gift is the donor's spouse, there shall be allowed as a deduction in computing taxable gifts for the calendar year an amount with respect to such interest equal to its value.

Section 1014(a) provides that the basis of property in the hands of a person acquiring the property from a decedent or to whom the property passed from the decedent is the fair market value of the property at the date of the decedent's death (or alternate valuation date).

Section 1014(b)(9) provides that, for purposes of IM section 1014(a), property acquired from the decedent includes property acquired from the decedent by reason of death, form of ownership, or other conditions, including property acquired through the exercise or non-exercise of a power of appointment, if the property is required to be included in determining the value of the decedent's gross estate for federal estate tax purposes.

Section 1014(e), however, provides an exception to the general rule of L section 1014(a). Under U section 1014(e), if appreciated property was acquired by the decedent by gift during the one-year period ending on the date of the decedent's death and the property is acquired from the decedent by, or passes from the decedent to, the donor of such property, the basis of such property in the hands of the donor is the adjusted basis of the property in the hands of the decedent immediately before the death of the decedent.

RULING #1. Grantor A and Grantor B propose to transfer property held as tenants by the entireties to Trust. The Grantors will each retain the power to terminate Trust by written notice to the other Grantor. If Trust is terminated, the trustee will deliver the trust property to the Grantors in both their names as tenants in common. We conclude that the initial contribution of assets to Trust as proposed will not constitute a completed gift by either Grantor under section 25.2511-2(c), since each will retain the right, exercisable unilaterally, to revoke their respective transfer, and revest title in themselves.

RULING #2. If either Grantor exercises the right to terminate Trust, each Grantor will receive an undivided 50% interest in the remaining balance of the Trust corpus, as a tenant in common. Therefore, distributions of Trust property to either Grantor during their joint lives will constitute a gift by the other Grantor to the extent of 50% of the value of Trust assets distributed. The gift will qualify for the gift tax marital deduction under section 2523.

RULING #3 AND #4. Upon the death of the first Grantor to die, he or she will possess a testamentary power exercisable alone and in all events, to appoint part or all of the assets of the Trust, free of trust, to such deceased Grantor's estate or to or for the benefit of one or more persons or entities, in such proportions, outright, in trust, or otherwise as the deceased Grantor may direct in his or her will.

We conclude that, on the death of the first Grantor to die, the portion of the Trust property attributable to the property the deceased Grantor transferred to Trust will be includible in the deceased Grantor's gross estate under section 2038. The balance of the property attributable to the property the surviving Grantor contributed to Trust will be includible in the deceased Grantor's gross estate under Section 2041.

Further, on the death of the first deceasing Grantor, the surviving Grantor is treated as relinquishing his or her dominion and control over the surviving Grantor's one-half interest in Trust. Accordingly, on the death of the first deceasing Grantor, the surviving Grantor will make a completed gift under U section 2501 of the surviving Grantor's entire interest in Trust. This gift will qualify for the marital deduction under L section 2523.

In addition, Section 1014(e) will apply to any Trust property includible in the deceased Grantor's gross estate that is attributable to the surviving Grantor's contribution to Trust and that is acquired by the surviving Grantor, either directly or indirectly, pursuant to the deceased Grantor's exercise, or failure to exercise, the general power of appointment. See H.R. Rept. 97201, 97th Cong., 1st Sess. (July 24, 1981).

RULINGS #5 AND #6. As discussed above, the surviving Grantor is treated as making a completed gift of his or her interest in Trust on the death of the first deceasing Grantor. Also, as discussed above, a portion of the Trust property will be subject to inclusion in the deceased Grantor's gross estate under Section 2038, and a portion will be subject to inclusion under Section 2041. Accordingly, to the extent the Credit Shelter Trust is funded, property passing to the trust is treated as passing from the deceased Grantor, and not from the surviving Grantor.

Similarly, any future payments from the Credit Shelter Trust to beneficiaries other than the surviving Grantor will not constitute a gift from the surviving Grantor to those beneficiaries. None of the assets held in the Credit Shelter Trust will be includible in the surviving Grantor's gross estate, since the surviving Grantor will possess only a special power of appointment with respect to the assets in the Credit Shelter Trust.

Similarly, any future payments from the Credit Shelter Trust to beneficiaries other than the surviving Grantor will not constitute a gift from the surviving Grantor to those beneficiaries. None of the assets held in the Credit Shelter Trust will be includible in the surviving Grantor's gross estate, since the surviving Grantor will possess only a special power of appointment with respect to the assets in the Credit Shelter Trust.

This ruling is directed only to the taxpayer who requested it. Section 6110(k)(3) provides that it may not be used or cited as precedent.

Sincerely yours,

Associate Chief Counsel (Passthroughs and Special Industries)
By: George Masnik Branch Chief Branch 4
Enclosure: Copy of letter for section 6110 purposes

Index